Proceedings of

The 17th International Symposium on Computer and Information Sciences

Edited by
Ilyas Cicekli • Nihan Kesim Cicekli • Erol Gelenbe

ISCIS XVII
October 28-30, 2002
Orlando, Florida USA

Organized by
Computer Science Program
School of Electrical Engineering and Computer Science
University of Central Florida

CRC Press
Taylor & Francis Group
Boca Raton London New York

CRC Press is an imprint of the
Taylor & Francis Group, an **informa** business

CRC Press
Taylor & Francis Group
6000 Broken Sound Parkway NW, Suite 300
Boca Raton, FL 33487-2742

First issued in hardback 2019

ISBN-13: 978-0-8493-1490-2 (pbk)
ISBN-13: 978-1-138-41394-8 (hbk)

Visit the Taylor & Francis Web site at
http://www.taylorandfrancis.com

and the CRC Press Web site at
http://www.crcpress.com

Library of Congress Cataloging-in-Publication Data

Catalog record is available from the Library of Congress

ISCIS XVII

The 17th International Symposium on Computer and Information Sciences

October 28-30, 2002
Orlando, Florida, USA

Supported by

University of Central Florida, Orlando, Florida, USA

Honorary Chair

Erol Gelenbe, University of Central Florida

Program Committee Chair

Ilyas Cicekli, University of Central Florida

Program Committee

Levent Akin
Bogaziçi University

Varol Akman
Bilkent University

Ethem Alpaydin
Bogaziçi University

Volkan Atalay
Middle East Technical University

Isik Aybay
Eastern Mediterraean University

Osman Balci
Virginia Tech

Mostafa Bassiouni
University of Central Florida

Ilyas Cicekli
University of Central Florida
(Chair)

Nihan Kesim Cicekli
University of Central Florida

Narsingh Deo
University Central of Florida

Asuman Dogaç
Middle East Technical University

Ron Dutton
University of Central Florida

Jean-Michel Fourneau
Université de Versailles
St. Quentin

Michael Georgiopoulos
University of Central Florida

Erol Gelenbe
University of Central Florida

Ratan Guha
University of Central Florida

Altay Güvenir
Bilkent University

Ugur Halici
Middle East Technical University

Emre Harmanci
Istanbul Technical University

Peter Harrison
Imperial College

Kien Hua
University of Central Florida

Alain Jean-Marie
University of Montpellier

Çetin Kaya Koç
Oregon State University

Takis Kasparis
University of Central Florida

Taskin Koçak
University of Central Florida

Selahattin Kuru
Isik University

Dan Marinescu
University of Central Florida

Philippe Nain
Institut National de Recherche
en Informatique et Automatique

Sema Oktug
Istanbul Technical University

Füsun Özgüner
Ohio State University

Meral Özsoyoglu
Case Western Reserve University

Tamer Özsu
University of Waterloo

Ramon Puigjaner
University of Balears

Guy Pujolle
University of Paris VI

Bülent Sankur
Bogaziçi University

Marek Sergot
Imperial College

Hadas Shachnai
Bell Labs

Andreas Stafylopatis
National Technical University
of Athens

Özgur Ulusoy
Bilkent University

Abdullah Uz Tansel
CUNY

Hakki Toroslu
Middle East Technical University

Adnan Yazici
Middle East Technical University

Advisory Board

Foreword

This symposium is the 17th in a long series of the International Symposia on Computer and Information Sciences (ISCIS).

The ISCIS has been held annually in Turkey since 1986, often in major resort areas along the Aegean or Mediterranean coast. ISCIS took place at the end of October to coincide with the few days of holiday offered by Republic Day in Turkey, which commemorates the foundation of the Turkish Republic on October 29, 1923.

This year the tradition was altered and the symposium was held at the University of Central Florida, in Orlando. This change has promoted the "international" nature of ISCIS and attracted participation by more U.S. scientists, as well as scientists from numerous European countries, including Turkey and other countries that have traditionally participated in ISCIS. But Orlando is also a resort town (as well as a hi-tech and university center), so we are still faithful to our goal of taking ISCIS participants to attractive geographic locations.

We believe we have achieved this goal of greater internationalization, given that our proceedings this year includes 76 papers from 14 countries. The papers in the program were selected either by invitation or after a careful and critical review process.

The symposium and the proceedings have been grouped into 18 sessions. The papers cover a wide range of research topics, such as Algorithms, Artificial Intelligence, Computer Graphics, Computer Networks, Databases, Evolutionary Computation, Graph Theory, Image Processing, Software Engineering, and Software Performance Engineering.

Given the continued growth in the response to this conference, ISCIS will be organized in the year 2003 by the Middle East Technical University in Turkey.

Finally, it is our pleasure to acknowledge the authors for choosing this avenue for the presentation of their work and thereby contributing to its success. We would also like to take this opportunity to thank the members of the program committee and the invited session chairs for their cooperation and support.

Ilyas Cicekli, Ph.D. (Bilkent University and University of Central Florida)
Nihan Kesim Cicekli, Ph.D. (Middle East Technical University and University of Central Florida)
Erol Gelenbe, Ph.D., D.Sc. (University of Central Florida)

Table of Contents

PLENARY TALKS

Gradient-Based Learning and Optimization 3
XI-REN CAO

Stochastic Fluid Models for Communication Networks 8
CHRISTOS G. CASSANDRAS

Stochastic Process Algebra, Reversed Processes and Product Forms 12
PETER G. HARRISON

Static Scheduling Strategies for Heterogeneous Systems 18
O. BEAUMONT, A. LEGRAND, and Y. ROBERT

SESSION 1-1: ADVANCED NETWORKING HARDWARE

Towards 10-100 Gbps Cryptographic Architectures 25
KHARY ALEXANDER, RAMESH KARRI, IGOR MINKIN, KAIJIE WU, PIYUSH MISHRA, and XUAN LI

Integrated Photonic Devices for Optical and Wireless Networking 31
FOW-SEN CHOA and JIE LIN

Splintering TCP 36
PATRICIA GILFEATHER and ARTHUR B. MACCABE

Network Processors: Origin of Species 41
N. SHAH and K. KEUTZER

SESSION 1-2: MULTIMEDIA TECHNOLOGY

Automatic Generation of Motion Activity Descriptors in Video Sequences 49
JUNG HWAN OH and VASAVI GAVIRNENI

ETCP: An Efficacy-Oriented Transport Protocol for Point-to-Point Connections 54
SIMON SHEU, SANG-FONG CHIEN, and PING-YI LIN

Buffer Management for Periodic Broadcast Servers 59
WALLAPAK TAVANAPONG and MINH TRAN

A Formal Treatment of the Sampling-Based Approach to Managing Image Databases 64
KHANH VU, KIEN A. HUA, and S.D. LANG

SESSION 1-3: IMAGE PROCESSING I

Measuring Female Facial Beauty by Calculating the Proportions of the Face 71
HATICE GUNES and M. YAHYA KARSLIGIL

Appearance Reconstruction of Three Dimensional Models from Real Images 76
ULAS YıLMAZ, ADEM Y. MÜLAYIM, and VOLKAN ATALAY

Texture Segmentation by Using Adaptive Polyphase Subband Decomposition 81
MUSTAFA YAMAN, VOLKAN ATALAY, MUSTAFA TÜRKER, A.ENIS ÇETIN, and ÖNER NEZIH GEREK

Multiscale Image Representation Using Switched Codebook Predictive Vector Quantization 86
MEHMET YAKUT

SESSION 2-1: COMPUTER NETWORKS I

A Parallel Algorithm for Global Optimisation and Semi-Infinite Programming 93
S. ASPREY, B. RUSTEM, and S. ZAKOVIC

Logical Performance of the Optical Packet Metropolitan Ring Architecture 98
T. ATMACA and D. POPA

Packet Selection in a Deflection Routing Algorithm 103
A. BORRERO, JEAN-MICHEL. FOURNEAU, and F. QUESSETTE

Geometrically Batched Networks 108
PETER G. HARRISON, DAVID THORNLEY, and HARF ZATSCHLER

SESSION 2-2: ALGORITHMS

A Polynomial-Time Algorithm for Allocating Independent Tasks on Heterogeneous Fork-Graphs 115
O. BEAUMONT, A. LEGRAND, and Y. ROBERT

An Experimental Evaluation of Modified Algorithms for the Graph Partitioning Problem 120
JURIZ SILC, PETER KOROSEC, and BORUT ROBIC

Bottleneck Perfect Domination on Some Classes of Graphs 125
W. CHUNG-KUNG YEN

Concept of and Experiments on Combining Compression with Encryption 130
MEHMET EMIN DALKILIC and EBRU CELIKEL

SESSION 2-3: COMPUTER GRAPHICS

Honeycomb Subdivision 137
ERGUN AKLEMAN and VINOD SRINIVASAN

A New Image-Based Lighting Method: Practical Shadow-Based Light Reconstruction 142
JAEMIN LEE and ERGUN AKLEMAN

Interactive Deformation with Triangles 147
JAMES DEAN PALMER, ERGUN AKLEMAN, and JIANER CHEN

Marker Mapping Techniques for Augmented Reality Visualization 152
FELIX G. HAMZA-LUP, LARRY DAVIS, CHARLES E. HUGHES, and JANNICK P. ROLLAND

SESSION 3-1: CODING AND WIRELESS COMMUNICATION

Resource Allocation for an Enterprise Mobile Services Platform 159
MATTI HILTUNEN, RITTWIK JANA, and YIH-FARN CHEN

Wireless MAC Protocols Supporting Real-Time Services in Wireless LANs 164
YOUNGGOO KWON, YUGUANG FANG, and HANIPH LATCHMAN

The Role of Error Control Coding in Joint Detection CDMA 169
CHRISTIAN SCHLEGEL

Sensivity to Timing Errors in EGC and MRC Techniques 174
YUNGJING YIN, JOHN P. FONSEKA, and ISREAL KORN

SESSION 3-2: ARTIFICIAL INTELLIGENCE

Visualizing Transition Diagrams of Action Language Programs 181
ÖZCAN KOÇ, FERDA N. ALPASLAN,and NIHAN K. ICEKLI

Turkish Natural Language Interface: CEVAPVER 187
ZEYNEP ALTAN and DOGAL ACAR

A Machine Translation System between a Pair of Closely Related Languages 192
KEMAL ALTINTAS and ILYAS CICEKLI

An Intelligent System Dealing with Nuanced Information 197
MAZEN EL-SAYED and DANIEL PACHOLCZYK

SESSION 3-3: IMAGE PROCESSING II

Robust Rotation Estimation from Three Orthogonally Oriented Cameras 205
SUNEIL SASTRI and RAYMOND KWONG

Computer Vision-Based Unistroke Keyboards 210
AYKUT ERDEM, ERKUT ERDEM, VOLKAN ATALAY, and A. ENIS CETIN

Camera Auto-Calibration Using a Sequence of 2D Images with Small Rotations and Translations 215
REZA HASSANPOUR and VOLKAN ATALAY

Biometric Security System Design Using Keystroke Rhythms Algorithm 220
AYKUT GUVEN and IBRAHIM SOGUKPINAR

SESSION 4-1: EVOLUTIONARY COMPUTATION

Evolutionary Computation: Current Research and Open Issues 227
KENNETH DEJONG

Mixing of Building Blocks and Single-Point Crossover 232
KUMARA SASTRY and DAVID E. GOLDBERG

Solution Stability in Evolutionary Computation 237
TERENCE SOULE, ROBERT B. HECKENDORN, and JIAN SHEN

A Comparison of Haploidy and Diploidy without Dominance on Integer Representations 242
AYSE S. YILMAZ and ANNIE S. WU

SESSION 4-2: COMPUTER NETWORKS II

Control of Lightpaths in Heterogeneous Optical Networks 249
JING WU and HUSSEIN T. MOUFTAH

The Link-Orientation Problem on Several Practical Networks 254
W. CHUNG-KUNG YEN and SHIN-JER YANG

Peer-to-Peer Cooperative Driving 259
ALINA BEJAN and RAMON LAWRENCE

Fairness in Differentiated Services Architecture 264
ERHAN ASIM OZTURK and CUNEYT F. BAZLAMACI

SESSION 4-3: DATABASES

Exploiting Semantic Constraints in a Database Browser 271
JIE ZHANG and DAVID L. SPOONER

Dispatching Java Agents to User for Data Extraction from Third Party Web Sites 276
DMITRIY BERYOZA, NAPHTALI RISHE, ANDREI SELIVONENKO, ALEJANDRO ROQUE, and IAN DE FELIPE

Incremental Maintenance of Object-Oriented Views in Data Warehouses 281
CHING-MING CHAO

Cortex-Based Mechanism for Discovery of High-Order Features 286
OLCAY KURSUN and OLEG FAVOROV

SESSION 5-1: GRAPH THEORY

Maximum Alliance-Free and Minimum Alliance-Cover Sets 293
KHURRAM H. SHAFIQUE and RONALD D. DUTTON

Offensive Alliances in Graphs 298
ODILE FAVARON, GERD FRICKE, WAYNE GODDARD, SANDRA M. HEDETNIEMI, STEPHEN T. HEDETNIEMI,
PETTER KRISTIANSEN, RENU C. LASKAR, and DUANE SKAGGS

Global Defensive Alliances 303
TERESA W. HAYNES, STEPHEN T. HEDETNIEMI, and MICHAEL A. HENNING

Introduction to Alliances in Graphs 308
PETTER KRISTIANSEN, SANDRA M. HEDETNIEMI, and STEPEHN T. HEDETNIEMI

SESSION 5-2: COMPUTER NETWORKS III

Case-Based Agents for Packet-Level Intrusion Detection in Ad Hoc Networks 315
R. GUHA, O. KACHIRSKI, D. G. SCHWARTZ, S. STOECKLIN, and E. YILMAZ

A Routing Solution for a Global, Space-Based Multimedia System 321
M. GUIZANI and I. G. SCHNELLER

Design and Implementation of Smart Packet Processor for the Cognitive Packet Network Router 327
TASKIN KOCAK and JUDE SEEBER

Dynamic Shortest Path Routing in 2-Circulants 332
TOMAZ DOBRAVEC, BORUT ROBIC, and BOSTJAN VILFAN

SESSION 5-3: SOFTWARE ENGINEERING

Measuring the Size of Object-Oriented Software Applications 339
JING-CHIOU LIOU

Net Class: A Multilingual, Web-Based Learning Management Tool 344
SEREN BASARAN, NESE YALABIK, and ÜMIT KIZILOGLU

How Human Factors Impact on Software Process Maturity 349
JING-CHIOU LIOU

A Mathematical Formalism for Specifying Design Patterns 354
DENVER R. E. WILLIAMS, CHARLES E. HUGHES, and ALI OROOJI

SESSION 6-1: NEW ISSUES IN NETWORKING

A New Wireless Archtecture for QoS, Security and Mobility 361
HAKIMA CHAOUCHI and GUY PUJOLLE

Bandwidth Allocation in Bluetooth Scatternets 367
ULF KÖRNER and NIKLAS JOHANSSON

Mobility and Multicast: Protocol Design and Analysis 372
ROLLAND VIDA, LUÍS H. M. K. COSTA, and SERGE FDIDA

Performance Modeling of an Edge Optical Burst Switching Node 377
LISONG XU, HARRY G. PERROS, and GEORGE N. ROUSKAS

SESSION 6-2: WEB-BASED SIMULATION

Educational Application of an Online Context Sensitive Speech Dictionary 385
G. BENGU, GUANGYU LIU, RITESH ADVAL, and FRANK SHIH

Using Computer Simulation to Optimize the Operations for an Automotive Manufacturing Facility 390
HALDUN ÇELIK and MURAT GÜVENTÜRK

A Web-Based Framework with Experimental Design Approach to Simulation Optimization 394
OSMAN NURI DARCAN and ALI RIZA KAYLAN

Evaluation of the Adaptivity of a Continuous Review Inventory Control Model 399
ASLI SENCER ERDEM and NURI BASOGLU

SESSION 6-3: SOFTWARE PERFORMANCE ENGINEERING

Performance Engineering Based on UML and SPNs: A Software Performance Tool 405
JUAN PABLO LÓPEZ-GRAO, JOSÉ MERSEGUER, and JAVIER CAMPOS

Extending MASCOT to a Component-Based Software Performance Engineering Methodology 410
ONOFRE MUNAR, CARLOS JUIZ, and RAMON PUIGJANER

Qualitative and Quantitative Evaluation Using Process Algebra 415
ADELMALEK BENZEKRI

Modeling Nodes of Communication Networks at the Bit and Packet Levels 419
GERARDO RUBINO

Author Index 425

Plenary Talks

Gradient-Based Learning and Optimization

Xi-Ren Cao*

Department of Electrical and Electronic Engineering
Hong Kong University of Science and Technology
Clear Water Bay, Kowloon, Hong Kong

Abstract

Recent research indicates that perturbation analysis (PA), Markov decision process (MDP), and reinforcement learning (RL) are closely related. Policy iteration in MDP can be viewed as a direct consequence of performance sensitivity analysis. Both sensitivity analysis and policy iteration depend on the concept of performance potentials. RL provides efficient on-line algorithms for estimationg potentials and other related quantities such as the Q-factors. The sensitivity point of view brings in some new insight to the area of learning and optimization. In particular, the gradient based optimization can be applied to parameterized systems without suffering the "curse of dimensionality", and can be applied to systems with correlated actions, etc.

Key words: gradient-based policy iteration, perturbation analysis, perturbation realization, Potentials, Poisson equations, Q-learning

1 Introduction

Recent research indicates that perturbation analysis (PA) [5, 8, 16], Markov decision process (MDP) [3, 18, 19, 20], and reinforcement learning (RL) [3, 4, 21, 22] are closely related. In this paper, we study the relations among these closely related fields. We show that the sensitivity point of view of PA brings in some new insight to the area of learning and optimization. The main ideas can be summarized as follows. Policy iteration in MDP can be viewed as a direct consequence of performance sensitivity analysis. Both sensitivity analysis and policy iteration depend on the concept of performance potentials. RL provides efficient on-line algorithms for

*Supported in part by a grant from Hong Kong UGC. Tel: (852) 2358-7048 Fax: (852) 2358-1485 Email: eecao@ee.ust.hk

estimationg potentials and other related quantities such as the Q-factors. The traditional approachs for estimating the potential of every state or the Q-factor of every state-action pair suffer the so-called "curse of dimensionality" problem because the number of states is usually too large. In addition, policy iteration can only be applied to problems with no constraints. In this paper, we show that the above difficulties can be avoided with the gradient-based optimization. In particular, for parameterized systems the performance sensitivities with respect to these parameters can be estimated based on a sample path. The gradient-based optimization may apply to systems with a large number of states and with various constraints. Single sample path based algorithms have been developed and will be reviewed. We will give an example to show a possible application in this direction.

2 Performance Sensitivity

The basic principle of PA (i.e., single sample path based sensitivity analysis) is as follows. Each change (small or large) in a parameter of a system induces a sequence of changes (small or large) in a sample path of the system; the effect of each change in a sample path (called a *perturbation*) of a system on its long-run performance can be measured by a quantity called *realization factor*; and the effect of a change in a system parameter on the system performance equals the sum of the effects of all the perturbations induced by this change in the parameter. This principle have been successfully applied to various queueing networks to obtain the performance sensitivities [5].

The same basic principle for PA can be applied to Markov processes to obtain performance sensitivity [8]. Consider an irreducible and aperiodic Markov chain $\mathbf{X} = \{X_n : n \geq 0\}$ on a finite state space $S = \{1, 2, \cdots, M\}$ with transition probability matrix

$P = [p(i,j)] \in [0,1]^{M \times M}$. Let $\pi = (\pi_1, \ldots, \pi_M)$ be the vector representing its steady-state probabilities, and $f = (f_1, f_2, \cdots, f_M)^T$ be the performance vector, where "T" represents transpose. We have $Pe = e$, where $e = (1, 1, \cdots, 1)^T$ is an M-dimensional vector whose all components equal 1, and $\pi = \pi P$. The performance measure is the long-run average defined as

$$\eta = E_\pi(f) = \sum_{i=1}^{M} \pi_i f_i = \pi f$$

$$= \lim_{L \to \infty} \frac{1}{L} \sum_{l=0}^{L-1} f(X_l) = \lim_{L \to \infty} \frac{F_L}{L}, \quad (1)$$

where

$$F_L = \sum_{l=0}^{L-1} f(X_l).$$

Let P' be another irreducible transition probability matrix on the same state space. Suppose P changes to $P(\delta) = P + \delta Q = \delta P' + (1 - \delta)P$, with $\delta > 0$, $Q = P' - P = [q(i,j)]$. We have $Qe = 0$. The performance measure will change to $\eta(\delta) = \eta + \Delta\eta$. Denote $\eta' = \eta(1)$ be the performance corresponding to P'. The derivative of η in the direction of Q is defined as $\frac{d\eta}{d\delta} = \lim_{\delta \to 0} \frac{\Delta\eta}{\delta}$. The discrete sensitivity is $\eta' - \eta$.

In this system, a perturbation means that the system is perturbed from one state i to another state j. For example, consider the case where $p(k,i) = 0.5$, $p(k,j) = 0.5$, and $p(k,l) = 0$ for all $l \neq i, j$. In computer simulation, to determine the next state that the Markov chain will jump into from state k, we generate a $[0,1)$ uniformly distributed random variable ξ. If $0 \leq \xi < 0.5$, then the Markov chain jumps into state i; otherwise, it jumps into state j. Now suppose that the transition probabilities are perturbed to $p'(k,i) = 0.5 - \delta$, $p'(k,j) = 0.5 + \delta$, and $p'(k,l) = 0$ (i.e., $q(k,i) = -1$, $q(k,j) = 1$, and $q(k,l) = 0$.) Assume that $0.5 - \delta \leq \xi < 0.5$, then the original Markov chain jumps into state i, but the perturbed one jumps into j. Therefore, a perturbation in such a system means state i changes to j. Thus, we study two independent Markov chains $\mathbf{X} = \{X_n; n \geq 0\}$ and $\mathbf{X}' = \{X_n'; n \geq 0\}$ with $X_0 = i$ and $X_0' = j$; both of them have the same transition matrix P. The realization factor is defined as [8]:

$$d(i,j) = \lim_{L \to \infty} E\left[\sum_{l=0}^{L-1} (f(X_l') - f(X_l))|X_0 = i, \ X_0' = j\right]. \quad (2)$$

Thus, $d(i,j)$ represents the average effect of a jump from i to j on F_L in (1).

The matrix $D \in \mathcal{R}^{M \times M}$, with $d(i,j)$ as its (i,j)th element, is called a *realization matrix*. From (2), we can prove that D satisfies the Lyapunov equation [8]

$$D - PDP^T = F, \quad (3)$$

where $F = fe^T - ef^T$. We can prove

$$\frac{d\eta}{d\delta} = \pi Q D^T \pi^T. \quad (4)$$

Next, from (2), we can define $d(i,j) = g(i) - g(j)$ and $D = ge^T - eg^T$. g is called a *performance potential vector* with $g(i)$ the potential at state i. From (3), it is easy to prove that g satisfies the Poisson equation

$$(I - P)g + \eta e = f. \quad (5)$$

We observe that if g is a solution to (5), then for any constant c, $g + ce$ is also a solution to (5). This is the same as the potential energy in physics. If we choose the constant in such a way that $\pi g = \eta$, then for this particular value of potential, the Poisson equation becauses

$$(I - P + e\pi)g = f. \quad (6)$$

From (4), it is easy to derive that

$$\frac{d\eta}{d\delta} = \pi Q g. \quad (7)$$

This is the continuous sensitivity formula; and

$$\eta' - \eta = \pi' Q g. \quad (8)$$

This is the discrete sensitivity formula. For more general cases, we assume that as P changes to P', the performance function also changes from f to f'. Let $h = f' - f$. It is easy to check that

$$\eta' - \eta = \pi'(Qg + h). \quad (9)$$

For continuous sensitivity, we set $f(\delta) = f + \delta h$. Together with $P(\delta) = P + \delta Q$, we have

$$\frac{d\eta}{d\delta} = \pi(Qg + h). \quad (10)$$

3 Policy Iteration and Reinforcement Learning

Policy iteration procedure is a natural consequence of (9): if P is the current policy, then the actions with the largest absolute value of Qg (componentwisely) are chosen as the policy for the next iteration. The diference between the continuous sensitivity (10) and the discrete

4

one (9) is only that π is replaced by π'. This clearly shows that at each step the policy iteration algorithm simply chooses the "steepest" direction to go for its next policy [6].

To know the exact value of the performance difference from (9), one needs to know π'. On the otherhand, if π' is known, one can get η' directly by $\pi' f$. In addition, it is impossible to calculate π' for all the policice since the policy space is usually very large. Fortunately, since $\pi' > 0$ (componentwisely), we can always determine which action is better at each state by using (9). Thus, we can perform policy iteration without knowing the exact value of the performance difference. This leads to the following discussion.

For two M-dimensional vectors a and b, we define $a = b$ if $a(i) = b(i)$ for all $i = 1, 2 \cdots, M$; $a \leq b$ if $a(i) < b(i)$ or $a(i) = b(i)$ for all $i = 1, 2 \cdots, M$; $a < b$ if $a(i) < b(i)$ for all $i = 1, 2 \cdots, M$; and $a \preceq b$ if $a(i) < b(i)$ for at least one i, and $a(j) = b(j)$ for other components. The relation $\leq$ includes $=$, $\preceq$, and $<$. Similar definitions are used for the relations $>$, $\succeq$, and $\geq$.

Next, we note that $\pi'(i) > 0$ for all $i = 1, 2, \cdots, M$. Thus, from (9), we know that if $Qg + h = (P' - P)g + (f' - f) \succeq 0$ then $\eta' - \eta > 0$. From (9) and the fact $\pi' > 0$, the proof of the following lemma is straightforward.

Lemma 1 If $Pg + f \preceq P'g + f'$, then $\eta < \eta'$.

In an MDP, at any transition instant $n \geq 0$ of a Markov chain $\mathbf{X} = \{X_n, n \geq 0\}$, an action is chosen from an action space $\mathcal{A}$ and is applied to the Markov chain. We assume that the number of actions is finite, and we only consider stationary policies. The actions that are available for $i \in \mathcal{S}$ form a nonempty subset $A(i) \subseteq \mathcal{A}$. A stationary policy is a mapping $\mathcal{L} : \mathcal{S} \to \mathcal{A}$, i.e., for any state i, $\mathcal{L}$ specifies an action $\mathcal{L}(i) \in A(i)$. Let $\mathcal{E}$ be the policy space. If action α is taken at state i, then the state transition probabilities at state i are denoted as $p^\alpha(i, j)$, $j = 1, 2, \cdots, M$. With a policy $\mathcal{L}$, the Markov process evolves according to the transition matrix $P^\mathcal{L} = [p^{\mathcal{L}(i)}(i, j)]_{i=1}^M |_{j=1}^M$. We use the superscript $*^\mathcal{L}$ to denote the quantities associated with policy $\mathcal{L}$.

The steady-state probabilities corresponding to policy $\mathcal{L}$ is denoted as a vector $\pi^\mathcal{L} = (\pi^\mathcal{L}(1), \cdots, \pi^\mathcal{L}(M))$. Suppose that at each stage with state i and control action $\alpha \in A(i)$, a cost $f(i, \alpha) = f(i, \mathcal{L}(i))$ is incurred. The long-run expected value of the average cost per stage corresponding to policy $\mathcal{L}$ is then

$$\eta^\mathcal{L} = \lim_{L \to \infty} \frac{1}{L} E\{\sum_{l=0}^{L-1} f[X_l, \mathcal{L}(X_l)]\},$$

For ergodic chains, the above limit exists and does not depend on the initial state. Our objective is to minimize this average cost per stage over the policy space $\mathcal{S}$, i.e., to obtain $\min_{\mathcal{L} \in \mathcal{E}} \eta^\mathcal{L}$.

Define $f^\mathcal{L} = (f[1, \mathcal{L}(1)], \cdots, f[M, \mathcal{L}(M)])^T$. (5) becomes

$$(I - P^\mathcal{L} + e\pi^\mathcal{L})g^\mathcal{L} = f^\mathcal{L},$$

The optimality equation can be easily derived from Lemma 1 and policy iteration algorithms for determining the optimal policy can be developed from Lemma 1. Roughly speaking, at the kth step with policy $\mathcal{L}_k$, we set the policy for the next step (the $(k+1)$th step) as $\mathcal{L}_{k+1} = arg\{\min[P^\mathcal{L} g^{\mathcal{L}_k} + f^\mathcal{L}]\}$, with $g^{\mathcal{L}_k}$ being the solution to the Poisson equation for $P^{\mathcal{L}_k}$. Lemma 1 implies that performance usually improves at each iteration. The minimum is reached when no performance improvement can be achieved. We shall not state the details here because they are standard.

Finally, potentials can be estimated on a single sample path. Efficient algorithms can be developed with stochastic approximation methods (see the next section). Sometimes when system structure, i.e., the transition probabilities, $p(i, j)s$, are completely unknown, we cannot apply policy iteration directly by using the potentials. In this case, we can estimate the Q-factor defined as [4, 22]

$$Q(i, \alpha) = \{\sum_{j=1}^M p^\alpha(i, j)g(j)\} + f^\alpha(i) - \eta, \qquad (11)$$

for every state-action pair (i, α). Smilar algorithms may be developed to estimate the performance gradients. These are the research topics in reinforcement learning.

One of the problems for the above approach is the "curse of dimensionality": when the number of state is too large, it is not feasible to estimate or calculate all the components for potential g or the Q-factor $Q(i, \alpha)$. Another problem is that the approach can only be applied to systems with the above described standard formulation; for example, it does not apply to systems with hidden state components or systems in which the action taken at one state may affect that of the other states.

4 Algorithms for Performance Gradients

The drawbacks suffered by the above approaches are because they are based on the fundamental equation (9), which depends on both π' (associated with P') and g (associated with P). The sample path of Markov process P does not directly contains information about π'. On the other hand, the performance sensitivity formula

5

(10) depends on π and P (both are assocaited with P). Therefore, we can develop on-line algorithms to estimate $\frac{d\eta}{d\delta}$ for any given $Q = P' - P$ on a single sample path of a Markov chain with transition probability P.

Now we present one of such algorithms developed in [9]. Denote a sample path as $\mathbf{X} = \{X_0, X_1, \cdots X_n, \cdots, \}$. Solving the Poisson equation (6) leads to

$$g(i) = E\{\sum_{n=0}^{\infty}[f(X_n) - \eta]|X_0 = i\}. \quad (12)$$

This can be approximated by

$$g_n(i) = \lim_{N \to \infty} \left\{ \frac{\sum_{k=0}^{N-n+1}\{\epsilon^i(X_k)[\sum_{j=0}^{n-1} f(X_{k+j})]\}}{\sum_{k=0}^{N-n+1} \epsilon^i(X_k)} \right.$$
$$\left. - \frac{n}{N}\sum_{k=0}^{N-1} f(X_k) \right\} \quad w.p.1, \quad (13)$$

where $\epsilon^i(x) = 1$ if $x = i$, and $\epsilon^i(x) = 0$ otherwise. Since the second term is a constant, we can remove it and obtain

$$g_n(i) = \lim_{N \to \infty} \frac{\sum_{k=0}^{N-n+1}\{\epsilon^i(X_k)[\sum_{j=0}^{n-1} f(X_{k+j})]\}}{\sum_{k=0}^{N-n+1} \epsilon^i(X_k)}. \quad w.p.1.$$

Based on this, it was proved in [9] that

$$\frac{\partial \eta}{\partial \delta} = \pi Q g = \lim_{N \to \infty} \frac{1}{N-n+1}$$
$$\sum_i \sum_j \left\{ \sum_{k=0}^{N-n} \epsilon^i(X_k)\epsilon^j(X_{k+1})\frac{q(i,j)}{p(i,j)}[\sum_{l=0}^{n-1} f(X_{k+l+1})] \right\}$$
$$= \lim_{N \to \infty} \frac{1}{N-n+1}$$
$$\left\{ \sum_{k=0}^{N-n} \{\frac{q(X_k, X_{k+1})}{p(X_k, X_{k+1})}\}[\sum_{l=0}^{n-1} f(X_{k+l+1})] \right\}, \quad w.p.1. \quad (14)$$

Algorithms can be developed based on (14) (see [9]). (14) has a significant meaning: we can estimate the performance sensitivity along any direction on a single sample path without estimating every component of g. Therefore, performance gradient based optimization approach do not suffer the "curse of dimensionality" problem. In general, we assume that the system transition probability matrix contains a parameter θ: $P = P(\theta)$. The system performance depends on θ: $\eta = \eta(\theta)$. When θ changes to $\theta + \Delta\theta$, $P(\theta)$ changes to $P(\theta) + \frac{dP}{d\theta}\Delta\theta$. Therefore, we can set $Q = \frac{dP}{d\theta}$. Along the direction of $Q\delta$ applying (14) yields the performance derivative $\frac{d\eta}{d\theta}$.

(14) was extended to the discounted cost problems and partially observable MDP in [1, 2].

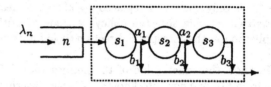

Figure 1: An M/G/1/N Queue

5 Gradient-Based Policy Iteration

In the standard policy iteration, at each iteration one chooses the policy with the largest $Qg + h$, componentwisely, as the policy in the next iteration. That is, policy iteration goes along the direction with the steepest performance gradient. Since policy iteration determines actions at every state separately, it does not apply to systems in which the action at one state may affect those of the others.

Motivated by the above observations, it was proposed in [11] a gradient-based policy iteration that may be applied to systems with correlated actions at different states. We treat the problem as performance optimization in a policy space with constraints for policy points. The main idea is to iterate policy along the steepest direction in the constrained region. Because performance derivatives can be obtained using π and g for the current policy, this approach avoids evaluating performance for every policy. The standard policy iteration is a special case of the gradient-based iteration. However, there are some theoretical issues remaining. For example, the proposed approach leads to a policy that is local optimal, i.e., at this point all the direction gradients to other policies are non-negative (in case of performance minimization). In addition, the convergence of the algorithms have to be proved. A complete study of this subject belongs to future research topic. Here, we simply use an example to illustrate the idea.

Consider an M/G/1/N queue, in which the service distribution is a Coxian distribution (cf. [12]). For simplicity, we assume in our problem that the distribution consists of three stages, each of them is exponentially distributed with mean s_i, $i = 1, 2, 3$ (see Figure 1). The state space of the system is $\{0, (n, s), n = 1, 2, \cdots 15, s = 1, 2, 3\}$, with s denoting the stage of the customer being served. In the standard MDP problem, the action taken at state (n, s) is $\alpha(n, s)$. The problem now is that for a real system, the stage is not observable; thus, for any n, we have the constraint

$$\alpha(n, 1) = \alpha(n, 2) = \alpha(n, 3) \equiv \alpha(n). \quad (15)$$

A detailed formulation of the problem and a gradient-based policy iteration algorithm is provided in [11].

6 Discussions

The concept of *performance potentials* plays a significant role in sensitivity analysis of Markov processes and MDPs. With the potentials estimated, performance derivatives can be obtained and policy iteration (i.e., MDPs) can be implemented based on a single sample path. The single sample path-based approach is practically important because it can be applied online to real engineering systems; in most cases, it does not require the system parameters to be completely known (see the examples in [7]). There are two ways to achieve the optimal performance with this approach: by perturbation analysis using performance derivatives, or by policy iteration, both can be implemented online. Stochastic approximation methods have to be used in these two cases to improve the convergence speeds and to reduce stochastic errors. For details, see [13, 17].)

Inspired by the potential-based sensitivity view of MDPs and the single sample path-based approach, a number of new research topics emerge. First, we observe that the performance derivatives along any direction Q can be estimated on a single sample path without estimating each individual component of the potential. Thus, for parameterized systems on-line optimization can be achieved by using the estimated performance gradients, which is not affected by the large size of the state space. Next, policy iteration can be implemented by using the performance derivatives. This leads to a new approach, the gradient-based policy iteration, to MDPs with correlated actions at different states [11]. A number of issues, such as the local minimal policy, the convergence of the algorithms, are yet to be addressed. This gradient-based policy iteration can be applied to problems such as MDPs with hidden state components and the distributed control of MDPs, the details are to be worked out. The other topics include the time aggregation of MDPs [10]. When the number of controllable states is small, this approach may save computations, storage spaces, and/or the number of transitions in sample-path-based approaches.

References

[1] J. Baxter and P. L. Bartlett, "Infinite-Horizon Policy-Gradient Estimation," *Journal of Artificial Intelligence Research*, Vol. 15, 319-350, 2001.

[2] J. Baxter, P. L. Bartlett, and L. Weaver "Experiments with Infinite-Horizon Policy-Gradient Estimation," *Journal of Artificial Intelligence Research*, Vol. 15, 351-381, 2001.

[3] D. P. Bertsekas, *Dynamic Programming and Optimal Control*, Vols. I, II, Athena Scientific, Belmont, Massachusetts, 1995.

[4] D. P. Bertsekas, and T. N. Tsitsiklis, *Neuro-Dynamic Programming*, Athena Scientific, Belmont, Massachusetts, 1996.

[5] X. R. Cao, *Realization Probabilities: The Dynamics of Queueing Systems*, Springer-Verlag, New York, 1994.

[6] X. R. Cao, "The Relation Among Potentials, Perturbation Analysis, Markov Decision Processes, and Other Topics," *Journal of Discrete Event Dynamic Systems*, Vol. 8, 71-87, 1998.

[7] X. R. Cao, "Single Sample Path-Based Optimization of Markov Chains," *Journal of Optimization: Theory and Application*, Vol. 100, 527-548, 1999.

[8] X. R. Cao and H. F. Chen, "Potentials, Perturbation Realization, and Sensitivity Analysis of Markov Processes," *IEEE Transactions on AC*, Vol. 42, 1382-1393, 1997.

[9] X. R. Cao and Yat-wan Wan, Algorithms for Sensitivity Analysis of Markov Systems through Potentials and Perturbation Realization, *IEEE Transactions on Control Systems Technology*, Vol. 6, 482-494, 1998.

[10] X. R. Cao, Z. Y. Ren, S. Bhatnagar, M. Fu, and S. Marcus, "A Time Aggregation Approach to Markov Decision Processes," *Automatica*, Vol. 38, 929-943, 2002.

[11] X. R. Cao and H. T. Fang, "Gradient-Based Policy Iteration: An Example," to appear in 2002 IEEE CDC.

[12] D.R. Cox, "A use of complex probabilities in the theory of stochastic processes," *Proceedings Cambridge Philosophical Society*, 51, 313-319, 1955.

[13] H. T. Fang and X. R. Cao, "Single Sample Path-Based Recursive Algorithms for Markov Decision Processes," *IEEE Trans. on Automatic Control*, submitted.

[14] P. Glasserman, *Gradient Estimation Via Perturbation Analysis*, Kluwer Academic Publisher, Boston, 1991.

[15] O. Hernandez-Lerma and J. B. Lasserre, "Error bounds for rolling horizon policies in discrete-time Markov control processes," *IEEE Transactions on AC*, Vol. 35, 1118-1124, 1990.

[16] Y. C. Ho and X. R. Cao, *Perturbation Analysis of Discrete-Event Dynamic Systems*, Kluwer Academic Publisher, Boston, 1991.

[17] P. Marbach and T. N. Tsitsiklis, "Simulation-based optimization of Markov reward processes," *IEEE Transactions on Automatic Control* Vol. 46, 191-209, 2001.

[18] S. P. Meyn, "The Policy Improvement Algorithm For Markov Decision Processes with General State Space," *IEEE Transactions on Automatic Control*, Vol. 42, 1663-1680, 1997.

[19] S. P. Meyn and R. L. Tweedie, *Markov Chains and Stochastic Stability*, Springer-Verlag, London, 1993.

[20] M. L. Puterman, *Markov Decision Processes: Discrete Stochastic Dynamic Programming*, Wiley, New York, 1994.

[21] R. S. Sutton, "Learning to Predict by the Methods of Temporal Differences," *Machine Learning*, Vol. 3, 835-846, 1988.

[22] R. S. Sutton and A. G. Barto, *Reinforcement Learning: An Introduction*, MIT Press, Cambridge, MA, 1998.

Stochastic Fluid Models for Communication Networks

Christos G. Cassandras[1]
Department of Manufacturing Engineering
and Center for Information and Systems Engineering
Boston University, Brookline, MA 02446
cgc@bu.edu

Abstract

A natural modeling framework for packet-based communication networks is provided through discrete event systems and, in particular, queueing models. However, the huge traffic volume that networks are supporting today makes such models highly impractical. An alternative modeling paradigm is based on Stochastic Fluid Models (SFM). The SFM paradigm allows the aggregation of multiple events, associated with the movement of individual packets over a time period of a constant flow rate, into a single event associated with a rate change. Using SFMs for the purpose of control and optimization rather than just performance analysis it has been recently shown that Perturbation Analysis (PA) techniques lead to simple unbiased sensitivity estimators that can be used not only in a simulation environment but also on line, driven by actual network data and requiring no knowledge of the traffic processes involved.

1 Introduction

A natural modeling framework for packet-based communication networks is provided through queueing systems. However, the huge traffic volume that networks are supporting today makes such models highly impractical. It may be impossible, for example, to simulate at the packet level a network slated to transport packets at gigabit-per-second rates. If, on the other hand, we are to resort to analytical techniques from classical queueing theory, we find that traditional traffic models, largely based on Poisson processes, need to be replaced by more sophisticated stochastic processes that capture the bursty nature of realistic traffic; in addition, we need to explicitly model buffer overflow phenomena which typically defy tractable analytical derivations.

---
[1]This work is supported in part by the National Science Foundation under Grants ACI-98-73339 and EEC-0088073, by AFOSR under contract F49620-01-0056, by ARO under grant DAAD19-01-0610, and by the NOKIA Research Center (Boston).

An alternative modeling paradigm, based on Stochastic Fluid Models (SFM), has been recently considered for the purpose of analysis and simulation. Introduced in [1] and later proposed in [2] for analysis of multiplexed data streams, SFMs have been shown to be especially useful for simulating various kinds of high-speed networks [3], [4], [5]. The efficacy of a SFM rests on its ability to aggregate multiple events over a time period of a constant flow rate, into a single event associated with a rate change. It forgoes the identity and dynamics of individual packets and focuses instead on the aggregate flow rate. For the purpose of *performance analysis*, especially in the presence of Quality of Service (QoS) requirements, the accuracy of SFMs depends on traffic conditions, the structure of the underlying system, and the nature of the performance metrics of interest. For the purpose of *control and optimization*, on the other hand, as long as a SFM captures the salient features of the underlying "real" system it is possible to obtain solutions to performance optimization problems even if we cannot estimate the corresponding performance with accuracy. In short, a SFM may be too "crude" for some performance analysis purposes, but able to accurately capture sensitivity information for control purposes. This point of view is taken in [6], where a SFM is adopted for a single traffic class network node in which threshold-based buffer control is exercised. For the problem of determining a threshold (measured in packets or bytes) that minimizes a weighted sum of loss volume and buffer content, it is shown that a solution based on a SFM recovers or gives close approximations to the solution of the associated queueing model. Since solving such problems usually relies on gradient information, estimating the gradient of a given cost function with respect to key parameters, such as the aforementioned threshold, becomes an essential task. Perturbation Analysis (PA) methods [7], [8] are therefore suitable, if appropriately adapted to a SFM viewed as a discrete-event system [9]. This approach has been used in [10], where incoming traffic rates were the parameters of interest, and in [6], where threshold parameters are optimized to solve buffer control problems. In [6], in particular, it was shown that Infinitesimal Perturbation Analysis (IPA) yields remarkably simple *nonparametric* sensitivity estimators for packet loss and workload metrics with respect to threshold or buffer size parameters in a single-node SFM with a single incoming traffic stream. In addition, the estimators obtained are unbiased under very weak structural assumptions on the defining traffic processes.

The remainder of this paper presents the basic SFM framework and summarizes results obtained through PA methods for gradient estimation and optimization problems involving loss volume and workload levels in communication networks. Details on these results may be found in [6], [9], [11], [12].

2 The Stochastic Fluid Model (SFM)

We view a communication network as consisting of nodes, each of which may be represented through a SFM as shown in Fig. 1. There are two "classes" of traffic: controlled (class 1) and uncontrolled (class 2). Uncontrolled traffic has a time-varying arrival rate $\alpha_2(t)$. A threshold θ is associated with class 1 traffic, which has a time-varying arrival rate $\alpha_1(t)$. A control policy is exercised so that when the total buffer content reaches a threshold θ, class 1 traffic is rejected, while class 2 traffic is not affected. The two traffic streams share a common FIFO buffer which has a finite capacity $b > \theta$. The service rate is also time-varying and denoted by $\beta(t)$. In addition, let $\gamma_1(\theta; t)$ be the loss rate of class 1 when the buffer content exceeds the designated threshold level θ, and let $\gamma_2(\theta; t)$ be the loss rate of class 2 when the buffer content exceeds the buffer size b. Finally, $x(\theta; t)$ denotes the buffer content at time t. The notational dependence on θ indicates that we will analyze performance metrics as functions of the given θ. For simplicity, we have limited ourselves to two traffic classes, but the model is readily extended to more controlled classes, each with its own associated threshold.

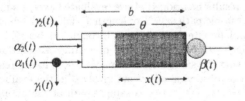

Figure 1: Stochastic Fluid Model (SFM) with two Traffic Classes

We are interested in studying sample paths of the SFM over a time interval $[0, T]$ for a given fixed $0 < T < \infty$. We assume that the processes $\{\alpha_1(t)\}$, $\{\alpha_2(t)\}$, and $\{\beta(t)\}$ are independent of θ (thus, we consider network settings operating with protocols such as ATM and UDP, but not TCP) and they are right-continuous piecewise continuously differentiable w.p.1.

Viewed as a discrete-event system, an *event* in a sample path of the above SFM may be either *exogenous* or *endogenous*. An exogenous event is any event that causes the difference function $[\alpha_1(t) + \alpha_2(t) - \beta(t)]$ or $[\alpha_2(t) - \beta(t)]$ to change sign. For our purposes, we identify the following exogenous events of interest: (e_1) an event where the buffer ceases to be empty, (e_2) an event where the buffer content leaves the value $x(\theta; t) = \theta$ after it has maintained it for some finite length of time, and (e_3) an event where the buffer content leaves the buffer limit b. An endogenous event is defined to occur whenever: (e_4) the buffer becomes empty, (e_5) the buffer content reaches the value $x(\theta; t) = \theta$ and then maintains it for some finite length of time, (e_6) the buffer content crosses the value $x(\theta; t) = \theta$ from either below or above, and (e_7) the buffer content reaches b. Observe that any exogenous event time is locally independent of θ, whereas any endogenous event time is generally a function of θ.

We assume that the real-valued parameter θ is confined to a closed and bounded (compact) interval Θ; to avoid unnecessary technical complications, we assume that $0 < \theta < b$ for all $\theta \in \Theta$. Let $\mathcal{L}(\theta) : \Theta \to \mathbb{R}$ be a random function defined over the underlying probability space $(\Omega, \mathcal{F}, P)$. Strictly speaking, we write $\mathcal{L}(\theta, \omega)$ to indicate that this sample function depends on the sample point $\omega \in \Omega$, but will suppress ω unless it is necessary to stress this fact. We consider three performance metrics, the *Loss Volume of Class 1*, $L_{1T}(\theta)$, the *Loss Volume of Class 2*, $L_{2T}(\theta)$, and the *Cumulative Workload* (or just *Work*) $Q_T(\theta)$, all defined on the interval $[0, T]$ as follows:

$$L_{iT}(\theta) = \int_0^T \gamma_i(\theta; t)dt, \quad i = 1, 2 \quad (1)$$

$$Q_T(\theta) = \int_0^T x(\theta; t)dt, \quad (2)$$

where, for simplicity, we assume that $x(\theta; 0) = 0$. We may then formulate optimization problems such as the determination of θ^* that minimizes a cost function of the form

$$J_T(\theta) = \frac{1}{T}E[Q_T(\theta)] + \frac{R}{T}\{E[L_{1T}(\theta)] + wE[L_{2T}(\theta)]\}$$

$$\equiv \frac{1}{T}J_Q(\theta) + \frac{R}{T}\{J_{1L}(\theta) + wJ_{2L}(\theta)\} \quad (3)$$

where R represents a rejection cost due to loss, and w is a weight factor to reflect the relative importance of class 1 and class 2 losses. In order to solve such problems, we rely on estimates of $dJ_{1L}(\theta)/d\theta$, $dJ_{2L}(\theta)/d\theta$ and $dJ_Q(\theta)/d\theta$ for use in stochastic gradient-based schemes. Henceforth we shall use the "prime" notation to denote derivatives with respect to θ.

3 Infinitesimal Perturbation Analysis (IPA) with respect to Threshold

Our objective is to estimate the derivatives $J'_{iL}(\theta)$, $J'_Q(\theta)$ through the sample derivatives $L'_{iT}(\theta)$ and $Q'_T(\theta)$ which are commonly referred to as the Infinitesimal Perturbation Analysis (IPA) estimators; comprehensive discussions of IPA and its applications can be found in [7], [8]. The IPA derivative-estimation technique computes the derivative of a sample function $\mathcal{L}(\theta)$ along an observed sample path ω.

In [6], the model of Fig. 1 was analyzed when there is a single controlled class (i.e., setting $\alpha_2(t) = 0$). In this case, only the loss $\gamma_1(\theta;t)$ is relevant, since the queue content is limited to $x(\theta;t) \leq \theta$. It has been shown that the expressions obtained for $L'_{1T}(\theta)$ and $Q'_T(\theta)$ are simple and nonparametric, i.e., they do not depend on any knowledge of underlying stochastic characteristics, including traffic and processing rates. Moreover, these estimators are shown to be unbiased under very mild technical conditions on the processes $\{\alpha_1(t)\}$ and $\{\beta(t)\}$. The following algorithm shows the simplicity of obtaining these estimates:

- Initialize a counter $\mathcal{C} := 0$ and a cumulative timer $\mathcal{T} := 0$.

- Initialize $\tau := 0$.

- If an overflow event is observed at time t and $\tau = 0$:

  - Set $\tau := t$

- If a busy period ends at time t and $\tau > 0$:

  - Set $\mathcal{C} := \mathcal{C} - 1$ and $\mathcal{T} := \mathcal{T} + (t - \tau)$
  - Reset $\tau := 0$.
  - If $t = T$, and $\tau > 0$:
      Set $\mathcal{C} := \mathcal{C} - 1$ and $\mathcal{T} := \mathcal{T} + (t - \tau)$.

The final values of $\mathcal{C}$ and $\mathcal{T}$ provide the IPA derivatives $L'_{1T}(\theta)$ and $Q'_T(\theta)$ respectively. We remark that the "overflow" and "end of busy period" events are readily observable during actual network operation: the former occurs when a packet is dropped and the latter when the queue content becomes empty. In addition, we point out once again that these estimates are independent of all underlying stochastic features, including traffic and processing rates.

In [11], the model of of Fig. 1 was analyzed with $b = \infty$. Compared to the nonparametric estimators derived for the single-class SFM in [6], the estimators in the two-class case generally depend on traffic rate information, but not on the stochastic characteristics of the arrival and service processes involved. They can once again be shown to be unbiased under mild technical conditions.

In [12], the analysis is further extended to include the case where the queue capacity b is finite. Interestingly, this model also captures the operation of the Differentiated Services (DS) protocol that has been proposed for supporting QoS requirements [13], [14], [15]. In a DS setting, packets arriving at a DS supporting domain are marked and aggregated into streams according to their classification. Subsequently, in all other nodes of the domain, all stream packets are treated according to that classification irrespective of the flow that they belong to. Thus, our model represents the handling of any one of the "assured forwarding" classes, where our two traffic classes correspond to different drop priorities; the uncontrolled stream corresponds to "green" packets which are dropped only if the total buffer capacity is exceeded, while the controlled stream corresponds to "yellow" packets which are dropped when the buffer exceeds a given threshold value θ. Otherwise, packets are treated alike.

4 Control and Performance Optimization

Based on the unbiased gradient estimates of $J'_{iL}(\theta)$, $J'_Q(\theta)$ in (3), optimization problems of this form can be solved using standard stochastic approximation algorithms (e.g., see [16]). The optimal threshold parameter, θ^*, may be determined through the iteration

$$\theta_{n+1} = \theta_n - \nu_n H_n(\theta_n, \omega_n^{SFM}), \qquad n = 0, 1, \dots \quad (4)$$

where $\{\nu_n\}$ is a step size sequence and $H_n(\theta_n, \omega_n^{SFM})$ is an estimate of $dJ_T/d\theta$ evaluated at $\theta = \theta_n$ and based on information obtained from a sample path of the SFM denoted by ω_n^{SFM}. In our case, the gradient estimator $H_n(\theta, \omega_n^{SFM})$ is the IPA estimator of $dJ_T/d\theta$ based on the results mentioned above, evaluated over a simulated sample path ω_n^{SFM} of length T, following which a control update is performed through (4) based on the value of $H_n(\theta, \omega_n^{SFM})$. The interesting observation here is that the same estimator may be used in the real system by observing all events involved in the evaluation of $H_n(\theta_n, \omega_n^{SFM})$ on a sample path of the actual system (denoted by ω_n^{DES}). Assuming that at these event times the arrival rates of both class 1 and class 2 traffic, as well as the service rate, are known (otherwise, they have to be measured on line), then the threshold parameter is updated as follows:

$$\theta_{n+1} = \theta_n - \nu_n H_n(\theta_n, \omega_n^{DES}), \qquad n = 0, 1, \dots \quad (5)$$

where the only difference from (4) is that data are obtained from ω_n^{DES} (a sample path of the "real" system) instead of ω_n^{SFM} (as sample path of the SFM which one can only simulate). In other words, the *form* of the IPA estimators is obtained by analyzing the system as a SFM, but the associated *values* are based on real data. Extensive numerical results on this approach may be found in [6], [11].

5 Network-wide Management

Ongoing research is geared towards the use of SFMs and IPA methods for network-wide control and optimization. This requires analyzing the effect of perturbation propagation across network nodes, each node modeled as shown in Fig. 1, with the ability to control incoming traffic while also accomodating interfering (uncontrolled) traffic that has originated elsewhere in the network. Thus, we envision an on-line network congestion control capability that does not require node decomposition and is general in the sense that it does not require knowledge of the traffic and service processes involved and only limited rate information. Towards the same goal, ongoing work is also considering how to develop IPA methods that include network feedback effects (i.e., allowing arriving traffic processes to depend on the buffer content in different ways) and how to allow for the possibility of packet processing other than through the usual first-in-first-out discipline.

References

[1] D. Anick, D. Mitra, and M. Sondhi, "Stochastic theory of a data-handling system with multiple sources," *The Bell System Technical Journal*, vol. 61, pp. 1871–1894, 1982.

[2] H. Kobayashi and Q. Ren, "A mathematical theory for transient analysis of communications networks," *IEICE Transactions on Communications*, vol. E75-B, pp. 1266–1276, 1992.

[3] G. Kesidis, A. Singh, D. Cheung, and W. W. Kwok, "Feasibility of fluid-driven simulation for ATM network," in *Proc. IEEE Globecom*, vol. 3, pp. 2013–2017, 1996.

[4] B. Liu, Y. Guo, J. Kurose, D. Towsley, and W. B. Gong, "Fluid simulation of large scale networks: Issues and tradeoffs," in *Proceedings of the International Conference on Parallel and Distributed Processing Techniques and Applications*, June 1999. Las Vegas, Nevada.

[5] A. Yan and W. Gong, "Fluid simulation for high-speed networks with flow-based routing," *IEEE Transactions on Information Theory*, vol. 45, pp. 1588–1599, 1999.

[6] C. G. Cassandras, Y. Wardi, B. Melamed, G. Sun, and C. G. Panayiotou, "Perturbation analysis for on-line control and optimization of stochastic fluid models," *IEEE Transactions on Automatic Control*, vol. AC-47, no. 8, pp. 1234–1248, 2002.

[7] Y. C. Ho and X. R. Cao, *Perturbation Analysis of Discrete Event Dynamic Systems*. Boston, Massachusetts: Kluwer Academic Publishers, 1991.

[8] C. G. Cassandras and S. Lafortune, *Introduction to Discrete Event Systems*. Kluwer Academic Publishers, 1999.

[9] Y. Wardi, B. Melamed, C. Cassandras, and C. Panayiotou, "IPA gradient estimators in single-node stochastic fluid models," *Journal of Optimization Theory and Applications*, 2001. To appear.

[10] Y. Liu and W. Gong, "Perturbation analysis for stochastic fluid queueing systems," in *Proc. 38th IEEE Conf. Dec. and Ctrl*, pp. 4440–4445, 1999.

[11] C. G. Cassandras, G. Sun, C. G. Panayiotou, and Y. Wardi, "Perturbation analysis of multiclass stochastic fluid models," in *Proceedings of 15th IFAC World Congress*, pp. 848–853, 2002.

[12] G. Sun, C. G. Cassandras, and C. G. Panayiotou, "Perturbation analysis of a multiclass stochastic fluid model with finite buffer capacity," in *Proceedings of 41st IEEE Conf. On Decision and Control*, 2002. To appear.

[13] S. Blake, D. Black, M. Carlson, E. Davies, Z. Wang, and W. Weiss, "An architecture for differentiated services," *RFC 2475*, Dec 1998. http://www.ietf.org/rfc/rfc2475.txt.

[14] J. Heinanen, F. Baker, W. Weiss, and J. Wroclawski, "Assured forwarding PHB group," *RFC 2597*, Jun 1999. http://www.ietf.org/rfc/rfc2597.txt.

[15] C. G. Panayiotou and C. G. Cassandras, "On-line predictive techniques for "differentiated services" networks," in *Proceedings IEEE Conference on Decision and Control*, pp. 4529–4534, Dec 2001.

[16] H. J. Kushner and D. S. Clark, *Stochastic Approximation for Constrained and Unconstrained Systems*. Berlin, Germany: Springer-Verlag, 1978.

Stochastic Process Algebra, Reversed Processes and Product-Forms

Peter G. Harrison

Department of Computing
Imperial College
180 Queen's Gate, London SW7 2BZ
England
Email: pgh@doc.ic.ac.uk

Abstract

The Stochastic Process Algebra (SPA) formalism for performance models of communicating systems is briefly reviewed, focussing on the subset of Markovian Process Algebra (MPA). MPA facilitates analytical solutions for equilibrium state probabilities, in principle, but direct methods are severely limited by the size of the state space. By considering the reversed process of a stationary Markov chain, product-forms are derived for the equilibrium state probabilities in stochastic networks defined by a collection of cooperating MPA agents. Key to the analysis is the property of compositionality. Under quite general conditions, the well known product-forms for networks of queues (Jackson's theorem) and G-networks (with both positive and negative customers) can be simply obtained. Two new product forms are also derived by systematically following this mechanical approach.

1 Introduction

The stochastic process algebra (SPA) formalism [9, 18, 1, 10, 17] describes both qualitative and quantitative aspects of communicating systems. In its Markovian subset, Markovian process algebra (MPA), e.g. [10, 17], all actions have an exponential duration, leading to a Markov model. A major *raison d'etre* of MPA is to facilitate a concise specification language from which the Markov state-transition graph can be generated mechanically and reliably. Hand-produced graphs for non-trivial systems are notoriously error-prone. However, very large state spaces can be generated for quite simple systems and the direct solution route therefore has limited value, although some important results have been obtained for state spaces of arbitrary structure [15, 16], using compositional minimisation and Markovian bisimulation [13], and via the Kronecker algebra [19]. Some transition graphs have special structures that facilitate efficient solutions, such as those of *product-form*. In general, it is difficult to establish that such structures exist, but if models are constructed in a certain hierarchical way, compositionality can be used to preserve the product-form properties of the constituent components [8, 20, 11, 2].

In section 2 Stochastic process algebra is motivated and a Markovian version, PEPA (Performance Evaluation Process Algebra, [10]), is defined. In Section 3 we briefly review the salient properties of reversed processes, as described in [14]. Section 4 states the Reversed Compound Agent Theorem (RCAT) that determines the reversed process of a certain type of cooperation between two agents [7], and hence a product-form for the stationary joint state probabilities. This theorem is applied to G-networks with triggers and resets in section 5 [3, 4, 5, 6]. These results are then extended with the introduction of negative triggers and more general resets. The paper concludes in Section 6 where we outline some directions for further work.

2 SPA and MPA

Stochastic process algebra (SPA) – see, for example, [9, 18, 1, 10, 17] – is a formalism developed over the last decade that can describe rigorously both the qualitative (functional) and quantitative (performance-related) behaviour of systems of interacting processes. The principal advantage of this algebraic approach to modelling is the property of *compositionality* possessed by all SPAs. This means that two or more fully specified systems can be combined together (as subsystems) into a more complex system in a simple way – both syntactically and semantically. The behaviours of the subsystems are not affected, except where they are explicitly connected to each other. Unfortunately, compositionality alone is, in general, insufficient to facilitate a hierarchical, inductive analysis of most properties. For example, absence of deadlock is not compositional in this sense. The practical advantage of compositionality is to precisely separate those properties which are local to the components of a system from those involved in interactions between them.

In the case of a Markovian process algebra, the Markov state-transition graph of a model can be computed, at least in principle, from which steady state probabilities and other quantities can be calculated by standard methods. However, this approach is intractable for state spaces of more than 10^8 states, which can describe only moderately complex systems. We therefore seek syntactic ways of identifying special structures in the Markov chain, leading in particlar to *product-form* solutions. We conduct our analysis using an abbreviated PEPA syntax, the full syntax and semantics of the PEPA language being given in [10]. We have just three constructions:

1. The prefix combinator defines an agent $(a, \lambda).P$ that carries out action (a, λ) of *type a* at *rate λ* and subsequently behaves as agent P.

2. The agent describing the cooperation of two agents P and Q which synchronise over actions with types in a specified set L is written $P \bowtie_L Q$.

3. A new *constant* agent A is defined by the assignment combinator $A \stackrel{\text{def}}{=} P$ to have the same behaviour as P.

Using this syntax, a *choice* (available in the full PEPA syntax) is expressed by multiple assignments:

$$A \stackrel{\text{def}}{=} P$$
$$A \stackrel{\text{def}}{=} Q$$

This is equivalent to $A \stackrel{\text{def}}{=} P + Q$ in conventional PEPA. Action hiding could easily be added to this syntax but will not be used in this paper.

In a cooperation $P \bowtie_L Q$, the agents P and Q proceed independently with any actions whose types do not occur in the cooperation set L. However, actions with types in L are only enabled in $P \bowtie_L Q$ when they are enabled in both P and Q. In standard PEPA, the shared action occurs at the rate of the slowest participant. Here, however, we require that for each action type in a cooperation set L, exactly one agent (either P or Q) is *passive* and effectively its synchronising action has rate $\top = \infty$. This means that the passive agent does not influence the rate at which a shared action occurs, essentially waiting for the other agent. This is not an undue restriction since choosing the slowest rate from a pair of active actions (with specified finite rates) is rarely meaningful. In a true synchronisation, the duration of the shared action is the longer of the two actions' durations in the cooperating agents. The mean value of this time is always *greater* than the maximum of the two constituent mean durations and only becomes a good approximation when one duration is much greater than the other. The probability distribution function of the joint action time is also not exponential but the product of the constituent exponential distribution functions. We call an agent defined using only assignments and prefixes *simple* and *compound* if it contains at least one instance of the cooperation combinator.

The set of actions which an agent P may next engage in – the *current actions* of P – is denoted by $Act(P)$, which can be defined inductively over the structure of P. When the system is behaving as agent P, these are the actions that are enabled. The states thus resulting from P are called the *derivatives* of P. If P can perform the action (a, λ) and then become P', we write $P \xrightarrow{(a,\lambda)} P'$ and say that P' is an *a-derivative* of P. The *derivative set*, denoted $ds(P)$, of an agent P is the transitive closure of all its derivatives and is defined by recursion. This defines a labelled transition system as a semantic model for PEPA. The *derivation graph*, formed by syntactic PEPA terms at the nodes, with arcs representing the transitions between them, determines the underlying Markov process of an agent P. The *transition rate* between two agents C_i and C_j, denoted $q(C_i, C_j)$, is the sum of the action rates labelling arcs connecting node C_i to node C_j.

The prefix combinator can describe every instantaneous transition rate between any two states of a Markov chain, and hence is sufficient alone to define *any* Markov chain. However, such specifications are usually no simpler than state transition matrices or graphs, and so we use the cooperation construct to facilitate hierarchical specifications. To clarify its usage, suppose an action with type $a \in L$ is active in P and passive in Q. It may be enabled in any of a subset of the states of P and Q; possibly in *every* state of P

13

and/or Q. For example, if P and Q represent queues, a might represent a departure from queue-P (enabled in every state of P with non-zero queue length) and an arrival to queue-Q (enabled in every state of Q). We denote reversed entities with an overbar.

3 Reversed Processes

A stochastic process $\{X_t \mid -\infty < t < \infty\}$ is *stationary* if $(X_{t_1}, X_{t_2}, \ldots, X_{t_n})$ and $(X_{t_1+\tau}, X_{t_2+\tau}, \ldots, X_{t_n+\tau})$ have the same probability distribution for all times $t_1, t_2, \ldots, t_n$ and τ. The reversed process of $\{X_t\}$ is the (necessarily) stationary process $\{X_{\tau-t}\}$ for any real number τ. It is straightforward to find the reversed process of a stationary Markov process if the stationary state probabilities are known.

Proposition 1 *The reversed process of a stationary Markov process $\{X_t\}$ with state space S, generator matrix Q and stationary probabilities π is a stationary Markov process with generator matrix Q' defined by*

$$q'_{ij} = \pi_j q_{ji}/\pi_i \quad (i, j \in S)$$

and with the same stationary probabilities π.

This proposition is standard, see for example [14], and immediately yields a product-form solution for π. This is because, in an irreducible Markov process, we may choose a reference state 0 arbitrarily, find a sequence of connected states, in either the forward or reversed process, $0, \ldots, j$ (i.e. with either $q_{i,i+1} > 0$ or $q'_{i,i+1} > 0$ for $0 \le i \le j-1$) for any state j and calculate

$$\pi_j = \pi_0 \prod_{i=0}^{j-1} \frac{q_{i,i+1}}{q'_{i+1,i}} = \pi_0 \prod_{i=0}^{j-1} \frac{q'_{i,i+1}}{q_{i+1,i}}$$

Proposition 1 opens up the possibility of computing the stationary probabilities using only the reversed rates and, in fact, it is possible to determine the q'_{ij} without recourse to first calculating π.

Proposition 2 *A stationary Markov process with state space S and generator matrix Q has reversed process with generator matrix Q' if and only if*

1. *$\sum_{\substack{j \ne i \\ i \in S}} q'_{ij} = q'_i = q_i = \sum_{j \ne i} q_{ij}$ for every state*

2. *For every finite sequence of states $i_1, i_2, \ldots, i_n \in S$,*

$$q_{i_1 i_2} q_{i_2 i_3} \cdots q_{i_{n-1} i_n} q_{i_n i_1} = q'_{i_1 i_n} q'_{i_n i_{n-1}} \cdots q'_{i_3 i_2} q'_{i_2 i_1}$$

This proposition, an extension of Kolmogorov's criteria for reversible processes [14], is proved in [7]. It can be used to find reversed rates in simple Markov processes and is the crux of the proof of the main theorem used in this paper, a compositional result for constructing reversed processes in a Markovian process algebra.

4 The RCAT

The key result, used extensively in this paper to derive product-forms, is that the reversed agent of a cooperation between two agents P and Q is a cooperation between the reversed agents of P and Q, after some re-parameterisation, under appropriate conditions. This result, derived in [7], is stated in the Reversed Compound Agent Theorem 1 (RCAT), below. We denote the subset of action types in a set L which are *passive* with respect to a process P (i.e. are of the form $(a, \top)$ in P) by $\mathcal{P}_P(L)$ and the subset of corresponding active action types by $\mathcal{A}_P(L) = L \setminus \mathcal{P}_P(L)$.

Theorem 1 *Suppose that the cooperation $P \underset{L}{\bowtie} Q$ has a derivation graph with an irreducible subgraph G. Given that*

1. *every passive action type in L is always enabled (i.e. enabled in all states of the transition graph);*

2. *every reversed action of an active action type in L is always enabled;*

3. *every occurrence of a reversed action of an active action type in $\mathcal{A}_P(L)$ (respectively $\mathcal{A}_Q(L)$) has the same rate in $\overline{P}$ (respectively $\overline{Q}$).*

the reversed agent $\overline{P \underset{L}{\bowtie} Q}$, with derivation graph containing the reversed subgraph $\overline{G}$, is

$$\overline{R}\{(\overline{a}, \overline{p_a}) \leftarrow (\overline{a}, \top) \mid a \in \mathcal{A}_P(L)\} \underset{L}{\bowtie}$$
$$\overline{S}\{(\overline{a}, \overline{q_a}) \leftarrow (\overline{a}, \top) \mid a \in \mathcal{A}_Q(L)\}$$

where

$$R = P\{\top_a \leftarrow x_a \mid a \in \mathcal{P}_P(L)\}$$
$$S = Q\{\top_a \leftarrow x_a \mid a \in \mathcal{P}_Q(L)\}$$

$\{x_a\}$ are the solutions (for $\{\top_a\}$) of the equations

$$\top_a = \overline{q_a} \qquad a \in \mathcal{P}_P(L)$$
$$\top_a = \overline{p_a} \qquad a \in \mathcal{P}_Q(L)$$

and $\overline{p_a}$ (respectively $\overline{q_a}$) is the symbolic rate of action type $\overline{a}$ in $\overline{P}$ (respectively $\overline{Q}$).

14

The proof of the theorem establishes Kolmogorov's criteria and is given in full in [7].

The enablement of action types is easily checked in each cooperating agent (conditions 1 and 2). The reversed processes of these agents is assumed known and so the reversed rate associated with each instance of a passive action (in its own participating agent) can be determined and checked if it is a constant (condition 3). The equations for the x_a can therefore be posed and the theorem applied. In an agent with a bundle of multiple transitions between two states, the reversed rate of the aggregate (summed) transition is distributed amongst the reversed arcs in proportion to the forward transition rates. Formally, we have:

Definition 1 *The reversed actions of multiple actions* (a_i, λ_i) *for* $1 \le i \le n$ *that an agent* P *can perform, which lead to the same derivative* Q, *are respectively*

$$(\overline{a_i}, (\lambda_i/\lambda)\overline{\lambda}))$$

where $\lambda = \lambda_1 + \ldots + \lambda_n$ *and* $\overline{\lambda}$ *is the reversed rate of the one-step, composite transition with rate* λ *in the Markov chain, corresponding to all the arcs between* P *and* Q.

This definition is needed to handle components that can either proceed independently or cooperate in a transition between the same two component-states. For example, a service completion at a queue can cause either an external departure or the transfer of a customer to another queue.

5 Gelenbe networks

We represent a single M/M/1 queue with negative customers (called a G-queue) by a normal M/M/1 queue with arrival rate λ^+ (that of the positive arrivals) and service rate $\mu + \lambda^-$ where μ is the usual rate of service and λ^- is the negative arrival rate. In other words, we split the departure arc from a busy queue into a 'service' component and a 'negative arrival' component. The reversed queue, with aggregated arrival streams, is then the same M/M/1 queue with arrival rate λ^+ and service rate $\mu + \lambda^-$. In this model, when the queue length is zero, we represent a negative arrival by an 'invisible' transition from state 0 to itself, with arbitrary rate, e.g. zero. In other words, negative arrivals to empty queues have no effect whilst still being enabled. The same invisible transitions will occur in the reversed process, which remains identical to the forward process.

In a network of G-queues, customers completing service normally at a node i may pass to a node j, as either a positive or a negative customer, with respective probabilities p_{ij}^+ or p_{ij}^-, or else leave the network. The generic single G-queue, for use in a network, and its reversed queue – identical apart from a redistribution of rates – is as shown in Fig. 1. Departures from the queue shown go to another queue with probability p (p^+ if positive, p^- if negative, $p^+ + p^- = p$) or leave the network with probability $1 - p$. External (positive) arrivals have rate λ_e^+ and arrivals from other queues have rate λ_i^+. Depending on the number of links to/from other queues, the rates λ_i^+, μp^+ and μp^- will have to be split further.

Gelenbe introduced 'triggers' in [5] as a generalisation of the concept of negative customers. A trigger is a negative customer that moves a (positive) customer to node j on arrival at node i with probability q_{ij}^+, with no effect on an empty queue. We call these *positive* triggers and extend this idea to include *negative* triggers also. On arrival at node i, a trigger may be either positive or negative. A negative trigger removes a (positive) customer and sends a *trigger* to node j with probability q_{ij}^-. We write $q_{ij} = q_{ij}^+ + q_{ij}^-$, so that the probability of a trigger being positive is $\sum_j q_{ij}^+$, negative is $\sum_j q_{ij}^-$ and a conventional negative customer is $1 - \sum_j q_{ij}$.

5.1 Generalised G-networks

We can try to apply the RCAT to any cooperation between two components defined on a flat state space (i.e. with no cooperations in these components); if its conditions are satisfied, there will be a product-form solution for an ergodic process. Starting with a pair of birth-death processes on the non-negative integers (e.g. the M/M/1 queue) suppose we split the arrival and departure streams, causing unit increments and decrements in the state respectively, so that a departure sub-stream cooperates with an arrival sub-stream in the other component, causing (internal) arrivals there, as well as departures locally. Now suppose that an internal arrival to (generalised) queue $m = 1, 2$ in local state i causes a state change $i \rightarrow j$ with probability $r_{m;ij}$, where $\sum_j r_{m;ij} = 1$ for all states i. Thus, $r_{m;ij} = \delta_{i+1,j}$ (the Kronecker-delta) defines a conventional queueing network, and $r_{m;ij} = \alpha_m \delta_{i+1,j} + (1 - \alpha_m)\delta_{i-1,j}$ can define a conventional G-network for appropriate choices of α_m, where we define $\delta_{-1,j} = \delta_{0j}$. Triggers can be incorporated similarly.

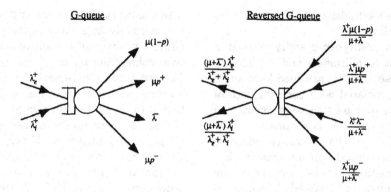

Figure 1: G-queue network node and its reversed queue

We consider an internal arrival in local state i of queue 1 (without loss of generality) to cause a transition to an *inserted state*, i' say, which transits to state j with probability $r_{1;ij}$. The first condition of the RCAT is always satisfied with the above definition of the $r_{1;ij}$ since they sum to 1 over j for all states i and so at least one is positive. The transition to the inserted state is therefore enabled. Condition 2 is satisfied if there are only cooperations in which departures, i.e. transitions that decrement the state, are active. In the reversed process, these become arrivals (state increments), which are always enabled.

It remains to check Condition 3, without loss of generality for queue 1. We assume that a departure (unit state-decrement) occurs with total instantaneous rate $\mu_1 + \lambda_1^-$, arising from a pair of transitions between every pair of states $i+1 \to i$, one transition of which cooperates with queue 2 and has active rate λ_1^-, the other representing a local departure at rate μ_1. Obviously we could also include conventional departures from queue 1 to queue 2 by further splitting the departure arc in the state transition graph. The reversed rates on the departure arcs are not at all obvious in this generalised queue, which is certainly not reversible. Since μ_1 and λ_1^- are constants, Condition 3 holds if and only if the reversed rate $q'_{i,i+1}$ of the double departure transition $i+1 \to i$ with rate $q_{i+1,i} = \mu_1 + \lambda_1^-$ is the same for all $i \geq 0$. Now, by Proposition 1, assuming the process is stationary, $q'_{i,i+1} = (\mu_1 + \lambda_1^-)\pi_{i+1}/\pi_i$. Hence Condition 3 holds if and only if π_{i+1}/π_i is constant, i.e. $\pi_i = \rho^i\pi_0$ for all $i \geq 0$ and some $\rho < 1$. In other words, we require a geometric equilibrium probability distribution for the local state space probabilities. It is straightforward to generalise this result to networks with an arbitrary number of nodes of this type.

Of course, the special cases of regular Jackson networks [12] and G-networks are known to satisfy the

above required property, but these networks are not unique in this. For example, consider a stationary generalised queue in which

$$r_{1;ij} = \delta_{i-1,j} \quad \text{if } i > 0$$
$$r_{1;0j} = \pi_j$$

where π_j is the equilibrium probability for state j. Then it can be shown, for example by direct solution of the balance equations, that

$$\pi_j = (1 - \rho_1)\rho_1^j$$

where $\rho_1 = \lambda_1^+/\mu_1$ and λ_1^+ is the external (positive) arrival rate. This result was derived by Fourneau and Gelenbe in [6], where the authors called this particular type of cooperating departure a *reset* since, on encountering an empty queue, a negative customer 'resets the queue to its steady state' rather than decrementing it, as when encountering non-empty queues. Resets therefore preserve the product-form solution of G-networks by the RCAT. Moreover, there are likely to be other birth-death processes with geometric stationary state distributions that would similarly yield product-form solutions through the RCAT.

It is also interesting to observe that, if a generalised queue does not cooperate actively with another, it does not violate Condition 3. Hence, assuming the other queues satisfy it, there is still a product-form regardless of the choice of $r_{1;ij}$. This is not entirely surprising since such a queue would then be largely detached from the rest of the network, acting essentially as a sink.

6 Conclusion

The use of Markovian Process Algebra and the RCAT of [7] introduces an entirely new approach to deriving the equilibrium state probabilities in separable Markov processes. This approach does not require balance equations to be solved but instead determines the reversed process whence a simple product-form solution ensues. The origins of the RCAT and the methodology based on it lie in a combination of MPA and the theory of reversed stationary processes. The presentation here has not used an MPA formalism explicitly, since a queueing network description is clearer to the human reader, but PEPA specifications are isomorphic and would be used for a mechanical implementation of the analysis and synthesis of product-forms.

The new approach identifies many known product-forms in a unified way, exemplified in this paper by the derivation of the solution of complex G-networks with triggers and resets. Moreover, significant new product-forms have been obtained, including extensions of G-networks to negative triggers and generalised resets, as well as, elsewhere (unpublished), a task-spawning arrival process.

By incorporating this methodology into a suitable support environment for process algebras, the derivation of many product-form theorems could be automated and new ones derived in a unified stochastic modelling framework.

References

[1] M. Bernardo and R. Gorrieri. A tutorial on EMPA: A theory of concurrent processes with nondeterminism, priorities, probabilities and time. *Theoretical Computer Science*, 202:1–54, 1998.

[2] G. Clark and J. Hillston. Product form solution for an insensitive stochastic process algebra structure. *Performance Evaluation*, 2002.

[3] E. Gelenbe. Random neural networks with positive and negative signals and product form solution. *Neural Computation*, 1(4):502–510, 1989.

[4] E. Gelenbe. Queueing networks with negative and positive customers. *Journal of Applied Probability*, 28:656–663, 1991.

[5] E. Gelenbe. G-networks with triggered customer movement. *Journal of Applied Probability*, 30:742–748, 1993.

[6] E. Gelenbe and J-M. Fourneau. G-networks with resets. In *Proceedings of PERFORMANCE '02*, Rome, 2002.

[7] Peter G Harrison. Turning Back Time in Markovian Process Algebra. *Theoretical Computer Science*, 2002, to appear.

[8] P.G. Harrison and J. Hillston. Exploiting quasi-reversible structures in Markovian process algebra models. *The Computer Journal*, 38(7):510–520, 1995.

[9] Peter G Harrison and Ben Strulo. Spades–a process algebra for discrete event simulation. *Journal of Logic and Computation*, 10(1):3–42, 2000.

[10] J. Hillston. *A Compositional Approach to Performance Modelling*. PhD thesis, University of Edinburgh, 1994.

[11] J. Hillston and N. Thomas. Product form solution for a class of PEPA models. *Performance Evaluation*, 35(3-4):171–192, 1999.

[12] J.R. Jackson. Jobshop-like queueing systems. *Management Science*, 10(1):131–142, 1963.

[13] J.P. Katoen. Markovian bisimulation. *Science of Computer Programming*, 202:1–54, 2000.

[14] F.P. Kelly. *Reversibility and Stochastic Networks*. Wiley, 1979.

[15] William Knottenbelt, Peter Harrison, Mark Mestern and Pieter Kritzinger. A Probabilistic Dynamic Technique for the Distributed Generation of Very Large State Spaces. *Performance Evaluation Journal*, 39(1-4):127–148, 2000.

[16] William Knottenbelt and Peter Harrison. Distributed Disk-based Solution Techniques for Large Markov Models. In *Proceedings of 3rd Int. Conference on the Numerical Solution of Markov Chains, NSMC '99*, pages 58–75, Zaragoza, September1999.

[17] N. Goetz, U. Herzog and M. Rettelbach. Multiprocessor and distributed system design: The integration of functional specification and performance analysis using stochastic process algebras. In *Proceedings of PERFORMANCE '93*, pages 121–146, Rome, 1993. Springer-Verlag, LNCS 729.

[18] J.P. Katoen P. D'Argenio and E. Brinksma. General purpose discrete event simulation using ♠. In *Proceedings of PAPM 1998*, pages 85–102, Nice, July 1998.

[19] B. Plateau and W. Stewart. Kronecker Algebra. *J. Assoc. Comput. Mach.*, 45(2):x–y, 1998.

[20] M. Sereno. Towards a product form solution for stochastic process algebras. *The Computer Journal*, 38(7):622–632, 1995.

Static scheduling strategies for heterogeneous systems

O. Beaumont
LaBRI, UMR CNRS 5800
Bordeaux, France
Olivier.Beaumont@labri.fr

A. Legrand and Y. Robert
LIP, UMR CNRS-INRIA 5668
ENS Lyon, France
{Arnaud.Legrand, Yves.Robert} @ens-lyon.fr

Abstract

In this paper, we consider static scheduling techniques for heterogeneous systems, such as clusters and grids. We successively deal with minimum makespan scheduling divisible load scheduling and steady-state scheduling. Finally, we discuss the limitations of static scheduling approaches.

1 Introduction

Scheduling computational tasks on a given set of processors is a key issue for high-performance computing. Although a large number of scheduling heuristics have been presented in the literature, most of them target only homogeneous resources. However, future computing systems, such as the computational grid, are most likely to be widely distributed and strongly heterogeneous. In this paper, we consider the impact of heterogeneity on the design and analysis of static scheduling techniques: how to enhance these techniques to efficiently address cluster and grid computing?

2 Minimum makespan scheduling

2.1 Framework

The traditional objective of scheduling algorithms is the following: given a task graph and a set of computing resources, find a mapping of the tasks onto the processors, and order the execution of the tasks so that: (i) task precedence constraints are satisfied; (ii) resource constraints are satisfied; and (ii) a minimum schedule length is provided.

Task graph scheduling is usually studied using the so-called *macro-dataflow* model, which is widely used in the scheduling literature. This model was introduced for homogeneous processors, and has been (straightforwardly) extended for heterogeneous computing resources. In a word,

there is a limited number of computing resources, or processors, to execute the tasks. Communication delays are taken into account as follows: let task T be a predecessor of task T' in the task graph; if both tasks are assigned to the same processor, no communication overhead is paid, the execution of T' can start right at the end of the execution of T; on the contrary, if T and T' are assigned to two different processors P_i and P_j, a communication delay is paid. More precisely, if P_i finishes the execution of T at time-step t, then P_j cannot start the execution of T' before time-step $t+\mathrm{comm}(T, T', P_i, P_j)$, where $\mathrm{comm}(T, T', P_i, P_j)$ is the communication delay, which depends upon both tasks T and T' and both processors P_i and P_j. Because memory accesses are typically one order of magnitude cheaper than inter-processor communications, it makes good sense to neglect them when T and T' are assigned to the same processor.

However, the major flaw of the macro-dataflow model is that communication resources are not limited. First, a processor can send (or receive) any number of messages in parallel, hence an unlimited number of communication ports is assumed (this explains the name *macro-dataflow* for the model). Second, the number of messages that can simultaneously circulate between processors is not bounded, hence an unlimited number of communications can simultaneously occur on a given link. In other words, the communication network is assumed to be contention-free, which of course is not realistic as soon as the processor number exceeds a few units.

2.2 Communication-aware models

Communication-aware models restrict the use of communication links in various manners. In the model proposed by Sinnen and Sousa [9], the underlying communication network is no longer fully-connected. There are a limited number of communication links, and each processor is provided with a routing table which specifies the links to be used to communicate with an other processor (hence the routing is fully static). The major modification is that at most one message can circulate on one link at a given time-step, so that contention for communication resources is taken into account.

Similarly, Hollermann et al. [7] and Hsu et al. [8] target networks of processors and introduce the following model: each processor can either send or receive a message at a given time-step (bidirectional communication is not possible); also, there is a fixed latency between the initiation of the communication by the sender and the beginning of the reception by the receiver. This model is rather close to the one-port model discussed below. Note that the extended version of this paper [2] contains many additional bibliographical references.

2.3 The one-port model

In this model, at a given time-step, any processor can communicate with at most another processor in both directions: sending to *and* receiving from another processor. The model also assumes communication/computation overlap. Several communications can occur in parallel, provided that they involve disjoint pairs of sending/receiving processors, which nicely models switches like Myrinet that can implement permutations, or even multiplexed bus architectures.

Serializing communications performed by the processors has a dramatic impact on the scheduling makespan. In fact, the one-port model turns out to be computationally even more difficult than the macro-dataflow model: scheduling a simple fork graph with an unlimited number of homogeneous processors is NP-hard [1]. Note that this problem has polynomial complexity in the macro-dataflow model; we have to resort to fork-join graphs to get NP-completeness in the macro-dataflow model [6].

Several heuristics have been introduced to deal with different-speed processors (see [2] for a comparison). Among them, the *Heterogeneous Earliest Finish Time* (HEFT) heuristic [10]. is a natural extension of list-scheduling heuristics to cope with heterogeneous resources. HEFT has been extended in [1] to fulfill the constraints of the one-port model. Furthermore, a new heuristic was introduced in [1], whose main characteristic is a better load-balancing at each decision step. This is achieved by considering a chunk of several ready tasks rather than a single one; the idea is to allocate to each processor a number of the tasks in the chunk whose overall processing time is proportional to its computing power.

Replacing the macro-dataflow by the one-port model is a first step towards designing realistic scheduling heuristics for heterogeneous clusters. However, such heuristics strongly depend upon an accurate knowledge of the whole task graph before execution, and they tend to require a precise estimation of the task and communication weights, which may limit their applicability to very regular problems

arising from dense linear algebra, digital signal processing or multi-media applications.

3 Steady-state scheduling

In this section we deal with large problems. In this context an absolute minimization of the total execution time is not really required. Indeed, deriving asymptotically optimal schedules is more than enough to ensure an efficient use of the architectural resources. In a word, the idea to reach asymptotic optimality is to relax the problem: (i) neglect the initialization and clean-up phases, and concentrate on steady-state operation; (ii) derive an optimal steady-state scheduling using linear programming; and (iii) prove the asymptotic optimality of the associated schedule.

3.1 Packet routing

The packet routing problem is the following: let $G = (V, E)$ be a non-oriented graph modeling the target architectural platform, and consider a set of same-size packets to be routed through the network. Each packet is characterized by a source node (where it initially resides) and a destination node (where it must be located in the end). For each pair of nodes (v_k, v_l) in G, let n_{kl} be the number of packets to be routed from v_k to v_l. Let $\mathcal{P} = \{(k, l) \in V^2, \ n_{kl} \neq 0\}$. Bertsimas and Gamarnik [3] introduce a scheduling algorithm which is asymptotically optimal when $n = \sum_{(k,l) \in \mathcal{P}} n_{kl} \to +\infty$. So to speak, temporal constraints have been removed in this algorithm: it is never written than a packet must have reached a node before leaving it.

Consider an arbitrary scheduling and let x_{ij}^{kl} be the number of packets circulating from v_k to v_l and using the edge (the communication link) between v_i and v_j, $\forall (i, j) \in E$, $\forall (k, l) \in \mathcal{P}$. The time needed to circulate a packet on any edge is assumed to be constant (equal to 1), but at most one packet can circulate on one edge at a given time-step. We obtain the following *relaxed* linear program:

$\textsc{Minimize} C_{\max}$,
$\textsc{subject to}$
$$\begin{cases} (1) \ \sum_{i,(k,i) \in E} x_{ki}^{kl} = n_{kl} & \forall (k,l) \in \mathcal{P} \\ (2) \ \sum_{i,(i,l) \in E} x_{il}^{kl} = n_{kl} & \forall (k,l) \in \mathcal{P} \\ (3) \ \sum_{j,(j,i) \in E} x_{ji}^{kl} = \\ \quad \sum_{r,(i,r) \in E} x_{ir}^{kl} & \forall (k,l) \in \mathcal{P}, \forall i \neq k, l \\ (4) \ C_{i,j} = \sum_{(k,l) \in \mathcal{P}} x_{ij}^{kl} & \forall (i,j) \in E \\ (5) \ C_{i,j} \leq C_{\max}, & \forall (i,j) \in E \\ (6) \ x_{ij}^{kl} \geq 0, \ C_{i,j} \geq 0, & \forall (k,l) \in \mathcal{P}, (i,j) \in E \end{cases}$$

The first two equations state that the number of packets of type (k, l) that leave node k and reach node l is n_{kl}. Equation (3) is the conservation law (conservation of the number of packets) at node i. Equation (4) defines the total occupation time of edge (i, j)., and equation (5) states that all these occupation times minor the makespan $C_{\max}$. Note that all temporal constraints have been left out, hence the name *relaxed*.

The solution of this linear program with $O(|E||P|)$ rational variables and $O(|V||P| + |E|)$ constraints can be obtained in polynomial time. The complexity does not depend on n, the total number of packets, which justifies its use when n is large. Now, to construct the actual scheduling, we split the execution into phases, and we reproduce a "rounded" version of the relaxed solution during each phases. Let Ω be the length of a phase (to be determined later) and let $a_{ij}^{kl} = \lfloor \frac{x_{ij}^{kl}\Omega}{C_{\max}} \rfloor$, $\forall (k, l) \in \mathcal{P}$, $(i, j) \in E$, be the number of packets (rounded from below) of type (k, l) which circulate on the edge (i, j) during Ω time-steps in the relaxed problem. The algorithm proposed in [3] is the following:

Input Compute the optimal value $C_{\max}$ from the relaxed linear program.

Step 1 During each phase $[l\Omega, (l + 1)\Omega]$, where $l = 0, \ldots, \lceil \frac{C_{\max}}{\Omega} \rceil - 1$, and for each edge $(i, j) \in E$, circulate on the edge as many packets of type (k, l) as available in node i at time $l\Omega$, but no more than a_{ij}^{kl}.

Step 2 At time-step $T = \lceil \frac{C_{\max}}{\Omega} \rceil \Omega$, all the packets that have not been fully routed are handled sequentially.

It can be proven that at time-step

$$(\frac{C_{\max}}{\Omega} + 1)\Omega + |E||V|(\frac{C_{\max}|P|}{\Omega} + |P| + \Omega),$$

all the packets have successfully been routed. The proof sketch is as follows. First the previous scheduling is shown feasible (during each phase, all the packets can indeed be transmitted). Next, at the end of Step 1, whose length is not larger than $(\frac{C_{\max}}{\Omega} + 1)\Omega$, the number of packets that have nor reached their destination is bounded by $|E|(\frac{C_{\max}|P|}{\Omega} + |P| + \Omega)$. These packets are routed sequentially on a path of length at most $|V|$, hence the duration of Step 2 is not larger than $|E||V|(\frac{C_{\max}|P|}{\Omega} + |P| + \Omega)$. If we choose Ω of the order of $\sqrt{C_{\max}}$, the makespan of the schedule is $C_{\max} + O(\sqrt{C_{\max}})$, hence the asymptotic optimality.

3.2 Mixed task/data parallelism

We consider here applications that consist of a suite of identical, independent problems to be solved. In turn, each problem consists of a set of tasks, with dependences between these tasks. A typical example is the repeated execution of the same algorithm on several distinct data samples: the task graph of the algorithm is executed several times, one for each problem instance. The application is executed using the master-slave paradigm: one particular processor holds (or produces) all the data that is initially needed. Tasks (or more precisely data files associated to them) are distributed to, and executed by, the other processors (the slaves). Note that different copies of the same task type (corresponding to different problem instances) may well be executed by different processors.

The objective is to derive an efficient scheme for the distribution and the scheduling of the tasks to the processors. We use the following notations:

- The task graph is $G = (T, C)$. Each vertex T_k represents a task type to be executed, and each edge $(T_k \rightarrow T_l)$ represents a communication between two tasks, and is weighted by $data_{k,l}$, the volume of communication to be exchanged (think of each edge as been associated to a file of type (k, l) to by sent from T_k to T_l).

- The platform graph is $G' = (P, L)$. Vertices represent computing resources and edges represent communication links. Each edge in L is weighted $c_{i,j}$, the time needed to transfer one data unit on the link from P_i to P_j.

- The time needed to execute (any copy of) task T_k on processor P_i is $w_{i,k}$. The time needed to communicate one file of type (k, l) (related to the edge from T_k to T_l in the task graph) along the communication link from P_i to P_j in the platform graph is $c_{i,j} \times data_{k,l}$

- We use the full-overlap one-port model of Section 2.3: at a given time-step, a processor can simultaneously execute a task, receive a message (at most one) and send a message (at most one).

This model is quite general, and deriving a minimum makespan schedule is hopeless. As in Section 3.1, we introduce a relaxed problem, which characterizes the optimal steady-state operation, i.e. the maximal throughput (total number of tasks executed per time-unit). We use the following notations:

- $s(P_i, P_j, T_k, T_l)$ is the fraction of time spent each time-unit by P_i to send to P_j data involved by the edge (T_k, T_l) of the task graph. Similarly, $\text{Sent}(P_i, P_j, T_k, T_l)$ is the number of data files of this type sent along the edge (P_i, P_j) per time-unit, with $s(P_i, P_j, T_k, T_l) = \text{Sent}(P_i, P_j, T_k, T_l) * data_{k,l} * c_{i,j}$.

- $\alpha(P_i, T_k)$ is the fraction of time spent each time-unit by P_i to compute tasks of type T_k. Similarly, $\text{Cons}(P_i, T_k)$ is the number of tasks of this type consumed by P_i each time-unit, with $\alpha(P_i, T_k) = \text{Cons}(P_i, T_k) * wi, k$.

20

- Finally, we add two fictitious tasks T_{begin} and T_{end} to the task graph. T_{begin} is the predecessor of all input tasks in G (tasks without any predecessor in G). The execution time of T_{begin} by any processor is equal to 0, and the communication volume along any edge from T_{begin} to an input task is also 0. Similarly, T_{end} is the successor of all output tasks in G.

Let P_{ms} be the master processor, and let $n(P_i)$ be the set of the neighbors of P_i in the platform graph. The following linear program summarizes the equations governing the activity of the processors and of the communication links within one time-unit, as well as conservation laws for each task file and each data file type:

MAXIMIZE $\sum_i \text{Cons}(P_i, T_{\text{end}})$,
SUBJECT TO
(1) $\forall i, \forall k, \quad 0 \leq \alpha(P_i, T_k) \leq 1$
(2) $\forall i, j, k, l, \quad 0 \leq s(P_i, P_j, T_k, T_l) \leq 1$
(3) $\forall i, j, k, l, \quad s(P_i, P_j, T_k, T_l) =$
$\qquad\qquad \text{Sent}(P_i, P_j, T_k, T_l) * data_{k,l} * c_{i,j}$
(4) $\forall i, k, \quad \alpha(P_i, T_k) = \text{Cons}(P_i, T_k) * wi, k$
(5) $\forall i, \quad \sum_{P_j \in n(P_i)} \sum_{(k,l) \in C} s(P_i, P_j, T_k, T_l) \leq 1$
(6) $\forall i, \quad \sum_{P_j \in n(P_i)} \sum_{(k,l) \in C} s(P_j, P_i, T_k, T_l) \leq 1$
(7) $\forall i, \quad \sum_{T_k \in T} \alpha(P_i, T_k) \leq 1$
(8) $\forall i, \quad \text{Cons}(P_i, T_{\text{begin}}) = 0$
(9) $\forall i, j, k, \quad s(P_i, P_j, T_k, T_{\text{END}}) = 0$
(10) $\forall i, k, l,$
$\sum_{P_j \in n(P_i)} \text{Sent}(P_j, P_i, T_k, T_l) + \text{Cons}(P_i, T_k) =$
$\quad \sum_{P_j \in n(P_i)} \text{Sent}(P_i, P_j, T_k, T_l) + \text{Cons}(P_i, T_l)$
(11) $\forall i, k \neq \text{begin}, l,$
$\sum_{P_j \in n(P_{\text{ms}})} \text{Sent}(P_j, P_{\text{ms}}, T_k, T_l) + \text{Cons}(P_{\text{ms}}, T_k) =$
$\quad \sum_{P_j \in n(P_{\text{ms}})} \text{Sent}(P_{\text{ms}}, P_j, T_k, T_l) + \text{Cons}(P_{\text{ms}}, T_l)$

The objective function is equal to the number of copies of task T_{end} executed per time-step. Because of the dependences, the availability of a copy of T_{end} means that the whole task graph instance has been executed. Equations (5) states that the fraction of time spent by P_i to send tasks cannot exceed 1; sending is sequential in the one-port model, hence the summation on the neighbors. Equation (6) is the counterpart for receptions, as well as equation (7) for computations. Equation (10), and its variant equation (11) for the master processor, is the most important: consider a given processor P_i, and a given edge (T_k, T_l) in the task graph. During each time unit, P_i receives from its neighbors a given number of files of type (T_k, T_l). Processor P_i itself executes some tasks T_k, thereby generating as many new files of type (T_k, T_l). What does happen to these files? Some are sent to the neighbors of P_i, and some are consumed by P_i to execute tasks of type T_l: we derive equation (10), which really applies to the steady-state operation. At the beginning of the operation of the platform, only in-

put tasks are available to be forwarded. Then some computations take place, and tasks of other types are generated. At the end of this initialization phase, we enter the steady-state: during each time-period in steady-state, each processor can simultaneously perform some computations, and send/receive some other tasks. This is why equation (10) is sufficient, we do not have to detail which operation is performed at which time-step.

Finally, we have derived a linear program whose complexity is polynomial in $|T|$, $|C|$, $|P|$ and $|L|$, and does not depend upon the number of problems (task graphs) to deal with. In this case, deriving a practical scheduling is easier than in Section 3.1. Having computed the solution of the linear program, we derive the time period T by computing the least common multiple of all denominators of the rational variables: we obtain an interval of length T during which the number of tasks executed and transmitted is an integer constant. Using a sequential initialization phase to feed the processors, and a sequential clean-up phase to process the very last tasks, we derive an asymptotically optimal schedule. More precisely, the number of tasks executed by this schedule is optimal, up to a constant that only depends upon the task graph and platform graph, not upon the total number of tasks.

4 Limitations of static scheduling

Replacing the macro-dataflow model by the one-port model is a first step towards designing realistic scheduling heuristics. In the extended version of this paper [2], we show that assuming a perfectly divisible load [4] greatly simplifies the task allocation problem. Dealing with steady-state operation instead of makespan minimization is a nice way to circumvent the computational complexity of scheduling problems while deriving efficient (often asympotically optimal) scheduling algorithms. However, several problems remain to be addressed.

4.1 Knowledge of the platform graph

Is it realistic to assume that all the information concerning the task graph is available from the very beginning of the scheduling? For some applications, tasks are only known *on-line*, as the computation progresses. But there are regular problems (e.g. a two-dimensional FFT, or a dense LU solver) for which the whole division into tasks, and the dependences between the tasks, is known a priori. For such problems, the *structure* of the task graph (nodes and edges) only depends upon the application, not upon the target platform. Problems arise from the weights, i.e. the estimation of the execution times and of the communication times. For instance, critical path scheduling relies on a precise knowledge of all these parameters to assign the next ready task to the adequate computing resource. Even the steady-state scheduling of independent tasks requires some static knowledge of the architecture.

A classical answer to this problem is borrowed from a simple paradigm used in dynamic strategies, namely *"use the past to predict the future"*, i.e. use the currently observed speed of computation of each machine and of each communication link to decide for the next distribution of work. There are too many parameters to accurately predict the actual speed of a machine for a given program, even assuming that the machine load will remain the same throughout the computation. The situation is even worse for communication links, because of unpredictable contention problems. When deploying an application on a platform, the idea is thus to divide the scheduling into phases. During each phase, all the machine and network parameters are collected and histogrammed, using a tool like NWS. This information will then guide the scheduling decisions for the next phase.

Moving from heterogeneous clusters to computational grids will cause further problems. Even discovering the characteristics of the surrounding computing resources may prove a difficult task. Still, even in the favorable case where the target platform graph has been well identified and is relatively stable, schedulers face two major difficulties: (i) providing an accurate modeling of the hierarchical structure of the platform and (ii) designing scheduling algorithms that are well-suited to this hierarchical structure.

4.2 Experiments versus simulations

Real experiments on the target platform are often involved to test or to compare heuristics. However, on a distributed heterogeneous platform, such experiments are technically difficult to drive, because of the genuine instability of the platform. For example, wide-area links are often shared with Internet traffic from other applications, and their performance is not as constant and reliable as the one of a dedicated cluster of workstations. In a word, it is almost impossible to guarantee that a platform which is not dedicated to the experiment, will remain exactly the same between two tests, thereby forbidding any meaningful comparison.

Simulations are then used to replace real experiments, so as to ensure the reproducibility of measured data. Being faster than real experiments, simulations will enable to test the algorithms in a variety of conditions. A key issue is the possibility to run the simulations against a realistic environment. The main idea of trace-based scheduling is to record the platform parameters today, and to simulate the algorithms tomorrow, against the recorded data: even though it is not the current load of the platform, it is realistic, because it represents a fair summary of what happened pre-

viously. A good example of such a trace-based simulation tool is SIMGRID [5].

5 Conclusion

The difficulty of scheduling for clusters and grids should not be underestimated. Data decomposition, task allocation and load balancing were known to be difficult problems in the context of classical parallel architectures. They become extremely difficult in the context of heterogeneous clusters, not to mention grid computing platforms. If the platform is not stable enough, or if it evolves too fast, dynamic schedulers are the only option. Otherwise, there is always the opportunity to inject some static knowledge into dynamic schedulers. Future work will decide whether this opportunity is a niche (the pessimistic answer) or whether it encompasses a wide range of applications (the expected answer!).

References

[1] O. Beaumont, V. Boudet, and Y. Robert. A realistic model and an efficient heuristic for scheduling with heterogeneous processors. In *HCW'2002, the 11th Heterogeneous Computing Workshop*. IEEE Computer Society Press, 2002.

[2] O. Beaumont, A. Legrand, and Y. Robert. Static scheduling strategies for heterogeneous systems. Technical Report 2002-29, LIP, ENS Lyon, France, July 2002.

[3] D. Bertsimas and D. Gamarnik. Asymptotically optimal algorithm for job shop scheduling and packet routing. *Journal of Algorithms*, 33(2):296–318, 1999.

[4] V. Bharadwaj, D. Ghose, V. Mani, and T. Robertazzi. *Scheduling Divisible Loads in Parallel and Distributed Systems*. IEEE Computer Society Press, 1996.

[5] H. Casanova. Simgrid: A toolkit for the simulation of application scheduling. In *Proceedings of the IEEE Symposium on Cluster Computing and the Grid (CCGrid'01)*. IEEE Computer Society, May 2001.

[6] P. Chrétienne, E. G. C. Jr., J. K. Lenstra, and Z. Liu, editors. *Scheduling Theory and its Applications*. John Wiley and Sons, 1995.

[7] L. Hollermann, T. S. Hsu, D. R. Lopez, and K. Vertanen. Scheduling problems in a practial allocation model. *J. Combinatorial Optimization*, 1(2):129–149, 1997.

[8] T. S. Hsu, J. C. Lee, D. R. Lopez, and W. A. Royce. Task allocation on a network of processors. *IEEE Trans. Computers*, 49(12):1339–1353, 2000.

[9] O. Sinnen and L. Sousa. Exploiting unused time-slots in list scheduling considering communication contention. In R. Sakellariou, J. Keane, J. Gurd, and L. Freeman, editors, *EuroPar'2001 Parallel Processing*, pages 166–170. Springer-Verlag LNCS 2150, 2001.

[10] H. Topcuoglu, S. Hariri, and M.-Y. Wu. Task scheduling algorithms for heterogeneous processors. In *Eighth Heterogeneous Computing Workshop*. IEEE Computer Society Press, 1999.

Session 1–1

Advanced Networking Hardware

Towards 10-100 Gbps Cryptographic Architectures[1]

Khary Alexander[1], Ramesh Karri, Igor Minkin, Kaijie Wu, Piyush Mishra, Xuan Li

[1]IBM Corporation, Poughkeepsie, NY, 12601, kalexa01@utopia.poly.edu

ECE Department, Polytechnic University, 5 Metrotech Center, Brooklyn, NY, 11201

ramesh@india.poly.edu, iminki01, kwu03, pmishr01, xli03 @utopia.poly.edu

Abstract

Support for secure transactions over insecure public communication networks, built atop high-speed optical infrastructure, requires cryptographic primitives with 10-100Gbps throughput. In this paper we present various hardware architectures for high-speed block and stream ciphers and study the associated throughput and area trade-offs. We demonstrate high-speed encryption architectures for Advanced Encryption Standard (AES) based block and stream ciphers and SNOW stream cipher with 4.7Gbp, 4.6Gbps and 2.12Gbps throughput rates respectively. We then present our ongoing work on high-speed architectures for tree-based stream cipher Leviathan.

Keywords: cryptography, encryption, block-cipher, stream-cipher, FPGA, VHDL, AES, Rijndael, SNOW, Leviathan

1 Introduction

Demand for high-speed encryption is rapidly increasing due to the large bandwidth requirements of the evolving network applications. These applications include Virtual Private Network (VPN) aggregation points, secure e-commerce web servers and Local Area Networks (LANs) with aggregate security protocol offload. As a result, cryptographic processing in software is proving to be inadequate, thereby fueling the industry's push towards hardware implementations of various cryptographic architectures. In this paper we present various hardware architectures for high-speed block and stream ciphers and study the associated throughput vs. hardware area trade-offs.

Cryptographic algorithms are classified as hash, private-key and public key algorithms. Hash algorithms operate on arbitrary length messages to create a fixed length digest or hash. Public key algorithms, also known as asymmetric-key algorithms, use the basic idea of one-way functions to generate encryption-decryption key pair to be used for data encryption. On the other hand, functionality and security of private-key algorithms, also known as symmetric-key algorithms, depend on the single private key. Private-key algorithms are basically of two types, block cipher and stream cipher, and can operate in various modes of operation such as Electronic Book Code (ECB), Output Feed Back (OFB), and Cipher Block Chain (CBC) mode.

Block ciphers process plaintext (ciphertext) messages in discrete blocks and encryption (decryption) of a particular plaintext (ciphertext) with a block cipher results in the same ciphertext (plaintext) when the same key is used. Examples of block ciphers include Data Encryption Standard (DES), triple-DES (3DES), and AES finalist algorithms - Rijndael, Twofish, RC6 and Serpent. After a thorough study of security and performance benchmarks NIST chose Rijndael as the winner. Stream ciphers, on the other hand, are practical approximations to the *one time pad*, operating with a time-varying transformation on individual elements as small as single bits. With a stream cipher, the transformation of these smaller units will vary, depending on when they are encountered during the encryption process. Stream ciphers can be created from dedicated key stream generators, such as Linear Feedback Shift Register (LFSR) and tree-based stream ciphers or by certain modes of operation of block ciphers. Examples of stream ciphers are SNOW, Leviathan and Rijndael in Integer Counter Mode (ICM).

Several hardware implementations of cryptographic algorithms have been described in literature, such as the algorithm-specific implementations of DES [[8], [9], [10], [11]], IDEA [12], Twofish [12], and Blowfish [12] and hardware-software co-design based crypto-processors, such as CryptoManiac [13]. In this paper we present our work on various hardware architectures for high-speed block and stream ciphers that achieve 10 to 100 Gbps throughput rates and study the associated throughput and area trade-offs.

Section 2 describes the implementation results of the four AES [7] finalist block ciphers on Field Programmable Gate Arrays (FPGAs). It also presents various high-speed architectures for these symmetric block ciphers and validates these using AES (Rijndael). Section 3 discusses high-speed architectures for stream ciphers - AES in ICM, SNOW, and Leviathan - followed by the corresponding implementation results. Section 4 concludes this study.

---

[1] This work is supported by CISCO University Research Program

2 Block Ciphers

A symmetric block cipher encrypts plaintext by iteratively applying a round transformation to the input block using different round-keys for each round. Round keys are derived from the private key by using a key-schedule transformation. Decryption is the reverse process of encryption. Usually the complexity of encryption and decryption operations is more significant than that of key generation operation. Hence, in this paper we only focus on optimizing the operations used by data encryption and decryption for better system performance.

Figure 1 shows the architecture for symmetric Rijndael [1] encryption and decryption. During encryption input block is exclusive-ored (XOR) with a round-key in the pre-processing step and the output is iteratively transformed N_r times using a round function where N_r denotes the total number of iterations and each iteration uses a different round key.

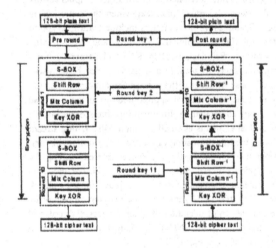

Figure 1: AES iterative block cipher

A round function consists of a series of operations (AES uses Substitution Box (SBox) - Shift Row (SRow) - Mix Column (MixCol) - Key XOR (KXor)). Number of rounds of encryption and decryption is a function of the data block size, user key size and the desired level of security. In most cases, increasing the number of encryption rounds improves security at the cost of system throughput and vice-versa. For example, AES processes data blocks of 128 bits, using cipher keys of 128, 192 or 256 bits. Table 1 shows the number of encryption/decryption rounds corresponding to these three different key sizes.

Table 1: Number of rounds of AES as a function of data blocks size and user key sizes

N_k	4	6	8
N_r	10	12	14
$N_b = 4$, N_k = key length/32, N_r = MAX (N_b, N_k) + 6			

2.1 FPGA Implementation of Block Ciphers

Table 2 shows the results of our implementation of four AES finalist block ciphers on Xilinx Virtex series XCV1000 FPGAs. All FPGA implementation were carried out using Synplicity® Synplify™ VHDL compiler, Modeltech® Modelsim™ VHDL simulator and Xilinx® Place and Route (PAR) tools. Details of these implementation results can be found in [3]. One Virtex slice contains two look-up tables (LUTs) and each LUT can implement four-input, one-output logic function. Throughput of a cipher represents the total number of bits encrypted per second and is calculated as *number of bits encrypted / (operation cycles * clock duration)*.

Table 2: Implementation results for AES finalists

	Area (Slices)	Frequency (MHz)	Throughput (Mbps)
Rijndael	3973	46.93	136.53
RC6	2397	23.99	73.11
Twofish	3262	20.16	75.9
Serpent	8073	28.638	57.28

An iterative looping architecture minimizes the hardware area requirements by implementing only one round over which the cipher iterates N_r times per block. This scheme however results in low throughput and can be costly in terms of the input and round key storage and multiplexing requirements. Throughput rates of all these implementations were less than 150 Mbps. Therefore advanced architectures need to be designed to achieve the target throughputs of 10Gbps and higher.

2.2 Advanced Architectures for Block Ciphers

Iterative block ciphers offer a variety of architectural options, each with the associated area and throughput tradeoffs. For example, a **loop-unrolled** architecture allows implementation of up to N_r rounds as a single combinational logic block, reducing the hardware for round key multiplexing and the number of clock cycles per block. However, this approach maximizes the hardware requirements and yields worst case register-register delay.

Another option for high-speed architectures is pipelining. A **partially pipelined** architecture achieves this by increasing the number of blocks of data that are being simultaneously operated upon. Each round is implemented as the atomic round element and the intermediate data are registered, decreasing the worst-case register-to-register delay. In the case of a full-length pipeline, the system will output a block at each clock cycle once the latency of the pipeline has been met. This architecture, however, also significantly increases the required hardware resources.

Basic pipelining can be extended by sub-pipelining to overcome these shortcomings. For example, AES can be sub-pipelined by partitioning the SRow and MixCol operations. This decreases the worst-case register-register delay and increases the number of data blocks that can be operated on simultaneously by a factor equal to the number of sub-divisions. However, these benefits come at the cost of an increase in the number of clock cycles, thereby requiring a corresponding decrease in the worst-case delay between the stages.

2.3 FPGA Implementation of Advanced Architectures for AES Block Ciphers

After analyzing these various architectures we decided to optimize the sub-pipelined AES block cipher with 128-bit block and 128-bit user key size to investigate the associated throughput vs. area tradeoffs. An important observation regarding AES is that the byte substitution is the most dominant operation. This operation is a non-linear transformation that operates independently on each byte using an 8-bit substitution table (SBox). As a result, a 128-bit data path requires sixteen copies of SBox module [3]. Therefore, round function was sub-pipelined to isolate it from SRow, MixCol and KXOR. Even though the second stage contained a multiplexer (to bypass MixCol during the last round of encryption) SBox operation still formed the critical path.

Two architectures were developed using this sub-pipelined round and in both cases key scheduling was performed a priori. First architecture (SP_1_1) [2] is built around one round with one sub-pipeline register to split it into 2-stages. Figure 2 shows that round-keys were stored in a key-RAM and 128-bit *TextIn* port was used to supply both user key and plaintext. Second architecture is a five stage partially pipelined (SP_5_1) loop unrolling of the sub-pipelined round, as shown in Figure 3. First four rounds were optimized by removing the bypass multiplexer in the second stage of the sub-pipeline since MixCol is always performed in these stages. In this case round keys were stored in a file of registers. This architecture resulted in a 10 stage pipeline (5 rounds * 2 stages per round) with 2.1 cycles ($2 + \frac{1}{10}$) per block.

Though we did not implement loop-unrolled and partially pipelined architectures, we performed a quantitative analysis of these architectures based on our study of the sub-pipelined architecture. Loop-unrolling is basically implementing up to N_r rounds as a single combinational block. A 5-stage loop-unrolled architecture can be implemented on a XC2V2000. It would require less hardware than the SP_1_1 implementation since sub-pipeline registers are eliminated. This would result in approximately five times decrease in frequency and (without pipelining) the cycles per block would increase from 2.1 to 3. Overall this would result in approximately seven times reduction in throughput with a small corresponding decrease in area.

If the sub-pipeline registers are removed from SP_5_1 to create a partially pipelined design, decrease in area would be even more negligible as only five registers

would be eliminated. The worst-case decrease in frequency would be about 50% but due to the mismatch between SBox operation and second stage in sub-pipeline the frequency would drop to about 75%. Changes, if any, in the cycles per block would be negligible since while half the number of blocks can be operated on at a given time there are also half as many stages to traverse. Therefore the worst case throughput would be half that of the SP_5_1 design.

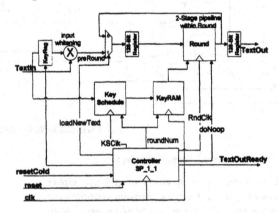

Figure 2: Single sub-pipelined round SP-1-1

2.4 Comparison with previous work

Table 3 shows the implementation results for these two AES architectures on Xilinx XC2V2000BG575-5 FPGA. The Five-stage loop unrolled implementation needs only a single copy of the key-schedule. This result in less than 4 times area overhead while achieving more than 4 times the throughput of one stage sub-pipelined design.

Table 3: FPGA implementation results of AES

	Area (slices)	Frequency (MHz)	Cycles/ Block	Throughput (Mbps)
SP_1_1	2128	90.55	10.5	1104
SP_5_1	8114	77.69	2.1	4735

Advanced architectures for AES were also implemented on Xilinx XCV1000 FPGA in order to compare them with their previous implementations at Worcester Polytechnic Institute (WPI). Unlike [2] our designs also implement the key scheduling function and use Xtime function to implement MixCol operation. Our implementations showed significant improvement over previous works, with a 50% increase in throughput a 20% decrease in hardware area and these results would improve further if we do not consider the key schedule overheads.

3 Stream Ciphers

A stream cipher generates a key stream that is usually combined with plaintext via bit-wise exclusive-or (XOR) operation for encryption and decryption. Following sections describe high speed architectures for AES-based, SNOW and Leviathan stream ciphers.

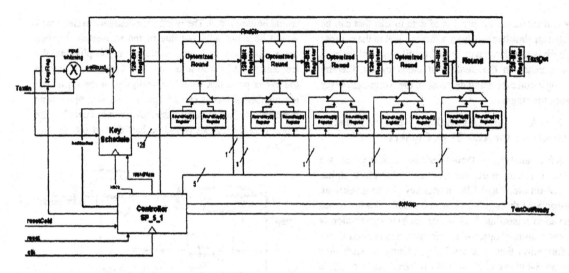

Figure 3: Five-stage sub-pipelined round SP-5-1

3.1 AES-based Stream Cipher

Certain modes of operation of a block cipher effectively transform it into a key stream generator and as such any block cipher can be used as a stream cipher. One such mode of operation is Integer Counter Mode (ICM) proposed in [4]. The key stream is generated from an ICM key and segment index and XORed with plaintext to generate the corresponding cipher text. Length of the ICM key is dependent on the block-length and the key-length parameters of the underlying block cipher.

The AES block cipher, presented in the prior section, was implemented in ICM mode to create an efficient synchronous key stream generator. Figure 4 shows that the generalized interface of our implementation facilitates easy IP reuse of AES block cipher architectures for AES stream cipher with some trivial modifications. The only additional components needed are the optimized count initializer and a counter with parallel load. Constant addition in parallel-load counter was faster (97MHz) than the block cipher. A multiplexer was used to drive the block cipher input from either the *keyIn* input for the ICM key or the counter.

ICM counter initialization algorithm required a 96-bit addition which turned out to be the main system bottleneck (see results corresponding to the un-optimized implementation in Table 5). Therefore, ICM counter initialization was optimized by folding the addition onto a single 32-bit carry-select adder operating at 108 MHz. This addition took three cycles, but was performed during key-schedule. Implementation results of these implementations are shown in Table 5.

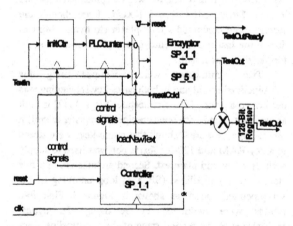

Figure 4: AES Integer Counter Mode stream cipher

3.2 SNOW Stream Cipher

A Linear Feedback Shift Register (LFSR) is a mechanism for generating a stream of binary bits [6]. The *register* consists of a series of cells that are initialized using the secret key. At each clocking instant the contents of the cells are shifted right by one position and a non-linear operation (e.g. XOR) is applied to a subset of the cell contents and fed back into the leftmost cell. This is an example of a many-to-1 feedback topology. Another way to implement an LFSR is with a 1-to-many topology where the most significant bit is used in all the taps. Regardless of the topology, LFSRs are fast and easy to implement in both hardware and software and with appropriate *feedback* the generated taps sequences can have a good statistical appearance.

Figure 5 shows SNOW, a LFSR based synchronous stream cipher that supports key sizes of 128 and 256 bits [6]. This architecture does not permit a straightforward tradeoff between area and throughput since it cannot be

28

broken into multiple rounds of computation to facilitate pipelining. Also, since there is a dependency between the generations of consecutive words in the key stream, they cannot be produced in parallel. Critical path consists of two 32-bit additions, two XORs and a left-shift by seven. Therefore in order to increase its performance we investigated a variety of high-speed architectures for adders.

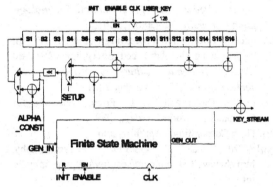

Figure 5: SNOW stream cipher implementation

Table 4 shows the results of this analysis based on which it was decided to employ 32-bit carry select adders using 8-bit carry look-ahead adders. Resulting design occupied 752 slices and operated at a frequency of 66.489 MHz. This is approximately three times faster than the fastest software implementation of SNOW stream cipher on Pentium III systems.

Table 4: Comparison of FPGA implementation of 32-bit adders on XC2V2000

	Frequency (MHz)
Ripple-Carry	31.6
Carry Look-ahead	43.9
Carry Look-ahead (8 slices)	76
Carry-Select (4-bit CLA)	72
Carry-Select (8-bit CLA)	89.2

3.3 Leviathan Stream Cipher

Leviathan is a complete binary-tree based stream cipher whose leaves are traversed consecutively from left to right to form a key stream [5]. A straightforward approach for generating 32-bit key values at all the leaf nodes entails $O(h2^h)$ computation time and at least $O(2^h)$ storage requirements where h denotes the height of the tree. For example, for a binary tree of height sixteen this translates to 2^{16} 32-bit memory locations for storing keys and $O(2^{20})$ computation time. In order to reduce this storage requirement key stream should be generated dynamically.

A simple approach for generating the key stream dynamically entails traversing a unique path from the root of the tree to the corresponding leaf node and executing the functions within each node. This scheme yields worst-case computation time which is equal to the height times the execution time of node function and the storage requirement of the order $O(1)$. Period between the generations of consecutive key values is

$$T_{key\ period} = \sum T_{A|B(15)} + T_C$$

thereby yielding low throughput.

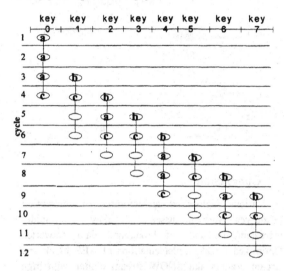

Figure 6: Pipelined traversal of computation tree

We investigated pipelined architectures to process paths leading to consecutive keys. Depth of the pipeline is determined by the height of the tree. This scheme offers fixed period between generations of consecutive keys. Figure 6 shows a tree of height five and its respective pipelined paths. Dataflow in the pipeline traverses the paths from either the intermediate node or the root node to the leaf nodes. Each path from the root to the leaf node is traversed by taking advantage of the shared intermediate nodes. All the node functions along the path traversed from the root to the leaf node are executed in successive stages of the pipeline and their results are stored in the pipeline registers.

Thus, when the data flow of the path traversing to the consecutive leaf node is pipelined these values need not be re-computed. This architecture can also efficiently implement power-aware pipeline in which clock gating is performed to disable specific data paths during empty pipeline slots.

3.4 FPGA Implementation of Stream Ciphers

Implementation results of the various stream ciphers on the Virtex-II series FPGAs are presented in Table 5. The particular FPGA packages and speed grades used were XC2V2000BG575-5 and XC2V250FG256-5 respectively. Optimized AES stream cipher operates at the same speed as the AES block cipher (Table 3), though it consumes 5% more area. 32-bit data path SNOW throughput approaches 3 Gbps. Expansion of this design to a 128-bit data path promises throughputs in the 12Gbps range.

Table 5: FPGA implementation results of stream ciphers

		Area (slices)	Frequency (MHz)	Throughput (Mbps)
AES ICM SP-1-1	Un-optimized	2282	74.251	905.155
	Optimized	2512	94.02	1146.149
AES ICM SP-5-1	Un-optimized	8326	40.025	2439.62
	Optimized	8631	76.159	4642.072
SNOW		752	66.489	2812.52

4   Conclusion

Various high-speed architectures of encryption primitives were discussed to satisfy the rapidly increasing demands of broadband data networks. Optimized FPGA implementations of AES block and stream ciphers and SNOW stream cipher with high throughput rates of 4.7 Gbps, 4.6 Gbps and 2.12 Gbps respectively were presented. Schemes exploiting parallelism cannot be directly extended to ciphers operating in the feedback modes such as CBC, CFB, and OFB. On the other hand, decryption in these feedback modes can utilize these high-speed architectures since they allow data path parallelism.

An analysis of the work under progress on the pipelined implementations of Leviathan stream cipher with optimized storage and computation requirements was also presented.

5   References

[1] J. Daemen, V. Rijmen, "AES proposal: Rijndael," *First Advanced Encryption Standard (AES) Conference*, CA, USA, 1998.

[2] A. J. Elbirt, W. Yip, B. Chetwynd, C. Paar, "An FPGA-based performance evaluation of the AES block cipher candidate algorithm finalists," *IEEE Transactions on VLSI Systems*, Vol. 9, No. 4, pp. 545–557, August 2001.

[3] R. Karri, K. Wu, P. Mishra, and Y. Kim, "Concurrent error detection of fault-based side-channel cryptanalysis of 128-bit symmetric block ciphers," *Proceedings, IEEE Design Automation Conference (DAC)*, NV, USA, June 2001.

[4] H. Lipmaa, P. Rogaway, and D. Wagner, "Comments to NIST concerning AES modes of operations: CTR-mode encryption," Symmetric Key Block Cipher Modes of Operation Workshop, MD, USA, October 2000.

[5] D. A. McGrew and S. R. Fluhrer "The stream cipher Leviathan," *New European Schemes for Signatures, Integrity and Encryption (NESSIE)*, October 2000.

[6] P. Ekdahl and T. Johansson, "SNOW: A new stream cipher," *Department of Information Technology, Lund University*, November, 2001.

[7] Federal Information Processing Standards (FIPS), "Announcing the Advanced Encryption Standard (AES)," *National Institute of Standards and Technology (NIST)*, November 2001.

[8] D. W. Davis and W. L. Price, "Security for Computer Networks," *Wiley*, 1989.

[9] HiFn Corporation. http://hifn.com

[10] S/390 and OS/390 Cryptography. http://www.s390.ibm.com/security/cryptography.html

[11] Shiva Corporation. http:/shiva/com

[12] X. Lai, "On the Design and Security of Block Ciphers," *Hartung-Gorre Veerlag*, 1992

[13] L. Wu, C. Weaver, and T. Austin, "CryptoManiac: A fast flexible architecture for secure communication," *International Symposium on Computer Architecture (ISCA)*, Sweden, June 2001.

Integrated Photonic Devices for Optical and Wireless Networking

Fow-Sen Choa and Jie Lin
Department of Computer Science and Electrical Engineering,
University of Maryland Baltimore County,
Baltimore, USA
choa@umbc.edu, jlin3@umbc.edu

Abstract

In this paper we described advanced photonic devices used for optical networking. We also summarized our recent works on optical frame switches, broadband optical access networks, and dense wavelength division multiplexing (DWDM) backbone networks for wireless application and access networks. Photonic integrated circuits will play a key role in modern communications and help to realize the vision of high bandwidth pervasive connectivity.

I. Introduction

With the great demand for bandwidth, optical fiber communication technologies are progressing at a very fast pace. The point-to-point transmission rate has increased quickly from much less than 1 Gb/s to 2.5, 10, and now towards 40 Gb/s [1]. The system capacity increases at an even faster speed due to the introduction of the wavelength-division-multiplexing (WDM) technology. The number of wavelengths in commercial systems has increased from 1 to 4, 8, 16, 40, and now towards several hundreds channels [2], and with the optical fiber low loss window increasing to 1.2-1.6 and even more, the operating wavelength will have a much more flexible choice, dramatically enrich the capacity of DWDM network. The requirement of the bandwidth will double every 6-9 months, and will achieve 10^3 Tbs (tera bits per second) in the next 10 years. The impact on the underlying networks is the challenge to build an optical infrastructure that can carry a widely heterogeneous mix of traffic.

Using photonic switches for routing, an all-optical network has the advantages of having bit rate, wavelength, and signal format transparencies. The signal formats can be IP, ATM, FDDI, etc. for digital signals and can be AM, FSK, QAM, DQPSK, etc. for analog signals. Within the transmission distance (transparency distance) that a signal can continue to have an acceptable S/N ratio, an all-optical packet network can be transparent to all types of signals. The advantage is obvious: one network can transport all different types of traffic.

Optical networks can also provide high-speed backbones for other broadband access technologies. We envisage that in the near future, wireless connectivity will be provided to users by (broadband) wireless networks, and that the mobile support stations will be connected by high-speed optical networks. That is to use DWDM system as wireless backbone networks and access networks.

For wireless backbone networks, we need intelligent scheme and devices to implement the desired functionalities like reconfigurability, bandwidth-on-demand, etc. We also need new schemes, like optics-assistant radio-frequency (RF)-beam forming techniques to help to achieve spatial-domain-multiple-access (SDMA), which can dramatically increase the capacity of wireless communications.

In the following sections we describe optoelectronic devices and subsystems used in wireless and optical networks that closely related to our recent research projects. We will then go over those projects and show how those devices and modules affect system performance in their corresponding networks.

II. Photonic devices

Transmitters, modulators, and receivers are basic terminal devices used in a link inside the optical network. For routing and signal switching in intermediate nodes, we need amplifiers, multiplexers, switches, wavelength converters, and all optical memories. In the following section we described these devices in detail.

2.1 Transmitter (integrated with modulator)

Traditional electrical to optical (E/O) conversion is to directly modulate the laser, the advantages of it is simple, small size/weight. However, this method will induce large RF insertion loss (~ 20 dB) due to the inefficient conversion of RF signals to amplitude-modulated optical signals. In order to solve this problem, we have developed frequency modulation techniques.

To achieve high FM efficiency and large modulation bandwidth (BW), we have developed a high-efficiency FM Laser, which consists of two sections: the DFB laser section and the EA (electronic absorption) modulation section. Fig. 1(a) shows the structure of the FM transmitter. Fig. 1(b) shows the real picture of the fabricated device. In this structure, the reflectivity of the EA modulator facet is not coated and the RF modulation contributes to the phase change of the laser and generates a high FM efficient [3] around 10 GHz/mA.

Using this device, combined with optical filter working as a FM discriminator, we can obtain a FM gain (RF to optical FM and then optical FM to optical AM), of more than 10dB gain. That means instead of big loss due to the modulation, by using this device, we can provide extra gain for the system, then we can extend the transmission distance. Since the EA modulator is a high-speed device, broadband transmitters with RF-photonic transmitting gain can be obtained.

To realize such a device in its integrated form, we have fabricated the FM laser and then further integrated it with a sharp edge filter (Mach-Zender interferometer). The device structure is shown in Fig. 2 (a) and (b).

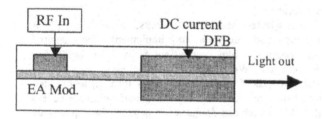

Fig. 1(a) FM transmitter structure

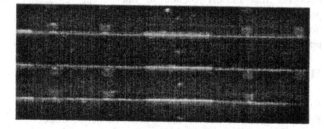

Fig. 1 (b) Fabricated FM transmitter

Fig. 2 (a) FM transmitter integrated with Mach-Zender

Fig. 2 (b) Fabricated integrated device

2.2 Integrated transceivers

Different from other transceivers, the device shown in Fig. 3 is a 4-section integrated coherent transceiver [4, 5]. The 4 sections are the gain section, the phase section, the grating section and the detector section. The gain section provides gain for the laser. The grating section and phase section provide wavelength tuning for this tunable laser. The detector section is made of the same material as the gain section but is negatively or zero biased under operations. This device has an extremely fine wavelength resolution and allows ultra-dense WDM operations. We can easily run multiple 155 Mb/s WDM signals with only 3 GHz optical channel spacing. By using this kind of device, we developed a broadband optical access networks with the characteristics of bandwidth-on-demand (BOD) and easy reconfigurability. Furthermore, by using this device to interconnect wireless base stations and mobile switching centers, we have demonstrated an intelligent wireless backbone network.

Fig. 3 4-section integrated transceiver

2.3 Switches

There are several types of switches, such as Micro Electro Mechanical Systems (MEMS), thermo-optic switches, electro-absorption switches and optical amplifier switches. MEMS are widely used in long haul communication due to its high extinction ratio and low transmission loss. But for packet switching applications, the speed of MEMS is too slow (~ ms) to be utilized. Fig. 4 (a) shows a 1x2 active/passive-waveguide switch, which is based on the semiconductor optical amplifier (SOA) technology [6]. The switch has a switching speed of 600 picoseconds as Fig.4 (b). This Y-junction switch is made on the InP substrate. At the input and output, we fabricated SOAs to amplify or absorb the transmitted signals. The signal switching is fulfilled by applying different currents to the output port to turn on/off the output. This kind of switch has several advantages: simple structure, fast switching speed, low insertion loss due to the gain provided by SOAs. By cascading several switch stages, we can obtain other functions like optical delay lines and NxN switches.

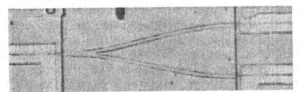

Fig 4(a) Fabricated 1x2 switches

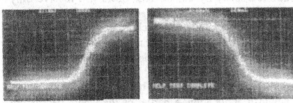

Fig. 4(b) Switch rising time and falling time

2.4 Wavelength converters

The ability to "imprint" digital information from one wavelength of light to another wavelength without passing the signal through electronics is a critical next step in the evolution of optical networks and photonic packet switching. We can make wavelength converter by using cross-gain and cross-phase modulation effects in SOA to do wavelength conversions. Fig. 5 shows two types of long-cavity ? converters: an all-active Y interferometer and an all-active Mach-Zender converter with separated injection branches. The conversion easily achieved 5 Gb/s (the speed limit of our BER testing set). The input 0-1 stream is complementarily converted to the output stream.

Fig. 5 Y interferometer and Mach-Zender converter

2.5 Fast Tunable Active Filters

Fast tunable filters are used in our experiments to as wavelength demultiplexers [7]. It has an insertion gain instead of insertion loss. Fig. 6 shows the experimental setup using the active filter. The DBR (Distributed Bragg Reflector) filter is composed of gain, phase, grating, and post-filter gain sections [4, 5]. Error signals for wavelength control and dynamic gain control are extracted from the gain section and feedback to the grating section and the gain section, respectively. The post-filter gain section can be used to switch the output on/off. The central wave-length of the DBR filter can be easily tuned

and locked to a desire wavelength by changing the grating bias current. Details of the controls can be found in reference [7]. 8-channel WDM signals with 0.8nm (100 GHz) spacing were coupled into the DBR gain section. Channel rejection ratio of 20 dB was achieved when the average input power of each channel was at -30dBm.

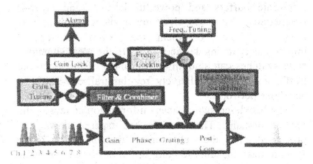

Fig. 6 Fast tunable active filter

2.6 WDM buffers

Figure 7 shows the structure of an 8-wavelength WDM buffer. The capacity of the memory is dependent on the number of wavelength and the optical frame size. Fixed length frames with different wavelengths are injected into the buffer and circulate in the loop. An 8-wavelength waveguide-grating-router (WGR) with 200-GHz channel spacing is used as the wavelength demultiplexer in the fiber loop. Semiconductor optical amplifiers (SOAs) are used to compensate the loss in the loop. Optical space switches are used to switch packets in or out the loop. The buffer can be operated as a random access memory [8] at the frame level to store and forward frames, not necessary following the input order. When the number of wavelengths and the circulation times increase, dispersion compensation and S/N ratio recovery in the loop will be required. Similar to the electronic dynamic random access memory (DRAM), we use a refresh circuit to regenerate the S/N ratio and write the signals back to the optical buffers before they seriously degrade.

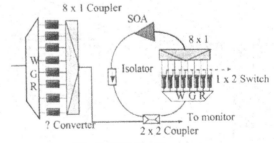

Fig. 7 WDM buffer

III. Optical network project

The above photonic devices have been used in our research projects: optical frame switches, broadband optical access networks, and DWDM wireless backbone networks as described below.

3.1 optical frame switches

An all-optical network consists of many edge switches and backbone switches. The edge switches have large electronic buffers and powerful layer-3 (and layer-4) functionality. They are electronic switches with optical interfaces. Some of them may even use optical interconnections inside the switch. In the ideal situation, edge switches can smooth out the burst of the incoming traffic and keep a relatively regular traffic within the backbone network.

The backbone switch keeps information always in the optical domain. The headers are tapered down and processed in the electronic domain for frame synchronization, table looking up, contention resolution, switching, and output controls. Since the buffers are made of a fiber delay line with a fixed length, it will be more convenient and efficient to handle frames with a fixed length [9].

The backbone switches have limited layer-3 capabilities. They accept or reject routing requests from edge switches according to its currently available capacity. However, they do not create routing path for a frame by themselves. The header contains labels to be specified at the edge switches. New labels are assigned to replace the old ones, switch-by-switch, when the frame passes through the network, similar to the VPI/VCI scheme in an ATM network. The header also contains information about the type, format, and bit rate of the payload. The payload can be either an analog or a digital signal. It can have an equal or a much higher bit-rate than that of the header.

3.2 Broadband access networks

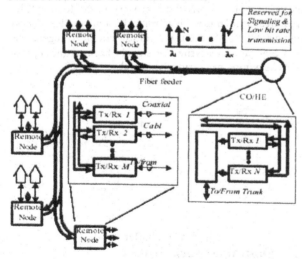

Fig. 8 Broadband access networks

Fig. 8 shows the basic architecture of a bandwidth-on-demand network. In the CO/HE (central office/head end), N coherent transceivers, which provide N fixed wavelengths to the system, are connected to several remote nodes through a bus or star fiber architecture. Each remote node supports 10 to 100 subscribers, who are connected to dedicated tunable coherent transceiver (TCT) modules in the remote node through dedicated copper coaxial cables. The tunable optical devices are controlled solely by the CO/HE. Users will receive only their own information and privacy is thus achieved. Since the channel switching and locking operation will cause millisecond scale latency, it is preferable that a group of users will TDM-share a specific optical channel, say, $?_N$, for signaling, low bit rate operations and network maintenance purposes [10]. When a user requests a high bandwidth application, a partial or the whole bandwidth of a new wavelength can be assigned to the user. According to the characteristics of the application, this channel capacity can be further partitioned between the up- and the down-stream signals if the half-duplex scheme is adopted. Consequently, a user occupies just-enough bandwidth and only when it is requested. This network is very similar to the AMPS [11] wireless system and can efficiently utilize the network resources to provide BoD services. When super-users emerge in the network, a number of wavelengths can be added for high bit rate operations and only the transceiver units for the specific users need to be upgraded. Unlike some specific SONET, ATM, IP networks, analog signals can also be accommodated in a coherent network [10]. This kind of network can easily scale up by adding more wavelengths. The number of wavelength can be increased according to the total number of users and grade of service following the Erlang B and C trunking models. It means that only a few added wavelengths are able to support a large number of additional users.

3.3 wireless backbone networks

We proposed and demonstrated a high-bandwidth, reconfigurable wireless communication system based on the WDM and TDMA techniques (not limited to TDMA only). The WDM backbone network has a tree structure. Capacity growth, using cell splitting, can be easily achieved by extending fibers from old ending points to each new ending point [12]. By using WDM techniques, a fully-connected logic topology can be deployed to the tree shape physical connection. Fine-granule tunable transmitters and receivers using the coherent technology are employed at each ending point. Using the broadcast and select scheme, the network configuration and its BW allocation can be dynamically rearranged. The micro cell site is composed of a RF antenna, RF circuits, and some optoelectronic devices. The majority part of the equipment will be sitting at the mobile switching center (MSC) and connected to each micro-cell through fibers.

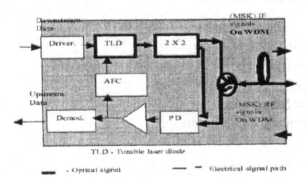

Fig. 9 The MSC structure

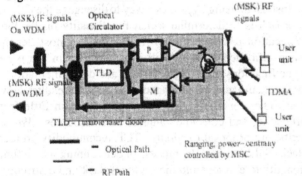

Fig. 10 The BS structure

We build the MCS and BS units using 4-section integrated coherent transceivers as shown in Fig. 9 and 10. Such a system has a fine granularity, which fits the broadband wireless applications very well. FSK modulation format is used to simulate the GSM signals. A down stream data at 100 Mb/s is sent to the phase section of the transceiver to generate FSK signals. RF beating signal is obtained from the detector and is amplified and sent to an antenna. Frequency locking is done at both ends to ensure a fixed RF frequency in 900 MHz band.

The reconfigurable broadband wireless backbone network using the fine-granule WDM technology, with characters of transparency, dynamic BW allocation, matched granularity, etc, becomes an excellent candidate for future broadband wireless networks.

IV. Conclusion

In this paper, we introduced some advanced and integrated photonic devices developed in our laboratory. We also envisage that in the near future, tetherless connectivity will be provided to users by (broadband) wireless networks and the mobile support stations will be connected by high-speed optical networks. To achieve this vision the key issue is to develop both system and device level integration technologies such that the cost of optical and RF systems can be greatly reduced and

become comparable to the electronic systems. Moreover, there is need for integrating the wireless and optical interfaces to achieve high efficiency and high performance signal conversion and distribution. To realize the vision, we need to further develop the integration technology. We expect high-performance, low-cost integrated photonic and RF-photonic chips will share a more important role with their electronic IC counter part in future broadband networks.

References:

[1] K. Suzuki et al.,"40 Gbit/s single channel optical soliton transmission over 70000 km using in -line synchronous modulation and optical filtering", Electron. Lett., Jan.1998, vol. 34, pp. 98-100.

[2] see, for example, Lucent product: "WaveStar. OLS 400G" at "http://www.lucent-optical.com/solutions/products".

[3] X.Huang, A.J.Seeds, et al,"Monolithically integrated Quantum-confined Stark effect tuned laser with uniform frequency modulation response", Photon. Technol. Lett., v. 10, pp. 1697-1699 (1998).

[4] M. Zirngibl, C. H. Joyner, L. W. Stulz, C. Dragone, H. M. Presby, I. P. Kaminow, "LARNet, a local access router network", IEEE Photon. Technol. Lett., Vol. 7, no. 2, pp.215-217, Feb. 1995.

[5] K.-Y. Liou, U. Koren, K. Dreyer, E. C. Burrow, J. L.Zyskind and J. W. Sulhoff, "A 24-Channel WDM Transmitter for Access System Using a Loop-Back Spectrally Sliced Light-Emitting Diode", IEEE Photon. Technol. Lett., vol. 10, no. 2, pp. 270-272, 1998.

[6] J. Fan et al., "Electrical control optical delay lines made of y-junction SOA switches," Conference on Lasers and Electro -Optics and International Quantum Electronics Conference Proceeding, (San Francisco, May 1998), paper CThO44

[7] J. H. Chen, Y. Chai, J. Y. Fan, F. S. Choa, T. Tanbun-Ek, P.Wisk, W. T. Tsang, C. A. Burrus, "WDM channel monitoring and signal power control/equalization using integrated tunable active filters,: Electronic Letters, vol. 34, pp. 1411-1413, 1998

[8] Y. Chai, J. H. Chen, F. S Choa, J. P. Zhang, J. Y. Fan, W.Lin, "Scalable and modularized optical random access memories" Conference on Lasers and Electro -Optics and International Quantum Electronics Conference Proceeding, (San Francisco, CA, May 1998), paper CThO17, pp. 397.

[9] F. S. Choa, H. Jonathan. Choa, "All-optical packet routing: Architecture and Implementation", Invited paper, Photonic Network Communications, vol. 1.4, pp. 303-311, 1999.

[10] Liming Wang, Fow-Sen Choa, Jye-Hong Chen, Yanjie Chai, Mei-Hao Shih, "Counter-receiving heterodyne detection with an integrated coherent transceiver and its applications in bandwidth-on-demand access networks", IEEE Journal of Lightwave Technology, vol. 17, pp. 1724-1731, Oct. 1999.

[11] see, for example, AT&T product "AMPS-based AUTOPLEX(R) System 1000".

[12] Jie Lin, F. S. Choa, "Demonstration of a broadband wireless backbone using ultra-dense WDM technology". (Long beach, May 2002), paper CtuS2, CLEO 2002, pp. 276.

Splintering TCP*

Patricia Gilfeather and Arthur B. Maccabe
Scalable Systems Lab
Department of Computer Science
University of New Mexico
pfeather@cs.unm.edu maccabe@cs.unm.edu

Abstract

In this paper, we describe a new approach to decreasing communication overhead: splintering. In contrast to OS bypass, the principle of splintering isn't that the operating system shouldn't be used, but that it should be used effectively. In the case of communication offload, the goal is to minimize the overhead associated with invoking the OS while still enabling the OS to control communication. We describe our initial experimentation with splintering defragment of IP datagrams. We follow this by a description of the approach we will take in splintering processing for TCP packets.

1 Introduction

Clusters built from commodity hardware and software have several advantages over more traditional supercomputers. Commodity clusters are cheap and ubiquitous. They are easier to design, program and maintain. However, as high-speed networks reach 10Gb/s and processors reach 2–3GHz, new commodity clusters are unable to harness increases in power.

One of the most effective tools for increasing the efficiency of high-performance computing has been the use of programmable Network Interface Cards (NICs). Offloading work to a programmable NIC has been an important tool in facilitating OS bypass. Improvements in networking technology have revealed the OS as a significant bottleneck in our ability to deliver low latency and high bandwidth to applications. The goal of OS bypass is to remove the OS from the communication path, thus eliminating costly interrupts and data copies between kernel space and user space. Ultimately, the OS must be involved in communication. As a minimum, the OS needs to be involved with the memory

used for communication, e.g., validating the use of memory and making sure that pages are "pinned."

Instead of using bypass as a way to disengage the OS, our approach is to determine which functionality in the communication protocol stack will give us the most benefits when offloaded. As we will illustrate later in the paper, some functions, like fragmentation and defragmentation or IP checksum, can be offloaded with positive results. However, other functions, like error handling, gain little from offloading and consume valuable NIC resources. We describe our proposal to *splinter* TCP, a commodity protocol stack. Splintering is the process of determining which functionality to extract from the protocol stack and distributing it. *By splintering the functionality of the TCP/IP stack, we expect to retain the advantages of commodity protocols and gain the performance efficiencies of appropriate offloading.*

Most importantly, splintering the communication stack means that communication rarely increases operating system activity. In other words, the act of communication doesn't cause the operating system to be invoked. First, we will discuss the advantages of commodity components. Second, we will discuss operating system bypass and its successes and disadvantages. Third, we will introduce splintering and finally, we will propose a method for splintering the TCP stack.

2 Advantages of Commodity Components

Commodity-based hardware and software, including communication protocols, provide several advantages. They have been extensively developed and tested, they are highly interoperable, and they represent inexpensive alternatives to specialized solutions. The cost advantages for the commodity approach reaches far beyond the savings realized at time of purchase. Often code has already been created in the community so there is little to no development cost. In the remainder of this section, we discuss the advantages of commodity-based hardware and communication protocols.

*Los Alamos Computer Science Institute SC R71700H-29200001 and Albuquerque High Performance Computing Center through IBM SUR

2.1 Hardware

Fast Ethernet is a great example of the trade-offs between inexpensive commodity hardware and more expensive specialized solutions. While Fast Ethernet is very inexpensive, it is capable of only 1/10th the bandwidth of Myrinet[2]. Ethernet is, additionally, saddled with a very small transmission unit (1500 bytes) which is becoming more and more of a problem. In 1999, Gigabit Ethernet offered bandwidth that was comparable to Myrinet, but the cost for switches and NICs was high. In the last six months, the price of Gigabit Ethernet NICs has dropped from around $1000/NIC to $200/NIC[4, 6]. This is the true advantage of commodity-based hardware. While Myrinet has out-paced Gigabit Ethernet in performance, it does not promise near the reductions in costs that we see when components become a true commodity.

2.2 Network Layer Protocol

Internet Protocol (IP) is a relatively old protocol and many of the assumptions underlying the design of IP are no longer valid. Generally speaking, IP's hierarchical, dynamic routing is inefficient although LANs can maintain route table information and alleviate this weakness. Additionally, IP checksums reside in the header rather than at the end of the packet so computing the checksum requires maintaining additional state[12]. Also, headers are of various size requiring a check of the length field of each header.

Despite these difficulties, it is unlikely that any protocol (with the possible exception of IPv6) will replace IP as the commodity network layer protocol. Additionally, IP routers remain the most cost-effective hardware choice and the IP routing mechanism is well-tested.

2.3 Transport Layer Protocols

Transport Control Protocol (TCP) contains a large amount of communication processing overhead to administer flow control, error discovery and correction, and to maintain connections. Many of these services are unnecessary to the high-speed network application. These networks are highly reliable with little to no errors so the error detection and recovery would be less intrusive if it were not on the main path for all messages. Congestion control is maintained by the application so it's existence in the transport layer is redundant.

On the other hand, TCP and its unreliable cousin User Datagram Protocol (UDP) are the most common transport layer protocols used today. TCP gives all of the advantages of a commodity protocol. Specifically, TCP is transparent to the layer above it, in this case the application layer. Thousands of applications are written based on the TCP protocol.

Interoperability would be severely limited without support for TCP.

3 Operating System Bypass

Operating system bypass (OS bypass) was developed to reduce latency by removing the host processor from the common path of communication. Additionally, OS bypass addresses the bottlenecks associated with memory copies and frequent interrupts. In most instances, OS bypass is achieved by moving OS policy onto the NIC and protocol processing into user space.

OS bypass achieves lower latency by eliminating interrupts and all copying of network data, including the final copy from kernel memory to user memory. Although this technique has been demonstrated successfully in some cases, zero-copy *to* user space has yet to be proven generally useful in an operating system standard release. The primary concern is that the overhead and special-casing in the page cache necessary to manage the transition between the two address spaces may exceed the overhead of a single memory copy into a user buffer.

3.1 VIA

The virtual interface architecture (VIA) is one of the best-known OS bypass solutions. VIA assigns a virtual NIC in user space. A virtual interface is created for each connection (much like a socket) and each virtual interface contains a send queue and a receive queue. The receive queue contains descriptors with physical addresses. These physical addresses are translated at initialization time and the memory pages are locked[11].

VIA decreases latency especially for small messages since the overhead involved with managing buffers is not counted in the latency. If the virtual interface is implemented in user space, CPU overhead associated with communication remains very high. If the virtual interface is implemented on the NIC, the CPU overhead surprisingly remains high since the application must still be invoked to pull messages off of the queue.

OS bypass is achieved by moving data directly from the NIC to application space. If the NIC knows where the application expects a message, it can DMA data directly into application space and avoid all memory copies. The application either needs to tell the kernel where it wants a message so the kernel can translate addresses and tell the NIC, or the application must ask the kernel for an address translation and tell the NIC directly [11, 10].

No matter how the NIC gets information about memory addresses, both the application and the kernel are involved. First, the application must become active in order to control addressing and this requires a context switch. Second, the operating system must be active in order to perform address translation which requires a trap into the kernel. Using OS bypass, communication traffic still increases operating system activity.

4 Splintering

The philosophy of splintering isn't that the operating system shouldn't be used, but that it should be used effectively. In the case of communication offload, the goal is to minimize the overhead associated with invoking the OS while still enabling the OS to control communication.

4.1 Splintering IP

The IP stack has been successfully splintered in the past. A great example of the splintering of the IP stack is checksum offloading. Many NICs will compute the checksum of an IP packet during the DMA of data from the NIC to the host processor.

We first splintered the IP stack in an attempt to relieve the interrupt pressure bottleneck associated with small frame sizes (1500 bytes) and high-speed networks (1Gb/s).

4.1.1 Reducing Interrupt Pressures

Interrupt pressure is the most significant concern for high-speed Ethernet networks, yet it is largely overlooked as a performance bottleneck. If the network interface generates an interrupt for each 1500-byte packet, a processor with a 1Gb/s network interface should be capable of handling an interrupt every 12 μsec. Modern systems require between five and ten μsec to process an empty interrupt handler [8].

Interrupt latencies, the time that it takes a processor to respond to an interrupt, may decrease with pipelining. However, interrupt overheads, the amount of time it takes a processor to process an interrupt, will remain steady. Even an extremely efficient system cannot hope to manage interrupts arriving at 12μsec, and the situation becomes utterly hopeless for 10 Gb/s networks.

4.1.2 Offloading Fragmentation

Fragmentation has been virtually nonexistent since Kent and Mogul [7] identified serious problems with intermediate fragmentation (where routers fragment packets too large for the outgoing MTU of the next link) and proposed path MTU discovery in order to avoid any fragmentation by intermediate routers between two endpoints. Endpoint fragmentation is the only kind of fragmentation allowed in IP version 6.

Endpoint fragmentation does not share most of the disadvantages of intermediate fragmentation. Endpoint fragmentation is already commonly used by applications such

as NFS that benefit from large datagrams being sent and received at higher levels of the protocol stack (in the case of NFS because disk blocks are the smallest unit of currency for disks). Moreover, fragmentation and reassembly are tasks that are extremely well-suited for implementation on a reasonably powerful NIC such as the Acenic[1]. They are easy to separate from the rest of the IP stack. This is accomplished by transparently accepting packets larger than the real MTU of the link and fragmenting on the card. Almost no modification of the driver is necessary. In fact the only change to the driver is configuring the driver to believe the MTU is 64000 bytes. The operating system and driver operate normally except that there are fewer interrupts.

In order to test the performance of splintered IP fragmentation, we used an unmodified copy of netperf 2.1pl3[9] to measure unidirectional UDP streaming bandwidth. We chose netperf as a testing platform because data from netperf are frequently cited by other high-performance projects. Additionally, among network performance measurement packages, netperf is one of few to have a reasonable UDP implementation. Netperf only reports the UDP bandwidth actually received, providing a reliable means of measuring bandwidth for an otherwise unreliable protocol. All reported measures are to within a 95% confidence interval.

We configured two 933 MHz, Linux 2.4.0(release) servers with version 0.49 of Jes Sorenson's Acenic driver (patched only to support tracedumps). The machines were connected by a cross-over fiber cable (with no switch). We tested splintered IP fragmentation against interrupt coalescing and jumbo frames, the two most common methods used to attempt to relieve interrupt pressure. See [5] for a complete discussion of the implementation, test methodology and results.

Figure 1 shows that offloading fragmentation and reassembly onto the NIC significantly increases the effective utilization of the host (where effective utilization is defined as bandwidth divided by CPU overhead).

We were able to implement fragmentation and reassembly on the NIC to demonstrate that it is possible to drastically impact the performance of a commodity protocol without significantly compromising its advantages[5]. Offloading a small part of the protocol led to a successful relieving of interrupt pressure while maintaining bandwidth, flexibility, interoperability and cost. Importantly, the OS remains in control of the communication, but it is only invoked upon the complete assembly of a datagram.

4.2 Splintering TCP

We have successfully splintered and offloaded part of the IP stack to reduce the interrupt pressures and to increase the effective utilization of compute nodes. Next, we will pro-

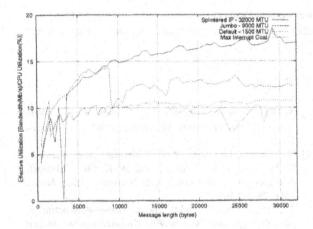

Figure 1. Effective utilization for unmodified firmware at 1500 byte MTU and offloaded fragmentation with driver MTU of 32000 bytes

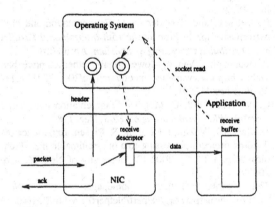

Figure 2. The Splintered TCP Architecture

pose to splinter and offload part of the TCP stack in order to reduce the communication costs associated with the protocol.

Figure 2 presents a graphical illustration of our approach to splintering the processing associated with the TCP protocol. In this case we only illustrate the processing done while receiving datagrams. In this illustration, solid lines indicate the paths taken by datagrams, while dashed lines represent control activities.

We start by considering the control path. In particular, we assume that the application issues a socket read before the data has arrived, i.e., a "pre-posted" read. Eventually, after traversing several layers of libraries, this read is transformed into a request that is passed to the operating system. The OS can then build a descriptor for the application buffer. This descriptor will include physical page addresses

for the buffer. Moreover, as the OS builds this descriptor, it can easily ensure that these pages will remain in memory (i.e., they will be pinned) as long as the descriptor is active in the NIC.

Now, we consider the handling of datagrams. When a datagram arrives, the NIC first checks to see if the incoming datagram is associated with a descriptor previously provided by the OS. If it finds such a descriptor, the NIC will DMA the data portion of the datagram directly to the application buffer, providing a true zero copy, and make the header available to the OS. In addition, the NIC will generate an acknowledgement, including the needed flow-control information, for this datagram. If the NIC does not find the needed descriptor, it will simply make the entire datagram available to the OS for "normal" processing.

Perhaps more interesting than the functionality that we intend to put on the NIC is the functionality that we plan to leave in the OS. As we have described, we will leave memory management in the OS and only provide the NIC with the mapping information that it needs to move data between the network and the application. We also plan to leave all failure detection and recovery in the OS.

With splintering, it is still necessary to invoke the OS to process the TCP headers, acknowledgements, and "unexpected" datagrams that have been queued by the NIC. Traditionally, the OS is invoked by the NIC, using an interrupt, for every datagram. This is needed to ensure the timely processing of datagrams. To avoid overrunning the processor with interrupts, many high-performance networks coalesce interrupts. That is, they wait until an number of packets have arrived or until a timer expires before they generate an interrupt. In standard environments, interrupt coalescing introduces a great deal of jitter in communication. In particular, packets that arrive shortly after the NIC has generated will have longer latencies.

Notice that this jitter is not as significant with TCP splintering. Connections that are sensitive to jitter can be managed by the NIC. This perspective leads to the possibility that the OS is never directly invoked to handle communication activities, but rather handles these activities after it has been invoked for another reason, e.g., the expiration of a quantum or an application I/O request.

Successful offloading of congestion control along with true zero-copy should substantially decrease the amount of CPU overhead associated with communication. Additionally, splintering allows the operating system to maintain appropriate control over resource management of the host processor and the NIC.

5 Related Work

Splintered TCP is similar to the EMP protocol[10] in that both push descriptors onto the NIC and achieve true zero-copy. EMP is different in that it's purpose is OS bypass for MPI whereas our work uses the TCP protocol. Additionally, EMP includes error handling on the NIC which potentially pushes too much processing onto the slower processor on the NIC. In our view, error handling should be treated as a special case and should not consume the limited resources that we would like to dedicate for high-performance activities.

Like splintered TCP, Trapeze[3] separates TCP headers from data. However, Trapeze sends both data and headers through the OS and uses page remapping to achieve zero-copy. Splintered TCP DMA's data directly to the application, thereby achieving a true zero copy. Also, splintered TCP avoids costly interrupts by offloading congestion control and ack generation to the NIC.

Splintered TCP is most similar to Wenbin Zhu's work on offloading parts of the RTS/CTS protocol of Portals[8]. While that work addressed the implementation of a specialized API, Portals, and a specialized protocol, reliable message passing protocol (RMPP), our work addresses a commodity API, sockets, and a commodity protocol, TCP. Moreover, we intend to extend the earlier work, by pushing descriptors onto the NIC on pre-posted reads.

6 Summary

OS bypass has been a popular philosophy aimed at relieving the performance pressures associated with high-performance communication. However, OS bypass attempts to fully disengage the operating system from the process of communication. This is not possible to achieve as the operating system must manage resources like memory and scheduling. Also, if work is pushed to the application, the application must be invoked, which is no more efficient than invoking the OS.

Splintering, on the other hand, attempts to more efficiently use the operating system to control communication. By moving select functions of communication onto the NIC, we can decrease the number of interrupts to the operating system while still allowing the operating system to manage resources.

There has long been a trend toward improving the performance of TCP/IP in high-performance computing while still maintaining its tremendous advantages. By creating a true zero-copy TCP, we can show that we can reduce overhead enough that TCP/IP becomes a viable protocol in the world of cluster computing. Furthermore, by appropriately offloading small parts of the protocols' functionality onto a NIC we have demonstrated the methods of splintering that will become more and more prevalent as we move into a distributed computing environment.

Here we have found that splintering the protocol stacks and offloading some implementation aspects of TCP/IP will lower communication overhead and increase performance without sacrificing the interoperability and cost advantages of the protocol.

References

[1] Acenic gigabit ethernet for linux. Web: 'http://jes.home.cern.ch/jes/gige/acenic.html', August 2001.

[2] N. J. Boden, D. Cohen, R. E. Felderman, A. E. Kulawik, C. L. Seitz, J. N. Seizovic, and W.-K. Su. Myrinet: A gigabit-per-second Local Area Network. *IEEE Micro*, 15(1):29–36, 1995.

[3] J. Chase, A. Gallatin, and K. Yocum. End-system optimizations for highspeed TCP. In *IEEE Communications, special issue on TCP Performance in Future Networking Environments*, volume 39, page 8, 2000.

[4] S. Elbert, Q. Snell, A. Mikler, G. Helmer, C. Csandy, K. Stearns, B. MacLeod, M. Johnson, B. Osborn, and I. Verigin. Gigabit ethernet and low cost supercomputing. Technical Report 5126, Ames Laboratory and Packet Engines, Inc., 1997.

[5] P. Gilfeather and T. Underwood. Fragmentation and high performance ip. In *Proc. of the 15th International Parallel and Distributed Processing Symposium*, April 2001.

[6] P. Hochmuth. Vendors lower gigabit ethernet price bar. Web: 'http://www.nwfusion.com/archive/2001/127651_11-26-2001.html', 2001.

[7] C. A. Kent and J. C. Mogul. Fragmentation considered harmful. *WRL Technical Report 87/3*, Dec. 1987.

[8] A. Maccabe, W. Zhu, J. Otto, and R. Riesen. Experience offloading protocol processing to a programmable nic. Technical Report TR-CS-2002-12, University of New Mexico, 2002.

[9] The public netperf homepage. Web: 'http://www.netperf.org/netperf/NetperfPage.html', 2001.

[10] P. Shivam, P. Wyckoff, and D. Panda. EMP: Zero-copy OS-bypass NIC-driven Gigabit Ethernet message passing. In ACM, editor, *SC2001: High Performance Networking and Computing. Denver, CO, November 10–16, 2001*, New York, NY 10036, USA and 1109 Spring Street, Suite 300, Silver Spring, MD 20910, USA, 2001. ACM Press and IEEE Computer Society Press.

[11] E. Speight, H. Abdel-Shafi, and J. K. Bennett. Realizing the performance potential of the virtual interface architecture. In *Proceedings of the 1999 Conference on Supercomputing*, ACM SIGARCH, pages 184–192, N.Y., June 20–25 1999. ACM Press.

[12] W. R. Stevens. *TCP/IP Illustrated, Volume 1; The Protocols*. Addison Wesley, Reading, 1994.

Network Processors: Origin of Species

Niraj Shah, Kurt Keutzer
University of California, Berkeley
{niraj,keutzer}@eecs.berkeley.edu

Abstract

Numerous programmable alternatives to network processing have emerged in the past few years to meet the current and future needs of network equipment. They all promise various trade-offs between performance and flexibility. In this paper we attempt to understand these new network processing alternatives. We present five major aspects of network processor architectures: approaches to parallel processing, elements of special-purpose hardware, structure of memory architectures, types of on-chip communication mechanisms, and use of peripherals. For each of these aspects, we include examples of specific network processor features.

1. Motivation

Many system designers are choosing to drop hard-wired ASIC solutions for system solutions in favor of application-specific instruction processors (ASIPs). Nowhere is this trend more apparent than in communication network equipment. The past four years have witnessed over 30 attempts at programmable solutions aimed at packet processing for communication networks. Classifying these architectures will help us to:

- evaluate the right match between an application and architectural features in a network processor
- develop a programming model that enables efficient programming of multiple network processors

More generally, understanding the evolution of network processors will help us understand the migration of programmable solutions to other application areas.

In this paper, we dissect the space of network processor architectures from five major perspectives. We first give our definition of a network processor (NPU). Then, we provide a number of perspectives from which to classify NPUs, drawing examples from the numerous NPUs currently on the market or in development. Lastly, we speculate on the future direction of these devices.

2. What is a Network Processor?

Top down, we define a network processor as any processor able to efficiently process packets for network communication. We purposely broaden the definition because we want to note that even general-purpose processors are used for packet forwarding.

Bottom up, we note that there are over 30 different processors self-identified as network processors [1]. As we shall see, self-identifying as network processor doesn't indicate any unique architectural features or approach. Thus, from the outset we emphasize that our approach to identifying network processors is *descriptive* and not prescriptive. Moreover, we claim that a descriptive approach is the only sensible approach to understanding network processors at this time and this descriptive approach makes the approach used to make the classification all the more important.

2.1. Means of Classification

To better understand the architectural space, we present five major strategies network processors have employed: approaches to parallel processing, elements of special-purpose hardware, structure of memory architectures, types of on-chip communication mechanisms, and use of peripherals.

2.2. Parallel Processing

To meet increasing line speed requirements, network processing systems have taken advantage of the parallelism present in various networking algorithms. NPU architectures exploit parallelism at three different levels: processing element level, instruction level, and word/bit level. It is important to note that while these approaches are orthogonal, a decision at one level clearly affects the others. Details on these three levels are given immediately below.

2.2.1. Processing Element Level

Before delving into different approaches to processing element level concurrency, we give our definition of a processing element:

A processing element (PE) is an instruction set processor that decodes its own instruction stream.

Most NPUs employ multiple PEs to take advantage of the data parallelism present in packet processing. Of those NPUs, there are two prevalent configurations:

- Pipelined: each processor is designed for a particular packet processing task
- Symmetric: each PE is able to perform similar functionality

In the pipelined approach, inter-PE communication is very similar to data-flow processing – once a PE is finished processing a packet, it sends it to the next downstream element. Examples of this architectural style include Cisco's PXF [2], EZChip's NP-1 [3], Vitesse's IQ2000 [4], and Xelerated Packet Devices [5]. In general, these architectures are easier to program since the communication between programs on different PEs is restricted by the architecture. However, there are timing requirements to be met by each program on every PE.

NPUs with symmetric PEs are normally programmed to perform similar functionality. They are often paired with numerous co-processors to accelerate specific types of computation. Arbitration units are often required to control access to the many shared resources. The Cognigine [6], Intel IXP1200 [7], IBM PowerNP [8], and Lexra NetVortex [9] are examples of this type of macro-

architecture. While these architectures have more flexibility, they are difficult to use, as programming them is very similar to the generic multi-processor programming problem.

2.2.2. Instruction Level

Many network processors have chosen not to implement multiple-issue architectures. This is likely based on the observation that most networking applications do not have the available instruction level parallelism to warrant it. This is in contrast to signal processing applications, for example. However, some architects have chosen to implement architectures that issue multiple instructions per cycle per processing element. For multiple issue architectures, there are two main tactics for determining the available parallelism: at compile time (e.g. VLIW) or at run time (e.g. superscalar). While superscalar architectures have had success in exploiting parallelism in general-purpose architectures (e.g. Pentium), VLIW architectures have been effectively used in domains like signal processing, where compilers are able to extract enough parallelism. VLIW architectures are often preferred because they are lower-power architectures. The success of VLIW architectures in networking will largely depend on their target applications. Control-plane code, for example, is largely control-dominated, and therefore lends itself more to a superscalar implementation.

The Agere Routing Switch Processor [10], Brecis' MSP5000 [11], and Cisco's PXF [2] use VLIW architectures. This allows them to take advantage of intra-thread instruction-level parallelism (ILP) at compile time by leveraging sophisticated compiler technology. Clearwater Networks takes another approach - they use a multiple

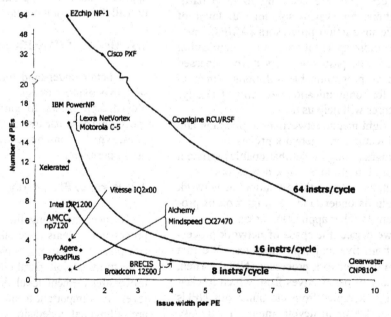

Figure 1. Trade-offs between number of PEs and issue width.

issue superscalar architecture in which a hardware engine finds the available ILP at runtime [12]. Cognigine also has multiple issue PEs (4-way), but they have a run-time configurable instruction set that defines data types, operations, and predicates [6].

2.2.3. Bit Level

Depending on the data types and operations present in an application, it is possible to exploit bit level parallelism. For example, some NPUs have circuitry to efficiently compute the CRC field of a packet header.

2.2.4. Summary

Figure 1 plots the number of PEs versus the issue width per PE. It is easy to see that NPU architects have faced a large trade-off between processing element level and instruction level concurrency. Clearwater Networks, at one extreme, has a single PE with 10 issue slots, while EZchip has 64 scalar PEs. On this chart, we have also plotted iso-curves of issuing 8, 16, and 64 instructions per cycle. While the clock speed and specialized hardware employed by network processors are not represented in this figure, it does illustrate the trade-offs NPUs have made between multiple levels of parallelism. Most NPUs have opted for more stripped down processing elements, instead of fewer multi-issue PEs. This severely complicates the programming model, as NPUs have more independent executing units in this approach.

2.3. Special-Purpose Hardware

Another strategy employed to meet increasing network processing demands is to implement common functions in hardware instead of having a slower implementation using a standard ALU. The major concern in having special-purpose hardware for NPUs is the granularity of the implemented function. There is a trade-off between the applicability of the hardware and the speedup obtained. The type of special-purpose hardware used can be broadly divided into two categories: co-processors and special functional units.

2.3.1. Co-Processors

A co-processor is a computational block that is triggered by a processing element (i.e. it does not have an instruction decode unit) and computes results asynchronously.

In general, a co-processor is used for more complicated tasks, may store state, and may have direct access to memories and buses. As a result of its increased complexity, a co-processor is more likely to be shared among multiple processing elements. A co-processor may be accessed via a memory map, special instructions, or bus transaction.

Most NPUs have integrated co-processors for common networking tasks; many have more than one co-processor. Operations ideally suited for co-processor implementation are well defined, expensive and/or cumbersome to execute within an instruction-set, and prohibitively expensive to implement as an independent special functional unit.

The functions of co-processors vary from algorithmic-dependent operations to entire kernels of network processing. For example, the Hash Engine in the Intel IXP1200 is only useful for lookup, if the algorithm employed requires hashing. For IP routing, the most common algorithms (trie table-based) do not use hash tables. This limits the freedom of software implementation on network processors – the software programmer is forced to implement a task using a specific algorithm that can make use of the co-processor.

The most common integrated co-processors execute lookup and queue management functions. The functionality of lookup is clear – given a key, lookup a value in a mapping table. The main design parameter is the size of the key. For additional flexibility, some co-processors also support variable sized keys. Since lookup often references large memory blocks, it needs to operate asynchronously from a processing element. Common uses of lookup are for determining next hop addresses and for accessing connection state. The global aspect of lookup operations (with respect to the device) requires the co-processor be shared by all processing elements. Queue management is another good candidate for an integrated co-processor as the memory requirement for packet queues is large and queues are relatively cheap to implement in hardware. The small silicon overhead eliminates many memory read and write operations that would otherwise be required. Other common co-processors are for pattern matching, computing checksum/CRC fields, and encryption/authentication.

2.3.2. Special Functional Units

A special functional unit is a specialized computational block that computes a result within the pipeline stage of a processing element.

Most network processors have special functional units for common networking operations like pattern matching and bit manipulation. The computation required for these operations is cumbersome and error-prone to implement in software (with a standard instruction set), yet very easy to implement in hardware. For example, Intel's IXP1200 has an instruction to find the first bit set in a register in a single cycle [7]. With a standard instruction-set, this would be quite tedious and take numerous cycles. As with co-processor candidates, the transistor overhead is well worth the convenience and speedup. Cognigine has a different approach – each PE has four execution units that can be dynamically reconfigured to match the appli-

43

cation. Their VISC (Variable Instruction Set Computing) "instruction" determines operand sizes, operand routing, base operation, and predicates [6].

2.4. Memory Architectures

A third strategy NPUs have employed is the structure of memory architectures. The major memory-related tactics of NPUs are: multi-threading, memory management, and task-specific memories.

For data-plane processing, it is unclear whether the overhead of an Operating System (OS) is warranted. NPUs have responded by including more hardware support for common OS functions, like multi-threading and memory management.

Hiding memory access latency is a key aspect to efficiently using the hardware of a network processor. The most common approach to hiding latency is multi-threading. Multi-threading is used to efficiently multiplex a processing element's hardware. The stalls associated with memory access are well known to waste many valuable cycles. Multi-threading allows the hardware to be used for processing other streams while another thread waits for a memory access (or a co-processor or another thread). Without dedicated hardware support, the cost of operating system multi-threading would dominate computation time, since the entire state of the machine would need to be stored and a new one loaded. As a result, many NPUs (Agere, AMCC, ClearSpeed, Cognigine, Intel, Lexra, and Vitesse) have separate register banks for different threads and hardware units to schedule threads and swap them with zero overhead. Clearwater Networks takes a slightly different approach – they have eight threads executing in parallel on the same processing element (which can issue 10 instructions per cycle) [12]. In addition, their processing element employs superscalar techniques to dynamically determine the available instruction-level parallelism and functional unit usage.

On the Intel IXP1200, memory management is handled in a similar fashion: the SRAM LIFO queues can be used as free lists, thus obviating the need for a separate OS service routine [7]. Some NPs have special hardware that handles the common I/O path (i.e. packet flow). Clearwater's Packet Management Unit copies data from a MAC device into a memory shared by the core [12]. IBM, Motorola, Intel, EZchip have similar units.

Like co-processors and special functional units are specializations of a generic computational element for a specific purpose, task-specific memories are blocks of memory coupled with some logic for specific storage applications. For example, Xelerated Packet Devices has an internal CAM (Content Addressable Memory) for classification [5]. On the Vitesse IQ2200, the Smart Buffer

Module manages packets from the time they are processed until they are sent on an output port [13].

In summary, most NPUs use hardware-supported multi-threading to hide latency. Some NPUs have taken this further to accelerate additional OS kernels (like memory management) and other common memory intensive tasks.

2.5. On-Chip Communication Mechanisms

In general, on-chip communication mechanisms are tightly related to the PE configuration. For NPUs with pipelined processing elements, most communication architectures are point-to-point, between processing elements, co-processors, memory, or peripherals. NPUs with symmetric PE configurations often have full connectivity with multiple busses. For example, Motorola's C-5 DCP has three buses with a peak bandwidth of 60Gbps that connect 16 channel processors and 5 co-processors. There's a Payload Bus for high bandwidth, fixed latency communication of packet payloads between channel processors, the buffer management co-processor, and the queue management co-processor. The Ring Bus provides bounded latency communication to and from the lookup co-processor. Lastly, the Global Bus provides access to most of the processor's memory through a conventional monolithic memory-mapped addressing scheme [14].

Brecis's communication architecture has taken an alternative approach of mapping application characteristics directly to their bus architecture. Their Multi-Service Bus Architecture has a 3.2Gbps peak bandwidth and connects the major devices of the network processor, including the DSPs, control processor, security co-processor, Ethernet MACs, and peripheral sub-system. It supports three priority levels, which correspond to the three types of packets their device processes: voice, data, and control. This allows programmers to handle the different latency and throughput requirements of these packet types. In addition, the bus interface for each processor consists of a packet classifier and three packet queues, which map directly to the three types of traffic handled by this device (voice, data, and control) [11]. This enables efficient implementation of Quality of Service applications, a key to supporting voice and data on the same processor.

2.6. Peripherals

In addition to performing layer 3+ tasks, NPUs also need to consider packet movement on to and off the chip. When placed in a line-card environment [15], there are two main interfaces a network processor has: network and switch. Some NPUs have integrated network interfaces on-chip (e.g. MAC devices). Ethernet is the most common protocol supported. SONET and ATM are also supported by a couple NPUs targeting higher line speeds as those protocols are used more in the core. For example, Brecis's MSP5000 has two on-chip 10/100 Ethernet MACs [11]. While this may limit the applicability of their chip, it makes integration into a system much easier. In addition, the tight integration of a MAC makes it less likely to be a bottleneck. For end-systems with more than one NPU in them, switch fabrics are necessary for their inter-communication. A few NPUs also include a dedicated switch interface (e.g. UTOPIA or SPI). For example, the IBM PowerNP has dedicated ingress and egress switch fabric interfaces to support higher line rates [8]. Those NPUs that do not have a network or switch interface normally handle these transactions on a high bandwidth shared bus. For example, the IX bus on the Intel IXP processors is used for communication with the MACs and switch fabric.

Some NPUs even have programmable peripherals to support multiple protocols. The Motorola DCP C-5 has two parallel Serial Data Processors (one for send, one for receive) that can be micro-coded to support a number of different layer 2 interfaces, like ATM, Ethernet, or SONET. These Serial Data Processors handle programmable field parsing, header validation, extraction, insertion, deletion, CRC validation/calculation, framing and encoding/decoding [14].

3. Whither Network Processors?

Although they are largely attacking the same applications, network processors are currently exhibiting tremendous architectural diversity. In this paper we have simply tried to capture and organize this architectural diversity that was spawned in a nutrient (venture capital) rich environment. That diversity has now led to survival strategies as the business environment has considerably worsened. We expect that pruning of the companies, and the architectural design space will, naturally occur. Nevertheless, the use of programmable processors for packet processing in communication networks is well motivated and we expect that at least a few hearty species will successfully adapt to specific market niches.

4. Acknowledgements

The authors would like to thank Chidamber Kulkarni, Christian Sauer, Scott Weber, the rest of the MESCAL team, and the anonymous reviewers for their invaluable feedback.

5. References

[1] N. Shah, "Understanding Network Processors", Master's thesis, Dept. of Electrical Engineering & Computer Sciences, Univ. of California, Berkeley, 2001.

[2] Cisco Systems, "Parallel eXpress Forwarding in the Cisco 10000 Edge Service Router", White Paper, October 2000.

[3] EZchip Technologies, "Network Processor Designs for Next-Generation Networking Equipment", White paper, December 1999.

[4] SiTera Corp, "PRISM IQ2000", Product Brief, February 2000.

[5] Thomas Eklund (Xelerated Packet Devices), "The World's First 40Gbps (OC-768) Network Processor", Presentation, Network Processor Forum, June 2001.

[6] Rupan Roy (Cognigine), "A Monolithic Packet Processing Architecture Monolithic Packet Processing Architecture", Presentation, Network Processor Forum, June 2001.

[7] Intel Corp., "Intel IXP1200 Network Processor", Product Datasheet, December 2001.

[8] IBM Corp, "IBM Network Processor (IBM32NPR161EPXCAC100)", Product Overview, November 1999.

[9] Bob Gelinas, Paul Alexander, Charlie Cheng, W. Patrick Hays, Ken Virgile, William J. Dally (Lexra), "NVP: A Programmable OC-192c Powerplant", Presentation, Network Processor Forum, June 2001.

[10] Agere, "PayloadPlus Routing Switch Processor", Preliminary Product Brief, Lucent Technologies, Microelectronics Group, April 2000.

[11] BRECIS Communications, "MSP5000 Multi-Service Processor", Product Brief, May 2001.

[12] Narendra Sankar (Clearwater Networks), "CNP810™ Network Services Processor Family", Presentation, Network Processor Forum, June 2001.

[13] Vitesse Semiconductor Corp., "IQ2200 VSC2232 Network Processor", Preliminary Data Sheet, 2001.

[14] Motorola Corporation, "Motorola C-5 DCP Architecture Guide", 2001.

[15] M. Tsai, C. Kulkarni, C. Sauer, N. Shah, K. Keutzer, "A Benchmarking Methodology for Network Processors", 1st Network Processor Workshop, 8th Int. Symp. on High Performance Computer Architectures (HPCA), Boston, MA, February 2002.

Session 1–2
Multimedia Technology

Automatic Generation of Motion Activity Descriptors in Video Sequences

JungHwan Oh   Vasavi Gavirneni

Department of Computer Science and Engineering
University of Texas at Arlington
Arlington, TX 76019-0015 U. S. A.
e-mail: {*oh, gavirnen*}@*cse.uta.edu*

Abstract

Recently, *motion activity* which is defined as amount of motion in a video sequence has been included as a descriptor in MPEG-7 standard. The motion activity descriptors (MADs) which describe this motion activity need to enable efficient content analyzing, indexing, browsing, and querying of video data. To address this issue, first, we propose a novel technique for automatic measurement of motion activity using accumulation of quantized pixel differences among the frames of given video segment. As a result, accumulated motions of shot are represented as a two dimensional *matrix*. Also, we investigate an efficient and scalable technique to compare these matrices and generate MADs that are representing various motions of shots effectively. Not only the degrees (amounts) but also the locations of motions are computed and presented accurately. Our preliminary experimental studies indicate that the proposed techniques are effective in capturing and comparing motion activities.

KEYWORDS: Motion activity, Motion activity descriptors, Video content analysis, Video similarity model, Video retrieval.

1 Introduction

As a result of the rapid advances in data compression, storage devices and communication networks, multimedia, in particular video media, has become an integral part in many fields including education, business and entertainment [1]. This brings about the researches on content analyzing and indexing of videos for effective browsing, retrieval, filtering, and summarizing [2, 1]. One of the most distinguishable features which video has is *motion*. However, this motion information is relatively less examined than the other features since the computation (i.e., optical flow) is expensive, and it is not easily applicable to natural video in which there are mostly little restrictions on camera operation, object(s) and background. The overall motion which is generated from camera motion and/or object(s) motion in video has been measured and manipulated for content analyzing and indexing purposes [3, 4, 5, 6].

Recently, *motion activity* which is defined as the perceived subjective degree of activity, or amount of motion, in a video sequence [7], has been included as a descriptor in MPEG-7 standard [8]. This motion activity which can give a little more detail information about motion than the overall motion estimation has been investigated in numerous researches. A combination of image and audio features [9], a mode of motion vector magnitudes [10], a tangent distance between consecutive frames [11], and mean, variance, and median of motion vector magnitudes [12] are used to determine the motion activity levels of video segments.

The motion activity descriptors (MADs) should be able to capture different characteristics from different video segments. To address this issue, first, we propose a novel technique for automatic measurement of motion activity using accumulation of quantized pixel differences among the frames of given video segment (i.e., shot which is defined as a collection of frames recorded from a single camera operation). As a result, accumulated motions of shot are represented as a two dimensional *matrix*. Also, we investigate an efficient and scalable technique to compare these matrices and generate MADs that are representing various motions of shots effectively. Their main contributions can be summarized as follows.

- This matrix is showing not only the amounts but

49

also the exact locations of motions. Therefore, we can get more accurate and richer motion information of shot.

- Because the proposed matrix comparison algorithm is very efficient and scalable, it can provide various ranges of clustering for shots which is essential tool for content analyzing, indexing, browsing, and querying of video data.

- It is very cost-effective because it uses accumulation of quantized pixel differences, and expensive computation (i.e., optical flow) is not necessary.

The remainder of this paper is organized as follows. In Section 2, we propose a novel technique for automatic measurement of motion activity, and discuss how to compute MADs automatically. The experimental results are discussed in Section 3. Finally, we give our concluding remarks in Section 4.

2 Computation and Description of Motion Activity

In this section, we introduce a novel technique for automatic measurement of *motion activity (MA)* in not only two consecutive frames but also whole shot which is a collection of frames. As a result, accumulated motions of shot are represented as a two dimensional *matrix*. Then, we discuss how to generalize and describe this matrix for the purpose of indexing and comparing each other.

2.1 Motion Activity Matrix

The MA for a shot with n frames is computed using the following steps. We assume that the frame size is $c \times r$ pixels.

Step.1 The color space of each frame is quantized (i.e., from 256 to 64 or 32 colors) to reduce false detection of motion by noise which is not actually motion but detected as motion.

Step.2 An empty two dimensional matrix which has the same size ($c \times r$) of the frame is created and initialized with zeros. For convenience, this matrix is called *Motion Activity Matrix (MAM)*.

Step.3 Compare all the corresponding pixels of two consecutive frames. If they have different color, increase the matrix value in the corresponding position by one (this value may be larger according to

the other conditions). Otherwise, it remains without any increasing or decreasing.

Step.4 Step.3 is repeated until all consecutive pairs of frames are compared.

To visualize the computed MAM, we can convert this MAM to an image which is called *Motion Activity Matrix Image (MAMI)*. Let us convert an MAM with the maximum value m into a 256 gray scale image as an example. If m is greater than 256, m and other values are scaled down to fit into 256 as maximum, otherwise, they are scaled up. But the value zero remains unchanged. An empty image with same size of MAM is created, and the corresponding value of MAM is assigned as a pixel value. For example, assign white pixel for the matrix value zero which means no motion, and black pixels for the matrix value 256 which means maximum motion in a given shot. Each pixel value for an $MAMI$ can be computed as follows if we assume that $MAMI$ is a 256 gray scale image.

$$Each\ Pixel\ Value = \frac{256}{Corresponding\ Matrix\ Value} \quad (1)$$

Figure 1 shows the first and the eighth frames in a shot, and the $MAMI$ for those frames #1 through #8. As seen in this figure, there is not much motion. The several frames and the $MAMI$ for whole shot (from the first frame (#1) to the last (#99)) are shown in Figure 2. These figures illustrate that the proposed technique can compute not only the exact amount (or degree) but also the region of motions in a shot.

#001   #008   #MAMI

Figure 1: Frames in a shot and its MAMI

2.2 Motion Activity Descriptors

For querying or indexing purpose, we basically need to compare shots, in other words, $MAMs$ need to be compared with other $MAMs$. In this subsection, we discuss a technique to compare shots in terms of amounts (degrees) as well as regions of motions.

The amount of motions can be compared by *Total Motion (TM)* computed from the corresponding MAM.

50

Figure 2: Frames in a shot and its $MAMI$

Assume that MAM_A and TM_A are motion activity matrix and total motion for shot A respectively. MAM_A and TM_A are defined and computed as follows (where, a_{ij} is obtained by Step.1 through Step.4 in the previous subsection).

$$MAM_A = \begin{pmatrix} a_{11} & a_{12} & a_{13} & ... & a_{1c} \\ a_{21} & a_{22} & a_{23} & ... & a_{2c} \\ ... & ... & ... & ... & ... \\ a_{r1} & a_{r2} & a_{r3} & ... & a_{rc} \end{pmatrix} \quad (2)$$

$$TM_A = \sum_{i=0}^{r} \sum_{j=0}^{c} a_{ij} \quad (3)$$

Also, if we cluster the shots (MAMs, eventually) based on the *Total Motion (TM)* computed from the corresponding MAM, we can reduce inappropriate comparisons among shots which have very different amounts of motions. Consequently, we can save the computation cost significantly.

However, comparing only by TM does not give very accurate results because it ignores the locality such that where the motions occur. We introduce a technique to capture locality information without using partitioning, which is described as follows. In the proposed technique, the locality information of MAM can be captured by two one dimensional matrices which are the summation of column values and the summation of row values in MAM. These two arrays are called as *Summation of Column (SC)* and *Summation of Row (SR)* to indicate their actual meanings. The following equations show how to compute SC_A and SR_A from MAM_A.

$$SC_A = (\sum_{i=0}^{r} a_{i1} \quad \sum_{i=0}^{r} a_{i2} \quad ... \quad \sum_{i=0}^{r} a_{ic})$$
$$SR_A = (\sum_{j=0}^{c} a_{1j} \quad \sum_{j=0}^{c} a_{2j} \quad ... \quad \sum_{j=0}^{c} a_{rj})$$

Figure 3 shows some examples such that how these SC

and SR can capture where the motions occur. Two SRs in Figure 3 (a) are same, which means that the vertical locations of two motions are same. Similarly, Figure 3 (b) shows that the horizontal locations of two motions are same by SCs. Figure 3 (c) is showing the combination of two, the horizontal and vertical location changes.

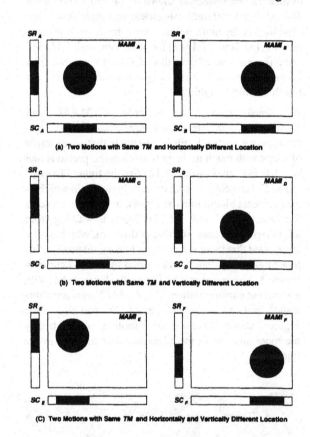

(a) Two Motions with Same *TM* and Horizontally Different Location

(b) Two Motions with Same *TM* and Vertically Different Location

(C) Two Motions with Same *TM* and Horizontally and Vertically Different Location

Figure 3: Comparisons of Locations of Motions

Therefore, we propose these TM, SC, and SR as Motion Activity Descriptors (MADs) in this paper. Now, we generalize shot similarity model using these three MADs. Assume that we compare MAM_A from shot A with MAM_B from shot B. The similarity ($Sim_{A,B}$) between MAM_A and MAM_B can be computed using the following equation.

$$Sim_{A,B} = \omega_1 \times (|TM_A \quad TM_B|)$$
$$+ \omega_2 \times (|SC_A \quad SC_B|) + \omega_3 \times (|SR_A \quad SR_B|) \quad (4)$$

where ω_1, ω_2, and ω_3 are weighted factors, and their summation ($\omega_1 + \omega_2 + \omega_3$) is 1.0. The computation of $|SC_A \quad SC_B|$ is that the summation of the differences of the corresponding matrix values.

51

3 Experimental Results

Our video clips in the test set were originally digitized in AVI format at 30 frames/second. Their resolution is 160×120 pixels. Our test set has 68 shots which consist of total 12,399 frames as shown in Table 1. They were divided into 5 different categories, and their details are explained in the table. In this experiment, we first compute MAM (and $MAMI$) for each shot, and TM, SC and SR are extracted from this MAM of each shot. The average values of TM per category is also shown in the fourth column of Table 1.

We already showed an example of MAM (and $MAMI$) of a shot in the category 3 (see Figure 2 in the previous section). Figure 4 shows that an example of a shot with much more motions than the previous one which is indicated by the $MAMI$ in the figure. To visualized SC and SR, we plot them in Figure 5, in which x-axis presents all columns and rows, and y-axis presents the values of SC and SR. An object is walking from left to right at a constant speed in this shot, which can be interpreted that there is a constant horizontal motion. Interestingly, this content is described by the SC curve in Figure 5. The last example (Figure 6) shows a shot with a zoom out camera motion. The $MAMI$ represents this camera motion clearly. Two curves (SC and SR) in the Figure 7 also show this camera motion, in which they are more motions in the edges and less motions in the middle.

Figure 4: Frames in Shot # 53 and its $MAMI$

4 Concluding Remarks

In this paper, first, we propose a technique to measure motion activity in a shot automatically using a two dimensional matrix. Not only the degree (amount) but also the location of motions are computed and presented

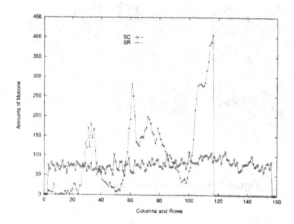

Figure 5: SC and SR for Shot # 53

Figure 6: Frames in Shot #66 and its $MAMI$

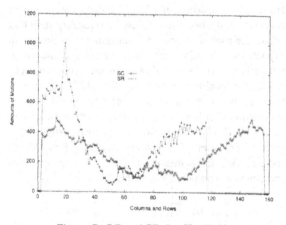

Figure 7: SC and SR for Shot# 66

52

Category No.	Total No. of Shots	Total No. of Frames	Average of TM	Category Description
1	7	1,115	10.1	No camera motion, and No specific object.
2	24	5,981	30.9	No camera motion, and One object which is not moving.
3	21	2,983	61.4	No camera motion, and One object which is moving a little.
4	12	567	462.1	No camera motion, and One or two objects which are moving much.
5	4	1,753	181.2	Camera zoom in and out
Total	68	12,399		

Table 1: Test Set of Shots and Its Results for Average of TM

accurately. The other technique to compare these matrices efficiently is also proposed. In the technique, the amounts and the locations of motions are compared with by TM, and SC and SR. Our preliminary experimental studies indicate that the proposed techniques are effective in capturing and comparing motion activity. We will perform further experiments in the future to study the effectiveness of matrix comparison technique using TM, SC and SR.

References

[1] R. Jain. Content-based multimedia information management. In *Proc. of 14th Int'l Conf. on Data Engineering*, pages 252–253, Orlando, Florida, February 1998.

[2] P. Aigrain, H. Zhang, and D. Petkovic. Content-based representation and retrieval of visual media : A state-of-the art review. *Multimedia Tools and Applications*, 3:179–202, 1996.

[3] Y. Tan, S. Kulkarni, and P. Ramadge. Rapid estimation of camera motion from compressed video with application to video annotation. *IEEE Transactions on Circuit and Systems for Video Technology*, 10(1):136–146, 2000.

[4] V. Kobla, D. Doermann, K. Lin, and C. Faloutsous. Compressed domain video indexing techniques using dct and motion vector information in mpeg video. In *Proc. SPIE Vol. 3022, Storage and Retrieval for Image and Video Databases VII*, pages 200–211, San Jose, CA, January 1997.

[5] E. Ardizzone et al. Video indexing using mpeg motion compensation vectors. In *Proc. IEEE International Conference on Multimedia Computing and Systems*, 1999.

[6] J. G. Kim, H. Chang, J. W. Kim, and H. Kim. Efficient camera motion characterization for mpeg video indexing. In *Proc. of 2000 IEEE International Conference on Multimedia and Expo.*, 2000, pages 1171–1174, New York, NY, July 2000.

[7] A. Divakaran, K. Peker, and H. Sun. A descriptor for spatial distribution of motion activity. In *Proc. of ICIP 2000*, Canada, 2000.

[8] International Organization for Standardization. Overview of the mpeg-7 standard. In *ISO/IEC/JTC1/SC29/WG11 N4031*, Mar. 2001.

[9] S. Pfeiffer, R. Lienhart, S. Fischer, and W. Effelsberg. Abstracting digital movies automatically. *Journal of Visual Communication and Image Representation*, 7(4):345–353, December 1996.

[10] W. Wolf. Key frame selection by motion analysis. In *Proc. of ICASSP 96*, pages 1128–1231, 1996.

[11] N. Vasconcelos and A. Lippman. Towards semantically meaningful features spaces for the characterization of video content. In *Proc. of ICIP 97*, 1997.

[12] K. Peker, A. Divakaran, and T. Papathomas. Automatic measurement of intensity of motion activity of video segments. In *Proc. of SPIE conf. on Storage and Retrieval for Media Databases 2001*, pages 341–351, San Jose, CA, Jan. 2001.

ETCP: An Efficacy-oriented Transport Protocol for Point-to-Point Connections

Simon Sheu[*]   Sang-Fong Chien   Ping-Yi Lin
Computer Science, National Tsing Hua University, Taiwan, R.O.C.
{sheu, sfchien, pylin}@cs.nthu.edu.tw

Abstract

Occasional congestions on the modern networks induce irksome packets dropping. This effect seriously challenges the protocol designs to preserve the integrity of information flows. While ARQ-variants precisely specify the exact data for retransmission, FEC-based schemes rectify the packet loss beforehand. They suffer either elongated correction time or excessive bandwidth consumption for delivery of supportive packets. This paper presents an idea from analytical evidences to improve the amount of data applicable to the receiver for every unit of data sent from the sender. Consequently, the derived transport protocol can achieve the superior efficiency close to ARQ-variants and offer punctual data correction capability like FEC-based approaches. The performance results from experimental investigations substantiate this favorable feature.

1. Introduction

With the advances of the network technologies, digital content distributions and exchanges are growing rapidly. Web surfing or edutainment-on-demand services offering course materials on line from corporations and academic institutes are ones of many such examples. In this paradigm, bit-level errata are detected and corrected using parity check mechanisms like FEC (*forward error correction*) coding [3]. The integrity of information datagram can be thus defended by incorporating the redundant bits inside each packet against the noises present in the transmission media [4, 5]. Likewise, packet erasures due to network congestion can be shielded by delivery of h more redundant packets beside k original ones against random h losses among every n ($= k + h$) packets. Several algorithms facilitate the encoding/decoding of "(n, k) erasure codes" to yield the code rate c ($= k/n$) and redundancy rate r ($= h/n$) for the network environments with the packet loss rate p ($\leq r$) [6, 7]. Noticeably, Tornado codes expedite coding process by orders of magnitude using simple XOR operations with a slightly increased c [8, 9].

These applausive efforts enable scalable media delivery protocols to resist packet erasures on broadcast streams [17, 18, 19]. For content-sensitive media streaming, different code rates can be applied to balance up the degrees of protection by intrinsic data dependency stemming from the compression schemes in charge [1, 2]. However, there are few, if any, investigations on the determination of suitable code rate over the end-to-end connections in practical network environments. Intuitively, the redundancy rate of some connections is chosen to be greater than the maximal possible packet loss rate. Even with prior knowledge about gross packet loss probability, this simple scheme can still suffer possibility of lost packets in occasional severe network congestion. Yet, most of packets are overprotected by excessive redundant codes as the networks are lightly loaded. To maintain the QoS (*quality of services*) specified by applications, ones would naturally increase the redundancy rate r to improve the success rate d of more than k packets arriving to the target applications [1, 2]. However, the overhead to deliver extra redundant packets competes for more bandwidth, and thus further worsens the network congestion, rendering higher packet loss rate in turns. To break this vicious spiral, each connection may graceful degrade its own QoS demand to also respect others' [2], like the fairness approach of TCP's AIMD [20]. An alternative is to employ the ARQ-like feedback to specify the transmission of further packets for the coding block of unrecoverable ones to make up k received packets [10, 11, 12]. As such, late-arriving packets by ARQ can be still useful for real-time applications [21]. Obviously, the degree of protection should strike a good balance between the success rate and extra round-trip delays for completion of recovering k packets. Particularly, the delivery efficiency e, the amount of data applicable to the receiver per unit of data sent from the sender, is an important factor to escape from the aforementioned spiral. Using the same amount of source traffics, a highly efficient delivery approach will bring more useful data to the receiver.

Park and Wang show that increasing redundancy rate beyond a certain point will contrarily decrease their recovery rate due to induced severer congestion [13]. They suggest using the feedback of x, the number of packets in a block arriving in time, to adjust on the fly the redundancy rate of the subsequent block of data packets [13]. Thus a

[*] This work is supported by the National Science Council, Project No. NSC 90-2213-E-007-038, and MOE Program for Promoting Academic Excellent of Universities, Grant No. 89-E-FA04-1-4, Taiwan, R.O.C.

desirable value of x can be approached well above the value of k. However, it is not clear how to deliberate the values of x and scale factor ε used in progressive adjustment. Severe oscillation around or slow convergence toward the desirable redundancy rate may stem from using improper ε's value. Choi and Shin examine the effects of bit-error rate and frame size for the wireless networks [14]. They suggest toggling between four redundancy rates to achieve good bit-rate efficiency, which is defined as the ratio of the amount of data applicable to the receiver over what were sent from the sender. However, none of these predetermined rates may yield the best efficiency.

In this paper, we propose a comprehensive analysis on how redundancy rate and packet loss rate jointly affect the delivery efficiency. Particularly, we derive an appropriate way to determine the optimal redundancy rate dynamically according to the packet loss rate fed back from the receiver along the connection session. To assess the effectiveness of our analysis, we design an efficacy-oriented transport protocol to exercise the dynamically chosen value for the redundancy rate. The experiments verify that our design can consistently achieve remarkable performance improvements. The rest of the paper is structured as follows. Section 2 describes the analysis on the determinant factors on delivery efficiency. Section 3 presents our proposed transport protocol. Section 4 carries out our performance study. Finally, we give concluding remarks in Section 5.

2. Analysis of Delivery Efficiency

For the delivery of every n packets over the network, we assume each packet has independent probability p of being lost [8]. Then, the probability of the network dropping x over n packets, $f(n, p, x)$, can be represented by a binomial random variable x [15] as:

$$f(n,p,x) = \binom{n}{x} p^x (1-p)^{n-x} \tag{1}$$

For large n, Eqn. 1 may be approached for fast computation by the *Demoivre-Laplace limit theorem* [15] as a normal density function with parameters $\mu = np$, $\sigma^2 = np(1-p)$, as:

$$f(n,p,x) \rightarrow \frac{1}{\sqrt{2\pi}\sigma} e^{\frac{-(x-\mu)^2}{2\sigma^2}} \tag{2}$$

For example, the probability of x lost packets for sending 100 packets over 10% packet loss rate network (n=100, p=10%) can be approximately computed as:

$$f(100,0.1,x) = \binom{100}{x}(0.1)^x (1-(0.1))^{100-x} \rightarrow \frac{1}{3\sqrt{2\pi}} e^{\frac{-(x-10)^2}{18}} \tag{3}$$

Fig.1(left) shows the density function of $f(100, 0.1, x)$.

For "(n, k) erasure code," a block of n packets is said to be "decodable" if the receiver obtains no less than k encoded packets, i.e. at most $n-k$ encoded packets can be dropped. With the redundancy rate r, the success rate or decodable probability $d(n, p, r)$ of this set can be derived as:

$$d(n,p,r) = \sum_{i=k}^{n} \text{Prob(Receiving } i \text{ packets)}$$

$$= \sum_{j=0}^{n-k} \text{Prob(Dropping } j \text{ packets)} \tag{4}$$

$$= \sum_{j=0}^{n-k} f(n,p,j) = \sum_{i=0}^{n \times r} f(n,p,i)$$

$$\approx \int_{0}^{(n \times r)+0.5} f(n,p,i)di = \int_{0}^{(n \times r)+0.5} \frac{1}{\sqrt{2\pi}\sigma} e^{\frac{-(x-\mu)^2}{2\sigma^2}} dx$$

$$= \int_{0}^{(n \times r)+0.5} \frac{1}{\sqrt{2\pi np(1-p)}} e^{\frac{-(x-np)^2}{2np(1-p)}} dx$$

Fig.1(right) sketches the decodable probability distribution of the previous example by a dotted line.

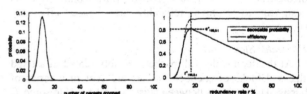

Fig. 1: The dropping (left) and decodable (right, dotted line) probability and efficiency (right, solid line) distribution of a block with n=100, p=10%.

Definitely more redundancy (larger r) can better resist the packet losses at a cost of increased network traffics. As shown in Fig.1(right, dotted line), as r increases, the success rate climbs up to reach its pinnacle at about $r = 16\%$, and saturate thereafter. Further augment of r will benefit no more since the success rate d has reached 100%. The delivery efficiency $e(n, p, r)$ can be calculated as:

$$e(n,p,r) = \frac{mks \cdot d(n,p,r)}{mns} = \frac{d(n,p,r)k}{n} = d(n,p,r)(1-r) \tag{5}$$

$$\approx (1-r) \cdot \int_{0}^{(n \times r)+0.5} \frac{1}{\sqrt{2\pi np(1-p)}} e^{\frac{-(x-np)^2}{2np(1-p)}} dx$$

where m is the number of code sets sent and s is the packet size. Fig. 1 (right, solid line) depicts its relationship with the code rate r by the same example (i.e. $e(100, 0.1, r)$.) As r increases, the delivery efficiency grows initially to reach its peak (~83%) at about r = 16%, as marked in the figure. Seeking for more protection against packet loss will only deteriorate the delivery efficiency, instead. That is, under this network state of p=10%, if encoding 16% out of a 100-packet block as redundancy, we can achieve the best efficiency with the probability of being decodable is about 98% (From Fig. 1 (right, dotted line).) It can be concluded that given any values of n and p ($n > 0$, $1 > p > 0$), there exists a best r^* corresponding to the optimal efficiency e^*.

Therefore, keeping using r^* under various network conditions dynamically will always choose the best way to efficiently deliver the information packets at a reasonable tolerance of success rate (nearly 100%). In the next section, we will discuss how this property can be incorporated in the proposed transport protocol based on the estimated network packet loss rate p. We note that r^* is slightly larger than p. A naïve selection of the redundancy rate exactly matching the packet loss rate is an unwise decision. Some blocks may win more packets than the others by probability distribution. Thus, the former are over-coded while the latter become not decodable. This fact can be pictured by the evidence $d(100, 0.1, 0.1)$ is just about 55% from Fig.1(right). The readers interested in the effect of block size n are referred to [16].

3. Transport Protocol

In this section, we design a network transport protocol, which benefit from optimizing delivery efficiency. This protocol provides reliability of transmitting source data using ARQ-like feedback to report the packet loss rate, and incorporates TCP-friendly AIMD [20] controls. It is designed to archive reliability and good efficiency simultaneously.

I. Sender Side

At the sender side, all packets are formulated of a fixed size s. Blocks of encoded packets are sent in a series of bursts. The intervals between bursts are all equal to some T. Burst i estimates its own allowable bandwidth $B(i)$ for data delivery and the packet loss rate $p(i)$, which will be discussed shortly after. In other words, in this Burst i, the sender could send traffic up to the amount of $T{\times}B(i)$ using the following steps.

Step1: *Retransmission*: Firstly, scan transmission table that logs the status of earlier delivered blocks. Enough packets are sent out to help reconstruct previously delivered blocks. We note that some of supplemental packets may be still possibly dropped. The optimal r^* is approximated to augment the number of packets to be retransmitted by a scaling factor $(1-r^*)^{-1}$.

Step2: *Encoding a block of erasure code*: Suppose the total number of retransmitted packets in Step 1 is R. In this step, the sender obtains k source packets and then encodes them into n encoded packets using erasure code. The value of n is computed as $n = T{\times}B(i)/s - R$. With the value of r^* from (4), the value of k can be determined as $k = (1 - r^*) \cdot n$.

II. Receiver Side

Upon receiving a packet of Block i in newer Burst t (either this packet belongs to a new block or is a retransmitted one), (re)start a timer. Packets for different blocks are attributed to the respective queues. Once the timer is expired, the receiver executes these steps:

Step1: *Check if decodable*: Check this block if it is decodable. If so, decode the block and pass it to the application. Or, mark it as *"need retransmission"*.

Step2: *NACKs*: Examine each block and send a NACK back to the sender if this block is marked. This message contains Burst ID, Block ID, and the number of additional packets required to decode the block.

Step3: *Network State*: Send back the information about current network state such as packet loss rate, which will be employed by the flow control to determine optimal redundancy rate r^*.

III. Flow Control

The objective of flow control is to estimate the available bandwidth $B(i)$ and the packet loss rate $p(i)$ in the coming i^{th} burst, and adjust the sending rate to be not so aggressive to overtake the bandwidth from other competitors sharing the same link. With $p(i)$, network efficiency in Burst i can be maximized by encoding a block with optimal redundancy rate r^*. This flow control is described as below:

$$\bar{p} = avg(p_1, p_2, \ldots, p_v), p(i) = \frac{p(i-1) + \bar{p}}{2}$$

$$\text{if } (\bar{p} > 0) \qquad B(i) = \frac{(1-\bar{p})}{(1-p(i))} \times B(i-1)$$

$$\text{else} \qquad B(i) = \beta \times B(i-1)$$

(9)

where v is the total number of feedbacks from the receiver during the burst $i-1$, p_i is the packet loss rate of the ith feedback, and β indicates the scale factor (1.02 is a empirical good value) to control how fast the sending rate adapts to current available bandwidth.

4. Performance Study

To examine the efficacy of the proposed transport protocol, we build its prototype for intensive simulations under the discrete event simulator *ns-2* [22]. Fig. 2 illustrates the network configuration in the experiments.

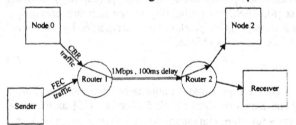

Fig. 2: The topology of experimental environment.

The bottleneck link interconnecting two routers has a bandwidth set to 1 Mbps of delay 100 ms. This link is shared by our transport protocol's traffic and the background traffic as well. The other links in this topology are all set to 10 Mbps with the delay 10 ms. The background traffic is modeled as the CBR at the rate of 400 kbps and travels through the bottleneck link from Node 0 to Node 2. It starts at the 30th sec and ends at the 120th sec during the simulation sessions. We keep track of the detailed actions taken by the experimental protocols in the entire duration of 200 seconds. To best observe the behaviors of the protocols, all the data packets and feedback messages are logged and summarized in the statistical tables and performance figures.

This study employs the following performance metrics to assess the quality of the protocols:

(1) Efficiency: the amount of data applicable to the receiver per unit of data sent from the sender,

(2) Success rate: the percentage of blocks decodable without any retransmission,

(3) Retransmissions: the average number of the times each block carries out retransmissions, and

(4) Bursts: the average number of bursts to complete delivery of each block.

We compare the proposed efficacy-oriented protocol T_e with other protocols using pre-determined code rates. For clarity, we use T_i to represent the protocol with the redundancy rate of i %. For instance, the protocol T_{10} employs the redundancy rate of 10 % to constantly protect each block of packets for delivery. Table 1 lists the other parameters used in these experiments for convenience of readers.

Table 1: Parameters used in experiments.

Parameter	Value	Unit
The interval between each burst T	1	Sec
The time α before blocks expires at the receiver.	1.5	Sec
Bandwidth scale factor β	1.02	N/A

To observe the effect of network congestion, we first disable the retransmission function and keep the sending rate constantly at 700 Kbps (no flow control) for all the protocols to compare their success rates in Exp-1. During $30^{th} \sim 120^{th}$ second, severe network congestion occurs in the presence of the background traffic. As shown in Table 2, only about 55% blocks can be decodable by T_0 & T_{10}. Albeit employing certain protection that matches the packet loss rate 10%, T_{10}'s efficiency is even worse than T_0 since some blocks may win more received packets than the others rendering fruitless of the latter. With excessive redundancy, T_{20} can sustain this severe condition. However, its efficiency is barely 79.55%. In vivid contrast, T_e dynamically adjusts its redundancy rate. As shown in Fig. 3(left), only blocks sent at 30th and 31st sec experience failures, while all the subsequent blocks are coded with proper redundancy rates. As such, T_e can best conserve delivery capacity to achieve the efficiency as high as 86.13%. With the retransmission function enabled, we would like to compare the average duration to complete delivery of a block. Table 3 summarizes the Exp-2's results shown in Fig. 4. T_{20} is the fastest yet at a considerable degradation of efficiency. T_0 is the other extreme. It takes a lot of retransmissions (0.91) and bursts (3.02) to complete. Our scheme T_e strikes best balance between efficiency and time. It achieves the efficiency close to T_0 at a speed like T_{20}.

To examine the behaviors of protocols in practice, the flow control is enabled in Exp-3 & Exp-4. Fig. 6 depicts how the sending rate is adjusted for TCP-friendliness: it initiates at 700 Kbps and grows by probing to reach

available bandwidth. When congestion occurs, it follows TCP's AIMD to adapt the sending rate. Since packet loss is used to signal the adaptation of sending rate, all the performances are degraded a little bit. Fig. 7 shows how T_e adapts each block's redundancy rate (i.e. r^*) according to the network state: a little more than packet loss rate is used to achieve the best efficiency and the favorable success rate about 95%. Other schemes evoking no reaction on the changes of the network conditions suffer the inferior delivery efficiency, worse success rate, or lengthy period to complete transmission of a block. The results from Table III & IV are consistent with those discussed before.

Table 2: (Exp-1) Constant sending-rate at 700kbps, retransmission disabled.

	T_e	T_0	T_{10}	T_{20}
Efficiency %	86.13	54.77	49.17	79.55
Success rate %	98.99	54.77	54.77	100.0

Table 3: (Exp-2) Constant sending-rate at 700kbps, retransmission enabled.

	T_e	T_0	T_{10}	T_{20}
Efficiency %	87.00	93.18	87.47	79.55
Retransmissions	0.02	0.91	0.49	0.00
Bursts	1.03	3.02	1.98	1.00

Table 4: (Exp-3) Dynamic sending-rate with retransmission.

	T_e	T_0	T_{10}	T_{20}
Efficiency %	88.63	95.67	88.49	79.46
Retransmissions	0.06	0.86	0.22	0.03
Bursts	1.12	2.89	1.43	1.05

Table 5: (Exp-4) Dynamic sending-rate without retransmission.

	T_e	T_0	T_{10}	T_{20}
Efficiency %	82.99	32.34	71.92	78.18
Success rate %	94.47	30.65	78.39	98.49

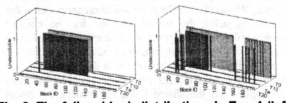

Fig. 3: The failure block distributions in Exp-1 (left) and Exp-4 (right).

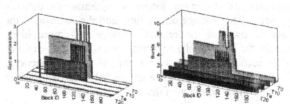

Fig. 4: Retransmissions (left), and bursts (right) for each block in Exp-2.

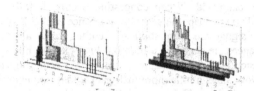

Fig. 5: Retransmissions (left), and bursts (right) for each block in Exp-3.

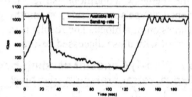

Fig. 6: The behavior of flow control.

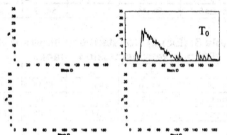

Fig. 7: The redundancy rate and packet loss rate of the protocols.

5. Concluding Remarks

Packet loss from network congestions can not be totally resolved simply by using higher redundancy rate to seek for more loss protection. This strategy of sending more redundant packets may further induce severer congestions and thus higher loss rate. Besides, higher redundancy rate also increases the time to deliver the same information under the same bandwidth capacity. In this paper, we present an idea from analytical investigations on the effectiveness of packet loss rate, code rate, success rate, and the like. We employ in the proposed transport protocol the strategy of using the redundancy rate for the optimal delivery efficiency throughout the connection sessions. As a result, we can dynamically adhere to the optimal utilization of the available delivery bandwidth in data transportation. While TCP's AIMD seeks for the fairness of bandwidth consumption on the shared links, our transport protocol tried to help resolve the network congestion from a more prospective viewpoint. The proposed efficacy-oriented approach allows every sender to optimize its delivery capacity. The savings on the time and the amount of the data to transmit the original message will more likely release the loads on the networks. As a whole, the networks will become more available for all the connections. Ultimately, every participant on the networks will benefit from the wide adoption of this efficacy-oriented feature.

References

[1] A. Albanese, J. Bloemer, J. Edmonds, M. Luby, M. Sudan, "Priority Encoding Transmission", *35th Annual Symposium on Foundations of Computer Science,* 1994.

[2] J. Bolot, S. Fosse-Parisis, D. Towsley. "Adaptive FEC-Based Error Control for Interactive Audio in the Internet." *IEEE INFOCOM 99:*

[3] A. J. McAuley, "Reliable Broadband Communication Using a Burst Erasure Correcting Code", *ACM SIGCOMM'90,* pp.297-306, Philadelphia, Sept. 1990.

[4] Rizzo, L., and Vicisano, L., "Effective Erasure Codes for Reliable Computer Communication Protocols," *ACM SIGCOMM,* 27(2):24-36, Apr 1997.

[5] R.E. Blahut, "Theory and Practice of Error Control Codes" *Addison Wesley,* MA, 1984.

[6] J. Hagenauer, "Rate Compatible Punctured Convolutional Codes (RCPC Codes) and their Applications," *IEEE Trans. Commun.,* Vol. 36, pp. 389-400, Apr. 1988,.

[7] C. Berrou, A. Glavieux, and P. Thitimajshima, "Near Shannon Limit Error-Correcting Coding and Decoding: Turbo Codes," in *Proc. ICC'93,* pp. 1064-1070, May. 1993.

[8] John W. Byers, Michael Luby, Michael Mitzenmacher, and Ashutosh Rege. "A Digital Fountain Approach to Reliable Distribution of Bulk Data." *In Proc. Of ACM SIGCOMM,* pp. 56–67, August 1998.

[9] Rizzo, L, "On the Feasibility of Software FEC." *DEIT TR,* http://www.iet.unipi.it/~luigi/softfec.ps, Jan 1997

[10] K. Park and W. Wang. "QoS-sensitive transport of real-time MPEG video using adaptive forward error correction." *In Proc. IEEE Multimedia Systems '99,* pages 426--432, 1999.

[11] B. Lamparter, Otto Bohrer, W. Effelsberg, and V. Turau. "Adaptable forward error correction for multimedia data streams", 1993.

[12] Daji Qiao, Kang G. Shin, "A Two-Step Adaptive Error Recovery Scheme for Video Transmission over Wireless Networks." *INFOCOMM 2000.*

[13] K. Park and W. Wang, "AFEC: An Adaptive Forward Error Correction Protocol for End-to-End Transport of Real-Time Traffic," *In Proc. of the IEEE IC3N,* pp. 196-205, 1998.

[14] Sunghyun Choi, Kang G. Shin, "Cost Effective Adaptive Error Control Using a Hybrid of FEC and ARQ in Wireless Networks," University of Michigan CSE-TR-402-99, 1999

[15] Sheldon Ross, "A First Course in Probability", *Prentice-Hall Inc,* 1998.

[16] Lettieri, P., Srivastava, M.B.: "Adaptive Frame Length Control for Improving Wireless Link Throughput, Range, and Energy Efficiency", *IEEE Infocom'98,* pp. 307-314, San Francisco, USA, March 1998.

[17] Kien A. Hua, Simon Sheu, "Skyscraper Broadcasting: A New Broadcasting Scheme for Metropolitan Video-on-Demand Systems," In Proc. Of ACM SIGCOMM, pp. 89-100, 1997.

[18] Ailan Hu, "Video-on-Demand Broadcasting Protocols: A Comprehensive Study," In Proc. Of IEEE INFOCOM 2001.

[19] A. Mahanti, D. L. Eager, M. K. Vernon, and D. S. Sundaram-Stukel, "Scalable On-Demand Media Streaming with Packet Loss Recovery," In Proc. Of ACM SIGCOMM'01, pp. 97-108, CA, 2001.

[20] J. Padhye and S. Floyd, "On Inferring TCP Behavior," In Proc. Of ACM SIGCOMM'01, Aug. 2001.

[21] I. Rhee, "Error Control Techniques for Interactive Low-bit Rate Video Transmission over the Internet," In Proc. Of ACM SIGCOMM '98.

[22] "The Network Simulator – ns-2," URL: http://www.isi.edu/nsnam/ns/.

Buffer Management for Periodic Broadcast Servers*

Wallapak Tavanapong   Minh Tran
The MiΔea Laboratory, Department of Computer Science
Iowa State University, Ames IA 50011-1040, U. S. A.
Email:{tavanapo,ttminh}@cs.iastate.edu

Abstract

The performance of video servers is limited by critical server resources. Periodic Broadcast has been shown to effectively utilize the server network I/O bandwidth, allowing the server to support a large number of concurrent users.

This paper investigates two more server resources that can prevent the server from broadcasting as many videos. These resources are disk bandwidth and memory space. In this paper, we model the relationship among them, propose a memory management technique, and evaluate its performance analytically with several periodic broadcast schemes.

Keywords: Periodic Broadcast, Video-on-Demand, Buffer Allocation, Multicast.

1 Introduction

Recent years have witnessed the increasing use of video data in several important applications such as distance learning, digital libraries, Movie-on-Demand, electronic commerce, etc. Existing video delivery techniques can be divided into two major approaches: "request-centric" and "video-centric". In the request-centric approach, the server allocates sufficient resources, namely disk I/O bandwidth, memory buffer, and network I/O bandwidth, to provide a continuous delivery for each arriving request or a batch of requests arriving closely in time for the same video [1, 2, 3]. As more requests arrive at the video server concurrently, longer initial delays are expected.

The video-centric approach aims to guarantee the worse initial delay for a particular video regardless of the request rate. Periodic broadcast techniques belong to this approach. The video server reserves a number of server channels for broadcasting a video; each channel is a unit of network I/O bandwidth needed to transmit video data. The server fragments the video into logical segments and periodically broadcasts them on the reserved channels. A large number of clients can tune into one or more channels concurrently to download the proper segments. The downloaded data are temporarily stored in the client disk buffer. As soon as the client receives the first few frames of the first segment, the playback can begin. While displaying the buffered frames, the client downloads subsequent segments typically from different channels. Since the first segment is broadcast periodically, the worst initial delay is the time interval between two consecutive broadcasts of the first segment. Because several channels are used for one video, this approach is recommended for popular videos.

In recent years, many server designs for the request-centric approach have been investigated. Among them, *buffer allocation* has been shown to reduce initial delays and increase server throughput noticeably. In Buffer Allocation, a memory buffer is allocated per user request [4, 5, 6, 7]. After the buffer for the request has been filled up for the first time, the playback can begin. More data are retrieved from disk to replace existing data in the buffer such that a jitter-free playback is guaranteed. The buffer size is determined by the disk bandwidth and the number of concurrent video streams that the server can support. Typically, each buffer is much smaller than the entire video. The design goal of the buffer allocation is to reduce the initial delay due to loading the data into the buffer.

Nonetheless, very little to none is mentioned about the effective use of memory and disk I/Os for servers in the video-centric approach. While server network I/O bandwidth has been the major research focus in recent years the server disk bandwidth and memory space can also limit the number of videos that can be broadcast. The problem of memory and disk management for periodic broadcast is different from that of the request-centric approach as follows.

- Reducing the initial delays is no longer the design objective since the worst initial delay is determined by broadcast techniques and parameters. The new design goal is to maximize the number of videos that can be broadcast given video characteristics, broad-

*This work is partially supported by the National Science Foundation Grant No. CCR 0092914.

cast parameters, and system configurations.

- The server knows exactly which videos to be broadcast and how they are broadcast. A new server design taking advantages of the broadcast pattern should perform better than those previously developed for the request-centric approach.

Since there is no absolute winner among the recent broadcast techniques, we aim to support any broadcast technique for constant-bitrate videos. We generalize these periodic broadcast techniques, formulate the problem of memory management, propose a buffer management technique for periodic broadcast. Finally, we develop an analytical model to assess the performance of the proposed technique with various broadcast techniques.

The remainder of this paper is organized as follows. In Section 2, we briefly summarize existing broadcast techniques. Section 3 describes the problem statement and our solution. Performance evaluation is presented in Section 4. Finally, we give our concluding remarks in Section 5.

2 Periodic Broadcast

Any periodic broadcast technique consists of four major components: (i) data fragmentation strategy, (ii) channel design, (iii) server broadcast strategy, and (iv) client downloading technique. These components altogether distinguish one broadcast technique from another. They also determine the worst service delay, server network I/O bandwidth requirement, and client capability. We generalize existing broadcast techniques according to the four components using video characteristics and broadcast parameters in Table 1.

Table 1: Parameters for a generic periodic broadcast technique

L	Playback duration of a video in seconds
p	Average playback rate in Mbps
K	Total number of segments per video
L_i	Playback duration of segment i (in seconds) where $\sum_{i}^{K} L_i = L$
$f(i)$	Function to compute L_i
W	Maximum segment size in terms of the playback duration of the first segment
C	Number of server channels reserved for broadcasting a video
r_i	Transmission rate of channel i (in Mbps) where $1 \leq i \leq C$

Data Fragmentation Strategy : A video file is logically fragmented into K segments denoted as

$S_1, \ldots, S_K$. A different broadcast technique employs a different function ($f(i)$) to determine the size of each segment i. For instance, $f(i)$ of Skyscraper Broadcast (SB) [8] produces a *broadcast series* of $[1, 2, 2, 5, 5, 12, 12, \ldots, W]$. That is, the playback duration of the 2nd and 3rd segments are each twice as long as that of the first segment. The next two segments each is five times as long, and so forth. The largest segment(s) each is W times as long. Other broadcast series are such as $[1, 1, 1, \ldots, 1]$ of Harmonic Broadcast (HB) [9] and its variants, or $[1, 2, 4, 8, 16, \ldots, W, W]$ of Striping Broadcast (STB) [10].

Channel Design : The server uses C channels to broadcast the K segments. Each channel bandwidth is r_i Mbps. The majority of periodic broadcast techniques allocate the channel bandwidth at the playback rate, and the number of channels is the same as the number of segments (i.e., $C = K$). These techniques are such as SB, STB, Greedy-Disk, and Conserving (GDB) [11]. The channel design, however, can be made more complicated. For instance, HB employs channels of decreasing bandwidth using Harmonic series (i.e, $r_i = \frac{p}{i}$).

Server Broadcast Strategy : The server repeatedly broadcasts each segment on one or more channels. Typically, one segment is repeatedly broadcast on one channel.

Client Downloading Strategy : A client employs *loader* threads to concurrently download video segments from different channels. There are as many loaders as the number of channels the client can listen to concurrently. The playback can begin as soon as one loader can access the beginning of the first segment[1]. While receiving the current segment, the client concurrently downloads subsequent segments typically from different channels. As the loaders fill up the client disk buffer, the playback thread consumes the data and renders them onto the screen. Different broadcast techniques have their own requirement for the number of loaders.

3 Memory Management for Periodic Broadcast Servers

Problem Statement: Given the video characteristics and the broadcast parameters in Table 1, and the server configuration in Table 2, maximize the number of videos that

---

[1]This is the case that $r_1 \geq p$; for $r_1 < p$, the download of the first segment must be finished before the playback is initiated.

a single video server with one disk can simultaneously broadcast given (a) the server network I/O bandwidth is sufficient to broadcast these videos; (b) all videos have the same characteristics and are equally very popular; and (c) the same broadcast technique and broadcast parameters are used for all videos.

Table 2: Server configuration

B	Memory space (in Mbits) available for the video server
TR	Disk transfer rate in Mbps
DL	Maximum seek overhead (in seconds) including rotational delay and seek time

We propose *Staging (SG)* to address the problem. Notations in Table 3 are used throughout our discussion. Note that the buffer size of the same segment of different videos is the same due to the assumption of same video characteristics and broadcast parameters. Due to space limitation, we discuss the basic case that the number of channels is equal to the number of segments. Other special cases can be mapped to the basic case as well.

Table 3: Notations

BS_i	Amount of memory buffer (in Mbits) reserved for S_i for each video
R	Total transmission rate (in Mbps) required to broadcast a video (i.e., $R = \sum_{i=1}^{C} r_i$)
n	Number of videos that can be broadcast

3.1 Staging for Periodic Broadcast (SG)

SG allocates a memory buffer for each segment of each video. For instance, if a video is partitioned into K segments, $n \cdot K$ buffers are needed to broadcast n videos. The size of each buffer is typically much smaller than the size of the segment. The formula to determine the segment size will be discussed shortly. The K buffers are deallocated when the broadcast of the video is terminated. Figure 1 depicts the architecture of the video server using SG.

A single retrieval thread retrieves video data for all the buffers in rounds. There are as many delivery threads as the number of segments per video since the same segment of different videos is broadcast at the same rate. Once the retrieval thread fills up the first buffer, the thread continues to retrieve the data for the second buffer until all buffers are filled up. Then, the delivery thread responsible starts broadcasting the data in its buffers simultaneously. The retrieval thread goes back to fill in the data in the buffers in the same order as in the previous round.

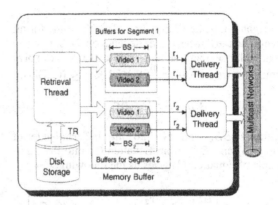

Figure 1: Staging when $n = 2$ and $K = 2$

To broadcast n videos, the server must have enough capacity to satisfy the following constraints.

- **Disk-Bandwidth Constraint**: The disk transfer rate must be enough to serve $n \cdot K$ segments concurrently. That is,

$$n \cdot R \leq TR. \qquad (1)$$

- **Memory-Space Constraint**: System memory must be large enough to support concurrent retrieval of $n \cdot K$ segments. That is,

$$n \cdot 2 \cdot \sum_{i=1}^{K} BS_i \leq B. \qquad (2)$$

The "2" in Equation (2) is due to the use of double buffering. It is needed since in the first round, the data in all the buffers must be filled up before the broadcast starts. When the delivery threads start broadcasting, the retrieval thread is ready to fill in the buffers for the 2nd round. Since the disk transfer rate is higher than the transmission rate of the broadcast channel, the memory space equal to the size of the buffer space is used to prevent the retrieval thread from overwriting the data that has not been broadcast.

In the following model, the thread scheduling time is assumed negligible, and one disk seek is assumed adequate to retrieve data into a buffer. This is typically the case when data blocks of one segment are stored contiguously on disk. To guarantee a continuous delivery, for each round, the time taken to transmit all the data in each buffer must be at least the time taken for the retrieval thread to retrieve the data into all the buffers for the next round. The memory space for each buffer (BS_i) must be enough to ensure this continuity principle that can be expressed mathematically as follows.

$$\frac{BS_i}{r_i} \geq n \cdot \sum_{j=1}^{K} \left[\frac{BS_j}{TR} + DL \right], \quad \forall i, 1 \leq i \leq K. \quad (3)$$

The right-hand-side of Equation (3) is the same for all segments, but the left-hand-side depends on the buffer size of a particular segment and the broadcast rate. To solve this equation, we let $\frac{BS_j}{r_j} = \frac{BS_1}{r_1}, \forall j, 1 < j \leq K$. Thus,

$$BS_j = \frac{r_j}{r_1} \cdot BS_1. \qquad (4)$$

Substituting BS_1 and r_1 into the left-hand-side of Equation (3) and BS_j from Equation (4) into the right-hand-side of Equation (3) gives us the following.

$$\frac{BS_1}{r_1} \geq n \left[\frac{BS_1}{TR} \cdot (1 + \frac{r_2}{r_1} + \ldots + \frac{r_k}{r_1}) + K \cdot DL \right]$$

$$\left[\frac{1}{r_1} - \frac{n \cdot R}{TR \cdot r_1} \right] \cdot BS_1 \geq n \cdot K \cdot DL.$$

To minimize the buffer size, we choose the lowest value of BS_1 that satisfies the above equation as follows.

$$BS_1 = \frac{n \cdot K \cdot DL \cdot TR \cdot r_1}{TR - n \cdot R}. \qquad (5)$$

After substituting Equations (4-5) in Equation (2), we get the following quadratic equation for the values of n that satisfy the memory-space constraint.

$$(2K \cdot DL \cdot TR \cdot R)n^2 + (B \cdot R)n - B \cdot TR \leq 0 \quad (6)$$

Therefore, the maximum number of videos that can be supported is the maximum value of n that satisfies the disk-bandwidth and memory-space constraints as expressed in Equation (7)[2].

$$n < \min \left(\frac{TR}{R}, \frac{-B \cdot R + \sqrt{B^2 \cdot R^2 + 8K \cdot DL \cdot B \cdot R \cdot TR^2}}{4K \cdot DL \cdot R \cdot TR} \right) \quad (7)$$

4 Performance Study

In this section, we evaluate the performance of SG using the maximum number of videos that can be broadcast as the performance metric. We perform sensitivity analysis to observe the effect of memory space, disk bandwidth and different broadcast techniques on SG. The system parameters and the video characteristics used in this study are presented in Table 4. The default values were used in the following studies unless stated otherwise.

To obtain the broadcast parameters for different broadcast techniques, we selected the values of K that guarantee the worst delay closest to the target worst delay. The value of W was set to the largest number determined by the function $f(i)$ of each broadcast technique. The number of the loaders of the client was at most three. We assume that the client has adequate disk buffer.

[2]For $ax^2 + bx + c = 0$, $x = \frac{-b \pm \sqrt{b^2 - 4ac}}{2a}$.

Table 4: Video characteristics and system parameters

Parameter	Default values	Variation
p (Mbps)	1.5	N/A
L (sec.)	3600	N/A
B (Mbytes)	512	$64 \sim 4096$
TR (Mbps)	240	$80 \sim 440$
DL (sec.)	0.02173	N/A
worst delay (sec.)	30	N/A

4.1 Effect of Memory Space

We varied the memory space from 64 to 4096 Mbytes and fixed the other parameters at the default values. The results are presented in Figure 2(a). As more memory is available, the performance of SG improves. Among the broadcast techniques, STB can broadcast the most number of videos. The performance of GDB and Optimized Periodic Broadcast (OPB) [12] are the same followed by those of SB, and HB. This is because STB uses the least number of channels to achieve the worst delay of 30 seconds. GDB and OPB use one more channel than STB does. HB uses the most number of channels with the least total disk bandwidth. Unlike the other broadcast techniques in which the disk bandwidth limits the number of videos that can be supported, HB is limited by the amount of the buffer space required to support these many channels. This is because, the size of each buffer increases exponentially as the number of channels increases linearly (see Equation (5)). Therefore, when the memory is large enough (beyond 2 GBytes), HB outperforms SB. Since memory space limits the number of videos supported by HB, more memory allows HB to broadcast more videos whereas the limiting factor of SB is the disk bandwidth.

4.2 Effect of Disk Bandwidth

We investigate the impact of disk bandwidth by varying the bandwidth between 80 and 440 Mbps and fixed the other parameters at their default value. The chosen range of the disk bandwidths captures the minimum disk-to-host transfer rate of current disk drives. Figure 2(b) shows that as the disk bandwidth increases, more videos can be broadcast. Comparing among the broadcast techniques, STB is best in taking advantage of more disk bandwidth. HB is almost insensitive to the increasing disk bandwidth since HB performance is bounded by the size of the memory.

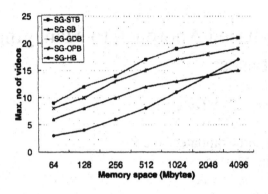

(a) Effect of memory space

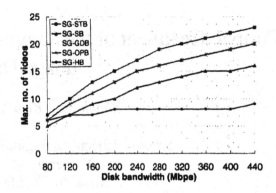

(b) Effect of disk bandwidth

Figure 2: Performance of SG

5 Concluding Remarks

We have presented the problem of memory management for periodic broadcast servers and provided a solution. An analytical model is presented to evaluate the proposed solution. Our performance study reveals the following conclusions.

- Memory buffer grows exponentially with the linear increase in the number of channels used to broadcast a video.

- Broadcast techniques have a significant impact on memory management. Despite a smaller disk bandwidth requirement, the broadcast technique that requires a large number of channels also demands a larger memory buffer than those using less channels. As a result, the server cost also increases.

References

[1] A. Dan, D. Sitaram, and P. Shahabuddin, "Scheduling policies for an on-demand video server with batching," in *Proc. of ACM Multimedia*, San Francisco, California, October 1994, pp. 15–23.

[2] Kien A. Hua, Ying Cai, and Simon Sheu, "Patching: A multicast technique for true video-on-demand services," in *Proc. of ACM Multimedia*, Bristol, UK, September 1998, pp. 191–200.

[3] A. Bary-Noy, J. Goshi, R. E. Ladner, and K. Tam, "Comparison of stream merging algorithms for media-on-demand," in *Proc. of SPIE MMCN'02*, January 2002.

[4] E. Chang and H. Garcia-Molina, "Effective memory use in a media server," in *Proc. of the 23r Int'l Conf. on Very Large Databases*, Athens, Greece, 496-505 1997.

[5] E. Chang and H. Garcia-Molina, "Bubbleup: Low latency fast-scan for media servers," in *Proc. of the 5th ACM Multimedia'97*, Seattle, Washington, 87-98 1997.

[6] T.-P. J. To and B. Hamidzadeh, "Dynamic real-time scheduling strategies for interactive continuous media servers," *ACM Multimedia Systems*, vol. 7, no. 2, pp. 91–106, 1999.

[7] S.-H. Lee, K-Y Whang, Y.-S. Moon, and I-Y. Song, "Dynamic buffer allocation in video-on-demand systems," in *Proc. of ACM SIGMOD*, May 2001, pp. 343–354.

[8] Kien A. Hua and Simon Sheu, "Skyscraper Broadcasting: A New Broadcasting Scheme for Metropolitan Video-on-Demand Systems," in *Proc. of the ACM SIGCOMM*, Cannes, France, September 1997, pp. 89–100.

[9] L. Juhn and L. Tseng, "Harmonic broadcasting for video-on-demand service," *IEEE Trans. on Broadcasting*, vol. 43, no. 3, pp. 268–271, Sept. 1997.

[10] S. Sheu, W. Tavanapong, and K. A. Hua, "Cost-effective periodic broadcast techniques for popular videos," *Submitted to ACM Multimedia Systems*, 2002.

[11] L. Gao, J. Kurose, and D. Towsley, "Efficient schemes for broadcasting popular videos," in *Proc. of Int'l Workshop on Network and Operating System Support for Digital Audio and Video*, July 1998.

[12] A. Mahanti, D. L. Eager, M. K. Vernon, and D. Sundaram-Stukel, "Scalable on-demand media streaming with packet loss recovery," in *Proc. of ACM SIGCOMM'01*, San Diego, CA, U. S. A., August 2001, pp. 97–108.

A Formal Treatment of the Sampling-based Approach to Managing Image Databases

Khanh Vu   Kien A. Hua   S.D. Lang

School of Electrical Engineering and Computer Science
University of Central Florida
Orlando, FL 32816-2362, U.S.A.
{khanh, kienhua, lang}@cs.ucf.edu

Abstract

Query-by-example is one of the most popular query models for today's image retrieval systems. A typical query contains not only relevant objects (e.g., Eiffel Tower), but also irrelevant image areas (e.g., the background). The latter, referred to as *noise*, has limited the effectiveness of existing image retrieval systems. One way to address this problem is to employ a sampling-based technique. Experimental results show that the system supports *noise-free queries* (NFQs) effectively, and is robust with respect to scaling and translation of the matching objects. In this paper, we develop the foundation of the sampling technique for supporting NFQ retrieval. The formal treatment of the approach allows its properties to be derived systematically. Its implementation is described under this formalism.

1 Introduction

Image databases can be queried in several ways. Query-By-Example (QBE), however, is by far the most widely supported model in research prototypes and commercial products such as [1], [2], [3], [4], [5]. In this environment, a user formulates a query by means of giving an example image selected from a pool of general image categories. A query image typically contains not only the objects of the user's interest, but also irrelevant image areas, referred to as *noise*.

We proposed a sampling-based approach [5], called *SamMatch*, to address this problem. SamMatch is able to determine similarity based on relevant regions specified *by the user at the query time*. SamMatch samples each image to obtain a large number of small blocks. At each sampling location, a number of its local features, such as color and texture, can be captured to represent the region. At query time, users can identify any combination of such regions as relevant, and only those will participate in the similarity measure.

Experiments have shown that SamMatch performs remarkably well for arbitrarily defined queries. This is attributed to many advantages including a noise-free similarity measure, robustness to scaling and translation, and an efficient indexing scheme. Nonetheless, the technique was presented in a descriptive format and its properties have not been formally established. In this paper, we provide a formal treatment of the sampling-based approach to image retrieval. In a unified framework, we prove the correctness of SamMatch's features including scaling handling, translation, and semantic constraints.

The remainder of this paper is organized as follows. We formalize the sampling-based approach to image retrieval and derive its properties based on the framework developed in Section 2. In Section 3, we discuss the SamMatch technique under this formalism. We conclude our work in Section 4.

2 The Sampling-Based Approach to Image Retrieval

We summarize in Table 1 the notations used in this section. Assuming that readers are already familiar with set notations, we explain the need for some of them in our environment. The extensive use of *member* ('$\in$'), rather than *subset* ('$\subseteq$'), of a set is exploited to facilitate function definitions. For example, in traditional settings, an image I contains a set of discrete points (pixels) along with a color value at each point, that is, $I \subset Z^2 \times C$. Since we will deal with pixels and their color values separately, we use $I \in (Z^2)^+ \equiv (Z^2) \cup (Z^2)^2 \cup (Z^2)^3 \cup \ldots$ That is, an image is an ordered list of pixels, each of which is a member of Z^2 whose color content can be obtained by accessing the image array. Likewise, a subimage S of I, $S \subseteq I$, is denoted as $S \in I^{[1..\|I\|]} \equiv I \cup I^2 \cup \ldots \cup I^{\|I\|}$; that is, S is an ordered list of pixels that belong to I.

Symbol	Description
k, r, m, n, t	Non-zero real constants
C	The set of color values
Z^2	The discrete space
$(Z^2)^+$	$(Z^2) \cup (Z^2)^2 \cup (Z^2)^3 \cup \dots$
$I, Q \in (Z^2)^+$	An image and a user-defined query
$(*)^{[1..\|I\|]}$	$\bigcup_{i \in [1..\|I\|]} (*)^i$
$\|(*)\|$	Size of $(*)$
$B \in I^m$	A block of m pixels of image I
$B[i]$	The ith pixel of block B, $i \in [1..m]$
$c(*) \in C$	Color value of pixel
$S \in I^{[1..\|I\|]}$	An arbitrary-shaped subimage of I
$S[i]$	The ith block of S
$b = T(B)$	Block transformation
$M(B)$	The block quantization function
$\{p, F\}$	Sampling scheme with sampling pattern p and frame F centered at each sampling location
$[\{p, F\}]$	Equivalence class of $\{p, F\}$
$'\cdot', '/'$	Multiplication, division operations on p, B, $\{p, F\}$
$T_{\{p,F\}}(*)$	Image transformation using sampling scheme $\{p, F\}$
$f(*)$	Feature vector

Table 1: *Symbols and their descriptions*

2.1 Block Transformation

Definition 1 *The block transformation $T(B)$ is defined as a mapping from an ordered list of pixels to a single pixel:*

$$T : I^m \to Z^2$$

where

$$T(B) = b$$

The transformation of a block can be viewed, reminiscent of the wavelet transformation, as a sequence of consecutive shrinking operations of the block to one pixel, see Figure 1. The most special feature of $T(B)$ is that blocks B originated from the same image are mapped to the same pixel. That is, the size of B, m, is arbitrary.

Definition 2 *The block quantization function M is defined as a mapping:*

$$M : I^m \to C$$

where

$$M(B) = c(T(B))$$

One important property of our block transformation and quantization is that a block and all its versions in different scales (i.e., resolutions) are evaluated to the same quantized value. We state this result in the following lemma.

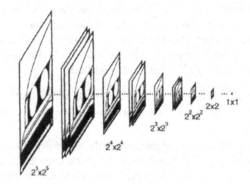

Figure 1: *Transformation of a block: consecutive shrinking of the block to one pixel*

Lemma 1 *All blocks that originate from the same image but are in different resolutions will produce the same quantization value.*

Proof Since all blocks that originate from the same image are transformed into a unique pixel, the quantization of it will result in only one number.□

Utilizing image processing techniques (bicubic, bilinear, HWT,...), it is easy to derive the formula to compute a block's quantization value, $M(T(B))$, which is given below:

$$M(B) = c(T(B)) = \left\lfloor \frac{\sum_{i=1}^m c(B[i])}{m} \right\rfloor \quad (1)$$

Equation 1 is defined for any block of one pixel or more. In general, block transformation and quantization do not impose any restriction on the shape and size of the transformed block. In this paper, we consider only square-shaped blocks.

2.2 Image Feature Vector

A sampling pattern p on an image is a 2-D spatial sampling on the image using pattern p (e.g., grid, checkerboard). Centered at each sampled location, we apply a square-shaped frame F to cover image pixels. Thus, two sampling schemes are said to be equal if they have the same p and F. The distance between two sampled locations is called a *span*. We use $p \cdot r$ to denote the same pattern but its sampling spans are multiplied by a real number r. Likewise, $F \cdot r$ denotes the square-shaped frame whose size is r times that of F. With those, we define the '$\cdot$' and '/' operations on sampling scheme $\{p, F\}$ as follows:

$$\{p, F\} \cdot r \equiv \{p \cdot \sqrt{r}, F \cdot r\} \quad (2)$$

and

$$\frac{\{p, F\}}{r} \equiv \{p, F\} \cdot \frac{1}{r}$$

It is easy to verify that such definitions imply that the ratios of the spans of p to $\sqrt{\|F\|}$ in a sampling scheme $\{p, F\}$ remain a constant when the '.' or '/' operation is applied to $\{p, F\}$. Indeed, suppose on the left side of (2), we have a span of $p = k \cdot \sqrt{\|F\|}$, then on the right side:

$$
\begin{aligned}
k \cdot \sqrt{\|F \cdot r\|} &= k \cdot \sqrt{\|F\| \cdot r} = k \cdot \sqrt{\|F\|} \cdot \sqrt{r} \\
&= \text{the span of } p \cdot \sqrt{r}
\end{aligned}
$$

In SamMatch, we are interested in the above dependency, although there can be other relationships between p and F. Figure 2 gives an example of the '.' operation on a sampling scheme.

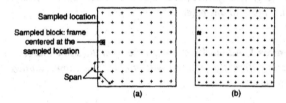

Figure 2: *Grid-pattern samplings $\{p, F\}$ and $\{p, F\} \cdot (3/4)$, respectively in (a) and (b), applied on the same image frame*

Definition 3 *The image transformation $T_{\{p,F\}}(I)$ of an image I is a mapping of I into an ordered set of l blocks $(B_1, \ldots, B_i, \ldots, B_l)$, $l \in [1..\|I\|]$, using sampling scheme $\{p, F\}$, followed by the application of the block transformation T on all members of that set:*

$$
T_{\{p,F\}} : (Z^2)^+ \to (Z^2)^+
$$

where $T_{\{p,F\}}(I) = (b_1, \ldots, b_i, \ldots, b_l)$ and $b_i = T(B_i)$, for $i \in [1..l]$.

Since the transformed blocks bs are members of Z^2, their spatial relationships are 2-D distances. The ordering of bs in $(b_1, \ldots, b_i, \ldots, b_l)$ depends on the sequencing strategy in use, e.g., left-right top-bottom, Hilbert-curve, or zigzag sequence. The subscript of b can be converted back to its coordinates for accessing the image array. In practice, we can compute the distance between b_i and b_{i+k} using their subscripts, and therefore, their spatial relationship is said specified by k.

We observe that when $\|F\| = \|I\|$, then $T_{\{p,F\}}(I) = T(I)$, i.e, I is represented by only one pixel. On the other hand, when $\|F\| = 1$ and p is a grid pattern in which the shortest span is equal to 1, then $T_{\{p,F\}}(I) = I$, or the image representation of I is at the pixel level. In general, the chosen sampling scheme decides how fine images (and its subimages) are represented. The matching probability, eventually the similarity measure, of subimages depends on the granularity of their representation. Generally, the finer granularity the image representation, the better the matching probability.

The feature vector f of I resulted from an image transformation $T_{\{p,F\}}(I)$ can be obtained by applying quantization on all image blocks at sampled locations:

$$
f(I) = (c_1, \ldots, c_i, \ldots, c_l) \in C^{[1..\|I\|]} \tag{3}
$$

where $c_i = M(B_i)$, $1 \le i \le l \le \|I\|$.

2.3 Object Representation

Any user-perceived object in an image I can be realized using an arbitrary-shaped subimage $S \in I^{[1..\|I\|]}$, where S is represented by its corresponding blocks in $T_{\{p,F\}}(I)$. That is,

$$
\begin{aligned}
T_{\{p,F\}}(S) &= (b_i, b_{i+k_1}, b_{i+k_1+k_2}, \ldots, b_{i+\ldots+k_{n-1}}) \\
&\in (T_{\{p,F\}}(I))^{[1..\|T_{\{p,F\}}(I)\|]}
\end{aligned} \tag{4}
$$

Similarly, the feature vector S of I can be derived from the image feature vector of I:

$$
\begin{aligned}
f(S) &= (c_i, c_{i+k_1}, c_{i+k_1+k_2}, \ldots, c_{i+\ldots+k_{n-1}}) \\
&\in C^{[1..\|T_{\{p,F\}}(S)\|]}
\end{aligned}
$$

We call $S[1] = c_i$, $S[2] = c_{i+k_1}, \ldots$, $S[n] = c_{i+\sum_{j=1}^{n-1} k_j}$ the content of S. As in the case for I, the parameters $k_1, k_2, \ldots, k_{n-1}$ in Formula 4 specify the (relative) spatial relationship between $S[i]$, $i \in [1..n]$. We call these ks the *traversal path* of S because we can trace along them to recover S.

We will use the terms *object* and *arbitrary-shaped subimage* interchangeably and use S to denote both of them. We first have the following trivial lemma.

Lemma 2 *The cardinality of an object representation cannot be larger than the number of pixels that compose the object. That is,*

$$
\|f(S)\| \le \|S\|
$$

Proof This is true because one block is mapped to only one pixel and the maximum number of transformed blocks cannot be larger than the number of the pixels that compose the object. $\square$

Lemma 2 makes it impossible to construct a representation whose size is larger that of the object itself. In practice, feature vectors are small, typically about one hundred components. Objects composed of fewer than such number of pixels are of no query interest by themselves. Thus, for the remainder of our discussion, we assume objects are sufficiently large that they can be mapped to practical representations.

2.4 Translation of Objects

In our framework, a translation of S can be defined as follows:

Definition 4 *Consider a subimage* $S \in I^{[1..\|I\|]}$, *and* $T_{\{p,F\}}(S) = (b_i, b_{i+k_1}, b_{i+k_1+k_2}, \ldots, b_{i+\ldots+k_{n-1}})$. *A subimage* S^t *is a translation of* S *if the following conditions are true:*

1. $S^t \in I^{[1..\|I\|]}$,

2. $T_{\{p,F\}}(S^t) = (b_j, b_{j+k_1}, b_{j+k_1+k_2}, \ldots, b_{j+\ldots+k_{n-1}})$,

3. $S[i] = S^t[i]$, $i \in [1..n]$.

In other words, the above definition requires that S^t: be in the same image I as S (condition 1), have an equivalent spatial relationship between its components with respect to sampling scheme $\{p, F\}$ (condition 2), and have the same color content as S (condition 3).

One important observation to note here is both S and S^t are applied upon by the same $T_{\{p,F\}}(*)$. As we will see in the next subsection, the use of different sampling schemes can produce equivalent representations for S which exists in multiple scales.

2.5 Scaling of Objects

The representation of an object can be altered by changing the applied sampling scheme. The question now is, if an object is in different scales, can we find related sampling schemes such that various versions of the object can be mapped to the same representation? We answer this question in the following lemma.

Lemma 3 *Consider an object* S *and its scaled version* S'. *If* S *is represented by a set of blocks under the application of some sampling scheme, there exists another sampling scheme that maps* S' *to that set.*

Proof Let $\{p, F\}$ be a sampling scheme and $T_{\{p,F\}}(S)$ be the corresponding transformation that maps S to an ordered set of blocks. We are required to find a sampling scheme $\{p', F'\}$ that maps S' to the identical set of blocks. It is easy to verify that the following scheme on S' will produce the same set of blocks: $\{p', F'\} = \{p, F\} \cdot (\|S\|/\|S'\|)$. □

We stress here an important distinction between $f(I)$ and $f(S)$ regarding to the applied sampling scheme. While we use different sampling schemes to achieve $f(S_1) = f(S_2)$, where S_1 and S_2 are subimages of the same object in different scales, we generally have different feature vectors of their containing images. Figure 3 shows an example of these

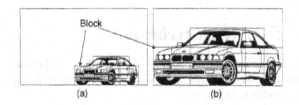

Figure 3: *Different scales of the same object are captured in a fixed-size representation*

mappings in which we use different sampling schemes on the images. Note that the size of the feature vector of the left image Figure 3(a) will be much larger than that of the right Figure 3(b) because the former is of a finer granularity representation. The object *car* S is captured in a unique representation for two scales.

Definition 5 *Consider an arbitrary set of sampling scheme* $\mathcal{U}$. *We can define a binary relation* $\mathcal{R}$ *as follows:*

$$\{p, F\} \mathcal{R} \{p', F'\} \text{ iff } \{p', F'\} = \{p, F\} \cdot r,$$

for some non-zero real number r.

It is easy to verify that relation $\mathcal{R}$ is an equivalence relation (i.e., it is reflexive, symmetric, and transitive). When the set of $\mathcal{U}$ is understood, we use the following notation for the equivalence classes:

$$[\{p, F\}] = \{\{p', F'\} \in \mathcal{U} \mid \{p', F'\} = \{p, F\} \cdot r.$$

We have the following lemma:

Lemma 4 *Given a fixed representation of an object* S *under a sampling scheme* $\{p, F\}$. *Any version of objects* S *in a different scale can be mapped to the fixed representation under the application of a proper member of* $[\{p, F\}]$.

Proof Let S_t be a version of object S and $T_{\{p_t, F_t\}}(S_t)$ produces the fixed representation of S. Consider any scaled version S_i of the object. Let $r = \frac{\|S_i\|}{\|S_t\|}$. Thus, $\{p_i, F_i\} = \{p_t, F_t\} \cdot r \in [\{p_t, F_t\}]$, and

$$\{p_i, F_i\} = \{p_t, F_t\} \cdot r = \{p_t, F_t\} \cdot \frac{\|S_i\|}{\|S_t\|}$$

By Lemma 3, $T_{\{p_i, F_i\}}(S_i)$ generates the representation as S_t's. □

Thus, for subimages which are of similar content but in different scales, Lemma 4 establishes the correctness of matching when we employ feature extraction schemes belonging to one equivalence class.

3 SamMatch Technique

We describe two central ideas of the SamMatch technique, which are the similarity model and scaling handling under the developed formalism.

3.1 Similarity Model

Assume we have a database DB containing images that are processed with sampling scheme $\{p, F\}$. We define the NFQ similarity model as follows:

Definition 6 *Given an NFQ Q, and its transformation $T_{\{p_Q, F_Q\}}(Q) = (b_i, b_{i+k_1}, b_{i+k_1+k_2}, \ldots, b_{i+\ldots+k_{n-1}})$ using a sampling scheme $\{p_Q, F_Q\} \in [\{p, F\}]$. A subimage S is said to be similar to Q with respect to the user-defined threshold δ if the following conditions are true:*

1. *$S \in I^{[1..\|I\|]}$, $I \in DB$,*

2. *$T_{\{p, F\}}(S) = (b_j, b_{j+k_1}, b_{j+k_1+k_2}, \ldots, b_{j+\ldots+k_{n-1}})$,*

3. *$\mathcal{D}(Q, S) = \sqrt{\sum_{i=1}^{n} |S[i] - Q[i]|^2} \leq \delta$*

In other words, a subimage S is similar to an NFQ Q if S is constructed in the same manner as Q and the difference in their content using the Euclidean distance is less than threshold δ.

3.2 Handling Scaling of Subimages

Lemma 4 enables matches of objects in different scales by using $\{p, F\}$ belonging in the same class $[\{p, F\}]$ provided we know the size of the compared objects. In reality, we know the size of one (e.g., the query) but not that of the others (e.g., objects in database images). To address this problem, we attempt to matches objects only selected scales. Figure 4 illustrates how SamMatch implements Lemma 4, assuming that we want to handle matching at three scales. We apply one $\{p_i, F_i\}$ for all database images (Figure 4 (a)) to produce one fixed-size image representation. Three $\{p, F\} \in [\{p_i, F_i\}]$ are applied to the query image: $\{p_{i-k}, F_{i-k}\}$ to find larger matching objects (Figure 4 (b)), $\{p_i, F_i\}$ to find matching objects of the same size (Figure 4 (c)), and $\{p_{i+k}, F_{i+k}\}$ to find smaller matching objects (Figure 4 (d)).

Based on empirical results, we can determine how many and which $\{p, F\}$ in order to achieve an excellent performance. Our selective feature extraction scheme is as follows:

$$[\{p, F\}^{SM}] = \{\{p_i, F_i\} | \{p_{i+1}, F_{i+1}\} = \{p_i, F_i\} \cdot 1.5,$$
$$i \in [1..4]\}$$

where p is the checkerboard pattern and F_{j+3} is a 16×16 block.

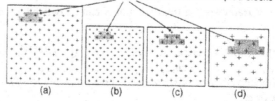

Matching areas with the same number of sampled blocks

(a) (b) (c) (d)

Figure 4: *One fixed sampling scheme for database images (a) and three schemes for the query (b, c, d)*

The size of the set $[\{p, F\}^{SM}]$ decides the number of feature vectors constructed for the query. Note that only one feature vector, determined by one $\{p_{j+3}, F_{j+3}\}$ is constructed for each database image. Multiple $\{p, F\}$ on the query will not incur storage penalty.

4 Concluding Remarks

The sampling-based approach has been shown to provide excellent retrieval performance for arbitrary-shaped queries. In this paper we establish the foundation for this approach in supporting image retrieval. The formal treatment of the approach allows its properties to be derived and proven. We are able to describe its implementation in this framework.

References

[1] W. Niblack, R. Barber, W. Equitz, M. Flicker, E. Glasman, D. Petkovic, P. Yanker, and C. Faloutsos. The qbic project: Query images by content using color, texture and shape. In *SPIE V1908*, 1993.

[2] W.Y. Ma and B.S. Manjunath. Netra: A toolbox for navigating large image databases. *Multimedia System*, 7:184–198, May 1999.

[3] Y. Gong, H.Chua, and X. Guo. Image indexing and retrieval based on color histogram. In *Proc. of the 2nd Int. Conf. on Multimedia Modeling*, pages 115–126, November 1995.

[4] M.E.J. Wood, N.W. Campbell, and B.T. Thomas. Iterative refinement by relevance feedback in content-based digital image retrieval. In *The Sixth ACM International Multimedia Conference*, pages 13–20, September 1998.

[5] K. A. Hua, K. Vu, and J. H. Oh. Sammatch: A flexible and efficient sampling-based image retrieval technique for large image databases. In *Proc. of the 1999 ACM International Multimedia Conference*, pages 225–234, Oct 1999.

Session 1–3
Image Processing I

Measuring Female Facial Beauty by Calculating the Proportions of the Face

Hatice Gunes[1]
Department of Computer Systems,
University of Technology, Sydney
Sydney, Australia
haticeg@it.uts.edu.au

M.Yahya Karsligil
Department of Computer Science and Eng.,
Yildiz Technical University
Istanbul, Turkey
yahya@ce.yildiz.edu.tr

Abstract

Facial attractiveness can be measured by using mathematical ratios provided by investigators in psychology, arts and image analysis. In this paper, we propose a feature-based measuring system for female facial beauty by calculating different proportions from the facial components automatically extracted from images [18]. We achieve a better feature extraction by generalization of features in the human face when obtaining the location of eyes, eyebrows, mouth, nose and chin in a portrait photograph. Using the principles of plastic surgeons and mathematical measurements we train our system to produce grades. We develop a grading algorithm that is based on the relationships between the facial components. This algorithm has been tuned on a set of data and validated by experiments on different people. We observe that the algorithm is able to handle a good range of decision making with the facial components properly extracted.

1. Introduction

The evaluation of facial beauty is generally assumed to be subjective, varying tremendously between individuals. However, beauty may not be limited to the eyes of a beholder. There is much evidence to suggest that there exist criteria for which facial attractiveness can be measured. [1.. 9] The science of measuring beauty existed for centuries. Through history and across different cultures, investigators in psychology, arts and image analysis have extensively studied the calculation of perfect dimensions of beauty. The Greeks and Egyptians stated that *all beauty is mathematics* and they used mathematics to analyze it. If this statement is true then perhaps there is a mathematical formula that describes facial beauty. Many formulas have been used in this attempt, the most famous of these being the Golden Proportion [11], Facial Thirds [12] and Facial Fifths [12]. Measuring the female facial beauty from an image is not a simple task since it involves multi-variable parameters that must be taken into consideration. For instance, the group from Marquardt Aesthetic Imaging Inc. has developed a method that measures facial beauty [13] using the Golden Ratio. However, that system requires a lot of manual measurements, while a fully automated procedure could be much faster and with more objective and repeatable results. While Aarabi and Hughes [19] provided an automated procedure their beauty grading system was not explicit. Therefore, in this paper, we measure the beauty of a face based on the mathematical ratios mentioned above, by providing automated proportion analysis. The experiment was performed for a female face within a given 24-bit color (RGB) portrait photograph.

The rest of the paper is organized as follows: Section 2 describes the general rules and our method for measuring facial beauty. Section 3 contains face detection process and step by step feature extraction, Section 4 describes the decision making process and Section 5 contains the results and finally, Section 6 is the conclusion.

2. Method Used for Measuring Beauty

In this section we provide information on the general rules applied and give an overview of the method.

2.1. General Rules Applied

The *Golden Proportions* and *Facial Thirds* are ratios derived from specific facial features [12,13,14].

---

[1] This work was developed in 2001 when the author was with the Department of Computer Science and Engineering, Yildiz Technical University, Istanbul, Turkey

The *Golden Proportion* is the ratio of 1 to 0.618 or the ratio of 1.618 to 1 as shown in Figure 1. For a perfect face, all of the proportions stated in Table 1 must fit the Golden Proportion 1.618.

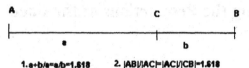

1. a+b/a=a/b=1.618   2. |AB|/|AC|=|AC|/|CB|=1.618

Figure 1: Golden proportion

Table 1: Ratios used for golden proportion comparison

2:4 Ratio of vertical distance between eyes and Chin to vertical distance between forehead and eyes
3:5 Ratio of vertical distance between forehead and Nose to vertical distance between nose and chin
6:7 Ratio of vertical distance between eyes and Lips to vertical distance between lips and chin
5:8 Ratio of vertical distance between nose and Chin to vertical distance between eyes and nose
8:9 Ratio of vertical distance between eyes and Nose to vertical distance between nose and lips
7:9 Ratio of vertical distance between lips and Chin to vertical distance between nose and lips

Facial Thirds states that, a well-proportioned face may be divided into roughly equal thirds by drawing horizontal lines through the forehead hairline, the brow, the base of the nose, and the edge of the chin [12,13,14].

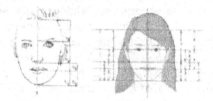

(a)   (b)
Figure 2 a) Facial thirds b) Template image with golden proportions

Table 2: Ratios used for facial thirds measurements

Segments used in Measurement	Measurement Type
Distance between forehead and eyebrow	"Facial Thirds" state that all of the three segments should be equal
Distance between eyebrow and nose	
Distance between nose and chin	
Distance between lip and chin	The ratio of vertical distance between lips and chin to vertical distance between nose and lips.
Distance between nose and lip	

A face is more attractive as it approaches the proportions shown in Table 2. Facial plastic surgeons have long been using these ratios as a guide for their work [10].

2.2. Overview of the Applied Method

In our research, the frontal view of the female face is used since we generally perceive each other from the front. It is easier to define relationships between the facial components in the frontal view.

The first step in measuring facial beauty is extracting the features of a female face. This face feature extraction task is accomplished in six phases: face localization by skin region detection, eye localization, pupil localization, eyebrow localization, lip localization by color segmentation, nose localization and finally, chin localization. The generalization of features in the human face is used to approximate the location of the eyes and the mouth. The last phase of our method involves estimating the proportions of the face from the features extracted and measuring the beauty of the face. This estimation is based on two facial beauty estimation methods described in Section 3. An example of a localized face and its features is shown in Figure 5.

3. Feature Extraction and Analysis

Following subsections will introduce the method we have used in order to detect the face and extract the features that are relevant to beauty estimation.

3.1. Detection of Facial Region

It is important to locate the facial region in order to remove irrelevant picture information. We detect the skin regions to obtain the exact location of the face. Experiments have shown that the skin tone among different races differs more in brightness than actual color. Skin regions are detected by hand segmenting out skin regions as proposed by Cheng [16] since this method simplifies skin region detection. The color-based approach is used to label each pixel according to its similarity to skin color, and subsequently label one sub-region as the face if it contains the largest blob of skin color pixels.

As a result of applied color segmentation, there are two possible outputs as the facial region: either a face without the neck component, in case chin line forms a strong contour and causes the neck to be a separate component, or the facial region with the neck component. In order to perform feature extraction on these facial regions, two different face models are proposed and used to obtain the localization of the eyes, eyebrows, nose, mouth and chin within certain sub-regions. The face is decomposed into 4 sub-regions as shown in Figure 3. These face models, take the Yow and Cipolla's Feature Based Model [15] as an example but create two different views only used with this particular beauty estimation algorithm.

Figure 3a,b Proposed face models

Decomposing the face model into 4 sub regions is related with the further processing of the image to improve the efficiency in localization of the facial features.

3.2. Eye Localization

After defining the location of the facial region, detecting the eye region is a much faster and simpler task. Using the decomposed face models explained above, we assume that in both models eyes are located in the second sub-region. After detecting the skin-colored regions in the image, all the pixels in each column are added to create

(a)   (b)

Figure 4 a) Facial region divided to 4 sub-regions b) Vertical histogram for skin regions

the vertical histogram [16] as shown in Figure 4. The two points, that have the local skin color minimums, are located in the second facial sub-region and these points are calculated from the histogram. Eyes are assumed to be located on these points.

3.3. Eyebrow Localization

After detecting a pair of possible eyes, which satisfies the geometrical constraints imposed by the face, it is easier to localize the eyebrows. Eyebrows are expected to be located in the upper part of the face and are the first components on the facial region down the forehead. We specify the position of eyebrows by checking if these components have pixels situated on the parallel location of eyes.

3.4. Lip Localization

We choose to locate the lips after having located the eyes because their horizontal position is between the two eyes and lips have a different color than the skin. For lip detection, the method in [17] is used in the search space between the third and fourth ¼ sub-region of the face. After obtaining the lip line, the location of the lips is saved later to be used for the proportion estimations.

3.5. Nose Localization

Nose anatomically is located between the eyes and the mouth. Once eye detection and lip detection is performed, searching for a nose is relatively easy due to the well-defined search space. The search space is arranged according to the lips and pupils. Vertical filter is applied on the binary image of the face since the nostrils and bottom surface of the nose are forming a line being darker than the rest of the nose due to shading. The starting point for the search is just above the lip line. The first component detected in the search area is assumed to be the tip of the nose.

3.6. Chin Localization

The chin detection process takes place after lip detection, as the chin anatomically is located between the lips and the neck. The search space is arranged according to the lip line and the horizontal lower limit of the facial region. The starting point for the chin detection process is just above the end of the facial region and the first component found in the search area is assumed to be the chin line.

4. Decision Making

Our decision making algorithm is based on the proportions calculated from the facial components

Figure 5 Result image for positions estimated after feature extraction

extracted. Each female face was scored by 5 independent females and 5 males on a 3-point scale (3 beautiful, 2 average, 1 unattractive) and the average of these scores was used as the human decision. A relation between the Golden Proportions, Facial Thirds and beauty of the face was obtained after this scoring process. Our method produces a score as the total of four independent grades as described below. Weighted grade 1 depends on the ratio of vertical distance between lips and chin to vertical distance between nose and lips. Weighted grade 2 depends on how well the face suits to "Facial Thirds". Weighted grade 3 depends on the positive correlation between the template image of Golden Proportions and the face tested. Weighted grade 4 depends on the total difference between all the ratios and Golden Proportion. Final score is the sum of weighted grades obtained in the first four phases. Determining the weight of these calculations in the whole marking scheme was based on changing each of the parameters rapidly while keeping the others invariant.

4.1. Calculating Weighted Grade 1

Taking the ratio of vertical distance between lips and chin to vertical distance between nose and lips as the input, the marking scheme shown in Table 3, is obtained:

Table 3: Ratios used for grading process 1

Type of measurement	Constraints	Weight
Ratio of (lip_to_chin)/ (nose_to_lip)	=2	5
(lip_to_chin) -(nose_to_lip)	< 1 pixels	4
(lip_to_chin) -(nose_to_lip)	<3 pixels and >1 pixel	2
(lip_to_chin) -(nose_to_lip)	<5 pixels and >3 pixels	0

4.2. Calculating Weighted Grade 2

Questioning how well the face suits to "Facial Thirds", we obtained the marking scheme shown in Table 4.

Table 4: Ratios used for grading process 2

Type of measurement	Constraints	Weight
All of the three segments of the face	Equal	5
Only two segments of the face	Equal	4
The difference between the three facial segments and the value of facial third	<3 pixels	3
The difference between the three facial segments and the value of facial third	<5 pixels and >3 pixels	2
None of the above apply		1

4.3. Calculating Weighted Grade 3

Considering the positive correlation between the template image of Golden Proportions and the face tested, following marking scheme is obtained:
1. Calculate the ratios for Golden Proportion checking
2. Calculate the mean ratio of all
3. Calculate the length and the width of the face. (Table5)

Table 5: Ratios used for grading process 3

Type of measurement	Constraints	Weight
The difference between the mean ratio and the Golden Proportion: 1.618	<0.050	3
	<0.090and >0.050	2
	<0.2 and >0.090	1
	>0.2	0

4.4. Calculating Weighted Grade 4

Considering the total difference between all the ratios and Golden Proportion, the marking scheme shown in Table 6 is obtained.

Table 6: Ratios used for grading process 4

Type of measurement	Constraints	Weight
Sum of the total difference between all the ratios and Golden Proportion	<0.60	5
	<1.0 and >0.60	4
	<1.5 and >1.0	3
	<2 and >1.5	1
	>2	0

4.5. Final Decision Process

The final decision function was defined as the total of weighted grade1, grade2, grade 3 and grade 4 in the decision making process. According to that marking scheme, the most beautiful face gets a total grade of 18 points and the most unattractive face gets a total grade of 1 point. 11-18 in this scale corresponds to attractive facial features. 6-10 corresponds to average feature set. 1-5 corresponds to facial features that exceed the parameters distort the face's aesthetic balance and may be seen as unattractive. This marking scheme is later adjusted to a simpler marking scheme over 3, as explained in Table 7, for a better usability and performance.

Table 7: Ratios used for final decision process

Type of measurement	Constraints	Grade	Final Decision
Total sum of grade 1,grade 2, grade 3 and grade 4	>10	3	Type 3: beautiful face
	>5 and <=10	2	Type 2: average face
	<=5	1	Type 1: unattractive face

5. Results and Analysis

We observe that the algorithm is able to handle a good range of decision making with the facial components properly extracted.

Table 8 and Figure 6 give an example of the experimental results of the test procedure. We try to demonstrate that human and system classifications do not differ to a large extent by comparing these two classification results with a cross correlation matrix as shown in Table 9. We achieved an overall efficient beauty measurement rate of 76% for 38 being out of 50 colored female images correctly classified (Table 9). For 12 images, due to overshooting or undershooting that the system performs in final decision process, the algorithm computes measurements that lead to slightly different results. The most common errors consist of the system making a mistake of one category only (See Table 9).

Table 8: Experimental Results

Original Face	Grades	Decision	Result
	G1: 2 G2: 3 G3: 3 G4: 5	>10	Beautiful face
	Score: 13		

Figure 6: Female faces that were ranked differently by the system

Table 9: Comparison of human and system classification with the cross correlation matrix

S.C. H.C.	Type 1	Type 2	Type 3
Type 1	4	2	1
Type 2	1	23	4
Type 3	1	3	11

H.C: Human Classification->True
S.C: System Classification->Correct/ Incorrect

For the time being, we worked on our experimental face database to train and test the method proposed, therefore it needs to be further verified by testing on larger databases like FERET [20]. Our future work will be aimed at training our system to measure female facial beauty within more refined classes to improve the capability of discriminating between different beauty grades.

We will also use the analysis done in this paper for providing solutions to improve female facial beauty, such as making suggestions to help women to apply makeup or hair style to provide them feedback to look more beautiful. Measurement of male facial attractiveness will also be investigated to find out the correlations between female and male facial beauty.

6. Conclusion

We have proposed a feature-based measuring system for female facial beauty by automatically calculating different proportions from the facial components extracted.

The mathematical measurements give a good foundation to what is appealing to the eye, but beauty is often seen in asymmetry, for example, Harrison Ford's crooked smile. Consequently, even plastic surgeons come to an understanding that science cannot be used to measure the esthetic value of beautiful faces completely. Beauty is still in the eye of the beholder to some extent, since the faces of people we love and admire become more beautiful to us because of what they mean to us.

References

[1] Bell, A. (1997), The Definition of Beauty, Nature October/November
[2] Perrett, D.I., May, K.A. & Yoshikawa, S. (1994). Facial shape and judgments of female attractiveness. Nature, 239-242.
[3] Langlois, J.H. & Roggman, L.A. (1990). Attractive faces are only average. Psychological Science, 1, 115-121.
[4] Cunningham, M.R., Roberts, A.R, Barbee, A.P., Druen, P.B et al. (1995). "Their ideas of beauty are, on the whole, the same as ours", Journal of Personality & Social Psychology, 68, 261-279.
[5] Jefferson, Y. (1993). Facial aesthetics--presentation of an ideal face. Journal of General Orthodontics, 4, 18-23.
[6] Mealey, L., Bridgstock, R, Townsend, G.C. (1999). Symmetry and perceived facial attractiveness: A monozygotic co-twin comparison.
[7] Landau, Terry. About Faces, Bantam Doubleday Dell Publishing Group, Inc. 1989. New York.
[8] Michiels, G. & Sather A.H. (1994). Determinants of facial attractiveness in a sample of white women. International Journal of Adult Orthodontics & Orthognathic Surgery, *9, 95-103.*
[9] Daibo, Ikuo, Suggestion from comparison research of facial beauty AASP 1999 Conference (third) in Taipei August 4 1999, Hokusei Gakuen University, Sapporo, Japan
[10] Parris, Cynara,The Bold and the Beautiful (According to Plastic Surgeons), Tyler Street Christian Academy, Dallas, Texas, Jack Robinson, Jr., Ph.D.
[11]http://www.bbc.co.uk/science/humanbody/humanface/beauy_golden_mean.shtml
[12] Farkas, Leslie G. et al., 1985,Vertical and horizontal proportions of the face in young adult North American Caucasians, Plastic and Reconstructive Surgery 75(3): 328-38.
[13] Marquardt Aesthetic Imaging Inc., http://www.beautyanalysis.com/index2_mba.htm
[14] Ricketts, M.D., 1982. Divine proportions in facial esthetics. Clinics in Plastic Surgery Vol. 9, No. 4.
[15] Yow, K.Choong, Cipolla, R. Feature-Based Human Face Detection (1996), CUED/F-INFENG/TR 249 August 1996
[16] Cheng, J., (2001), Boston University, CS585 Image and Video Computing
[17] M.A.Sid-Ahmet, (1992), Image Processing, Color Image Processing
[18] Gunes, H., Karsligil,Y., (July,2001), "Measuring Female Facial Beauty by Calculating the Proportions of the Face", YTU, Istanbul, BEng
[19] Aarabi, P., Hughes, D., The automatic measurement of facial beauty, 2001 IEEE International Conference on Systems, Man, and Cybernetics, Page(s): 2644 -2647 vol.4, 2001
[20] The Facial Recognition Technology Database

Appearance Reconstruction of Three Dimensional Models from Real Images *

Ulaş Yılmaz, Adem Y. Mülayim, Volkan Atalay
Department of Computer Engineering
Middle East Technical University
TR-06531, Ankara, Turkey

Abstract

An image based model reconstruction system is described. Real images of a rigid object acquired under a simple but controlled environment are used to recover the three dimensional geometry and the surface appearance. Based on a multi-image calibration method, an algorithm to extract the rotation axis of a turn-table has been developed. Furthermore, this can be extended to estimate robustly the initial bounding volume of the object to be modeled. The coarse volume obtained, is then carved using a stereo correction method which removes the disadvantages of silhouette based reconstruction by photoconsistency. The concept of surface particles is adapted in order to extract a texture map for the model. Some metrics are defined to measure the quality of the reconstructed models.

1 Introduction

An image-based model reconstruction method is described. Using an off-the-shelf camera, considerably realistic looking models of a 3D rigid object can be reconstructed from its 2D images [1, 2, 3, 4, 5, 6]. The goal of this study is to investigate the image-based reconstruction of 3D graphical models of real objects in a controlled imaging environment and present the work done in our group for such a reconstruction. Although many parts of the whole system have been well-known in the literature and in practice, there are contributions of this study which can be stated as follows: developing a vision based calibration algorithm and its compari-

son, extraction of the rotary axis, estimation of the initial bounding cube of the acquired object, removing the disadvantages of the reconstruction approach based on silhouettes and volume intersection using photoconsistency, use of particles for a smooth appearance recovery.

The organization of the paper is as follows: we first describe our geometry reconstruction process in the following section. Section 3 gives the detailed description of our appearance recovery algorithms. Results obtained in the framework of our study are given in Section 4. The paper concludes with Section 5.

2 Geometry reconstruction

The purpose of camera calibration is to obtain an estimate of the parameters which determine the transformation of a point in 3D world to a point in a 2D image by a camera. This is necessary in order to be able to associate a 3D world point with a 2D image point. In order to compute the parameters of the camera, we use a multi-image calibration approach [5]. Our acquisition setup is made up of a rotary table with a fixed camera as shown in Figure 1. The rotation axis and distance from the camera center to this rotation axis remain the same during the turns of the table. Based on this idea, we have developed a vision based geometrical calibration algorithm for the rotary table [7]. Furthermore, we can compute very easily the distance between the rotation axis of the table with respect to the camera center which in fact facilitates the calculation of the bounding cube [4].

Once the bounding volume is obtained, carving this volume by making use of the silhouettes, a coarse model of the object is computed. This volume has some extra voxels which in fact should not exist. In this context, we have implemented a stereo correction algorithm which removes these extra voxels using photo-

---

*This study is partially supported by TÜBİTAK (Scientific and Technical Research Council of Turkey) under the grant EEEAG-199E024, by METU Graduate School of Natural and Applied Sciences and by METU Research Grant. Adem Y. Mülayim's study is supported by TÜBİTAK Integrated PhD Program.

Figure 1. System setup.

consistency [5]. Algorithm 1 which is mostly inspired from Matsumoto et. al. [8] outlines the process.

Algorithm 1 Computing the photoconsistent voxels.

reset all photoconsistency values of the voxels in V_{object} to max photoconsistency value
for all image i in the image sequence **do**
    for all visible voxels in image i **do**
        produce a ray from camera optic center
        find max photoconsistent voxel on the ray
        for all voxels between the max photoconsistent
        voxel and camera optic center **do**
            reduce voxel photoconsistency votes
        end for
    end for
end for
for all voxel v in voxel space V_{object} **do**
    if the photoconsisency of v is less than a threshold
    then
        remove v from V_{object}
    end if
end for

In the algorithm, each voxel in the object voxel space V_{object}, starts with a high photoconsistency vote value; that is each voxel on the model generated by the silhouette based reconstruction is assumed to be on the real object surface. Each view i is then processed in the following manner. For each view i, rays from the camera center c_i through the voxels seen from that view i are traversed voxel by voxel. Each voxel on the ray is projected onto the images $i-1$, i, $i+1$ and the voxel's photoconsistency value is calculated using texture similarity measures among the projection regions on the images $i-1$, i, $i+1$. Then, the voxel with maximum photoconsistency value is found and all the voxels existing between this voxel and the camera center c_i loose votes in an increasing order as they become closer to c_i. This process is repeated for all the rays which can be generated from the view i. When the process is

performed for all the views, excess voxels caused by the silhouette based reconstruction lose most of their initial photoconsistency votes. Then by thresholding, this excess volume is carved. Figure 2 explains better the idea. In this figure, darkest colored voxels get the highest voting; i.e. they have the maximum texture similarity according to the algorithm. The color of voxel shows its vote.

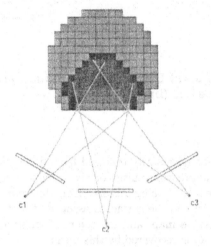

Figure 2. Darkest colored voxels get the highest voting.

3 Appearance reconstruction

There exist several studies for appearance reconstruction of 3D models from real images [9, 10, 11, 12]. In most of these studies, the model is represented as a triangular wireframe, and each triangle is associated with one of the images for texture extraction. The method causes discontinuities on the triangle boundaries as shown in Figure 3-a, since adjacent triangles can be associated with different source images. Applying low pass filter on the boundaries cannot come up with a global solution.

In this study, 2D texture mapping is used but to reduce the drawbacks due to the lack of third dimension information, the concept of surface particles is adapted [6, 13]. An abstraction is done on the actual representation of the model: the model is considered to be a surface composed of particles with three attributes: position, normal and color. While reconstructing the appearance of the model, instead of associating triangles to images, particles are associated with images for texture extraction. This is what makes the proposed method superior to the others: since a tri-

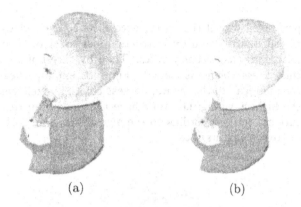

(a)   (b)

Figure 3. (a) Discontinuities on the triangle boundaries, (b) reconstruction using particles.

angle is not necessarily textured from a single image, there are not discontinuities on the triangle boundaries due to the fact of being textured from different images. Each particle on the surface is associated with a pixel on the texture map, and the color information of the texture map is recovered by this means.

A particle is not necessarily visible in all of the images in the sequence, it can be occluded or a back face in some of them. So, the extraction takes place at two steps: visibility check and color retrieval. Visibility check is performed using the particle normal and the particle position by simple hidden surface removal and occlusion detection algorithms. The particle is projected on the source images in which it is visible, and a set of candidate color values, $C = \{c_0, ..c_{M-1}\}$ are collected. In this study, the candidate color values are fused in order to produce the most photoconsistent appearance. Before assigning a color value to a particle, it is decided whether the information extracted from the source images is photoconsistent or not. The photoconsistency is defined in Definition 1. The value of Θ is empirical and set to 60. It is expected that the values of a photoconsistent set concentrates around the view-independent color of the particle. This method is very suitable for removing illumination artifacts as shown in Figure 3-b. However, if the geometry of the object is not constructed precisely, the photoconsistency criteria will fail for most of the particles, which will cause irregularities on the surface appearance.

Definition 1 *Let the extracted color values for a given particle be $C = \{c_0, c_1, ..c_{M-1}\}$ for an image sequence $S = \{I_0, I_1, ..I_{N-1}\}$. The color of the particle for this sequence is photoconsistent if*

1. There exists at least two images in S in which the

particle is not occluded.

2. The particle is not on the background in any of the images in S.

3. $C_\sigma < \Theta$ where C_σ is the standard deviation of intensity values of the colors in C.

The overall appearance reconstruction process is described in Algorithm 2: by projecting the particle on the source images, a set of candidate colors is extracted. If the reconstructed set is photoconsistent then the color of the particle is selected as the median of this set. If a particle is occluded in all of the images or a photoconsistent color cannot be extracted from the sequence, there occurs regions whose appearance cannot be recovered on the model. The colors of the particles in these regions are interpolated using the colors of the adjacent particles.

Algorithm 2 Recovering the color of a particle.

reset the candidate color set of the particle to empty set
for all images in the sequence **do**
   if particle is visible in the image **then**
      project particle on the image
      insert the extracted color in C
   end if
end for
if C is photoconsistent **then**
   set the color of the particle to the median of C
else
   set the color of the particle to the color of the nearest particle whose color is consistent.
end if

---

4 Error analysis and experimental results

In addition to visual comparison, the quality of the reconstructed models is measured with a set of methods. These methods are based on the comparison of original images of the object with rendered corresponding images using the reconstructed model. The images that are used for reconstruction (training images) should not be used for quality measurement (test images). If the training images are also used as the test images, the measurements will be biased. Instead, some of the acquired images are not used in reconstruction but kept as test images to obtain more reliable quantitative analysis. Generally, visual similarity cannot be described by computational similarity. Although there is no universal and accepted method to tell how similar two images are, there still exists in the literature the following methods: Hausdorff distance (HD), root-mean-square error ($RMSE$), direct difference error (DDE), and normalized cross correlation ratio (CO) [14].

The experiments are performed on a personal computer with 512 MB of RAM, Intel PIII 800Hz CPU and 32MB frame buffer. The images are captured with a 2/3" Color Progressive scan CCD camera at a resolution of 1294x1030. While rendering the final model, texture mapping is performed using the routines provided by OpenGL. As shown in Figure 4, the algorithms are successful in removing the highlights. Some further results for two objects are shown in Figure 5. Also the error analysis for the "box" object is given in Table 1.

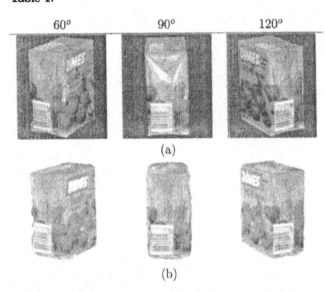

(a)

(b)

Figure 4. (a) Sample images, (b) sample reconstructions for the "box" object.

Table 1. Error analysis for the "box" object.

	HD_{chess}	HD_{city}	$NCCR$	$RMSE$	DDE
$Error$	14.50 %	24.46 %	1.17 %	12.26%	7.38 %

5 Conclusion

In this paper, we describe an image based model reconstruction system using real images of rigid and static objects. In fact, it is an end-to-end system for reconstructing 3D object models using a camera and calibrated turntable. The described system can be used as an inexpensive scanner. The acquisition in this work

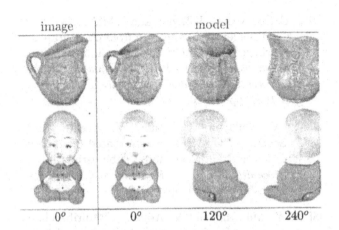

Figure 5. Sample reconstructions.

is not performed in a very well controlled environment: camera makes a controlled motion around the object and the images are acquired in daylight. The improvements contributions described in this study can be stated as follows. A vision based camera calibration algorithm is developed and it is used in the extraction of the rotation axis. The bounding cube of the object is estimated using the extracted rotation axis. To eliminate the drawbacks of the silhouette based reconstruction, a shape from photoconsistency algorithm is implemented to correct the disadvantages of the previous steps. The concept of surface particles is adapted in order to extract a texture map for the model. Futhermore, the assessment of the constructed models is peformed visually and also by using some metrics to measure the quality of the reconstructed models. Although parts of the system have been described in the literature before, we beleive that it is important to put together a complete system. Furthermore, the choice of the method and the way is implemented is described in detail and could be of interest to other researchers.

References

[1] U. Yılmaz, A. Y. Mülayim, and V. Atalay, "Reconstruction of three dimensional models from real images," in *International Symposium on 3D Data Processing Visualization and Transmission*, G. M. Cortelazzo and C. Guerra, Eds., Padova, Italy, June 2002, pp. 554–557, IEEE Computer Society.

[2] W. Niem and J. Wingbermühle, "Automatic reconstruction of 3d objects using a mobile monoscopic camera," in *Proceedings of International Conference on Recent Advances in 3D Imaging and Modeling*, May 1997, pp. 173–180.

[3] P. E. Debevec, C. J. Taylor, and J. Malik, "Modeling and rendering architecture from photographs: A hybrid geometry and image-based approach," in *Proceedings of SIGGRAPH'96, Computer Graphics Proceedings, Annual Conference Series*, August 1996, pp. 11–20.

[4] A. Y. Mülayim, O. Özün, V. Atalay, and F. Schmitt, "On the silhouette based 3d reconstruction and initial bounding cube estimation," in *Proceedings of Vision Modeling and Visualisation*, November 2000, pp. 11–18.

[5] A. Y. Mülayim and V. Atalay, "Multibaseline stereo coreection for silhouette-based 3d model reconstruction from multiple images," in *Proceedings SPIE, Three-Dimensional Image Capture and Applications IV*, January 2001, pp. 24–25.

[6] F. Schmitt and Y. Yemez, "3d color object reconstruction from 2d image sequences," in *Proceedings of International Conference on Image Processing*, October 1999, pp. 65–69.

[7] A. Y. Mülayim, Y. Yemez, F. Schmitt, and V. Atalay, "Rotation axis extraction of a turn table viewed by a fixed camera," in *Proceedings of Vision Modeling and Visualisation*, November 1999, pp. 35–42.

[8] Y. Matsumoto, K. Fujimura, and T. Kitamura, "Shape-from-silhouette/stereo and its application to 3-d digitizer," in *Discrete Geometry for Computer Imagery Conference, Lecture Notes in Computer Science 1568*, 1999, pp. 177–188.

[9] W. Niem and H. Broszio, "Mapping texture from multiple camera views onto 3d object models for computer animation," in *Proceedings of International Workshop on Stereoscopic and Three Dimensional Imaging*, September 1995, pp. 99–105.

[10] S. Genç and V. Atalay, "Texture extraction from photographs and rendering with dynamic texture mapping," in *Proceedings of the 10th International Conference on Image Analysis and Processing*, September 1999.

[11] H. P. A. Lensch, W. Heidrich, and H-P. Seidel, "Automated texture registration and stitching for real world models," in *Proceedings of Pacific Graphics*, October 2000, pp. 317–337.

[12] J. P. Neugebauer and K. Klein, "Texturing of 3d models of real world objects from multiple unregistered photographic views," *Computer Graphics Forum*, vol. 18, no. 3, pp. 245–256, September 1999.

[13] R. Szelisky and D. Tonnesen, "Surface modeling with oriented particles," *Computer Graphics (SIGGRAPH'92)*, vol. 26, no. 2, pp. 185–194, July 1992.

[14] V. Di Gesu and V. Starovoitov, "Distance-based functions for image comparison," *Pattern Recognition Letters*, vol. 20, no. 2, pp. 207–214, 1999.

Texture Segmentation by Using Adaptive Polyphase Subband Decomposition

Mustafa Yaman, Volkan Atalay
Department of Computer Engineering,
Middle East Technical University,
Ankara, Turkey
e106201@ceng.metu.edu.tr
volkan@ceng.metu.edu.tr

Mustafa Türker
Department of Geodetic and Geographic
Information Technologies,
Middle East Technical University,
Ankara, Turkey
mturker@metu.edu.tr

Enis Çetin
Department of Electrical Engineering
Bilkent University,
Ankara, Turkey
cetin@ee.bilkent.edu.tr

Öner Nezih Gerek
Department of Electrical Engineering
Eskişehir Anadolu University,
Eskişehir, Turkey
ongerek@anadolu.edu.tr

Abstract

In this study, a new texture segmentation method is proposed for texture analysis applications. The technique makes use of an adaptive polyphase subband decomposition to analyze textural blocks and extract the discriminating feature sets for segmentation of the images. The subband decomposition treats the texture blocks as 2-d signals having correlated spectral properties and the filter banks used split this signal into several frequency regions which are decorrelated by the decomposition. The filter coefficients are not static but modified through the process for adaptively analyzing the signal. The feature sets constructed according to the filter coefficients and the error image are fed to the classifier functions. Since the method decomposes the signal optimally, the feature extraction capability is boosted. The method is tested on artificial images produced by using Brodatz textures and texture blocks cut from IRS Pan satellite imagery.

1. Introduction

Today, texture analysis has a very wide range of application areas in computer vision and digital image processing such as medical imaging, remote sensing, document segmentation and content based search etc. Texture segmentation is one of the main components of analysis by texture and is defined as assigning a label to each pixel of the image based on the properties of the pixel and its relationship with its neighbours.

For analyzing images by texture several approaches have been proposed [1] : These are statistical, geometric, model-based and signal-processing. Statistical approaches use several statistical measures to define textural properties of an image. In [2], the cooccurance matrix is proposed by computing the relative frequencies of gray-level pixels at relative displacements. Haralick suggests 14 features, including correlation, entropy, contrast and angular second moment etc., describing two dimensional probability density function. Geometric approaches include the least used features because of the limited practical capability. Since textures confronted in real life are neither totally deterministic nor stochastic, the tight assumptions on the image are the disadvantage of these methods. In [3], voronoi tessellation features are used for texture segmentation. Model based methods make an assumption of an image model to describe texture. Petland introduces a fractal-based texture analysis system using the fractal dimension as the texture description in [4]. Lastly, signal-processing approaches use spatial and spatial frequency filters, filter banks and frequency transforms such as Fourier transform, wavelet transforms and wavelet models [2].

In this paper, a new texture analysis method is proposed which can be categorized as a signal processing method. The technique makes use of an adaptive polyphase subband decomposition to analyze textural blocks and extract the discriminating feature sets for segmentation of the images. The subband decomposition [5] treats the texture blocks as 2-d signals having correlated spectral properties and the filter banks used split this signal into several frequency regions, which are decorrelated by the decomposition. While the polyphase filter banks [6] enable the signal be separated into m-phase m subbands, the filter coefficients give us an important clue about the relation between the corresponding pixels in these subbands which are the neighbouring pixels in the original image.

Within the context of subband decomposition and filter banks adaptive filtering appears to be an emerging method for achieving more efficient decomposition of signals [7]. In the recent study of Gerek and Cetin [8], a new adaptation scheme is used for estimating an unknown system, in which the filter coefficients are updated to remove unnecessary information among the neighbouring subsignals. Therefore, a significant improvement in the coding and compressing the image data is achieved while the perfect reconstruction property is preserved. Inspired by this study, we analyzed the texture discrimination property of adapted filter coefficients and the error signal produced by this model and propose a new method to define and segment images by texture using this property.

In Section II, the adaptive polyphase subband decomposition concept is reviewed. The filter bank structure and the adaptation algorithm is presented. In Section III, the feature extraction scheme and the implementation details is explained. The experiments and results are placed in Section IV and in Section V the conclusions are presented and the future work is defined.

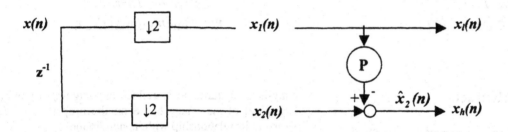

Figure 1: Adaptive Filter Bank Structure Analysis Stage

2. Adaptive Polyphase Subband Decomposition

As mentioned in the introduction section, the main aim of decomposing the signal into its subbands adaptively is finding the relationship between the neighbouring pixels by using the coefficients of the filter which are modified during the decomposition by the input image and the error image which is the optimization criterion. In Figure 1, the structure of the adaptive filter bank used for the analysis is presented.

In this structure, after the input signal is separated into its even and odd subbands, the first polyphase component x_1 is used to predict the second polyphase component x_2. The aim is to remove the correlation between the two subbands. So prediction filtering is used to achieve this decorrelation between subbands. Since images can be modeled as 2-d signals and they are nonstationary in nature, the predictor should be adaptive; i.e. the prediction filter adapts itself to minimize correlation.

2.1 Adaptation Scheme by Using Recursive Least Squares Algorithm

In Figure 1, the predictor **P** is assumed to minimize $x_h(n)$ which is the error subsignal defined as:

$$x_h(n) = x_2(n) - \hat{x}_2(n) \tag{1}$$

where $\hat{x}_2(n)$ is obtained by

$$\hat{x}_2(n) = \sum_{k=-N}^{N} w_{n,k} x_1(n-k) = \sum_{k=-N}^{N} w_{n,k} x(2n-2k) \tag{2}$$

The filter coefficients $w_{n,k}$'s are updated using a Recursive Least Squares (RLS) type adaptation algorithm [7,9]. According to this algorithm, an index of performance $\varepsilon(n)$ is defined as the minimization criterion. Thus, we write

$$\varepsilon(n) = \sum_{k=1}^{n} \beta(n,k) |e(k)|^2 \tag{3}$$

where $e(k)$ is the difference between desired signal $x_2(k)$ and the predicted signal $\hat{x}_2(k)$. Therefore, $e(k)$ is defined as

$$e(k) = x_h(k) = x_2(k) - \tilde{x}_n^T(k)\hat{w}(n) \tag{4}$$

82

where $\hat{w}(n) = \left[w_{n,-N}, \cdots, w_{n,N} \right]$ is the weight vector at time instant n and $\widetilde{x}_n$ input vector at time instant k,

$$\widetilde{x}_n = \left[x_1(k-N), x_1(k-N+1), \cdots, x_1(k+N-1), x_1(k+N) \right]^T \quad (5)$$

The $\beta(n,k)$ in Equation 3 is the weighting factor which is between 0 and 1 and the use of this weighting factor enables decreasing and/or eliminating the effect of the distant data in the past while operating the filter.

For computing the optimum value of $\hat{w}(n)$ weight vector, the performance index $\varepsilon(n)$ is minimized by the normal equation,

$$\Phi(n)\hat{w}(n) = \Theta(n) \quad (6)$$

where $\Phi(n)$ is the M-by-M correlation matrix defined by

$$\Phi(n) = \sum_{k=1}^{n} \beta(n,k) \widetilde{x}_n(k) \widetilde{x}_n^T(k) \quad (7)$$

and $\Theta(n)$ is the estimated M-by-1 cross correlation vector

$$\Theta(n) = \sum \beta(n,k) \widetilde{x}_n(k) x_2^*(k). \quad (8)$$

The solution of Equation 6 is

$$\hat{w}(n) = \Phi^{-1}(n)\Theta(n). \quad (9)$$

Solving this equation needs matrix inversion $\Phi^{-1}(n)$ which is $O(N^3)$. In order to decrease this high computational cost, a "recursive" method is developed which computes $\hat{w}(n+1)$ directly from $\hat{w}(n)$ in $O(N^2)$ time.

Here, it is observed that

$$\Phi(n+1) = \Phi(n) + \widetilde{x}(n+1)\widetilde{x}^T(n+1) \quad (10)$$

and

$$\Theta(n+1) = \Theta(n) + x(n+1)x_2^*(n+1) \quad (11)$$

Then, by using the matrix inversion lemma
$$(a+bcd)^{-1} = a^{-1} - a^{-1}b(c^{-1}+da^{-1}b)^{-1}da^{-1} \quad (12)$$
we get

$$\Phi(n+1)^{-1} = \Phi(n)^{-1} \frac{\Phi(n)^{-1}\widetilde{x}(n+1)\widetilde{x}^T(n+1)\Phi(n)^{-1}}{1+\widetilde{x}^T(n+1)\Phi(n)^{-1}\widetilde{x}(n+1)} \quad (13)$$

allowing us to compute $\Phi^{-1}(n+1)$ from $\Phi^{-1}(n)$ in $O(N^2)$ time. Thus, using these equations Equation 9 can be redesigned in a recursive manner as :

$$\hat{w}(n+1) = \hat{w}(n) + (\Phi^{-1}(n+1)\widetilde{x}(n+1).(x_2^*(n+1) - \widetilde{x}^T(n+1)\hat{w}(n))$$
(14)

where $(x_2^*(n+1) - \widetilde{x}^T(n+1)\hat{w}(n)) = e(n+1)$, i.e. error value as defined in Equation 4 and $(\Phi^{-1}(n+1)\widetilde{x}(n+1))$ is called as the "kalman gain vector" [7].

2.2. Two Dimensional Extension of the Filter Bank Structures

In our implementation we deal with images and we have to extend the idea of the adaptive filter bank structure presented in 2.1. for two dimensional case. The conventional method to implement multidimensional filters with one dimensional modules is the separable prediction method. First the rows of the image are filtered, and then this data is column-wise processed.

3. Texture Feature Extraction and Segmentation

In Equation 2, we model texture as the linear combination of the neighbouring pixels plus the prediction error. So after adaptive filtering the computed weights $w_{n,k}$ and the error image x_h are used as the parameters describing texture. Since images to be segmented include several textures, we need to compute these parameters in a region of support with predefined radius.

In our implementations, a radius N for the region of support is defined which reflects the properties of the textural block. For every pixel to be segmented firstly the weights are computed from the adaptive polyphase subband decomposition structure explained in Section 2. A $Nx4$ matrix of coefficients $w_i(x,y)$ are computed in addition to the error image $e(x,y)$. Later, the feature set for the corresponding pixel is constructed from these parameters. The feature sets are constructed by using the energy $\in$ and variance σ^2 measures computed from the coefficients and the error signal defining the relationship between the pixels in the region of support where this feature set is stored as the attribute of the pixel being predicted. The same operation is repeated for every pixel in the image to be segmented and a new image $featmap(x,y,F[1..k])$ containing the feature sets is constructed. Lastly, the $featmap$ is clustered by using k-means [11] algorithm, i.e. the number of texture classes and their initial class means are first guessed and an after iterative process of assigning every feature set to the class label with nearest distance and checking the consistency of class means the image is classified.

4. Experiments and Results

This section shows a part of our experiments applied on images having textural information as the significant discriminating property of the desired classes. The images are both artificial images produced by Brodatz [12] textures and image blocks cut from IRS Pan [13] satellite images. In all experiments, radius of 12 pixels is chosen for the region of support and 4 coefficients are used for the prediction.

In Figure 2, there are 3 sample texture pairs and their corresponding segmented images. The texture pairs are 50x100 – 8 bit images containing two types of 50x50 texture blocks pasted next to each other. The performance of the algorithm reaches to 97 % for the tested images as shown in Table I by their figure number. In Figure 3, we extracted 2 image blocks from IRS Pan images [13] of several cities in Turkey. These 100x200 – 8 bit image blocks are assumed to contain two types of texture classes and segmented by this assumption. The results for these and similar images display a mean percentage of correct segmentation of 93 % at city boundaries and inner city segmentations. Especially, the noisy spots and irregular road network tend to decrease the texture discrimination and increase the convergence between the textural properties for the city blocks.

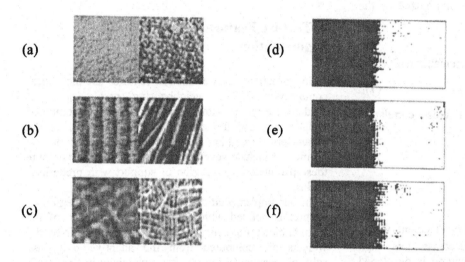

(a)　(d)
(b)　(e)
(c)　(f)

Figure 2 : Sample texture pairs (a), (b), (c) and their corresponding segmentations (d), (e), (f)

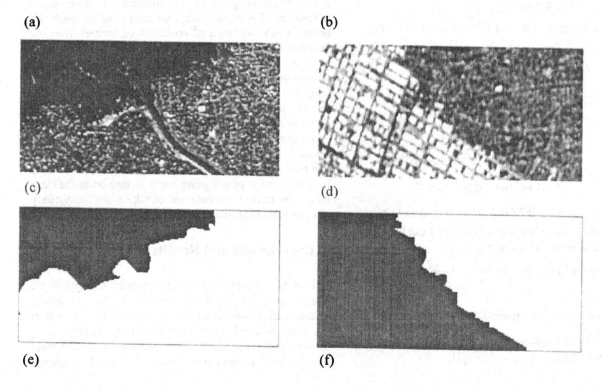

(a)　(b)
(c)　(d)
(e)　(f)

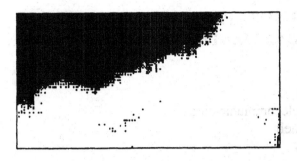 

Figure 3: Sample image blocks (a), (b) extracted from IRS Pan images; (c),(d) the of the images ; (e), (f) achieved segmentation of the images

Table 1 : Segmentation Results For the Test Images	
Test Images by figure number	Percent of Correct Segmentation
2(a)	97.76 %
2(b)	97.06 %
2(c)	95.00 %
3(a)	93.73 %
3(b)	93.41 %

5. Conclusion

A texture segmentation scheme for analysis of images by texture using adaptive polyphase subband decomposition is presented. The performance of the algorithm is demonstrated for both synthesized texture blocks and image blocks extracted from urban areas. The results are computed for the desired segmentations and percentage of the correctly segmented pixels are listed.

The method displays promisingly accurate results for segmenting images by texture. Several improvement techniques like implementing the fast filter algorithms and testing and comparing with several other segmentation algorithms are on the agenda.

References

[1] T. Randen, Filter and Filter Bank Design for Image Texture Recognition, Ph.D. Thesis, Norwegian University of Science and Technology Stavanger College, Stavanger, Norway, 1997.
[2] R. M. Haralick, Statistical and Structural Approaches to Texture. Proc. IEEE, 67(5):786-804, 1979

[3] A. K. Jain. Fundamentals of Digital Image Processing. Prentice-Hall, Englewood Cliffs, 1989.
[4] A.P Pentland, Fractal-based description of natural scenes, IEEE Trans. on Pattern Analysis and Machine Intelligence, 6:661-674, 1984.
[5] A. N. Akansu and R. A. Haddad, Multiresolution Signal Decomposition, Academic Press, San Diego, 1992
[6] G. Strang and T. Nguyen, Wavelets and Filter Banks, Wellesley – Cambridge Press, Wellesley, MA, 1996.
[7] S. Haykin, Adaptive Filter Theory, Englewood Cliffs, NJ, Prentice Hall, 1986,
[8] Ö. N. Gerek and A. E. Çetin, Adaptive Polyphase Subband Decomposition Structures for Image Compression, IEEE Trans. on Image Proc., 9(10):1649-1660, Oct. 2000.
[9] Ö. N. Gerek, Image Coding for Digitized Libraries, Ph.D. Thesis, Bilkent University, Ankara, Sept. 1998.
[10] M. Unser. Texture classification and segmentation using wavelet frames. IEEE Trans. on Image Proc., 4(11):1549-1560, Nov. 1995.
[11] R. Schalkoff. Pattern Recognition: Statistical, Structural and Neural Approaches. Wiley, New York, 1992.
[12] P. Brodatz. Textures: A Photographic Album for Artists and Designers. Dover, NY, 1966.
[13] IRS - Indian Remote Sensing Satellite http://www.eurimage.com/Products/irs.shtml

MULTISCALE IMAGE REPRESENTATION USING SWITCHED CODEBOOK PREDICTIVE VECTOR QUANTIZATION

Mehmet Yakut

Department of Electronics and Telecommunications

University of Kocaeli

Kocaeli, Turkey

myakut@kou.edu.tr

Abstract:

In this study different vector formation is proposed for mutiscale image representation similar to pyramidal representation. Using the vector formation described here higher predictability assured between successive vectors. Switched codebook predictive vector is developed for the proposed vector formation. User selectable high resolution images are obtained using the information carried on low resolution vector quantized images. The method used here is useful for applications like fast search on criminal database over low rate transmission lines and user selectable progressive wieving of images on slow internet services.

Indexing terms: Vector , pyramid coding, multiscale image representation, switched codebook VQ, predictive VQ, feature based quantization, self organising feature map (SOFM).

1. Introduction:

Vector quantisation is a powerfull tool for data compression according to rate distortion theory. A better performance can always be achieved by coding vectors instead of scalars even if the source is memoryless [2]. Vector quantizer provides arbitrarily shaped quantisation regions in higher dimension. VQ methods have potential of redundancy removal beyond linear dependencies by optimal placement of codevectors [3]. However cost for generation optimisation of codebooks increase exponantially with the vector dimension. Most of the VQ applications are restricted to small vector sizes due to these facts [6].

The transmission of still images is an important field in interactive image compression. With raster scan transmission techniques a digital image is transmitted as a sequence of rows or lines impliying that to be able to appreciate the image, the wiever must wait for the complete transmission. Multiscale image representation and compression (like pyramidal representation) will alleviate this problem by first transmitting a lower scale approximate image, if wiever requests for better image quality lower scale image can be improved to higher scale (original scale) image by transmitting the differences of the two scales of images [11]. Obviously lower scale image represents global characteristics of the original image while higher scale image represents local image properties (such as small changes, and details).

Multiscale image representation and progressive image transmission is very important subject when we are required for featured images to scan or fast object searching in a large image database, similarly when accessing large criminal image database for recognition of the suspect from a telephone line etc. Vector quantisation of the lower scale and higher scale representation of the large image database will highly reduce the required transmission bit rate. If needed errors between the higher scale image and the original can be transmitted using Huffman coding to achieve the original image.

VQ is an appealing coding technique since the rate distortion bound can be approached as the vector dimension is increased [3,5]. Most of the compression applications suffer from complexity, computational and storage needs. Computational and storage complexity increases exponantially with rate and distortion. For unstructured VQ applications codebooks are trained to represent whole characteristics of the image database [13]. Most of the time local characteristics are ignored. When multiscale image representation is used lower scale image carry global information about image, while having rough local properties. Generally fine image details have small amplitudes which can be seen as differences of the original and the lower scale image [1]. In our study, lower scale image has deterministic role on the detail image codebooks. Rough local characteristics determines the codebooks for fine details by use of neural network codebook selector. Average intensity, activity of the vector components, directional variances of the rough image could be used instead of neural network [12]. Using self organizing feature mapping neural networks, bit assignment problem of the above properties is solved in self classification manner. Otherwise desicion rule for the bit assignment to the rough local properties of the image will be troublesome.

86

2. Use of Predictive Vector Quantisation with Novel Vector Formation Scheme

In our application predictability between successive vectors is increased using different vector formation scheme. Although intervector correlation is reduced in our new vector form, there is scalar predictability for the difference vector components and there exists clustering for the difference codebooks. Initially encoded vector has a natural codebook selector function for the difference codebooks. Since all vector components for successive vectors are next to each other, each vector component can be predicted from the previosly encoded vector components. Number of the vectors used in prediction can be chosen as far as computational needs do not overload the system. Instead of complex vector prediction schemes, which inhales computational resouces, using simple prediction, like lossles JPEG type will be important avdantage of the proposed vector formation. Selection of the difference codebooks does not require extra computational cost. Since the difference codebooks are trained independently training period required is not too long. Best matching codevector is searched only in the SOFM selected codebook that increases the codevector searching performance. In this study SOFM codebook selection is done only for the initial code vector and same difference codebook is used for encoding the next 15 vectors. If SOFM codebook selector is used continiously at each step of vector quantisation, we can select any of the difference codebooks to find the best matching code vector at every step of the quantisation. Continiously codebook selection increases computational cost slightly and requires some additional time for training. Number of difference code books can be up to number of code vectors for lower scale image encoding. If training set size is small, using more difference codebooks than required, causes many dummy or randomly distributed code vectors. Training period will last too long, if large size of training set is selected. Use of SOFM codebook selector enable efficient use of codebook memory and flexibility on the selection of the distortion level beside codebook size measure. We can increase number of difference code books up to number of lower scale codebook size if needed.

2.1. Vector formation:

Vector formation method used in this study is described in figure 1. The boxes numbered with 0 show initial vector, 1 show the next vector and 2.3...and so on. Using this vector formation method, there is a higher and simpler predictability between successive vectors. Also the first vector serves as difference codebook selector since it carries some structural information about the next 15 vectors. Initial vector can be selected from the top left corner or any other corner and following vectors

are formed by using zig zag, rowwise or columnwise scanning.

9	10	11	12	9		11	12	9	10	11	12	9	b	11	12
8	1	2	13	8	1	2	13	8	1	2	13	8	1	2	13
7	0	3	14	7	0	3	14	7	0	3	14	7	0	3	14
6	5	4	15	6	5	4	15	6	5	4	15	6	5	4	15
9	10	11	12	9		11	12	9	10	11	12	9	10	11	12
8	1	2	13	8	1	2	13	8	1	2	13	8	1	2	13
7	0	3	14	7	0	3	14	7	0	3	14	7	0	3	14
6	5	4	15	6	5	4	15	6	5	4	15	6	5	4	15
9	10	11	12	9		11	12	9	10	11	12	9	10	11	12
8	1	2	13	8	1	2	13	8	1	2	13	8	1	2	13
7	0	3	14	7	0	3	14	7	0	3	14	7	0	3	14
6	5	4	15	6	5	4	15	6	5	4	15	6	5	4	15
9	10	11	12	9		11	12	9	10	11	12	9	10	11	12
8	1	2	13	8	1	2	13	8	1	2	13	8	1	2	13
7	0	3	14	7	0	3	14	7	0	3	14	7	0	3	14
6	5	4	15	6	5	4	15	6	5	4	15	6	5	4	15

Figure 1. Spiral type vector formation

2.2 SOFM codebook selector:

SOFM's are special class of Artificial Neural Networks based on competitive learning in which only one neuron is active for the same class of inputs [16]. The competition rule is also known as winner takes all. The neurons in SOFM are selectively tuned to various classes of the input patterns through the competitive learning process [15]. In our study SOFM's are trained to select difference codebooks using the information contained in the previously encoded codevector. SOFM's can be wieved as a neural network vector quantizer, usually named as learning vector quantizer [14]. Winning neuron is found by euclidian distance between input x and weights w_j Eq.(1), and the weights of the winning neuron which has the minimum euclidian distance are updated using Eq.(2)

$$i(x) = \arg\min \|x(n) - w_j\| \quad \text{for } j = 1, 2, \ldots N \tag{1}$$

$$w_j(n+1) = \begin{cases} w_j(n) + \eta(n)[x - w_j(n)] & \text{if neuron } j \text{ is active} \\ w_j(n) & \text{otherwise} \end{cases} \tag{2}$$

16 input and 4,8,16, 32, 64 output SOFM's are trained and used as code book selector in this study. Learning rate is initially selected as 0.05 and is reduced up to 0.0001 during training iterations. The restriction of sum of weights to any neuron should be 1 used in the weight update process. The weights and inputs are assumed to be normalized to 1 also.

3. Predictive Switched VQ (PSVQ) for Multiscale Image Representation

The image first decomposed into lower and higher scale images. The lower scale image is low pass filtered and subsampled version of the original image. Original image is subsampled at every 4 samples after low pass filtering. As the low pass filter Gaussian type seperable filter is used [7]. Lower scale image is VQ encoded, after training the codebook using generalized Lloyd algorithm [8]. Minimum Euclidian distance is used to search the best matching codevector in the code book.

If (di < dj) for all j where di = ‖ x - xi ‖ then encode vector x, by using the codevector x_i. Once first vector

$$1 \quad \hat{X}(m,n)=X(m-1,n)$$
$$2 \quad \hat{X}(m,n)=X(m,n-1)$$
$$3 \quad \hat{X}(m,n)=X(m-1,n-1)$$
$$4 \quad \hat{X}(m,n)=X(m,n-1)+X(m-1,n)-X(m-1,n-1)$$ (3)
$$5 \quad \hat{X}(m,n)=X(m,n-1)+(X(m-1,n)-X(m-1,n-1))/2$$
$$6 \quad \hat{X}(m,n)=X(m,n-1)+(X(m,n-1)-X(m-1,n-1))/2$$
$$7 \quad \hat{X}(m,n)=(X(m-1,n)+X(m,n-1))/2$$

Table 1. Vectors used in prediction scheme

Vector to be encoded	linear prediction vectors	JPEG type prediction vectors
0	No	no
1	0	0 mod1
2	0,1	0,1 mod7
3	0,1,2	0,1,2 mod5
4	1,2,3	0,3 mod7
5	2,3,4	0,3,4 mod5
6	3,4,5	0,5 mod7
7	4,5,6	0,5,6 mod5
8	5,6,7	0,1,7 mod5
9	6,7,8	1,8 mod7
10	7,8,9	1,8,9 mod 5
11	8,9,10	1,2,10 mod5
12	9,10,11	2,11 mod 7
13	10,11,12	2,11,12 mod 5
14	11,12,13	2,3,13 mod 5
15	12,13,14	3,4,14 mod5

encoded, difference codebook is selected using SOFM and next vector is predicted from the previosly encoded vector and difference between the predicted value and the original image is vector encoded. One of the suitable simple JPEG prediction mode is used for vector prediction as shown in Eq.(3) [4].

First vector in the subsampled image is vector quantized (Eqn 4),

$$\hat{X}_{LP} = Q(X_{LP})$$ (4)

and index i_n is fed to SOFM and transmitted to receiver. Next vector to be encoded is predicted (Eq.5) from previosly encoded vectors shown at Table 1.

$$\widetilde{X}(n+1) = P(\hat{X}_{LP}(n), \hat{X}_{LP}(n-1), \hat{X}_{LP}(n-1))$$ (5)

The most suitable difference codebook is selected by means of SOFM fed with i_n. Residual vector is vector quantized (Eq.6) using the selected difference codebook by index i_n.

$$\hat{X}(n+1) = Q[X(n+1) - \widetilde{X}(n+1)], \quad using\, Cb[F(i_n)]$$ (6)

Consequently index of the best matching difference code vector k_{n+1} is transmitted. Since only the indexes and code vectors are used for prediction and codebook selection, there is no overhead bit/s to transmit.

4. L2 norm MR PSVQ

The vector formation method can easily be applied to L2 norm pyramid represantation. In the L2 norm pyramid representation image is sub sampled by a factor of two in both x and y dimension at each step. The lowest scale image (32x32) is vector quantized first, then the difference between the first level and second level is vector quantized using the prediction scheme in figure 2. First level is used as initial information source and code book selector for the second level vector quantizer. As seen in equations 7, 8, 9, 10 information carried on previously encoded vectors is used to predict the current vector to be encoded. Vector components are precisely predicted using our vector formation method since only the neighboring pixels are used for prediction. As seen in eqn. 7 for the prediction of the vector component a_0, previously quantized level vector component a is used. Prediction of the next vector component a_1 is found by utilizing the previosly quantized vector components a_0, b_0, e_0 and f_0 as seen in eqn 8. For next two vectors, the components a_2 and a_3 are predicted as in eqn. 9 and 10 in similar way using the neigboring pixels..

In L2 norm approach viewer at the far end of transmission channel can decide to transfer the next level of the image, which avoids transmission of unnecessary information. Many lower sacale images are browsed together at one screen view, and the one we are interested in is viewd at higher scales to see the details of the image. Therefore efficient use of transmission channel is achieved. The new modular predictive vector formation method can easily be applied to L2 norm. The same block diagram seen in figure 5 is used for L2 norm vector quantisation and the same decoder used in MR PSVQ. Results of L2 norm application to our method are seen in table 2.

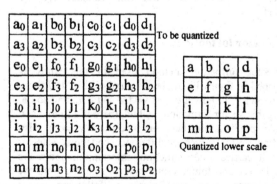

Figure 2. Vector formation for L2 norm pyramid representation

88

$$\tilde{a}_0 = a \tag{7}$$

$$\tilde{a}_1 = \frac{2\hat{a}_0 + 2\hat{b}_0 + \hat{e}_0 + \hat{f}_0}{6} \tag{8}$$

$$\tilde{a}_2 = \frac{2\hat{a}_1 + 2\hat{b}_1 + \hat{a}_0 + \hat{b}_0 + \hat{e}_0 + \hat{f}_0}{8} \tag{9}$$

$$\tilde{a}_3 = \frac{\hat{a}_0 + \hat{a}_1 + \hat{a}_2 + \hat{e}_0 + \hat{e}_1}{5} \tag{10}$$

Block diagram of the system is seen in Figure 5. which performs above operations. The decoding system can be easily estimated from Figure 5.

Figure 3. Example of browsing multiple images and training set images

4. Results and Conclusion:

Multiscale image representation is realized via predictive vector quantisation and better image qualities are obtained when compared to ordinary vector quantisation. Using the method described here better results are reached when codebook sizes are greater than 64 for 16 diference codebooks. Results using 16 different codebooks are shown in table 2. Table is organised with respect to codebook sizes. For the exact comparison of the results including overhead bits required for lower scale images, bold results should be used for Lena image, and similar row shifts for the other images. The lost correlation by selecting apart code vector elements is recovered using the multiple codebooks between 8 and 16. Use of more than 16 difference codebooks increases PSNR performance up to 2dB depending on the image to be encoded when codebook size is 256 and there still we have a chance to stop dummy image transfer. As the number of codebooks is increased, then the number of the dummy codevectors in the codebooks also increase, which results in inefficient use of memory. Multiscale image representation is advantageous especialy if unnecessary information transfer would dump the system performance. When the wiever decides not to see the details of the image, after seeing the lower scale one, then, about 15 lower scale image transmission time is gained, that means cost of detail wiev is 15 times higher. JPEG type simple prediction scheme gives better results which do not need multiplication. If the method is

trained on a large training set, sub optimal global codebook can be obtained which will obviously perform better than ordinary vector quantizer.

Table 2. Results of the MR PSVQ encoding system with 16 codebooks (PSNR in dB)

Codebook size	Image	GLA VQ (dB)	MR PSVQ (with 16 CB)	L2 norm MR PSVQ (with 16 CB)
32	Elaine	26.40dB	28.38dB	31.35dB
32	Lena	24.86dB	26.25dB	28.52dB
32	Boat	24.22dB	25.43dB	27.26dB
64	Elaine	27.16dB	29.15dB	31.93dB
64	Lena	25.80dB	27.18dB	**29.18dB**
64	Boat	24.86dB	26.07dB	27.87dB
128	Elaine	28.20dB	30.36dB	32.60dB
128	Lena	26.70dB	**28.13dB**	29.71dB
128	Boat	25.73dB	26.87dB	28.34dB
256	Elaine	29.18dB	30.96dB	33.39dB
256	Lena	**27.59dB**	29.32dB	30.31dB
256	Boat	26.49dB	27.72dB	28.87dB

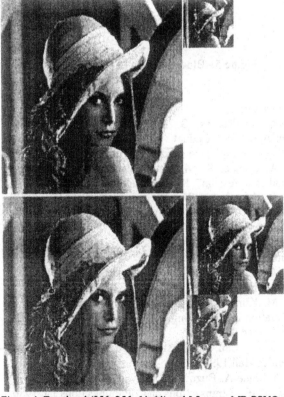

Figure 4. Two level (256x256, 64x64) and L2 norm MR PSVQ (256x256, 128x128, 64x64, 32x32) results for Lena using 64 codebooks with 256 codevectors

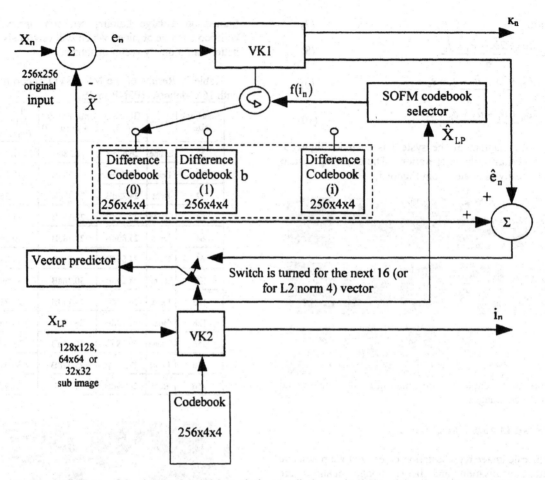

Figure 5. Block diagram of the developed multi resolution predictive switched codebook vector quantizer

References:

[1] C. F. Barnes, S. A. Rizvi, N. M. Nasrabadi, "Advances in residual vector quantisation" IEEE transactions on image processing Feb 1996,

[2] A. Gersho, R. M. Gray, "Vector quantisation and signal compression" Kluwer academic publishers, 1992

[3] R. M. Gray, "Vector quantisation" IEEE ASSP magazine 1984

[4] H.M. Harry J.W. Woods, "Predictive vector quantisation of images" IEEE transactions on Communications Nov 1985.

[5] A. K. Jain, "Image data compression; A review " Proceedings IEEE March 1981, p349-389

[6] M. Kunt, A. Ikonomopoulos, M. Kocher, "Second generation image coding techniques", Proceedings IEEE vol.73 no.4 April 1985

[7] J. S. Lim, "2-D signal and image processing" Prentice Hall 1990

[8] Y.Linde A. Buzo R.M. Gray, "An algorithm for VQ design" IEEE transactions on Communications Jan 1980.

[9] N. M. Nasrabadi, R. A. King, "Image coding using vector quantisation: A review" IEEE transactions on Comm. vol.36 no.8 Aug 1988.

[10] S. Panchanatan M. Goldberg, "Mini-max algorithm for image adaptive VQ", IEEE Proceedings Feb 1991.

[11] L. Wang, M. Goldberg "Progressive image transmission using vector quantisation in pyramid form" IEEE Transactions on Comm. V 37, no:12, p1339-1349, Dec. 1989

[12] L. Wang, S. A. Rizvi N.M. Nasrabadi, "A modular neural network vector predictor for predictive image coding" IEEE Transactions on image processing, v.8, no.7, p1198-1217, Aug. 1998

[13] B. Wegmann C. Zetzche, "Feature spesific vector quantisation of images" IEEE transactions on image processing Feb 1996.

[14] Kohonen T. "Learning vector quantisation for pattern recognition" Helsinki University of Technology, Finland 1986

[15] Kohonen T. "Self organisation and associative memory" Springer Verlag, Newyork 1988.

[16] Kohonen T "The self-organizing map" IEEE Proceedings 1990.

Session 2–1
Computer Networks I

A Parallel Algorithm for Global Optimisation and Semi–Infinite Programming

S. Asprey
CPSE
Imperial College of Science,
Technology and Medicine
London, SW7 2BY
S.Asprey@ic.ac.uk

B. Rustem and S. Žaković
Department of Computing
Imperial College of Science,
Technology and Medicine
London SW7 2BZ
B.Rustem@ic.ac.uk

Abstract

In this paper, we report results of the implementation of an algorithm designed to solve semi–infinite programming problems. Due to its computational intensity, parallelisation is used in two stages – for evaluating the global optimum and for checking the feasibility of constraints. We parallelise the algorithms by using MPI - the message passing interface. The algorithms are then applied to engineering and macroeconomic modelling problems, including designing robust optimally informative experiments for dynamic model identification, and robust macroeconomic policies for inflation targeting.

1. FORMULATION OF THE PROBLEM

In this paper parallelisation of the following semi–infinite problem is considered:

$$
\begin{aligned}
&\min_{x \in X} \quad f(x) \\
&s.t. \quad G(x,y) \leq 0, \quad \forall y \in Y \\
&\qquad X = \{x \in \mathcal{R}^n | g_i(x) \leq 0, \quad i = 1, ..., k\} \\
&\qquad Y = \{y \in \mathcal{R}^m | q_i(y) \leq 0, \quad i = 1, ..., l\} \\
&\qquad G : \mathcal{R}^{n+m} \to \mathcal{R}^{n_G}, \qquad (1)
\end{aligned}
$$

where X and Y are nonempty compact subsets of $\mathcal{R}^n$ and $\mathcal{R}^m$ and f and G are continuously differentiable on X and $X \times Y$ respectively. The term semi–infinite programming arises from the fact that $G(x,y) \leq 0, \quad \forall y \in Y$ represent an infinite set of constraints on x.

Problem (1) was first considered by John [6] who gave necessary and sufficient conditions for its solution. Since then, it has been extensively studied in the literature. Other efforts in this direction include Blankenship and Falk [2], Gustafson [5] and, more recently, Lawrence and Tits [8].

Certain minimax and saddle point problems, as well as problems of optimal engineering design can be formulated as in (1). An application to computer–aided design is presented in [9], whereas in [7] Kwak and Haug consider parametric optimal design. In such problems, $f(x)$ in (1) may present the cost function associated with the design, x is a vector of control variables and y is a vector of uncertain parameters. The formulation ensures that the resulting design will fulfil the constraints $G(x,y) \leq 0$ for all $y \in Y$.

In this paper, we solve (1) using the algorithm based on the work of Blankenship & Falk [2], where a two-phase procedure is employed to guarantee feasibility for the general nonlinear constraints.

1.1. Global Optimisation

For global optimisation in (1) we use a stochastic algorithm, developed by Rinnooy Kan and Timmer [12]. The algorithm starts local optimisations from numerous different points, and keeps a list (X_{max}) of maxima encountered. As a stopping rule it uses Bayesian estimate of the total number of maxima, based on the numbers of local optimisations performed, and local solutions found. In step 4 we define $x_{max}(x_{st}) = arg \max_x \{f(x)\}$ as a local maximum of $f(x)$, obtained when search was started from x_{st}. The algorithm is outlined below.

1. Set $X_{max} = \emptyset$, $n_{loc} = 0$, $n_{max} = 0$.

2. **DO**

3.   Choose a random starting point x_{st}

4. $x_{max}(x_{st}) = arg\max_x\{f(x)\}$

5. $n_{loc} = n_{loc} + 1$

6.   **IF**$(\text{not}(x_{max}(x_{st}) \in X_{max}))$**THEN**

7. $X_{max} = X_{max} \cup x_{max}(x_{st})$

8. $n_{max} = n_{max} + 1$

9.   **END IF**

10. $n_{tot} = \frac{n_{max}(n_{loc}-1)}{n_{loc}-n_{max}-2}$

11.   **IF**$(n_{tot} \leq n_{max} + 0.5)$**EXIT**

12. **END DO**

13. $x_{glob} = \{x_{glob} \in X_{max} | f(x_{glob}) \geq f(x), \quad \forall x \in X_{max}\}$

The constrained nonlinear programming problems which appear in (1), and also in the above algorithm, are solved using standard nonlinear programming packages, in this case NAG subroutine e04ucf [10]. The subroutine computes the minimum of a general smooth function which may include simple bounds as well as linear and nonlinear constraints.

The full semi-infinite algorithm (SIP), for solving (1) is given below.

1. Set $k = 0$, $Y_0 = \{y_0\}$, $F_k = \{x \in X | G(x,y) \leq 0, \quad \forall y \in Y_k\}$.

2. **PHASE 1**

3. $x_k = arg\min_x\{f(x)|x \in F_k\}$

4.   **IF**(infeasible)**STOP** : original problem infeasible

5. **PHASE 2**

6.   OK = **true**, $\hat{Y} = \emptyset$

7.   **DO** $j = 1, n_G$

8. $y_k^j = arg\max_{y \in Y}\{G_j(x_k, y)\}$ (global)

9.   **IF**$\{G_j(x_k, y_k^j) \geq 0\}$**THEN**

10.   OK = **false**

11. $\hat{Y} = \hat{Y} \cup \{y_k^j\}$

12.   **END IF**

13.   **END DO**

14.   **IF**(NOT OK) **THEN**

15. $Y_{k+1} = Y_k \cup \hat{Y}$

16. $k = k + 1$

17.   **GOTO** 2

18.   **ELSE**

19.   **STOP**:optimal feasible solution found

20.   **END IF**.

The feasibility check in step 9 depends on the nature of the constraints, whether they are hard or soft, and on the application being considered. Hard constraints indicate situations where no constraint violation can be tolerated by the physical system. This requires feasibility for all realizations of y, which may further increase the price of computation.

2. MESSAGE PASSING INTERFACE — MPI

To parallelise the algorithms mentioned in the previous section the Message Passing Interface MPI is used. It is a specification for a library of routines to be called from C or Fortran programs. MPI was first developed in 1993 when a group of computer vendors, software writers, computational scientists, etc. collaborated on setting a standard portable message–passing library.

2.1. Basic MPI Concepts

The message-passing model can be simply described by figure 1. The master process, enumerated Process 0, sends data to the slave processes enumerated 0 to $n-1$. After the data is processed it is sent back to the master process.

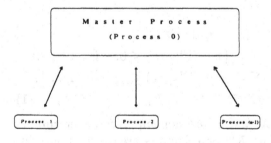

Figure 1. The message–passing model.

94

2.2. Parallelising Semi–infinite Programs

There are two subprocedures in the full SIP algorithm that can be parallelised, namely the global optimisation and checking for violation of the constraints.

In the case of global optimisation parallelisation, is done as follows – the master process chooses N_{st} starting points x_{st} and distributes them evenly ($\approx \frac{N_{st}}{n-1}$ points) to each of the remaining $n-1$ processors. Local optimisation procedure shall be started from x_{st}. The results are then passed back to the master process, where it is checked if the newly obtained point is to be disregarded or added to the list of local minima.

A similar procedure is performed for constraint violation. n_G constraints are present and they can be sent to different processors, which return the information about violation. Then, again, the master process decides whether to add a new constraint to the feasible region.

3. APPLICATIONS

To illustrate the application of the algorithm, two examples are presented. One from macroeconomic and the other from engineering.

3.1. An Application in Macroeconomic

In a recent paper, Orphanides and Wieland [11] use a simple macroeconomic model of inflation, output and interest rates for inflation targeting. The policy instrument is the short term nominal interest rate. The dynamic structure of the model is represented by a single lag of inflation in the Phillips curve and a single lag of the output gap in the aggregate demand equation. It is appropriate, therefore, to interpret the length of a period to be rather long, say half a year to a year.

In every period, the policymaker sets the interest rate, r. To describe the policymaker's welfare loss during a period t a per–period loss function is specified as a weighted average of the deviation of inflation π from its desired target π^* and the output deviation from the economy's natural level y

$$l_t = l(\pi_t, y_t) = \omega(\pi_t - .\pi^*)^2 + (1-\omega)y_t^2,$$

where $\omega \in (0,1)$. The state variables y_t and π_t,

are defined by the linear Phillips curve:

$$
\begin{aligned}
y_t &= \delta + \rho y_{t-1} - \xi r_{t-1} + u_t, \\
\pi_t &= \pi_{t-1} + \alpha y_t + e_t,
\end{aligned}
\tag{2}
$$

where $\alpha, \xi > 0, \rho \in [0,1)$ and e_t, u_t are zero–mean random shocks.

An alternative approach in this framework is that the policymaker chooses the parameters x_1 and x_2 of the feedback law $r_t = x_1 \pi_t + x_2 y_t$ to minimise welfare losses that are maximised over w_t. The objective function is defined in terms of a sum of per–period losses:

$$f(x_1, x_2, u, e) = \sum_{s=0}^{\infty} \beta^s l_{t+1+s}, \quad \beta \in (0,1), \tag{3}$$

where β is the discount factor.

Results for the following two problems are presented:

Problem Macro–1

$$
\min_{x_1, x_2} \quad \max_{u,e} \quad
\begin{array}{l}
f(x_1, x_2, u, e) \\
-0.05 \le u_t, e_t \le 0.05.
\end{array}
\tag{4}
$$

Problem Macro–2
($w = (u, e, \alpha, \rho, \xi)^t$).

$$
\min_{x_1, x_2} \quad \max_w \quad
\begin{array}{l}
f(x_1, x_2, w) \\
-0.05 \le u_t, e_t \le 0.05 \\
0.21 \le \alpha \le 0.47 \\
0.66 \le \rho \le 0.88, \\
0.3 \le \xi \le 0.5.
\end{array}
\tag{5}
$$

In both examples three worst cases are found. Each of the worst cases actually present possible outcome a different scenario. However, for all of the possible worst–case scenarios the feedback rule is the same:

$$r_{t-1} = 1.30\pi_t + 1.14y_t \tag{6}$$

for problem Macro–1, and

$$r_{t-1} = 1.26\pi_t + 1.75y_t, \tag{7}$$

for Macro–2. The advantage of the minimax formulation is that performance is guaranteed at the worst case level and will improve if the worst case is not realised. Feedback rules, together with CPU times and speed-ups are presented in Table 1.

The best speed–up is achieved for problem Macro–1, where computational time has been reduced from almost 42 hours to less than 4 hours.

95

Table 1
Numerical results (Macro–1 and Macro–2)

Problem Macro–1			
procs.	time	speed–up	solution
1	150872	–	$x = (1.30, 1.14)$
4	57585	2.62	$x = (1.30, 1.14)$
8	26876	5.61	$x = (1.30, 1.14)$
16	13366	11.29	$x = (1.30, 1.14)$
Problem Macro–2			
procs.	time	speed–up	solution
1	27898	–	$x = (1.26, 1.75)$
4	9559	2.92	$x = (1.26, 1.75)$
8	4596	6.07	$x = (1.26, 1.75)$
16	2557	10.91	$x = (1.26, 1.75)$

3.2. Robust Optimal Design of Dynamic Experiments

To obtain predictive models of processing systems, we are faced with the problem of having to estimate several freely-varying parameters within the model from collected experimental data in order to validate the model. Due to the nonlinearity of these models, the ease at which this can be accomplished not only depends on the parameterisation of the model (*i.e.*, the mathematical form of the model), but also on "where" in the experiment space the data have been collected. The main questions that arise when designing optimally informative experiments are – how should we adjust time–varying controls, initial conditions or the duration of the experiment to generate the maximum amount of information for parameter identification?

The predicted amount of information contained within a set of experimental data can be used to design future experiments that are optimally rich in information for parameter estimation purposes. To quantify this, an information matrix for dynamic experiment design is defined as:

$$M_I(\theta, \phi) \equiv \sum_{r=1}^{M} \sum_{s=1}^{M} \tilde{\sigma}_1^{rs} Q_r^T Q_s, \qquad (8)$$

where ϕ is a vector of experiment decision variables (*i.e.*, sampling times of response variables to be predicted by the model, time–varying controls

to be applied to the process, etc.) and θ is the vector of model parameters to be estimated from data. The $(n_{sp} \times p)$ matrix Q_r is the matrix of first–order dynamic sensitivity coefficients of the rth response variable in the model computed at each of n_{sp} sampling points (the number of which is chosen *a priori*):

$$Q_r \equiv \begin{bmatrix} \frac{\partial y_r(\theta, \phi, t_1)}{\partial \theta_1} & \cdots & \frac{\partial y_r(\theta, \phi, t_1)}{\partial \theta_p} \\ \cdots & \cdots & \cdots \\ \frac{\partial y_r(\theta, \phi, t_{n_{sp}})}{\partial \theta_1} & \cdots & \frac{\partial y_r(\theta, \phi, t_{n_{sp}})}{\partial \theta_p} \end{bmatrix} \qquad (9)$$

To design future experiments in the face of uncertainty in the parameters, θ, we solve the following max-min optimisation problem:

$$\phi_R = \arg \max_{\phi \in \Phi} \{ \min_{\theta \in \Theta} \{ \det(M_I(\theta, \phi)) \} \}. \qquad (10)$$

Problem (10) may be rewritten as:

$$\begin{aligned} \max_{\phi \in \Phi, \Psi \in R} \quad & \Psi \\ s.t. \quad & \Psi \leq \phi_R, \quad \forall \theta \in \Theta. \end{aligned} \qquad (11)$$

where, $\Phi \subset \mathcal{R}^n$ and $\Theta \subset \mathcal{R}^m$ represent feasible regions (upper and lower bounds on each element of ϕ and θ, respectively), and thus there are no functional constraints on the variables. In a typical situation, the dimension n of Φ is much larger than the dimension m of Θ, indicating that the problem of maximising Ψ is much more complex.

A typical example is presented to illustrate the application of the robust optimal experiment design. Consider a fed-batch reactor in which the fermentation of baker's yeast is carried out. To model this process the following model is proposed

$$\begin{aligned} \frac{dy_1}{dt} &= (r - u_1 - \theta_4) y_1 \\ \frac{dy_2}{dt} &= -\frac{ry_1}{\theta_3} + u_1(u_2 - y_2) \qquad (12) \\ r &= \frac{\theta_1 y_2}{\theta_2 + y_2}. \end{aligned}$$

Within this process, there are two time-varying controls (u_1, u_2) and two measured concentrations (y_1, y_2). Here, we have $\Phi \subset \mathcal{R}^{29}$ and

$\Theta \subset \mathcal{R}^4$ as there are four model parameters to be estimated from experimental data. In problems such as these, it seems rather obvious that the use of parallelisation will not gain much improvement as the most expensive computation is that of the **max** problem which is done sequentially.

Table 2
Intermediate solutions for problem (11).

iteration		results	No. of processors	
			1	4
I	**max**	39.39		
	min	-51.78	1517 s	1365 s
II	**max**	4.57		
	min	-6.74	1677 s	1543 s
III	**max**	4.48		
	min	-4.07	1864 s	1640 s
IV	**max**	4.47		
	min	0.00	2564 s	2179 s
	total time		7622 s	6727 s

In Table 2 we show the solution to (10) for the model describing the semi-batch fermentation of baker's yeast [1]. As can be seen, usage of 4 processors gained about 10% improvement in the computational time, reducing it from 127 minutes to approximately 112 minutes.

4. CONCLUSIONS

A way to parallelise semi–infinite programming algorithm has been presented in this paper. Two different subprocedures – global optimisation and checking of constraint violation have been parallelised. The parallelisation has been done within the MPI (Message passing Interface) framework [4]. The hardware used is a 80 node Fujitsu AP3000 parallel server with 15.5GB of memory and 336GB of local disk storage, at Imperial College Parallel Computing Centre (ICPC).

Two sets of complex problems arising from macroeconomic and optimal process design are presented. Speed–up for the macroeconomic example is more significant due to the nature of the design problem, where the non–parallised part is of much bigger dimension and complexity than the parallised one.

REFERENCES

1. Asprey, S. P. and Macchietto, S., "Statistical tools for optimal dynamic model building", Comp. Chem. Eng. 24(2000) 1261–1267.
2. Blankenship, J. W. and Falk, J. E., "Infinitely Constrained Optimization Problems", JOTA, vol. 19, pp. 261–281, 1976.
3. Danskin, J. M., The Theory of Max–Min, Springer Verlag: Berlin, 1967.
4. Gropp, W., Lusk, E. and Skjellum, A., Using MPI, The MIT Press, Cambridge, Massachusetts, 1994.
5. Gustafson, S. A., "A three–phase algorithm for semi–infinite programming". In Fiacco, A. V. and Kortanek, O.(eds.), "Semi–infinite Programming and applications", pp. 138–157, Lecture Notes in Economics and Mathematical Systems (vol 215.), Springer: Berlin, 1981.
6. John, F., "Extremum Problems With Inequalities as Subsidiary Condition", Studies and Essays, Courant Anniversary Volume, John Wiley and Sons, New York, 1948.
7. Kwak, B. M. and Haug, E. J., "Optimum Design in the Presence of Parametric Uncertainty", JOTA, vol. 19, pp. 527–546, 1976.
8. Lawrence, C. T. and Tits, A. L.,"Feasible Sequential Quadratic Programming for Finely Discretized Problems from SIP". In Reemtsen, R. and Ruckmann, J. J.(eds.), "Semi–infinite Programming", pp. 159–193, Kluwer Academic Publishers, 1998.
9. Mayne, D.Q., Polak, E. and Trahan, R., "An Outer Approximation Algorithm for Computer–Aided Design Problems", JOTA, vol.28, pp. 331–352, 1979.
10. N. A.G., Library, "Subroutine E04UCF.", http://www.nag.co.uk
11. Orphanides, A. and Wieland, V., "Inflation Zone Targeting", European Economic Review, pp. 1351–1387, vol. 44, 2000.
12. Rinnooy Kan, A., and Timmer, G. T., "Stochastic Global Optimization Methods. Part II: Multilevel Methods", Mathematical Programming, vol. 78, pp. 39–57, 1987

Logical Performance of the Optical Packet Metropolitan Ring Architecture

Tulin Atmaca
Département Réseaux et Services de Télécom,
Institut National des Télécomunications,
Evry, France,
Tulin.Atmaca@int-evry.fr

Daniel Popa
Département Réseaux et Services de Télécom,
Institut National des Télécomunications,
Evry, France,
Daniel.Popa@int-evry.fr

Abstract

An important trend in networking is the migration of packet-based technologies from Local Area Networks (LAN) to Metropolitan Area Networks (MAN). The rapidly increasing volume of data traffic in metro networks is challenging capacity limits of existing transport infrastructures based on circuit-oriented technologies like SONET and ATM. In this paper we consider a WDM metro ring architecture using optical packet switching. A network architecture study based on optical fixed length packet has been done and two optical packet-filling strategies are proposed. Their performance is analyzed by simulation.

Keywords: Optical packet switching, ring, MAN, packet filling algorithms, access protocol, performance.

1. Introduction

The exponential growth of traffic caused by the explosion of Internet use requires new technologies and more scalable backbone networks. Ethernet, and more specifically Gigabit-Ethernet, is expected to be the interface of choice connecting users to the public network due to its low cost, native LAN connectivity, synergism with IP, high bandwidth granularity and planned bandwidth scalability. Wavelength division multiplex (WDM) appears to be the solution to provide a faster networking infrastructure that can meet the explosive growth of the Internet. Since this growth is mainly fueled by IP data traffic, wavelength-routed optical networks [3] which employ circuit switching may not be the most appropriate for the emerging optical Internet. Packet-based transport technology is considered by many [7, 8, 10] to be an alternative for scaling metro networks to meet the demand. The main researches and the development lines converge to an all-optical [1] or an opto-electronic [2] packet switching network. However, at this moment the technology is not mature enough to provide a viable solution.

Optical packet switching [4] is a switching technique, which is opposite to the circuit switching, and delivers a completely new functionality. The transmission unit is an *optical packet*, which can contain one or several electronic packets.

In this paper, we show the interest for the optical metro network. In our work we study optical packet filling algorithms for synchronous ring networks. Our focus on ring topologies is motivated by the wide deployment of SONET/SDH rings. These networks represent a significant investment on the part of carriers, and are currently being upgraded to support WDM.

This paper is organized as follows. Section 2 describes the considered ring network architecture. Section 3 describes the model under study and provides detailed description of the optical packet-filling strategies. Section 4 presents simulation results on the performance of these strategies and finally Section 5 provides some concluding remarks.

2. The Ring Network Architecture

2.1. Ring and Node Architecture

MAN (Metropolitan Area Network) ring architecture is shown in Figure 1. The network architecture is organized around a hub, connecting the metro network to the backbone [6]. This hub can be a Layer 2 or Layer 3 electronic switch (IP router, a Label switch/router, or an Ethernet switch) with interfaces to encapsulate client packets (eg. Ethernet variable length packets) into optical packets. The ring nodes (S_i) use Optical Add/Drop Multiplexers (OADM) to insert/extract optical packets on the wavelengths shared between several nodes.

This architecture results from a spectral separation of upstream bus and downstream bus flows from/toward a hub node. Moreover, we have a separation of downstream wavelengths, generated on the hub to distribute packets to the ring nodes, from upstream wavelengths, generated in

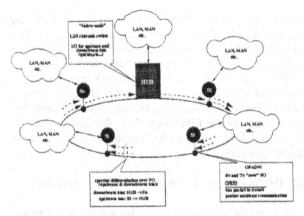

Figure 1: Metro ring architecture

OADMs and received at the hub. Transparent ring nodes (S_i) can both read data on a downstream bus and write on an upstream bus. On this architecture a network node is in direct communication with the hub. The communication between ring nodes is made via hub. No optical buffers are presented on the OADM transit path, hence no packet can be dropped once the packet is on the ring. A very simple collision avoidance mechanism is implemented through photodiode power detection on each locally accessible upstream wavelength. Voids are detected and a fixed delay (slightly larger than the packet size allowed on the network) ensures collision free packet insertion on the upstream bus from the add port.

2.2. Optical Packet Format

The optical packet format adopted in our study is illustrated in Figure 2. It is based on network physical and hardware constraints.

Figure 2: Optical packet format

An optical framing includes a minimum guard band, named *Inter Packet Gap (IPG)* and equals to 20 *ns*, allowing packet insertion. At the hub is used a novel design of burst mode receiver [6] for the packet-by-packet detection of upstream bus wavelengths, requiring a limited preamble (*Pr*) of 16 bytes in the optical packet. Then, the optical frame is composed of header with routing information and of payload field. The packet length is defined in time (eg. ~1,3 μs, 2 μs,).

2.3. MAC (Medium Access Control) Protocol

Transporting packets across a shared medium is a problem typically handled on the MAC layer of a protocol stack. In this paper we are interested in upstream bus access problems. The ring nodes should listen to transmission medium, similarly to Ethernet, before sending a packet. In a slotted architecture (synchronous

network), the gap length is a multiply of optical packet length. It means that a free space is detected at least one packet can be send. The access protocol is reduced to simple void(s) detection on upstream bus.

3. The Network Model Under Study

3.1. Ring and Node Model

The ring network architecture and node structure was described in the previous section. This architecture is analyzed within our study and obtained results are presented in the next section.

We consider *n* upstream bus nodes (*n*+1 with hub) in a unidirectional ring. The upstream bus can support *K* wavelengths between two consecutive ring nodes. A number λ_i of wavelengths is accessible for each node S_i for transmission packets path (with $\lambda_i < K$).

Each node is attached to one or more wavelengths on upstream bus. In the direction from the access networks to the ring, the ring node acts as a concentrator. It collects and buffers electronically data packets, transmitted by the users over the access networks, which need to be transported over the ring. Buffered packets can be grouped together and transmitted in an optical packet to the hub. The considered optical packet length is larger than 1,3 μs.

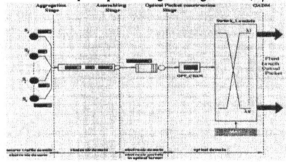

Figure 3: Edge node model under study

The logical architecture of an edge node is shown in Figure 3. Each node is equipped with one OADM and several transceivers. Each node has dedicated wavelengths to send packets. Packets, waiting for transmission, are organized in transmission buffer. The serving policy of the buffered packets is FIFO (First In First Off).

3.2. Optical Packet-Filling Strategy

The access networks for a metro network are Local Area Networks (LAN). Usually the LAN is an Ethernet network. The Ethernet frame size is variable with a length between 64 and 1500 Bytes [11]. Since fixed length optical packet has a fixed payload length, to fill up completely an optical packet seems to be difficult.

The strategies can be classified in two classes, as follows, depending on performance:

a) In the first one, a node can segment the IP datagram to fill up the optical packet.

b) In the second one, a node fills up the optical packet without segmenting access networks packets.

We propose two packet-filling strategies, namely: *Segmenting-FIFO Strategy* and *FIFO Strategy*. The first algorithm belongs to the "segmenting" class and the last one belongs to the "no segmenting" class.

3.2.1. Segmenting-FIFO Strategy

The first strategy we consider could break incoming IP datagrams to fill up the remaining free space in optical payload. The remaining segment (the segment that is not inserted) stays in the queue at the same place and is inserted in the next optical packet. Thus, we call this strategy *Segmenting FIFO Strategy*. The aim of this strategy is to increase the optical packet-filling ratio. More specifically, the operation of the strategy at node i is as follows.

At the transmitting side, node i maintains a variable *threshold*, which specifies the smaller segment length that could be obtained breaking IP datagrams. It appends at resulting segments control information (electronic overhead) used at ring output (hub) for reassembly process. Two situations can prevent IP datagrams to be segmented and inserted:

a) If the length of the remaining free space in optical payload is below the *threshold* then the space will be never used.

b) If the remaining segment length is less than *threshold* the IP datagrams are not segmented

3.2.2. FIFO Strategy

The *FIFO Strategy* is opposed to Segmenting FIFO Strategy. The operation of this strategy at node i is as follows.

At the transmitting side, if is not enough remaining free space in optical payload to insert an entire electronic packet, the last one should wait the next optical packet to be transmitted. The segment/reassembly process is avoided.

Compared to Segmenting FIFO Strategy, *FIFO Strategy* is simple since only the optical packet construction is operated at the transmitting side. The reverse process occurs at the receiving side.

4. Numerical Results

In this section, the algorithms described bellows are compared. In our simulation study we consider 10 nodes, each one with an electronic buffer of 10 Mbits. The distance between nodes (and implicit) the propagation delay is neglected. We assume that we have one wavelength and the wavelength runs at 10 Gbps. We

model the packet arrival process to each node by exponential sources and using Ethernet traces [11]. The emitted source packet length is variable between 64 and 1500 Bytes. The exponential source bit rate is 10 Mbps.

In section 4.1 we present the network performance of the Segmenting-FIFO algorithm with different optical packet size (i.e. ~1,3 μs, 2 μs). In section 4.2 we study the performance for the FIFO algorithm. We also investigate the impact of the optical packet length on the performance of the algorithms.

4.1. Performance of Segmenting-FIFO Strategy

In this section we are interested in several performance measures, namely: optical packet filling ratio, loss ratio, mean buffer delay and buffer requirement.

Figure 4 plots the mean optical packet-filling ratio versus *threshold* size for two optical packet lengths. The mean optical packet-filling ratio is defined as the average number of bits used to fill up the optical payload in a unit

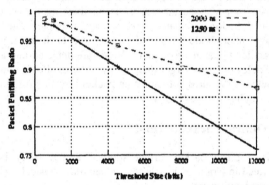

Figure 4: Mean optical packet filling ratio vs. threshold size

time divided by the length of optical packet. We observe that with the increase of threshold the filling ratio decreases. A small threshold (64 Bytes) assures a very good packet-filling ratio (99%). In the case of greatest threshold performance in term of packet filling ratio is worst (76%). It means that an optical packet is in average 24% empty and in average 24% of wavelength bandwidth is wasted. On the other hand, Figure 4 shows the impact of packet length on the algorithm performance. For the greatest *threshold* the larger optical packet gives better results than the smallest optical packet length.

The impact of the algorithm on the network performance is shown in next two figures. The results are obtained for a ring load $\rho = 0.95$ and a *threshold* size equal to the mean packets length incoming from access networks (~576 Bytes). In Figure 5, it can be seen the buffer occupancy distribution on the upstream bus node. For the first upstream bus nodes, the buffer occupancy degree appears to be the same. Up to the sixth node the free spaces on the upstream bus are enough for each node

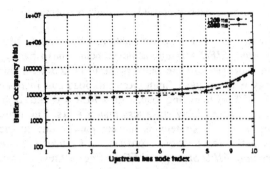

Figure 5: Buffer Occupancy vs. Upstream Bus Node Rank

to send its packets. For these nodes, buffer occupancy degree is given by the last electronic packet arrival that ills up the optical payload. The use of same traffic profile for all ring nodes explains these results. Moving forward on bus, for the upstream nodes (eg. 9,10) is difficult to find free spaces and the number of buffered packets increases. Buffer occupancy for the last node is less than 1% of total buffer size. We observe that the buffer occupancy degree, at last node, seems to be the same for all optical packet lengths. This is due to the fact that the largest optical packet has a better optical packet-filling ratio, so the optical packets are filling up better.

Because the buffer occupancy degree for ring nodes is less than 1% the packets loss ratio at ring access is zero.

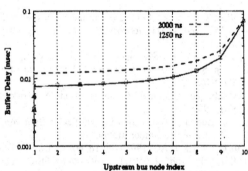

Figure 6: Mean buffer delay vs. upstream bus node rank

Figure 6 plots the mean buffer delay versus the upstream bus node rank. We observe that, as the rank node increase, the mean buffer delay increase. This is due to the fact that the network load is low for the first nodes (up to the 5 node) and the waiting time, in this case, is give only by the last arrived packet used to fill up an optical packet. Because the firstly nodes on upstream bus occupy the bus bandwidth, the packets transmission of the last nodes become more difficult. Buffering time for these node increases. Waiting time, at last node, seems to be the same for 1.2 μs and 2 μs optical packet length respectively. For all the ring nodes the buffer delay is less than 100 μs.

Simulation results showed that an increase in optical

packet length leads to an increase of buffer occupancy and buffer delay. Comparing the largest optical packet to the smallest optical packet, we observe that first one gives a buffer occupancy and a buffer delay slightly lowers than the second one.

4.2. Performance of FIFO Strategy

In this section we focus to obtain the maximum input LAN load (electronic load) that assure no packet loss at ring network access. The ring load is limited up to $\rho = 0.95$.

Figure 7 shows the mean optical packet-filling ratio versus optical payload length. We observe that with the increase of payload length the filling ratio increases. The smaller optical packet length assures a filling ratio equal to 76%. For the largest optical packet the filling ratio is slightly lower than 90%.

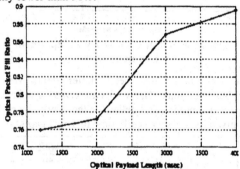

Figure 7: Mean packet filling ratio vs. optical payload length

Figures 8 plots the PLR (Packet Loss Ratio) versus the input LAN load for the last upstream bus node. We observe that the largest optical packet equal to 4 μs, achieves the highest input LAN throughput for that the PLR on the ring is zero.

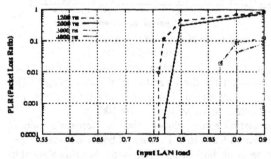

Figure 8: PLR vs. input LAN load

In our simulation experiments, we observed that the largest optical packet guarantees a throughput for the access networks equals to 90% percent of total upstream bus throughput, and so one. Next figures show buffer delay and buffer occupancy versus upstream bus node rank. We keep the same input LAN load as obtained in Figure 7, for the next simulation results.

101

In Figure 9 it can be seen that increasing the optical packet length is important for "non segmenting" filling algorithms class. We observe that, as the node rank increases, the buffer occupancy increasing is important. For the last upstream bus node the largest optical packet length assures the lower buffer occupancy. This is due to fact that with increase of packet length the packet filling ratio increases.

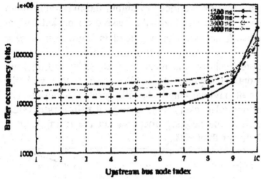

Figure 9: Buffer occupancy vs. upstream bus node rank

Figure 10 shows the mean buffer delay versus upstream bus node rank. The results are gives for different optical packet lengths. The delay for the lastly upstream nodes is given by the necessarily time to detect gap(s) on

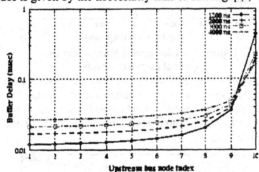

Figure 10: Mean buffer delay vs. upstream bus node rank

the upstream bus. The buffer delay for the last upstream node is lowest for the largest optical packet length. The buffering delay for this last node is less than 400 μs. For the first nodes the delay stays under 100 μs.

Simulation results showed that an increase in optical packet length leads to a decrease of buffer occupancy and buffer delay at the last upstream node. For this algorithm (without IP datagram segmentation) the optical packet length has an important impact on the network performance.

5. Conclusions

This paper described a WDM metro ring architecture with optical packet switching. Two packet-filling

strategies have been proposed and their performance was analyzed.

Based on our experimentation, we found that, *Segmenting-FIFO Strategy* achieves better mean packet-filling ratio (99%). The network performance with this strategy is quite good. Input electronic load can increase up to ~95% of total ring load, with a PLR = 0 and mean buffering packet delay stays less than 100 μs. The main drawback of this strategy is the complexity due to the segmentation/reassembly process. Compared to *Segmenting FIFO Strategy*, *FIFO Strategy* achieves lower performance. The mean packet-filling ratio is less than 90%. The input maximum LAN load, for a ring PLR = 0, is limited up to 85% of the total ring load. The mean buffer delay increases up to 400 μs at last ring node. The main strategy advantage is the simplicity. The complexity of the segmentation/reassembly process is avoided.

We also observed that the *FIFO Strategy* is more sensitive to optical packet length than *Segmenting FIFO Strategy*. The *FIFO Strategy* performance is comparable to *Segmenting FIFO Strategy* performance when the optical packet length is rather large.

Finally we note that if we set the *threshold* to a greater value (for example, set threshold to 1500 bytes) the strategy converges to FIFO Strategy.

References:

[1] I. Kotuliak, T. Atmaca, "Logical Performances of the Optical Switch in MAN and WAN Networks", In *Proceedings*, April 2002, *Colmar*, France.
[2] R. Ramaswami, K. Sivarajan, "Optical Networks – A practical Perspective", *Morgan Kaufmann* Publisher, Inc., 1998, ISBN 1-55860-445-6.
[3] B. Mukherjee, "Optical Communication Networking", *McGraw-Hill*, 1997.
[4] GambiniP. and al., "Transparent Optical Packet Switching – Network Architecture and Demonstration" in
KEOPS project, IEEE JSAC, 1998, vol. 16, no. 7, pp 1245-1258.
[5] L.G Kazovsky and al., WU1, *proceedings* OFC 20001, March 2001, Anahcim, CA USA
[6] N. Le Sauze, A. Dupas, E. Dotaro and al., "DBORN: A Shared WDM Ethernet Bus Architecture for Optical Packet Metropolitan Networks", In *Proceedings*, July 2002, Cheju Island, Korea.
[7] "An Introduction to Resilient Packet Ring Technology", *A White Paper* by the Resilient Packet Ring Alliance, October 2001.
[8] C. Qiao: "Labeled Optical Burst Switching for IP-over-WDM Integration", *IEEE Comunication Magazine*, September 2000, Vol. 38, No. 9, pp. 104-114.
[9] K. M. Sivalingam, S. Subramaniam, "Optical WDM Network – Principle and Practice", *Cluver Academic* Publisher, 2000, ISBN 0-7923-7825-3.
[10] L. Xu, H.G. Perros, and G. R. Rouskas, "A Simulation Study of Access Protocols for Optical Burst-Switching Ring Networks", In *Proceedings*, Second International (IFIP-TC6) Networking Conference, Pisa, Italy, May 2002.
[11] http://w³.caida.org/analysis/AIX/plen_hist/

Packet Selection in a Deflection Routing Algorithm

A. Borrero, J.M. Fourneau, F. Quessette
PRiSM,
Université de Versailles Saint-Quentin en Yvelines,
45 Av. des Etats Unis,
78000 Versailles, France
{arbor,jmf,qst}@prism.uvsq.fr

Abstract

Deflection routing is the usual algorithm for all-optical networks. Here, we study the selection of packets which must be misdirected since resources are not sufficient. Using graph and algorithmic arguments, we prove some properties of optimal selection which can be easily taken into account in fast heuristics.

1. Introduction

Due to the high bandwidth they could offer, all optical packets networks have received considerable attention during the last years. One of the major drawback of this technology is the lack of large buffers which can be used to store packets queues waiting for a free link during the routing. Fiber delay loops allow to provide some computation time for the routing algorithms but they are not designed to store a large amount of packets. Therefore routing algorithms are quite different of the algorithms designed for store and forward networks based on electronic buffers. Several packet routing strategies without intermediate storage of data packets have been designed [1,9] and deflection routing is clearly one of the easiest solution [2,3,10]. In shortest-path Deflection Routing, switches attempt to forward packets along the shortest hop path to their destinations. Each link can send a finite number of packets per time-slot (the link capacity). No packets are queued. At each slot, incoming packets have to be sent to their next switch along the path. If the number of packets requesting a link is larger than the link capacity, then there is some contention. Only some of the packets will receive the link they ask for and the other ones have to be misdirected or deflected. Thus, deflected packets have to travel through longer paths to their destination. These routing algorithms are known to clearly avoid deadlocks (packets in the network do not move) but livelocks could occur (packets move but never reach their destination), except for some cases of deflection routing in some classes of networks such as trees [5]. Deflection routing algorithms do not explain how to chose the packets to be misdirected, or even the number of such packets. The selection and the routing decision arc local choices without global knowledge and must be made in every node and at each slot. Several heuristics or greedy algorithms have been proposed for the packets assignment to direction. However, this selection process is very important as the network goodput is strongly decreasing with the average number of deflections [4]. There exist efficient graph algorithms which provide optimal solutions in term of number of deflections during each time slot. However these algorithms are quite complex to implement for the control of optical switches. Although their complexity is polynomial, they do not fulfill the time requirements of the optical switches.

In this paper we study several theoretical aspects of this selection algorithm to improve the heuristics currently used. Furthermore these properties may be used to study the performance of deflection routing networks with uniform traffic [4]. In section 2, we present the graph framework for this selection algorithm. Section 3 is devoted to theoretical properties of the best selection while in section 4 we present an optimal algorithm for network with a link capacity equal to 1.

2. Graph Framework

The routing problem has several graph formulation. Usually, we consider a bipartite directed graph G=(V1, V2, E). V1 and V2 are two sets of nodes while E contains the directed edges. The nodes of V1 represent the incoming packets while the nodes of V2 are associated to outputs. The directed edges represent the directions that a packet may use to follow a shortest path to its destination. Thus the edges are directed from V1 to V2. In the sequel such a graph will be denoted as a configuration. Here, we consider 2D meshes for the network topology [6]. But most of the theoretical results obtained here can be easily extended to other topologies.

Current Node ☐   Destination Node ●
O Poss.posit. (fav.)   Poss. posit. (deflected)

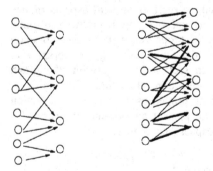

Fig 1 : Routing in a 2D Mesh

The nodes of V1 have a degree upper bounded by 2 since packets have one or two available directions for a shortest path in a grid (see Fig. 1) . This is also true for odd torus but in an even torus, some packets may have 4 possible directions. The nodes of V2 have an arbitrary degree but every node i of V2 has a capacity capa (i). This integer number is the maximal number of packets which may use the output link represented by node i. Let v the number of links and f the number of wavelengths multiplexed on the link, we have:

$$|V\_1| \leq v f, \quad |V\_2| \leq v \text{ and } capa(i) \leq f$$

Fig 2 : a configuration (left), a graph after transformation and a matching in bold (right)

So the selection algorithm has to optimize the number of packets which are directed in a direction they request. First, we can slightly transform the problem to find a classical graph problem and a known algorithm.

Let us consider graph H built from original graph G. H is also bipartite. The first set of nodes is V1. The second set is denoted as W2. Every node of V2 is divided into f nodes in W2. The nodes of W2 are indexed by (y, l) where y is the link number and l is the wavelength index. It exists a directed edge in H between x and (y,l) if and only if it exists a directed edge in G between x and y (see both parts of Fig. 2 and notice that f=2). Thus the selection of the packets which join their wished output is a matching, and the optimal choice is a maximal matching.

Definition 1 [Matching] : A matching of a bipartite graph is a regular subgraph of degree 1.

The maximal matching in a bipartite graph is a well known graph problem with several applications. A polynomial algorithm based on alternating paths is known for long (see [7], section 1.5.2). However the complexity of this algorithm is $O(|V| |E|)$. This is quite important for a time-constrained applications for optical switches. In the following, we turn back to the initial representation of the routing requested by the graphs we have called configurations. d(j) will denote the degree of node j. Let x be an arbitrary node, s(x) will denote an arbitrary successor or predecessor of x, without confusion as we consider bipartite graph.. If G is a graph and x a node of G, G - {x} will denote the graph where node x and edges incident to x are removed. Similarly, if x and y are nodes, G + {(x,y)} will represent the graph where the edge (x,y) has been added. Finally, e(x) will be a null vector except component indexed by x which is equal to 1.

3. Theoretical results

We prove some results for the optimal number of deflections for an arbitrary configuration. These properties imply some simple heuristics to minimize the number of deflections.

Definition 2 : Let G be an arbitrary configuration and capa be an arbitrary capacity vector, we denote as dfx(G,capa) the minimal number of deflected packets for configuration G and capacity capa.

Lemma 1 : Let G be a configuration which is composed of two connected components G1 and G2 which are configurations. Let capa1 and capa2 be the corresponding decomposition for vector capa, we have clearly:

dfx(G,capa) = dfx(G1,capa1) + dfx(G2,capa2)

Lemma 2 [Sub-additivity]: Let G be an arbitrary configuration. Let W and U be a partition of V1. We divided of edges of E according to this partition of the nodes to obtain two sets E1 and E2. We have decomposed the configuration G into G1 = (W, V2, E1) and G2 = (U, V2, E2). Let capa1 and capa2 be two arbitrary capacity vectors. We have:

dfx(G,capa1+capa2) ≤ dfx(G1,capa1) + dfx(G2,capa2)

Then we introduce some technical lemmas which have strong implications:

Lemma 3 [Saturation]: Let j be an arbitrary node of V2, if d(j)<capa(j), we can decrease capa(j) to d(j) while the optimal number of deflections is kept constant: dfx(G,capa) = dfx(G,min(capa, d)) where the min operator is applied componentwise.

Lemma 4 : Let x be an arbitrary node of V2, we have :

dfx(G,capa) ≤ dfx(G,capa - e(x)) ≤ 1 + dfx(G,capa)

Proof : The first part of the relation is obvious. To prove the last part, we consider an optimal solution for configuration G. We have two cases:

- node x is saturated (i.e. the number of accepted incoming edges is equal to the capacity). Thus decreasing capa(x) by one creates a new deflection for a packet which was already accepted in the previous solution.

- If node x is not saturated, we can decrease capa(x) by one without increasing the number of deflections (a simple consequence of Lemma 3).

Thus, we have a solution with an upper bound of 1 + dfx(G, capa) deflections. Of course the best solution for configuration G and capacity capa-e(x) will be smaller than this upper bound. And, the second part of the relation is established.

Corollary 1 : Consider an arbitrary node x of V2, we have:

dfx(G,capa) - 1 ≤ dfx(G,capa+e(x)) ≤ dfx(G, capa)

Lemma 5 : Let G be a configuration such that there exist a saturated node y of V2 (i.e. d(y)> capa(y)) and a degree 1 node x in V1, then we can add the edge (x,y) while the optimal number of deflections is kept constant:

dfx(G,capa) = dfx(G+{(x,y)},capa)

We can now derive several properties of optimal algorithms. First, if a packet has only one possible direction, we must accept its request.

Lemma 6: Let x be a node V1 such that d(x)=1 and capa(s(x)) >0, we have:

dfx(G,capa) = dfx(G - {x},capa - e(s(x)))

Proof : We have two choices for node x: we can accept (x, s(x)) or deflect node x.

- If we deflect node x, we add one deflection and then we have to consider a modified graph G-{x} and the same capacity vector. Thus after this choice the optimal number of deflections will be equal to 1 + dfx(G - {x},capa).

- If we decide to route x to s(x), we do not increase the deflection number at this step. The graph becomes G-{x} and the capacity vector is now capa - e(s(x)). Thus the optimal number of deflections is equal to dfx(G-{x},capa-e(s(x))).

According to Lemma 4, the last value is not larger than the first one. Thus, it is better to accept (x,s(x)) and the relation is proved.

Lemma 7 : Let y be a node of V2 such that d(y) ≤ capa(y), we have for s(y), arbitrary predecessor of y:

dfx(G,capa) = dfx(G - {s(y)}, capa- e(y))

Proof: Let x be an arbitrary predecessor of y. The degree of x may be 1 or 2. If it is 1, according to Lemma 6, we accept (x,y), and the relation is established. Let us now consider that the degree of x is 2 and let z be the other successor of x. The algorithm has three choices: deflect x, accept (x,y) or accept (x,z). For all choices, the configuration at the next step becomes G-{x}.

- If x is deflected, the capacity vector is still capa. Therefore if we apply an optimal algorithm on this subproblem we get 1+dfx(G-{x},capa) deflections.

- If one accept (x, y), the capacity vector becomes capa - e(y). So using an optimal algorithm at the next step, we get dfx(G-{x},capa-e(y)) deflections.

- Similarly, the last choice leads to dfx(G-{x},capa-e(z)) deflected packets.

According to Lemma 4 the first choice is the worst solution. We have now to compare the last two choices. Assume that we accept (x,z), the capacity vector is now

105

capa-e(z). As the node x is removed, we also delete the edge (x,y) and the degree of y is decreased by 1. Thus we now have: $d(y) < capa(y)$. According to Lemma 3, we can remove one wavelength from y:

$$dfx(G-\{x\},capa-e(z)) = dfx(G-\{x\},capa-e(z) -e(y))$$

And we apply Lemma 4:

$$dfx(G-\{x\},capa-e(z)-e(y)) \geq dfx(G-\{x\},capa-e(y))$$

Therefore it is better to chose (x,y) than (x,z).

This two properties state that we can iterate on accepting node with one possible destination and node without conflict. After each accepted request, the configuration is updated and the degrees are decreased. Accepted nodes of V1 are removed. Similarly, nodes of V2 with null capacity are removed and edges incident to removed nodes arc also removed. Thus nodes which satisfy Lemma 6 or 7 may appear. However this is not always sufficient to complete the selection process.

Lemma 8 : Let G be a configuration such that V2 has only two nodes y and z and all nodes of V1 are connected to y and z (ie. $G=K\{n,2\}$). Clearly:

$$dfx(G,capa) = max(0, (|V1| - capa(y) -capa(z)))$$

And this value is reached by any feasible random assignment.

Lemma 9 : Let G be a connected configuration such that every node of V1 have a degree 2, assume that the capacities are all equal to 1. Then:

$$dfx(G,capa) = max(0,(|V1| - |V2|))$$

And the assignment is detailed in the proof.

Proof : by induction of the size of |V1 and |V2| (note that $dfx(G,capa) \geq max(0,(|V1| - |V2|))$ is clear):

If $|V2|=2$, then the relation is directly obtained from Lemma 8 as $capa(y) = capa(z) = 1$.

If $|V2|>2$, due to the assumptions, we have $|V2| \leq |V1| +1$. The proof made by induction is omitted. We have to consider two cases based on the degree of the nodes of V2.

- There exists a node y in V2 such that d(y)=1, we accept the assignment (s(y),y) since Lemma 6 proves that it is the best solution. Once the assignment is done, the graph has (|V1|-1) and (|V2|-1) nodes in the two sets of nodes. We can now apply the induction assumption.

- If every node of V2 has a degree larger than 2, then we can prove that it exists a node z in V2 such that G-{z} is still connected. The proof of this technical lemma is omitted due to space limitation. We accept (x,z) where x is an arbitrary predecessor of z. We remove nodes x and z. Thus the graph is still connected and it has less nodes but the assumption on the degree of nodes in V1 is not satisfied. We add new edges from the nodes in V1 to a saturated node in V2 (all the nodes of V2 are saturated when capa=1) since Lemma 5 insures that we do not change the number of deflected packets. Thus we can apply the induction.

4. Algorithm and Heuristics

First we consider that the capacity is equal to one. This restriction is true if the switches do not allow the wavelength conversion. This algorithm operates for D directions and C packets, $C \leq D$. Every packet has at most 2 favorable directions and capa=1 for all directions. The algorithm is mainly based on Lemmas 6, 7 and 9..

- Each packet is marked as not routed.
- While it remains some packets marked not routed
    - If there is a packet no still routed with 0 available favorable direction, then we mark it as being routed to X (this packet will be deflected at the end of the algorithm).
    - Else if there is a packet not yet routed with only 1 available favorable direction, then we mark it as being routed to this direction, and we mark this direction as being not available.
    - Else if there is one available direction which is requested by only one packet, we route this packet to that direction. We mark it as being routed and the direction as being not available.
    - Otherwise we select a random compatible assignment for a packet and a direction. We route the packet and do the marks.
- End While
- Each one of the packets marked X (to be deflected) is routed to a different available direction, since $C \leq D$ it always remains some available directions.

Theorem 1 : The algorithm provides the minimal number of deflected packets.

This algorithm has been generalized to more complex topologies and the optimality has been proved in this more general framework [8].The complexity of the algorithm is $O(|V|+|E|)$ if one use an appropriate data structure to store the nodes of degree 0 or 1 and to find them in a constant time. As $|E| \leq 2|V|$, we obtain a linear complexity which is significantly better than the alternating path method. However the heuristic of random choice cannot be extended to arbitrary number of wavelengths with an optimality guarantee. Consider the following example depicted in Fig. 3.

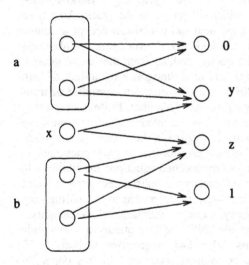

Fig 3 : a configuration where a random choice fails

Assume that capa(0) + capa(y) = a and capa(1) + capa(z) = b+1. Note that a and b are the sizes of the two sets of incoming packets. Clearly, it is better to select (x,z) rather than (x,y). Indeed, the first choice leads to no deflection (apply Lemma 1 and 8), while the last choice imply one deflected packet. The configuration does not satisfy any of the first three cases of the algorithm. Thus we accept a random assignment. And this random assignment could be a bad solution such as (x,y).

5. Bibliography

[1] P.Baran, "On distributed communication networks", IEEE Trans. on Communication Systems, CS-12, 1964.

[2] J. C. Brassil and R.L. Cruz, "Bounds on maximum delay in networks with deflection routing", IEEE Trans. on Parallel and Distributed Systems}, 6(7), pp 724--732, 1995.

[3]T. Chich, « Optimisation du routage par déflexion dans les réseaux de télécommunications métropolitains », PhD thesis, ENS-Lyon, December 1997.

[4] T.Czachorski,, J.M.~Fourneau, S. Nowak, and F. Quessette, "Performance of Deflection and Mixed Routing Algorithms", Second Germano-Polish Teletrafic symposium, Gdansk, 2002.

[5] U.Feige and R. Krauthgamer., "Networks on which hot-potato routing does not livelock", Distributed Computing, 13, pp 53--58, 2000.

[6] P. Gravey, S. Gosselin, C. Guillemot, D. Chiaroni, N. Le Sauze, A. Jourdan, E. Dotaro, D. Barth, P. Berthomé, C. Laforest, S. Vial, T. Atmaca, G. Hébuterne, H. El~Biaze, R. Laalaoua, E. Gangloff, and I. Kotuliak, "Multiservice optical network: Main concepts and first achievements of the ROM program", Journal of Ligthwave Technology, 19, pp 23--31, January 2001.

[7] J. Mchugh. "Algorithmic Graph Theory", Prentice Hall, 1990.

[8] S. Mneimeh and F. Quessette, "Minimum Deflection Routing Algorithm", Alcatel Patent Application \#135945, 2002

[9] Y. Ofek and M. Yung, "Principles for high speed network control: loss-less and deadlock-freeness, self-routing and a single buffer per link". ACM Symposium On Principles of Distributed Computing, pp 161--175, 1990.

[10] A. Schuster, "Optical Interconnections and Parallel Processing: The Interface", chapter Bounds and analysis techniques for greedy hot-potato routing, pp 284--354, Kluwer Academic Publishers, 1997.

Geometrically batched networks

Peter Harrison, David Thornley, Harf Zatschler
Department of Computing,
Imperial College London,
UK
{pgh|djt|hz3}@doc.ic.ac.uk

Abstract

We develop approximate solutions for the equilibrium queue length probability distribution of queues in open Markovian networks by considering each queue independently, constructing its arrival process as the join of each contributing queue's departing traffic. Without modulation and non-unit batches, we would only need to consider mean internal traffic rates, modelling each queue as M/M/1 to give an exact result by Jackson's theorem. However, bursty traffic significantly affects steady state queue lengths; for given throughput, mean queue length varies linearly with mean batch size. All batch sizes are geometrically distributed, so each queue is Markovian and has known analytical solution. Our analysis is based on properties of the output processes of these queues, their superposition and splitting, to form the arrival processes at all queues. In general, this leads to a fixed-point problem for the network's equilibrium. The numerical results of our approach are compared with simulation and show promising accuracy.

1. Introduction

Batched processes provide enhanced descriptive power in queueing models; see [9], for example. This can be especially important for modelling the kind of bursty traffic typically observed in present day communication systems [1]. We have an automated formulation and solution mechanism that incorporates batches of geometrically distributed size in Markov modulated multiprocessor queues of finite or infinite capacity. Geometric distributions can be scaled and superimposed to produce a class of monotonic, unbounded convex probability density functions. Networks of such queues can be analysed by considering each queue in isolation, with an arrival process formed by the superposition of the departure processes from all connected queues, together with any external arrivals. A key issue is to approximate accurately this superposition.

More specifically, we are developing a Markov modulated queue in which all jumps in the queue length are geometrically distributed and which can accept a number of independent batched arrival processes. Unbounded transitions in the queue resulting from the use of geometric batch arrivals lead to Kolmogorov equations of 'infinite range'. Our method produces an ensemble of transformed balance equations of minimal, finite range, a large region of which can be represented as a linear homogeneous matrix recurrence relation in the vectors of the modulation state occupation probabilities at each queue length. This localization of the batched equations facilitates solution of unbounded queues via matrix geometric or spectral expansion methods, and is crucial to producing manageable complexity in queues with large, finite capacity.

We find that the ability of this queue to allow independent streams rather than aggregated arrivals [5,10] improves network solution accuracy. In this paper, we outline the formulation of the queue, describe the iterative solution of a network of such queues and examine the effect of different traffic approximation schemes.

2. Queue formulation

The Kolmogorov equations of a queue which includes geometrically batched processes (arrivals and/or service completions) can involve terms corresponding to an infinite range of queue lengths, but their structure allows transformation of the balance equations into a form that includes terms only from a small, local set of queue lengths. The original motivating algebraic concept behind this approach can be found in [3], where particular instances of batched queues are considered.

The transformation procedure has similar goals to Gaussian elimination, which *per se* is inapplicable to unstructured infinite systems. The balance equations are effectively diagonalised, but using an efficient procedure which takes advantage of the structure of their formulation.

Our general formulation solves queues with multiple processors, multiple service streams (multiple streams per processor allow the mixing of batches to construct more complex batch distributions in a Poisson point process), breakdowns and repairs, and both positive and negative arrivals. All the processes are modulated by an independent, finite state Markov chain. Each process may be independently described in every modulation state, and all parameters can be specified (as a constant) within each of a finite number of ranges of queue lengths.

Independent work by Chakka formulates solutions to queues with multiple arrival streams, based on the methods first used in [3]. Although these yield a satisfying theoretical motivation for the underlying algebraic approach, we develop an alternate, algorithmic approach. Problematically, the original methods have difficulty where multiple arrival (or departure streams) in a given modulation state have the same batch size distribution, or if there are different numbers of streams in different modulation states. Our new methods automatically take account of these effects during the construction of the balance equations.

2.1. A Repeating Region

It is well known that over a large range of queue lengths, the probability flux pattern does not change. In this region, the balance equations are of the form:

$$\sum_{i=-u}^{d} \mathbf{v}_{j+i} A_i = \mathbf{0}$$

Where $\mathbf{v}_j$ is the vector of modulation state occupation probabilities at queue length j, and A_i is the matrix of rates into state j with jump size i. We refer to this range of queue lengths, where the coefficients in the (transformed) Kolmogorov equations form a linear homogeneous recurrence relation, as the *repeating region*. The matrix geometric literature often refers to *non*-linear equations – this describes the polynomial in the matrix R used to generate the solution, of the form $\mathbf{v}_j = \mathbf{u}.R^j$.

3. Network Solution

We solve networks of geometrically batched queues iteratively using approximated departure traffic at each queue. The aggregate arrival process at each queue is then the superposition of the approximated departure processes of the feeding queues.

We initialise the solution with a coarse approximation based on the traffic equations of the network. For a network of M/M/c queues, this traffic would yield the correct solution for every queue, by Jackson's theorem. The presence of batches, modulation, finite queues and negative customers renders this procedure approximate. We therefore refine this solution in an iterative process in-volving three stages: re-approximating the departure link traffic of each queue, solving each individual queue based on that new traffic, then assessing convergence criteria and repeating if they are not met.

There is a wide range of methods for approximating link traffic, as has been widely explored in the literature. In [5], the traffic arriving at a queue is generally a single geometrically batched stream which has been calculated to approximate the *aggregate* behaviour of all the contributing departure processes. Our queue formulation allows us to treat the departure processes (which have been approximated) as individual streams, arriving independently at target queues.

3.1. Departure Process Approximation.

Our queues employ geometrically batched processing, which leads to bursty departures, and hence a requirement for batched link traffic. The distribution of batch sizes in the departure process of a queue with batched processing is not exactly geometrically distributed. The batch size distribution from a queue with length j is necessarily bounded above by j. If we approximate this with a geometric distribution which matches the mean batch size of the departures, this over-estimates the contribution of large batch sizes. The effect on subsequent queues is to cause an over-estimate of mean queue length. We find that the mean queue length resulting from geometrically batched arrivals increases linearly with the mean batch size for fixed throughput.

To improve the traffic approximation, we superpose the batched traffic with unbatched traffic (of unit batch size) to form an *enriched* approximation, as unbatched traffic tends to cause an under-estimate of mean queue length. The (per job) throughputs of these two approximating departure sub-streams sum to the throughput determined for individual jobs at the queue. There are a number of regimes that could be followed to make use of the two streams, and of course we could choose more streams. In this initial investigation, we seek to verify that the model of the network can be improved by superposition of departure traffic to form arrival processes.

When using single batched Poisson streams to approximate the departure processes, we compute the mean batch size, d_i say, of departures from each queue i. Each batch size distribution parameter is then set to give the same mean d_i, and each rate parameter to give the correct throughput, λ_i say. The enriched departure approximation at each queue is a superposition of a batched Poisson stream with mean batch size d_i and rate $\beta\lambda_i/d_i$ and an independent unbatched Poisson stream with rate $(1-\beta)\lambda_i$. This yields a different (smaller) mean batch size. The weights are chosen heuristically, for example in terms of node utilisation.

The arrivals to any given queue in a network are formed by the assumed independent superposition of the feeding queues' approximated departure processes. This superposition is simply achieved by presenting each link's traffic as an independent arrival stream to the queue. Each traffic component can be independently modulated, so the modulation structure of the target queue becomes the Cartesian product of those of the feeding departure process approximations, and any modulation of the queue's processing rate.

3.2. Solution of Individual Queues

Once the departure process approximations have been constructed at the beginning of an iterative step, we can solve the component queues based on the new arrival processes constructed as described earlier.

We formulate the equations using localizing transformations, which yield a finite recurrence relation for the repeating region (which is infinite in an unbounded queue), and explicit equations that impose the necessary boundary conditions at the empty and full (if finite capacity) queue. The solution to such a homogeneous linear matrix recurrence relation is formed as an inner product of a number of geometric terms and a set of basis vectors. These series can be represented explicitly, as in spectral expansion techniques [11], or implicitly using optimized matrix geometric methods [2,4,12].

Spectral expansion provides for an arbitrary number of components to the solution – in fact the exact number required. Matrix geometric methods provide a square M by M matrix, where M is the number of modulation states. This can have the correct number of degrees of freedom (free variables bound by the transformed equations), more than sufficient, or too few to give a solution. In queues using geometric batches and multiple arrival streams, we may find that the number d of eigenvalues is greater than M^2. To represent the solution using matrix geometric methods, we therefore would require $n > 1$ matrices R_i ($1 \le i \le n$).

$$\mathbf{v}_j = \sum_{i=1}^{n} \mathbf{u}_i R^J, \text{ in matrix geometric terms}$$

$$= \sum_{i=1}^{d} \alpha_i \psi_i \lambda_i^j, \text{ in spectral expansion terms}$$

where the α_i are constants and (λ_i, ψ_i) are the eigenvalue-eigenvector pairs of a certain characteristic equation corresponding to the transformed Kolmogorov equations for the repeating region.

We use spectral expansion in the examples provided here, as we do not yet have an efficient means for finding a set of independent generator matrices R_i. We speculate that using the previous iteration's solution for an ensemble of independent R_i matrices at each queue as a starting point in the new iteration will improve efficiency.

The queues in our network take multiple independent arrival streams, leading to a matrix recurrence relation of degree $C+A$, where C is the number of independent batched service completion streams, and A is the number of independent batched arrival streams. With M modulation states, we therefore find up to $M(C+A)$ eigenvalues with independent eigenvectors associated with the characteristic equation. This number of eigenvalues is reduced by one for each instance of an arrival or departure process having a zero rate in a given modulation state, or a pair of processes having the same batch size distribution parameter. For example, with a single unreliable processor, in the modulation state corresponding to the inactive processor, there is no service completion stream, so there is one less eigenvalue than the maximum.

4. Results

We have taken a small class of network topologies and examined the effect different approximation strategies have on the accuracy of the steady state solution of the network. We compare our approximated results with simulation of the network in a standard fashion. The approximation method has a marked effect on queue length distributions, and we have found that a single target measure, mean queue length, sheds light on this effect.

The range of approximation methods are referred to in the graphs as follows: "simulated" comes from simulation, "Poisson" comes from using a single (unbatched) Poisson stream for departures, "aggregated" refers to the use of a single geometrically batched stream for arrivals, aggregating the behaviour of all contributing queues, "batched" refers to our use of independent batched streams from each contributing queue, and "weighted" refers to the use of enriched departure streams, in this case Poisson superposed with batched in appropriate proportion. In the networks considered, λ is the external arrival rate to server S, ρ_i is the load at queue C_i and ϕ_i is the service completion batch size distribution parameter at queue C_i. All of our analytical solutions were implemented in Mathematica® [13].

4.1. Simple Feed Forward

A feed forward network (figure 4, when $n=1$ and $p_1=0$) does not require iteration for its solution. In the following examples, $\lambda=1$.

Figures 1 and 2 show the results, in terms of the error in the mean queue length at C_1, of solving the network using Poisson, batched and weighted approximations. The batched approximation tends to overestimate the mean queue length, and the Poisson traffic leads to a serious underestimation. A combination of these two approximations can be used to correct these deficiencies, as

110

in the weighted result. Our initial approach has been to share throughput between the batched and unbatched streams in a ratio $\rho:(1-\rho)$, where ρ is the utilization of the queue in the current iteration. We chose this, as a relatively idle queue tends to produce small batches, and the busy queue, larger ones. The results are promising, and could be improved with a more sophisticated ratio.

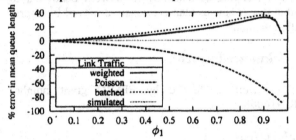

Figure 1. Percentage error in mean queue length of C_1 against ϕ_1 with ϕ_2=0.5.

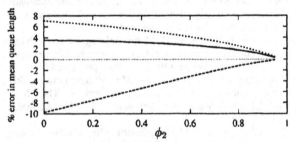

Figure 2. Percentage error in mean queue length of C_1 against ϕ_2 with ϕ_1=0.3.

4.2. A Tandem Queue

Consider a tandem queue with feedback, as obtained using the structure in figure 4, setting n=1, p_1>0, and λ=1. This is the simplest network that requires iteration for its solution.

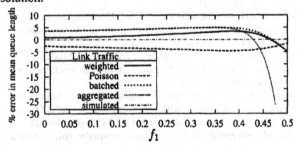

Figure 3. Error in mean queue length of C_1 for all strategies when varying feedback fraction f_1.

The Poisson underestimation continues up to a point where that approximation does not cause sufficient losses in the finite queue, where the real traffic often occurs in large batch sizes. Note that our use of independent input

streams does not fare significantly better than the aggregation approximation in this case, as there are few streams. In this example, C_1 is saturated at f_1=0.5, which means that the distribution of departure batch sizes is closer to geometric, and the use of independent batched streams becomes more accurate.

4.3 Multiple Clients Feeding Back

We now take a single server node with external Poisson arrivals, and split its output between a number of heterogeneous clients which feed back a proportion of their output to the server. We use six client-nodes with independent processing characteristics. The server receives six independent arrival processes, as any independent Poisson streams aggregate to a single stream with the summed rate, and one client is unbatched. For the example results, we vary only f_6. The remaining parameters ϕ_1 through ϕ_6 are 0.0, 0.1, 0.3, 0.4, 0.5, 0.2 and f_1 through f_5 are all 0.4. The processor rate for each client is chosen so that its capacity is 1. The server has rate 4, batch parameter 0.3, and λ=3.

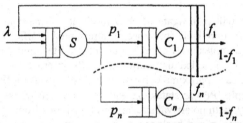

Figure 4. A network comprising a server S taking external Posson arrivals rate λ, and a proportion f_i fed back from n clients C_i, $1 \le i \le n$.

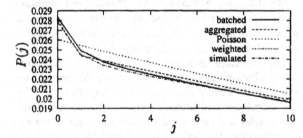

Figure 5. Queue length distribution at server for f_6=0.75.

Figure 5 shows part of the queue length distribution at the server. The arrival process is quite complex, yet all three batched approximations fare similarly, although enriched does best, and aggregated does least well. However, if we look at the mean queue length error at the server, aggregation looks most accurate. In contrast, the mean queue length error at C_6 is best approximated using enriched traffic, especially at higher feedback probabilities.

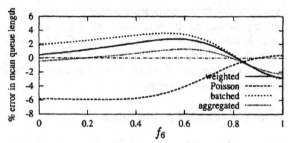

Figure 6. Mean queue length error for S, varying f_6.

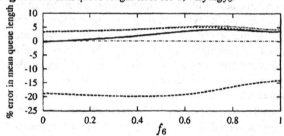

Figure 7. Mean queue length error for C_6, varying f_6.

5. Further work

We will investigate Markov modulated behaviour, to express unreliable processors, interrupted traffic, and more complex traffic behaviour (e.g. finite approximations to long tailed distributions), e.g. the internet.

We can approximate instantaneous batches using IPPs. A simple IPP has states *on*, with Poisson arrivals rate λ, and *off*, with no arrival stream, and transitions from *off* to *on* at rate a, and back at rate b. An arrival occurs on a transition from *off* to *on*, which we implement using an unusual 'diagonal transition' in the 2D Markov chain, so the mean number of arrivals in one visit to the active state is $(b+\lambda)/b$. As b increases to infinity (with constant $(b+\lambda)/b$) the process converges to a Poisson point arrival process with geometrically distributed batch sizes, rate a, and batch size distribution parameter $\lambda/(b+\lambda)$.

This structure increases the number of modulation states, which gives a single matrix R for the matrix geometric method more degrees of freedom, allowing solution for more arrival streams using a single matrix. Small inaccuracies are introduced because the batches are not instantaneous: the effect is to introduce over-sized batches in some circumstances. We are looking at the use of negative customers [6,7] to counteract this.

We also intend to address the question of response time distributions. This has been solved in [8] for a Markov modulated M/M/1 queue with batches, negative customers and infinite capacity. Our iterative method could therefore be applied immediately to the sojourn time distribution at a single such queue in a network, but the accuracy of the approximation would be more questionable, this metric being notoriously less robust.

6. Conclusions

Geometrically batched processes allow us to express burstiness in a network, and we expect to produce efficient and accurate means for solving for the steady state of such networks. Our superposition of modified batched streams has enabled matching of network behaviour to within closer bounds than previously achieved by aggregation methods.

7. Acknowledgements

This work is funded by EPSRC grant number GR/N16068.

References

[1] M. Bhabuta and P.G. Harrison. Analysis of ATM traffic on the London MAN, In *Proceedings of the 4th International Conference on Performance Modelling and Evaluation of ATM Networks*, Ilkely, Chapman and Hall, 1997.

[2] D.A. Bini, G. Latouche, B. Meini. Solving matrix polynomial equations arising in queueing problems *Linear Algebra and its Applications* **340**, 1 Jan 2002, pp 225-244

[3] R. Chakka and P.G. Harrison. A Markov modulated multi-server queue with negative customers - The MM CPP/GE/c/L G-queue. *Acta Informatica* **37**: (11-12), 2001, pp. 881-919.

[4] W. Fisher and K.S. Meier-Hellstern. The (Markov Modulated Poisson Process) MMPP Cookbook, *Performance Evaluation*, **18**, 22-July 1996, pp.149-171

[5] R.J. Fretwell and D.D. Kouvatsos. Correlated Traffic Modelling and Batch Renewal Markov Modulated Processes, In *Proc. 4th IFIP Workshop on Perf. Modelling and Evaluation of ATM Networks*, Chapman & Hall, 1997, pp. 20-44.

[6] E. Gelenbe. Product form queueing networks with negative and positive customers, *Journal of Applied Probability*, **28**, 1991, pp. 656-663.

[7] E. Gelenbe. G-Networks with signals and batch removal, *Probability in the Engineering and Informational Sciences*, 7, 1993, pp. 335-342.

[8] P.G. Harrison. The MM CPP/GE/c/L G-queue: sojourn time distribution, *Queueing Systems: Theory and Applications*, **41**(3), 2002, pp 271-298.

[9] P.G. Harrison and N.M. Patel, Performance Modelling of Communication Networks and Computer Architectures, Addison-Wesley, 1993.

[10] D.D. Kouvatsos and S.G. Denazis, ``Entropy Maximised Queueing Networks with Blocking and Multiple Job Classes", *Performance Evaluation* 17, 1993, pp.189-205

[11] I. Mitrani and R. Chakka. Spectral expansion solution for a class of Markov models: Application and comparison with the matrix-geometric method, *Performance Evaluation*, **23**, 1995, pp. 241-260.

[12] M. Neuts. Matrix-Geometric Solutions in Stochastic Models: An Algorithmic Approach, Dover Publications, 1995.

[13] Stephen Wolfram. The Mathematica Book, 4th ed., Wolfram Media/Cambridge University Press, 1999.

Session 2–2
Algorithms

A polynomial-time algorithm for allocating independent tasks on heterogeneous fork-graphs

O. Beaumont
LaBRI, UMR CNRS 5800
Bordeaux, France
Olivier.Beaumont@labri.fr

A. Legrand and Y. Robert
LIP, UMR CNRS-INRIA 5668
ENS Lyon, France
{Arnaud.Legrand,Yves.Robert}@ens-lyon.fr

Abstract

In this paper, we consider the problem of allocating a large number of independent, equal-sized tasks to a heterogeneous processor farm. We assume communication-computation overlap capabilities for each slave (and for the master), but the communication medium is exclusive: the master can only communicate with a single slave at each time-step. We give a polynomial-time algorithm to solve the following scheduling problem: given a time-bound T, what is the maximal number of tasks that can be processed by the master and the slaves within T time-units?

1 Introduction

In this paper, we deal with the problem of allocating a large number of independent, equal-sized tasks to a heterogeneous processor farm. This master-slave scheduling approach is motivated by applications that are addressed by collaborative computing efforts such as SETI@home [17], factoring large numbers [7], the Mersenne prime search [15], and those distributed computing problems organized by companies such as Entropia [9].

The master processor P_0 can process a task within w_0 time-units: it communicates a task in d_i time-units to its i-th slave P_i, $1 \le i \le p$, which requires w_i time-units to process it. We assume communication-computation overlap capabilities for each slave (and for the master), but the communication medium is exclusive. In other words, the master can only communicate with a single slave at each time-step. We state the communication model more precisely:

1. a given communication from P_0 to P_i lasts d_i units of time

2. P_0 cannot be involved in any other communication during these units of time

3. P_i cannot start the execution of the task before the communication is completed.

We give a polynomial-time algorithm to solve the following scheduling problem (to be stated more formally in Section 2: given a time-bound T, what is the maximal number of tasks that can be processed by the master and the p slaves within T time-units? The polynomial complexity of this scheduling problem is established in Sections 3 and 4. This result is rather surprising: indeed, two variants of the problem are shown NP-complete in Section 5. Finally, we survey several related problems from the literature in Section 6.

2 Problem statement

We consider a fork-graph (see Figure 1) with a master-processor P_0 and p slaves P_i, $1 \le i \le p$. The master processor P_0 owns an arbitrarily large number of independent, equal-size, non-preemptive tasks; it can process a given task within w_0 time-units; in parallel, it can send tasks to the p slaves, but only to a single slave at a given time-step.

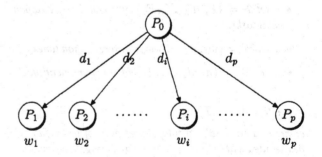

Figure 1. Heterogeneous fork-graph

It takes d_i time-units for slave P_i to receive a task. More precisely, if P_0 sends a task to P_i at time-step t, P_i cannot start executing this task before time-step $t + d_i$, while P_0 cannot initiate another communication before time-step

$t + d_i$. P_i can process a task within w_i time-units; while computing a given task, P_i can receive another task from P_0.

We deal with the following scheduling problem: given a time bound T, determine the scheduling and allocation of tasks to processor which maximize the total number of tasks whose execution is completed no later than T. Informally, we have to determine the best ordering of the messages sent by the master, together with the identity of the processors which execute the corresponding tasks, so as to maximize the total number of executed tasks. Note that this scheduling problem is called the NOW-Exploitation problem in [16].

Clearly, because the master processor can compute and communicate in parallel, it should be kept busy; within T time-units, P_0 can execute $\lfloor \frac{T}{w_0} \rfloor$ tasks. To deal with the case where the master processor P_0 has no processing capability, simply let $w_0 = +\infty$. Similarly, to deal with the case where the master cannot overlap its own computations with the communications to the slaves, add a new child P_{-1} such that $d_{-1} = w_0$ and $w_{-1} = w_0$, and then let $w_0 = +\infty$.

To state our complexity result, we have to be more precise about the problem specification. The expected output of the scheduling algorithm includes the list of tasks to be processed by each slave. The size of this list will be linear in the time-bound T, therefore exponential in the problem size if we only let T in the input (because it can be encoded with $O(\log T)$ bits). Rather, we let the input include the original list of all tasks owned by the master. Such an hypothesis makes full sense in practice: even though we assume equal-size tasks, each task will correspond to a different file, and to a different computation, and we must keep track of which task is executed on which computing resource.

We are ready to formally state our scheduling problem (in view of the previous remarks, we omit the computations performed by the master processor):

Definition 1 (MAX-TASKS($n, \mathcal{F}, p, \mathcal{W}, \mathcal{D}, T$)). *Given*

- *a set $\mathcal{F} = \{F_1, F_2, \ldots, F_n\}$ of n equal-size independent tasks,*

- *a set $\mathcal{W} = \{w_1, w_2, \ldots, w_p\}$ of p execution times,*

- *a set $\mathcal{D} = \{d_1, d_2, \ldots, d_p\}$ of p communication delays,*

- *a time-bound T,*

compute a maximal-cardinal subset of $\mathcal{F}$ of tasks that can be executed within T time-units on a heterogeneous master-slave platform made up with p slaves P_i of computation time w_i and communication time d_i, $1 \leq i \leq p$.

Theorem 1. *MAX-TASKS($n, \mathcal{F}, p, \mathcal{W}, \mathcal{D}, T$) can be solved in polynomial time.*

The proof is constructive. In the following, a (somewhat sophisticated) greedy algorithm is shown to be optimal.

3 Reduction to a problem with at most one task per slave

Proposition 1. *Any instance MAX-TASKS($n, \mathcal{F}, p, \mathcal{W}, \mathcal{D}, T$) can be polynomially reduced to an instance MAX-TASKS-SINGLE($n, \mathcal{F}, p', \mathcal{W}', \mathcal{D}', T$) where each slave is constrained to execute at most one task.*

Proof. Each slave P_i can be dealt with separately, so let i be fixed. We use duplicate slave nodes to simulate the taking of successive nodes by the original node P_i, which we replace by a collection of l_i slaves $P_{i,j}$, $1 \leq j \leq l_i = \min(n, \lfloor \frac{T - w_i - d_i}{M_i} \rfloor + 1)$, where $M_i = \max(d_i, w_i)$. See Figure 2: all the new slaves have the same communication capability d_i as P_i, but $P_{i,j}$ processes a task in $w_{i,j} = w_i + (j-1) \cdot M_i$ time-units. In the new instance of the problem, each slave $P_{i,j}$ will execute a single task, namely the $(j+1)$-th task (if any) that was executed by P_i in the original problem instance. The bound l_i need not be tight, it is simply computed from the constraint $d_i + w_{i,l_i} \leq T$.

After the transformation, the total number of slaves is bounded by $p \times n$, which is indeed polynomial in the size of the input (because $\mathcal{F}$ is of size at least $O(n)$ and $\mathcal{W}$, or $\mathcal{D}$, of size at least $O(p)$). ■

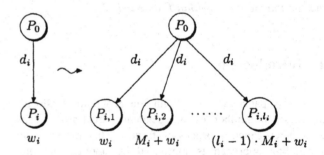

Figure 2. Replacing a slave by a collection of uni-task slaves

4 With at most one task per slave

In this section, we solve MAX-TASKS-SINGLE($n, \mathcal{F}, p, \mathcal{W}, \mathcal{D}, T$), the problem where each slave is limited to executing at most one-task. The problem is reduced to deciding which slave to communicate with, and in which order. For simplicity, we still use the notations $p, \mathcal{W}, \mathcal{D}$ while in fact there are $p' = O(pn)$ slaves after the transformation of Section 3. We start with a technical lemma:

Lemma 1. *Consider a set of k slaves capable of executing k tasks (one each) within T units with some scheduling. Then, if we sort these slaves by computation times (largest first),*

116

and if we schedule the communications from the master P_0 in that order, we can also execute k tasks within T time-units.

Proof. To simplify notations, let $P_1, P_2, \ldots, P_k$ be the sorted slaves: $w_1 \geq w_2 \geq \ldots \geq w_k$. Let $(P_{i_1}, \ldots, P_{i_k})$ be the ordering of the communications from P_0 in the original schedule. The following set of equations is satisfied:

$$
\begin{aligned}
(L_1) \quad & d_{i_1} + w_{i_1} & \leq T \quad & \text{first task} \\
(L_2) \quad & d_{i_1} + d_{i_2} + w_{i_2} & \leq T \quad & \text{second task} \\
& \vdots \quad \ddots & \vdots \quad & \vdots \\
(L_k) \quad & d_{i_1} + d_{i_2} + \cdots + d_{i_k} + w_{i_k} & \leq T \quad & \text{last task}
\end{aligned}
$$

Let $j_1, \ldots, j_k$ be the indices of the tasks of the sorted slaves in the original schedule: $i_{j_1} = 1$, $i_{j_2} = 2$, ... and $i_{j_k} = k$. $i_{j_1} = 1$ means that processor P_1 is assigned the j_1-th task in the original schedule. We prove by induction that tasks can be assigned in the ordering $1, 2, \ldots, k$ of sorted computation times:

i) For the first task, we have $d_1 + w_1 \leq T$. Indeed, see equation L_{j_1}: $d_{i_1} + \cdots + d_{i_{j_1-1}} + d_1 + w_1 \leq T$.

ii) For the second task, we have $d_1 + d_2 + w_2 \leq T$. Indeed, there are two possibilities: if $j_2 > j_1$, then the inequality L_{j_2} contains the quantity $d_{i_{j_1}} + d_{i_{j_2}} + w_{i_{j_2}}$, hence $d_1 + d_2 + w_2 \leq T$; otherwise, if $j_2 < j_1$, then the inequality L_{j_1} contains the quantity $d_{i_{j_1}} + d_{i_{j_2}} + w_{i_{j_1}}$; because $w_2 \leq w_1$, we derive that $d_1 + d_2 + w_2 \leq T$.

iii) For the general case, let $i < k$. Assume that for all $l \leq i$ we have $d_1 + \cdots + d_l + w_l \leq T$. We aim at proving that $d_1 + \cdots + d_{i+1} + w_{i+1} \leq T$. Let $m_i = \max(j_1, \ldots, j_i)$.

- Either $j_{i+1} > m_i$; then we consider the inequality $L_{j_{i+1}}$, which contains the terms $d_1, d_2, \ldots, d_i$ (because $j_{i+1} > m_i$) as well as the term $d_{i+1} + w_{i+1}$. Hence $d_1 + \cdots + d_{i+1} + w_{i+1} \leq T$.

- Or $j_{i+1} < m_i$; then we consider the inequality L_{m_i}, which contains the terms $d_1, d_2, \ldots, d_{i+1}$ as well as the term $d_i + w_i$. Hence $d_1 + \cdots + d_{i+1} + w_i \leq T$. Because $w_i \geq w_{i+1}$, we finally derive that $d_1 + \cdots + d_{i+1} + w_{i+1} \leq T$. ∎

We introduce the following greedy algorithm:

```
MASTER-SLAVE((P_1, ..., P_p), T)
1:   Sort slaves such that d_1 ≤ d_2 ... ≤ d_p
2:   L ← ∅
3:   For i = 1 To p Do
4:      If L ∪ {P_i} can be scheduled
            within T time-units
5:      Then L ← L ∪ {P_i}
6:   Return (L)
```

The condition at line 4 can be checked using Lemma 1: sort the current list L according to the computation times and verify that all inequalities are satisfied.

Proposition 2. *The* Master-Slave *algorithm returns a maximal set of tasks that can be processed within T time-units.*

Proof. To simplify notations, we say that a set of indices $\mathcal{I} = \{i_1, \ldots, i_k\}$ is *schedulable* if there exists a valid scheduling executing k tasks within T time-units, with processors $\{P_{i_1}, \ldots, P_{i_k}\}$.

Assume that the set $\mathcal{I} = \{i_1, \ldots, i_k\}$ is schedulable, and further (without loss of generality) that $d_{i_1} \leq d_{i_2} \leq d_{i_k}$. We show that the MASTER-SLAVE algorithm returns at least k values, i.e. a schedulable set $\mathcal{G} = \{g_1, \ldots, g_k\}$, which will conclude the proof. We proceed by induction.

i) Let $\mathcal{I}_0 = \{i_1, \ldots, i_k\}$. The set $\mathcal{I}_0$ is schedulable. Each subset of $\mathcal{I}_0$ is schedulable. In particular, each singleton $\{i_j\}$ is schedulable. By construction of the MASTER-SLAVE algorithm, g_1 exists and $g_1 \leq \min(i_1, \ldots, i_k)$. This is because the MASTER-SLAVE algorithm selects the smallest index of a schedulable task. Now we show that there exists a schedulable set $\mathcal{I}_1$ of k elements which contains g_1. If $g_1 \in \mathcal{I}_0$ we are done: $\mathcal{I}_1 = \mathcal{I}_0$. Otherwise consider the ordering $i_{j_1}, i_{j_2}, \ldots, i_{j_k}$ in which $\mathcal{I}_0$ is scheduled: we have the set of inequalities:

$$
\begin{aligned}
(L_1) \quad & d_{i_{j_1}} + w_{i_{j_1}} & \leq T \\
(L_2) \quad & d_{i_{j_1}} + d_{i_{j_2}} + w_{i_{j_2}} & \leq T \\
& \vdots \quad \ddots & \vdots \\
(L_k) \quad & d_{i_{j_1}} + d_{i_{j_2}} + \cdots + d_{i_{j_k}} + w_{i_{j_k}} & \leq T
\end{aligned}
$$

We replace the first scheduled index i_{j_1} by g_1 to build I_1: we let $I_1 = I_0 \setminus \{i_{j_1}\} \cup \{g_1\}$. The first inequality $d_{g_1} + w_{g_1} \leq T$ holds because g_1 is schedulable. The other inequalities (L_2) to (L_k) still hold because $d_{g_1} \leq d_{i_{j_1}}$. Hence $\mathcal{I}_1 = \{g_1, i_{j_2}, \ldots, i_{j_k}\}$ is schedulable.

ii) Therefore there exists a schedulable set $\mathcal{I}_1 = \{g_1, i'_1, \ldots, i'_{k-1}\}$. For all j, $1 \leq j \leq k_1$, the pair $\{g_1, i'_j\}$ is schedulable, which establishes that the MASTER-SLAVE algorithm does select an index g_2 after selecting g_1. Furthermore, $g_2 \leq \min(i'_1, \ldots, i'_{k-1})$. Now we show that there exists a schedulable set $\mathcal{I}_2$ of k elements which contains g_1 and g_2. If $g_2 \in \{i'_1, \ldots, i'_{k-1}\}$ let $\mathcal{I}_2 = \mathcal{I}_1$. Otherwise, consider the ordering in which $\mathcal{I}_1$ is scheduled. There is no reason that g_1 should be scheduled first in $\mathcal{I}_1$, hence we have two cases:

- g_1 is indeed the first task in $\mathcal{I}_1$ to be communicated by P_0. Let f be the index of the second

117

task in $\mathcal{I}_1$ to be communicated by P_0. Because the pair $\{g_1, g_2\}$ is schedulable, we can replace f by g_2: the first two inequalities (L_1) and (L_2) are satisfied (maybe we have to swap g_1 and g_2, but anyway this pair can be scheduled), and the following $k-2$ inequalities still hold true because $d_{g_2} \le d_f$.

- The index f of the first task in $\mathcal{I}_1$ to be communicated by P_0 is different from g_1. Then we replace f by g_2: the first inequality (L_1) is satisfied because $\{g_2\}$ is schedulable, and the following $k-1$ inequalities still hold true because $d_{g_2} \le d_f$.

We conclude that $\mathcal{I}_2$ is schedulable.

iii) For the general case, assume we have a schedulable set $\mathcal{I}_{j-1} = \{g_1, \ldots, g_{j-1}, i'_1, \ldots, i'_{k-j+1}\}$ For every l, $1 \le l \le k - j + 1$, the subset $\{g_1, \ldots, g_{j-1}, i'_l\}$ is schedulable, hence the the MASTER-SLAVE algorithm does select an index g_j after selecting $g_1, \ldots, g_{j-1}$. Furthermore, $g_j \le \min(i'_1, \ldots, i'_{k-j+1})$. Now we show that there exists a schedulable set $\mathcal{I}_j$ of k elements which contains $\{g_1, g_2, \ldots, g_j\}$. If $g_j \in \{i'_1, \ldots, i'_{k-j+1}\}$ let $\mathcal{I}_j = \mathcal{I}_{j-1}$. Otherwise, consider the ordering in which $\mathcal{I}_{j-1}$ is scheduled. We pick up the first task f to be scheduled that is different from the MASTER-SLAVE indices $g_1, g_2, \ldots, g_{j-1}$. We replace this index f by g_j to derive $\mathcal{I}'_j$. We claim that $\mathcal{I}_j$ is schedulable. To see this, consider the scheduling of $\mathcal{I}_{j-1}$, and let l be such that the first l inequalities (L_1) to (L_l) deal with MASTER-SLAVE indices $g_{i_1}, g_{i_2}, \ldots, g_{i_l}$, while (L_{l+1}) deals with index f:

(a) $\{g_{i_1}, \ldots, g_{i_l}, g_j\}$ is schedulable as a subset of $\{g_1, \ldots, g_j\}$: a valid ordering of these $l+1$ tasks provide the first $l+1$ inequalities.

(b) inequalities (L_{l+2}) to (L_k) still hold because $d_{g_j} \le d_f$.

This establishes Proposition 2. ∎

Proof of Theorem 1. First we note that the complexity of the Master-Slave algorithm is quadratic in the number of slaves: each task is processed once, and the test for its insertion in the returned scheduled is easily implemented in time linear in the number of already selected tasks. To see this, simply maintain the list of already selected tasks together with their current termination time. When a new task F_i is inserted, we increment by d_i the termination times of all tasks F_j whose w_j is smaller than w_i, and we check on the fly that these termination times still do not exceed T.

Going back to the original problem, the complexity is thus bounded by $O(n^2 p^2)$: after the transformation of Section 3, the number of uni-task slaves is bounded by $O(n.p)$,

and the complexity of the greedy algorithm is at most quadratic in that quantity. This concludes the proof of Theorem 1. ∎

5 Extensions

In this section we briefly mention two variants which are natural extensions of the MAX-TASKS$(n, \mathcal{F}, p, \mathcal{W}, \mathcal{D}, T)$ problem. The first variant deals with a two-port communication model, where the master can communicate to at most two slaves simultaneously. The second variant still uses the one-port model (each processor is capable of sending to or receiving from at most another processor at any time-step), but now there are two masters sharing slaves. Both variants turn out to be NP-complete. Due to the lack of space, the formal statement of both variants and the NP-completeness proofs are to be found in [4].

6 Related problems

This paper is a follow-on of two previous papers that study the same scheduling problem. In [3], communication links are assumed to be homogeneous. In other words, $d_i = d$ for $1 \le i \le p$. We use a matching algorithm to compute the optimal solution in this context. In [2] we deal with master-slave tasking on more general tree-structured networks: in other words, the underlying architecture is a tree, it is no longer restricted to a fork graph. We do not know the complexity of the master-slave scheduling problem on a general tree graph, which seems to be a challenging open problem. Rather than searching a solution to this problem, we characterize in [2] the best steady-state for various operation models (i.e. we neglect the initialization and termination phases).

We classify several related papers along the following lines:

Scheduling fork graphs The complexity of scheduling fork graphs has been widely studied in the literature. Given a task graph, the standard macro data-flow model [14] assumes that: (i) processors are homogeneous; (ii) communication delays are paid each time a task and one of its successors are not assigned to the same processor. In this model, scheduling a fork graph with an infinite number of processors is a polynomial problem [10], while scheduling a fork-join graph is NP-complete [6].

Extensions of the standard macro data-flow model includes the one-port model [13] (just as in this paper, each processor can communicate with at most another processor at a given time-step) and the LogP model [8]. Scheduling fork graphs in the one-port model [1] or in the LogP model [20] remains NP-complete, even for an infinity of resources.

Scheduling divisible load Instead of scheduling several communications, one for each task, the divisible load approach consists in scheduling a single communication at the beginning of the operation. The cost of this communication is proportional to the amount of computation performed. A fork-graph (also called a single-level tree, or star network) is targeted in [19], with homogeneous links and different-speed processors. The extension to heterogeneous links is dealt with in [5].

Master-slave on the computational grid Master-slave scheduling on the grid can be based on a network-flow approach [18] or on an adaptive strategy [12]. Enabling frameworks to facilitate the implementation of master-slave tasking are described in [11, 21].

7 Conclusion

In this paper, we have shown that master-slave tasking using heterogeneous fork-graphs can be solved in polynomial time, using a non-trivial greedy algorithm. The complexity of this scheduling problem for arbitrary tree graphs is a challenging open problem. A first step to solving this problem would be to study the complexity for a linear chain of processors.

References

[1] O. Beaumont, V. Boudet, and Y. Robert. A realistic model and an efficient heuristic for scheduling with heterogeneous processors. In *HCW'2002, the 11th Heterogeneous Computing Workshop*. IEEE Computer Society Press, 2002.

[2] O. Beaumont, L. Carter, J. Ferrante, A. Legrand, and Y. Robert. Bandwidth-centric allocation of independent tasks on heterogeneous platforms. In *International Parallel and Distributed Processing Symposium IPDPS'2002*. IEEE Computer Society Press, 2002. Extended version available as LIP Research Report 2001-25.

[3] O. Beaumont, A. Legrand, and Y. Robert. The master-slave paradigm with heterogeneous processors. In D. S. Katz, T. Sterling, M. Baker, L. Bergman, M. Paprzycki, and R. Buyya, editors, *Cluster'2001*, pages 419–426. IEEE Computer Society Press, 2001. Extended version available as LIP Research Report 2001-13.

[4] O. Beaumont, A. Legrand, and Y. Robert. A polynomial-time algorithm for allocating independent tasks on heterogeneous fork-graphs. Technical Report 2002-07, LIP, ENS Lyon, France, Feb. 2002.

[5] S. Charcranoon, T. G. Robertazzi, and S. Luryi. Optimizing computing costs using divisible load analysis. *IEEE Transactions on computers*, 49(9):987–991, Sept. 2000.

[6] P. Chrétienne and C. Picouleau. Scheduling with communication delays: a survey. In P. Chrétienne, E. G. C. Jr., J. K. Lenstra, and Z. Liu, editors, *Scheduling Theory and its Applications*, pages 65–89. John Wiley & Sons, 1995.

[7] J. Cowie, B. Dodson, R.-M. Elkenbracht-Huizing, A. K. Lenstra, P. L. Montgomery, and J. Zayer. A world wide number field sieve factoring record: on to 512 bits. In K. Kim and T. Matsumoto, editors, *Advances in Cryptology - Asiacrypt '96*, volume 1163 of *LNCS*, pages 382–394. Springer Verlag, 1996.

[8] D. Culler, R. Karp, D. Patterson, A. Sahay, K. Schauser, E. Santos, R. Subramonian, and T. von Eicken. LogP: A practical model of parallel computation. *Communications of the ACM*, 39(11):78–85, 1996.

[9] Entropia. URL: http://www.entropia.com.

[10] A. Gerasoulis and T. Yang. On the granularity and clustering of directed acyclic task graphs. *IEEE Trans. Parallel and Distributed Systems*, 4(6):686–701, 1993.

[11] J. P. Goux, S. Kulkarni, J. Linderoth, and M. Yoder. An enabling framework for master-worker applications on the computational grid. In *Ninth IEEE International Symposium on High Performance Distributed Computing (HPDC'00)*. IEEE Computer Society Press, 2000.

[12] E. Heymann, M. A. Senar, E. Luque, and M. Livny. Adaptive scheduling for master-worker applications on the computational grid. In R. Buyya and M. Baker, editors, *Grid Computing - GRID 2000*, pages 214–227. Springer-Verlag LNCS 1971, 2000.

[13] S. L. Johnsson and C.-T. Ho. Spanning graphs for optimum broadcasting and personalized communication in hypercubes. *IEEE Trans. Computers*, 38(9):1249–1268, 1989.

[14] C. H. Papadimitriou and M. Yannakakis. Towards an architecture-independent analysis of parallel algorithms. *SIAM Journal on Computing*, 19(2):322–328, 1990.

[15] Prime. URL: http://www.mersenne.org.

[16] A. L. Rosenberg. Sharing partitionable workloads in heterogeneous NOWs: greedier is not better. In D. S. Katz, T. Sterling, M. Baker, L. Bergman, M. Paprzycki, and R. Buyya, editors, *Cluster Computing 2001*, pages 124–131. IEEE Computer Society Press, 2001.

[17] SETI. URL: http://setiathome.ssl.berkeley.edu.

[18] G. Shao, F. Berman, and R. Wolski. Master/slave computing on the grid. In *Heterogeneous Computing Workshop HCW'00*. IEEE Computer Society Press, 2000.

[19] J. Sohn, T. G. Robertazzi, and S. Luryi. Optimizing computing costs using divisible load analysis. *IEEE Transactions on parallel and distributed systems*, 9(3):225–234, Mar. 1998.

[20] J. Verriet. *Scheduling with communication for multiprocessor computation*. PhD thesis, Dept. of Computer Science, Utrecht University, 1998.

[21] J. B. Weissman. Scheduling multi-component applications in heterogeneous wide-area networks. In *Heterogeneous Computing Workshop HCW'00*. IEEE Computer Society Press, 2000.

An Experimental Evaluation of Modified Algorithms
for the Graph Partitioning Problem

Jurij Šilc, Peter Korošec
Computer Systems Department
Jožef Stefan Institute
Ljubljana, Slovenia
{jurij.silc, peter.korosec}@ijs.si

Borut Robič
Faculty of Computer and Information Science
University of Ljubljana
Ljubljana, Slovenia
borut.robic@fri.uni-lj.si

Abstract

Graph partitioning problem has an important role with a wide range of applications in many different areas including numerical computation, geographical information systems, data-mining, database design, scientific simulation, and the design of VLSI circuits. By using partitioning, we are concentrating on trying to reduce the costs of designing systems and to speed up system operations. In this article we present a comparison and an evaluation of different, modified algorithms for solving the graph-partitioning problem.

1. Introduction

The *partitioning problem* is a family of problems that have in common a set of elements that need to be partitioned into several subsets so that a given cost function is optimized (maximized or minimized). The partitioning problem finds applications in numerical computation, geographical information systems, data-mining, database design, scientific simulation, the design of VLSI circuits, etc. [1, 14].

In this paper we are interested in a specific version of this problem called the *graph-partitioning problem*, which involves partitioning a graph into a given number of parts such that each part has roughly the same number of vertices, and the number of edges that straddle the parts is minimized. The graph-partitioning problem appears very frequently in various areas [4]. One such area is the (co)design of hardware and software, where, for example, chip planning, memory paging, and the reduction of communication (while balancing workload) in a multiprocessor, are three topical fields.

Unfortunately, graph-partitioning problems are often NP-hard [5], which makes it impossible to find optimal solutions for them in time, which is polynomial in the length of the input (unless P = NP). As a result, heuristic approaches are normally used to solve graph-partitioning problems.

In general, there are two types of heuristic graph-partitioning methods. Informally, *constructive methods* start with one vertex and progress to the final partition by adding vertices to parts, one at a time, while *iterative-improvement methods* start with an initial partition and then iteratively progress to the final partition by moving the vertices between parts.

The goal of this paper is to investigate selected iterative-improvement algorithms for graph partitioning, to suggest modifications to improve these algorithms, and to evaluate them experimentally.

2. Graph Partitioning Problem

2.1. Problem Definition

A graph $G(V, E)$ consists of a non-empty set V of vertices and a set E of edges, which are unordered pairs of elements of V. A k-partition of G comprises k mutually disjointed subsets $D_1, D_2, ..., D_k$ (called domains) of V whose union is V; $D = \{D_1, D_2, ..., D_k\}$. The set of edges that connects the different domains of a partition is called an edge-cut. A partition is balanced if the sizes of the domains are roughly the same. The graph-partition problem is to find a balanced partition with a minimal edge-cut $\zeta(D)$.

2.2. Problem Solving

Since the space of feasible solutions for the graph-partitioning problem is prohibitively large we are forced

120

to recourse to heuristic approaches, which reduce or bound the space to be searched. Unfortunately, heuristics cannot usually guarantee optimal or even close-to-optimal solutions. Indeed, relying on ad hoc approaches, they are often used without any theoretical guarantee that they will even return feasible solutions. On the other hand, they may return very good solutions, sometimes even optimal, so they can be acceptable if one is willing to give up the "all-or-nothing" principle.

For the graph-partitioning problem there are two basic classes of heuristic methods: *constructive* and *iterative-improvement* methods. Constructive methods partition a given graph by starting with one or more seed vertices and then adding other vertices to the seeds, one at a time. Iterative-improvement heuristic methods start with some initial partition of the given graph and then iteratively improve successive partitions by moving the vertices between domains.

In the following, we will focus on iterative-improvement graph-partitioning methods. In particular, we will describe four new heuristic algorithms that we developed using four iterative-improvement algorithms: min-cut, simulated annealing, tabu search, and genetic algorithm.

3. Iterative-Improvement Algorithms

3.1. Min-Cut: MC and MC'

The Kernighan-Lin partitioning algorithm is a greedy algorithm that iteratively interchanges two sets of vertices between two domains of equal size to produce maximal improvement in the edge-cut [9]. The complexity of the basic algorithm is $O(n^2 \log(n))$, where n is the number of nodes. Since the Kernighan-Lin algorithm was originally designed to solve the two-way partitioning problem, we customized it for solving general k-way partitioning problems. The resulting algorithm is called the min-cut algorithm (**MC**). The algorithm uses a recursive procedure, which on every call divides a domain into two domains of appropriate sizes, so that, in a finite number of recursion calls, it divides the given graph into k domains of approximately the same size.

We introduced several improvements to the **MC** algorithm, which resulted in the modified min-cut algorithm called **MC'**. First, we used a more efficient procedure for searching the best pair of vertices to swap. To do this we applied the Compact_Col_Scan procedure [3]. While the time complexity of the original procedure used in the Kernighan-Lin algorithm is $O(p^2)$, the complexity of the Compact_Col_Scan is $O(d^2)$, where $d = \lceil 2E/V \rceil$, and p is the size of the domain. Another modification that we made is based on the assumption that we have previously randomly generated k domains

and then run the **MC** (with Compact_Col_Scan) algorithm over them. We repeat this procedure until there is no improvement in the domains. Since the time complexity of the **MC** algorithm with the Compact_Col_Scan procedure is $O(dn/k \log(n/k))$ [3], the time complexity of the body in the while loop of the **MC'** is bounded above by $O(dnk \log(n/k))$.

3.2. Simulated Annealing: SA and SA'

The simulated-annealing algorithm **SA** is a very general optimization method. The algorithm works by iteratively proposing changes and either accepting or rejecting each change [7, 10]. The main idea is in the analogy between a combinatorial optimization problem and the problem of determining the lowest-energy ground state of a physical system with many interacting atoms. At each temperature during the annealing process, slow cooling enables the system to achieve equilibrium. Several heuristic approaches have been developed to control the simulated-annealing process [11]. In general, the **SA** algorithm returns good results (even optimal) if the temperature reduction is slow enough.

Instead of using the original **SA** algorithm (which is potentially too slow) once, we decided to run an *accelerated version* of the **SA** several times (m times), and then pick the best of the results obtained. Notice, that the acceleration is achieved by large temperature reduction at each step. The modified algorithm is called **SA'**.

3.3. Tabu Search: TS and TS'

Tabu search [6, 8] is a strategy for guiding known heuristics to overcome local optima. It is an iterative-improvement method that uses a limited list of past moves (called the tabu-list) to help diversify the search and avoid becoming trapped in local optima. Each time a move is made it is placed on the tabu-list. A move already on the tabu-list is deemed forbidden, and is typically removed from the tabu-list after a time t_{hold}. For the graph-partitioning problem we started with the usual choice, i.e., tabu search with a fixed t_{hold} [2], and adapted it for solving general k-way partitioning problems. We chose $t_{hold} = \lfloor ap \rfloor$ with $0 < a < 1$. In addition, we used the Compact_Col_Scan procedure instead of the original procedure for searching out the best pair of vertices to swap. We call the resulting algorithm the **TS** algorithm.

Unfortunately, a bad value of t_{hold} in the **TS** may end with poor results. We avoided this in the *randomized tabu-search* algorithm [2] called **TS'**. The **TS'** algorithm starts several times, each time with a different initial partition (in our case obtained by **MC'**). Given an initial partition, **TS'** improves it by iteratively applying the **TS** algorithm, each time with a randomly chosen t_{hold}.

3.4. Genetic approach: GA and GA'

Genetic algorithms are based on ideas and techniques from genetic and evolutionary theory. Genetic algorithms simulate an evolutionary process with N individuals that represent points in a search space. For our problem we used the ideas of the parallel genetic algorithm (**GA**) applied to the k-way graph-partitioning problem [8, 13].

The weakest feature of our main algorithm is its slow convergence. To remedy this we added an *adaptation step* and designed an adaptation genetic algorithm called **GA'**. The adaptation step is executed after the mutation step. During the adaptation step a fast algorithm (in our case **MC'**) improves the solution created by the mutation.

4. Experimental Results and Discussion

In this section, we present and discuss the results of the experimental evaluation of the **MC'**, **SA'**, **TS'**, and **GA'** algorithms as well as the original **MC** [3], **SA** [7], **TS** [8], and **GA** [13] algorithms.

4.1. Workload, metrics and the experimental environment

The workload for testing the algorithms consists of a number of randomly generated graphs. We have generated 40 graphs: 10 graphs for each size $n = 100$, 200, 300, and 400. Half of these are sparse graphs (i.e., $n < e < 2n$), while the others are dense (i.e., $2n < e < 3n$). The graphs' descriptions, based on their sizes and the numbers of edges, are given in Table 1.

Table 1: Graphs sizes and number of connections

Number of vertices	Sparse graphs			Dense graphs		
	Minimal number of edges	Maximal number of edges	Average number of edges	Minimal number of edges	Maximal number of edges	Average number of edges
100	146	191	170.2	204	262	238.0
200	270	390	329.6	403	478	436.6
300	355	567	442.8	630	897	729.4
400	499	769	617.2	815	1199	1032.8

We have decided to partition the graphs into $k = 2, 4$, 16 and 32 domains. By doing so, we were trying to cover the whole spectrum of domain granularity, from coarse ($k = 2$ and 4) to fine ($k = 16$ and 32). We optimally tuned the parameters for each of the algorithms by making preliminary runs. In this way we ensured that each algorithm performs best in all possible situations in a reasonable execution time. Then we ran each algorithm 50 times on each test graph for all possible values of k. As a result, each of the algorithms was run 8.000 times.

For each run of the algorithm we measured *time* (in seconds) and *cost* (edge-cut size, i.e., $\zeta(D)$) to produce a graph partition.

The algorithms were implemented in Borland® Delphi™. The experiments were made on a computer with an AMD Athlon™ XP 1800+ processor running the Microsoft® Windows® XP operating system.

4.2. Performance Results

In what follows, we discuss the algorithms that have been selected for this experiment. First, let us compare each of the original algorithms with the corresponding modified algorithm (Table 2).

4.2.1. Min-Cut. As we can see, the **MC'** algorithm performs much better than the original **MC** algorithm. The achieved *cost* values of the two algorithms are almost the same, but the **MC'** is much faster than the **MC**, and the difference in the *time* consumptions quickly increases with n. This makes **MC'** attractive for solving bigger problems (in terms of graph size n, and partition granularity k).

4.2.2. Simulated Annealing. The **SA'** algorithm is the most disappointing one. With a small k (coarse partitions) it is quite competitive with the original **SA**, but as k increases (fine partitions) the algorithm performs worse in terms of *cost*, although it is faster. The reason for this is that it is very difficult to find the optimal cooling schedule and the degree of acceleration.

4.2.3. Tabu Search. The most consistent method is tabu search, since its overall performance is relatively good under all conditions. The *cost* values achieved by our **TS'** were better than those achieved by the **TS**, but *time* consumption on the large graphs was higher. Notice, however, that **TS'** does not need any parameter tuning. This can be an advantage in cases where we have an unknown, or a very wide, problem definition (e.g., graph size, density, etc.).

4.2.4. Genetic Algorithm. The improvements achieved by the **GA'** in terms of *cost* and *time*, compared with the **GA**, are relatively large. Another noticeable feature is the **GA'**'s behavior. We can see that time consumption decreases at $n = 400$. The reason for this is in the setting of the value that determines after how many iterations without improvement the algorithm is to be terminated. With larger k and n the probability that we will find a better solution in the next m iterations decreases. In order to prevent this we should increase m. The result would be a slightly better *cost* at the expense of a much higher *time* consumption.

Table 2: The average *cost* and *time* values for each of the tested algorithm

Domain granuality	k	n	Sparse graphs				Dense graphs			
			cost	time	cost	time	cost	time	cost	time
Algorithm			MC		MC'		MC		MC'	
coarse	2	100	31	0.01	32	0.01	55	0.01	55	0.01
	2	200	59	0.11	59	0.02	93	0.12	94	0.02
	2	300	70	0.41	71	0.05	165	0.45	166	0.06
	2	400	102	1.26	103	0.12	238	1.42	241	0.16
	4	100	54	0.02	54	0.01	92	0.02	91	0.01
	4	200	101	0.13	99	0.03	157	0.15	155	0.04
	4	300	121	0.49	122	0.08	276	0.55	273	0.10
	4	400	175	1.47	174	0.17	399	1.68	394	0.21
fine	16	100	88	0.02	91	0.01	144	0.02	145	0.01
	16	200	157	0.15	159	0.04	239	0.15	241	0.04
	16	300	189	0.52	190	0.08	413	0.58	413	0.09
	16	400	269	1.52	270	0.16	591	1.77	589	0.18
	32	100	109	0.02	110	0.02	170	0.02	170	0.02
	32	200	181	0.15	185	0.05	272	0.16	277	0.05
	32	300	216	0.53	222	0.10	462	0.58	468	0.10
	32	400	304	1.57	311	0.19	656	1.77	664	0.20
Algorithm			SA		SA'		SA		SA'	
coarse	2	100	22	6	22	9	45	8	45	11
	2	200	41	24	42	31	73	28	74	36
	2	300	47	74	52	78	136	84	140	97
	2	400	73	131	80	143	201	162	210	172
	4	100	41	6	42	7	78	7	78	9
	4	200	75	26	85	23	129	29	138	26
	4	300	88	68	119	47	234	82	263	6
	4	400	132	123	192	85	344	164	406	10
fine	16	100	78	2	94	3	132	3	145	
	16	200	139	11	210	9	217	13	288	1
	16	300	179	27	307	23	383	39	523	2
	16	400	279	46	454	45	565	73	778	5
	32	100	107	1	126	2	166	2	182	2
	32	200	190	7	262	8	275	8	351	8
	32	300	269	16	369	20	480	22	614	22
	32	400	403	30	529	39	707	41	893	43
Algorithm			TS		TS'		TS		TS'	
coarse	2	100	23	2	22	5	47	2	45	5
	2	200	46	7	40	20	78	7	71	20
	2	300	56	19	45	51	147	19	133	51
	2	400	85	46	70	122	217	46	198	123
	4	100	40	2	40	7	77	3	76	7
	4	200	74	10	73	28	127	10	126	29
	4	300	87	25	86	67	231	25	231	70
	4	400	128	51	129	138	337	53	340	145
fine	16	100	82	4	77	10	136	4	131	10
	16	200	140	13	131	36	221	13	211	36
	16	300	156	31	152	83	381	31	369	84
	16	400	228	65	221	174	540	65	533	176
	32	100	106	6	102	15	166	6	162	15
	32	200	175	16	165	42	265	16	255	42
	32	300	203	34	189	92	448	34	433	93
	32	400	283	72	269	198	637	73	618	198
Algorithm			GA		GA'		GA		GA'	
coarse	2	100	27	9	22	3	51	9	45	3
	2	200	53	50	41	15	87	51	73	15
	2	300	64	148	48	48	156	165	137	50
	2	400	94	325	71	150	223	350	202	161
	4	100	50	10	40	5	88	11	76	5
	4	200	98	57	72	27	154	62	125	26
	4	300	122	161	84	74	274	197	228	79
	4	400	175	361	122	228	399	426	335	218
fine	16	100	83	13	75	13	138	13	129	13
	16	200	153	74	136	14	236	80	214	15
	16	300	190	209	166	19	415	252	380	22
	16	400	275	548	233	60	605	593	542	62
	32	100	106	16	100	17	167	16	160	19
	32	200	175	98	161	64	267	101	248	70
	32	300	211	275	192	97	457	296	427	124
	32	400	305	531	280	53	665	522	621	59

5. Conclusion

Graph partitioning has useful applications in many disciplines. In this paper we improved and evaluated several algorithms for the graph-partitioning problem. In particular, we focused on the following iterative-improvement algorithms: min-cut, simulated annealing, tabu search, and genetic algorithm.

We tested the algorithms on randomly generated sparse and dense graphs containing up to 400 vertices, each of which was divided up into 32 partitions (domains). None of the algorithms was a clear winner and the graph density itself does not have a significant impact on the algorithm's execution.

However, we found experimentally that the modified min-cut algorithm (**MC'**) is a good choice when the execution time is of primary importance. When the quality of the result (*cost*) is more important, however, our modified genetic algorithm (**GA'**) is a better choice. Slightly slower, but exhibiting a similar quality, is the modified tabu-search algorithm (**TS'**). The advantage of this algorithm is that no fine tuning is needed. This tuning becomes crucial in the modified simulated-annealing algorithm (**SA'**), where it is very difficult to find the best cooling schedule. We suspect that this might be the reason why this algorithm performs relatively poorly compared with the other competing algorithms. Interestingly, the relative performance of these algorithms (either in terms of *time* or *cost*) is not affected by the graph density or by the domain granularity.

References

[1] Alpert, C. J. and A. B. Kahn, "Recent Direction in Netlist Partitioning: A Survey", Integr., The VLSI J., 19, 1995, pp. 1-81.

[2] Battiti, R. and A. A. Bertossi, "Greedy, Prohibition, and Reactive Heuristics for Graph Partitioning", IEEE Trans. Comp., 48, 1999, pp. 361-385.

[3] Dutt, S., "New Faster Kernighan-Lin-type Graph-partitioning Algorithms", In *Proceedings IEEE/ACM Int'l Conf. CAD*, November 1993, pp. 370-377.

[4] Fjällström, P. –O., Algorithms for Graph Partitioning: A Survey. Linköping Electronic Articles in Computer and Information Science, 3(10), 1998.

[5] Garey, M. R. and D. S. Johnson, Computers and Intractability: A Guide to the Theory of Incompleteness, W. H. Freeman and Company, New York, 1979.

[6] Glover, F., E. Taillard, and D. de Werra, "A User's Guide to Tabu Search", Ann. Oper. Res., 41, 1993, pp. 3-28.

[7] Johnson, D. S., C. R. Aragon, L. A. McGeoch, and C. Schevon, "Optimization by Simulated Annealing: An Experimental Evaluation; Part 1, Graph Partitioning", Oper. Res., 37, 1989, pp. 865-892.

[8] Kadluczka, P. and K. Wala, "Tabu Search and Genetic Algorithms for the Generalized Graph Partitioning Problem", Cont. Cyb., 24, 1995, pp. 459-476.

[9] Kernighan, B. W., S. Lin, "An Efficient Heuristic Procedure for Partitioning Graph", Bell Sys. Tech. J., 49, 1970, 291-307.

[10] Kirkpatrick, S., S. D. Gelatt Jr., and M. P. Vecchi, "Optimization by Simulated Annealing", Science, 220, 1983, pp. 671-680.

[11] van Laarhoven, P. J. M. and E. H. L. Aarts, Simulated Annealing: Theory and Applications, Kluwer Academic Publishers, Dordrecht, 1989.

[12] Lagnese, E. and D. Thomas, "Architectural Partitioning for System Level Synthesis of Integrated Circuits", IEEE Trans. CAD Integr. Circ. Sys., 10, 1991, pp. 847-860.

[13] von Laszewski, G. (1991) "Intelligent Structural Operators for the k-way Graph Partitioning Problem", In *Proceedings 4th Int'l Conf. Gen. Algorithms*, 1991, pp. 45-52.

[14] Schloegel, K., G. Karypis, and V. Kumar, "Graph Partitioning for High Performance Scientific Simulations", In Dongarra, J. et al. (eds.), CRPC Parallel Computing Handbook, Morgan Kaufmann, 2000.

Bottleneck Perfect Domination on Some Classes of Graphs

William Chung-Kung Yen

Department of Graphic Communications and Technology,
Shih Hsin University, Taipei, Taiwan
email: ckyen001@ms7.hinet.net

Abstract

Suppose that $G(V, E, C)$ denotes a graph with vertex-set V and edge-set E, where each vertex v is associated with a real cost $C(v)$. This paper studies the Bottleneck Perfect Dominating Set problem (the BPDS problem) on G. For each subset Q of V, the bottleneck cost of Q is defined as $\max\{C(x) \mid x \in Q\}$. The goal is to find a perfect dominating set with the minimum bottleneck cost.

This paper first proves that the BPDS problem is NP-hard on planar-bipartite graphs. Second, the NP-hardness property on chordal graphs is shown and an $O(m)$ time greedy algorithm on split graphs is designed. Finally, a linear-time optimal algorithm on weighted interval graphs is proposed by the dynamic programming strategy.

Keywords: bottleneck cost, perfect dominating set, planar-bipartite graph, chordal graph v.s. split graph, interval graph

1. Introduction

Let $G(V, E, C)$ be a connected and undirected graph with n-vertex-set V and m-edge-set E, and each vertex v is associated with a real cost $C(v)$. The concept of *dominating sets* has natural and wide applications in many real situations such as resource allocations on computer networks [10, 11]. In various facilities locating problems, facilities will be allocated at some vertices. It is reasonable and natural to arrange the facilities so that each vertex with no facility is adjacent to at least one vertex with facility. Since placing a facility at different vertex costs differently, the basic objective is to identify a set of vertices at which to build facilities such that the *sum cost* is minimized. For dominating problems and their related problems, many previous works deal with this research issue [10, 11, 24]. In real world applications, another key issue is to minimize the *"most largest cost"* of building these facilities. It is important to keep the largest amount *as small as possible* for different investors. This type of cost is termed *bottleneck cost* herein. Some papers consider bottleneck measurements on some graph problems, e.g., the Bottleneck Traveling Salesman Problem [3, 18], the Bottleneck k-Supplier Problem [12], the Bottleneck Spanning Tree Problem and the Bottleneck Maximum Cardinality Matching Problem [5], and the Bottleneck

Graph Partition Problem [13], etc. This paper focuses on finding a perfect dominating set with the minimum bottleneck cost.

A *dominating set* Q of a graph $G(V, E)$ is a subset of V in which each vertex $v \in (V - Q)$ is adjacent to at least one vertex $u \in Q$. Many useful types of dominating sets have been proposed and studied, such as connected dominating sets (the subgraph induced by Q is connected), independent dominating sets (Q is independent, i.e., $(u, v) \notin E$, for all $u, v \in Q$), total dominating sets (no isolated vertex in Q), and perfect dominating sets (every vertex $u \in V - Q$ is adjacent to exactly one vertex in Q) [10, 11, 15, 23, 24]. Most of these previous researches are to identify a set D of certain type of dominating sets such that $\sum_{x \in D} C(x)$ is minimized. For any $H \subseteq V$, the *bottleneck cost*, denoted by $\beta(H)$, is defined as $\max_{x \in H}\{C(x)\}$. The problem studied in this paper is defined precisely as follows:

The Bottleneck Perfect Dominating Set problem (The BPDS problem): Given a graph $G(V, E, C)$, determine a perfect dominating set (PD set) D such that $\beta(D) \leq \beta(H)$, for all PD sets $H \neq D$.

In the weighted graph shown in Figure 1, the sets $\{b, e, f\}$ and $\{a, f\}$ are two PD sets. The set $\{b, e, f\}$ is a PD set with the minimum bottleneck cost which is equal to $\max\{W(b), W(e), W(f)\} = \max\{1, 1, 3\} = 3$.

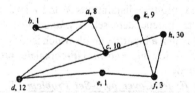

Fig. 1. A instance of the BPDS problem.

In [24], the significance and motivations of finding various dominating sets with minimum bottleneck costs have been addressed. We have proven that the BDS problem, the problem of finding a dominating with the minimum bottleneck cost, is $O(n\log n + m)$ time solvable on general graphs and $O(n)$ time solvable on weighted trees. Meanwhile, the BIDS problem (the Bottleneck Independent Dominating problem) has been proven to be NP-hard on planar graphs and an $O(n)$ time algorithm for the BIDS problem on weighted interval graphs has been proposed. In [26, 27], we have proven that the BIDS problem is NP-hard on chordal graphs and bipartite graphs, but linear-time solvable on weighted trees and polynomial-time solvable on weighted permutation graphs. In [25], we have shown that the BPDS problem is NP-hard on bipartite graphs and $O(n)$ time solvable on trees. In the rest of this paper, we first prove that the BPDS problem is NP-hard on planar-bipartite graphs. Then, an $O(n)$ time algorithm is proposed on weighted interval graphs. The strategy used is the dynamic programming strategy [1, 15, 17, 23, 24]. The lower bound of the BPDS problem is $O(n)$ since each vertex must be examined at least once in order to derive an optimal solution. Thus, our algorithm is time-optimal in worst case.

2. NP-hardness on Planar-Bipartite Graphs

A corresponding decision problem of the BPDS problem and one of its variants are introduced, respectively.

The Bottleneck Perfect Dominating Set decision problem (The BPDS decision problem): Given an undirected and connected graph $G(V, E, C)$ and a positive real constant η, determine whether a PD set D exists such that $\beta(D) \leq \eta$.

The Constrained BPDS decision problem (The CBPDS decision problem): Given an undirected and connected graph $G(V, E)$ and a subset V' of V, determine whether there exists a PD set D such that $D \subseteq (V - V')$.

The following lemma can be derived via setting V' $= \{v \mid C(v) \leq \eta\}$ and $\eta = \max\{C(v) \mid v \in (V - V')\}$, respectively.

Lemma 1: The BPDS decision problem is polynomially equivalent to the CBPDS decision problem.

This section examines the complexity of the BPDS problem on planar-bipartite graphs. A graph $G(V, E)$ is said to be *planar* if we can draw G in the plane so that the edges of G intersect only at end vertices [9]. In another, G is called a *bipartite graph*, denoted by $G(X \cup Y, E)$, if V can be partitioned into two disjoint sets X and Y such that both X and Y is an independent set. A *planar-bipartite graph* $G(X \cup Y, E)$ is just a bipartite graph which is also planar.

The following known NP-complete problem is used for reduction.

The Planar Exact Cover by 3-Set Problem (The Planar X3C Problem) [7]: Let $F = \{S_1, ..., S_p\}$ be a family of sets where each S_i is a 3-element subset of a set $X = \{x_1, ..., x_{3n}\}$. In addition, the bipartite graph $G_{X3C}(V_{X3C}, E_{X3C})$, where $V_{X3C} = X \cup F$ and $E_{X3C} = \{(x_i, S_j) \mid x_i \in S_j, 1 \leq i \leq 3n$ and $1 \leq j \leq p\}$, is planar. Does there exist a subfamily F' of F such that each element of X occurs in exactly one member of F'?

Lemma 2: The CBPDS decision problem is NP-complete on planar-bipartite graphs.

Proof. The tasking for showing that the CBPDS decision problem belongs to the NP class of problems can be achieved using the same technique in [24]. The following

will show that the Planar X3C problem can be polynomially reduced to the CBPDS decision problem on planar-bipartite graphs. Given an instance of the Planar X3C problem in which $F = \{S_1, ..., S_p\}$ and $X = \{x_1, ..., x_{3n}\}$, the instance of the corresponding CBPDS decision problem is merely the bipartite graph $G_{CBPDS}(V_{CBPDS}, E_{CBPDS})$, where $V_{CBPDS} = X \cup F$ and $E_{CBPDS} = \{(x_i, S_j) \mid x_i \in S_j, 1 \leq i \leq 3n$ and $1 \leq j \leq p\}$ and V'_{CBPDS} is just equal to the set X. It has been known that G_{CBPDS} is a planar-bipartite graph.

Now, it is easily verifiable that a subfamily F' of F such that each element of X occurs in exactly one member of F' iff F' is a PD set contained in $(V_{CBPDS} - V'_{CBPDS})$.

Based on the discussions so far, a perfect dominating set $F' \subseteq (V_{CBPDS} - V'_{CBPDS})$ exists in the planar-bipartite graph G_{CBPDS} iff there exists a subfamily F' of F such that each element of X occurs in exactly one member of F'. This implies that the CPDS decision problem is NP-complete on planar-bipartite graphs. □

Based upon Lemma 1 and Lemma 2, the NP-Completeness of the CBPDS decision problem implies the NP-Completeness of the BPDS decision problem. Consequence, the following main theorem holds.

Theorem 1: The BPDS problem is NP-hard on planar-bipartite graphs.

3. Complexities on Chordal Graphs and Split Graphs

This section will prove that the BPDS problem is NP-hard on chordal graphs. Given a graph $G(V, E)$, an edge is called a *chord* of a cycle if it connects two nonconsecutive vertices of the cycle. G is called a *chordal graph* [6] if every cycle with length greater than three has a chord. Also, a known NP-complete problem is introduced.

The Exact Cover problem (The EC problem) [7]: Given a family of $F = \{S_1, ..., S_p\}$ of sets where each S_i is a subset of a set $X = \{x_1, ..., x_q\}$, does there exist a subfamily of pairwise disjoint sets of F whose union is equal to X?

Lemma 3: The CBPDS decision problem is NP-complete on chordal graphs.

Proof. Checking that the CBPDS decision problem belongs to the class of NP problems can also be done using the similar reasoning in [24]. We now show that the EC problem can be polynomially reduced to the CBPDS decision problem on chordal graphs. Given an instance of the EC problem in which $F = \{S_1, ..., S_p\}$ and $X = \{x_1, ..., x_q\}$, a graph $G(V, E)$ is constructed by the following transformation rules.

$V = \{x_1, ..., x_q\} \cup \{S_1, ..., S_p\} \cup \{a_1, ..., a_p\}$ and
$E = \{(x_z, S_t) \mid x_z$ belongs to $S_t\} \cup \{(S_j, a_j) \mid j = 1, ..., p\}$
$\cup$

$\{(x_z, x_s) \mid$ for all $z \neq s\}$

Let $\Phi = \{v_1, v_2, v_3, v_4\}$ be any cycle of G. Either one of the following possibilities should occur. (1) All of

126

the four vertices in Φ belong to $\{x_1, ..., x_q\}$ (2) Two vertices in Φ belong to $\{x_1, ..., x_q\}$ and the other two vertices belong to $\{S_1, ..., S_p\}$. A chord must exist in these two cases since $\{x_1, ..., x_q\}$ forms a clique. Therefore, G is a chordal graph. It is easy to see that the time-complexity of the transformation procedure is polynomial.

Let $V' = X$. Then, $(V - V')$ corresponds to the set $\{S_1, ..., S_p\} \cup \{a_1, ..., a_p\}$. Suppose that K is a solution of the EC problem. Without a loss of generality, we can assume that $K = \{S_1, ..., S_\alpha\}$, $1 \leq \alpha \leq p$. Then, $S_z \cap S_t = \varnothing$, for all S_z and S_t in K. It implies that each x_h in X will be dominated by one vertex in K exactly. It is clear that a_j is only dominated by S_j, $j = 1, ..., \alpha$. This implies that $R = K \cup \{a_{\alpha+1}, ..., a_p\}$ must form a perfect dominating set.

Next, if R is a perfect dominating set and $R \subseteq (V - V')$, then each x_h in X must be dominated by exactly one vertex in R, denoted by $x^{(R)}_h$. This means that $x^{(R)}_h \in F$, for all h, and either $x^{(R)}_z \cap x^{(R)}_s = \varnothing$ or $x^{(R)}_z = x^{(R)}_s$, for all $z \neq s$. Therefore, $K = \cup_{1 \leq h \leq q}\{x^{(R)}_h\}$ is a solution of the EC Problem.

From the above discussions, a perfect dominating set $R \subseteq (V - V')$ exists in the chordal graph G iff there exists a subfamily of pairwise disjoint sets of F such that its union is equal to X. This implies that the CBPDS decision problem is NP-complete on chordal graphs. $\square$

Theorem 2: The BPDS problem is NP-hard on chordal graphs.

The next class of graph considered is the class of split graphs. A graph $G(V, E)$ is called a *split graph* [26] if V can be separated into two disjoint sets K and I such that K forms a clique and I is an independent set. Let $SG(V, E)$ denote a split graph with the vertex-set $V = K \cup I = \{k_1, ..., k_s\} \cup \{i_1, ..., i_t\}$. Denote that $\beta(SG) = \min\{\beta(R) \mid R$ is a PD set of $SG\}$.

Since K is a clique, at most one vertex in K can be included in any PD set. Let V^0 be any PD set. Either $K \cap V^0 = \{k_j\}$, for some k_j, or $K \cap V^0 = \varnothing$. The following two new problems are introduced and Formula (3.1) can be obtained.
(P0) Compute $\beta_K(SG) = \min\{\beta(R) \mid K \cap R = \{k_j\}$, for some k_j, and R is an PD set$\}$.
(P1) Compute $\delta_{K'}(SG) = \min\{\beta(R) \mid K \cap R = \varnothing$ and R is an PD set$\}$.

$$\delta(SG) = \min\{\delta_K(SG), \delta_{K'}(SG)\} \text{ -- (3.1)}$$

Let us first consider Problem (P0). For any vertex k_j in K, define Neighbor_$I(k_j) = \{i_q \in I \mid (i_q, k_j) \in E\}$. The set Neighbor_$K(i_q)$ can be defined similarly, for any vertex $i_q \in I$. The following property holds.

Property 1. For any optimal solution V^* of Problem (P0), it must contain all vertices belonging to I – Neighbor_$I(k_j)$, when $k_j \in V^*$.

Property 1 indicates that an optimal solution of Problem (P0) can be found by examining each vertex k_j in K, all vertices in I, as well as each edge once. Therefore, the time-complexity needed is $O(m)$.

Lemma 4: Problem (P0) can be solved in $O(m)$ time.

Now, turn to Problem (P1). If R is a proper subset of I, then the vertices in $I - R$ are not dominated by R. Thus, if R is an PD set of SG and $K \cap R = \varnothing$, then R must be equal to I. So, in order to solve Problem (P1), the only task is to check whether every vertex in K is adjacent to exact one vertex in I and the time-complexity is only $O(n)$.

Lemma 5: Problem (P1) can be solved in $O(n)$ time.

Lemma 4 and Lemma 5 imply that the total time-complexity is $O(m) + O(n) = O(m)$.

Theorem 3: The BPDS problem can be solve in $O(m)$ time on weighted split graphs.

4. An $O(n)$ Time Algorithm on Weighted Interval Graphs

This section resolves the BPDS problem on weighted interval graphs. A graph $G(V, E)$ is called an *interval graph* if its vertices can be put into a one-to-one correspondence with a set F of intervals on the real line R so that two vertices are adjacent in G iff their corresponding intervals have a nonempty intersection [8].

This section uses a tree structure, called clique path, to represent any interval graph [2, 6, 22]. Indeed, interval graphs is a subclass of the class of chord graphs. Chordal graphs are intersection graphs if the sets are restricted to subtrees of a tree [6]. In [6], Gavril also demonstrated that the intersection models could be selected so that the nodes of the tree are always the *maximal cliques* of the original graphs. Each vertex then corresponds to the subtree comprised of exactly those cliques to which it belongs. Such an intersection model is termed a *clique tree* of the graph. If the intersection model is further restricted such that the clique tree itself is a path, called a *clique path*, it defines the class of interval graphs [4, 14]. A clique tree of a chordal graph can be constructed in linear-time [21].

Suppose that the clique path of the input interval graph G has z cliques, $C_1, ..., C_z$, where C_j denotes the jth clique from left to right in the clique path. Define $C_i < C_l$ iff C_i stands to the left of C_j. C_{j+1} is said to the *immediate successor* of C_j in this ordering scheme for any $1 \leq j < z$, and we use the notation $IS(C_j)$ to denote the immediate successor of C_j hereafter. The *index number* of C_j, denoted by $INDEX(C_j)$, is just the number j. Each interval v can belong to more than one clique, say $C_{v_1}, ..., C_{v_p}$, $p > 1$.

Property 2 [24]: For any interval v, if $v \in C_{v_1}, ..., C_{v_p}$, $p > 1$, then these p cliques form a subpath in the clique path.

Assume that $<LC(v), RC(v)>$ denotes the leftmost and the rightmost cliques in the subpath, respectively. If v only belongs to some clique C_v, then $<LC(v), RC(v)> = <C_v, C_v>$. For any two vertices u and v, we define $u \leq v$ iff $LC(u) < LC(v)$ or ($LC(u) = LC(v)$ and $RC(u) \leq RC(v)$). Without a loss of generality, the vertices are assumed to be sorted according to this order in the rest of the paper.

Efficient algorithms exist for finding dominating sets [19], path covering [20], and Hamiltonian circuits [16] on interval graphs. This section will design an $O(n)$ time algorithm for solving the BPDS problem on weighted interval graphs.

Now, for any vertex v, v is called a *black vertex* if v must be included in any optimal solution; and v is called a *white vertex* if v must be excluded in any optimal solution. For any pair s, h in which $1 \leq s < h \leq z$, $C_{s,h}$ represents the subgraph induced by the vertices belonging to C_s, C_{s+1}, ..., C_{h-1}, and C_h hereafter. Let $\delta(C_{s,h})$ be the bottleneck cost of all optimal solutions on $C_{s,h}$, i.e., $\delta(C_{s,h}) = \min\{\beta(D) \mid D$ is PD set of $C_{s,h}\}$. The major objective of the BPDS problem is to compute $\delta(C_{1,z})$.

Since each node of the clique path corresponds to a maximal clique of the original interval graph, there must exist exactly one black vertex in each clique C_s, $1 \leq s \leq z$.
Property 3: For each $v \in C_s$, if v is black, then all the following properties hold. (1) All vertices $x \in ((C_s \cup ... \cup RC(v)) - \{v\})$ must be white. (2) Let y be the vertex with the largest index value in $RC(v)$. Then, all vertices $u \in (IS(RC(v)) \cup ... \cup RC(y))$ must also be white.

Lemma 6: Suppose that there exists a black vertex v in any clique C_s. Let y be the vertex with the largest index value in $RC(v)$. If there exists some $u \in RC(y)$ such that $RC(u) = RC(y)$, then no PD set exists on the original input graph.

Let us first consider the node C_1. Suppose that v^* is the only black vertex in C_1. Let y be the vertex with the largest index value in $RC(v)$. Assume that C_t is the immediate successor of $RC(y)$. Let $H = RC(y) \cap C_t$ and $B = RC(y) - H$. Based on Property 2, in $C_{t,z}$, all vertices in H must be white. The original BIDS problem on $C_{t,z}$ with the additional constraint that all of the vertices in H must be white is first recursively solved. This problem can be formulated in general as follows:
(P_R) Compute $\delta_{R'}(C_{t,z}) = \min\{\beta(D) \mid D$ is PD set of $C_{t,z}$ and $x \notin D$, for all $x \in R$, where $R \subset C_t\}$.

After solving the problem $(P_{R'})$ on $C_{t,z}$ in which $t =$ INDEX(IS(RC(v^*))) and R is given to be RC(y) $\cap$ IS(RC(y)), for each $v^* \in C_1$ and y be the vertex with the largest index value in RC(v^*). The following formulas can be derived.
$$\delta(C_{1,z}) = \min_{v^* \in C_1}\{\max\{W(v^*), \delta_{R'}(C_{t,z})\}\}, \text{ where}$$

for each $v^* \in C_1$, $t =$ INDEX(IS(RC(v^*))) and R is given to be RC(y) $\cap$ IS(RC(y)), for each $v^* \in C_1$ and y is the vertex with the largest index value in RC(v^*) -- (4.1)

The task left is to solve the problem $(P_{R'})$ on $C_{t,\beta}$, $t > 1$, for some given $R \subset C_t$ in which each vertex in R must be white. Using the similar reasoning again, the following formula can then be obtained.
$$\delta_{R'}(C_{t,z}) = \min_{u^* \in (C_t - R)}\{\max\{W(u^*), \delta_Q(C_{q,z})\}\},$$

where for each $u^* \in (C_t - R)$, $q =$ INDEX(IS(RC(u^*))) and

Q is given to be RC(y) $\cap$ IS(RC(y)), for each $u^* \in (C_t - R)$ and y is the vertex with the largest index value in RC(u^*) -- (4.2)

The boundary conditions of the problem occur when the interval graph only contains the maximal clique C_z. Verifying the correctness of the following two formulas is a simple matter.
$$\delta(C_z) = \min_{v^* \in C_z}\{W(u^*)\} \text{ -- (4.3)}$$
$$\delta_{R'}(C_z) = \min_{u^* \in (C_z - R)}\{W(u^*)\}, \text{ for any nonempty}$$

set $R \subset C_z$ -- (4.4)

Based upon the computational results so far, an algorithm can be easily designed for identifying a PD set with the minimum bottleneck cost on a weighted interval graphs by the dynamic programming strategy [1, 17]. The time-complexity of this algorithm is analyzed as follows:

Let $T(P_{R'}, C_{t,z})$ denote the time-complexity for solving the problem $(P_{R'})$ on $C_{t,z}$ and $T(\text{BIDS}, C_{1,z})$ denote the time-complexity of the proposed algorithm. Summarizing the results till now, the following formulas can be easily derived.
$$T(\text{BIDS}, C_{1,z}) = \sum_{v^* \in C_1}(T(R', C_{t,z}) + 1),$$

where for each $v^* \in C_1$, $t =$ INDEX(IS(RC(v^*))) and R is given to be RC(y) $\cap$ IS(RC(y)), for each $v^* \in C_1$ and y is the vertex with the largest index value in RC(v^*) -- (4.5)
$$T(P_{R'}, C_{t,z}) = \sum_{u^* \in (C_t - R)}(T(Q, C_{y,z}) + 1), \text{ where}$$

for each $u^* \in (C_t - R)$, $q =$ INDEX(IS(RC(u^*))) and Q is given to be RC(y) $\cap$ IS(RC(y)), for each $u^* \in (C_t - R)$ and y is the vertex with the largest index value in RC(u^*) -- (4.6)

Formula (4.3) and (4.4) can derive the following formula.
$$T(\text{BPDS}, C_z) = T(P_{R'}, C_z) = O(|C_z|) \text{ -- (4.7)}$$

It is easy to ascertain that each vertex will be examined in constant time. This implies that $T(\text{BIDS}, C_{1,z}) = O(n)$.
Theorem 4: The BPDS problem can be solved in $O(n)$ time on weighted interval graphs.

5. The Conclusions

This paper addresses the Bottleneck Perfect Dominating Set problem on graphs with real costs on vertices. It first proves that the time-complexity on planar-bipartite graphs is NP-hard. Then, the NP-hardness property on chordal graphs and $O(m)$ time greedy algorithm on split graphs are shown. Finally, an $O(n)$ algorithm for the problem on weighted interval graphs is proposed by the dynamic programming strategy.

The followings are possible worthy research directions in the future.
1. Solving the problem on other classes of graphs, such as cactuses and block graphs.

2. Finding out the properties and relationships between bottleneck problems and summation problems on graphs.

3. Extending the cost measurements for considering communication costs simultaneously.

Acknowledgement

This research was supported by National Science Council, Taiwan, R.O.C., under contract number NSC-89-2213-E-159-001.

References

[1] R. E. Bellman and S. E. Dreyfus, Applied Dynamic Programming, Princeton University Press, Princeton, N. J., 1962.

[2] P. Buneman, "A Characterization on Rigid Circuit Graphs", *Discrete Mathematics*, Vol. 9, 1974, pp. 205-212.

[3] G. Carpaneto, S. Martello, and P. Toth, "An Algorithm for the Bottleneck Traveling Salesman Problem", *Operations Research*, Vol. 32, 1984, pp. 380-389.

[4] D. R. Fulkerson and O. A. Gross, "Incidence Matrices and Interval Graphs", *Pacific Journal of Mathematics*, Vol. 15, 1965, pp. 835-855.

[5] H. N. Gabow and R. E. Tarjan, "Algorithms for Two Bottleneck Optimization Problems", *Journal of Algorithms*, Vol. 9, 1988, pp. 411-417.

[6] F. Gavril, "The Intersection Graphs of Subtrees in Tree Are Exactly the Chordal Graphs", *Journal of Combinatorial Theory*, Vol. 16, 1974, pp. 47-56.

[7] M. R. Garey and David S. Johnson, Computers and Intractability: A Guide to the Theory of NP-Completeness, Bell Laboratories, Murray Hill, Freeman & Co., N. J., 1978.

[8] M. C. Golumbic, Algorithmic Graph Theory and Perfect Graphs, Academic Press, New Work, 1980.

[9] R. Gould, Graph Theory, The Benjamin/Cummings Publishing Company, Inc., Menlo Park, California, 1988.

[10] T. W. Haynes, S. T. Hedetniemi, and P. J. Salter, Fundamentals of Dominations in Graphs, Marcel Dekker, Inc., Yew York, Basel, Hong Kong, 1998.

[11] T. W. Haynes, S. T. Hedetniemi, and P. J. Salter, Dominations in Graphs: Advanced Topics, Marcel Dekker, Inc., Yew York, Basel, Hong Kong, 1998.

[12] D. S. Hochbaum and D. B. Shmoys, "A Unified Approach to Approximation Algorithms for Bottleneck Problems", *Journal of the ACM*, Vol. 33, 1986, pp. 533-550.

[13] D. S. Hochbaun and A. Pathria, "The Bottleneck Graph Partition Problem", *Networks*, Vol. 28, 1996, pp. 221-225.

[14] C. G. Kekkerkerker and J. CH. Boland, "Representation of a Finite Graph by a Set of Intervals on the Real Line", *Fundament Mathematicae*, Vol. 51, 1962, pp. 45-64.

[15] Y. C. Liu and M. S. Chang, Polynomial Algorithms for Various Weighted Perfect Domination Problems on Some Classes of Graphs, Master Theses, Dept. of Computer Sciences and Information Engineering, National Chung Cheng University, 1993.

[16] G. K. Manacher, T. A. Mankus and C. J. Smith, "An Optimum $\Theta(n\log n)$ Algorithm for Finding a Canonical Hamiltonian Path and a Canonical Hamiltonian Circuit in a Set of Intervals", *Information Processing Letters*, Vol. 35, 1990, pp. 205-211.

[17] G. L. Nemhauser, Introduction to Dynamic Programming, Wiley, New York, 1966.

[18] R. G. Parker and R. L. Rardin, "Guaranteed Performance Heuristics for the Bottleneck Traveling Salesperson Problem", *Operations Research Letters*, Vol. 2, 1984, pp. 269-272.

[19] G. Ramalingam and C. P. Rangan, "A Unified Approach to Domination Problems on Interval Graphs", *Information Processing Letters*, Vol. 27, 1988, pp. 271-274.

[20] A. S. Rao and C. P. Rangan, "Linear Algorithm for Optimal Path Cover Problem on Interval Graphs", *Information Processing Letters*, Vol. 35, 1990, pp. 149-153.

[21] D. J. Rose, R. E. Tarjan and G. S. Lueker, "Algorithmic Aspects of Vertex Elimination on Graphs", *SIAM Journal on Computing*, Vol. 5, 1976, pp. 266-283.

[22] J. R. Walter, Representation of Rigid Cycle Graphs, Ph.D. Theses, Wayne State University, 1972.

[23] C. C. Yen and R. C. T. Lee, "The Weighted Perfect Domination Problem", *Information Processing Letters*, Vol. 35, 1990, pp. 295-299.

[24] W. C-K Yen, "Bottleneck Domination and Bottleneck Independent Domination on Graphs", *Journal of Information Science and Engineering*, Vol. 18: March 2002, pp. 311-331.

[25] W. C-K Yen, "Domination and Perfect Domination under Bottleneck Cost Minimization with Extensions", in *Proceedings of National Computer Symposium*, 2001, pp. A135-A146.

[26] W. C. K. Yen, "Bottleneck Independent Dominating on Some Classes of Graphs", in *Proceedings of International Computer Symposium, Workshop on Algorithms and Theory of Computation*, 2000, pp. 1-8.

[27] W. C. K. Yen and C. Y. Tang, "The Bottleneck Independent Dominating on Permutation Graphs", in *Proceedings of International Computer Symposium*, Vol. I, 1992, pp. 455-462.

Concept of and Experiments on Combining Compression with Encryption

Mehmet Emin Dalkilic
International Computer Institute,
Ege University,
35100 Bornova/Izmir, Turkey
dalkilic@bornova.ege.edu.tr

Ebru Celikel
International Computer Institute,
Ege University,
35100 Bornova/Izmir, Turkey
celikel@bornova.ege.edu.tr

Abstract

Compression reduces storage and communication costs by decreasing data size while encryption provides security by making data unintelligible to everyone but the key holder. We present a novel concept that combines these distinct research areas of Computer Science to sum up the benefits of the two. This work adds a security dimension to compression. We also present the results of some experiments on the way of efficiently implementing the concept.

1. Introduction

Both Compression and Cryptography had their theoretical roots in Information Theory. Nevertheless, these two research areas followed distinct paths. Maybe it is time to join both of these areas of Information Science to obtain the mutual advantage of the two.

Compression removes redundancy in the data and thus reduces its size considerably. That, in turn, leads to communication and storage cost savings. On the other hand, Cryptography provides security and privacy for the data. If both services are required, one after the other is applied; usually compression followed by encryption. (Since good encryption tends to remove redundancy completely, it is useless to compress encrypted data.)

Both compression and cryptography are also related to Coding Theory. Many compression techniques such as Huffman's Algorithm, Arithmetic Coding, Interval or Recency Rank Encoding [1] generate and use codes shorter than the original encoding (usually ASCII). The basic building block which is relied upon by most cryptosystems use substitution where a key dependent code table is employed. Further information can be found in the following references: Compression [1, 2] and Encryption [3, 4].

In this paper we introduce a novel concept that combines compression with encryption. Furthermore, the framework presents a tradeoff to be explored: One may obtain better compression by giving up security to some extend; or, obtain improved security by tolerating a smaller compression ratio.

2. Compression with Encryption

The only *unconditionally secure cryptosystem*[1] is the one-time pad where a Vigenère cipher with a random key equal to the length of the plaintext is used. Therefore, any cryptosystem either with a key shorter than the length of the plaintext or a key with any statistical relationship to the plaintext can be broken assuming that enough ciphertext together with the necessary computing resources and time are available. This fact is the driving force behind the compression with encryption concept.

The following example[2] is a Vigenère cipher with a repeating key and it uses Table 1 as the encoding matrix.

```
Plaintext:  we~are~discovered~save~yourselves
Key:        operationoperationoperationoperat
Ciphertext: JTDRRXHRVFRSLEJMRMFPZV~QWHDFTPLEK
```

Each plaintext letter is coded by the key letter beneath. For example, using key letter o, the plaintext letter w is encrypted to ciphertext letter J because that is the letter at the intersection of the row labeled o and the column labeled w. Both the ciphertext and the key are sent to the receiver where he/she can easily decrypt J into w given the key letter o using Table 1. Even when the key is not available the plaintext can be obtained using well known cryptanalytical methods [5].

---

[1] The ciphertext generated by the cryptosystem does not contain the minimum necessary information to determine uniquely the corresponding plaintext, no matter how much ciphertext is available [4]
[2] Example plaintext is from [4]. Space is represented by ~. Uppercase letters are used for Ciphertext while plaintext and key sequences are presented in lowercase letters.

Table 1. Plain Vigenère Encoding Matrix.

	a	b	c	d	e	f	g	h	i	j	k	l	m	n	o	p	q	r	s	t	u	v	w	x	y	z	~
a	A	B	C	D	E	F	G	H	I	J	K	L	M	N	O	P	Q	R	S	T	U	V	W	X	Y	Z	~
b	B	C	D	E	F	G	H	I	J	K	L	M	N	O	P	Q	R	S	T	U	V	W	X	Y	Z	~	A
c	C	D	E	F	G	H	I	J	K	L	M	N	O	P	Q	R	S	T	U	V	W	X	Y	Z	~	A	B
d	D	E	F	G	H	I	J	K	L	M	N	O	P	Q	R	S	T	U	V	W	X	Y	Z	~	A	B	C
e	E	F	G	H	I	J	K	L	M	N	O	P	Q	R	S	T	U	V	W	X	Y	Z	~	A	B	C	D
f	F	G	H	I	J	K	L	M	N	O	P	Q	R	S	T	U	V	W	X	Y	Z	~	A	B	C	D	E
g	G	H	I	J	K	L	M	N	O	P	Q	R	S	T	U	V	W	X	Y	Z	~	A	B	C	D	E	F
h	H	I	J	K	L	M	N	O	P	Q	R	S	T	U	V	W	X	Y	Z	~	A	B	C	D	E	F	G
i	I	J	K	L	M	N	O	P	Q	R	S	T	U	V	W	X	Y	Z	~	A	B	C	D	E	F	G	H
j	J	K	L	M	N	O	P	Q	R	S	T	U	V	W	X	Y	Z	~	A	B	C	D	E	F	G	H	I
k	K	L	M	N	O	P	Q	R	S	T	U	V	W	X	Y	Z	~	A	B	C	D	E	F	G	H	I	J
l	L	M	N	O	P	Q	R	S	T	U	V	W	X	Y	Z	~	A	B	C	D	E	F	G	H	I	J	K
m	M	N	O	P	Q	R	S	T	U	V	W	X	Y	Z	~	A	B	C	D	E	F	G	H	I	J	K	L
n	N	O	P	Q	R	S	T	U	V	W	X	Y	Z	~	A	B	C	D	E	F	G	H	I	J	K	L	M
o	O	P	Q	R	S	T	U	V	W	X	Y	Z	~	A	B	C	D	E	F	G	H	I	J	K	L	M	N
p	P	Q	R	S	T	U	V	W	X	Y	Z	~	A	B	C	D	E	F	G	H	I	J	K	L	M	N	O
q	Q	R	S	T	U	V	W	X	Y	Z	~	A	B	C	D	E	F	G	H	I	J	K	L	M	N	O	P
r	R	S	T	U	V	W	X	Y	Z	~	A	B	C	D	E	F	G	H	I	J	K	L	M	N	O	P	Q
s	S	T	U	V	W	X	Y	Z	~	A	B	C	D	E	F	G	H	I	J	K	L	M	N	O	P	Q	R
t	T	U	V	W	X	Y	Z	~	A	B	C	D	E	F	G	H	I	J	K	L	M	N	O	P	Q	R	S
u	U	V	W	X	Y	Z	~	A	B	C	D	E	F	G	H	I	J	K	L	M	N	O	P	Q	R	S	T
v	V	W	X	Y	Z	~	A	B	C	D	E	F	G	H	I	J	K	L	M	N	O	P	Q	R	S	T	U
w	W	X	Y	Z	~	A	B	C	D	E	F	G	H	I	J	K	L	M	N	O	P	Q	R	S	T	U	V
x	X	Y	Z	~	A	B	C	D	E	F	G	H	I	J	K	L	M	N	O	P	Q	R	S	T	U	V	W
y	Y	Z	~	A	B	C	D	E	F	G	H	I	J	K	L	M	N	O	P	Q	R	S	T	U	V	W	X
z	Z	~	A	B	C	D	E	F	G	H	I	J	K	L	M	N	O	P	Q	R	S	T	U	V	W	X	Y
~	~	A	B	C	D	E	F	G	H	I	J	K	L	M	N	O	P	Q	R	S	T	U	V	W	X	Y	Z

Let us rearrange the plaintext "we~are~discovered ~save~yourselves" as shown.

Plaintext: w~r~icvrdsv~orevs
Key: eaedsoee~aeyuslex
Ciphertext: ~~VC~QZVCSZXHIPZO

If the key is known, decryption is done using Table 1. If the key is not known, even a message this short can be solved with the aid of the n-gram (n-letter) statistics of the source language since only a small percentage of n-grams are used in the text and that percentage goes down with increasing n. For example, about half of the 2-grams occur in English text and that ratio shrinks to less than 5% for 4-grams and less than 1% for 5-grams [6].

In the ciphertext the first letter ~ corresponds to one of the digrams in: {~a, zb, yc, xd, we, vf, ug, th, si, rj, qk, pl, om, nn, mo, lp, kq, jr, is, ht, gu, fv, ew, dx, cy, bz, a~}.

Most of these digrams can easily be eliminated because they are not word starters. The most probable ones are {we, ug, th, si, pl, om, mo, is, gu, ew}.

The next cipher letter is also ~. Thus, the likely (meaningful or could lead to a meaningful sequence) 4-letter sequences may be marked as {we~a, thug, this, sinn, simo, omis, moth, is~a, gulp}.

For the third letter v candidates are {va, ub, tc, sd, re, qf, pg, oh, ni, mj, lk, kl, jm, in, ho, gp, fq, er, ds, ct, bu, av, ~w, zx, yy, xz, w~}. Plausible sequences are {we~are, tugh~w, this~w, mother, is~ava, is~aho, gulp~w}.

The choices "we~are" and "mother" are much more likely than the rest. The point here is that only a very small subset of the $27^3 = 19,683$ choices decrypt into meaningful words and the receiver could decrypt the ciphertext. This is cryptanalysis and we do not expect the receiver of a compressed text to do cryptanalysis because it is time consuming and error-prone.

What if an auxiliary message is received telling us which alternative is the correct one at every step of the decryption? This would make things easier and in fact it would turn the decryption process into a decoding process. Using an auxiliary message (i.e., help string) to turn decryption into decoding is one of the central ideas to the compression with encryption concept. There are two more central ideas to this concept. The first is to use a decoding table (Vigenère) which is the basis of encryption for compression; thereby, opening up the possibility to provide security within compression. The second is to use one part (out of n parts) of the plaintext as the key to encrypt the remaining parts of the plaintext; thereby, cutting the ciphertext size to $1/n^{th}$ although some of these savings will be offset by the help string cost increase.

2.1. Definitions

Encoding. Given a plaintext[3] P from a source alphabet A, and n > 1 (Note that $|X|$ denotes the cardinality of X):

• Divide the plaintext into n disjoint parts.

• Create an encryption table E of size $|A|^n$ where each entry is a symbol from a ciphertext symbol set S.

• Encrypt the (n −1) parts using the last part as the key.

• Create a help string, H for decoding process.

• (optional) Compress ciphertext and help string, $C \parallel H$ using a conventional compression algorithm e.g., Huffman, Lempel-Ziv, GZIP, PPM, etc.

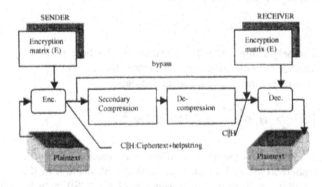

Figure 1. Compression with Encryption Diagram

Decoding. Given a ciphertext C of $|P|/n$ symbols from a ciphertext symbol set S, the encryption table E (or a key to recreate it), n, the help string H, and the optional conventional compression algorithm:

• If compression applied during encoding, decompress.

• Decrypt the ciphertext C using the encryption table E and the help string H.

In our example, $|P| = 33$, source and ciphertext alphabets are the English Alphabet plus the space (~)

---
[3] We describe the concept for text compression. It easily extends to other data types like images, etc. by simply extending the input symbol set.

symbol, i.e., $|A|=|S|=27$, $n=2$, and the Encryption matrix (Table 1) contains $27^2=729$ entries. A simple help string for this example would be 5,1,5,4,... because the correct decoding for the first ciphertext letter ~ is the 5th choice (e.g., we), for the second letter, coincidentally again ~, is the 1st choice (e.g., ~a), and so on.

An alert reader would observe that the sequence 5,1,5,4... is in fact an encoding of the key eaed....; this is only one of the many help string encoding alternatives. Another choice would be 23,27,18,27,... i.e., w~r~... that correspond to an encoding of the plaintext. In Section 3 we will see that help string does not have to be either an encoding of the plaintext or the key. It is simply an encoding of an identifier of the correct choice.

2.2. Analysis

Compression. Let $m=|P|/n$ and C_i is the number of bits necessary to encode the ith ciphertext symbol The ciphertext size $|C|$ is:

$$|C| = \sum_{i=1}^{m} C_i \le \sum_{i=1}^{m} \lceil \log_2|S| \rceil = m \times \lceil \log_2|S| \rceil \quad (1)$$

At worst, $\lceil \log_2|S| \rceil$ bits are needed to encode a ciphertext symbol. On one extreme, $|S| = 1$ (i.e., all n-grams are encoded with the same symbol), and $|C| = 0$. On the other extreme, $|S|=|A|^n$ (i.e., each n-gram encoded uniquely), and $|C| = |P| \times \lceil \log_2|A| \rceil$. Thus,

$$0 \le |C| \le |P| \times \lceil \log_2|A| \rceil \quad (2)$$

The help string size $|H|$ is given in Eq. 3 where H_i is the number of bits necessary to encode the correct choice number for the ith n-gram in the plaintext.

$$|H| = \sum_{i=1}^{m} H_i \le \sum_{i=1}^{m} \lceil \log_2|S_i| \rceil \le m \times \lceil \log_2 (|A|^n /|S|) \rceil \quad (3)$$

In Eq. 3, S_i is the number of n-grams represented by the ciphertext symbol which represents the ith n-gram in the plaintext with sum of all distinct S_j ($1 \le j \le |S|$) must be equal to the number of the entries in E that is $|A|^n$.

$$\sum_{j=1}^{|S|} S_j = |A|^n \quad (4)$$

At worst, $\lceil \log_2 (|A|^n /|S|) \rceil$ bits are needed to encode the correct one among $|A|^n/|S|$ possibilities. On one extreme, $|S| = 1$ (i.e., all n-grams are encoded by the same symbol), and $|H| = |P| \times \lceil \log_2|A| \rceil$. On the other extreme, $|S|=|A|^n$ (i.e., each n-gram encoded uniquely), and $|H|=0$. That is,

$$0 \le |H| \le |P| \times \lceil \log_2|A| \rceil \quad (5)$$

As expected, the best case for the ciphertext size is the worst case for the help string size and vice versa. Since each plaintext symbol can be encoded using at most $\lceil \log_2|A| \rceil$ bits, the following equation gives the upper bound for the sum of the ciphertext and the help string.

$$|C| + |H| \le |P| \times \lceil \log_2|A| \rceil \quad (6)$$

Security. For small n values (e.g., 2,3,4), if the encryption matrix is public and the help string coding is static, system provides only weak security. However, even this "weak" encryption would stop over 90% of the intruders since most of them are not capable of passing this barrier. With larger n, the search space for each n-gram ($|A|^{n-1}$) gets very large (e.g., for n = 6 and $|A|=27$, it is 14,348,907) stopping more people. Nevertheless, the security is only moderate because the statistics is out there to work with.

Stronger security can be achieved through two modifications.

• Let a shared key between the sender and the receiver determine the Encryption matrix. This is easy to implement for instance using a pseudo-random number generator (PRNG). The key determines the seed to the generator, and the pseudo-random sequence generated determines the Encryption matrix layout. Even though, both the PRNG and the algorithm to create the Encryption matrix given a PRNG sequence are public, no one can create the Encryption matrix without knowing the seed to the PRNG i.e., the key. If Encryption matrix is secret, the key space for a single n-gram increases to $|A|^n$.

• Use multiple iterations through the Encryption matrix. Multiple rounds increase the strength of the cryptosystem. With each iteration, the language (n-gram) statistics dissipate and cryptanalysis gets more and more difficult while the help string stays unaffected.

3. Experiments

The purpose of these experiments is to answer some questions on the way to efficiently implement the compression with encryption concept. Here, we will look for answers to the questions as how compressible the ciphertext, C, is as compared to the plaintext P; what the impacts of different Encryption matrices are; and what the influence of various Help String encoding schemes is.

For the experiments, we have used two text files (bib and book1) from the Calgary Corpus that is available at *ftp.cpcs.ucalgary.ca/pub/projects/text.compression.corpus* and a number of conventional compression algorithms including Arithmetic Encoding (ARTH) [7], Huffman Coding (HUFF) [1,2,3], Lempel-Ziv (LZ77) [8], PPM* [9], Burrows-Wheeler (BWMN) [10]. We have confined the experiments to n=2.

132

3.1 Ciphertext vs. Plaintext Compressibility

For given test files, bib and book1, we generated the ciphertext using Table 1. Then, we applied the compression algorithms both to the plaintext and ciphertext files. Because encryption removes much of the redundancy, ciphertext files are compressed to much poorer rates as compared to plaintext files. The last row of Table 2 shows this difference (Δ). In terms of compressing encrypted text there is not too much difference between the algorithms; roughly speaking all compress around 4 bits per character except LZ77 which performs worse. This means that any fast conventional compression algorithm can be employed as the Secondary Compression Algorithm in our framework.

Table 2. Compressibility of Ciphertext as Compared to Plaintext under Different Algorithms

	ARTH		HUFF		LZ77		PPM*		BWMN	
	bib	book1	bib	book1	bib	book1	bib	book1	bib	book1
P	4.15	4.09	4.15	4.12	3.19	3.73	1.91	2.16	2.16	2.58
C	4.72	4.61	4.71	4.63	5.05	6.00	3.58	4.27	3.83	4.46
Δ	-13,73%	-12,71%	-13,49%	-12,38%	-58,31%	-60,86%	-87,43%	-97,69%	-77,31%	-72,87%

3.2 Hard vs. Easy Encryption Matrices

Suppose we fix $|S|$ at $|A|$ i.e. we will use each ciphertext symbol for $|A|^n/|S| = |A|$ (n=2) entries in the Encryption table, E. If we deliberately assign one symbol to the most frequently used $|A|$ n-grams, then assign the next symbol to the next most frequently used $|A|$ n-grams, and so on, symbols assigned to frequently used n-grams will occur with a much higher ratio than the average. Thus, the average entropy of the ciphertext decreases, allowing it to be compressed better. If we choose to make Encryption matrix as part of the key (i.e., keep it secret), this Encryption matrix is "easy" to break; because, high frequency ciphertext symbols represent high-frequency n-grams. However, if we assign ciphertext symbols randomly to the entries of the Encryption matrix, frequency data dissipates in the ciphertext and cryptanalysis becomes more difficult.

We have created an easy (to break) Encryption matrix which we call *DiFreq* short for digram frequency and a hard Encryption matrix, *Random* (each symbol is randomly assigned to $|A|$ digrams). We compressed the sample texts for both matrices using each algorithm (see Table 3). As expected, *DiFreq* provided improvement on the compression rate for all algorithms averaging about 16%. Results for *Random* matrix are almost the same as the results given in Table 2 for the plain Vigenère matrix on encrypted text. In fact, the plain Vigenère is a *Random* Encryption matrix.

To estimate the (uncompressed) help string costs for both encryption matrices we employed a context dependent encoding using a precompiled ordered 4-gram list for English. Suppose we will encode the $(i+1)^{th}$ digram of the input text, and its ciphertext symbol is ∂. We use the previous (i.e., i^{th}) digram as the "context". That is, we first determine the number of 4-grams, x, beginning with the ith digram and encrypted by ∂. Then, we encode the index of the $(i+1)^{th}$ digram, y, among these 4-grams using $\lceil \log_2 x \rceil$ bits. Note that, $\lceil \log_2 27 \rceil = 5$ bits are added to the estimation if the searched 4-gram is not found.

For the ongoing example, under the *Random(DiFreq)* encryption matrix, the 3rd digram re is encrypted by W(A) and the 2nd digram ~a is used as its context. Since there are 7(16) 4-grams starting with ~a as well as encrypted by W(A) and re's index is 3(10) among them, and 011 (1010) would be the binary help string entry.

The help string bpc (bits per character) values for bib and book1 files are 2.91 and 2.56 for *Random* and 3.58 and 3.42 for *DiFreq* encryption matrices, respectively. Using these values, total output sizes (C ‖ H) are computed and given in Table 3 for both *Random* and *DiFreq* matrices. It is seen that compression rates around 3.5 bpc are achieved for PPM* and BWMN.

Table 3. Performances of Random and Digram Frequency (DiFreq) Encryption Matrices

		ARTH		HUFF		LZ77		PPM*		BWMN	
		bib	book1	bib	book1	bib	book1	bib	book1	bib	book1
Random	C	4.70	4.56	4.70	4.58	5.02	5.92	3.56	4.22	3.82	4.42
	C‖H	3.81	3.56	3.81	3.57	3.97	4.24	3.24	3.39	3.37	3.49
DiFreq	C	3.88	3.5	3.88	3.52	4.38	4.86	3.18	3.68	3.50	3.84
	C‖H	3.73	3.46	3.73	3.47	3.98	4.14	3.38	3.55	3.54	3.63
Δ(%)	C	17,45%	23,25%	17,45%	23,14%	12,75%	17,91%	10,67%	12,80%	8,38%	13,12%
	C‖H	1,97%	2,81%	1,97%	2,80%	-0,38%	2,36%	-4,48%	-4,72%	-5,20%	-4,01%

The last row on Table 3 shows that the total output sizes do not vary much for *Random* or *DiFreq* encryption matrices. That is, use of a Random type matrix which provides additional security, does not adversely affect the compression quality.

3.3. Flexible Encryption Matrices

Here, we experiment with some "flexible" Encryption matrix layouts that exploit the digram statistics of the source language. Our purpose is to demonstrate that with an intelligent Encryption matrix layout, we can achieve better overall compression. We use the digram statistics (partially shown in Table 4) compiled by G. Dalkilic [6].

Table 4. Ordered Digram Frequencies (%) for English.

1	e~	3.48	5	d~	2.21	9	an	1.56	13	er	1.24	17	~o	1.13
2	~t	2.85	6	~a	2.08	10	n~	1.48	14	~i	1.18	18	~w	1.06
3	th	2.65	7	s~	1.96	11	~s	1.43	15	nd	1.16	19	r~	1.05
4	he	2.24	8	t~	1.78	12	in	1.31	16	~h	1.13	20	y~	1.03

In this part of the study, the essential idea is to represent high frequency digrams with as much distinct ciphertext symbols as possible. For instance, if we represent the most frequent digram e~ (~ stands for space) with a distinct ciphertext symbol, then there is no need to add a help symbol for that digram. Similarly, if we assign one cipher symbol to two digrams say er and ~i, then any occurrence of that symbol needs only a single help string bit. If we assign one cipher symbol to 4 different digrams, those digrams need two help string bits to be resolved (i.e., uniquely decoded). In general, if a symbol represents K digrams we need $\lceil \log_2 K \rceil$ bits to uniquely decode it.

Table 5. Help String Cost Estimates for two Flexible Encryption Matrix Designs

		Flexible Coding 1					Flexible Coding 2	
i	|Si|	|Ei|	Freq.%	cost (bpc)	i	|Si|	|Ei|	Freq.%	cost (bpc)
1	12	12	25,03	0	1	26	26	39,33	0
2	10	20	18,94	0,1894	2	30	60	31,64	0,3164
3	10	40	22,01	0,4402	3	30	120	21,96	0,4392
4	10	80	20,16	0,6048	4	20	160	6,40	0,1920
5	10	160	12,28	0,4912	5	20	320	0,67	0,0268
6	10	320	1,58	0,0790	6	2	64	1,23E-06	6,15E-08
7	2	128	2,99E-05	1,79E-06					
Σ	64	760	100,00	1,80	Σ	128	750	100,00	0,97

Table 5 shows two Encryption matrix designs using the principle outlined above. $|S_i|$ shows the number of symbols where each represents 2^{i-1} distinct digrams. For instance, in the first design, each of the 12 symbols is assigned to a unique digram, while the next 10 to two digrams, and the following 10 to four digrams each, and so on. $|E_i|$ is the total number of digrams represented by symbols in $|S_i|$. Column labeled *Freq* shows the sum of digram frequencies represented by symbols in $|S_i|$. Finally, the column *cost (bpc)* shows the help string cost estimation due to the encoding of each group of digrams. For instance, estimated cost due to the use of the 3rd group in Flex-2 (digrams 87 through 206) is 0,4392 bpc. Overall, the Flex-2 design is expected to require 46% less help string bits than that of the Flex-1 design. However, since Flex-2 uses twice as many cipher symbols (128 to 64), its ciphertext compression rate will be worse than that of the first design.

As shown in Table 6, the Flex-2 design has inferior ciphertext compression rates. However, the help string savings easily offset for that inferiority and Flex-2 gives better overall compression rates well under 3 bpc for PPM* and BWMN. Note that for bib and book1, uncompressed help string costs are 2.14 and 1.76 bpc for Flex-1 and 1.20 and 0.94 for Flex-2 respectively, matching well with our expectation of 46% improvement.

Table 6. Performances of Flexible Encryption Matrices

		ARTH		HUFF		LZ77		PPM*		BWMN	
		bib	book1	bib	book1	bib	book1	bib	book1	bib	book1
Flex-1	C	5,76	5,70	5,76	5,70	5,42	6,54	3,84	4,34	4,16	4,72
	C||H	3,95	3,73	3,95	3,73	3,78	4,15	2,99	3,05	3,15	3,24
Flex-2	C	6,64	6,50	6,66	6,52	5,56	6,76	4,06	4,44	4,44	4,94
	C||H	3,92	3,72	3,93	3,73	3,38	3,85	2,63	2,69	2,82	2,94

It is fair to note that the best conventional compression algorithms perform close to 2 bpc for text files. Our compression with encryption approach with better Encryption matrices and encoding schemes can be competitive. Furthermore, it provides security which is a unique feature for a compression algorithm.

4. Conclusion

We have introduced a novel concept that combines compression with encryption adding a security dimension to the compression. Static conventional compression is a special case of the Compression with Encryption concept where all n-grams are encoded with distinct symbols. Moreover, the formulation provides alternatives where one may adjust parameters for better compression or better security.

We have carried out some experiments to better understand the features of this new concept. Although the concept is new, and there are more to be addressed for an efficient implementation, the results that we have presented are very encouraging. Future work will concentrate on larger *n* values (n > 2) in addition to devising better Encryption matrix layouts and more efficient help string encoding/decoding schemes.

References

[1] Hankerson, D., G.A. Harris, and P.D. Johnson, Introduction to Information Theory and Data Compression. CRC Press. (1998).

[2] Witten, I.H., A. Moffat, and T.C. Bell, Managing Gigabytes: Compressing and Indexing Documents and Images, 2nd ed. Morgan & Kaufmann. (1999)

[3] Stinson, D. R., Cryptography Theory and Practice. CRC Press. (1995).

[4] Stallings, W., Cryptography and Network Security: Principles and Practice. 2nd ed. Prentice Hall. (1998).

[5] Dalkilic, M.E., and C. Gungor, "An Interactive Cryptanalysis Algorithm for Vigenère Cipher" *Lect.Notes Comput. Sci.* Vol. 1909 (2000), pp. 341-351.

[6] Dalkilic, G., Statistical Properties of Contemporary Turkish and a Text Compression Application. (In Turkish) Master Thesis. Ege Univ., Turkey (2001).

[7] Nelson, M., "Arithmetic Coding + Statistical Modeling = Data Compression Part 1 - Arithmetic Coding" *Dr. Dobb's Journal.* (1991).

[8] Ziv, J. and A. Lempel, "A Universal Algorithm for Sequential Data Compression" *IEEE Trans. On Information Theory.* Vol. 23 No. 3 (1977), pp. 337-343.

[9] Cleary, J.G. and I.H. Witten, "Data Compression Using Adaptive Coding and Partial String Matching" *IEEE Trans. On Communications.* Vol.32 No.4 (1984), pp. 396-402.

[10] Burrows, M. and D.J. Wheeler, "A Block-sorting Lossless Data Compression Algorithm" *Digital Systems Research Center (SRC) Report.* (1994).

Session 2–3
Computer Graphics

Honeycomb Subdivision

Ergun Akleman*and Vinod Srinivasan
Visualization Sciences Program,
Texas A&M University

Abstract

In this paper, we introduce a new subdivision scheme which we call honeycomb subdivision. After one iteration of the scheme each vertex becomes exactly 3-valent and with consecutive applications regular regions strongly resembles a honeycomb. This scheme can be considered as a dual for triangle schemes. The major advantage of the new scheme is that it creates a natural looking mesh structure.

1. Introduction

Although subdivision surfaces were introduced more than 20 years ago by Doo, Sabin, Catmull and Clark[5, 8], they were ignored by the computer graphics industry until they were used in 1998 Academy Award-winning short film *"Geri's Game"* by Pixar [7, 20]. Since then subdivision surfaces have become increasingly popular in the computer graphics and modeling industry. This is not a surprise since subdivision methods solve the fundamental problem of tensor product parametric surfaces [12, 13] without sacrificing the speed of shape computation [5, 8, 11, 9, 18, 7]. Unlike tensor product surfaces, with subdivision surfaces, control meshes do not have to have a regular rectangular structure. Subdivision algorithms can smooth any 2-manifold (or 2-manifold with boundary) mesh [20, 21].

Subdivision surfaces assume that users first provide an irregular 2-manifold control mesh, M_0. By applying a set of subdivision rules, a sequence of finer and finer 2-manifold meshes $M_1, M_2, \ldots, M_n, \ldots$ are created. These meshes eventually converge to a "smooth" limit surface M_∞ [10].

One way to classify subdivision schemes is based on what kind of regularity emerges with the application of the scheme [16]. In other words, the pattern of regular regions can be used to characterize the scheme. Based on regular regions, existing subdivision schemes can be classified into three major categories:

- Corner cutting schemes such as Doo–Sabin [8, 3]: after one iteration all vertices [1] become 4-valent and the number of non-4-sided faces remains invariant after the first refinement.

- Vertex insertion schemes such as Catmull-Clark [5]: after one iteration all faces become 4-sided and the number of non-4-valent vertices is constant after the first refinement.

- Triangular schemes such as $\sqrt{3}$-subdivision [10, 11]: after one iteration all faces become 3-sided and the number of non-6-valent vertices is constant after the first refinement.

Notice that in this list vertex insertion and corner cutting schemes are dual, i.e., one of them makes every face 4-sided, the other one makes every vertex 4-valent. There is currently no dual for triangular schemes. The scheme we present in this paper provides the missing dual for triangular schemes:

- Honeycomb schemes: after one iteration all vertices become 3-valent and the number of non-6-sided faces is constant after first refinement.

We call such schemes honeycomb since the resulting meshes strongly resemble honeycombs, which our dictionary defines as (1) A structure of hexagonal, thin-walled cells constructed from beeswax by honeybees to hold honey and larvae, (2) Something resembling this structure in configuration or pattern.

Figure 1 shows five iterations of our honeycomb scheme. In this example, the control mesh M_0 is a dodecahedron, M_1 is a truncated icosahedron or soccer ball [19]. More interestingly, the mesh strucures from M_2 to M_5 can be found in virus structures [17]. As seen in this example, the most important property of the new scheme is that the resulting mesh structures strongly resemble natural structures such as cells or honeycombs. It is also interesting to note that their structure looks similar to Voronoi diagrams.

---

*Corresponding Author: Address: 216 Langford Center, College Station, Texas 77843-3137. email: ergun@viz.tamu.edu. phone: +(979) 845-6599. fax: +(979) 845-4491.

[1] Vertices and faces are also called vertets and facets in order to avoid confusion with the vertices and faces of a solid model [16].

The remainder of this paper is organized as follows. In the next section, we provide refinement rules for our general honeycomb scheme. In Section 3, we introduce the coefficients of our honeycomb algorithm that are used to create the meshes shown in Figure 1. Section 4 explains how to implement a remeshing algorithm for honeycomb subdivision. Section 5 discusses implementation and results. Finally, our conclusion is given in Section 6.

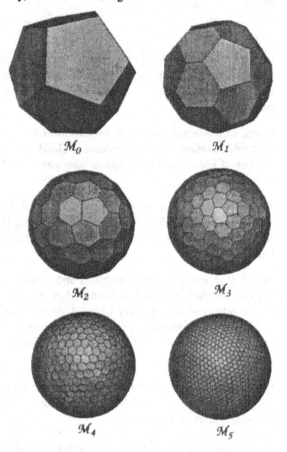

Figure 1. Five iterations of our honeycomb scheme over a dodecahedron.

2. Refinement Rules for Honeycomb Schemes

We give the refinement rules for a general honeycomb algorithm as follows (The algorithm is also illustrated in Figure 2, where the black vertices and edges are new and constitute the new mesh, and the gray vertices and edges are in the old mesh and are removed by the algorithm.):

- **Step 1** : For each edge e_n of a face $f = \{e_0, e_1, \ldots, e_n, \ldots, e_{N-1}\}$ of the mesh, create a new

vertex v'_n (See Figure 2.B) (we assume that the vertex and edge indices are given in the order of a face traversing). Compute the position of each new vertex as a linear combination of the old vertex positions $\{v_0, v_1, \ldots, v_n, \ldots, v_{N-1}\}$. Note that since v'_n's correspond to edges instead of vertices, in order to derive the coefficients of a honeycomb scheme, it will be useful to use the following linear equation:

$$v'_n = \sum_{m=0}^{N-1} a_{n,m} \left((1-t)v_m + tv_{(m+1) \ (\text{mod} \ N)} \right) \quad (1)$$

where the $a_{n,m}$'s are real coefficients, N is the valence of the face and t is a real number between 0 and 1.

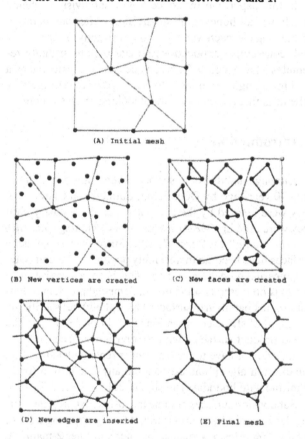

Figure 2. Illustration of honeycomb process.

Remark 1. Note that $(1-t)v_m + tv_{(m+1) \ (\text{mod} \ N)}$ is a point on the edge e_m. In our examples we generally use $t = 0.5$.

- **Step 2** : For each face, create a new face by connecting all the new points that have been generated by that face (See Figure 2.C);

- **Step 3** : For each edge of the mesh, connect the two new points that have been generated for that edge (See

138

Figure 2.D);

- **Step 4** : Remove all old vertices and edges (See Figure 2.E).

Remark 2. Let F_n, E_n and V_n denote the number of faces, edges and vertices created by n_{th} iteration. It is straightforward to show that $F_n = F_{n-1} + V_{n-1}$, $E_n = 3E_{n-1}$ and $V_n = 2E_{n-1}$. Based on these equations, it follows that

$$\lim_{n \to \infty} \frac{F_n}{F_{n-1}} \longrightarrow 3.$$

In other words, this honeycomb subdivision scheme increases the number of faces 3-fold at each iteration. Therefore, regular haneycomb scheme can also be called a $\sqrt{3}$ honeycomb algorithm [10].

Remark 3. The support region of our honeycomb scheme (the region that is influenced by a given control vertex [16]) has a fractal boundary, a Koch island [15].

Remark 4. It is difficult to identify the precision set of any honeycomb scheme (comparing the scheme with a parameteric surface) since the regular regions of the honeycomb scheme do not correspond correspond known to any parameterization scheme such as the tensor product or box-spline parameterizations.

3. The Coefficients of Our Honeycomb Algorithm

Like any subdivision scheme relying on approximation, in honeycomb subdivision the coefficients $a_{n,m}$ in step 1 in the above algorithm must satisfy the following conditions:

1. $a_{n,m} \geq 0$ for all n and m and

2. for all n $\sum_{m=0}^{N-1} a_{n,m} = 1.$

These conditions guarantee convergence of the algorithm and provide C^0 continuity and affine invariance properties.

The coefficients of our scheme are inspired by the coefficients of the Doo-Sabin scheme. Let vertex indices in a face be given in rotation order. We use the following formula to compute the coefficients $a_{n,m}$ which are needed to compute the position of v'_n.

$$a_{n,m} = \begin{cases} a & \text{if } n = m \\ \beta \dfrac{1-a}{3N-5} & \text{otherwise} \end{cases} \quad (2)$$

where

$$\beta = 3 + 2\cos\left(\frac{2(n-m)\pi}{N}\right).$$

In these equations, the parameter a in equation (2) is provided by the users and is as a tension parameter [4]. Note that the value of a controls the speed of convergence. We suggest making a a decreasing function of N, i.e, for higher-sided faces (larger values of N) the algorithm must converge faster. In all the examples in this paper we use the following function for a

$$a = 0.45 + \frac{1.25}{N}.$$

It is easy to verify that in this scheme, each coefficient $a_{n,m}$ is always greater than zero if $1 > a > 0$, and the coefficients do add up to 1. By using Fourier analysis, similar to Doo-Sabin's approach, we can show that the new scheme also has three distinct but complex eigenvalues[2]. The complex part comes from the phase shift introduced by the term $v_m + v_{(m+1) \pmod{()N}}$. Absolute values of the other eigenvectors will be smaller than one if $a < 1$, regardless of the value of N. Similar to Doo-Sabin's scheme, only one eigenvector corresponds to the eigenvalue 1, two eigenvectors correspond to the second largest (in absolute value) eigenvalue and the rest of the eigenvectors correspond to the smallest eigenvalue. Because of this property our scheme provides tangent plane continuity.

4. Implementation and Results

The remeshing algorithm explained in the section 2 has been implemented in a C++ program. We applied the honeycomb algorithm to the various control shapes. Figure 3 shows examples of applying our honeycomb scheme. The images at the left in Figure 3 show the control meshes and images at the right show the mesh after four iterations of our honeycomb algorithm. It is interesting to note that the honeycomb algorithm creates a very natural looking mesh structure. It therefore can be used after other subdivision schemes to create natural looking meshes.

The honeycomb algorithm can create lateral artifacts [16]. Figure 4.(B) shows such an artifact. Although the hexagonal prism control mesh shown in Figure 4.(A) is a convex shape, we see smooth but periodic lumps and bumps across the height as shown in Figure 4.(B). These periodic bumps are created during the first iteration hexagonalization and smoothed after one more iteration. We call this periodic bumping *"Bricklayers' Problem"* since a straight boundary cannot be obtained with hexagonal tiles. Bricklayers solve this problem quite simply: they cut hexagonal

---

[2]We want to point out that it is possible to derive coefficients that give real eigenvalues. In fact, we tested various sets of coefficients that gave real eigenvalues. However, the visual quality of the shapes turned out better with complex eigenvalues. Based on this information, we deduce that it is better to use complex eigenvalues because of the rotation inherent in the scheme.

tiles along the borders. To implement their solution: (1) convert the faces of the control mesh into hexagons, (2) cut hexagonal faces at the boundaries as bricklayers. As shown in Figure 4.(D), when we use a control shape shown in Figure 4.(C) periodic bumps disappear.

Figure 3. Examples of honeycomb subdivision. The images at the left show the control meshes and images at the right show the mesh structures after four iterations of our honeycomb algorithm.

5. Discussion, Conclusion and Future Work

In this paper, we introduced a new subdivision algorithm. The algorithm provides a tension parameter to control the shape of subdivided surface. We implemented a honeycomb algorithm, over the DLFL structure. We observed that honeycomb schemes can create natural looking mesh structures.

The main problem with honeycomb schemes are the lateral artifacts. Our current solution requires user intervention which may not be desirable for many applications. We

expect that this problem can be solved with non-stationary planarization schemes. We are currently working on the development of such a scheme.

Another problem we face is that it is very difficult to identify the precision set for any given honeycomb scheme. Unfortunately, we still do not have a promising approach to solve this problem.

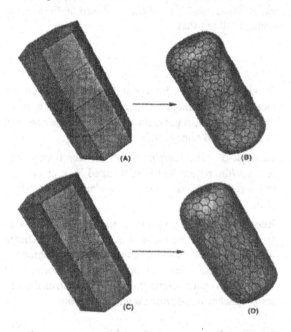

Figure 4. Lateral artifacts and bricklayer's solution.

6. Acknowledgments

We are very grateful to the Malcolm Sabin who gave us encouragement when we first identified the honeycomb remeshing scheme. We are thankful to Gary Greenfield for his helpful suggestions. This work was partially funded by the Research Council of College of Architecture and the Interdisciplinary Program of Texas A&M University .

References

[1] E. Akleman and J. Chen, "Guaranteeing the 2-Manifold Property for meshes with Doubly Linked Face List", *International Journal of Shape Modeling* Volume 5, No 2, pp. 149-177.

[2] E. Akleman, J. Chen, and V. Srinivasan, "A New Paradigm for Changing Topology During Subdivision Modeling," *Pacific Graphics 2000*, October 2000, pp. 192-201.

[3] E. Akleman, J. Chen, F. Eryoldas and V. Srinivasan, "Handle and Hole Improvement with a New Corner Cutting Scheme with Tension," *Shape Modeling 2001*, May 2001, pp. 183-192.

[4] R. H. Bartels, J. C. Beatty, and B. A. Barsky, *An Introduction to Splines for use in Computer Graphics and Geometric Modeling*, Morgan Kaufmann Publishers, Los Altos, CA, 1987.

[5] E. Catmull and J. Clark, "Recursively Generated B-spline Surfaces on Arbitrary Topological Meshes", *Computer Aided Design*, No. 10, September 1978, pp. 350-355.

[6] J. Chen, "Algorithmic Graph Embeddings", *Theoretical Computer Science*, No. 181, 1997, pp. 247-266.

[7] T. DeRose. M. Kass and T. Truong, "Subdivision Surfaces in Character Animation", *Computer Graphics*, No. 32, August 1998, pp. 85-94.

[8] D. Doo and M. Sabin, "Behavior of Recursive Subdivision Surfaces Near Extraordinary Points", *Computer Aided Design*, No. 10, September 1978, pp. 356-360.

[9] M. Halstead, M. Kass, and T. DeRose, "Efficient, fair interpolation using Catmull-Clark surfaces", *Computer Graphics*, No. 27, August 1993, pp. 35-44.

[10] Kobbelt L., "$\sqrt{3}$-Subdivision", *Computer Graphics*, No. 34, August 2000, pp. 103-112.

[11] C. Loop, "Smooth Subdivision Surfaces Based on Triangles", Master's Thesis, Department of Mathematics, University of Utah, 1987.

[12] C. Loop and T. DeRose, "Generalized B-spline surfaces with arbitrary topology", *Computer Graphics*, No. 24, August 1991, pp. 101-165.

[13] C. Loop, "Smooth spline surfaces over irregular meshes", *Computer Graphics*, No. 28, August 1994, pp. 303-310.

[14] M. Mantyla, *An Introduction to Solid Modeling*, Computer Science Press, Rockville, Ma., 1988.

[15] B. Mandelbrot, *The Fractal Geometry of Nature*, W. H. Freeman and Co., New York, 1980.

[16] M. Sabin, "Subdivision: Tutorial Notes", *Shape Modeling International 2001, Tutorial*, May 2000.

[17] I. Stewart, *Game, Set and Math: Enigmas and Conundrums*, Penguin Books, London, 1991.

[18] T. W. Sederberg, D. Sewell, and M. Sabin, "Non-Uniform recursive Subdivision Surfaces", *Computer Graphics*, No. 32, August 1998, pp. 387-394.

[19] R. Williams, *The Geometrical Foundation of Natural Structures*, Dover Publications, Inc., 1972.

[20] D. Zorin and P. Schröder, co-editors, *Subdivision for Modeling and Animation*, ACM SIGGRAPH'99 Course Notes no. 37, August, 1999.

[21] D. Zorin and P. Schröder, editor, *Subdivision for Modeling and Animation*, ACM SIGGRAPH'2000 Course Notes no. 23, July, 2000.

A New Image Based Lighting Method:
Practical Shadow-Based Light Reconstruction

Jaemin Lee and Ergun Akleman*
Visualization Sciences Program
Texas A&M University

Abstract

In this paper we present a practical image based lighting method. Our method is based on a simple and easily constructible device: a square plate with a cylindrical stick. We have developed a user-guided system to approximately recover illumination information (i.e. orientations, colors, and intensities of light sources) from a photograph of this device. Our approach also helps to recover surface colors of real objects based on reconstructed lighting information.

1. Motivation

The compositing, which can be defined as the integration of computer-generated images (CG) and live-action photographs, has been an essential part of movie making. Currently, there exist a number of large special effect companies specialized mainly in compositing. For a succesful compositing it is crucial to seamlessly integrate real and CG components. It is well known that such a seamless integration requires solving a set of extremely difficult problems. Most of these problems are related to recovering the following real world information: **1.** Illumination information to simulate the same lighting environment for both CG and real objects, **2.** Camera positions and parameters, **3.** Shapes, material properties, and motion of real objects. The special effect companies solve these problems by employing a large number of computer graphics experts and mathematicians. Since most small special effect firms can not afford to employ large number of computer graphics experts and mathematicians, for such small companies there is a need for simple and effective methods to recover the real world information.

In this paper, we present a image based lighting method. Our method does not require any specific expertise in computer graphics or mathematics. The usability of our method was tested in a graduate level compositing course. Based on our method each student was able to seamlessly integrate

CG characters into complicated real scenes. Figure 1 shows a frame from a composited animation created by one student. Based on this experience, we claim that our method can easily be used even by very small special effect firms and individuals.

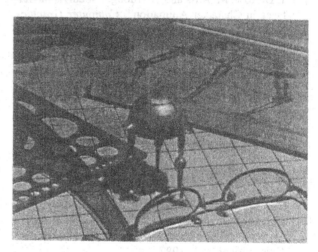

Figure 1. : A frame from a composited animation by Han Lei.

2. Introduction and Related Work

Image based techniques have recently been developed to achieve solutions to the problems addressed in the previous section. These techniques include camera calibration, image based lighting, and image based modeling. Among these techniques, we focuce on image based lighting that is used to recover illumination information from photographs of the real world. There are three major image based lighting approaches: **1.** Fisheye lens: Uses fisheye lense photographs that give a 180 degree field of view [9]. **2.** Gazing ball: Uses a photograph of a mirrored ball placed for catching the reflected view on its surface [1, 12]. (This method is generally used by special effect companies.) **2.** Shadow based: Uses shadows in the photographs [7, 8, 9].

*Corresponding Author: Address: 216 Langford Center, College Station, Texas 77843-3137. email: ergun@viz.tamu.edu. phone: +(409) 845-6599.

Our method we present is shadow based. Shadow based methods have been proven to be reliable in recovering illumination information [7, 8, 9]. Shadow irradiance contains illuminant information such as intensities and orientations of light sources [11, 6].

Despite their power, existing shadow based methods are not very useful for practical applications. There are two major problems with these methods. **1.** For any given photograph, basic shapes and material properties of real objects have to be reconstructed by the users. **2.** The illumination information is computed by solving a large matrix. Solution of such a large matrix may be computationally expensive .

The main advantages of our method over previous shadow based approaches are the followings: **1.** We use photographs of a simple device that can easily be constructed. Since the shape of the device is simple, it is easy to create its CG model. Moreover we can use the very same CG model for different projects, because it is the only object that our method requires to retrieve illumination information. **2.** We observed that only a few characteristic pixels are sufficient to recover illumination information. The rest of the pixels in the image is redundant. We have developed a user-assisted software to choose the characteristic pixels. Using these characteristic pixels we can drastically reduce the size of the matrix to be inverted. **3.** Parameters of the shaders can be adjusted to create the same surface colors of objects.

The limitations of our method can be summarized as follows: **1.**The illumination information recovered by the proposed method does not include indirect illumination such as reflections from adjacent surfaces in a scene. **2.** Initial intensities of lights from our software can be too strong to use them without readjustment. These high intensities are caused by physical inaccuracies in widely used lighting and shading models in computer graphics. This paper also presents solutions to these limitations without sacrificing quality and practicality of our method.

3. Methodology

To provide a simple and practical image based lighting method, we first simplify the complexity of illumination by classifying illumination information into three categories: **1.** Key illumination: It represents main lighting sources in a scene (key lights). Key lights are the lights that produce visible shadows on floor surfaces. **2.** Direct illumination: It represents all the lights that do not create visible shadows. It also includes reflections coming from environment except adjacent surfaces. These lights are often called fill lights in computer graphics and movie industry. **3.** Indirect illumination: It includes reflections from adjacent surface.

In this work, we propose to recover both key and direct illumination from photographs of a simple device that is

shown in Figure 2. This device consists of a wooden plate with a cylindrical stick in the center. Using color values of the pixels corresponding to the surface of the plate it is possible to derive a set of linear equations to estimate key and direct illumination as follows:

$$A.L = C \qquad (1)$$

where A is a matrix whose coefficients are computed from the visibility of an incoming light source, L is a vector that includes the unknown values of light intensities for given set of light positions, and C is a vector that includes the color value of selected surface points [9].

Solving the equation 1 can be computationally difficult if the number of selected surface points are extremely large. For instance, the plate surface Figure 2 consists of approximately 75,000 pixels. Therefore, if we consider the entire region of this white plate, it will be difficult to solve the equation 1. Fortunately, most of these pixels are redundant and their number can easily be reduced.

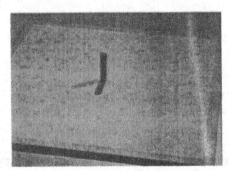

Figure 2. A photograph of the device under studio lighting.

To simplify the problem we only consider two types of regions on the plate[1]. **1.** Shadows cast by the stick on the painted white surface and **2.** the rest of the white surface of the plate. Notice that the colors in each one of these regions are almost constant in most cases. Thus, a few number of samples from each of shadow regions and the rest of the plate is enough to recover the lighting information. By using samples from only these particular regions, the size of the matrix A drastically reduces, and it becomes very easy to solve the equation 1. We further observe that **1.** key illumination can be recovered only from shadow colors cast by the stick and **2.** direct illumination can be recovered from the color of the rest of the plate.

---

[1]As seen in Figure 2, there are small blue squares painted on the white surface of our geometric model. We use these squares to identify a camera orientation relative to the device. They are not be used in collecting color samples.

In order to collect the samples (or in other words to choose characteristic pixels), we use a user-assisted approach. In our approach, the users select the ends of the shadows to compute the orientations, colors and intensities of key lights. We collect one color sample for each shadow and get one key light for each distinct shadow region. An additional color sample is collected from anywhere on the unshaded white surface to compute direct illumination, i.e. the intensity and color values of fill lights.

The orientation of a key light is identified based on a surface point selected in the end of a shadow for a color sample as shown in Figure 3. This surface point is used to create a line passing through both the surface point and the top of the stick. Then, an intersection point between the line and an imaginary hemisphere over the model is defined as the location of a key light. With this system, the distance of the key light can be adjusted by changing the size of the dome without affecting its direction.

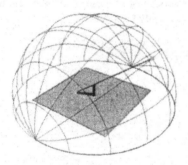

Figure 3. Computing the orientation of a key light from shadow positions.

Initial lighting information directly computed by solving the linear equation based on the color samples may not always work. This is because shader models that are used in 3D modeling and animation systems are generally crude approximations of the real physical behaviors. Our solution to work around this problem is to adjust colors of all the lights in a scene according to the ratios of pixel values on the white surfaces in a rendered image and a photograph. This process can be performed iteratively until the both color values are close enough. In addition to the intensity adjustment, fill lights need to be improved further for better results. Since our method does not include indirect illumination caused by adjacent surface reflectances, we add another set of lights to the scene on the ground level. These lights simulate indirect light rays bouncing off from the adjacent surfaces. Then, the overall intensity of those lights is adjusted based on a sample photograph.

Under a reconstructed lighting environment, we can also recover material colors of real objects assuming that the recovered illumination is the same as real one in the photo-

graph. In general we can define colors only in relative ways based on lighting environments, for instance white in daylight might look yellowish in incandescent lights. Therefore, if colors of synthetic objects need to be matched with real ones in a photograph, we have to find a common factor first, which affects color rendition under a specific lighting condition. This common factor is found from a reconstructed lighting condition with an arbitrary surface color, then it is used for color matching according to the following linear model. $c_p = a.c_o$

where, c_o is an unknown color value before being illuminated by the current lights, a is an illumination factor of the current lights, and c_p is a color after being illuminated by the current lights.

4. Procedure

We have developed a C++ program that be called *lightRecon* to compute locations and intensities of light sources based on pixel values selected by users from a given photograph. We have a N x N size nonsingular matrix from the data, and find its solution through matrix inversion using elementary operation. We also use a commercial software, namely Maya, to recover camera information by matching a virtual scene with a camera view from live footage. The virtual scene contains a CG model of our physical device and light sources that take lighting data from lightRecon to illuminate the scene. We also use Maya to render the scene with a recovered illumination information.

The overall process of our method consists of six steps.

1. Field record: This step consists of five stages: **1.1.** Survey data: It is to record measurements of a real scene, such as lighting condition, surface information of objects in the scene, camera height and angle, dimension of the device, distance between camera and the device, film format and size, lens size, and exposure information. **1.2.** Photograph of the real scene: This is an image without any reference objects in a scene. We use this photograph to composite with CG objects as final outputs. **1.3.** Photograph of a gazing ball: This is an image with a gazing ball. We use this photograph to have an additional information about environment. **1.4.** Photograph of the device: An image of the device is used to obtain pixel values of the white surface of the device as illumination data. And it also helps us to set up a camera view based on the picture. **1.5.** Photograph of material samples: We use this picture to find proper parameters of our shaders to match colors of synthetic and real objects. The Figures 4, 5 and 6 shows the images that are needed for a field record.

No shadows should be cast on the white surface of the device except ones from the cylindrical stick in the center of the plate. Multiple exposures are recommended to be able to choose ideal pictures.

2. Camera parameter reconstruction: We build a 3D replica of a real scene based on the survey data using a 3D application. A virtual model of the device is used to find a camera orientation. Note that the blue squares on the white surface of the device is designed to help us to identify the orientation of a camera.

Figure 4. An example of background.

3. Illumination reconstruction: Compute lighting information by using lightRecon. Our software allows to select pixels, constructs a matrix from selected pixel values and computes orientations and intensities of lights by using this matrix. T

4. Illumination adjustment: To improve initial light intensities, which are computed by lightRecon, we readjust them based on pixel values of both a rendered image and a background photograph. The overall process of this stage as follows: **4.1.** Render the virtual model of the device with initial light intensities. **4.2.** Open both the rendered image and the background photograph in any image prossing software and collect a pixel value from each image. **4.3.** Find a ratio of each color of two selected pixels. **4.4.** Multiply the initial intensities by the ratios to compute new intensities of the light sources. **4.5.** Render the scene with new illumination information. Go to 4.1 until the ratio values approach near to one.

5. Material colors: Parameters of shader colors for synthetic objects are estimated from the photographs of material samples taken in a real scene. The overall process of this stage is the following: **5.1.** Render a scene with synthetic objects using shader colors that are chosen from the photographs of material samples. **5.2.** Open the rendered image in a image processing program, then collect color values of the synthetic objects. We need these color values including initial shader colors as data in order to find an unknown factor value of the linear equation as we introduced in the methodology. This factor represents a lighting environment of the real scene, which affects the rendition of the material samples. **5.3.** Estimate an unknown factor of the linear equation with the given data, then find new parameters of

the shader colors by applying the obtained factor values and the material colors in the photographs to the same equation. **5.4.** Rerender the same scene with the updated shader colors. If necessary, conduct the process iteratively until you get right colors.

Photograph of a gazing ball

Photograph of our device

Material samples

Figure 5. An example of field record based on the backgound image in the Figure 4.

5. Conclusion

Image based ligting is essential for realistic compositing. Although many image based ligting methods have been introduced, they require a substantial amount of computer graphics experience and mathematical knowledge. In this work, we present a simple method to overcome this disadvantage with existing techniques.

We tested our method in a graduate level compositing course. Based on our method each student was able to seamlessly integrate CG characters into complicated real scenes. Based on this experience, we claim that our method can easily be used even by small firms and individuals.

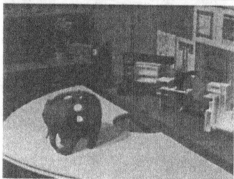

Figure 6. Two examples of compositing based the information given in Figure 5.

References

[1] P. E. Debevec, "Rendering Synthetic Objects into Real Scenes: Bridging Traditional and Image-based Graphics with Global Illumination and High Dynamic Range Photography", *Proc. SIGGRAPH 98*, pp. 189-198, July, 1998.

[2] A. Fournier, A. Gunawan and C. Romanzin, " Common Illumination between Real and Computer Generated Scenes", *Proc. Graphics Interface '93*, pp. 254-262, 1993.

[3] B. K. P. Horn, "Obtaining shape from shading information", Chapter 4, *The Psychlogy of Computer Vision*, McGraw-Hill Book Co., New York, N. Y., 1975.

[4] B. K. P. Horn, "Understanding image intensities", *Artificial Intelligence*, 8(2), pp. 201-231, 1977.

[5] K. Ikeuchi and K. Sato, "Determining Reflectance using Range and Brightness Images", *Proc. IEEE Intl. Conference on Computer Vision 90*, pp. 12-20, 1990.

[6] J. R. Kender and E. M. Smith, "Shape from Darkness: Deriving Surface Information from Dynamic Shadows", *Proc. IEEE Intl. Conference on Computer Vision 87*, pp. 539-546, 1987.

[7] I. Sato, Y. Sato and K. Ikeuchi, "Illumination Distribution from Shadows", *Proc. IEEE Conference on Computer Vision and Pattern Recognition 99*, pp. 306-312, June 1999.

[8] I. Sato, Y. Sato and K. Ikeuchi, "Illumination distribution from brightness in shadows: adaptive estimation of illumination distribution with unknown reflectance properties in shadow regions", *Proc. IEEE Conference on Computer Vision and Pattern Recognition 99*, pp. 875-882, September 1999.

[9] I. Sato, Y. Sato and K. Ikeuchi, "Acquiring a Radiance Distribution to Superimpose Virtual Objects onto a Real Scene ", *IEEE Transactions on Visualization and Computer Graphics*, vol. 5, no. 1, pp. 1-12, March 1999.

[10] Y. Sato, M. D. Wheeler and K, Ikeuchi, "Object shape and reflectance modeling from observation", *Proc. of SIGGRAPH 97*, pp. 379-387, August, 1997.

[11] S. A. Shafer and T. Kanade, "Using Shadows in Finding Surface Orientations", *Computer Vison, Graphics, and Image Processing*, 22(1), pp. 145-176, 1983.

[12] Y. Yu, P. Debevec, J. Malik and T. Hawkins, "Inverse global illumination: Recovering reflectance models of real scenes from photographs", *Proc. of SIGGRAPH 99*, pages 215–224, August 1999.

Interactive Deformation with Triangles

James Dean Palmer and Ergun Akleman*
Visualization Sciences Program
Texas A&M University

Jianer Chen
Department of Computer Science
Texas A&M University

Abstract

In this paper, we present a new deformation technique based on triangular deformers. One of the advantage of triangles over lines is that triangles uniquely define three linearly independent vectors in 3D. These three vectors can be used as a local coordinate system. Deformation is described by a set of source and destination triangles. For each source and destination triangle and for any point 3D space, we can compute a unique transformation vector for any given source and destination triangles.

We combine these transformation vectors described by each deformer pair, by using a weigted average that is a function of the distance to the source traingle. In the paper, we provide a set of blending functions to effectively interpolate these transformation vectors from each triangle to compute a combined transformation. To obtain a deformation of a given polygonal mesh, we simply translate each vertex of the polygonal mesh with a combined transformation vector that is computed by using the position of the vertex.

Our technique can be used for both 2D and 3D deformation. We have implemented systems for interactive 2D and 3D deformations. In our 2D implementation, we use line and point deformers in addition to triangles.

1. Introduction and Motivation

This paper presents a new deformation technique that is based on triangle deformers. The first deformation method in computer graphics was introduced by Alan Barr in 1984 [2]. In 1986, Sederberg and Parry introduced *Free-Form Deformations* (FFD), which involves a mapping from one coordinate space to another through a trivariate tensor product Bernstein polynomial [12]. Over the years a number of variations on FFD have been introduced. These include Coquillart's *Extended Free-Form Deformation* (EFFD) [6]

and Lazaris, Coquillart and Jansene's *Axial Deformations* [8]. Jin, Li and Peng used generalized metaballs for general constrained deformations [10]. Borrel and Rappoport introduced *Constrained Deformations* [4], Singh and Fiume proposed *Wires* [13] and Crespin introduced *Implicit Free-Form Deformations* (IFFD). IFFD provides a frame work in which most of the Free-Form Deformation techniques can be used but is based on deformers defined by a local tool and a blending function [7]. Within the IFFD model, a set of deformers act on a model. Each deformer is characterized by a local coordinate space, an invertible mapping function, an invertible transformation function and a potential function. These deformers are then applied to geometry using a process similar to FFD [7].

Crespin's work inspired our initial investigations with using implicit functions and simplicial complexes to deform geometry. We also observed a number of similarities between our technique and the *Feature-Based Image Metamorphosis* (FBIM), which is introduced in 1992 by Beier and Neely [3] and has been used as a visual effect in a number of motion pictures as well as the Michael Jackson's video *Black and White*. FBIM uses line deformers to deform the location of pixel with inverse mapping [3]. Although, FBIM is not really a deformation approach, the underlying transformation algorithm shares many similarities to deformation algorithms.

Mathematically, there are two differences between our technique and FBIM technique:

- Our deformations are based on trangles instead of lines.

- Our technique is a forward mapping instead of inverse.

Line deformers are appropriate for only 2D deformations; For 3D deformations, triangle deformers are needed. The main advantage of triangles over lines in 3D is that triangles uniquely define three linearly independent vectors. These three vectors can be used as a local coordinate system to compute a unique transformation vector for any given source and destination triangles. Another advantage of using triangle deformers is that triangles can effectively ex-

---
*Corresponding Author. Address: 216 Langford Center, College Station, Texas 77843-3137. email: ergun@viz.tamu.edu. phone: +(979) 845-6599. fax: +(979) 845-4491. Supported in part by the Texas A&M, Interdisciplinary Program.

press non-uniform scaling and shear from the source to the destination.

By using a weigted average, we combine the transformation vectors described by each deformer pair. The weights are functions of the distance to the source traingle. They are similar to implicit blending functions. For predictable results, they must be always positive and monotone decreasing. In the paper, we provide a set of blending functions. To obtain a deformation of a given polygonal mesh, we simply translate each vertex of the polygonal mesh with a combined transformation vector that is computed by using the position of the vertex.

We have implemented systems for interactive 2D and 3D deformations. In our 2D implementation, we use line and point deformers in addition to triangles. In 2D, instead of using FBIM's inverse mapping technique, we use forward mapping functions to manipulate the geometry of the grid. The deformation of the grid also deforms the texture that is mapped to the grid. This approach takes the advantage of 3D acceleration hardware that supports texture mapping and provides interactive deformations in 2D. Our 3D implementation uses exactly the same deformation concept as the 2D implementation but in 3D we only support triangle deformers to uniquely define a local coordinate system.

2. Methodology

Our approach is based on functions that are constructed by the operations that are used in implicit surface construction. The overall deformation is described by a set of deformer pairs (point, line and triangle pairs). Each deformer pair consists of one source and one destination. For each source and destination shape a local coordinate is computed to describe the transformation described by the change of position and shape between the source and destination. In addition, for each shape a weight function that is described by the distance to the shape is given. Then, the transformations are combined by using these weight function.

In our framework, to describe a deformation, the users defines a set of deformer pairs. Each deformer pair consists of two shapes: the source shape and the destination shape. Each one of these pairs uniquely describe a transformation vector for any given point in the source image. In this section, we discuss the effect of different types of deformer pairs.

The simplest of these deformers are point pairs. A point deformer can uniquely define transformation in any dimension. As can be observed from Figure 1.A, point deformer can only implement translations, but not allow scaling, rotating, or shearing.

Beier and Neely uses line deformer pairs [3]. An advantage of using lines over a simple point deformer is that one can describe scaling and rotation up to 360 degree. Fig-

ure 1.B shows a source image is translated, rotated, and scaled from the source line to the destination line by changing the coordinate system to be relative to the source and destination lines. As can be observed from the image, the line primitive doesn't allow us to shear the image and we can only scale the image uniformly. We cannot, for example, scale only the width or scale only the height. Another problem with line deformers is that in 3D deformation not uniquely defined.

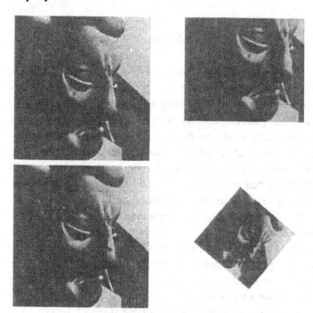

Figure 1. Examples of point and line deformers.

On the other hand, triangular deformers allow us to effectively translate, rotate, scale, and shear an image and uniquely describe a transformation. Moreover, unlike line deformers, deformations uniquely defined by triangle deformers in 3D. Figure 2.A shows the effect of triangle deformers. The source image is translated, rotated, scaled and sheared from the source triangle to the destination triangle by changing the coordinate system to be relative to the source and destination triangles. Figure 2.B shows an example of 3D deformation of a teapot by a single triangle deformer pair.

If there exists more than one deformer, the problem is to appropriately combine the transformations described by each deformer pair. In order to compute the combined transformation, we simply calculate a weighted average of transformations given by each simplex pair. Weights are computed based on the distance of a deformer to a given point.

Figure 3.A illustrates how two triangles can be used together to deform an image. One application of image deformation is caricature. Akleman, Palmer and Logan have

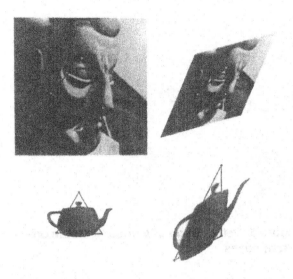

Figure 2. 2D and 3D examples of triangle deformers.

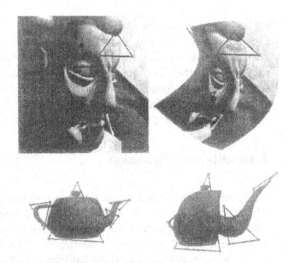

Figure 3. 2D and 3D examples of blended triangle deformers.

recently used the 2D deformation system for generating extreme caricatures [1]. Figure 3.B shows 3D deformations with multiple deformers. In this example, we have added a small deformer to the teapot handle while using another deformer to actually make the teapot body longer. We then used two deformers on the spout to make it large at the base of the spout but small and narrow at the tip of the spout.

In 2D, if we use only line primitives, FBIM's weight function and inverse maps instead of forward ones, our deformation technique will be exactly the same as the FBIM technique. In other words, our technique can be considered as a generalization of the FBIM technique. Our generalization comes from (1) using triangle and point primitives in addition to line primitives, (2) using new weight functions and (3) using forward maps instead of inverse ones. By using triangles in addition to lines, we provide users with shear transformations in addition to translation, scaling and rotation. And by using forward maps, we are able to develop an interactive system by taking advantage of texture mapping hardware.

Our 3D approach can be considered a straight generalization of FBIM to 3D since lines are natural simplest deformers for 2D and triangles are natural deformers for 3D.

3. Implementation

Several important implementation choices had to be made in developing software to test and analyze the algorithms we have developed. These issues include what language to write the application in, what user interface toolkit to use, and what graphic toolkit to use.

Our implementation is written in C++ which is an object oriented language. By using an object oriented approach in writing this software we were able to abstract the deformers into pluggable objects. In 2D, a triangle deformer can work seemlessly with a point or line deformer. Furthermore, new deformers can be added to this system without having to change much existing code and the new objects can work seemlessly with the deformers we have already developed.

We chose to use OpenGL as the graphic toolkit since OpenGL supports hardware texture and 3D acceleration. By using forward mapping functions to manipulate texture mapped grids, we can harness the hardware accelerated texture mapping support to interactively deform 2D images. While hardware accelerated texture mapping and 2D/3D transformations are used extensively in games and 3D applications, most 2D applications don't utilize the functionality that is becoming standard in the newest generation of consumer display adaptors. The application we have developed is a good example of using hardware acceleration generally intended for use in 3D within a 2D application. And of course, OpenGL was an excellent choice when we extended our 2D deformation engine to 3D as well.

Fltk was chosen as the GUI (graphic user interface) toolkit, because it is very portable and has excellent OpenGL support. The applications we have developed have been compiled under Irix and Linux. Porting them to other platforms, such as MS Windows, should not be difficult.

2D user interface that we have developed supports point, line, and triangle primitives. It also supports several different blending functions and it is extremely easy to add other blending functions. We can also vary the blending constants in these equations to gauge their effect. 3D user interface supports loading OBJ format 3D models instead of 2D images. The interface also provides convenient tools to navigate about the object or scene being deformed. It also supports multiple "frames" so one can do simple key framed animation. The 3D implementation also supports all of the same blending features that our 2D implementation does.

4. Results and Discussion

Figure 4.A shows that drastic deformations can be obtained with only a few deformers. In this example, we changed a neutral character into a grumpyone by turning down the nose and manipulating the mouth into a frown. Figure 4.B demonstrates a head that has been deformed into a happy character. We have used the deformers to change the mouth into a smile and we have moved the forehead and brow higher. Figures 4.A and 4.B also show that we don't necessarily need to be extremely accurate in bounding features with triangle deformers. Figure 5.A shows a nose feature that has been closely bounded by a triangle deformer. The deformed feature stays relatively close to the destination triangle. Figure 5.B shows a nose feature that has been loosely bounded by a triangle deformer. Since the deformer is effectively deforming all of the space that it bounds, it will not pull the nose feature out as far as the closely bounded example did.

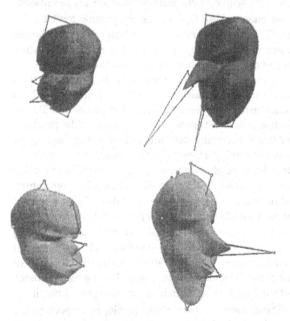

Figure 4. Deformation of a human head model to create grumpy and happy characters.

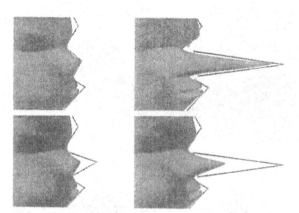

Figure 5. Deformation of a nose to create different noses.

5. Future Work and Conclusion

We developed a new interactive deformation technique. This technique improves on existing techniques and provides a powerful framework for future work. The simplicial complex based deformation algorithms that we are working with should work well across n dimensions and have a plethora of applications. Applications for this work include 2D morphing and warping, as well as 3D warping, modeling, and animation.

One limitation of the local coordinate based approaches such as this technique or FBIM is that the coordinate transformation can not express a rotation of more than 360 degrees. If we had defined a coordinate mapping transformation in terms of scale rotation and translation we could have expressed rotations more than 360 degrees. We have already developed and have had some initial successes in using this alternate mapping framework, but future work is necessary to extend it to 3D and to compare and contrast it to the local coordinate based approach.

By using C++'s object oriented inheritance we can easily define new deformers that can be plugged into our application and will blend seamlessly with existing deformers. We intend to extend our current work to higher dimensions and then we intend to define distance functions for more complex simplicial complexes. Simplicial complexes and operations on simplicial complexes are well defined in higher dimensions. By building our algorithms' framework on these structures our algorithm should easily extend from 2D to 3D and potentially to even higher dimensions.

More generally our algorithm should be applicable to simplicial complexes. A simplex is a set of d+1 points whose convex hull has dimension d. The points of the simplex may exist in a space whose dimension is larger than d. In 2D, simplexes includes points, lines and triangles. A simplicial complex is composed of a number of simplices.

The intrinsic dimension of the complex is the dimension of each simplex in the complex. The embedded dimension of the simplicial complex is the dimension of the space of the points in the simplicial complex.

Simplicial complexes represent a straightforward and well defined data structure that allow one to take advantage of linear programming methods for the solution of geometric problems, boundary evaluation, affine transformations, subdivision, and constructive solid geometry operators. Simplicial complexes also provide a very simple and general method for expressing geometry in n-dimensional space. [11]

Using this technique with simplicial complexes instead of the more specific cases we have used in this research would allow a more general framework of deformation tools that scale to N dimensions and can represent more complex deformations.

References

[1] E. Akleman, J. D. Palmer, R. Logan. Making Extreme Caricatures with a New Interactive 2D Deformation Technique with Simplicial Complexes. *Visual 2000 Proceedings*, 100-105, Sept. 2000.

[2] A. H. Barr. Global and local deformations of solid primitives. *Computer Graphics SIGGRAPH '84 Proceedings*, 18(3):21-30, 1984.

[3] Beier and Neely. Feature-Based Image Metamorphosis. *Computer Graphics*, 26(2):35-42, 1992.

[4] P. Borrel and A. Rappoport. Simple constrained deformations for geometric modeling and interactive design. *ACM Transactions on Graphics*, 13(2):137-155, 1994.

[5] E. Brisson. Representing geometric structures in d dimensions: topology and order *ACM Symposium on Computational Geometry*, 218-227, 1989.

[6] S. Coquillart. Extended Free-Form Deformation : A Sculpturing Tool for 3D Geometric Modeling. *Computer Graphics SIGGRAPH '90 Proceedings*, 24(4):187-196, 1990.

[7] B. Crespin. Implicit Free-Form Deformations. *Implicit Surfaces*, 1999.

[8] F. Lazarus, S. Coquillart, and P. Jancene. Axial deformations: an intuitive deformation technique. *Computer Aided Design*, 26(8):607-613, 1994.

[9] R. Logan. *Automated Interactive Facial Caricature Generation*. Masters Thesis: Texas A&M University. December 2000.

[10] X. Jin, Y. Li and Q. Peng. General Constrained Deformations Based on Generalized Metaballs. *Computers & Graphics*, 24:219-231, 2000.

[11] A. Paoluzzi, F. Bernardini, C. Cattani and V. Ferrucci. Dimension-independent modeling with simplicial complexes. *ACM Transactions on Graphics*, 12(1):56-102, 1993.

[12] T. W. Sederberg, S. R. Parry. Free-form Deformations of solid geometric models. *Computer Graphics SIGGRAPH '86 Proceedings*, 20(4):151-160, 1986.

[13] K. Singh and E. Fiume "Wires: a geometric deformation technique" *Computer Graphics SIGGRAPH '98 Proceedings*, 405-414, 1998.

[14] B. Wyvill and G. Wyvill. Field Functions for Implicit Surfaces. *Visual Computer*, 5:75-82, 1989.

Marker Mapping Techniques for Augmented Reality Visualization

Felix G. Hamza-Lup[1], Larry Davis[1], Charles Hughes[1], and Jannick P. Rolland[1,2]
[1]School of Electrical Engineering and Computer Science
[2]School of Optics-CREOL
University of Central Florida
Orlando, FL 32816
{fhamza, ceh}@cs.ucf.edu, {davis, jannick}@odalab.ucf.edu

Abstract

The requirements for tracking in augmented reality environments are stringent because of the need to register real and computer-generated virtual objects. Driven by the need to track real objects within these environments, we propose two algorithms to distribute markers on complex rigid objects. The proposed algorithms employ an optimization technique with a spherical or cylindrical intermediary surface. The validity and effectiveness of the algorithms are tested heuristically by simulation.

1. Introduction

Placing real and computer-generated objects into register is a challenging problem in augmented reality (AR). Because virtual and real objects must be placed into register, i.e. spatial coincidence, the need for accurate tracking not only for the head of the user but also for other objects is predominant [1][2].

The research presented in this paper is a component in the development of a comprehensive framework for the Distributed Augmented Reality Collaborative Environment referred as DARE. Applied to medical visualization, DARE allows human anatomical 3D models to be overlaid on real patient models or human patient simulators, and the data to be shared across remote locations. At remotely dispersed locations users obtain an enhanced view of the real environment, by wearing see-through head-mounted displays (HMDs) to observe three-dimensional computer-generated objects superimposed on their real-world view [3]. The position and orientation of the real objects must be computed to render the computer-generated objects from the correct viewpoint at the correct depth.

Thus, the requirements for tracking in DARE as in other AR environments are extremely stringent whether the specific application is a training tool, a diagnosis tool or an aid to guided surgery [4]. An approach to tracking real objects is marker-based, optical tracking technology where markers are distributed on the object's surface. However, in the case of complex objects, *ad hoc* methods for marker distribution may waste resources and/or restrict tracking performance.

We propose two algorithms for marker mapping on complex rigid objects. The first algorithm, referred to as the *quiescent algorithm*, approximates a uniform distribution for a specified number of markers on the surface of the object. An iterative optimization process determines the number of markers.

The second algorithm, referred to as the *viewpoint algorithm*, minimizes the number of markers while keeping the constraint that at least k markers are seen (detected) from different viewpoints. The number of markers required to determine an object's position and orientation from each viewpoint is dependent on the tracking system used.

2. The quiescent algorithm

In this section, we describe a three-step algorithm for placing sets of markers onto complex rigid objects. The name of the algorithm is derived from the second step. Quiescence refers to the minimum potential energy (resting) state of a set of points that can be achieved via optimization.

The algorithm requires the availability of a three-dimensional triangular mesh model of the object. The problem of mapping from 2D surfaces onto complex 3D objects is encountered in texture mapping [5]. Conceptually, the texture mapping process is simple. A small area of the texture pattern maps onto the area of a geometric surface. However, in the case of a complex 3D object, its surface equations can be difficult to approximate. To solve this problem, a two-part, texture-based mapping technique is used. The technique uses intermediary three-dimensional regular surfaces.

The first step determines whether to use a cylinder or a sphere as an intermediary surface. The decision is based upon the application tracking requirements and the elongation of the object. If the object is elongated, the principle axis of symmetry is determined by eigenvector analysis and a cylinder is used as the intermediary surface. Otherwise, a sphere is used as an intermediary surface.

The extent of elongation of a complex object can be quantified by an assessment of the eigenvalues of the dispersion matrix computed from the vertices of its 3D triangular mesh. For a complex object, the ratio between the largest and the smallest eigenvalue is considered. If this ratio is greater than or equal to 10, we choose a cylinder over a sphere for the mapping.

Once the object elongation has been quantified, the main axis of symmetry is determined by the eigenvector corresponding to the strongest eigenvalue.

Let p be the centroid of the triangular mesh that represents the complex object. We compute the Cartesian coordinates of the centroid in the global coordinate system. Let n be the total number of vertices (points) in the three-dimensional triangular mesh that approximates the complex object. Let p_i be the position of the ith vertex in the mesh. Let $d_i = d_i - p$, $i \in [1,n]$ the vectors between the centroid and each vertices in the mesh. The 3x3 symmetrical dispersion matrix is:

$$A = \sum_{i=1}^{n} d_i d_i^T \quad \text{,where } d_i^T \text{ is the transpose of } d_i.$$

To determine the eigenvectors of this matrix, we diagonalize it, given that A is real and symmetric. The diagonalized A can be written as:

$$D = V^{-1}AV$$

where $D_{ij} = \lambda^{[i]}$, $i=j$ is the matrix of eigenvalues and V is the matrix of eigenvectors.

In the second step of the quiescent algorithm, we use an optimization procedure to uniformly distribute the markers on the cylinder or on the sphere. Using optimization, an initial number of markers are distributed on the intermediary surface. Then, the minimum number of markers that meet the tracking system detection requirements is computed in an iterative process [6]. Simulated annealing lends itself well to this approach because of the well-specified criteria for point movement to an optimal solution during iterations of the algorithm [7]. Furthermore, during optimization, simulated annealing includes methods for escaping some local minima. It is important to note, however, that other optimization methods can be used to solve this problem. As such, it is not our intention to explore the advantages of using one optimization algorithm versus another.

In the third step, the markers are mapped from the intermediary surface to the desired complex 3D object in an approach similar to two-way texture mapping. This can be done using the normal from the intermediary surface, the normal from the object's surface, or the center or principal axis of the object. The algorithm we developed uses the center or principal axis of symmetry of the object in the mapping process. A description of the geometrical formulae for cylindrical and spherical intermediary surfaces is given in Appendix A and B, respectively.

The inputs of the quiescent algorithm are:
1. A 3D Model: the set of n points defined in Cartesian coordinates (X_i, Y_i, Z_i), where $i \in [1,n]$, n being the number of vertices in the three dimensional triangular mesh approximating the complex object onto which the markers are mapped.
2. A set of intermediary marker positions: the set of k points defined in Cartesian coordinates (X_{Mi}, Y_{Mi}, Z_{Mi}), where $i \in [1,k]$, k being the number of points that describe the initial positions of the marker centers on the intermediary surface after the annealing procedure from the second step.

The output is a set of k points describing the final positions of the marker centers on the object's surface. Each point is defined by the Cartesian coordinates (X_{Fi}, Y_{Fi}, Z_{Fi}), where $i \in [1,k]$, k being the number of markers.

3. The viewpoint algorithm

Similar to the quiescent algorithm, the purpose of this algorithm is to distribute a finite number of markers on a complex 3D object. The improvements over the previous algorithm are twofold. First, this algorithm further minimizes the number of markers. Second, it guarantees that at least k markers are visible from each viewpoint, where k is the minimum number of markers that are necessary for a given tracking system.

The viewpoint algorithm can be described in four steps:
1. A triangular mesh is generated for the complex 3D object. Each triangle of the mesh is assigned a different number.
2. The number and the positions of the viewpoints arround the complex object are selected. A higher number of viewpoints will give better results because this is equivalent to analyzing the object from more angles. Hence, more viewpoints will give better marker positions on the complex object. Moreover, the probability that at least k markers are visible will increase when the object changes

153

position and orientation in the tracking frame of reference. To distribute the viewpoints around the object, we place them uniformly on the sphere that surrounds the object and has a radius two times the maximum distance between any two points in the triangular mesh. All the viewpoints are added to the ViewpointsList.

3. For each triangle, the number of viewpoints from which it can be seen is computed. We create the TrianglesList. If two triangles have the same viewpoint count we sort them by the number assigned in step 1. We create a list having in each node the triangle number and the number of viewpoints from which this triangle can be seen.

4. As long as the ViewpointsList is not empty:
   4.1 Select the triangle with the highest viewpoint count that is next in the TrianglesList and add a marker on its surface.
   4.2 If fewer than k markers from that viewpoint are seen, step 4.1 is repeated.
   4.3 Else the viewpoint is removed from the ViewpointsList and the TrianglesList is updated.

The algorithm assures that from each viewpoint at least k markers are visible and minimizes the number of markers.

4. Experimental Results

To heuristically test the validity of the algorithms, software simulations were performed. Computer-generated, random, three-dimensional triangular meshes representing the complex objects were used.

4.1 The quiescent algorithm

The markers on the intermediary surface after annealing are represented as small spheres on the transparent surface. The small spheres on the object represent the final positions of the markers on the surface of the complex object.

The first set of simulations was performed with a sphere as an intermediary surface, shown as a transparent surface in Figure 1.

The 3D scene contains:
- a randomly generated 3D triangular mesh consisting of 10 triangles
- 30 markers
- a sphere of radius R as an intermediary surface, where R is greater then the maximum distance between any two points in the triangular mesh.

Figure 1: Sphere as intermediary surface

The second set of simulations was performed with a cylinder as an intermediary surface, shown as a transparent surface in Figure 2.

The 3D scene contains:
- a randomly generated 3D triangular mesh consisting of 10 triangles
- 24 markers
- a cylinder of radius R and height H as an intermediary surface, where $2R$ and H are greater then the maximum distance between any two points in the triangular mesh.

The validity of the algorithm on complex objects was tested heuristically. We aligned the tracking system camera with the scene camera and rotated the object. We observed that at least 3 markers per viewpoint were seen and that there was a fairly uniform distribution of markers on the surface of the object.

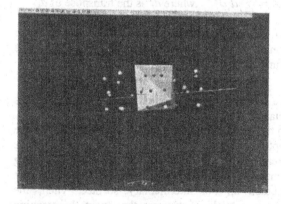

Figure 2: Cylinder as intermediary surface

4.2 The viewpoint algorithm

The uniformly distributed viewpoints on the surface of the sphere surrounding the 3D object are represented as small cubes in Figure 3. The small spheres on the object represent the final position of the markers.

154

The 3D scene contains:
- a randomly generated 3D triangular mesh consisting of 10 triangles
- 30 viewpoints uniformly distributed on the bounding sphere that surrounds the complex object.
- a sphere of radius *R*. *R* is greater than double the maximum distance between any two points in the triangular mesh.

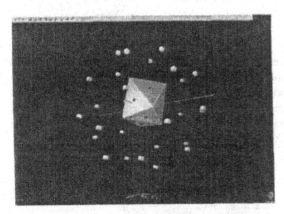

Figure 3: The viewpoint approach

The current implementation places the markers at the center of mass (centroid) of the triangles. Most optical tracking systems require at least 3 markers visible from each viewpoint to correctly determine the position and orientation of the object. If only one triangle is seen from a viewpoint, the other markers are distributed on the vertices that form the triangle.

5. Conclusions

Two algorithms are proposed for marker distribution on complex rigid objects. The experiments demonstrate the success of the algorithms applied on randomly generated complex rigid objects.

In addition to further verification, there are several issues that still need to be addressed. One issue is the type of markers: active versus passive. Another issue is accounting for the cones of emission for different type of active markers and investigating their impact on the marker distribution and orientation.

6. Acknowledgements

This work was supported in part by the US ARMY Simulation, Training, and Instrumentation Command (STRICOM) and by the National Science Foundation under grant EIA 9986051.

7. References

[1] Welch G., and G. Bishop "SCAAT: incremental tacking with incomplete information," Proceedings of SIGGRAPH '97, in Computer Graphics Proceedings, Annual Conference Series, ACM SIGGRAPH, 333-344, 1997.
[2] Argotti, Y, L. Davis, V. Outters, and J.P. Rolland "Dynamic superimposition of synthetic objects on rigid and simple-deformable real objects," *Computers and Graphics*, 26/6/2002.
[3] Rolland, J.P., and H. Fuchs, "A comparison of optical and video see-through head-mounted displays", Chap. 4 in Wearable Computers and Augmented Reality, T. Caudell and W. Barfield. (Eds.), Lawrence Erlbaum Associates, Mahwah, 113-156, 2001.
[4] Holloway, R., An analysis of registration errors in a see-through head-mounted display system for craniofacial surgery planning, Ph.D. dissertation, University of North Carolina at Chapel Hill, 1995.
[5] Blinn, J.F, M.E. Newell, "Texture and reflection in Computer Generated Images", CACM, 19(10), 542-547, 1976.
[6] Davis L, J.P. Rolland, R. Parsons, E. Clarkson, "Methods for designing head-tracking probes", Proceedings of the Joint Conference on Information Sciences (JCIS), 498-502, 2002.
[7] Kirkpatrick, S., C.D. Gelatt, and M.P. Vecchi, "Optimization by simulated annealing", *Science*, 220, 671-680, 1983.

Appendix A
Cylinder as intermediary surface

1. We align the principal symmetry axis of the object with the cylinder axis, e.g. the OX axis.
2. Let $(X_{Marker}, Y_{Marker}, Z_{Marker})$ be the Cartesian coordinates of a point in the markers intermediary position file (i.e. after the annealing algorithm has been applied on the cylinder). For each point, we find the equation of the section plane (SP) that is parallel to the OZY plane and passes through the point. This plane is unique.
3. From the triangular mesh that represents the 3D complex object we isolate the set of triangles (TS) that are intersected by SP using a range factor (RF) based on the granularity of the triangular mesh.
4. For each triangle we isolate its section segment by computing the intersection point between a line segment determined by two vertices of the triangle and the SP.

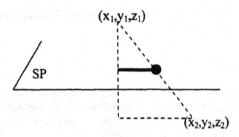

Figure A1: Section segment

Using the plane equation, we identify the coefficients. In this case SP is parallel with the OZY axis and passes through the point $(X_{Marker}, Y_{Marker}, Z_{Marker})$ hence we have: A=1, B=0, C=0 and D= (-)X_{Marker}. The SP equation is given by:

$$x - x_{Marker} = 0 \quad (A1)$$

The parametric equations of the line that passes through two points (x_1, y_1, z_1), (x_2, y_2, z_2) are:

$$x = x_1 + (x_2 - x_1)t$$
$$y = y_1 + (y_2 - y_1)t$$
$$z = z_1 + (z_2 - z_1)t$$

Substituting equation A1 into the first parametric equation for the line yields:

$$x_{Marker} = x_1 + (x_2 - x_1)t$$
$$y = y_1 + (y_2 - y_1)t$$
$$z = z_1 + (z_2 - z_1)t \text{ , unknowns: t, y, z.}$$

The solution of this system is given by:

$$t = \frac{x_{Marker} - x_1}{x_2 - x_1}$$

$$y = y_1 + (y_2 - y_1)\frac{x_{Marker} - x_1}{x_2 - x_1}$$

$$z = z_1 + (z_2 - z_1)\frac{x_{Marker} - x_1}{x_2 - x_1}$$

5. We repeat step 4 for each triangle in TS until we obtain all the section segments.

6. We repeat step 2 for each point in the markers intermediary positions file.

Appendix B
Sphere as intermediary surface

1. The centroid of the general shape is computed by applying the arithmetic mean on each dimension:

$$x_c = (x_1 + x_2 + ... + x_n)/n$$
$$y_c = (y_1 + y_2 + ... + y_n)/n$$
$$z_c = (z_1 + z_2 + ... + z_n)/n$$

2. Let $(X_{Marker}, Y_{Marker}, Z_{Marker})$ be the Cartesian coordinates of a point in the markers intermediary position file (i.e. after the annealing algorithm has been applied on the sphere). The parametric equations of the line that passes through the points (X_c, Y_c, Z_c), $(X_{Marker}, Y_{Marker}, Z_{Marker})$ are given by:

$$x = x_c + (x_{Marker} - x_c)t$$
$$y = y_c + (y_{Marker} - y_c)t$$
$$z = z_c + (z_{Marker} - z_c)t$$

3. For each triangle, the intersection between the plane generated by the triangle and this line is computed. Having three points: (X_1, Y_1, Z_1), (X_2, Y_2, Z_2), (X_3, Y_3, Z_3), the equation of the plane that passes through them is given by: Ax+By+Cz+D=0, where:

$$A = y_1(z_2 - z_3) + y_2(z_3 - z_1) + y_3(z_1 - z_2)$$
$$B = z_1(x_2 - x_3) + z_2(x_3 - x_1) + z_3(x_1 - x_2)$$
$$C = x_1(y_2 - y_3) + x_2(y_3 - y_1) + x_3(y_1 - y_2)$$
$$D = x_1(y_3 z_2 - y_2 z_3) + x_2(y_1 z_3 - y_3 z_1) + x_3(y_2 z_1 - y_1 z_2)$$

From the plane equation and the parametric equation of the lines we can find the intersection point $(X_{Sol}, Y_{Sol}, Z_{Sol})$. Then we check whether each point is inside the triangle. While this operation can be done in several ways, we check if the point is inside 2 angles of the triangle.

4. Step 3 is repeated for each marker in the input file.

156

Session 3–1

Coding and Wireless Communication

Resource Allocation for an Enterprise Mobile Services Platform

Matti Hiltunen, Rittwik Jana, Yih-Farn Chen

AT&T Labs - Research

180 Park Ave

Florham Park, NJ, 07932.

email: hiltunen,rjana,chen@research.att.com

Abstract— With rapid technological advances being made in the area of wireless communications it is expected that, in the near future, mobile users will be able to access a wide variety of services that will be available over a heterogeneous network. The qualities of these services are essential to the overall end user experience and it is the responsibility of the network and the mobile service platform to deliver on these expectations. In the context of mobile computing environments, limited and dynamically varying available resources, stringent application requirements and user mobility make it difficult to provide sustained quality of service to applications. This paper addresses the above issues, in particular a) a queuing model is derived for a mobile service platform (iMobile) to identify its resource allocation needs, b) a network simulation of a mobile service platform is provided for estimating the expected response time and c) a testbed implementation of a mobile service platform to negotiate adaptive service support.

I. INTRODUCTION

Recent years have witnessed explosive research in the development of indoor/outdoor mobile computing environments, which seek to provide the mobile user a wide array of advanced applications such as multimedia, WWW browsers, distributed file systems and databases. A fundamental problem is that the wireless medium is a scarce shared resource which has very different characteristics from wireline networks. There are many research papers in the literature that discuss efficient resource management techniques to provide an acceptable Quality of Service (QoS) below the network layer, i.e. transport, link and physical layers [1] [2]. In this paper we investigate QoS issues that are central to a mobile service platform. In its broadest definition, a mobile service platform can be thought of as a proxy that enables rapid development and deployment of mobile services [3][4]. The proxy maintains user, device and transmission profiles, accesses and processes internet/intranet data on behalf of the user, keeps track of user interactions by means of sessions, performs content transformations appropriate to the user and device needs and last but not least performing AAA (authentication, authorization and accounting) services.

Figure 1 shows a reference architecture of such a mobile service paltform, iMobile. A mobile device always interacts with an iMobile gateway before accessing iMobile services. A gateway authenticates a mobile user and puts each service request on the message queue. Any iMobile server can then pick up the request. Each server hosts a set of infolets for backend connections to corporate services. Both iMobile gateways and servers interact with the service profile database, which governs the transcoding and content delivery processes.

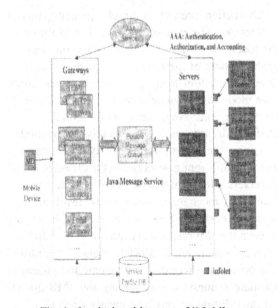

Fig. 1. Logical architecture of iMobile.

This paper addresses the resource allocation and

159

performance issues in iMobile. Specifically, it attempts to provide a methodology for answering the questions such as

• How many gateways, JMS providers, and IM engines are required to satisfy the client load?

• What is the expected response time of the system? Given the complexity of the system and all the unknown variables (e.g., other load on the system components), it is not realistic to expect highly accurate results, rather, the purpose is to provide methods of estimating the answers to these questions. Specifically, we envision that this analysis is only used to determine initial resource allocation for an iMobile installation and dynamic resource allocation is used during the system execution for fine-grain resource reallocation.

The paper is organized as follows. In section II we present a queuing model of iMobile. In section III we simulate a large scale network using a network simulator, ns and obtain the expected queuing delay at the messaging channel and the response time distribution for a mix of web related traffic source. Section IV summarizes our major findings and discusses the potential benefits of introducing a QoS architecture in a mobile service platform.

II. A SIMPLE QUEUEING MODEL FOR IMOBILE

This section presents a simple queueing model for iMobile. The goal of this model is to illustrate the process of modeling iMobile, while providing a rough estimate of the resources required to support a specified system load. In this model, see figure 2, we model the iMobile servers as M/M/N queues and all the other components as (potentially replicated) M/M/1 queues, see [5]. In this simple model, we assume the system load is evenly distributed between the different gateways and the different external servers. Note that the use of JMS [6] as the communication mechanism between the iMobile gateways and servers provides automatic load balancing between the iMobile servers (and thus, the iMobile servers are modeled as M/M/N queue). If multiple JMS queues are required, we assume the gateways distribute requests evenly among the JMS queues and the iMobile servers read evenly from all of the JMS queues. Note that this simple queueing model does not consider the impact of the network.

We use the following notation in the model. The system load, i.e., the request arrival rate, is denoted by λ. The number of gateways, JMS queues, iMobile servers, and external servers are denoted by G, J, I, and S, respectively. The average service time at an iMobile components x for a request is denoted by $T_{x_{in}}$ and for a reply is denoted by $T_{x_{out}}$. The average service time at the external server is denoted by T_s. Note that all the service times are the average times over different request types. If the service times are measured individually for each different request type, we should estimate the frequency of each type and use these frequencies to calculate the overall average service time as a weighted average.

The model assumes the gateways, queues, and servers are independent from one another. In particular, it assumes the components that process requests are independent from the components that process the corresponding replies. In principle, it would be possible to configure the system so that this assumption is true, but in practice in the iMobile system, the same components process both the requests and the replies. Therefore, our model must factor how much this sharing affects the service time (for requests and replies) at these components. This impact, denoted by c, can be calculated based on the fact that each component typically processes the same number of replies as it processes requests, that is, the total arrival rate at the component is 2 times the arrival rate in the abstract model. Furthermore, assuming that processing a request takes approximately as long as processing a reply, we can solve c to be $\frac{1}{1-\lambda T}$, where λ is the arrival rate at the component and T is the average measured service time for a request or reply in an unloaded system.

Given the service times and arrival rates at each of the components, queuing analysis provides formulas for calculating the utilization, ρ, and the delay, T_R (residence time) at each component. For brevity, we will not repeat the basic formulas for M/M/1 and M/M/N queues in this paper, but they can be found in any queuing analysis text book, for example [5]. Since our model consists only of M/M/1 and M/M/N components, we can use Jackson's Theorem to calculate the mean response time of the whole system. Based on Jackson's Theorem, the average response time of the system is then the sum of the delays at each component in the queuing model.

160

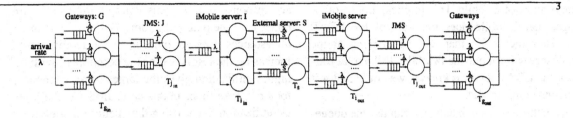

Fig. 2. Queuing model for iMobile.

A. Required measurements

A number of system measurements are required before the analysis can be performed. Typically, it is not possible to instrument the JMS implementation or the external servers, but it is possible to instrument the iMobile gateways and servers as well as some client devices for the experiments. Therefore, we can perform the measurements indicated in figure 3.

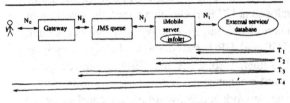

Fig. 3. Required measurements.

In this figure, T_1 reflects the response time of the external server, including the processing at the external server and the network transmission between the iMobile server and the external server. T_1 is best measured by instrumenting the infolets, but can be estimated by instrumenting the iMobile server. T_2 reflects the response time of the iMobile server. T_2 can be measured by instrumenting the iMobile server to take a time stamp when it receives a request from the JMS and just before it sends its reply to the JMS. T_3 reflects the response time of the JMS. This measurement can be taken by instrumenting the gateway to take a time stamp just before sending a request to the JMS and just after receiving the corresponding reply. Finally, T_4 reflects the response time of iMobile and it can be measured by using an instrumented iMobile client application. Although many iMobile clients can be intrumented (e.g., an HTTP client), some cannot (e.g., a cell phone), in which case T_4 must be estimated. Furthermore, we

have to measure the network transmission times on the different network links. The average one-way network transmission times between the client and the gateway, gateway and JMS, JMS and iMobile server, and iMobile server and the external server are denoted by N_c, N_g, N_j, and N_i, respectively.

Based on these measurement, we can calculate the share of the total time taken by each of the components:

- External server: $S_s = T_1 - 2 * N_i$
- iMobile server: $S_i = T_2 - T_1$
- JMS queue: $S_j = T_3 - T_2 - 2 * N_g - 2 * N_j$
- Gateway: $S_g = T_4 - T_3 - 2 * N_c$

These shares are used to calculate the service times at each component. Since the shares at the gateways, JMS, and iMobile servers include the processing of both the request and reply, we divide the share in half and use the adjustment factor c to calculate the average service time at the component.

B. Case study

To illustrate the use of the model, let us consider a case study based on measurements on an experimental iMobile installation. The specifics of the experimental setup are not important for this example, but the client, gateway, JMS provider, and iMobile server were executing on separate desktops, all connected by a 100Mb Ethernet, and the client used a web browser (http protocol) to access the iMobile service. The external server in this case was a LDAP server providing employees' contact information. Based on using the *ping* program, we estimate the one-way delay between any two machines in this network to be 0.1ms. We estimate that the response times are as follows, LDAP server 200ms (T_1), iMobile server 205ms (T_2), JMS 211ms (T_3), and iMobile client 219ms (T_4).

The LDAP server is an external server from the

point of view of iMobile. This implies, among other things, that iMobile does not control the LDAP server nor the traffic that will be arriving at the LDAP server from outside iMobile. If the total traffic for the LDAP server is known, we could factor it in the queueing model.

Given these measurements, we can use the queueing model to analyse the resource requirements and the response time at different system loads. For example, consider the case where the system requirements state that the system must support upto 150 requests per second ($\lambda = 150$) and the average response time must be less than 250ms. Using the model, we can determine that one gateway is not able to handle this load, that is, if we only have one gateway, at this request rate its service queue would grow indefinitely and thus, the response time of the whole system would grow indefinitely. If we set the number of gateways to two ($G = 2$), the system is able to handle the load without any component getting overloaded. Figure 4 provides the results of the queueing analysis given a configuration with two gateways, one JMS server, and one iMobile server. The column *rate* is the request/reply arrival rate at the component, *serv time* is the adjusted service time that accounts for the fact that the same component processes requests and replies, ρ is the utilization at the component, and T_r is the delay at the component including processing and queueing. Note that the network time for communication between the iMobile server and LDAP server is included in the LDAP response time, so the network time in the table only includes the other network hops.

Component	rate (reg/sec)	serv time (ms)	ρ	T_r (ms)
Gateway	75	5.51	0.41	9.40
JMS	150	4.83	0.72	17.50
iMobile server	150	4.00	0.60	10.00
LDAP server	150	200	n/a	200.00
iMobile server	150	4.00	0.60	10.00
JMS	150	4.83	0.72	17.50
Gateway	75	5.51	0.41	9.40
Network				0.6
Total				274.40

Fig. 4. Analysis results for one configuration.

The results in the table 4 indicate that the aver-

age response time for this configuration is 274ms rather than the required 250ms. Thus, the given set of resources does not quite meet the requirements. Increasing the resources for the component with the highest utilization gives the largest improvement in total response time. In this case, JMS has the highest utilization. Now, using the queuing model, if we increase the number of JMS replicas to 2 ($J = 2$), the average service time at JMS drops to 3.54ms and the average total response time of the system drops to 249ms. Thus, based on thsi queueing model, we can determine that the system requirements can be satisfied with an installation of two gateways and two JMS servers.

III. LARGE SCALE NETWORK DYNAMICS OF IMOBILE

Figure 5 presents a network simulation environment of iMobile. The simulation was performed using NS [7]. NS is an event driven network simulator developed at UC Berkeley that simulates a variety of IP networks. It implements network protocols such as TCP and UPD, traffic source behavior such as FTP, Telnet, Web, CBR and VBR and queue management mechanisms.

The network topology simulated consists of 10 gateways and 10 iMobile servers connected via a link between two concentrators. The concentrator can be thought of as the message queue in our platform. The JMS queue is modeled as a TCP link, $n0 - n1$ employing a FIFO queue with a 1.5Mbps link with a 50 msec delay. The duplex links between the gates and n0 are modeled as TCP with a bandwidth of 10Mbps and 10 msec delay. This is mirrored between n1 and the iMobile server instances. Each node uses a DropTail queue. The source model is typical of an internet request-response mechanism. The number of pages per session is varied. The average response time and the queuing delay at the JMS is studied. The parameters distributions that define the source model are a) inter-arrival time for pages are Exponentially distributed and is set to 1 every second and b) inter-arrival time for objects per page is also exponentially distributed and is set to t10 and c) the average object size has a Pareto distribution of 10 packets per object.

Figure 6 shows the expected queuing delay in seconds at the concentrator as a function of concurrent

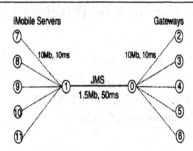

Fig. 5. Detailed queuing model for iMobile.

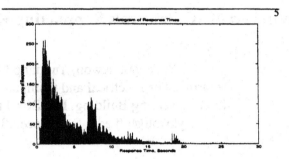

Fig. 7. Histogram of Response Times, 30 sessions, 5 gates, 5 servers.

sessions.

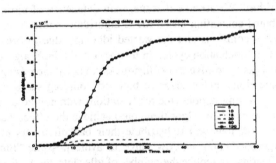

Fig. 6. Queuing delay as a function of sessions.

Figure 7 shows the histogram of response times in seconds for a 30 session simulation. The mean response time is 4.44 seconds and a standard deviation of 3.6 seconds. Note that the end to end delays is from an iMobile gateway to an iMobile server and back. Notionally in an enterprise the gateways and serves are usually colocated within a local area network.It is possible for an iMobile gateway to be deployed close to the edge of the network (closest to the user). In this case the requests would travel across the Internet or tunelled Internet to get back to the iMobile server. The dynamics of the network will change since the bottleneck can no longer be represented as a 10 Mbps link. However, this example illustrates the relative queuing delays and average response times as a function of offered load.

IV. CONCLUSION

Three factors motivate the work in this paper. Firstly, it is essential to evaluate the mobile service platform system capacity of a cluster of servers with respect to a particular configuration set. Secondly, how can we analyze the performance of such a sys-

tem under varying load conditions? Thirdly, from an implementation point of view, what is the appropriate architecture to introduce QoS? This paper has proposed a queuing model for a mobile service platform. In particular, the use of this queuing model will allow engineers to obtain an estimated number of servers and gateways to accommodate a particular load. We also present a network simulation environment which illustrates the dynamics of the mobile service platform performing under a realistic load. Last but not least, as future work we are investigating the possiblity of using the queuing model and the measured request arrival rates and server response times to dyanmically allocate new servers or resources. This would allow us to handle sudden surges in service requests ("flash crowds").

REFERENCES

[1] S.Floyd and K.Fall, "Promoting the use of end to end congestion control in the internet," *IEEE/ACM Trans. on Networking*, pp. 458–472, Aug 1999.
[2] L. Breslau and S.Shenker, "Best-effort versus reservations: A simple comparative analysis," in *Proc. of SigComm*, Oct 1998.
[3] H. Rao, Y.-F. Chen, D.-F. Chang, and M.-F. Chen, "iMobile: A proxy-based platform for mobile services," in *Proceedings of the 1st ACM Workshop on Wireless Mobile Internet (WMI 2001)*, (Rome, Italy), Jul 2001.
[4] Y.-F. Chen, H. Huang, R. Jana, T. Jim, R. Muthumanickam, S. John, S. Jora, and B. Wei, "iMobile EE - an enterprise mobile service platform," *ACM Journal on Wireless Networks*, to appear.
[5] L. Kleinrock, *Queueing Systems, Volume I: Theory*. New York, NY: Wiley, 1975.
[6] Sun Microsystems, *Java Message Service Documentation, Version 1.0.2b*. Sun Microsystems, Inc., Mountain View, CA, Aug 2001.
[7] "The network simulator:ns-2." http://www.isi.edu/nsnam/ns.

Wireless MAC Protocols Supporting Real-time Services in Wireless LANs *

Younggoo Kwon, Yuguang Fang and Haniph Latchman
Department of Electrical and Computer Engineering, University of Florida
435 Engineering Building, P.O.Box 116130, Gainesville, FL 32611-6130
ykwon@ufl.edu, fang@ece.ufl.edu, latchman@list.ufl.edu

Abstract

Design of efficient medium access control (MAC) protocols which provide high throughput for data traffic and good quality of service (QoS) for real-time traffic is one of major thrusts in wireless mobile networks and has received considerable attention in both academic research and industrial deployment. In this paper, we investigate a new efficient contention algorithm for wireless local area networks, namely the Fast Collision Resolution (FCR) algorithm, which attempts to provide significantly high throughput performance for data services. To support QoS for real-time services, we incorporate the priority algorithm based on service differentiations with the FCR algorithm, and show that this prioritized FCR algorithm can simultaneously achieve high throughput and good QoS support for real-time and data services.

1. Introduction

A good medium access control (MAC) protocol for wireless local area networks (LANs) should provide an efficient mechanism to share limited spectrum resources, together with simplicity of operation and high throughput. Distributed contention-based MAC protocol research in wireless networks started with ALOHA and slotted ALOHA in the 1970s. Later, MACA, MACAW, FAMA and DFWMAC were proposed by incorporating the carrier sense multiple access (CSMA) technique as well as handshake mechanism for collision avoidance (CA) ([2, 5, 7] and references therein). The most popular contention-based wireless MAC protocol, the carrier sense multiple access/collision avoidance (CSMA/CA), becomes the basis of the MAC protocol for the IEEE 802.11 standard([8]). However, it is observed that if the number of active users increases, the throughput performance of the IEEE 802.11 MAC protocol degrades significantly because of the excessively high collision rate. Although many innovative distributed contention-based MAC protocols have been proposed, it is not an easy task to satisfy

all desirable properties while preserving the simplicity of implementation in real wireless LANs. In [10] and [11], we propose a new efficient distributed contention-based MAC algorithm, namely, the *fast collision resolution* (FCR) algorithm. We observe that the main deficiency of most distributed contention-based MAC algorithms comes from the packet collisions and the wasted idle slots due to backoffs in each contention cycle. In this regard, the FCR algorithm attempts to resolve the collisions quickly by increasing the contention window sizes of both the colliding stations and the deferring stations (the ready stations with non-zero backoff timers). This algorithm could achieve the effect that all active stations will redistribute their backoff timers in the large contention window range to avoid possible "future" collisions. To reduce the number of idle slots, the FCR algorithm gives a small idle backoff timer for the station with a successful packet transmission. Moreover, when a station detects a number of idle slots, it will start to reduce the backoff timer exponentially, comparing to the linear decrease in backoff timer. In this paper, we extend the FCR algorithm by incorporating the priority algorithm based on service differentiations([1, 6]) to support QoS for real-time and data services. The prioritized FCR algorithm can achieve high throughput for best-effort data traffic while at the same time supporting QoS for real-time applications.

This paper is organized as follows. In the next section, we describe the newly proposed *fast collision resolution* (FCR) algorithm. In Section 3, we present the prioritized FCR algorithm with QoS support for real-time services and its performance evaluation. Conclusions are given in the final section.

2. Fast Collision Resolution

There are two major factors affecting the throughput performance in all MAC protocols: the transmission failures (due to packet collisions or other channel conditions) and the idle slots due to the backoff procedures. In IEEE 802.11 wireless LANs, due to the difficulty of collision detections in wireless environments, the Ethernet typed CSMA/CD is no longer effective any more. The collision avoidance (CA) in combination with the CSMA is proposed. Any station with a data packet will have to sense the channel before it is transmitted. If the channel is sensed busy, all nodes sensing the

*This work was supported in part by the Office of Naval Research Young Investigator Award under grant N000140210464.

164

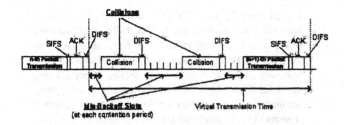

Figure 1. Basic Packet Transmission Structure of CSMA/CA

status will have to wait until the channel is idle. The collision resolution is done via backoff. Detailed operation for IEEE 802.11 MAC (CSMA/CA) can be founded in [8]. According to the operations used in CSMA/CA, the packet transmission cycle can be characterized in Figure 1.

We observe that in order to increase the throughput, we have to reduce the average number of idle slots, the average number of collisions and increase the average packet length. While the packet length may be transmission dependent, the natural way to boost the throughput is to reduce the other two factors. To better reduce the collisions, one may want to choose the backoff timers in a larger range (corresponding to the situation that the contention window size is larger), this would be effective when the number of active stations is large, however, in doing so, the average number of idle slots will increase when the number of active stations is small as most stations are slowly counting down the backoff timers (in deferring modes). In the IEEE 802.11 MAC protocol, it has been observed that there are too many collisions due to the smaller range in choosing the backoff timers, hence the throughput degrades dramatically when the number of active stations is large. Another observation is that in most MAC backoff algorithms, when a node is deferring its transmissions, its backoff timer is decreasing one slot at a time whenever an idle slot is detected. If there are too many active stations in deferring, with high probability there will exist at least two nodes assuming the same backoff timers, which causes much predictable "future" collisions. This problem is particularly serious because backoff timers will be suspended when the busy channel is detected, thus the decrease of backoff timers will be much slower, leading to more collisions (many new deferring nodes may pick the backoff timers which have been used by previously deferring stations). One intuitive idea to overcome this dilemma is to actively expand the range of backoff timers when a node "discovers" that the channel is overloaded! In distinction to all traditional MAC protocol design, we ([10]) proposed the *Fast Collision Resolution (FCR)* algorithm in which we require all deferring nodes to repick their backoff timers in a larger range, the net effect is that all deferring nodes will redistribute their backoff timers for better collision resolution. To overcome the consequence of more wasted idle slots, we propose to use the exponentially fast decrease of the backoff

timers whenever a pre-assigned number of consecutive idle slots is detected. Based on this argument, we propose the following more efficient MAC algorithm.

2.1 Fast Collision Resolution Algorithm

Based on the previous argument, we proposed the following backoff algorithm ([10] and [11]).

1. *Backoff Procedure*: All active stations will monitor the medium. If a station senses the medium idle for a slot, then it will decrement its backoff time (BT) by a slot time, i.e., $BT_{new} = BT_{old} - aSlotTime$ (or the backoff timer is decreased by one unit in terms of slot). When its backoff timer reaches to zero, the station will transmit a packet. If there are $[(minCW + 1) \times 2 - 1]$ consecutive idle slots being detected, its backoff timer should be decreased much faster (say, exponentially fast), i.e., $BT_{new} = BT_{old} - BT_{old}/2 = BT_{old}/2$ (*if* $BT_{new} < aSlotTime$, *then* $BT_{new} = 0$) or the backoff timer is decreased by a half. The net effect is that the unnecessary wasted idle backoff time will be reduced when a station, which has just performed a successful packet transmission, runs out of packets for transmission or reaches its maximum successive packet transmission limit.

2. *Transmission Failure (Packet Collision)*: If a station notices that its packet transmission has failed possibly due to packet collision (i.e., it fails to receive an acknowledgment from the intended receiving station), the contention window size of the station will be increased and a random backoff time (BT) will be chosen as follows: $CW = \min[maxCW, ((CW + 1) \times 2 - 1)]$, $BT = uniform(0, CW) \times aSlotTime$, where $uniform(a, b)$ indicates an integer randomly drawn from the uniform distribution between a and b, and CW is the current contention window size.

3. *Successful Packet Transmission*: If a station has finished a successful packet transmission, then its contention window size will be reduced to the initial (minimum) contention window size $minCW$ and a random backoff time (BT) value will be chosen accordingly, i.e., $CW = minCW$, $BT = uniform(0, CW) \times aSlotTime$. If a station has performed successive packet transmissions for the maximum successive transmission limit ($T_{PkTrans}$), then it will perform the following actions to give opportunities for the medium access to other stations: $CW = maxCW$, $BT = uniform(0, CW) \times aSlotTime$.

4. *Deferring State*: For a station which is in deferring state, whenever it detects the start of a new busy period, which indicates either a collision or a packet transmission in the medium, the station will increase its contention window size and pick a new random backoff

time (BT) as follows: $CW = \min[maxCW, ((CW + 1) \times 2 - 1)]$, $BT = uniform(0, CW) \times aSlotTime$.

In the FCR algorithm, the station that has successfully transmitted a packet will have the minimum contention window size and a small value of the backoff timer, hence it will have a higher probability to gain access of the medium, while other stations have relatively larger contention window size and larger backoff timers. After a number of successful packet transmissions for one station, another station may win a contention and this new station will then have higher probability to gain access of the medium for a period of time. We notice that in IEEE 802.11, there is no limit for successive packet transmissions, while in FCR, we do.

2.2 Prioritized Fast Collision Resolution (FCR) Algorithm with Quality of Service (QoS) Support

In order to cope with the QoS requirements of real-time applications, many algorithms have been proposed in contention-based MAC protocols for wireless LANs ([1, 6]). The most popular approach is to use a priority scheme for each traffic type, i.e., real-time traffic has higher priority for medium access than best-effort data traffic. With higher priority for medium access, real-time traffic will be served earlier than best-effort data traffic, which results in relative performance improvements for real-time traffic over data traffic. In the distributed contention-based MAC, the priority for QoS support can either using the inter-frame spacing (IFS) in which real-time traffic using shorter IFS ([6]), or using the different contention window size, in which real-time nodes will be assigned smaller contention window sizes ([1]). The latter gives statistical guarantee instead of absolute guarantee as many reservation-based scheme, i.e., smaller contention window size only provides higher probability to gain access of the medium. Due to the simplicity of this approach, we will focus on the statistical QoS based on the provisioning of contention window sizes. The novelty is on the backoff algorithm used for different traffic. We observe that for voice traffic, IEEE 802.11 backoff algorithm (i.e., binary exponential backoff) gives better performance in terms of packet dropping ratio, while FCR works better for data traffic in terms of throughput. Such difference is due to the traffic characteristics. Therefore, we will use IEEE 802.11 backoff algorithm for voice traffic with smaller contention window size while use the FCR for video traffic and data traffic with different contention window size assignments. The details are described as follows:

1. *Voice Packet*: IEEE 802.11 MAC algorithm with the minimum contention window size of 7 and the maximum contention window size of 255 is used for a station with voice traffic. It has the access guaranteed initial backoff range [0, 7], which gives the highest priority to voice traffic for accessing the medium. Voice traffic needs repeated packet transmissions in constant time intervals (e.g., only one packet transmission is needed every 30 ms). The FCR algorithm works with high efficiency for best-effort data traffic transmission, where each active station has more than one packets to transmit. However, in voice traffic transmissions where only one packet transmission is needed every 30 ms, the IEEE 802.11 MAC is more suitable because it does not increase the contention window sizes of the deferred stations. That is, after one station succeeds in transmitting a packet, and leaves the contention session, the remaining stations still keep the same contention window sizes and contend again (in the FCR algorithm, these remaining stations increase the contention window sizes). This results in small wasting idle slots in voice traffic transmissions.

2. *Video Packet* : Fast collision resolution (FCR) algorithm with the minimum contention window size of 3 and the maximum contention window size of 31 is used for video packet transmissions. It starts the contention for video packet transmissions after the initial backoff range of voice traffic. The smaller maximum contention window size of video traffic (MaxCW=31) than that of best-effort data traffic (MaxCW=2047) gives video traffic higher priority for the medium access over best-effort data traffic.

3. *Best-Effort Data Packet*: Fast collision resolution (FCR) algorithm with the minimum contention window size of 3 and the maximum contention window size of 2047 is used for best-effort data traffic. It starts the contention for best-effort data packet transmissions after the initial backoff range of voice traffic. FCR scheme with the large maximum contention window size achieves the high throughput for best-effort data traffic in addition to providing the opportunity for the medium access to voice or video traffic.

3 Performance Evaluation

We consider three different types of traffic: constant bit rate (CBR) voice traffic, variable bit rate (VBR) video traffic, and best-effort data traffic. The detailed source models used in our simulations are described as follows:

1. *Voice Model*([4]): A voice source has two states, talkspurts and silent gaps identified by a speech activity detector. The probability that a principal talkspurt, with mean duration t_1 second, ends in a time slot of duration τ seconds is $\gamma = 1 - exp(-\tau/t_1)$. The probability that a silent gap, of mean duration t_2 seconds, ends during τ seconds time slot is $\sigma = 1 - exp(-\tau/t_2)$. Measured mean values for t_1 of principal talkspurts and t_2 of principal silent gaps are 1.00 and 1.35 seconds. We use 32 kbps voice traffic sources which generate one 120 byte payload voice packet every 30 msec during talkspurts period, and we assign the deadline for voice packet delay as 30 msec (i.e., the maximum voice packet delay is 30 msec).

166

2. *Video Model*([4, 9]): We use the H.263 video traffic with 40 msec interframe period, i.e., 25 frames per second. During an interframe period, each video source generates a frame consisting of a variable number of packets. As soon as packets become available from the coder, they could be transmitted at the maximum rate the channel allows. The video packet size is 120 bytes and the mean rate of video traffic is 48 kbps and the maximum rate is 480 kbps. That is, there are 2 packets per frame for the mean rate and the maximum number of packets per frame is 20. We use the deadline for video packet delay as 120 msec.

3. *Best-effort Data Model*([3]): It is assumed that best-effort data sources always have packets to transmit. We use the parameter $q = 0.975$ from the geometric distribution for best-effort data packet length, which implies that the average packet length of best-effort data traffic is 40 slots.

We first present the results for FCR with all best-effort data stations, which generate traffic with packet lengths geometrically distributed. We assume that the best-effort data packets are always available at all stations and that the maximum successive packet transmission limit in the FCR algorithm is set to 10. Figure 2 shows the throughput performance for both IEEE 802.11 MAC and our MAC with FCR.

The result show that our proposed FCR outperforms the IEEE MAC protocol in terms of throughput and average delay.

Next, we present the simulation results of the prioritized FCR algorithm for 10 and 100 best-effort data traffic stations with varying the number of CBR voice traffic stations up to 15. We compare the results of the prioritized FCR algorithm with those of the IEEE 802.11 MAC algorithm. The ratio of the dropped voice packets to the total generated voice packets is shown in Figure 3(a), and the throughput for the best-effort data traffic transmissions is shown in Figure 3(b). In Figure 3(a), the IEEE 802.11 MAC algorithm loses over 40% of voice packets with 10 best-effort data stations and over 90% with 100 best-effort data stations. This is expected because the IEEE 802.11 DCF mode treats real-time traffic the same as the best-effort data traffic. The ratios of dropped voice packets for the prioritized FCR algorithm are close to zero for both cases. The prioritized FCR algorithm shows very low voice packet dropping ratio while still preserving high throughput performance for best-effort data traffic, which is obvious in Figures 3(a) and 3(b).

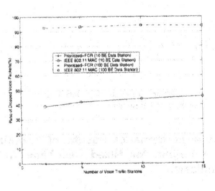

(a) Ratio of Dropped Voice Packets

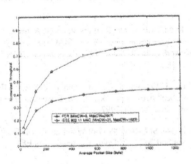

(a) Throughput for 100 BE data stations wireless LAN

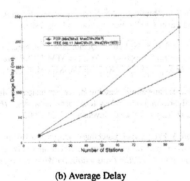

(b) Average Delay

Figure 2. Delay performance

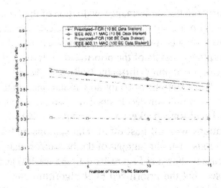

(b) Throughput of Best-Effort Data Traffic

Figure 3. Performance Results of Prioritized FCR Algorithm for Voice and Data Traffic

167

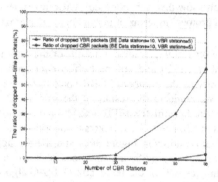

(a) Ratio of Dropped Real-Time Packets vs. Number of CBR Stations

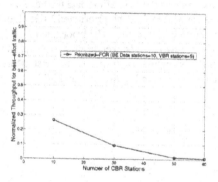

(b) Throughput of Best-Effort Data Traffic vs. Number of CBR Stations

Figure 4. Performance Results of Prioritized FCR Algorithm for Mixed Real-Time Traffic Transmissions

We carry out the performance evaluation of the prioritized FCR algorithm for the integration of three different traffics: voice, video, and best-effort data. Figure 4(a) and 4(b) show the performance results of the prioritized FCR algorithm for the integration of three different traffics. The number of best-effort data stations is 10 for all simulations. Figure 4(a) shows that the ratio of the dropped real-time packets to the generated real-time packets vs. various numbers of CBR voice stations with 10 best-effort data stations and 5 VBR video stations. The throughput of the best-effort data traffic for this case is shown in Figure 4(b). In Figure 4(a) and 4(b), we can see that the prioritized FCR algorithm can support the desired QoS for real-time applications upto 30 CBR stations with 10 best-effort data stations and 5 VBR stations. Figure 4(a) shows that voice traffic has much higher priority for channel access over video and best-effort data traffics, so the ratio of dropped packet for voice traffic is close to zero for most cases. The ratio of dropped packet for video traffic is affected by best-effort data traffic as the number of CBR

stations increases. From the simulation results, we can conclude that the QoS for voice traffic is highly satisfied and the QoS for video traffic is satisfactory in the prioritized FCR algorithm. While providing QoS for real-time traffic, the prioritized FCR algorithm achieves high throughput for best-effort data traffic when the channel is available for best-effort data traffic transmissions between real-time traffic transmissions, which is shown in Figure 4(a) and 4(b).

4 Conclusions

In this paper, we study new contention-based medium access control algorithms with and without QoS support for real-time applications. Performance results show that the proposed schemes can achieve high throughput performance for non-real-time traffic while still maintaining good QoS for real-time applications.

References

[1] I. Aad and C. Castelluccia, "Differentiation mechanisms for IEEE 802.11," *IEEE INFOCOM*, Anchorage, Alaska, April 2001.

[2] V. Bharghavan , "MACAW: A Media Access Protocol for Wireless LAN's," *SIGCOMM'94*, pp.212-225, London, England, Aug. 1994.

[3] F. Cali, M. Conti, and E. Gregori, "Dynamin Tuning of the IEEE 802.11 Protocol to Achieve a Theoretical Throughput Limit," *IEEE/ACM Trans. on Networking*, vol. 8, NO. 6, pp.785-799, Dec. 2000.

[4] J. Chen, K. M. Sivalingam, P. Agrawal, and R.Acharya, "Scheduling Multimedia Services in a Low-Power MAC for Wireless and Mobile ATM Networks," *IEEE Trans. on Multimedia*, Vol.1, NO.2, pp.187-201, June 1999.

[5] B. P. Crow, I. Widjaja, J. G. Kim, and P. T. Sakai, "IEEE 802.11 Wireless Local Area Networks," *IEEE Communications Magazine* Vol.35, pp.116-126, Sep. 1997.

[6] J. Deng and R. S. Chang, "A Priority Scheme for IEEE 802.11 DCF Access Method," *IEICE Trans. Commun.*, Vol.E82-B, NO.1, Jan. 1999.

[7] C. Fullmer and J. Garcia-Luna-Aceves, "Floor acquition multiple access (FAMA) for packet-ratio networks," *Proc. SIGCOMM'95*, pp.262-273, Cambridge, MA.

[8] IEEE 802.11 Wireless LAN Medium Access Control (MAC) and Physical Layer (PHY) specifications, *IEEE*, 1997.

[9] Y. Kwok and V. K. N. Lau, "A Quantitative Comparison of Multiple Access Control Protocols for Wireless ATM," *IEEE Trans. on Vehicular Technology*, Vol.50, NO.3, pp.796-815, May, 2001.

[10] Y. Kwon, Y. Fang and H. Latchman, "Fast collision resolution (FCR) MAC algorithm for wireless local area networks," *IEEE Globecom'2002*, Taipei, Taiwan, November 17-21, 2002.

[11] Y. Kwon, Y. Fang and H. Latchman, "Design of MAC protocols with fast collision resolution for wireless local area networks," Revised and resubmitted to *IEEE Transactions on Wireless Communications*.

The Role of Error Control Coding in Joint Detection CDMA

Christian Schlegel
University of Alberta
Edmonton, AB, CANADA

Abstract

It is well known that joint detection of CDMA signals has many advantages and can significantly improve the spectral efficiency of a system. In this paper we examine the role of error control coding in such CDMA systems and compare performance of novel iterative detection schemes with the information theoretic capacity limits of the CDMA channel. We conclude that powerful error control codes are not necessary to overcome the multiple access interference, and that simple error control schemes can have superior performance in terms of achievable spectral efficiency.

1 System Model

The code-division multiple-access (CDMA) channel is a linear channel where the signals of different users superpose and cause mutual interference due to the usual lack of orthogonality between the signature sequences of the different terminals which access the channel. Error control coding can be used to overcome this interference, as is currently the state of the art in IS95 and CDMA2000. On the other hand, joint detection of the CDMA signal exploits the structure of the interference and jointly decodes all users. Several such joint detectors [4, 15] have in the past been studied, including the maximum-likelihood detector [13] whose complexity is, however, prohibitive for implementation.

However, maximum likelihood detection is not a requirement to achieve the capacity of a communications channels, and, recently, the application of forward error control coding and the integration of FEC in a serial concatenated fashion with iterative decoding has proven to be a very effective methodology to attain high performance [11]. This method can be seen as an appliction of the "turbo decoding principle" [3] to CDMA systems. The method is based on realization that CDMA combined with forward error control coding can be viewed as the serial concatenation of two "coding systems", and serial turbo decoding principles have been applied, first used in [7, 1, 6]. Such systems break joint decoding into two operations, viz. CDMA a

posteriori probability (APP) estimation, or an approximation thereof, and a bank of K single-user FEC APP decoders. These two components form a closed loop around which updated soft information is exchanged in the form of extrinsic a posteriori probabilities.

Figure 1 shows the receiver set-up for this iterative method, where Π_k is the interleaver for user k. The extrinsic a posteriori information from the error control decoder is typically transformed into a softbit $\tilde{d}_i^{(k)}$, given by

$$\tilde{d}_i^{(k)} = E\left[d_i^{(k)}|y\right] = \tanh\left(\frac{\lambda_i^{(k)}}{2}\right)$$

where $\lambda_i^{(k)}$ is the log-likelihood ratio of the i-th bit of the k-th user, and, importantly, $\tilde{d}_i^{(k)}$ the minimum variance estimate of $d_i^{(k)}$.

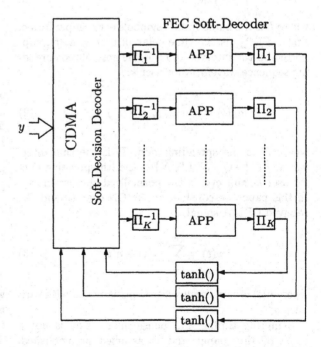

Figure 1: Block diagram of the joint iterative decoder

The FEC soft-ouput decoder is well understood [8]. It transforms a noisy input signal into probability estimates of the transmitted symbols, usually given in the form of log-likelihood ratios (LLR). The CDMA soft-decision decoder [6] is very complex if exact a-posteriori probabilities are to be calculated, however, efficient linear decoders exist. Alexander et.al. [2], for example, use a simple cancellation operation and achieved surprisingly good results. Wang and Poor [14] augmented the canceller with an MMSE filter to perform improved interference suppression. The decorrelator has also been used [9], however, decorrelation linearly eliminates all interference at the cost of a power loss in the target user, and it can easily be shown that iterative processing is no benefit in this case. The proposed detectors using decorrelation (projection receivers) operate on a one-path processing only.

The system model considered is that of asynchronous CDMA with K transmitters which generate independent binary information bits $u_k \in \{0, 1\}$, $k = 1, \ldots, K$ and encode these bits by K parity check codes. Random interleavers separate the encoders from the spreading operation as is customary in serial concatenation. The outputs of the encoders are mapped into BPSK, and modulated by the K spreaders. Assuming equal powers, the signal from the kth spreader is

$$x_k(t) = \sum_{j=0}^{L-1} d_k(j) a_k(t - jT - \tau_k) \qquad (1)$$

where L is the number data symbols per user per frame, $\{\tau_k (< T)\}_{k=1}^{K}$ is the time delay of user k, $a_k(t)$, supported on the interval $[0, T]$, is the normalized spreading sequence waveform for user k:

$$a_k(t) = \sum_{l=0}^{N-1} a_{k,l} g(t - lT_c) \qquad (2)$$

where N is the spreading gain, T_c is the chip interval, $a_{k,l} \in \{-1/\sqrt{N}, 1/\sqrt{N}\}$ is the lth spreading chip for user k, and $g(t)$ is the normalized chip waveform. In this paper we consider an AWGN channel and the received CDMA signal is

$$y(t) = \sum_{k=1}^{K} x_k(t) + n(t) \qquad (3)$$

where $n(t)$ is zero mean white Gaussian noise with variance σ^2.

Acquiring timing and phase information is not a topic of this paper and is assumed accomplished, e.g., by any of the well-known algorithms proposed in [5]. With this the received signal is sampled by chip matched filters, leading to the discrete channel model

$$y = Ad + n \qquad (4)$$

where n is an $(L + 1)N$ vector of sampled white noise with variance σ^2, A is an $(L + 1)N$ by LK matrix whose j-th column is $a_{|j/K|,k} = [\underline{0}_{iN + \frac{\tau_k}{T_c}}, a_{k,i}^T, \underline{0}_{(L-i)N-k}]^T$; $k = j - |j/K|$ where $j = iK$, and $\underline{0}_l$ is a length-l all-zero row vector, and $d = [d_1(1), \ldots, d_K(1), d_1(2), \ldots, d_K(L)]^T$ is a vector of encoded symbols.

2 Soft Information Exchange

2.1 The CDMA Decoder

The CDMA interference resolution function is to generate soft outputs of the encoded symbols $d_i^{(k)}$ given a received frame of symbols y. Since the CDMA channel is a linear channel, it can be shown that the optimal processing given knowledge of the interfering signals is simply to subtract the interference from the received signal. In an iterative decoder this subtraction is incomplete since the estimates of the interfering symbols may be inaccurate. Each user, e.g., user k, can view the received signal y after cancellation as its own, contaminated with residual interference, i.e.,

$$y = \sum_{i=1}^{L} \sqrt{P_k} d_k(i) a_{i,k}$$

$$+ \overbrace{\sum_{i=1}^{L} \sum_{\substack{j=1 \\ (j \neq k)}}^{K} \sqrt{P_k} (d_j(i) - \tilde{d}_j(i)) a_{i,j}}^{I_k} + n \quad (5)$$

where $\tilde{d}_i(k)$ was generated during a previous iteration, and is now used to partially cancel the interference from users $j \neq k$. The term I_k in (5) is then the *residual interference* after cancellation. Viewing multiaccess interference as noise, the signal-to-noise ratio maximizing filter is the matched filter. Thus the i-th sample for user k is given by

$$z_k(i) = \sqrt{P_k} d_k(i) +$$

$$\sum_{l=1}^{L} \sum_{\substack{j=1 \\ (j \neq k)}}^{K} \sqrt{P_j} h_{kj}(i, l)(d_j(l) - \tilde{d}_j(l)) + n_k \quad (6)$$

where $h_{kj}(i, l)$ is the crosscorrelation between the k-th user's signature sequence used to spread bit i, and the j-th user's signature sequence used to spread bit l. These values can be arranged in a tri-diagonal correlation matrix, given by $H = A^T A$. The operation in (6) is called simple *interference cancellation* whereby the correlated interference is estimated and subtracted from the output of the matched filter front-end.

As mentioned above, $z_k(i)$ can be subject to further noise suppressing by a minimum mean square error (MMSE) filter

$$
\begin{aligned}
w_k(i) &= \arg \min_{w \in \mathbb{R}^N} E\left[(d_k(i) - w^T(i)z)^2\right] \\
&= \frac{P_k}{1 + P_k a_{i,k}^T K^{-1} a_{i,k}} K^{-1} a_{i,k} \quad (7)
\end{aligned}
$$

where $K = A_k^T D_k A_k$, D_k is a diagonal matrix of the *residual* power of the interfering users, and $A_k = [a_1, \cdots, a_{k-1}, a_{k+1}, \cdots, a_K]$. The MMSE filter is considerably more complex than simple interference cancellation due to the inverse of K, but provides some performance gain as shown below.

Both $z_k(i)$ and $w_k(i)z$ are well approximated by Gaussian statistics, and the single-user soft-output FEC decoders do in essence simply see an AWGN channel with a certain variance. The whiteness of the noise is due to the interleavers which elimninate correlation between samples. The performance for large systems of (6) and (7) can now be measured by the normalized variance $\sigma_k^2 = E[\frac{\sigma_{z,k}^2}{\mu_{z,k}^2}]$, where $\mu_{z,k}$ and $\sigma_{z,k}^2$ are expected signal amplitude and variance of z_k respectively. Alexander et. al. [1] have shown that for equal coded symbol powers $P_1 = \cdots = P_K = P$, for simple cancellation

$$
\sigma_k^2 = \frac{\sigma^2}{P} + \frac{K-1}{N} \sigma_d^2 \quad (8)
$$

where $\sigma_d^2 = E[(d - \tilde{d})^2]$ is the variance of the residual interference stemming from the incomplete cancellation of the previous iteration, and for MMSE cancellation [11, 12]

$$
\frac{1}{\sigma_k^2} = -\frac{\sigma^2 + \sigma_d^2(\alpha-1)P}{2\sigma_d^2 \sigma^2} + \frac{\sqrt{\sigma^4 + \sigma_d^4(\alpha-1)^2 P^2 + 2\sigma_d^2(\alpha+1)\sigma^2 P}}{2\sigma_d^2 \sigma^2} \quad (9)
$$

Equation (8) is linear in the residual interference power, and (9) is nearly linear (it becomes linear as $E_b/N_0 \to \infty$).

Figure 2 shows the *variance transfer* curves of these two detectors for two values of the signal-to-noise ratio. As can be shown, the slope of (9) equals $\alpha - 1$, whereby the slope of (8) equals α, and we can conclude already at this point that the MMSE detector can support N more users than simple cancellation, where N is the processing gain. It is therefore clear that MMSE is efficient in this context only for systems with small load K/N.

Little is currently known about the transfer behavior of the APP CDMA decoder, however, it can be shown that it intersects with the two IC cancellation transfer curves at the vertical axis at $\sigma_d^2 = 0$. This means that the FEC decoder must be capable of overcoming the channel noise alone, irrespective of which CDMA decoder is used, since the ordinate value at $\sigma_d^2 = 0$ is the Gaussian channel noise. This also means that none of these interference cancellation methods can outperform single user decoding. In retrospect this seems obvious, but was not so in light of the serial concatenated view of the system.

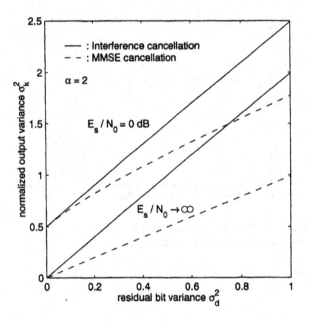

Figure 2: Asymptotic VTR for MMSE and simple cancellation detectors at $\frac{E_s}{N_0} = 0$dB and $\frac{E_s}{N_0} \to \infty$ respectively

2.2 The Error Control Decoder

The role of the error control code is analogous. It receives $z_i(k)$, a signal embedded in Gaussian noise with an aprori LLR

$$
\lambda_A(d_i^{(k)}) = \log \frac{\Pr(d_i^{(k)} = 1|z_i(k))}{\Pr(d_i^{(k)} = -1|z_i(k))} = \frac{2}{\sigma^2} z_i(k) \quad (10)
$$

The single user APP decoders produce extrinsic LLR values $\lambda_E(d_i^{(k)})$ of the coded bits $d_i(k)$, from which the soft bits $\tilde{d}_k(i) = \tanh(\lambda_E(d_k(i))/2)$ are generated for cancellation (see Figure 1), or fed directly to an APP CDMA decoder. The soft-output transfer characteristics of the error control code is currently not yet well understood, however, experiments vindicate the folklore that powerful codes do well close to their decoding limit, whereas weak codes do better for high input noise in improving the output variance. Figure 3 shows the transfer curves of some powerful concatenated error control curves, while Figure 4 shows the transfer curves of relatively weak FEC codes. The strong codes are given in the table at the end of the paper.

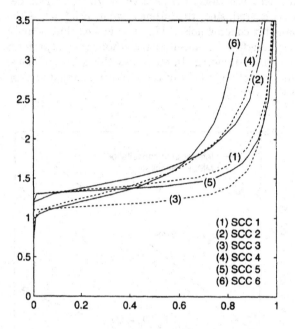

Figure 3: Variance transfer curves of some strong concatenated error control codes.

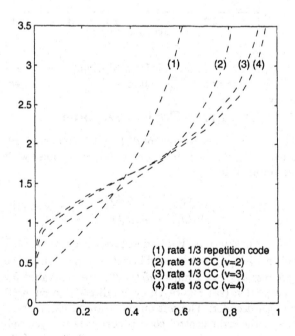

Figure 4: Variance transfer curves of weak codes.

Putting the transfer behavior of the CDMA detec-

tor and the FEC decoders together, iterative decoding can be viewed as an exchange of variances between these two components. This is otherwise known as density evolution, and becomes increasingly accurate as the block size and thus the interleaver sizes increase. Figure 5 shows an example of a "measured" variance exchange and demonstrates that it fits well into the predictions by these two transfer curves. Decoding is therefore possible only if there is an open channel through with these iterations can proceed, and the "cutoff point" is where the two transfer curves intersect. This analysis gives therefore an accurate tool to examine coded CDMA systems and their potential.

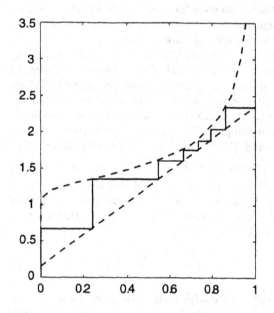

Figure 5: Variance transfer example between a simple interference canceller and FEC code SCC 2 for $K = 23, N = 10$ at $E_b/N_0 = 10$dB.

The distinction between the strong and the weak codes leads to the following conclusion: Strong codes are preferable only if channel noise is the dominant impairment, while weak codes support a larger slope and thus a larger system load.

Figure 6 shows a compilation of the performance of a large number of coded systems which supports this conclusion. As can be seen by careful inspection, the weaker codes fare better in cancelling the interference but require a higher signal-to-noise ratio since their performance in overcoming channel noise is poorer, while strong codes overcome the channel noise but do not support very large system loads due to their "threshold"-like behavior of the variance transfer curve. For an extremely efficient system using only a [2,1,2] parity check code see [10].

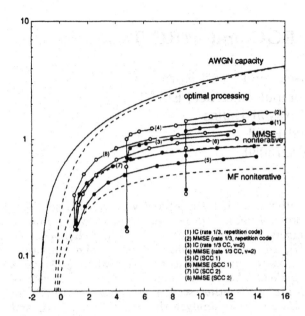

Figure 6: Attainable spectral efficiencies of iterative decoders compared to the capacity limit of both joint and single path decoding.

3 Conclusion

We have presented a density evolution analysis of coded CDMA systems to gain insight into the role of both the CDMA soft detector and the soft-output FEC decoders. We have shown that in order to overcome multiple access interference, simple error control codes are preferable and indeed more efficient. We have also shown that overcoming the channel noise is the sole responsibility of the FEC code. This gives guidelines to the application of error control coding in high-interference linear channels where joint iterative decoding is used.

References

[1] P.D. Alexander, M.C. Reed, J.A. Asenstorfer and C.B. Schlegel, "Iterative Multiuser Interference Reduction: Turbo CDMA", *IEEE Trans. Commun.*, vol. 47, no. 7, July 1999.

[2] P.D. Alexander, A. Grant and M.C. Reed, "Iterative Detection in Code-Division Multiple-Access with Error Control Coding", *European Transaction on Telecommunications*, vol. 9, pp. 419-426, Sep. 1998.

[3] C. Berrou and A. Glavieux, "Near Optimum error correcting coding and decoding: turbo-codes", *IEEE Trans. Commun.*, vol. 44, pp. 1261-1271, Oct. 1996.

[4] R. Lupas and S. Verdu, "Linear multiuser detectors for synchronous code-division multiple access channels", *IEEE Trans. Inform. Theory*, vol. 35, pp. 123–136, January 1989.

[5] H. Meyr, M. Moeneclaey and S. Fechtel, *Digital Communication Receivers*, Wiley, New York, 1998.

[6] M. Moher, "An Iterative Multiuser Decoder for Near-Capacity Communications", *IEEE Trans. Commun.*, vol. 47, pp. 870–880, July 1998.

[7] M.C. Reed, C.B. Schlegel, P.D. Alexander and J.A. Asenstorfer, "Iterative Multiuser Detection for CDMA with FEC: Near-Single-User Performance", *IEEE Trans. Commun.*, vol 46, no. 12, Dec. 1998.

[8] C. Schlegel, *Trellis Coding*, IEEE Press, Piscataway, New Jersey, 1997.

[9] C. Schlegel, S. Roy, P. Alexander, and Z. Xiang, "Multi-user projection receivers", *IEEE J. Select. Areas Commun.*, vol. 14, October 1996.

[10] C. Schlegel and Z. Shi, "A low-complexity efficient iterative CDMA multiuser detector", submitted to *IEEE Comms. Letters*, July 2002.

[11] Z. Shi and C. Schlegel, "Joint Iterative Decoding of Serially Concatenated Error Control Coded CDMA", *IEEE Journal on Selected Areas in Communications*, pp1646-1653, August 2001.

[12] D. Tse and S. Hanly, "Linear Multiuser Receivers: Effective Interference, Effective Bandwidth and User Capacity", *IEEE Trans. Inform. Theory*, Mar. 1999.

[13] S. Verdu, "Minimum probability of error for asynchronous Gaussian multiple access channels", *IEEE Trans. Inform. Theory*, vol. 32, pp. 85–96, January 1986.

[14] X. Wang and H.V. Poor, "Iterative (Turbo) Soft Interference Cancellation and Decoding for Coded CDMA", *IEEE Trans. Commun.*, vol. 47, no. 7, July 1999.

[15] Z. Xie, R. Short, C.K. Rushforth, "A family of suboptimum detectors for coherent multiuser multiuser communications", *IEEE J. Select. Areas Commun.*, vol. 8, pp. 683–690, May 1990.

	Inner Code	Outer Code	R_i	R_o
SCC 1	$g_1 = [1 \ \frac{1+D^2}{1+D+D^2}]$	$g_2 = \begin{bmatrix} 1 & 0 & \frac{1+D^2}{1+D+D^2} \\ 0 & 1 & \frac{1+D}{1+D+D^2} \end{bmatrix}$	$\frac{1}{2}$	$\frac{2}{3}$
SCC 2	$g_1 = [1 \ \frac{1+D^2}{1+D+D^2}]$	$H = [111]$	$\frac{1}{2}$	$\frac{2}{3}$
SCC 3	$g_1 = \frac{1}{1+D}$	$g_2 = \begin{bmatrix} 1+D^2 & 1+D+D^2+D^3 & 1+D+D^2+D^3 \end{bmatrix}$	1	$\frac{1}{3}$
SCC 4	$g_1 = \frac{1}{1+D}$	rate 1/3 repetition code	1	$\frac{1}{3}$
SCC 5	$g_1 = \begin{bmatrix} 1 & 0 & \frac{1+D^2}{1+D+D^2} \\ 0 & 1 & \frac{1+D}{1+D+D^2} \end{bmatrix}$	$g_2 = [1 \ \frac{1+D^2}{1+D+D^2}]$	$\frac{2}{3}$	$\frac{1}{2}$
SCC 6	$g_1 = \begin{bmatrix} 1 & 0 & \frac{1+D^2}{1+D+D^2} \\ 0 & 1 & \frac{1+D}{1+D+D^2} \end{bmatrix}$	rate 1/2 repetition code	$\frac{2}{3}$	$\frac{1}{2}$

Sensitivity to Timing Errors in EGC and MRC Techniques

Yunjing Yin, John P. Fonseka and Israel Korn*
School of Engineering and Computer Science, EC 33
The University of Texas at Dallas
2601, N. Floyd Road
Richardson TX 75080

Abstract

The effect of imperfect timing is analyzed in EGC and MRC techniques over Rayleigh and Nakagami-m fading channels with BPSK modulation. In the case of EGC the bit error probability is derived, while in the case of MRC error rate bounds are presented. Theoretical results are justified by computer simulation. Numerical results demonstrate that both EGC and MRC are fairly sensitive to timing errors, and comparatively, MRC is more sensitive.

Index Terms - Diversity combining, Imperfect fading estimates, Error rate analysis

1. Introduction

In maximal ratio combining (MRC) and equal gain combining (EGC), the signals on different channels are processed in such a way that the signal to noise ratio (SNR) for the combined signal is

$$\gamma = \begin{cases} \sum_{k=1}^{L} \gamma_k, & \text{MRC} \\ \frac{1}{L}\left[\sum_{k=1}^{L} \sqrt{\gamma_k}\right]^2, & \text{EGC} \end{cases} \quad (1)$$

where, γ_k is the SNR on the kth diversity channel and L is the number of diversity branches. These expressions are valid only under perfect conditions. In particular, perfect estimates of fading parameters and perfect estimates of timing information on every branch are required. In MRC both the amplitude and the phase, while in EGC the phase, of all fading components are required at the receiver. Hence, it is important to investigate the sensitivity of the diversity combining techniques to system impairments. Several studies in the literature have reported the sensitivity to various estimation errors under different conditions [1,4-6]. The effect of phase errors with BPSK and QPSK signals has been presented in a Rayleigh channel

without diversity in [4] and with EGC in [5]. Few other studies [6] deal with the sensitivity to phase errors in CDMA systems in fading channels. In [7], the combined effect of phase and amplitude estimates has been considered with QAM in a Rayleigh channel without diversity. A review of some of the other studies are presented in [1]. In this study, we analyze the sensitivity of EGC and MRC techniques to timing errors. We consider BPSK signaling with coherent demodulation in a Nakagami-m fading channel which corresponds to a Rayleigh channel when $m = 1$. We analyze the system with EGC theoretically, and present theoretical bounds with MRC. We also verify the theoretical results by computer simulation. This study differs from [6] primarily because (a) it considers Nakagami-m fading as opposed to Rayleigh fading considered in [6] (b) it considers a Tikhonov distribution for the timing error, which is known to be a better model in practice [8], as opposed to a uniform distribution considered in [6] and (c) in the case of MRC, it presents performance bounds in integral form as opposed to approximations presented in series form.

2. System Model

Fig. 1

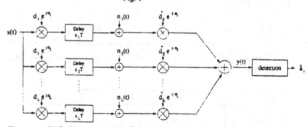

Fig. 1 EGC and MRC with imperfect timing.

Fig. 1 shows the conceptual low-pass equivalent model of EGC and MRC with imperfect timing. The quantities $\epsilon_1 T$, $\epsilon_2 T,...\epsilon_L T$ represent the associated timing errors of the individual diversity branches respectively (ϵ_k represents the normalized timing error on the kth branch normalized to the bit duration T). It is assumed here that $\epsilon_1, \epsilon_2,...\epsilon_L$ are independent and identically distributed with a Tikhonov probability density function (pdf) [8]

$$f_\epsilon(\epsilon_k) = \frac{exp[(\cos(2\pi\epsilon_k))/(2\pi\sigma_\epsilon)^2]}{I_0(1/(2\pi\sigma_\epsilon)^2)}, \quad |\epsilon_k| \le 0.5 \tag{2}$$

where σ_ϵ is the standard deviation of ϵ_k, and $I_0(.)$ is the zeroth order modified Bessel function of the first kind. Using the complex envelope notation, the transmitted BPSK signal is

$$s(t) = \sqrt{\frac{2E}{T}} \sum_i a_i u_T(t - iT) \tag{3}$$

where E is the bit energy, $a_i \in \{+1,-1\}$ is the ith bit, and $u_T(t)$ is the unit magnitude rectangular pulse over $[0,T]$. Assuming a flat and slow fading channel with additive white Gaussian noise (AWGN), the received signal on any kth diversity branch in presence of the timing error ϵ_k can be written as

$$r_k(t) = s(t - \epsilon_k T)\xi_k(t) + n_k(t), \quad k = 1, 2, ..., L \tag{4}$$

where $\xi_k(t) = d_k(t)e^{j\alpha_k(t)}$ is the complex fading process with unity variance, magnitude $d_k(t)$ and phase $\alpha_k(t)$, $n_k(t)$ is the channel noise which is modeled by a complex zero mean Gaussian process with power spectral density N_0 and L is the total number of diversity branches. It is assumed that the fading processes and the noise components on different diversity branches are all mutually independent. Denoting $\xi_k(t)$, $d_k(t)$ and $\alpha_k(t)$ over a duration of T by ξ_k, d_k and α_k respectively (which is justified under slow fading), the received signal $r_k(t)$ during any ith interval, $iT \le t < (i+1)T$, can be written as

$$r_k(t) = \begin{cases} \begin{cases} a_i\sqrt{\frac{2E}{T}}d_k e^{j\alpha_k} + n_k(t), \\ \quad iT \le t < (i+1)T + \epsilon_k T \\ a_{i+1}\sqrt{\frac{2E}{T}}d_k e^{j\alpha_k} + n_k(t), \\ \quad (i+1)T + \epsilon_k T \le t < (i+1)T \end{cases} & \epsilon_k < 0 \\ \begin{cases} a_{i-1}\sqrt{\frac{2E}{T}}d_k e^{j\alpha_k} + n_k(t), \\ \quad iT \le t < iT + \epsilon_k T \\ a_i\sqrt{\frac{2E}{T}}d_k e^{j\alpha_k} + n_k(t), \\ \quad iT + \epsilon_k T \le t < (i+1)T \end{cases} & \epsilon_k > 0 \end{cases} \tag{5}$$

For Nakagami-m fading, the pdf of d_k, $f_d(d_k)$ is [1]

$$f_d(d_k) = \frac{2}{\Gamma(m)} d_k^{2m-1}(m)^m e^{-md_k^2} \tag{6}$$

where $\Gamma(m)$ is the standard Gamma function.

3. EGC with Timing Errors

In EGC, with perfect knowledge of phases α_k, the input to the detector is (see Fig. 1)

$$y(t) = \sum_{k=1}^{L} r_k(t)e^{-j\alpha_k}. \tag{7}$$

Considering a correlator type BPSK demodulator, the decision variable of the ith symbol can be obtained from $y(t)$ as

$$D_i = \sqrt{\frac{1}{N_0}}\text{Re}\{\int_{iT}^{(i+1)T} \sqrt{\frac{1}{T}}y(t)dt\}$$
$$= a_i\sqrt{\frac{2E}{N_0}} \sum_{k=1}^{L} d_k c_k + \sum_{k=1}^{L} w_k \tag{8}$$

where $\text{Re}\{.\}$ denotes the real part of the argument,

$$c_k = \begin{cases} 1 & \text{if } a_i = a_{adj} \\ (1 - 2|\epsilon_k|) & \text{if } a_i \ne a_{adj}, \end{cases} \tag{9}$$

and w_k follows from the real part of the noise component in (5) and is zero mean Gaussian with unit variance. It is seen from (5) and (8) that timing errors introduce intersymbol interference (ISI) in the decision variable. It follows from (5) and (8) that the effect of the timing error on D_i from any kth branch depends on the effective adjacent symbol a_{adj}, which for the symbol a_i is a_{i+1} if $\epsilon_k < 0$, and a_{i-1} if $\epsilon_k > 0$. It is noticed from (5), (8) and (9) that if $a_i = a_{adj}$, ϵ_k has no effect on D_i, and if $a_i \ne a_{adj}$, the effect of ϵ_k is to reduce the signal component from the kth branch by a factor $(1 - 2|\epsilon_k|)$. The term $1/\sqrt{N_0}$ in D_i which does not affect the decision has been used simply to express it in terms of E/N_0. It is also seen from (8) that the instantaneous signal to noise ratio (SNR) of the decision variable is

$$\gamma = \frac{2E\left[\sum_{k=1}^{L} d_k c_k\right]^2}{LN_0} = \frac{1}{L}[\sum_{k=1}^{L} \sqrt{\gamma_k}c_k]^2 \tag{10}$$

where $\gamma_k = 2Ed_k^2/N_0$ is the SNR on the kth branch without a timing error.

In this study, the BEP is calculated by extending the analysis of EGC with perfect conditions presented in [3] using the characteristic function (CHF) of the decision variable. In [3], the BEP has been found as

$$P_e = \frac{1}{2} - \frac{1}{2\pi} \int_{-\infty}^{\infty} \frac{\text{Im}\{\phi_D(\omega)\}}{\omega} d\omega \tag{11}$$

where $\phi_D(\omega)$ is the CHF of the decision variable D_i in (8) and $\text{Im}\{.\}$ represents the imaginary part of the argument. Since D_i depends on the values of c_ks, its CHF $\phi_D(\omega)$ is calculated by conditioning on the number of terms l in (8) for which $c_k = 1$. For any given l, assuming independent diversity branches, $\phi_D(\omega)$ follows from (8) as

$$\phi_{D|l}(\omega) = \overline{e^{j\omega D|l}} = \phi_1^l\left(\sqrt{\frac{2E}{N_0}}\omega\right)\phi_2^{(L-l)}\left(\sqrt{\frac{2E}{N_0}}\omega\right)\phi_{w_k}^L(\omega) \quad (12)$$

the overline denotes the averaging operation, $\phi_1(\omega)$ is the CHF of d_k,

$$\phi_1(\omega) = \int_{-\infty}^{\infty} e^{jd_k\omega} f_d(d_k) dd_k \quad (13)$$

which can be expressed as

$$\phi_1(\omega) = \begin{cases} {}_1F_1(1;\frac{1}{2};\frac{-\omega^2}{4}) + j\omega\sqrt{\frac{\pi}{4}}exp(-\frac{\omega^2}{4}) & m=1 \\ {}_1F_1(m;\frac{1}{2};\frac{-\omega^2}{4m}) + \\ j\omega\frac{\Gamma(m+\frac{1}{2})}{\Gamma(m)}\sqrt{\frac{1}{m}} {}_1F_1(m+\frac{1}{2};\frac{3}{2};-\frac{\omega^2}{4m}) & m\neq 1, \end{cases} \quad (14)$$

$\phi_2(\omega)$ is the CHF of $d_k(1-2|\epsilon_k|)$ which is

$$\phi_2(\omega) = \overline{e^{j\omega d_k(1-2|\epsilon_k|)}} = 2\int_0^{0.5} \phi_1[\omega(1-2|\epsilon_k|)]f_\epsilon(\epsilon_k)d\epsilon_k \quad (15)$$

and $\phi_{w_k}(\omega)$ is the CHF of w_k which follows from the Gaussian distribution as [3]

$$\phi_{w_k}(\omega) = \overline{e^{j w_k \omega}} = \int_{-\infty}^{\infty} e^{j w_k \omega} f(w_k) dw_k = e^{-\frac{\omega^2}{4}}. \quad (16)$$

In the above equations, ${}_1F_1(a,b,z)$ is the confluent hypergeometric function [9]. Combining Eqns. (11), (12) and (16), the BEP can be expressed as

$$P_e|_l = \frac{1}{2} - \frac{1}{2\pi}\int_{-\infty}^{\infty} \frac{\text{Im}\left[\phi_1^l(\sqrt{\frac{2E}{N_0}}\omega)\phi_2^{(L-l)}(\sqrt{\frac{2E}{N_0}}\omega)\right]}{[\omega exp(\frac{L\omega^2}{4})]}d\omega. \quad (17)$$

The overall BEP is calculated by averaging $P_e|_l$ over l which requires averaging over all combinations of symbols (a_{i-1}, a_i, a_{i+1}). Noticing that (i) $c_k=1$ for all k when $a_{i-1} = a_i = a_{i+1}$ (which occurs with probability 1/4) (ii) $c_k = (1-2|\epsilon_k|)$ for all k when $a_{i-1} = a_{i+1} \neq a_i$ (which occurs with probability 1/4) (iii) in all other cases, $a_{i-1} = a_i \neq a_{i+1}$ or $a_{i-1} \neq a_i = a_{i+1}$ (which occurs with probability 1/2), the number of branches with $c_k = 1$ can vary between 0 and L, the overall BEP can be expressed using the binomial expansion as

$$P_e = \frac{1}{4}(P_e|_0 + P_e|_L) + \frac{1}{2^{(L+1)}}\sum_{l=0}^{L}\binom{L}{l}P_e|_l$$

$$= \frac{1}{4}(P_e|_0 + P_e|_L) + \frac{1}{2^{L+1}}\left(2^{L-1} - \frac{1}{2\pi}\int_{-\infty}^{\infty}\frac{\text{Im}[\phi_1(\sqrt{\frac{2E}{N_0}}\omega) + \phi_2(\sqrt{\frac{2E}{N_0}}\omega)]^L}{[\omega exp(\frac{L\omega^2}{4})]}d\omega\right) \quad (18)$$

For the special case when $L=1$ with Rayleigh fading, (18) can be simplified using standard integrals [9] as

$$P_e = \frac{1}{2} - \frac{1}{4}\sqrt{\frac{2}{2+\frac{N_0}{E}}} - \frac{\sqrt{E/N_0}}{2I_0(1/(2\pi\sigma_\epsilon)^2)}$$

$$\int_0^{0.5}\frac{(1-2\epsilon)exp[(\cos(2\pi\epsilon))/(2\pi\sigma_\epsilon)^2]}{\sqrt{(1-2\epsilon)^2 E/N_0 + 1}}d\epsilon. \quad (19)$$

4. MRC with Imperfect Timing

We analyze the effect of timing errors in MRC assuming that both amplitude and phase estimates of fading components are available at the receiver. The decision variable with MRC in presence of timing errors during any ith interval, similar to (8), follows from Fig. 1 as

$$D_i = a_i\sqrt{\frac{2E}{N_0}}\sum_{k=1}^{L}d_k^2 c_k + \sum_{k=1}^{L}d_k w_k \quad (20)$$

Further, the SNR of D_i can be expressed as

$$\gamma = \frac{2E\left[\sum_{k=1}^{L}d_k^2 c_k\right]^2}{N_0\sum_{k=1}^{L}d_k^2} \quad (21)$$

which reduces to (1) for the case with perfect timing (i.e., $c_k=1$ for all k).
We obtain upper and lower bounds of γ as

$$\gamma^{(1)} = \sum_{k=1}^{L}\gamma_k^{(1)} \leq \gamma \leq \gamma^{(2)} = \sum_{k=1}^{L}\gamma_k^{(2)} \leq \gamma^{(3)} = \sum_{k=1}^{L}\gamma_k \quad (22)$$

where

$$\gamma_k^{(1)} = \gamma_k e_k, \gamma_k^{(2)} = \gamma_k c_k^2,$$
$$e_k = \begin{cases} [1-4|\epsilon_k|], & 0 \leq |\epsilon_k| \leq 0.25 \\ 0 & 0.25 < |\epsilon_k| \leq 0.5. \end{cases} \quad (23)$$

$\gamma^{(2)}$ is obtained from (21) using Schwartz inequality, while $\gamma^{(3)}$ is the case without timing errors. $\gamma^{(1)}$ is obtained in three steps; (1) writing $c_k = 1 - p_k$, where p_k has values 0 and $2|\epsilon_k|$, (2) taking the square and ignoring the term $(\sum_{k=1}^{L}d_k^2 p_k)^2$ and (3) observing that no term in the sum can be negative. Thus the error probability is bounded by

$$P_{e3} \leq P_{e2} \leq P_e \leq P_{e1}, P_{ex} = \overline{P_e(\gamma^{(x)})}. \quad (24)$$

Following the analysis in [1,2] for $\gamma = \sum_{k=1}^{L}\gamma_k$ with independent γ_k

$$\overline{P_e(\gamma)} = \frac{1}{\pi}\int_0^{\pi/2}\prod_{k=1}^{L}M_{\gamma_k}\left(-\frac{1}{\sin^2\phi}\right)d\phi. \quad (25)$$

176

Thus conditioning on the number of terms l for which $e_k = c_k = 1$, we get

$$P_{ex|l} = \frac{1}{\pi} \int_0^{\pi/2} M_\gamma^l\left(-\frac{1}{\sin^2\phi}\right) M_{\gamma^{(x)}}^{L-l}\left(-\frac{1}{\sin^2\phi}\right) d\phi \quad (26)$$

where
$$M_{\gamma^{(1)}}(s) = q + 2\int_0^{0.25} M_\gamma[s(1-4\epsilon_k)]f(\epsilon_k)d\epsilon_k$$

$$q = 2\int_{0.25}^{0.5} f(\epsilon_k)d\epsilon_k \quad (27)$$

$$M_{\gamma^{(2)}}(s) = 2\int_0^{0.5} M_\gamma[s(1-2\epsilon_k)^2]f(\epsilon_k)d\epsilon_k \quad (28)$$

and for Nakagami-m fading

$$M_\gamma(s) = \left(1 - \frac{2sE}{mN_0}\right)^{-m}. \quad (29)$$

We have already established that with probability 0.25 $\epsilon_k = 0$ for all k, with probability 0.25 $\epsilon_k = 1$ for all k and with probability 0.5 $\epsilon_k = 0$ for some values of k and 1 for the others. Thus for $x = 1$ and 2,

$$P_{ex} = \frac{1}{4}(P_{ex|0} + P_{ex|L}) + \frac{1}{2^{L-1}}\sum_{l=0}^L \binom{L}{l} P_{ex|l}$$

$$= \frac{1}{4}(P_{ex|0} + P_{ex|L}) + \frac{1}{\pi 2^{L-1}} \int_0^{\pi/2}$$

$$\left[M_\gamma\left(-\frac{1}{\sin^2\phi}\right) + M_{\gamma^{(x)}}\left(-\frac{1}{\sin^2\phi}\right)\right]^L d\phi \quad (30)$$

where we have again used the binomial expansion. For x=3,

$$P_{e3} = P_{e3|L} = \frac{1}{\pi}\int_0^{\pi/2} M_\gamma^L\left(-\frac{1}{\sin^2\phi}\right) d\phi. \quad (31)$$

Hence, P_e with MRC can be upper and lower bounded using (27), (28) and (30) for any value of L. It is mentioned here that the upper bound in (24) has a limitation as it has a floor due to q whereas the actual error probability monotonically decreases with increasing SNR. Specifically, the error floor associated with the upper bound follows from (24), (27) and (30) as $\frac{1}{8}[1 + 2^{-(L-1)}]q^L$. Hence, the upper bound in (27) and (30) can be effectively used for error probabilities higher than the above floor.

5. Numerical Results and Discussion

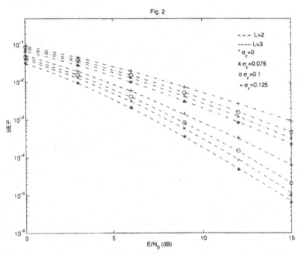

Fig. 2 BEP variation of EGC in presence of timing errors in a Rayleigh channel when $L = 2$ and 3.

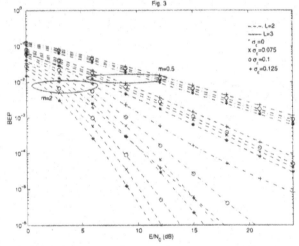

Fig. 3 BEP variation of EGC in presence of timing errors in a Nakagami-m channel with $m = 0.5$ and 2 when $L = 2$ and 3.

Fig. 2 shows the BEP variations of EGC at different values of σ_ϵ over a Rayleigh channel. In Fig. 2 (and also in Figs. 3) the lines represent the theoretical results while the specially marked points represent simulated results. Similarly, Fig. 3 shows the BEP variations with EGC over a Nakagami-m channel with $m=2$ and $m = 0.5$. It is seen that the theoretical results match well with the simulations. It is further seen that BEP is fairly sensitive to timing errors, and as one can expect, the sensitivity increases with increasing L.

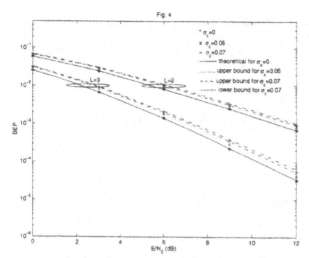

Fig. 4 BEP variation of MRC in presence of timing errors in a Rayleigh channel when $L = 2$ and 3.

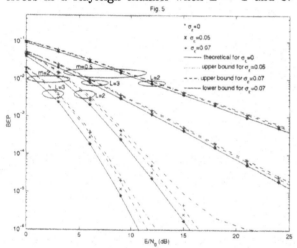

Fig. 5 BEP variation of MRC in presence of timing errors in a Nakagami-m channel with $m = 0.5$ and 2 when $L = 2$ and 3.

Figures 4 and 5 show similar BEP variations with MRC in presence of timing errors. Simulated results, the theoretical variations with perfect estimates, variations of the upper bound according to (27) and (30), and selected cases of lower bound according to (28) and (30) are plotted separately. It is seen that the bounds match well with the simulated results particularly at lower values of σ_ϵ. Fig. 5 also demonstrates the effect of the error floor of the upper bound when $m = 2$, $L = 2$ and $\sigma_\epsilon = 0.07$. Comparing with Figs. 2 and 3, it is seen from Figures 4 and 5 that MRC is more sensitive to timing errors than EGC. Comparing different channels, it is seen that the sensitivity to timing errors increases with increasing m both in EGC and MRC.

6. Conclusions

The effect of imperfect symbol timing has been analyzed in EGC and MRC techniques over Rayleigh and Nakagami-m fading channels. BPSK modulation with coherent demodulation has been considered. Timing errors on different diversity branches have been assumed to be independent and identically distributed according to a Tikhonov distribution. In the case of EGC, the effect of timing errors has been theoretically analyzed and justified by computer simulation. In the case of MRC, error rate bounds have been derived and justified by simulation. It has been numerically demonstrated that both EGC and MRC are fairly sensitive to timing errors, and comparatively, MRC is more sensitive.

References

[1] M.K. Simon and M.-S. Alouini, "Digital Communication over Fading Channels," John Wiley and Sons Inc., New York, 2000

[2] M.-S. Alouini and A.J. Goldsmith, "A unified approach for calculating error rate of linearly modulated signals over generalized fading channels," *IEEE Trans. on Commun.*, COM-47, pp. 1324-1334, Sept. 1999

[3] Q.T. Zhang, "Probability of error for equal-gain combiners over Rayleigh channels: some closed-form solutions", *IEEE Trans. Commun.*, COM-45, pp.270-273, Mar. 1997

[4] M.K. Simon and M.-S. Alouini, "Simplified noise reference loss evaluation for digital communication in presence of slow fading and carrier phase error", *IEEE Trans. Veh. Technol.*, vol.50, pp. 480-486, March 2001

[5] M.A. Najib and V.K. Prabu, "Analysis of equal-gain diversity with partially coherent fading signals," *IEEE Trans. Veh. Technol.*, vol. 49, pp. 783-791, May 2000

[6] M.O. Sunay and P.J. McLane, "Probability of error for diversity combining in DS CDMA system with synchronization errors", *European Transactions on Telecommunications*, vol. 9, pp. 449-463, Oct. 1998

[7] X. Tang, M.-S. Alouini and A.J. Goldsmith, "Effect of channel estimation error on M-QAM BER performance in Rayleigh fading", *IEEE Trans. on Commun.*, COM-47, pp. 1856-1864, Dec. 1999

[8] M.K. Simon, "A simple evaluation of DPSK error probability performance in the presence of bit timing error", *IEEE Trans. on Commun.*, COM-42, pp.263-267, Feb-Apr 1994.

[9] I.S. Gradshteyn and I.M.Ryzhik, Table of Integrals, Series, and Products, New York: Academic, 1980

Session 3–2
Artificial Intelligence

Visualizing Transition Diagrams of Action Language Programs

Özcan Koç, Ferda N. Alpaslan, Nihan K. Çiçekli
Department of Computer Engineering
Middle East Technical University,
06531 Ankara, TURKEY
Phone: +90–312–210–2080
Fax: +90–312–210–1259
okoc@udel.edu, alpaslan@ceng.metu.edu.tr, nihan@cs.ucf.edu

Abstract

The subject of action languages is one of the prominent research topics in current Artificial Intelligence (AI) research. One of the problems in teaching and learning action languages as well as writing causal theory expressions is the difficulty of visualizing transition diagrams in mind. A tool, called TDV, which extends CCALC [GL98b] and uses GraphViz[KN91] software, is developed to visualize transition diagrams of $\mathcal{C}$ programs.

Keywords : Action Languages, causal theories, transition diagrams, visualization.

1 Introduction

The subject of action languages is one of the prominent research topics in current Artificial Intelligence (AI) research. An action language allows its users to study the change and properties of actions by means of fluents and causal relations among them. A *fluent* is a judgement about the status of objects in the world—*i.e.* a logical world model. Causal relationships among fluents are expressed using logical propositions. For example,

Shoot(gun) causes ¬*Alive* if *loaded(gun)*

describes the effect of *Shoot* action on *Alive* fluent. Action languages and related research are discussed in many recent papers [GL98a], [BG97]. $\mathcal{C}$ is an action language developed by Enrico Giunchiglia and Vladimir Lifschitz[GL98b] and uses the idea of causal theories. $\mathcal{C}$ is a language having two kinds of *laws*. Static laws are of the form

caused F if G

and dynamic laws are of the form

caused F if G after H

where F and G are propositional combinations of fluent names and H is a propositional combination of fluent and action names. The dynamic laws are used to show the direct effects of the actions. The $\mathcal{C}$ language also has some additional expressions that can be written in the form of static and dynamic laws. These are itemized below:

U causes F if G

inertial F

always F

nonexecutable U if F

default F if G

U may cause F if G

where F and G are propositional combinations of fluent names and U is a propositional combination of fluent and action names. Examples of simple planning problems that are solved using $\mathcal{C}$ can be found in [McC99]. A $\mathcal{C}$ program defines a *transition system* which consists of sets of fluents and relationships among these fluent sets. Although $\mathcal{C}$ offers a complete system in formalizing action language domains, it lacks a tool to obtain a visual appearance of the resulting transition systems. Drawing a transition diagram is the best way of representing the whole state space of the problem domain. Doing it manually is time consuming and open to errors. Moreover, an automated tool would be helpful for the learners and teachers of action languages.

The Causal Calculator (CCALC) [McC99] is a system, written in Prolog, for query answering and satisfiability in the context of planning. It is developed for the language of causal theories [MT97]. The input to CCALC is given in C which is translated to causal theory by using rewrite rules. The causal theory is grounded to obtain a ground causal theory. The ground causal theory is translated to propositional logic by means of literal completion. Then, the propositional logic formulas are put into the conjunctive normal form (CNF). To find a model of the system, CCALC uses a so-called *satisfiability solver* (SAT). These are propositional provers based on Davis–Putnam method and expect their input in CNF. The models found by SATs are then used for planning. The idea behind this approach can be found in [KS92].

We have developed a software, called TDV(Transition Diagram Visualizer), to draw transition diagrams defined by programs written in action language C. TDV extends the CCALC package and uses GraphViz[KN91] package for drawing.

The rest of this paper is organized as follows: Section 2 explains transition diagrams, Section 3 discusses implementation details, Section 4 compares the performance of algorithms, Section 5 presents the visual customizations and Section 6 contains the conclusion.

2 Transition Diagrams

Programs written in action languages consist of causal clauses which constitue a causal theory. Every causal theory defines a transition system. A *transition system* is a set of transitions of the form $<s, A, s'>$, where s is initial state A is a set of states and s', is resulting state

At each state, every fluent has a value of *true* or *false*. Hence, a state s is a set of all literals, *i.e.* positive or negative fluents. A is a, possibly empty, set of concurrent actions that a causal theory allows to execute concurrently. If we assume that there are n fluents and m actions, there are $2^n \times m \times 2^n$ possible transitions for non–concurrent case and $2^n \times 2^m \times 2^n$ possible transitions for the concurrent case. Among these, some are *causally explained*[1]. A *transition diagram* refers to a set of

---

[1]A transition $< s, A, s' >$ is *causally explained* if its resulting state s' is the only interpretation of σ^{fl}, *i.e* fluent symbols, that satisfies all formulas caused in this transition[GL98b].

```
:- include 'C.t'.
:- sorts latch.
:- variables L    :: latch.
:- constants
  l1, l2          :: latch;
  up(latch)       :: defaultFalseFluent;
  open            :: inertialFluent;
  toggle(latch)   :: action.
caused open if up(l1) && up(l2).
caused -open if -up(l1) ++ -up(l2).
toggle(L) causes up(L) if -up(L).
toggle(L) causes -up(L) if up(L).
```

Figure 1: C code for suitcase domain

causally explained transitions.

We can represent transition diagrams by means of labeled directed graphs. In such a representation, nodes correspond to states and edges represent transitions. Figure 2 presents the transition diagram of Lin's suitcase domain [Fan95] whose code is presented in Figure 1 as an example. In the suitcase domain, there is a spring–loaded suitcase with two latches. The suitcase is open whenever both latches are up. According to Figure 2, the domain has 3 fluents—*open, up(l1)* and *up(l2)*—and 2 actions—*toggle(l1)* and *toggle(l2)*. Since this is a concurrent example[2], there are $2^3 \times 2^2 \times 2^3 = 256$ possible transitions. Among these 14 of them are causally explained. In C, states may change (or remain same) without executing any action. Transitions labeled with 0 represent such null actions. Note that *up(l1)* and *up(l2)* fluents are defined as defaultFalseFluent. If we modify this definition as up(latch) :: inertialFluent; then, we would obtain a transition diagram as illustrated in Figure 3. In this case, transition diagram has again 14 causally explained transitions with certain differences, *i.e.* some of the transitions are different. These two figures emphasize the importance of formalization.

Although the Figures 2 and 3 are strongly connected directed graph, transition diagrams may be unconnected. A directed graph is said to be strongly connected if and only if there is a path—in the sense of graph theory—between every two vertices in the graph. Figure 4 illusrates a transi-

---

[2]C assumes that any program is concurrent unless it contains a noconcurrency—or equivalently nonexecutable _A && _A1 if _A@<_A1—statement.

182

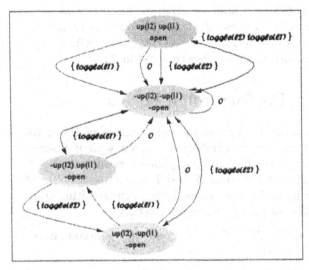

Figure 2: Transition diagram of suitcase example

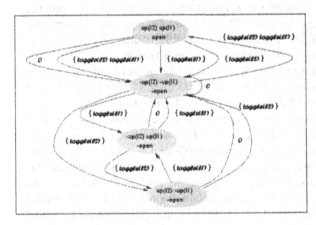

Figure 3: Transition diagram of suitcase example (with inertial fluents)

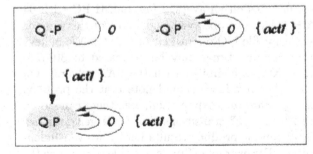

Figure 4: A transition diagram which is not strongly connected.

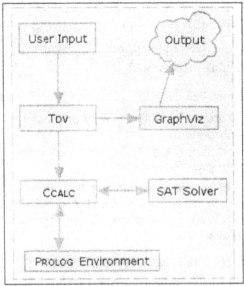

Figure 5: TDV architecture

tion diagram which is not strongly connected. This graph is not strongly connected, because it is not possible to reach $\{\neg P \ \neg Q\}$, or any other node, from $\{P \ Q\}$.

3 Visualization of Transition Diagrams

In order to visualize the transition diagram of a C program, TD software extends the CCALC software as illustrated in Figure 5. CCALC passes the information about the nodes and transitions among the nodes to TDV. After extracting the node and transition information, the result is written to a file in a format readable by AT&T's GraphViz software and the file is sent to dot^3 as input. dot produces the transition diagram. CCALC neither produces nodes or transitions, nor uses this information. Hence, this information is obtained by posing planning problems to CCALC as outlined in algorithm, named **algorithm 1**, below:

Algorithm

1. Ask CCALC to find a plan of length 1 with initial condition **true** and goal **true**. CCALC

$^3 dot$ is a part of GraphViz package.

produces a plan with an initial state s_0, a final state s_1 and a set of actions A_0.

2. While there are more transitions, construct a new planning problem with

   - current state is s,
   - goal state s' is different from previously found goals,
     i.e. $s' \neq s_1 \wedge s' \neq s_2 \wedge \ldots s' \neq s_n$ where s_i are goals found so far,
   - set of actions A is different than previously found action sets, i.e. $A \neq A_1 \wedge A \neq A_2 \wedge \ldots A \neq A_n$ where A_i are actions found so far.

   After finding the new transition $< s, A, s' >$, add s' to the set of non-processed nodes if we see this node for the first time.

3. When there are no more transitions, mark current state s as processed, take another non-processed node as new s, and go to step 2.

4. Repeat step 3 until all nodes are processed.

5. Output the resulting nodes and transitions to a file.

As we discussed before, a state may change, or remain same, without performing any action. In such a case, how to specify that at least one action should be used in order to get a different transition is a problem needs special handling. This is formulated by the following statement:

```
0: \/V_A1: o(V_A1,0)
```

This statement specifies that at least one action should occur, and it solves the problem. Although the algorithm outlined above is correct, transition diagrams produced by the algorithm may be incomplete. As we discussed in the previous section, transition diagrams may be unconnected. The above algorithm, however, finds only a connected subgraph of the transition diagram. To overcome this difficulty, we can generate all states by taking permutations of 2^n literals beforehand, and use them as non-processed nodes. This algorithm is named `algorithm 2`. However, this would decrease the performance considerably for graphs which are not fully connected. A hybrid of these two algorithms, named `algorithm 3`, is also possible. In this case, a set of desired nodes is given to the system as non-processed nodes. System discovers the remaining nodes by applying the first algorithm. All of these 3 algorithms were implemented in TDV.

4 Performance Issues

In order to discuss the complexities of the algorithms, let us consider a domain with n fluents, m actions, T causally explained transitions and N nodes. We assume N and T are actual number of nodes and edges, respectively, in the resulting transition diagrams, hence they satisfy

- $0 \leq N \leq 2^n$ (concurrent and non–concurrent case)

- $0 \leq T \leq N \times 2^m \times N$ (concurrent) or $0 \leq T \leq N \times (m+1) \times N$ (non-concurrent case)

Therefore, `algorithm 1` runs in $O(T)^4$ in general and in $O(N \times 2^m \times N)$ for the worst case. `Algorithm 2` first discovers *all* possible nodes ($O(2^n)$), then it finds all causally explained transitions ($O(T)$). So, `algorithm 2` runs in $O(2^n) + O(T)$, which impiles a worst case of $O(2^n \times 2^m \times 2^n)$ and a best case of $O(2^n)$. `Algorithm 3`, like `algorithm 1`, runs faster than `algorithm 2`. This algorithm runs in $O(T_1 + T_2 + T_3 + \cdots + T_n)$, where each T_i denotes the number of causally explained transitions in discovered subgraph i. As we can easily see, the summation satisfies the $0 \leq T_1 + T_2 + T_3 + \cdots + T_n \leq T$ inequality, since the summation of number of causally explained transitions in subgraphs cannot exceed the total number of causally explained transitions.

Our experiments, *see* appendix, showed that our program runs reasonably fast for domains with 2^{11} or less nodes. Each of the examples took less than six minutes on an average Pentium II PC with 64 MB RAM. We observed that, most of this time is spent for file I/O operations of CCALC. We believe that running times may be decreased to 30–75% if CCALC is compiled with the SAT solvers. On the other hand, we should note that the problem is, *by definition*, exponential; i.e. there can be up to $2^n \times 2^m \times 2^n$ transitions. So, for larger domains, TDV cannot produce results fastly, or even indefinitely. For example, TDV is not able to produce the

---

[4]If the graph is not connected, T is the number of causally explained transitions in the subgraph discovered by the algorithm.

transition diagram of airport problem[LMRT00], since there are 42 fluents—which impiles $2^{42} = 4.398.046.511.104$ possible nodes.

5 Visual Customizations

GraphViz package offers some customizations about the visual appearance of graphs, and we have an interface for these options. TDV supports the customizations of shape of nodes, node and edge fonts, size/color of node and edge fonts, multi-line labels for nodes and edges, thickness of edges, scale of graphs and it is able to produce a smaller version of transition diagrams by merging[5] bi–directional edges, *etc.*

In addition to these customization, *dotty* program of GraphViz package allows its users to modify the layout of the graph.

6 Conclusion and Suggested Work

Action laguages is one of the important topics in current AI research. In order to help the study of action languages research a tool which is capable of displaying the transition diagrams of C programs is developed. We will improve our tool by implementing algorithm 3. Three different algorithms were developed to achieve speed and completeness. Also, several visual customizations are offered for convenience. System is tested in SWI–Prolog under Windows NT/2000. Minor revisions may be done to run the program under different operating systems. Furthermore, we believe that it would be useful to develop a web based interface to achive a cross–platform system.

Acknowledgements

We are grateful to Vladimir Lifschitz and Esra Erdem for their suggestions and useful comments.

---

[5]If there are two nodes X and Y such that there is a transition from X to Y with action set A and another transition from Y to X with the same set of actions , *i.e.* A, TDV can display a single edge with two arrowheads which reduces the number edges displayed. Such kind of edges are called bi–directional edges.

Appendix

Yale Shooting Domain

```
:- sorts gun.
:- variables G :: gun.
:- constants
 g1, g2                    :: gun;
 load(gun), shoot(gun) :: action;
 alive, loaded(gun)      :: inertialFluent.
load(G) causes loaded(G).
shoot(G) causes -alive if loaded(G).
shoot(G) causes -loaded(G).
```

C code for yale shooting example

References

[BG97] Chitta Baral and Michael Gelfond. Reasoning about effects of concurrent actions. *Journal of Logic Programming 31*, 1997.

[Fan95] Lin Fangzhen. Embracing causality in specifying the indirect effects of actions. *Proc. of IJCAI-95*, pages 1985–1991, 1995.

[GL98a] Michael Gelfond and Vladimir Lifschitz. Actions languages. *Electronic Transactions on AI*, page 3, 1998.

[GL98b] Enrico Giunchiglia and Vladimir Lifschitz. An actions language based on causal explanation: Preliminary report. *Proc. AAAI-98*, pages 623–630, 1998.

[KN91] Eleftherios Koutsofios and Stephen North. Drawing graphs with dot. Technical report, AT&T Bell Laboratories, Murray Hill, NJ, September 1991.

[KS92] H. Kautz and B. Selman. Planning as satisfaibility. *Proc. of ECAI-92*, pages 359–379, 1992.

[LMRT00] Vladimir Lifschitz, Norman McCain, Emilio Remolina, and Armando Tacchella. Getting to the airport: the oldest planning problem in AI. *Logic-Based Artificial Intelligence*, pages 147–165, 2000.

[McC99] Norman McCain. Using the causal
         calculator with the $\mathcal{C}$ input language.
         Technical report, 1999.

[MT97]   Norman McCain and Hudson Turner.
         Causal theories of action and change.
         Proc. AAAI-97, pages 460–465, 1997.

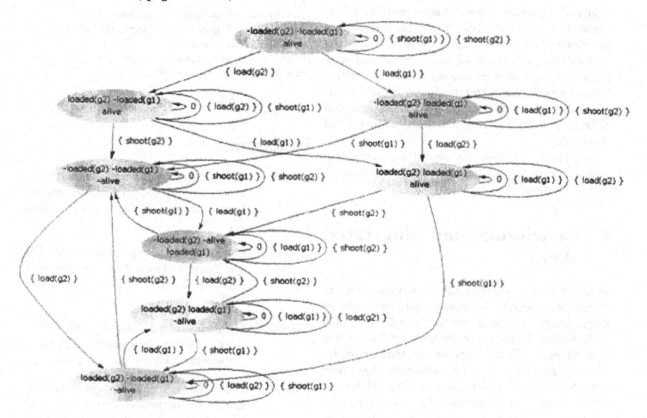

Transition diagram of yale shooting example

TURKISH NATURAL LANGUAGE INTERFACE: CEVAPVER

Zeynep Altan
Istanbul University
Department of Computer Engineering,
34850, Avcılar, Istanbul, Turkey
zaltan@istanbul.edu.tr

Dogal Acar
Istanbul University
Department of Computer Engineering,
34850, Avcılar, Istanbul, Turkey
dogal@istanbul.edu.tr

Abstract

In this paper we developed the system CevapVer presenting a new Natural Language Interface to Database System for Turkish. CevapVer is a portable system, which answers native Turkish questions by translating them into SQL query. It takes questions from a Turkish subset, parses them using a Unification-Based Tree Substitution Grammar into a semantic representation like prolog description, and then translates that model into SQL query. The study also involves the explanations about the morphological analysis, syntactic analysis, semantic analysis and database query modules, which has originally been developed for the CevapVer system.

1. Introduction

It is possible to divide database applications into three groups as the programs including graphic interface, text interface and sound interface. While windows-based operating systems use the graphic interface, DOS and Unix systems use the text interface. Moreover, sound interface has widely been utilized in recent applications. The Natural Language Interface to Database (NLIDB) system is the program that has been used to make queries on databases with natural language questions.

The first NLIDB study was the "Baseball System" [1], which was developed in 1961 by utilizing a syntactic grammar. This system was answering the natural language questions about American Baseball league. Ladder [2] was another famous NLIDB system, which a semantic grammar has been used. The studies analyzing NLIDB systems have begun to increase from the beginning of 1990s. The "Masque Project" developed as master thesis at the University of Edinburgh [3], and the "Squirrel Project" generated at the University of Essex [4] have really contributed to extend those studies. Darcan's Master Thesis called "An Intelligent Database Interface for Turkish" was the first Turkish study about NLIDB systems [5]. Cetionoglu (2001) developed a prolog-based tool in her Master Thesis called "A Prolog Based Natural Language Processing Infrastructure for Turkish" [6].

Finally, NLIDB systems became applicable to the dialog systems, which were achieved by sound technology. The "ATIS Project" developed in Holland [7] is an example of Dialog-System studies in recent years.

2. NLIDB System Architectures

NLIDB systems can be divided into two groups with two different architectures as one level & multilevel NLIDB systems, and syntax based & nonsyntax-based systems.

The systems developed as one layer analyze the sentence, and then translate the result into a database query. That is a direct and simple method for those systems. But one level system does not allow the program to be modified for new applications. For that purpose, a new grammar and a new system must be modeled.

Multilevel systems are generally composed of two fundamental levels as the grammar system and logical intermediate level. Although these two modules depend on each other, they act as independent modules. Such systems are generally preferred because of the independency from the application. The first level usually holds the morphological and syntactic analysis, and then the parsing tree obtained in the first stage is transformed into an intermediate language that

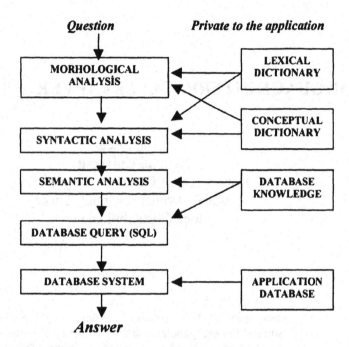

Figure 1. The architecture of the CevapVer System

Figure2: The combination operation of
a tree structure
[a]IO noun phrase, I noun, C initial rule representing
the sentence, EO verb phrase

is called logical language or semantic representation. This representation is later translated into database query. Intermediate language is normally independent from the application and database, but it depends on to a modifiable database knowledge, which can be configured for different databases and applications. The NLIDB systems generally use classical grammars for syntactic analysis like context-free structure. There are also different methods to analyze the sentences other than classical systems such as pattern matching and semantic grammar systems.

In a pattern matching system, special words or word groups in a sentence are matched, and those groups are used to produce the database query without syntactic analysis.

Semantic grammar systems use the same methods as in syntax-based systems. The difference from others is that they do not use syntax-based grammar categories as NP, VP etc. They use nonterminals, which are applied to semantic concepts and structures. The "Lifer System" [8], developed for American navy with a semantic grammar, was designed to answer the questions about ships.

Most of the recent applications have developed by utilizing Unification Grammar (UG). Context-Free Grammars (CFGs) are usually used by these systems. UG defines the words, phrases and sentences in a more detailed manner compared with the traditional grammar systems. Some commonly used unification grammar systems include Lexical-Functional Grammar (LFG) and Tree-Adjoining Grammar (TAG). LFG developed by

Joan Bresnan and Ron Kaplan [9] using the unification process at the second half of 70s. LFG has been applied to Turkish at Bilkent University to realize the language translation [10]. Joshi [11] firstly used TAG in 1975 and Shabes [12] developed its lexical structure in 1988. Lexicalized-Tree-Adjoining Grammar (LTAG) systems generally use CFG structure of which the basic structures are tree items. LTAG was used in XTAG project to parse the English sentences [13]. We can confer that TAGs are fairly suitable for Turkish applications. Since the syntactic structure of Turkish sentences is rather free, inverted sentences are often used, and they are also accepted as grammatical. Moreover, the utilization of phrases is so flexible.

3. The CEVAPVER System

CevapVer is a Turkish NLIDB system, which answers the Turkish questions using a relational database. Firstly, it translates the Turkish sentences into SQL (Structured Query Language), and then queries the database. The system has been developed by using Visual Basic 6.0 programming language. That is also a portable system, which can easily be modified for new applications.

The system firstly performed the morphological analysis of identified words in the question sentence, and then the syntactic analysis has been constructed. Afterwards the parse tree has been converted into semantic representation, and then into SQL query. The consequence of the SQL query has been returned to the end-user. The architecture of the CevapVer system can be seen in Figure 1.

3.1. Morphological Analysis

Turkish words include more complicated morphological structure than English words. In general, both the Turkish verbs and nouns comprise more than one suffix; therefore we have to divide them into smaller parts to determine their meanings. The vowels of any suffix change according to the last vowel of the root word; therefore it is fairly difficult to analysis the Turkish words morphologically. This property has usually been used for the softening of consonants grammar rule [14].

The CevapVer System, at the morphological level, analyzes the words of the input sentence. For example, Cem *Yavuz'un 12/01/1995'den önce yayınlanmış "Algoritma Analizi" konusundaki makalelerini listele* sentence has morphologically been analysed as follows:

Cem Yavuz'un (proper name) ⇒ Yavuz+un
("un" affix is determining suffix)
12/01/1995'den (date) ⇒. ...+den
("den" is an ablative suffix)
önce (before) ⇒ adverb of time
yayınlanmis (printed) ⇒ yayınla+n+mis
("n+mis "represents past definite participle)
"Algoritma Analizi" ⇒ excluded from the analysis because of the quotation marks.
konusundaki (subject)⇒ konu+s+un+da+ki
("s"is fusion letter, "un" is a genitive, "da" is a locative, and " ki" is a genitive suffix)
makalelerini (papers) ⇒ makale+ler+i+n+i
("ler' is plural case, "i" is determinated, 'n' is fusion letter, "i" is accusative
listele *(list)* ⇒ root: listele.

Although the system analyzes each suffix of the nouns, it only parses a subset of the verbs, because the NLIDB system merely uses the question and imperative sentences. Therefore we have implemented the partial parsing for the verbs.

3.2. Syntactic Analysis

Syntactic analysis of the sentences has been realized by a special Turkish grammar called Unification-Based Tree Substitution Grammar (UBTSG), which parses all imperative and interrogative sentences in Turkish. We defined a set of trees that symbolize the Turkish phrases such as noun, adjective and adverb phrases. These are the elementary phrases, which construct the whole sentence. More complex phrases obtained from the elementary phrases have not been defined in the grammar. They are constructed from the combination of elementary phrases during parsing.

The tree notation of the system does not represent the meaning of the words. The symbol "↓" means that the incorporated nonterminal can take a tree below it. If the related rules do not conflict, the trees are combined under these symbols. The IO tree at the left side of Figure 2 replaces to the under of IO↓ node at the right side. So a new tree will be formed by the combination of two trees.

3.3. Vocabulary

The system CevapVer uses two kinds of vocabulary: one is the application database and the other one is its vocabulary database. In the application database the words that can be used in the query sentences have been determined, and the columns that correspond to these words have been introduced to the system. Besides, the words that cannot be in the application database such as verbs, adverbs etc. have also been instituted to the system together with their types such as noun, adjective etc. Since the system uses the application database more comprehensively than the system database, this property enables a simple modification for new applications. During the parsing of syntactic analysis module, the words of the sentences have firstly been searched in the system database. If anyone of the words cannot be found there, then the application database module has been sought. If this quest results in a failure again, then an error message has been written by the system. The concepts used to establish the words to CevapVer system for the portability are as follows:

Columns: The fields of tables in database have been defined as "*columns*". They represent the related fields in the system. For example, *subj* is a column name in an application database involving the subject of the books, and we can define *subj* field as a column.

Sets: In an application, it is possible to possess same column names. The sets have been used to distinguish the same columns from each other. The columns that get same names have been assigned to sets being a logical or table based relationship. For example, both the name of a writer and a department has been represented with the word "name".

189

Objects: Objects involve the set of words in a sentence. We usually used only one word to represent a group of words. Therefore we have instituted the objects that can be used in an application, and the fields of words that the object represents.

Words: Words stay out of groups above. They do not exist in the application database, and were not defined as *set, column* or *object*. Verbs, particles, adjectives that do not affect the database query are defined as "*word*" in the system.

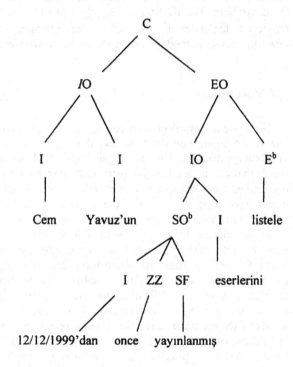

Figure 3: The parsing tree of a Turkish sentence.
[b]: SO adjective phrase, E verb, ZZ adverb of time, SF participle

3.4. Semantic Analysis

This step transforms the parsing tree into a semantic representation. This illustration forms the intermediate level between database queries and parsing tree. During the translation, the words that are useless for the database query have been eliminated, and the field names of words, objects, columns and sets have been obtained. The parsing tree in Figure 3 is then translated into the following semantic representation:

listele (eserler ((Cem Yavuz'un), (12/12/1999'dan önce yayınlanmış)).

The object "eserler" in this sentence represents the articles, books and all attributes of these words. These words represent the following fields in the database:

eser.eserturu, konu.konu, tarih.basimtar , yazar.adi , yazar.soyadi.

3.5. Database (SQL) Query

Semantic representation has been translated into SQL query as the last step. The field names of the words for semantic representation have been obtained during the syntactic analysis, and the application database has been used as the vocabulary and the field names have been determined at this stage. The construction of the SQL sentence have been completed after organizing the relationships according to the tables of the application database as follows:

*SELECT **Eser**.eseradi, **eser**.eser.turu, **tarih**.basimtar, **yazar**.adi, yazar.soyadi FROM eser, tarih, yazar WHERE yazar.adi= 'Cem' and yazar.soyadi ='Yavuz' and tarih.basimtar < {12/12/1999} and eser.eserno = yazar.eserno and tarih.eserno = eser.eserno*

Finally, CevapVer System can make query from the database to get answer to the question asked by the end user with the SQL sentence constructed above. The parsing result can be seen in Figure 4.

4. Conclusion

In this study we presented the CevapVer System that is an alternative Natural Language Interface to Database system for Turkish. The modules of that system have originally been built up and, they are fairly independent from each other. Therefore other programs analyzing Turkish can use these individual modules. Most important module of CevapVer System is the syntactic analysis module. In the study, we developed a Substitution Grammar with unification- based features, which holds Turkish sentences successfully. Another important innovation is the explanation of new concepts such as columns, sets, objects and words for the portability of the system. In this way, it is rather simple to modify CevapVer for new applications. CevapVer uses the application database more than the system database, so it is also simple to build and modify the system vocabulary. Our study on CevapVer System has been lasting, and it is a necessity to improve the grammar to analyze more complicated Turkish sentences. The system doesn't parse all suffixes of verbs in the morphological analysis, which are needless for NLIDB systems.

References

[1] Krulee G.K., Computer Processing of Natural Language, Prentice-Hall, New Jersey, 1991.

[2] Androutsopulos J., Rithic G.D., Thanisch P., "Natural Language Interfaces to Databases an Introduction", *Journal of Natural Language Engineering*, Camb. Univ. Press, 1994.

[3] Androutsopulos J., Rithic G.D., Thanisch P., "Masque/SQL: An Efficient and Portable Natural Language Query Interface for Relational Databases", *In proceedings of 6th Inter. Conference on Industrial and Engineering Applications of Artificial Intelligence*, 1994.

[4] Barros, Flavia A. and Roeck A., "Anaphora Resolution in Squirrel, A Natural Language Interface to Databases", in *AISB Quarterly*, No 88, 1994.

[5] Darcan N.O.,"An Intelligent Database Interface for Turkish". Master Thesis, Bogazici University, 1991.

[6] Cetinoglu O., "A prolog Based Natural Language Processing Insfructure for Turkish", Master Thesis, Bogazici University, 2001.

[7] Bod R., Beyond Grammar, CSLI Publ., 1998.

[8] Allen J.,Natural Language Understanding, 2.Edition., Benj./Cum.Publ.Co., 1995.

[9] Kaplan R.M., Bresnan J.," LFG: A formal system for grammatical representation", *In* The Mental Representation of Grammatical Relations, MIT Press, pp.173-281, 1982.

[10] Güngördü Z., A Lexical-Functional Grammar for Turkish, Master Thesis , Bilkent University, 1993.

[11] Joshi A.K., Levy L.S., Takahashi M., "Tree Adjunct Grammars", Journal of Computer and System Sciences v: (10)1, pp.136-63, 1975.

[12] Schabes, Y., Abeille A. and Joshi A.K. "Parsing strategies with lexicalized grammar ", In *Proceedings of COLING'88*, pp.578-583, 1988.

[13] XTAG, http://www.cis.upenn.edu/~xtag

[14] Altan Z., "The Role of Morphological Analysis in Natural Language Processing", Anadolu University Journal of Sciences and Technology, v: 3(1),pp. 59-79, 2002.

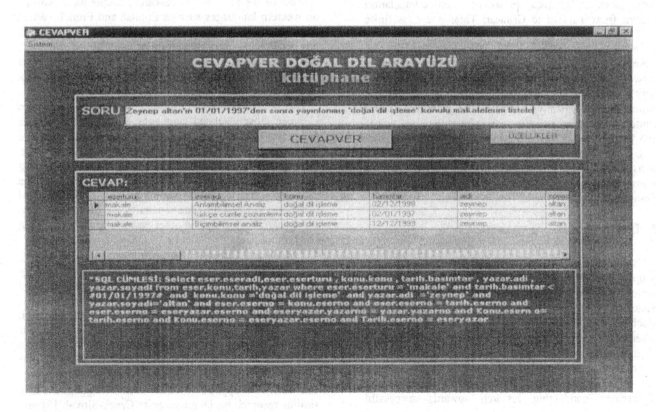

Figure 4: The interface of CevapVer System

191

A Machine Translation System Between a Pair of Closely Related Languages

Kemal Altintas [1,3]

[1] Dept. of Computer Engineering
Bilkent University
Ankara, Turkey
email:kemal@ics.uci.edu

Ilyas Cicekli [1,2]

[2] Dept. of Computer Science
University of Central Florida
Orlando, Florida, USA
email: ilyas@cs.ucf.edu

Abstract

Machine translation between closely related languages is easier than between language pairs that are not related with each other. Having many parts of their grammars and vocabularies in common reduces the amount of effort needed to develop a translation system between related languages. A translation system that makes a morphological analysis supported by simpler translation rules and context dependent bilingual dictionaries may suffice most of the time. Usually a semantic analysis may not be needed. This paper presents a machine translation system from Turkish to Crimean Tatar that uses finite state techniques for the translation process. By developing a machine translation system between Turkish and Crimean Tatar, we propose a sample model for translation between close pairs of languages. The system we developed takes a Turkish sentence, analyses all the words morphologically, translates the grammatical and context dependent structures, translates the root words and finally morphologically generates the Crimean Tatar text. Most of the time, at least one of the outputs is a true translation of the input sentence.

Keywords: Natural Language Processing, Machine Translation.

1. Introduction

Using computers for translation has been interesting for people since the invention of computers. During the period after the Second World War, both the United States and the Soviet Union supported projects on machine translation in order to be able to read each other's documents. Later, the importance of machine translation for the replacement of human translators was discovered due to economic reasons. Parties from industry supported and implemented MT systems. Today, many researchers conducting research towards successful machine translation systems among many world languages.

Traditionally, human translators helped people to understand written documents and speech in a foreign language. However, it is not always possible to find a human translator, who can do the job for us. Also, the amount of written material that one person can translate in unit time is very limited. Moreover, having a human translator is costly. For this reason, people and companies are in the search of finding alternative methods for the translation process.

Most of the time, at MT research, people have worked on western languages such as English and French. When other languages are included, again most of the research has been trying to translate from or into English. Machine translation between close pair of languages was left rather untouched and Turkish [2] and Turkic languages have not attracted too much attention.

This paper explains a finite state method for translation between closely related languages, which we believe, is needed to construct language domains that will make the translation process from other languages possible. Developing such a system is easier than developing independent systems between language pairs. Also, the process by nature will take some of the issues like word order and most of the time semantics out of the scene, so the research can focus on other issues like the translation of grammar.

Turkish and Crimean Tatar, being two close languages, may be a model for machine translation between closely related languages. Most parts of the grammars and vocabulary of the two languages are common. Usually, the differences in grammars are at the morpheme level, where the morphemes for a specific grammar construct or the order of appearance of morphemes may differ. Most of the root words are used in both languages with smaller differences. Methods developed for this pair of languages can easily be applied to other Turkic languages. Also, similar research on language pairs Czech-Slovak [5] and Spanish-Catalan [2] show that the methods described in

---

[3] His current address is Information & Computer Science Dept., Univ. of California, Irvine, CA 92697

this paper are applicable to other closely related language pairs.

The rest of the paper is organised as follows: Section 2 explains the details of the translation process between closely related languages. The translation system is explained in Section 3. Implementation and limitations are discussed in Section 4. Section 5 concludes the paper.

2. MT Between Closely Related Languages

Translation is a hard job due to various reasons. First of all, different societies have different cultures. The concepts that each society has in mind and the names that they give to objects and abstract concepts may be different. Some languages may not have certain grammatical structures that are present in the target language. For example, Turkish does not have an explicit perfect tense and translation of perfect tense from English to Turkish may cause some problems. Another problem with translation is the ambiguity. Since one word may have many meanings, the process of choosing the correct sense among the alternatives is not an easy task.

However, for languages that are very close to each other, some of these problems are not present. These languages are almost always the languages of people who have similar cultures and common historical roots. Cultural differences between people speaking closer languages are not very significant most of the time. Even when they have different cultures and concepts, the concepts of the other culture is usually present in the language since they have great interaction. Also, when the two languages are closer to each other, the grammatical differences and inexistence of some words are limited. Ambiguities are usually preserved in the two languages. For example, in the sentence "John saw the girl with binoculars", the part 'with the binoculars' is ambiguous since it may belong to John or the girl. This may be a problem while translating this sentence into Turkish. However, the ambiguity is preserved in French and it is not a problem for a translation into French [4]. As a result, the closer the languages of people, the easier to make translation between them.

People usually have worked on translation systems for languages that are not directly related. However, translation of closely related languages is also very important. First of all, the research for translation between similar languages will contribute a lot to the overall machine translation techniques. Since the structures of the languages are similar, many features of the two languages may be ignored. For example, Turkish is a free word order language whereas English is more strict in the word order. In the translation process from Turkish to English, we have to consider the word order. On the other hand, the translation from Turkish to Kazakh, which is also a free word order language, would usually not require

consideration of word order. Thus, research may focus on other features of translation process.

Another advantage of translation between closely related languages is its creating a domain of interchangeable languages. In other words, having a system that is capable of successfully translating between Turkish and Uzbek, any machine translation system translating from English to Turkish will also enable us to translate from English to Uzbek. Implementing a system translating from Turkish to Uzbek is easier than developing a system translating from English to Uzbek. So, with lesser effort, we can have a system that is capable of translating from English to several Turkic languages.

In MT of close languages, most of the time a lexical analysis supported by some translation rules may be sufficient, and a semantic analysis may not be required. The number of translation rules is smaller than those of translation between unrelated languages. As a result, hand coding the rules is easier.

A translation system for closely related languages may need morphological analysis and morphological disambiguation tools for the source language, domain specific and general translation lexicons, and morphological generator for the target language. In this case, it will be a word-for-word translation system and it will suggest no translation rules for the grammar. However, even when the languages are very close to each other, there are some differences in the grammars in addition to vocabularies. Otherwise, it would be hard to say the two languages to be different and we could only talk about the same language written with different word domains. We believe that a module to make the necessary translations for the grammars should be included in the system.

Two other systems, [2,5] claim to be using similar methodologies in their translations between closely related languages. The system translating between Czech and Slovak [5] claims to be using a translation memory which stores the previously translated sentence pairs. When a human translator starts translating a new sentence, the system checks the translation memory for the sentence. If it appears in the memory, it is suggested to the user. The user is free to use, modify or reject it. The Spanish-Catalan system [2] uses a similar idea that we used in our system. The basic difference is that they apply the bilingual dictionary before the grammatical translation module. It is a matter of choice and as long as the grammatical translation rules are crafted accordingly, and it does not affect the system performance.

3. Translation System

Translation from Turkish to Crimean Tatar is in general disambiguated word-for-word translation. The grammars of the two languages are very similar, and each morpheme usually has a corresponding morpheme with or without change. Finite state transducers, which can transfer the grammar differences, context dependent structures and roots, are most of the time sufficient. Ambiguities in Turkish are usually preserved in Crimean Tatar.

The steps of the translation process can be listed as follows:

- Morphological analysis of Turkish text
- Morphological disambiguation
- Application of context dependent and grammatical translation rules
- General one-to-one translation of words.
- Morphological generation of Crimean Tatar text

After the input text is morphologically analysed, it needs to be disambiguated. Then the phrases and the context dependent structures of the disambiguated text are translated. Phrases that consist of more than one word and words that depend on the previous and following words must be translated before the roots in order not to lose the context information. In the following step, one-to-one translation of words is done using a bilingual dictionary between Turkish and Crimean Tatar. The morphological generation of the processed text is the last step.

Turkish morphological analyser [7] used in the accepts single word inputs and gives all possible analyses of the input word without considering the context information. A typical output of the morphological analyser can be seen in the analysis of the word "evlerimizden" (from our houses):

    evlerimizden
    ev+Noun+A3pl+P1pl+Abl

This result indicates that this word is a third person plural noun with possessive 1st person plural and in ablative case.

The translation system was developed using XEROX Finite State Tools (XFST) so it uses the XFST syntax for the translation rules [6]. The general structure of the rules is context dependent replacement. The corresponding phrase or word in a given context replaces one phrase or a word. The structure of a translation rule is as follows:

    [source -> target || LeftContext _ RightContext];

The source is mapped to target if it appears in the given context. The underscore character determines the position of the source word(s). Context information is not obligatory and if it is not given, the source text is always mapped to target in any context.

We can categorize the translation rules into the following categories:

1. Most Trivial – No Change

This set of rules includes no change in the roots or in the morphemes. All the roots and the morphemes in Turkish are conserved. No translation rules are applied for these cases

2. Root Change

Only the root is changed, and the rest of the morphemes are not changed. These rules are basically from the bilingual dictionary.

3. Morpheme Change

Some of the morphemes are to be changed without touching the root of the word. For example, Turkish "FeelLike" morpheme is to be changed into "FutPart" without effecting the other parts of the word in lexical form.

4. Root and Morpheme Change

In addition to the root of the source structure, some of its morphemes are changed too. Actually, these are mostly the word, which are expressed different word category in the target language. The root and the related morphemes are mapped to target morphemes.

5. Verbs That Effect Its Object

Some verbs change the case of their objects. In other words, the same verb is used with different cases of its object in the two languages. For example, in Turkish something is asked to a person whereas something is asked from someone in Crimean Tatar. In this case, the dative morpheme of a noun is changed into ablative if it precedes the certain verbs such as "sormak" (to ask) and "ısmarlamak" (to order) in Turkish.

6. Grammar Structures That Effect the Previous and Following Words

These are the rules that effect the previous and following words. For example, the past participle morpheme –dik in Turkish corresponds to –gen in Crimean Tatar and the possessive morpheme is added to the verb in Turkish but it is added to the noun in Crimean Tatar. Another such rule is that the noun coming after the word "çok" (many) can be singular in Turkish but it cannot be singular in Crimean Tatar.

7. More than One Word Maps to One Word

Sometimes more than one word should be expressed with a single word or one word corresponds to two or more words. For example, "yırlamak" (to sing) in Crimean Tatar is expressed as "şarkı/türkü söylemek" in Turkish.

8. One Word Maps to More than One Words

In Crimean Tatar, the compound tenses are written separately. Whenever a second tense follows the first one, it is separated from the first one. Also, sometimes one Turkish word should be translated as a group of words such as "sunmak" (to present) translated as "taqdim etmek".

The order of rules normally is not important. Mostly, they can be applied in any order. However, the rules that change the roots must be applied at the last step. The system is dependent on the Turkish roots and it checks the Turkish roots and morphemes when it checks the previous and next tokens. Thus, to have a reliable system, the rules that change the roots must be applied at the end.

If, at anywhere, a rule order is important, it can be placed in the correct position in the rules. The architecture of the system is such that it applies the first rule to the input, then applies the second rule to the output of the first and so on. Parallel rules are applied in parallel at the same time in the order that they appear in the rules. If for any reason, it is possible to give more than one output for the given input, all possible generations are given. This is helpful, especially in parallel runs, since more than one rule may effect the input.

Before this output is fed to Crimean Tatar morphological generator, one final transformation is possible. Many of the words in Turkish and in Crimean Tatar are the same except that they are written with 'k' in Turkish and with 'q' in Crimean Tatar. The rule is strict and any 'k' that precedes or follows any of "a, ı, o, u" are to be changed into a 'q'. In addition, since the system we developed does not operate on Turkish characters and special upper case characters are used instead of them, we need to change the Turkish characters into the form recognised by the morphological processor. As a result, we can apply this rule to the input so that many words that are not covered by the translation lexicon can be recognised by the generator.

After the grammar rules and the root words are translated, the lexical form should be changed to the surface form using a morphological processor [1] for Crimean Tatar. The morphological processor was developed as a part of this project and it runs in both ways. Given the surface form, the lexical form is produced by the program. Similarly, when the lexical form is given, the corresponding surface form is produced. The mappings are not one to one due to ambiguities in the language, so it is always possible to get more than one result.

4. Evaluation – Results

4.1 Implementation

The system is implemented using XEROX Finite State Tools for language engineering [6]. Xerox finite-state tool (XFST) is a general-purpose utility for computing with finite-state networks. It enables the user to create simple automata and transducers from text and binary files, regular expressions and other networks by a variety of operations. The user can display, examine and modify the structure and the content of the networks. The result can be saved as text or binary files. TWOLC is a compiler that converts two-level rules into deterministic, minimized finite-state transducers. The Finite-State Lexicon Compiler (LEXC) is an authoring tool for creating lexicons and lexical transducers. It is designed to be used in conjunction with transducers produced with the Xerox Two-level Rule Compiler (TWOLC).

The interface of the translation system was written in Java language. It reads the input from a text file and extracts the tokens. The tokens are organised and fed to XEROX tools, which are launched as external applications. The output of each transducer is fed to the next one and the final result is shown on the screen.

The input sentence for the translation system is first read from the input device and divided into its words, then each word is passed through Turkish morphological analyser. All possible analyses are generated by the FST and then they are again joined so that the context information, the original order in which the words appeared is not lost. As a result, we get all possible combinations of the sentences derived from the morphological analyses of the input words.

These sentences are then given to the translation FST that checks the sentences for compatibility with Crimean Tatar grammar. All necessary grammar changes and context dependent transformations are made by this FST. The output of the translation FST is again broken down to its words and this time each word is given to the FST that translates the roots. After the roots are translated, the output is given to the Crimean Tatar morphological processor to generate the surface form.

4.2 Examples

The followings are example translations by the system. The numbers in front of each sentence shows how many times this sentence was generated from separate lexical forms. For example, a 2 in front of a sentence says that two different lexical forms led to the same surface form. The correct translations are marked with a *.

akşam eve geleceğiz
(We will come home in the evening)
2 aqSam evge kelecekmiz *
1 aqSam evge istiqbalmIz

çiçeği suladıkça büyüyor
(The flower/his flower is growing as it is watered)
1 CeCegi suvarGan sayIn Ose *
1 CeCeklni suvarGan sayIn Ose *

4.3 Limitations

In Turkish, many of the words are ambiguous, that is there are more than one meaning for many of the words. Usually only one of them is true and acceptable in a given sentence. Which one of these should be accepted is totally dependent on the context. Morphological disambiguators use context information and statistical processing to guess the correct analysis for a word. The coverage of our morphological disambiguator should be improved.

Another limitation of the system is that, although the languages are very similar, there are some problems, which cannot be overcome with a finite state translation tool. Turkish and Crimean Tatar are free word order languages and theoretically words of a sentence may be organised in many different ways to give the same meaning. It is better for the object to be close to the verb, but it is not a must. As we explained in a previous section, the cases for objects of some verbs are different in two languages. When the object does not come just before the verb, it cannot be covered by our system. Consider the sentence "Rus kızıyla evlendi" (He got married to a Russian girl). The system will successfully translate it to "Rus qızına evlendi". However, the sentence "Rus kızıyla Moskova'da evlendi" (He got married to a Russian girl in Moscow) cannot be easily covered without a parse. Similarly, the sentence "Rus qızıyla memnuniyetle evlendi" (He got married to a Russian girl with pleasure) will probably generate a wrong result since the noun in instrumental case that precedes the verb "evlenmek" (get married) is "memnuniyet" (pleasure).

The use of present progressive for simple present meaning is more common in Crimean Tatar. The sentence "Siz giderseniz ben de gel_ir_im" (If you go, I will come) can be translated as "Siz ketseñiz men de kel_ir_im". However, the same verb in the same tense in the sentence "Ben de bazen gel_ir_im" (I also sometimes come) is translated into "Men de kimerde kel_e_m" (I also am sometimes coming [may not be grammatically correct in English]). There is not a rule for this and it cannot be determined easily even with a parse of the sentence.

One problem with Turkic languages is that verbs do not have regular phonetic rules to get the aorist, causative and passive morphemes. The verb "bakmak" (to look) in Turkish and in other Turkic languages is made causative by –tır as in "baktırmak" (to have/cause somebody look). However, the verb "akmak" (to flow) is made causative by –ıt as "akıtmak" (to cause something flow) although phonetically it is similar to "bakmak".

5. Conclusion

Although there is much influence of Anatolian Turkish over Crimean Tatar, it is a prototype for Kipchak oriented Turkic languages. Finite state rules and systems developed for Crimean Tatar may be applied to other Kipchak languages such as Kazan Tatar, Kazakh or Kirgiz. Having morphological processors and other resources ready in hand, we expect machine translation among these languages to be relatively easy.

Experiments with two other systems show that similar methods may be applied to other closely related languages. Provided that the rules are ready in hand, coding them is not very difficult. Finite state transducers for morphological process, translation of grammar rules

and bilingual dictionaries may be coded relatively easily with finite compilers.

Close languages are languages of people who usually share a historical background and a common culture. The grammars of such languages do not differ very much. For agglutinative languages, the differences may be expected at the morpheme level. For other languages, it is expected that for any word or morpheme in the source language, a corresponding word and/or morpheme can be found using finite state techniques. Since the cultures and the way of thinking of the people who are speaking close languages are similar, the concepts and terms are usually similar. Both morphological and semantic ambiguities are usually preserved and a morphological disambiguator is usually sufficient. A semantic analyser and a parser may not be needed most of the time.

To sum up, Crimean Tatar language is similar to Turkish, although it has many variations. We tried to cover largest possible rules for a simple pure Crimean Tatar text, without any rule abiding proper names or foreign words.

We believe that Crimean Tatar machine translation system may be a prototype for translation systems between close pair of languages, especially for Turkish and other Turkic languages. They have similar properties with Crimean Tatar and we believe rules and methods developed for Crimean Tatar may be applicable to other languages with relatively little changes.

References

[1] Altintas, Kemal, Cicekli, Ilyas: 2001, A Morphological Analyser for Crimean Tatar. In *Proceedings of Turkish Artificial Intelligence and Neural Network Conference (TAINN2001)*, North Cyprus
[2] Canals, Raül, Esteve, Anna, Garrido, Alicia et.al.: 2000, interNOSTRUM: A Spanish-Catalan Machine Translation System, *Machine Translation Review*, Issue No.11, December 2000 - pp 21-25.
[3] Cicekli, Ilyas, Guvenir, H. Altay: 2001, Learning Translation Templates from Bilingual Translation Examples, *Applied Intelligence*, Vol. 15, No. 1, pp: 57-76.
[4] Jurafsky, Daniel, Martin, James H.: 2000, *Speech and Language Processing*, Prentice Hall.
[5] Kubon, Vladislav, Hajic, Jab, Hric, Jan: 2000, Machine Translation of Very Close Languages, in *ANLP-NAACL2000*, Washington.
[6] MLTT Finite State Homepage, (http://www.xrce.xerox.com/research/mltt/fst/home.en.html)
[7] Oflazer, Kemal: 1994, Two-level Description of Turkish Morphology, *Literary and Linguistic Computing*, Vol. 9, No:2.

An Intelligent System Dealing with Nuanced Information

Mazen El-Sayed and Daniel Pacholczyk

University of Angers, 2 Boulevard Lavoisier, 49045 ANGERS Cedex 01, France

{elsayed,pacho}@univ-angers.fr

Abstract

This paper presents a symbolic model for handling *nuanced information* expressed in the affirmative form "x is m_α A". In this model, *nuanced information* are represented in a qualitative way within a symbolic context. For that purpose, vague terms and linguistic modifiers that operate on them are defined. The model presented is based on a symbolic M-valued predicate logic and provides a new deduction rule generalizing the classical Modus Ponens Rule.

1 Introduction

In this paper, we present a model dealing with *nuanced information* expressed in an affirmative form "x is m_α A" where m_α and A are labels denoting respectively a nuance and a vague term. There are two formalisms for handling with nuanced information. The first one refers to *fuzzy logic* introduced by Zadeh [12, 13] and which is used when the imprecise information is evaluated in a *numerical way*. In this formalism, each vague term, like "red" and "young", is represented by a fuzzy set. This one is defined by a *membership function* that characterizes the gradual membership to the fuzzy set and indicates some properties of the term like *precision, imprecision and fuzziness*. Zadeh [13] uses a fuzzy modifier m_α for representing, from the fuzzy set A, the fuzzy set "m_α A". So, "x is m_α A" is interpreted by Zadeh as "x is (m_α A)" and regarded as many-valued statement. The *fuzzy modifiers* [3, 4, 11] are defined in such a way that operate on fuzzy sets by modifying some of their properties. The second formalism refers to a symbolic many-valued logic [9, 11] which is used when the imprecise information is evaluated in a *symbolic way*. This logic is the logical counterpart of *multiset theory* introduced by De Glas [9]. In this theory, the term m_α linguistically expresses the degree to which the object x satisfies the term A. So, "x is m_α A" is interpreted by De Glas [9] as "x is (m_α A)", and then regarded as boolean statement. Agreeing on this idea, Pacholczyk [11] considers nevertheless that some nuances of natural language can not be interpreted as satisfaction degrees and must be instead defined such as *linguistic modifiers*. The modifiers have not been studied within a multiset context. The introduction of linguistic modifiers constitutes the main idea of our work. The modifiers operate on the term by modifying its meaning. Within a multiset context, there are no concepts used to represent the properties of a term. So, before defining linguistic modifiers we have to propose a new representation model based on multiset theory. This will be our first contribution in this paper. The new model generalizes the results of fuzzy sets theory, namely when the domains are not necessarily numerical scales. Our basic idea has been to associate with each vague term a new *symbolic* concept called *"rule"*. This symbolic concept is equivalent to the membership function within a fuzzy context. In other words, its geometry (1) modelizes the gradual membership to the multiset representing the term, and (2) indicates the precision, imprecision and the fuzziness of this term. Our second contribution in this paper is to propose a deduction rule dealing with nuanced information. For that purpose, we propose a deduction rule generalizing the classical *Modus Ponens* rule in a many-valued logic proposed by Pacholczyk [11]. Note that the first version of this rule has been proposed in a fuzzy context by Zadeh [13] and has been studied later by various authors [3, 5, 10]. In section 2, we present briefly the basic concepts of the M-valued logic which forms the backbone of our work. Section 3 introduces our new approach for the symbolic representation of vague terms. In section 4, we define new linguistic modifiers in a purely symbolic way. In section 5, we propose a new *Generalized Modus Ponens* rule.

2 M-valued predicate logic

According to De Glas [9], the statement "x is v_α A" means "x (is v_α) A". Within a multiset context, to a vague term A and a nuance v_α are associated respectively a multiset A and a symbolic degree τ_α. So, the statement "x is v_α A" means that x belongs to multiset A with a degree τ_α. The M-valued predicate logic [11] is the logical counterpart of the multiset theory. In this logic, to each multiset A and a membership degree τ_α are associated a M-valued predicate A and a truth degree τ_α−true. In this context, the following equivalence holds: x is v_α A $\Leftrightarrow x \in_\alpha$ A $\Leftrightarrow$ "x is v_α A" is true $\Leftrightarrow$ "x is A" is τ_α−true.

One supposes that the membership degrees are symbolic degrees which form an ordered set $\mathcal{L}_M = \{\tau_\alpha, \alpha \in [1, M]\}$. This set is provided with the relation of a total order: $\tau_\alpha \leq \tau_\beta \Leftrightarrow \alpha \leq \beta$, and whose smallest element is τ_1 and the largest element is τ_M. We can then define in $\mathcal{L}_M$ two operators $\wedge$ and $\vee$ and a decreasing involution $\sim$ as follows: $\tau_\alpha \vee \tau_\beta = \tau_{max(\alpha,\beta)}, \tau_\alpha \wedge \tau_\beta = \tau_{min(\alpha,\beta)}$ and $\sim \tau_\alpha = \tau_{M+1-\alpha}$. One obtains then a chain $\{\mathcal{L}_M, \vee, \wedge, \leq\}$ having the structure of De Morgan lattice [11]. On this set, an implication $\rightarrow$ and a T-norm T can be defined respectively as follows: $\tau_\alpha \rightarrow \tau_\beta = \tau_{min(\beta-\alpha+M,M)}$ and $T(\tau_\alpha, \tau_\beta) = \tau_{max(\beta+\alpha-M,1)}$.

Example 1 *For example, by choosing M=9, we can introduce:* $\mathcal{L}_9 = \{$not at all, little, enough, fairly, moderately, quite, almost, nearly, completely$\}$.

3 Representation of vague terms

Let us suppose that our knowledge base is characterized by a finite number of concepts C_i. A set of terms P_{ik} is associated with each concept C_i, whose respective domain is denoted as X_i. The terms P_{ik} are said to be the *basic terms* connected with the concept C_i. As an example, basic terms such as *"small"*, *"moderate"* and *"tall"* are associated with the particular concept *"size of men"*. A finite set of *linguistic modifiers* m_α allows us to define *nuanced terms*, denoted as *"$m_\alpha P_{ik}$"*. Linguists distinguish [6] three signed terms: a negative term like "small", a positive term like "tall" and a neutral term like "moderate".

3.1 Representation with *"rules"*

In the following, we propose a symbolic representation to modelize the vague terms which define a "concept". We suppose that a domain of a vague term, denoted by X, is not necessarily a numerical scale. It can for example be "set of men", "set of animals", etc. This domain is simulated by a *"rule"* (cf. Figure 1) representing an arbitrary set of objects. Thus, the set {small, moderate, tall} can be represented as follows:

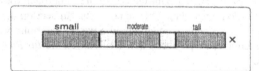

Figure 1: Representation with *"rule"* of a domain X

The basic idea is to associate with each multiset a object which represents a symbolic equivalent to the membership function in the fuzzy set theory. In our work, we focus only on vague terms which can be represented by a membership L-R function. The new object, called "rule", has a geometry similar to a membership L-R function and its role is to illustrate the membership graduality to the multisets. In order to define the geometry of this "rule", we use concepts similar to those defined within a fuzzy context like the core, the support and the fuzzy part of a fuzzy set [13].

Definition 1 *The core of a multiset P, denoted as Core(P), is defined by:* $Core(P) = \{x \in X \mid x \in_M P\}$.

Definition 2 *The fuzzy part of a multiset P, denoted as F(P), is defined by:* $F(P) = \{x \in X \mid x \in_\alpha P$ *and* $\alpha \in [2, M-1]\}$.

Definition 3 *The support of a multiset P, denoted as Sp(P), is defined by:* $Sp(P) = \{x \in X \mid x \in_\alpha P$ *and* $\tau_\alpha > \tau_1\}$.

We associate with each multiset a "rule" that contains the elements of its support (cf. Figure 2). This "rule" is the union of three disjoined subsets: *the left fuzzy part, the right fuzzy part* and *the core*. For a multiset P_i, they are denoted respectively by L_i, R_i and C_i. In order to define formally the concept of directions (left and right) between subsets, we introduce a relation of strict order whose role is to order classical subsets in the universe X.

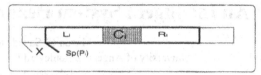

Figure 2: Parts of a *"rule"*

Definition 4 *Let A and B be two disjoined subsets of X. A is said to be on the left compared to B, denoted as* $A \prec B$, *if and only if, by traversing the "rule" X of left on the right, one meets A before meeting B.*

We use the relation which has been just introduced to define the fuzzy parts L_i and R_i. We want to say by the left fuzzy part of a multiset the subset of $F(P_i)$ located on the left of the core of this multiset. This part is maximal in the meaning of it contains all elements of $F(P_i)$ which are on the left of C_i. In other words, it represents the largest subset of $F(P_i)$ located on the left of C_i. In the same way, we can define the right fuzzy part of P_i as the largest subset of $F(P_i)$ located on the right of C_i. We define them formally as follows.

Definition 5 *Let L_i be a subset of $F(P_i)$. Then, L_i is called left fuzzy part of P_i if and only if:* $\forall A, A \subset F(P_i)$, *if* $A \prec C_i$ *then* $A \subset L_i$.

Definition 6 *Let R_i be a subset of $F(P_i)$. Then, R_i is called right fuzzy part of P_i if and only if:* $\forall A, A \subset F(P_i)$, *if* $C_i \prec A$ *then* $A \subset R_i$.

We recall that each fuzzy part contains the elements belonging to P_i with degrees varying from τ_2 to τ_{M-1}. We thus suppose that each fuzzy part L_i and R_i is the union of M-2 subsets which partition it and of which each one contains the elements belonging to P_i with the same degree (cf. Figure 3). These subsets are defined in the following way:

Definition 7 *The set of elements of L_i belonging to P_i with a τ_α degree, denoted as $[L_i]_\alpha$, is defined as follows:* $[L_i]_\alpha = \{x \in L_i \mid x \in_\alpha P_i\}$.

Definition 8 *The set of elements of R_i belonging to P_i with a τ_α degree, denoted as $[R_i]_\alpha$, is defined as follows:* $[R_i]_\alpha = \{x \in R_i \mid x \in_\alpha P_i\}$.

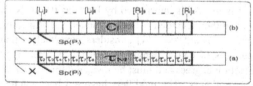

Figure 3: Graduality in a *"rule"*

In order to keep a similarity with the fuzzy sets of type L-R, we choose to place, in a "rule" associated with a multiset, the subsets $[L_i]_\alpha$ and $[R_i]_\alpha$ so that the larger α is, the closer the $[L_i]_\alpha$ subsets and $[R_i]_\alpha$ are to the core C_i (cf. Figure 3). That can be interpreted as follows: the elements of the core of a term represent the typical elements of this term, and the more one object moves away from the core, the less it satisfies the term. Finally, we can propose the definition of a multiset represented by a "rule".

Definition 9 *A multiset P_i is defined by (L_i, C_i, R_i), denoted as $P_i = (L_i, C_i, R_i)$, such that:*

- *$\{L_i, C_i, R_i\}$ is totally ordered by the relation $\prec$ and partitions $Sp(P_i)$,*

- *$\{[L_i]_2, ..., [L_i]_{M-1}\}$ is totally ordered by the relation $\prec$ and partitions L_i,*

- *$\{[R_i]_{M-1}, ..., [R_i]_2\}$ is totally ordered by the relation $\prec$ and partitions R_i.*

One supposes that the "rules" associated with multisets have the same geometry but the position of each "rule" and the sizes (or the cardinalities) of its parts depend on the semantics of the term with which it is associated. In the paragraph 3.3, we introduce symbolic parameters to represent these "rules". These parameters are symbolic values using essentially the notion of symbolic cardinality of a subset. This notion is introduced briefly in the next paragraph.

3.2 Symbolic quotient of cardinalities

In order to qualify the cardinality of an ordinary subset, we use a binary predicate called *Rcard* which is defined on boolean formulas of the logic language. The definition of this predicate and some properties governing it are presented in [7, 8]. This predicate allows to define the *Quotient of Cardinalities* of two subsets. Given two subsets A and B such as the cardinality of B is bigger than the cardinality of A, we can express the cardinality of A compared to the cardinality of B in a qualitative way by using linguistic terms like *"approximately the quarter"*, *"approximately the half"*, etc. Then, we can say "the cardinality of A is *"approximately the half"* among that of B". These terms constitute a set of M symbolic degrees of quotient of cardinalities: $Q_M = \{Q_\alpha, \alpha \in [1, M]\}$. More generally, we can say "the cardinality of A is Q_α among that of B" which will be denoted as $A \trianglelefteq_\alpha B$.

Example 2 *For M=9, we can introduce the following set:* $Q_9 = \{$nothing at all, less of the quarter, approximately the quarter, approximately the third, approximately the half, approximately the two thirds, approximately the three quarters, near to equal, equal$\}$.

3.3 Symbolic parameters for a multiset

Within a symbolic context, we want to define a multiset P_i by a symbolic parameter set. These parameters are given by experts which describe the "rule" associated with P_i in a qualitative way. We distinguish two types of parameters: parameters describing the sign of the term and the internal geometry of the "rule". The description of the internal geometry concerns the relative sizes of the fuzzy parts and the core compared to the "rule". The second type of parameters relates to the size of the "rule" and its position in the domain. The position of a *"rule"* is given compared to another, known as multiset or "rule" of reference. For example, for the concept "size of men" described by {small, moderate, tall}, we can say that *"moderate"* is on the right compared to *"small"* and *"tall"* on the right compared to *"moderate"*. Equivalently, we can say that *"moderate"* is

on the left compared to *"tall"* and *"small"* on the left compared to *"moderate"*. So, to locate a "rule" representing a multiset P_i, we introduce two parameters that indicate: (1) the position of this "rule" compared to a "rule" representing a multiset of reference P_r and (2) to what degree these "rules" overlap.

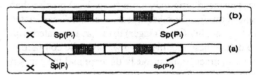

Figure 4: Relative position for a *"rule"*

We can introduce the parameters to represent a multiset:

- $Q_{l_i} \in Q_M$: indicates the relative size of the left fuzzy part compared to the "rule" i.e. $L_i \trianglelefteq_{l_i} Sp(P_i)$.

- $Q_{r_i} \in Q_M$: indicates the relative size of the right fuzzy part compared to the "rule" i.e. $R_i \trianglelefteq_{r_i} Sp(P_i)$.

- $Q_{c_i} \in Q_M$: indicates the relative size of the core compared to the "rule" i.e. $C_i \trianglelefteq_{c_i} Sp(P_i)$.

- $Q_{\epsilon_i} \in Q_M$: indicates the relative size of the *"rule"* compared to the domain X. In other words, we have: $Sp(P_i) \trianglelefteq_{\epsilon_i} X$.

- $\sigma_i \in \{-1, 0, +1\}$: indicates the sign of P_i. $\sigma_i = -1$ if P_i is negative, $\sigma_i = 0$ if P_i is neutral and $\sigma_i = +1$ if P_i is positive.

- $s_i \in \{"l", "r"\}$: indicates the position of P_i compared to P_r. $s_i = "l"$ if P_i is on the left compared to P_r and $s_i = "r"$ if P_i on the right compared to P_r.

- $Q_{\rho_i} \in Q_M$: indicates the relative size of the intersection between the "rules" representing respectively P_i and P_r i.e. $Sp(P_i \cap P_r) \trianglelefteq_{\rho_i} Sp(P_r)$.

Finally, we will represent a multiset P_i by:

$$P_i = \{< P_r, Q_{\rho_i}, s_i, Q_{c_i} >, < \sigma_i, Q_{l_i}, Q_{c_i}, Q_{r_i} >\}.$$

Example 3 *We consider the concept "size of men" which is described by the three following basic terms:* $\mathbb{C} = \{P_i | i \in [1..3]\} = \{$small, moderate, tall$\}$ *which are considered respectively as negative, neutral and positive terms. We can define them as follows:*

- *small:* $P_1 = \{< P_1, Q_M, "r", Q_4 >, < -1, Q_1, Q_6, Q_4 >\}$
- *moderate:* $P_2 = \{< P_1, Q_4, "r", Q_4 >, < 0, Q_4, Q_3, Q_4 >\}$
- *tall:* $P_3 = \{< P_2, Q_4, "r", Q_4 >, < +1, Q_4, Q_6, Q_1 >\}$.

4 Linguistic modifiers

We have noted previously that some nuances can not be interpreted as symbolic degrees and they must be defined as *linguistic modifiers* [3, 4, 11]. These modifiers provide new vague terms starting from a vague basic term. In this section, we define linguistic modifiers in a completely symbolic way and we are interested in some modifiers known as precision modifiers and translation modifiers. We define these modifiers by using the *"rule"* concept.

4.1 Precision modifiers

The *precision modifiers* make it possible to increase or decrease the precision of the basic term. We distinguish two types of precision modifiers: contraction modifiers and dilation modifiers. A contraction (resp. dilation) modifier m produces nuanced term mP_i more (resp. less) precise than the basic term P_i. In other words, the "rule" associated with mP_i is smaller (resp. bigger) than that associated with P_i. We define these modifiers in a way that the contraction modifiers contract simultaneously the core and the support of a multiset P_i, and the dilation modifiers dilate them. The amplitude of the modification (contraction or dilation) for a precision modifier m is given by a new parameter denoted as τ_γ. The higher τ_γ, the more important the modification is.

Definition 10 *Let P_i be a multiset. m is said to be a τ_γ-contraction modifier if, and only if it is defined in the following way:*

1. if $P_i = (L_i, C_i, R_i)$ then $mP_i = (L_i', C_i', R_i')$ such as $L_i' \trianglelefteq_M L_i$ and $R_i' \trianglelefteq_M R_i$

2. $\forall x, x \in_\alpha P_i$ with $\tau_\alpha < \tau_M \Rightarrow x \in_\beta mP_i$ such as $\beta = max(1, \alpha - \gamma + 1)$

Definition 11 *Let P_i be a multiset. m is said to be a τ_γ-dilation modifier if, and only if it is defined in the following way:*

1. if $P_i = (L_i, C_i, R_i)$ then $mP_i = (L_i', C_i', R_i')$ such as $L_i' \trianglelefteq_M L_i$ et $R_i' \trianglelefteq_M R_i$

2. $\forall x, x \in_\alpha P_i$ with $\tau_\alpha > \tau_1 \Rightarrow x \in_\beta mP_i$ such as $\beta = min(M, \gamma + \alpha - 1)$

In this paper, we use $\mathbb{M}_6 = \{m_k | k \in [1..6]\} = \{exactly, really, \emptyset, more\ or\ less, approximately, vaguely\}$ which is totally ordered by $j \leq k \Leftrightarrow m_j \leq m_k$ (cf. Figure 5). $\mathbb{M}_6$ contains a modifier by default, denoted as $\emptyset$, which keeps unchanged the basic term. The modifiers situated after $\emptyset$ are *dilation modifiers* and those preceding it are *contraction modifiers*.

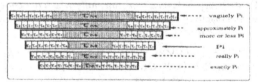

Figure 5: Precision modifiers

4.2 Translation modifiers

The *translation modifiers* operate both a translation and precision variation on the basic term. We define translation modifiers similar to those defined by Desmontils and Pacholczyk [4] within a fuzzy context. In this work, we use $\mathbb{T}_9 = \{t_k | k \in [1..9]\} = \{extremely\ little, very\ very\ little, very\ little, rather\ little, \emptyset, rather, very, very\ very, extremely\}$ totally ordered by $k \leq l \Longleftrightarrow t_k \leq t_l$ (cf. Figure 6). $\mathbb{T}_9$ contains a particular modifier, denoted as $\emptyset$, which keeps

unchanged the multiset P_i to which it operates. The modifiers preceding $\emptyset$ produce dilations as well as translations on the right if P_i is negative and translations on the left if P_i is positive. The modifiers following $\emptyset$ produce contractions as well as translations on the right if P_i is positive and translations on the left if P_i is negative. The translation amplitudes, the contraction or dilation amplitudes are calculated in such a way that the multisets $t_k P_i$ cover the universe X.

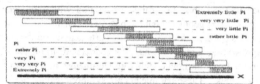

Figure 6: Translation modifiers (P_i is positive)

Within a fuzzy context, a modifier operates on the membership function associated to a fuzzy set and modifies the numerical parameters defining it. In a similar way, we define a translation modifier t_k which operates on multisets by modifying their symbolic parameters. So, we can define the translation modifiers as follows:

Definition 12 *Let P_i be a multiset such as $P_i = \{< P_r, Q_{\rho_i}, s_i, Q_{\epsilon_i} >< \sigma_i, Q_{l_i}, Q_{c_i}, Q_{r_i} >\}$. The nuanced multiset $t_k P_i$ is defined in the following way:*

- $t_k P_i = P_i = \{< P_r, Q_{\rho_i}, s_i, Q_{\epsilon_i} >< \sigma_i, Q_{l_i}, Q_{c_i}, Q_{r_i} >\}$ *if $\sigma_i = 0$ or k=5*
- $t_k P_i = \{< t_{k+1} P_i, Q_{\rho_k}, s_i', Q_{\epsilon_i'} >< \sigma_i', Q_{l_i}, Q_{c_i}, Q_{r_i} >\}$ *if $1 \leq k < 5$*
- $t_k P_i = \{< t_{k-1} P_i, Q_{\rho_k}, s_i', Q_{\epsilon_i'} >< \sigma_i', Q_{l_i}, Q_{c_i}, Q_{r_i} >\}$ *if $5 < k \leq 9$, with:*

1. $\sigma_i' = -1$ if $\{\sigma_i = -1$ and $k > 5\}$ or $\{\sigma_i = +1$ and $k < 5\}$ and $\sigma_i' = +1$ otherwise,

2. $s_i' = "r"$ if $\{\sigma_i = -1$ and $k > 5\}$ or $\{\sigma_i = -1$ and $k < 5\}$ and $s_i' = "l"$ otherwise,

3. $Q_{\epsilon_i'} \leq Q_{\epsilon_i}$ if $k > 5$ and $Q_{\epsilon_i'} \geq Q_{\epsilon_i}$ otherwise.

5 Exploitation of vague knowledge

In this section, we treat the exploitation of nuanced information. In particular, we are interested to propose a generalization of the Modus Ponens rule within a many-valued context [11]. This generalization may have the following form: If we know that {If "x is A" then "y is B" is τ_β-true and "x is A'" is τ_ϵ-true} and that {A' is more or less near to A}, what can we conclude for "y is B", in other words, to what degree "y is B" is true?

This form of the *Generalized Modus Ponens* rule has been studied firstly by Pacholczyk in [11] and later by El-Sayed in [7, 8]. In Pacholczyk's versions, the concept of nearness binding multisets A and A' is modelled by a similarity relation which is defined as follows:

Definition 13 *Let A and B be two multisets. A is said to be τ_α-similar to B, denoted as $A \approx_\alpha B$, if and only if: $\forall x | x \in_\gamma A$ and $x \in_\beta B \Rightarrow min\{\tau_\gamma \rightarrow \tau_\beta, \tau_\beta \rightarrow \tau_\gamma\} \geq \tau_\alpha$.*

This relation generalizes the equivalence relation in a many-valued context as the similarity relation of Zadeh [13] has been in a fuzzy context. It is (1) reflexive: $A \approx_M A$, (2) symmetrical: $A \approx_\alpha B \Leftrightarrow B \approx_\alpha A$, and (3) weakly transitive: $\{A \approx_\alpha B, B \approx_\beta C\} \Rightarrow A \approx_\gamma C$ with $\tau_\gamma \geq T(\tau_\alpha, \tau_\beta)$ where T is a T-norm.

By using the similarity relation to modelize the nearness binding between multisets, the inference rule can be interpreted as: {more the rule and the fact are true} and {more A' and A are similar}, more the conclusion is true. In particular, when A' is more precise than A ($A' \subset A$) but they are very weakly similar, any conclusion can be deduced or the conclusion deduced isn't as precise as one can expect. This is due to the fact that the similarity relation isn't able alone to modelize in a satisfactory way the nearness between A' and A. For that, we add to the similarity relation a new relation called *nearness relation* and which has as role to define the nearness of A' to A when $A' \subset A$. In other words, it indicates the degree to which A' is included in A.

Definition 14 *Let A and B be two multisets such as $A \subset B$. A is said to be τ_α-near to B, denoted as $A \sqsubset_\alpha B$, if and only if $\{\forall x \in F(B), x \in_\gamma A \text{ and } x \in_\beta B \Rightarrow \tau_\alpha \rightarrow \tau_\beta \leq \tau_\gamma\}$.*

Proposition 1 *The nearness relation satisfies the following properties:*

1. *Reflexivity: $A \sqsubset_M A$*
2. *Weak transitivity: $A \sqsubset_\alpha B$ and $B \sqsubset_\beta C \Rightarrow A \sqsubset_\gamma C$ with $\tau_\gamma \leq min(\tau_\alpha, \tau_\beta)$.*

In the relation $A \sqsubset_\alpha B$, the less the value of α is, the more A is included in B. Finally, by using similarity and nearness relations, we propose our *Generalized Modus Ponens* rule.

Proposition 2 *Let A and A', B and B' be predicates associated respectively with the concepts C_i and C_e. Given the following assumptions:*

1. *it is τ_β-true that if "x is A" then "y is B"*
2. *"x is A'" is τ_ϵ-true with $A' \approx_\alpha A$.*

Then, we conclude : "y is B" is τ_δ-true with $\tau_\delta = T(\tau_\beta, T(\tau_\alpha, \tau_\epsilon))$. If the predicate A' is such as $A' \sqsubset_{\alpha'} A$, we conclude: "y is B" is τ_δ-true with $\tau_\delta = T(\tau_\beta, \tau_{\alpha'} \longrightarrow \tau_\epsilon)$.

Example 4 *Given that "really red" $\approx_8$ "red" and "really red" $\sqsubset_8$ "red", from the following rule and fact:*
- it is true that if "the tomato is red" then "it is ripe"
- "the tomato is really red" is quite-true,
we can deduce: "the tomato is ripe" is almost-true. With the Pacholczyk's inference rule presented in [11] one obtains: "the tomato is ripe" is fairly-true. Given that almost-true > fairly-true, we can remark clearly that, when A' is more precise than A, our new result is more precise than that obtained with the old Pacholczyk's inference rule. For the other cases, the two results are identical.

6 Conclusion

In this paper, we have proposed a model symbolically dealing with nuanced information. In this model, we defined a term by symbolic parameters provided by the expert in a qualitative way. Based on this representation method, we defined some linguistic modifiers in a purely symbolic way. Lastly, we presented a new *Generalized Modus Ponens* rule for exploiting nuanced information. With this rule, we obtain satisfactory results.

References

[1] J. F. Baldwin. A new approach to approximate reasoning using fuzzy logic. *Fuzzy sets and systems*, 2:309 – 325, 1979.

[2] B. Bouchon-Meunier and L. Valverde. A ressemblance approach to analogical reasoning function. *Lecture notes in comp. sc.*, 1188:266–272, 1997.

[3] B. Bouchon-Meunier and J. Yao. Linguistic modifiers and imprecise categories. *Int. J. of intelligent systems*, 7:25–36, 1992.

[4] E. Desmontils and D. Pacholczyk. Towards a linguistic processing of properties in declarative modelling. *Int. J. of CADCAM and Comp. Graphics*, 12:351–371, 1997.

[5] D. Dubois and H. Prade. Fuzzy sets in approximate reasoning: Inference with possibility distributions. *Fuzzy sets and syst.*, 40:143–202, 1991.

[6] O. Ducrot and J-M. Schaeffer. Nouveau dictionnaire encyclopédique des sciences du langage. *Editions du Seuil*, 1995.

[7] M. El-Sayed. Une approche logico-symbolique des connaissances nuancees via des modificateurs linguistiques. *RJCIA'00, France, 113-126*, 2000.

[8] M. El-Sayed. *Une approche logico-symbolique des connaissances nuancees via des modificateurs linguistiques*. PhD thesis, Univ. of Angers, 2001.

[9] M. De glas. Knowladge representation in fuzzy setting. Technical Report 48, LAFORIA, 1989.

[10] L. D. Lascio, A. Gisolfi, and U. C. Garcia. Linguistic hedges and the generalized modus ponens. *Int. J. of intelligent systems*, 14:981–993, 1999.

[11] D. Pacholczyk. *Contribution au traitement logico-symbolique de la connaissance*. PhD thesis, University of Paris VI, 1992.

[12] L. A. Zadeh. Fuzzy sets. *Information and control*, 8:338–353, 1965.

[13] L. A. Zadeh. A theory of approximate reasoning. *Int. J. Hayes, D. Michie and L. I. Mikulich (eds); Machine Intelligence*, 9:149–194, 1979.

Session 3–3
Image Processing II

Robust Rotation Estimation From Three Orthogonally-Oriented Cameras

Suneil Sastri
S. Rogers Sr. Dept. of Electrical and Computer
Engineering, University of Toronto
sastri@control.utoronto.ca

Raymond Kwong
S. Rogers Sr. Dept. of Electrical and Computer
Engineering, University of Toronto
kwong@control.utoronto.ca

Abstract

This paper presents the novel ORThogonally-oriented CAMeras (ORTCAM) algorithm that robustly estimates rotation of a set of three orthogonally-oriented cameras undergoing motion. Orthogonally-oriented cameras are any set of divergently-facing cameras where the cameras are oriented 90° to one another. The ORTCAM algorithm robustly estimates rotation using feature correspondences between two views from each camera. The ORTCAM algorithm is shown to both resolve planar and rotation degeneracies and yield rotation estimates superior to those obtained by averaging the rotation estimates from all cameras.

1. Introduction

It is well known that two views from a camera must satisfy the epipolar constraint [6]. Specifically, a correspondence $\mathbf{x} \rightarrow \mathbf{x}'$ must satisfy the constraint:

$$\mathbf{x}'^{\mathrm{T}} E \mathbf{x} = 0, \qquad (1)$$

where E is the essential matrix. Since the essential matrix is solely composed of the rotation and translation of the camera relative to the scene [4], one can determine ego-motion by estimating the essential matrix. Unfortunately, certain point correspondence configurations can lead to multiple interpretations for the essential matrix. These point correspondence configurations are known as degenerate configurations and in the presence of these configurations the epipolar constraint is said to suffer *degeneracy*.

Degeneracy can be classified into two types: motion-dependent degeneracy and motion-independent degeneracy. Motion-dependent degeneracy occurs when the camera undergoes pure rotation. In such a case, the epipolar constraint is undefined and the correspondences satisfy a homography

$$\mathbf{x}' = R\mathbf{x}, \qquad (2)$$

where the homogeneous matrix R is constrained to be a rotation matrix. Motion-independent degeneracy occ-

urs when both the object points and the two camera centers lie on a quadric surface as described by Maybank [7]. When such a surface is a plane-pair with all object points lying on one plane and both camera centers lying on the other, the correspondences satisfy a homography [2]

$$\mathbf{x}' = H\mathbf{x}, \qquad (3)$$

where H is a general homogeneous matrix. In this paper we focus our attention on degeneracies due to two views related by rotation (rotation degeneracy) and due to two views of a plane (planar degeneracy) only. The reason for this is that these degeneracies are the most likely to occur[1].

To address the problem of degeneracy, Kanatani proposed using a model selection criterion, known as the Geometric Information Criterion (GIC) [5], to establish whether point correspondences are best described by the epipolar constraint, a homography, or any other model one may choose to fit to the data. Torr extended Kanatani's research and "robustified" the GIC into the Geometric Robust Information Criterion (GRIC) [12].

While the GRIC can help us identify rotation and planar degeneracies, only pure rotation can be recovered uniquely from a rotation homography. Motion of the camera relative to a plane, on the other hand, cannot be recovered uniquely from the planar homography describing the data since, in general, the planar homography will yield two solutions for motion: one real and one virtual [14].

To overcome this problem we present the novel ORThogonally-oriented CAMeras (ORTCAM) algorithm to estimate robustly the rotation of a set of three orthogonally-oriented cameras using point correspondences from each camera. Orthogonally-oriented cameras are any set of divergently-facing cameras that are oriented 90° to one another. A picture of this configuration is shown in Figure 1.

If the three orthogonally-oriented cameras undergo motion where each camera sees one plane, then none of the cameras alone can reliably determine rotation.

---

[1] Planar degeneracies are especially common in human-made environments since most walls can be interpreted as planes

Figure 1. Picture of three orthogonally-oriented cameras.

The ORTCAM algorithm overcomes this limitation by exploiting the configuration of the cameras in order to reliably recover the rotation of the orthogonally-oriented cameras. The ORTCAM algorithm has the further advantage of improving rotation estimation over what can be achieved by the simple averaging of the rotation estimates from all cameras.

This paper begins with a brief introduction to quaternions. Next, the model of the orthogonally-oriented cameras is presented. This section discusses how we can compare the rotation estimate(s) from each camera. Subsequently, a description of the ORTCAM algorithm is presented along with simulation results. Finally, the ORTCAM algorithm's performance with experimental data is presented.

2. Quaternions

A quaternion is a 4×1 vector representation of rotation. The entries of the 4×1 vector are a function of the axis of rotation, $\mathbf{a}=[X,Y,Z]^T$, and the rotation angle about the axis, θ. One advantage of using quaternions is that they are simpler to work with than matrices, since we need to deal with six nonlinear constraints to ensure that a matrix is a rotation matrix. Another benefit is that rotation with respect to other coordinate systems can easily be determined when the rotation is in the quaternion form (this is exploited in Section 3).

The form of the quaternion is fairly straightforward. If we let $\mathbf{q}$ be a quaternion representation of rotation then $\mathbf{q} = \sin\theta/2 \; [\mathbf{a}^T, \cos\theta/2]^T$. Descriptions of how to decompose a quaternion into a rotation matrix and vice versa are presented in [3] and [15], respectively.

3. Three Orthogonally-Oriented Cameras Model

The model that we consider is the set of three orthogonally-oriented cameras whose camera centers are offset from a common center as shown in Figure 2. The subscripts F, S and B in Figure 2 denote the motion parameters for the front, side and bottom cameras, respectively. The key to resolving rotation ambiguity is obtaining rotation consensus among the rotation estimates from all cameras. In order to do this we must compare the rotations in a common coordinate system. While such a coordinate system can be chosen arbitrarily, for convenience we will choose the front camera's coordinate system. From Figure 2, we observe the following equality among the axes for the front, side and bottom cameras: $Z_F = X_S = Y_B$, $Y_F = Y_S = -Z_B$ and $X_F = -Z_S = X_B$. In matrix form the equality is written as follows.

$$\begin{bmatrix} X_F \\ Y_F \\ Z_F \end{bmatrix} = \begin{bmatrix} 0 & 0 & -1 \\ 0 & 1 & 0 \\ 1 & 0 & 0 \end{bmatrix}\begin{bmatrix} X_S \\ Y_S \\ Z_S \end{bmatrix} = \begin{bmatrix} 1 & 0 & 0 \\ 0 & 0 & -1 \\ 0 & 1 & 0 \end{bmatrix}\begin{bmatrix} X_B \\ Y_B \\ Z_B \end{bmatrix}. \qquad (4)$$

Let

$$[S \rightarrow F] = \begin{bmatrix} 0 & 0 & -1 \\ 0 & 1 & 0 \\ 1 & 0 & 0 \end{bmatrix} \;\&\; [B \rightarrow F] = \begin{bmatrix} 1 & 0 & 0 \\ 0 & 0 & -1 \\ 0 & 1 & 0 \end{bmatrix}. \qquad (5)$$

be the transformations that convert the coordinates in the side camera's and bottom camera's coordinate system, respectively, to the front camera's coordinate system. $[\alpha \rightarrow \beta]$ denotes that a parameter in camera α's coordinate system has been converted to camera β's coordinate system.

To convert the rotations for the side and bottom cameras' coordinate systems to the front camera's coordinate system, we cannot simply multiply the matrix form of the rotations by the transformations in (5). To address this problem we make use of the quaternion form of rotation. Recall from the previous section that a quaternion $\mathbf{q}$ consists of 4 components; the first three of which represent a scaled axis about which rotation occurs. By subjecting the first three components of the quaternions for the side and bottom cameras to transformations in (5) while leaving the fourth components unchanged, we can specify these rotations with respect to the front camera's coordinate system. Relating the side and bottom cameras' rotations to the front camera's coordinate system we get:

$$\mathbf{q}_{[S \rightarrow F]} = \begin{bmatrix} [S \rightarrow F] & \mathbf{0} \\ \mathbf{0}^T & 1 \end{bmatrix}\mathbf{q}_S \;\&\; \mathbf{q}_{[B \rightarrow F]} = \begin{bmatrix} [B \rightarrow F] & \mathbf{0} \\ \mathbf{0}^T & 1 \end{bmatrix}\mathbf{q}_B. \; (6)$$

where $\mathbf{0}$ is a 3×1 zero vector.

A detailed discussion of the reconstruction of the translation of the common center of the orthogonally-oriented cameras and the ambiguity with such a reconstruction is presented in [11].

4. The ORTCAM algorithm

The ORTCAM algorithm consists of three sequential steps: *Model Identification, Resolution of Rotation*

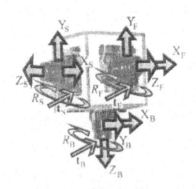

Figure 2. The orthogonally-oriented cameras model. Axes are superimposed onto the front (F), side (S) and bottom (B) cameras. R_F, R_S, and R_B **represent the rotations as seen by the front, side and bottom cameras, respectively.** t_F, t_S, and t_B **represent the translations as seen by the front, side and bottom cameras, respectively.**

Ambiguity and *Improved Rotation Estimation.*

The assumptions made in the ORTCAM algorithm are that the cameras are exactly oriented 90° apart, the images have been calibrated, the correspondences are perturbed by zero-mean, isotropic, Gaussian noise on all coordinates and the maximum percentage of outliers between two views is 50%.

4.1. Model Identification

In order to resolve planar and rotation degeneracies, we first identify them using the GRIC. The three models that we attempt to fit to the data are the rotation homography, the planar homography and the epipolar constraint shown in (2), (3) and (1), respectively. For convenience we will refer the rotation homography, planar homography and epipolar constraint models as the R, H and E models, respectively.

To use the GRIC we first obtain a robust estimate for each model using the RANdom SAmple Consensus (RANSAC) algorithm [1]. The main draw-back with the RANSAC algorithm is that we require *apriori* knowledge of the noise level, σ. To overcome this limitation it was suggested in [13] that the noise level be estimated by the Least Median of Squares (LMS) algorithm [9] under the assumption that the most general model (i.e. the E model) describes the data even if the data is described by a less general model (i.e. the H model or the R model). The reason for this is that the E model can always fit data from the H and R models well, whereas the reverse is not true. When estimating σ from two views of a plane or related by pure rotation, the LMS algorithm has a tendency to underestimate σ. Fortunately, GRIC model selection seems to be fairly immune to small fluctuations in σ [11]. If the H or R model is selected, we can then re-estimate the selected model using the LMS algorithm and obtain a better estimate for σ.

To properly constrain the essential and rotation matrices during estimation, we parameterize them using their quaternion decompositions [11]. The iterative minimization algorithm used within the RANSAC and LMS algorithms is the Sampson error minimization algorithm [10]. This iterative minimization algorithm was chosen due to the simplicity of its implementation. Estimation using Sampson error minimization works well provided that the errors are small compared to the measurements [2]; this is generally the case when correspondences are picked using feature tracking software.

The above procedure outlines *Model Identification* for one camera alone. This procedure must be repeated for all cameras. Notice that *Model Identification* alone has allowed us to resolve rotation degeneracy. The main drawback with *Model Identification* is that LMS algorithm cannot be used to determine σ if more than 50% of the data are outlying.

4.2. Resolution of Rotation Ambiguity

To resolve rotation ambiguity for any cameras suffering planar degeneracy we use rotation consensus among the rotation estimates from all cameras. The use of this strategy stems from the fact that, in general, only estimates of real rotation are consistent for all cameras. It is straightforward to show that two cameras cannot always resolve rotation ambiguity due to planar degeneracy. Consider the case where both cameras view planes whose normals to the cameras are identical. If both cameras undergo rotation about the axis perpendicular to the direction of orientation of the cameras and translation parallel to the planes, then the homogeneous matrices describing the correspondences for both cameras are identical. Consequently, both the real and virtual solutions for rotation for the cameras are identical and no rotation consensus can be achieved. If, however, we add a third camera orthogonal to the other two, then rotation ambiguity can be resolved. Thus, it is recommended that three orthogonally-oriented cameras be used instead of two to resolve rotation ambiguity.

To identify the estimates of the real rotation, we begin by converting all rotations to the front camera's coordinate system using the transformations in Section 3. Those cameras whose data are represented by the R or E model have one estimate for rotation and the remainder of the cameras whose data are represented by the H model have two solutions for rotation. To identify the estimates of the real rotation, we identify which estimates minimize the cost function:

$$C(R', R'', R''') = \|R' - R''\|_F^2 + \|R'' - R'''\|_F^2 + \|R''' - R'\|_F^2 \quad (7)$$

where R', R'' and R''' represent an estimate from the front, side and bottom cameras, respectively, and $\|\cdot\|_F$ represents the Frobenius norm. All possible combinations of rotations for the three cameras are substituted into (7) and the combination that minimizes (7) is selected as the estimates of the real rotation. The Frobenius norm is used because estimates of the real rotation from different camera are not the same, however, the error between these estimates should be small.

The simulation results for *Resolution of Rotation Ambiguity* are shown in Figure 3. Notice that the estimates for the real rotation are selected everytime for all cameras.

4.3. Improved Rotation Estimation

We can further improve the estimates of rotation by using a single parameterization of rotation, relating it to all cameras and subsequently running an iterative minimization algorithm. The motivation behind this stems from the fact that when the cameras are related via a single parameterization of rotation, the cameras are no longer independent from one another. As a result, the data from all cameras can contribute to improving the estimate of rotation.

To relate the single parameterization of rotation to all cameras we parameterize the rotation as a quaternion. In quaternion form, rotation can be easily related to all cameras using the transformations described in Section 3. Once the single parameterization has been related to all cameras, we use an iterative minimization algorithm to improve the estimate of rotation. The iterative minimization algorithm chosen for *Improved Rotation Estimation* is the Sampson error minimization algorithm.

In order to use the Sampson error minimization algorithm we need an initial solution for the parameters that constitute the Sampson error. The parameters are the motion parameters, and possibly a normal to a plane, for each camera. The initial solution chosen for the translation parameter, and possibly a normal to a plane, for each camera is the real estimate that each camera obtained during *Model Identification*. To determine an initial value for rotation we substitute the real rotation estimates from all cameras into the single parameterization and select the rotation that yields the largest set of inliers[2] over all cameras.

Since the Sampson errors for all cameras are related via rotation, we can simultaneously minimize the errors for all cameras. Once Sampson error minimization has converged, we can reassess the inliers over all cameras and repeat iterative minimization until the

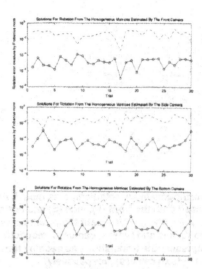

Figure 3. Resolution of rotation ambiguity using (7) over 30 trials with σ=1 and no outliers present. All cameras undergo motion relative to a plane. For each camera's estimate of the homogeneous matrix two solutions for rotation exist: one real (—) and one virtual (- -). Notice that the rotation selected (o) by (7) always coincides with the real solution for rotation.

inlier set has converged.

The simulations results in Figure 4 show the performance of *Improved Rotation Estimation* in comparison to the simple averaging of the rotations from all cameras and to the individual estimates of rotation obtained by the front, side and bottom cameras. Notice that *Improved Rotation Estimation* yields rotation estimates superior to those obtained by simple averaging or by the individual cameras.

The ORTCAM algorithm is also robust to deviations in the orthogonality of cameras. Simulations illustrating this robustness are presented in [11].

5. Experimental results

A preliminary experiment was conducted to test the ORTCAM algorithm. The experiment consisted of

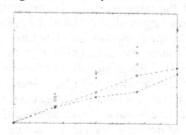

Figure 4. Simulation results illustrating the estimation error for *Improved Rotation Estimation* (-☆-), simple averaging (·-▽-·), the front camera (.+.), the side camera (.o.) and the bottom camera (.✖.). Mean rotation error was calculated at each value of σ over 50 trials. 200 correspondences were established for each camera at each trial. The simulations are shown for σ ={0..1}, 0-30% outliers.

---

[2] Inliers are assessed for each camera using each camera's estimate of σ obtained in *Model Identification*.

subjecting the three orthogonally-oriented cameras, shown in Figure 1, attached to an experimental stand, to random motion over six frames (a description of the experimental stand is available in [11]). The stand is capable of two degrees of freedom of rotation – rotations about the front camera's Y and Z axes. Rotation was measured using a pair of optical encoders on the stand. 69 correspondences were established between consecutive frames by hand[3].

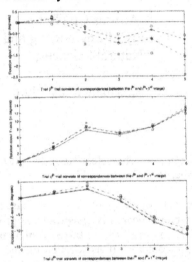

Figure 5. Cumulative rotation about the front camera's X, Y and Z axes for the estimates from *Improved Rotation Estimation* (-☆-), simple averaging (-∇-), the front camera (.+.), the side camera (.o.) and the bottom camera (.✖.), and for the measurements (—) over 6 frames.

Figure 5 shows the cumulative rotation about the front camera's X, Y and Z axes as estimated by *Improved Rotation Estimation*, simple averaging and each camera, and as measured by the encoders. Unfortunately, we see that significant rotation about the front camera's X axis was estimated when, according to the measurements, there should be no such rotation present. The reason for this stems from the fact that there was misalignment of the orthogonally-oriented cameras and the stand [11]. While this misalignment means that the rotations measured by the encoders and those experienced by the orthogonally-oriented cameras differed slightly, nonetheless we use the measurements to compare the mean rotation error from each estimate. The results for rotation error are shown in Figure 6. Notice that ORTCAM algorithm gave the best estimates for rotation.

6. Conclusion

---

[3] Establishing correspondences by hand was done for simplicity. Future experiments will establish correspondences using feature tracking software.

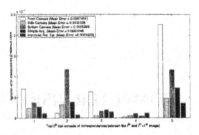

Figure 6. Rotation error associated with *Improved Rotation Estimation*, simple averaging and the front, side and bottom cameras over 6 frames.

This paper illustrated the ORTCAM algorithm's ability to both improve rotation estimation and resolve both rotation and planar degeneracies. Preliminary experimental results demonstrated the ORTCAM algorithm's improved rotation estimation. However, due to slight design flaws in the preliminary experiment, further experiments are needed to thoroughly verify the ORTCAM algorithm's performance. Furthermore, more accurate estimates can be achieved if a maximum likelihood estimator (MLE) is used in the algorithm. Currently, integrating the quaternion form of rotation into an MLE is an outstanding issue. In addition, while justification was given for using three cameras over two to resolve planar degeneracy, a theory establishing the minimum number of orthogonally-oriented cameras necessary to always resolve planar degeneracy is needed.

References

[1] Fischler, M. A. and Bolles, R. C., "Random Sample Consensus. ...", *Comm. of the Assoc. of Comp. Mach.*, 24(6):381-395, 1981.
[2] Hartley, R. I. and Zisserman, A., *Multiple view geometry in computer vision*, Cambridge Univ. Press, 2000.
[3] Horn, B. K. P., "Closed-form solution of absolute orientation using unit quaternions.", *J. Opt. Soc. of Amer.*, 4(4):629-642, 1987.
[4] Huang, T. S. and Faugeras, O. D., "Some properties of the E ...", *IEEE Trans. Patt. Anal. & Mach, Intel*, 11(12):1310-1312, 1989.
[5] Kanatani, K., *Statistical Optimization for Geometric Computation: Theory and Practice*, Elsevier Sciences B. V., 1996.
[6] Longuet-Higgins, H. C., "A computer algorithm for reconstructing a scene from two ...", *Nature*, 293:13-26, 1981.
[7] Maybank, S. J., "The angular velocity associated with the optical flow field ...", *Proc. R. Soc. Lond.*, B227:399-410, 1985.
[8] Maybank, S. J., "Properties of essential matrices. ", *Int. J. Imag. Sys. & Tech.*, 2:380-384, 1990.
[9] Rousseeuw, P. J. and Leroy, A. M., *Robust regression and outlier detection*, John Wiley & Sons, 1987.
[10] Sampson, P. D., "Fitting conic sections to "very scattered" data an iteration ...", *Comp. Graphics & Imag. Proc.*, 18:97-108, 1982.
[11] Sastri, S., *Robust Rotation Estimation From Three ...*, M.A.Sc. Thesis, University of Toronto, 2002.
[12] Torr, P. H. S., "An assessment of information criterion for ...", *IEEE Proc. Comp. Vision & Patt. Rec.*, 47-53, 1997.
[13] Torr, P. H. S. *et al.*, "Robust detection of degenerate...", *Comp. Vision & Imag. Understanding*, 71(3):312-333, 1998.
[14] Tsai, R. Y. and Huang, T. S., "Estimating three-dimensional...", *IEEE Trans. Acoustics, Speech & Sig. Proc.*, 30(4):525-534, 1982.
[15] Wheeler, M. D. and Ikeuchi K., "Iterative estimation of...", Technical Report, Carn. Mellon Univ., CMU-CS-95-215, 1995.

COMPUTER VISION BASED UNISTROKE KEYBOARDS

Aykut ERDEM[1], Erkut ERDEM[1], Volkan ATALAY[1]
[1]Dept. of Computer Engineering,
Middle East Technical University,
Ankara, Turkey
{aykut, erkut, volkan}@ceng.metu.edu.tr

A. Enis CETIN[2]
[2]Faculty of Engineering and
Natural Sciences,
Istanbul, Turkey
cetin@sabanciuniv.edu.tr

Abstract

In this paper we present a unistroke keyboard based on computer vision. The keyboard can be made of paper containing an image of the keyboard which has an upside down U-shape. Each character is represented by a nonoverlapping rectangular region. The user enters a character to the computer by covering the character region with a stylus. The actions of the user are captured by a camera and the covered key is recognized. During the text entry process the user need not have to raise the stylus from the keyboard and this leads to faster data entry rates. In a companion system the user imitates writing on a surface using a pointer or a stylus. In this case the trace of the pointer is analyzed and the characters are recognized. The character set of the continuous hand writing system is based on the Graffiti alphabet to achieve very high recognition rates.

1. Introduction

In this paper we address the problem of entering ASCII text to a wearable computer or a mobile communication device. Mobile communication and computing devices currently have tiny keyboards which are not easy to use. Furthermore such keyboards occupy a large part of the screen in tablet computers and touch screen systems. Computer vision may provide alternative, flexible and versatile ways for humans to communicate with computers. In this approach the key idea is to monitor the actions of the user by a camera and interpret them in real-time. For example, character recognition techniques developed in document analysis [4,6,12] can be used to recognize hand-writing or sketching. In [4] we developed a vision based system for recognizing isolated characters drawn by a pointer or a stylus on a flat surface or the forearm of a person. The user's actions are captured by a head mounted camera. To achieve very high recogniton rates characters are restricted to a single stroke alphabet as in Graffiti in [4] .

The concept of computer vision based regular QWERTY type keyboards is independently proposed by us [13] and Zhang et.al.[8]. In this system a character is entered to the computer if its location on the keyboard image is covered by a finger. In this approach the keyboard is a passive device. Therefore it can be made out of paper, fabric or foldable plastic having an image of a QWERTY or other type of regular size keyboard. However, the realization of 10-finger typing on a vision based keyboard is very difficult due to the occlusion of some key locations by unused fingers. We believe that the occlusion problem can be solved by tracking the finger tips in a parallel manner. However the computational cost of such a system may be too high.

Unistroke keyboards provide a good trade off between 10-finger typing and continuous handwriting recognition. In this paper, we present a computer vision based unistroke Cirrin type keyboard [14] which is designed for tablet computers and the user draws one stroke per word. The key locations are placed circularly and to enter a word the user traces out a path determined by the characters forming the word using a stylus. Whenever the stylus enters a key location the corresponding character is recognized by the tablet computer. In this paper we place our key locations on an upside down U like curve instead of a circle as shown in Figure 1. In this layout design the user can place his or her hand in the middle which elliminates the occlusion problem. In this way the camera can be placed on the users' forehead or shirt pocket.

In a companion system we develop a continuous Graffiti-like script based text entry system. This is an

210

extension of the text entry system described in [4]. Instead of drawing isolated characters the user sketches the Graffiti alphabet in a continuous manner on his or her left arm using a pointer or a stylus or a finger. In this approach the alphabet is also based on Graffiti™ alphabet. However, some letters of the Graffiti alphabet has to be modified to increase the recognition accuracy. By restricting the alphabet to Graffiti-like characters very high recognition rates can be achieved.

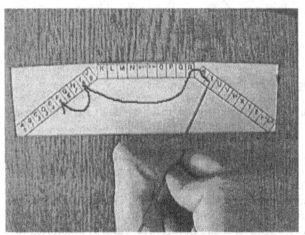

Figure 1: Up side down U shaped keyboard. The word "first" is entered in this example.

We describe the vision based keyboard system in Section 2, and in Section 3 we present the continuous Graffiti recognition system.

2. Unistroke Keyboard System

Practical computer vision based human-machine communication systems can be developed by taking advantage of the advances in computer technology. It is now feasible to process video in real-time in a standard PC without requiring any special purpose hardware.

In Figure 1 a Cirrin-type unistroke keyboard image drawn on regular paper is shown. The stylus is simply a pointer with a red mark at the tip. The system is implemented using a 550 MHz Intel Pentium-III personal computer and a web camera.

The Cirrin keyboard is circular whereas our keyboard consists of three rectangles each divided into 10 key regions as shown in Figure 1. The main reason for this keyboard topology is to eliminate the occlusion problem. In this way the camera can be placed on the users' forehead or shirt pocket. In Cirrin there are no keys for "space", "enter", "shift", etc. and word boundaries are determined by pen up and down action. In our case we placed "space", "enter", and "shift" keys. As a result the

user need not have to lift the stylus from the keyboard during the ASCII text entry process.

In the first step of the recognition algorithm, the system detects the position of the keyboard in the initial video frame. This process is performed by finding the edges of the image with the Canny edge detection algorithm. The corners of the keyboard is detected from the binary image obtained via the edge detection process. Rectangles in the keyboard picture produce quadruples in the observed image. After finding the corners, each quadruple in the image frame is mapped to a rectangle by using the boundary information of the rectangles in the keyboard picture. In this way pixels belonging to each character region is determined. In the current keyboard system it is assumed that the keyboard is placed on a planer surface. In the future versions we will handle foldable keyboards as well.

The tip of the stylus is determined by detecting the moving pixels in the image and the color information (the tip of the stylus is red). The moving pixels are determined by taking the image difference of two consequitive image frames. Since the corners of the keyboard are detected in the previous steps the differencing operation is performed only inside of the quadruple corresponding to the keyboard. To robustify the detection process color information is also used. The red pixels among the moving pixels are determined as the tip of the stylus. This also robustifies the system against the small movements of the users' forearm.

A character is entered to the computer when the tip of the stylus enters the corresponding key region. The stylus has to stay in a key region at least in two image frames for recognition.

3. Vision Based Continuous Character Recognition

Unistroke isolated character recognition systems are successfully used in personal digital assistants in which people feel easier to write rather than type on a small size keyboard [8,9]. In this approach it is assumed that each character is drawn by a single stroke as an isolated character. One of the alphabets that has this property is the Graffiti™. In [4] we developed a vision based system for recognizing isolated Graffiti characters drawn by a pointer or a stylus on a flat surface or the forearm of a person. The advantages of our computer vision based text entry system compared to other vision based systems [10-12] are the following:

- The background is controlled by the forearm of the user. Furthermore, if the user wears a unicolor fabric then the tip of the finger or the beam of the pointer can be detected in each image of the video by a simple image processing operation such as thresholding.

- It is very easy to learn a Graffiti-like alphabet. Only a few characters are different from the regular Latin alphabet. Although it may be easy to learn other text entry systems such as [5,10,11], some people are reluctant to spend a few hours to learn unconventional text entry systems. Furthermore, in addition to the regular characters other single stroke characters can be defined by the user to be used as bookmarks, pointers to databases etc.

- Computationally efficient, low power consuming algorithms exist for the recognition of unistroke characters and they can be implemented in real time with very high recognition accuracy. After a few minutes of studying the Graffiti alphabet, about 86% accuracy is possible. After some practice, accuracy improves to about 97%. Almost 100% accuracy seems to be possible [9]. Therefore the accuracy is very high compared to regular handwriting recognition method described in [12].

- Computer vision based text entry systems are almost weightless.

In this paper, we extend the isolated Graffiti recognition problem to continuous Graffiti recognition as a companion system to the unistroke keyboard system. Graffiti alphabet cannot be directly extended to continuous handwriting. The characters of the alphabet has to be modified to increase the recognition accuracy. For example, the unistroke characters corresponding to "o" and "q" may be confused very easily in continuos hand writing.

In our unistroke alphabet, handwriting version of Greek letter phi is used for "q", the Graffiti character gamma for "t" is replaced by the character shown in Figure 2. Other modified characters are "X" and "L".

In this handwriting method, the transitions from character to character are also restricted to the three strokes shown in the middle row of Figure 2. Transition from one character to another can be done with a horizontal line segment, a monotonically decreasing convex curve or a monotonically increasing convex curve. The last authors's name "Cetin" is written in continuous Graffiti in the bottom row of Figure 2. For example, the character "C" is connected to the character "E" with the convex up curve and the character "I" is connected to "N" via the horizontal stroke.

Figure 2: The characters for "t", "q", "x" and "L" in continuous Graffiti alphabet (upper row); the letter to letter transition strokes (middle row); the last author's name written in continuous Graffiti (the bottom row).

3. 1 Continuous Graffiti Recognition Algorithm

The characters can be drawn using a stylus, finger or a laser pointer on the forearm of the user. In the current system the user writes in continuos Graffiti using a laser pointer on the forearm captured by a camera mounted on the forehead or a shirtpocket. The video is segmented to image sequences corresponding to each word. The image sequence starts with a laser pointer turn-on action and terminates when the user turns off the laser pointer.

In our system unistroke characters are described using a chain code which is a sequence of numbers between 0 and 15 obtained from the quantized angle of the beam of the laser pointer in an equally time sampled manner as shown in Figure 3. The chain code is extracted from the relative motion of the beam of the laser pointer between consequtive images of the video and it is applied as an input to the recognition system which consists of finite state machines (FSM) corresponding to individual characters together with possible connections to the next character. In general, there are two different FSM's for each character. Some characters can be combined to the other characters in three ways: e.g., the Graffiti character "G" thus there are three FSM's representing "G". The input is applied to all FSM's corresponding to all of the characters and the FSM generating the minimum error determines the recognized character.

Step1. Extraction of chain code.
- The position of the red mark produced by the laser pointer is found in each frame.
- A chain code is generated according to the angle between two consecutive laser mark positions.

212

Step 2. Analysis using finite state machines.

- The chain code is applied as input to each finite state machine.
- State changes are determined in addition an error counter is increased by one, if a change is not possible according to the current FSM.
- If a chain code does not terminate in the final state, the corresponding character is eliminated.
- Errors in each state are added up to find the final error for each character.
- Character with the minimum error is the recognized one.

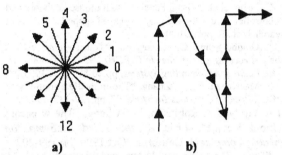

Figure 3. a) Chain code values for the angles, b) a sample chain coded representation of the character "N"=4,4,4,1,14,14,13,4,4,4,0,0.

In Figure 3 (b), the character "N" is characterized by the chain code *4,4,4,1,14,14,13,4,4,4,0,0*. The first three inputs, 4, 4, and 4, do not produce any error when applied to the first state of the two FSM's representing the character "N". The forth number or the chain code, 1, leads to an error and an increase in the error counter by 1. The next input 14 makes the FSM to go to the next state and the subsequent 14, and 13 let the machine to remain there. Whenever the input becomes 4, the FSM moves to the third state. The machine stays in this state until the input 0 appears and this makes FSM to go to the final state. The rest of the input data being 0 makes the machine to stay in the final state, and when a new input is encountered the FSM terminates with an error value of 1. (the other FSM representing the character "N" corresponding to monotonically decreasing connection terminates with an error value of 3). The next input is applied to the first states of all of the FSM's to determine the next character.

Both the time and space complexity of the recognition algorithm are O(n), n being the number of elements in the chain code.

It is observed that the FSM based recognition algorithm is robust as long as the user does not move his arm or the camera during the writing process of a letter.

Characters can be also modeled by Hidden Markov Models which are stochastic FSM's instead of the deterministic FSM's to further increase the robustness of the system at the expense of higher computational cost. In addition, in order to prevent noisy state changes, look-ahead tokens can be used which acts as a smoothing filter on the chain code.

3.2 Video Processing

The images corresponding to a character are to be processed to extract the marker positions for chain code extraction. If the position of the marker is found in the initial frame, it can be tracked in the consecutive images. In our experiments, we use a red laser pointer to write the characters. The images are decomposed into red, green and blue components and the red mark can be found by thresholding followed by a connected component analysis in the red image. If hand gestures are to be used, a skin filter may be necessary. Other pointers such as the tip of a pen can be also extracted and traced in a similar manner. Clearly, a laser pointer is the most robust text entry device to changing lighting and background conditions. Our current system handles only the laser pointer. We are currently working on finger and ordinary pointer based text entry.

An image sequence is segmented according to words which are separated from each other by discontinuous pointer movements, e.g, a sudden jump from the beginning of the left hand to the ankle. In the case of a laser pointer, at the end of each word the user turns off the light. This marks the end of each word. Segmentation of the video for each word is based on the jumps of the red mark of the laser pointer. A new word starts when the user turns on the laser pointer.

There are mainly two problems during the image capture and processing steps: distortion due to perspective projection and occlusion of the marker. Distortion in the characters occurs when the drawing or hand gestures are done in a non-orthographic manner. It is observed that such perspective distortion up to about 22.5 degrees of difference between the camera and the forearm does not affect the recognition as all of the captured and processed data are in two dimensions. However, if a more robust system is desired, a self-calibration algorithm or video orbits algorithm can be applied. However, these algorithms are too complex for current wearable computational power. Thus, a simplified version based on similar principles should be implemented. For example, the system can be calibrated by initially drawing two hypothetical lines on the forearm. Occlusion is not considered in this system, since the camera is assumed to capture the images in front of the marker.

4. Experimental Results and Conclusions

The experimental setup is composed of a red laser pointer, a dark background fabric and a commercial camera with an capturing card. The camera produces 320 pixel by 240 pixel color images at about 13 frames per second. All of the processing is performed on a Celeron 600 processor with 64MB of memory in real time.

The user draws continuous Graffiti characters using the red pointer on the dark background material. In Graffiti like recognition systems, very high recognition rates are possible [9]. In our system, in spite of the existence of perspective distortion, it is possible to attain a recognition rate of 90% at about 12 word per minute (wpm) writing speed. It is also observed that the recognition process is writer independent with little training. We believe that we can achieve higher writing speed rates with the advances in digital camera and wearable computer technology.

The perspective distortion plays some role in the recognition accuracy of the system. In our experiments, we have observed that the degradation in recognition is at most 10% around 30 degree difference between the plane on the which writing is performed and the camera.

Several tests are also carried out under different lighting conditions. In day (incandescent) [fluorescent] light the pixel value of the background is about 50 (180) [100] whereas the pixel value of the beam of the laser pointer is about 240 (250) [240]. In all cases the beam of the laser pointer can be easily identified from the dark background.

The current writing speed of the handwriting recognition system is lower than the 35 to 40 wpm transcription speeds of septambic keyer Twiddler [5]. However, regardless of the keyboard the composition writing speed is below 20 wpm for most people. We believe that in a wearable computing environment the composition speed rather than the transcription speed is important.

The unistroke keyboard is implemented using an ordinary web camera attached to the USB port of the computer. This system has a higher recognition accuracy (96%) than the handwriting recognition system. In fact with some training in an optimized keyboard the user can get close to the 20 wpm writing speed.

5. References

[1] D. Hall, J. Martin, and J.L. Crowley, "Statistical Recognition of Parameter Trajectories for Hand Gestures and Face Expressions", *Computer Vision and Mobile Robotics Workshop*, Santorini, Greece, September 17-18, 1998.

[2] I. Laptev and T. Lindeberg, "Tracking of multi-state hand models using particle filtering and a hierarchy of multi-scale image features", *Tech. Rep*, KTH , Sweden, March 2000.

[3] F. Quek et.al, "Gesture cues for conversational interaction in monocular video", *Proc. ofRecognition, Analysis, and Tracking of Faces and Gestures in Real-Time Systems*, Greece, Sept1999.

[4] O. F. Ozer, O. Özün, C. O. Tüzel, V. Atalay, A. E. Cetin, "Vision Based Single-Stroke Character Recognition for Wearable Computing", *IEEE Intelligent Systems*, Vol. 16, No. 3, pp. 33-37, May/June 2001

[5] www.handykey.com

[6] O.N. Gerek , A.E. Cetin , A. Tewfik, and V. Atalay, "Subband Domain Coding of Binary Textual Images for Document Archiving", *IEEE Trans. on Image Processing*, Vol.8, No.10, pp.1438-1446, October 1999.

[7] Z. Zhang. et.al. "Visual Panel: Virtual mouse keyboard and 3d controller with an ordinary piece of paper". Microsoft Research Tech. Report, 2000.

[8] D. Goldberg and C. Richardson, "Touch-typing with a stylus", *Proceedings of the INTERCHI '93 Conference on Human Factors in Computing Systems*, pp.80-87, N.Y, 1993.

[9] I.S. MacKenzie and S. Zhang, "The immediate usability of Graffiti", *Proc. of Graphics Interface '97*, pp.129-137, 1997.

[10] A Vardy, J A Robinson, L-T Cheng, "The wristcam as Input Device", *Proc. of the Third Int.Symp. on Wearable Computers*, California, Oct 1999, pp 199-202.

[11] Starner, Thad, Weaver, Joshua, and Pentland, Alex. "A Wearable Computing Based American Sign Language Recognizer", *Proc. of the First Int. Symp. on Wearable Computers*, Cambridge, MA, IEEE Press, Oct. 13-14, 1997.

[12] M.E. Munich and P. Perona, "Visual input for pen-based computers", *13th Int. Conf. Pattern Recognition*, pp.33-37, Vienna, 1996.

[13] Y. Yardimci, A. E. Cetin, "Computer Vision Based Keyboard", Patent Application, Sept. 2000.

[14] Jennifer Mankoff and Gregory D. Abowd. Cirrin: A word-level unistroke keyboard for pen input. In *Proceedings of UIST '98*. Technical note. pp.213-214.

Camera Auto-Calibration using a Sequence of 2D Images with Small Rotations and Translations

Reza Hassanpour
Department of Computer Engineering,
Cankaya University,
Ankara, Turkey
reza@cankaya.edu.tr

Volkan Atalay
Department of Computer Engineering,
Middle East Technical University,
Ankara, Turkey
volkan@ceng.metu.edu.tr

Abstract

3D model generation needs depth information of the object in the input images. This information can be found using stereo imaging but it needs camera parameters. Camera calibration is not possible without some knowledge about the objects in the scene or assuming fixed or known values for the camera parameters. When using fixed camera parameters, however, small rotation angles or small translation in camera position can degenerate the results. The degeneracy can be omitted by adding new restrictions to the a-priori knowledge about the camera parameters. The calibrated data may be used to reconstruct 3D model of the scene.

1. Introduction

There is a significant body of work on three dimensional (3D) analysis of images in recent years [1,2,3,4,5]. Many application areas such as computer animation, medical imaging and teleconferencing require 3D information of the environment that can be simulated on our machines. The first step in 3D analysis is modeling 3D objects. This step, in general has been proven to be a difficult task to accomplish. The reason for the difficulty is the need for very sensitive and reliable measurements that can either be obtained by using complicated measuring devices to find the range data (depth information) or by developing algorithms to extract this information from two dimensional (2D) images using different features of the objects. To deal with these problems, the researchers have either limited the 3D objects to be modeled to a small and known class of natural or artificial entities [4] or imposed restrictions on the parameters of the problem [2,3]. These restrictions make possible to incorporate the knowledge about the objects or the camera into the system. However, if the camera rotation is not about at least two non-parallel axes, it is not be possible to find the aspect ratio of scene and camera. To avoid this problem some new restrictions such as known aspect ratio or knowledge about scene should be incorporated. In this study, assuming fixed values for camera internal parameters, we develop an algorithm to compute intrinsic parameter matrix when the rotation is only about the vertical axis and translation is small. This type of rotation is quite common when the images are taken with a handheld camera by a person standing in (almost) a fixed place. In this study, we describe an auto-calibration algorithm with fixed but unknown camera parameters which is initially proposed by Triggs [2]. We have modified Triggs' algorithm to incorporate known aspect ratio and skew values to make it applicable for small rotation around a single axis.

2. Image Formation Process

A single image, despite its rich content, does not contain enough information to reconstruct the 3D scene. This is because of the image formation process which maps a 3D scene onto a 2D image. In this mapping process, the depth data is lost, however if two or more images are available, the 3D point can be obtained from the intersection of sight lines as demonstrated in Figure 1.

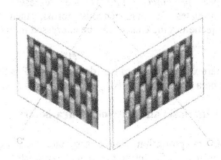

Figure 1. 3D location of a point from the intersection of sight lines.

In this process, we need to know:

- corresponding points in the images,
- orientation and relative location of the camera,
- internal camera parameters.

Corresponding points in the images may be found by detecting interest points in both images and matching them by means of some similarity measure [6]. Camera orientation and location, is called as the extrinsic parameters of camera, which relate the external position of camera to the structure of the corresponding sets of image points. Intrinsic camera parameters define the physical properties of the camera.

3. Camera Model

A simple model of a CCD camera may be defined by the pinhole camera. The geometric process for image formation in a pinhole camera is illustrated in Figure 2.

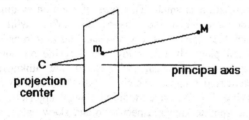

Figure 2. Image formation in a pinhole camera.

In the simplest model, we can assume that the center of projection is the origin of a Euclidean coordinate system and the plane on which the image is created lies at distance f along the z axis from the x-y plane and parallel to it. This plane is called *image plane*. In this model, the center of projection is called the camera center, the line passing from the camera center and perpendicular to image plane is called the *principal axis*. The intersection of principal axis and image plane is called *principal point*. If we represent the coordinates in homogeneous forms, then the projection in the camera can be expressed in matrix form as:

$$x=PX \qquad (1)$$

where x is the image of world point X and P is the camera projection matrix.

3.1 Intrinsic and Extrinsic Parameters

Camera projection matrix associates the world coordinates of points to the image coordinates. This means that the association process is affected by the physical properties of the camera. First property in this regard is the focal length f of the camera. In addition, the coordinates on the image plane depends on the scanning process in the camera and shape and size of the pixels. Camera pixels may be non-rectangular which then includes a skew effect in the projection. Furthermore, the projection center may not correspond to the origin of the coordinate system in the image plane. Therefore, the image coordinates should be scaled with pixel width and height. All these physical properties of the camera are called intrinsic parameters. A projection matrix considering the intrinsic parameters is given by Equation 2.

$$K = \begin{vmatrix} \alpha_x & s & x_0 \\ 0 & \alpha_y & y_0 \\ 0 & 0 & 1 \end{vmatrix} \qquad (2)$$

where α_x and α_y are the focal length of the camera in terms of pixel dimensions in x and y directions respectively, s is the skew parameter and x_0 and y_0 are location of the principal point. The coordinate system of the camera is related to the world coordinate system via a translation and a rotation. The coordinates of a point in the camera frame is related to its coordinates in the world frame with the Equation 3 where C is the coordinates of camera projection center in world coordinates and R is rotation matrix.

$$X_{cam}=R(x-C) \qquad (3)$$

The location and direction of the camera are given by the *extrinsic* parameters.

3.2 Camera Matrix

Considering both camera position and orientation and its physical features, the mapping from world coordinates to image plane coordinates is given by the following equation:

$$P=KR[I \mid -C] \qquad (5)$$

which can be simplified as:

$$P=K[R \mid t] \qquad (6)$$

This equation combines the intrinsic and extrinsic parameters of a projective camera and is called camera matrix. K and R matrices can be found from camera matrix by decomposing it to an upper-triangulation matrix and an orthogonal matrix using RQ decomposition.

4. 3D Reconstruction and Auto-calibration

Given two images and a set of matching points such as x_i and x_i', we want to find point set X_i such that its mappings in first and second images are x_i and x_i' respectively. From definition of a camera matrix we have $x_i = PX_i$ and $x_i' = P'Xi$. Therefore, our first step should be the computation of camera matrices P and P'. To find these matrices, we need to establish a geometrical relation between the corresponding points in the images. This relation is

216

given by a matrix called *fundamental matrix*. Mathematically the matrix is defined as:

$$x'Fx=0 \quad (7)$$

In this relation, F (fundamental matrix) is a 3x3 matrix and x_i and $x_i{}'$ are the points from the images. This equation shows that given any point from first image, its corresponding point in the second image should lie on a line which is called *epipolar line*. The reason for this restriction is that the camera centers c and c' and world point X lie in a plane, *epipolar plane* which also includes the sight lines form X to image planes and the line connecting two camera centers together (*baseline*) as shown in Figure 3.

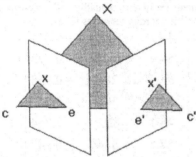

Figure 3. Camera centers and sight lines lie in the epipolar plane.

Given a point x and the camera centers, it is possible to find the intersection line of epipolar plane with the second image plane which is a line passing through point x'. The relationship defined by fundamental matrix is only dependant on projective coordinates of the points in the images and not on the Euclidean measurements like angles and lengths. This means F does not depend on the choice of a coordinate frame and any projective transformation of world points will not affect it. But these transformations will affect camera projection matrices P and P'. Thus although a pair of camera matrices like P and P' uniquely determine the fundamental matrix, the reverse in not true. So given a set of corresponding points in the two images, the camera matrices and 3D scene can be reconstructed up to a projective transform. To upgrade a projective reconstruction to a more realistic one with a geometric structure we need an orthogonal transformation plus a translation. This transform leaves the plane at infinity unchanged and transforms the *absolute conic* which is a specific conic, into itself. The absolute conic is defined as follows:

The absolute conic Ω is a degenerate point conic on the plane at infinity π_{inf}. Since π_{inf} is defined as $[0\ 0\ 0\ 1]^T$ the points on Ω satisfy

$$x^2+y^2+z^2=0$$
$$w=0 \quad (11)$$

Every known angle or ratio of lengths imposes a constraint on the absolute conic and if enough constraints are available it can be uniquely determined. If the absolute conic is identified it can be used to upgrade an Affine structure to a metric one. The matrix for upgrading from a projective reconstruction to a metric one is called a *Homograohy* matrix. Dual of the absolute conic *DAC* is related to the camera intrinsic parameters via Equation 12.

$$\Omega^* = KK^T \quad (12)$$

DAC and π_{inf} are encoded in a concise form using a degenerate dual quadric which is called the *absolute dual quadric* Q^*_{inf} . The relationship between Ω^* and Q^*_{inf} is given in Equation 13. π_{inf} is the null vector of Q^*_{inf} .

$$\Omega^* = P\ Q^*_{inf}\ P^T \quad (13)$$

5. Proposed Method

Camera projection matrix maps absolute dual quadric to *DAC* via Equation 13. This means that any assumption about the intrinsic parameters of the camera can be transferred to a restriction on the value of the entries of *DAC* and absolute dual quadric. By imposing constraints on the entries of camera intrinsic matrix such as constant values for focal length, skew, aspect ratio and so on, we may define equations on unknown dual absolute quadric entries. This set of equations, if solved gives us the absolute dual quadric which may be used to find the camera intrinsic parameters. The only problem here is that, the method is applicable if there are rotations about at least two non-parallel axes in the images with at least 30 degrees in each rotation axis and some translations in each direction. To avoid this problem, we have added two more restrictions: skew is 0 and aspect ratio is 1. These restrictions are reasonable assumptions in most real systems. The relationship between the elements of Ω^* and Q^*_{inf} are given in Equation 14.

$$\Omega^*_{ij} = (P\ Q^*_{inf}\ P^T)_{ij} \quad (14)$$

Here i and j subscripts show the element at row i and column j. For each image, we have a set of equations of type 14. Since the Equation 14 is given in homogeneous coordinates, it is valid only up to a scale factor. In order to eliminate this scale factor, cross product of the entries of Ω^* can be used. Here to solve the equations in an iterative form, we preferred to use a cost function and minimize it subject to some restrictions. The cost function is given in Equation 15.

$$\sum_i (\Omega^* \wedge P_i\ Q^*_{inf} P_i^T) \quad (15)$$

The restrictions imposed on the equations are

- rank 3 restriction for Q^*_{inf} by putting its determinant equal to zero,
- $\|\Omega^*\| = 1$,
- $\|Q^*_{inf}\| = 1$,

- skew is zero,
- aspect ratio is known and equal to one.

After adding skew=0 and aspect ratio=1 restrictions the Ω^* matrix have the following values in terms of camera intrinsic parameters

$$\begin{bmatrix} \alpha^2 + x_0^2 & x_0 y_0 & x_0 \\ x_0 y_0 & \alpha^2 + x_0^2 & y_0 \\ x_0 & y_0 & 1 \end{bmatrix}$$

where x_0 and y_0 are camera principle point coordinates and α is the camera resolution in the unit of length in both x and y directions. (we have assumed that they are equal). To solve this set of equations we have used quadratic sequential programming functions provided by MATLAB.

6. Experimental Results

The algorithm given in previous section is implemented using MATLAB. We have imposed the restrictions as equality constraints and used quadratic sequential programming to solve them. The algorithm is tested on a sequence of images taken from an object on a rotating plate. In each image, we have rotated the plate for 20 degrees and change the location of the camera to have some translation (although small) in the location of the object. Three views chosen from the sequence are shown in Figure 5.

Figure 5. Sequence of input images.

The camera calibration matrix K is computed after finding the fundamental matrix from matching points using 8 points algorithm [10] and then determining the camera projection matrices [11]. Camera intrinsic matrix K is given below.

$$\begin{bmatrix} 1234 & -0.002 & 657.1 \\ 0 & 1234.01 & 519.6 \\ 0 & 0 & 1 \end{bmatrix}$$

We have also reconstructed some corner points of the object and find their 3D coordinate values. The homography matrix converting projective camera matrices into a metric one was found from the Equation 15.

$$Q^*_{inf} = H\hat{I}H \quad (15)$$

H^{-1} obtained from Equation 14 is a 3D point homography taking the projective coordinate to Euclidean coordinates. Decomposition of Q^*_{inf} may be done by eigenvalue decomposition method [11]. The homography matrix H is given as follows.

$$\begin{bmatrix} 15478 & 0.4867 & -0.9853 & -0.2779 \\ -89451 & 0.8472 & -0.1704 & 0.3032 \\ 280.9 & 235 & -0.0008 & 182.7 \\ -563.2 & -1214.8 & -0.0017 & 35.351 \end{bmatrix}$$

Figure 6 shows the corner points we have selected to find their 3D coordinates. These points in our experiment are given manually. The reconstructed values of the coordinates are as follows.

$$\begin{bmatrix} 44.7 & 28.5 & -0.841 \\ 57.9 & 31.7 & -0.723 \\ 66.9 & 28.1 & -0.958 \\ 80.3 & 30.5 & -0.859 \\ 45.1 & 83.7 & -0.864 \\ 57.5 & 88.0 & -0.749 \\ 67.2 & 83.6 & -0.981 \\ 78.9 & 87.0 & -0.869 \end{bmatrix}$$

Metric reconstruction is valid up to a scale factor which may be found only from some a-priori knowledge about the objects in the image. This fact is clear from the values given above, but other than this, despite the small rotation angle about only a single axis and a small translation value, the results are satisfactory. If the matching pairs are reliable (which is the case in natural images with a good texture) this algorithm may be followed by a bundle adjustment to increase accuracy in point location in 3D.

Figure 6. Location of reconstructed points.

Figure 7 demonstrates reconstructed corner points marked in Figure 6 from top and front views.

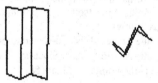

Figure 7. Reconstructed points from top and front views.

218

7. Conclusion

An auto-calibration method for a sequence of images with small rotations and translation is described and preliminary experimental results are demonstrated. We intend to apply the described method for three dimensional head modeling as the next step. Three dimensional positions of known facial features computed from two dimensional images will be used to deform a generic head model by using a spring based energy minimization method.

References

[1] Faugeras, O. and Robert, L.: 1994, What can two images tell us about a third one?, in J.-O. Eklundh(ed.), Proceedings of the 3rd European Conference on Computer Vision, Vol. 800-801 of Lecture Notes in Computer Science, Springer-Verlag, Stockholm, Sweden. also INRIA Technical report 2018.

[2] Triggs, B., "Autocalibration and the absolute quadric", In CPVR97, pages 607-614, 1997

[3] Zhang, Z. and Isono, K. and Akamatsu, S.,"Euclidean Structure from Uncalibrated Images Using Fuzzy Domain Knowledge: Application to Facial Images Synthesis",ICCV98, 1998,pp. 784-789

[4] Fua, P., 2000, "Regularized bundle-adjustment to model heads from image sequences without calibration data", International Journal of Computer Vision, 38(2).

[5] Faugeras, O.: 1995, Stratification of 3-D vision: projective, affine, and metric representations, Journal of the Optical Society of America A12(3), 465_484.

[6] Zhang, Z., Deriche, R., Faugeras, O. and Luong, Q.-T.: 1995, A robust technique for matching two uncalibrated images through the recovery of the unknown epipolar geometry, Artificial Intelligence Journal 78, 87_119.

[7] Shan, Y. and Zhang, Z., "Corner Guided Curve Matching and its Application to Scene Reconstruction", CVPR00, 2000, pp. 796-803

[8] C. Harris and M. Stephens, "A combined corner and edge detector", Fourth AlveyVision Conference, pp.147-151, 1988.

[9] O. Faugeras, "What can be seen in three dimensions with an uncalibrated stereo rig", Computer Vision - ECCV'92, Lecture Notes in Computer Science, Vol. 588, Springer-Verlag, pp. 563-578, 1992.

[10] Hartley, R.:1995, In defence of the 8-point algorithm, Proceedings of the 5th International Conference on Computer Vision, IEEE Computer Society Press, Boston, MA, pp. 1064_1070

[11] Hartley, R, Zisserman, A "Multiple View Geometry in Computer Vision" Cambridge University press, 2000.

Biometric Security System Design Using Keystroke Rhythms Algorithm

Aykut GUVEN
Dogus University
Department of Computer Engineering
aguven@dogus.edu.tr

Ibrahim SOGUKPINAR
Gebze Institute of Technology
Department of Computer Engineering
ispinar@bilmuh.gyte.edu.tr

Abstract

Biometric technologies are becoming a vital part of computerized security systems. It is likely that biometric security technologies will be of greater importance in the light of terrorism, threads to computer systems. Biometric principals can be generalized as the automatic detection of a person's suitable physical or neuro physical characteristics. Furthermore physical characteristics refer to the physical properties or attributes of a person that are inherited and neuro physical characteristics are those that depend on person's behavior. This paper presents the idea of Keystroke Identification classified as a neuro physical characteristics for the purposes of a security system. Pattern recognition in neuro physical security systems have often proof to be difficult. To date two methods are deployed for keystroke pattern recognition. These are based on statistical or vector algorithms. This paper extends the domain of vector based biometric algorithms with a view to increase recognition frequency and reliability.

Keywords: Keystroke Identification, Pattern Recognition, Computer Security.

1. Introduction

Computers are used heavily in social and business life, especially during the last 30 years. Computer based systems are used all around the world in both the private and public domains.

Although computers systems have been making our lives easier, there is a down-side in that computer systems need to be protected. There are millions of computers in the world and they are connected with each others either using a public network, like internet, or using private networks, like intranet or extranet. Security is the process to safe guard valuable objects against unauthorized used and access. There are many proven and commercially available security hardware and software systems in used today to ensure data security.

Today cryptology that converts the original row data into cryptic bit patterns is proving to be an important security measure against unauthorized access. In such systems data access prevention is not the key concern for even the possession of cryptic data does not necessarily result in the availability of the original data.

In contrast to securing a system using cryptology one can achieve the same objectives by designing a system that uses access control.

Another important point to keep security is to design systems that are able to know their users. The latter could be made to use biometric properties of its users in providing secure access authentication.

Biometric access control systems, referred to online systems [1], deploy suitable databases that contain user biometric properties. There are a lot of biometric properties to design a security system.

In this paper, we briefly introduce biometric systems and explain our keystroke identification system. As a biometric identification system, Keystroke is also used in many different areas. Not just as a security, also as an analysis method of users' performance even in many engineering areas such as analyzing user performance [2]. Researches on the biometric systems are still going on and the number of the research in this area is increasing rapidly[3]. For Instance, The group of companies and universities involved in this research include the **Institute for Criminal Investigation and Crime Science** ICICS), the **University of Huddersfield** in the UK and the **University of Delft**'s TNO/TPD department in Holland [3].

1.1 Biometric Systems

Biometric systems can be grouped into 2 main categories. First category depends on peoples' physical properties like finger prints, iris and retina patterns. Other important category is neuro physical properties [4] that depend on behavior of people like sign recognition, keystroke recognition. There are also new properties that are still being studied by researchers. In Table 1 failure rates of the Biometric methods are given [5]. It easily is can be seen that Retina and Iris recognition systems have the lowest failure rate. Physical property based recognition systems have always a high secure level.

Biometric Method	Failure Rate
Retina Recognition	1:10.000.000
Iris Recognition	1:131.000
Fingerprint Recognition	1:500
Hand Geo. Recognition	1:500
Sign Recognition	1:50
Voice Recognition	1:50
Face Recognition	No Data Available
Vascular Patterns Rec.	No Data Available

Table 1-Ratio of Wrong Recognition

Behavior property based recognition systems have more low security level. This is because peoples' physiological conditions are always changing, so, it is difficult to catch a pattern about peoples' physiological conditions. On the other hand, for physical biometric properties, there is not any conditional state for people. Because, everybody has the same fingerprint pattern during all of their lives time. And using a sensor to read someone's fingerprint pattern and to match it with a known pattern is enough to set up a security system. There is no extra algorithm and computing requirement for this. One of the biggest disadvantages of using physical biometric systems is their high costs. Although retina scan has the highest reliability it also has the highest cost. For a network with 100 computers this costs may be much for many companies. To reduce costs, software based solutions are preferred. Behavior based biometric systems do not need to have extra hardware devices. This is the biggest advantage of these systems although they have low reliability. Another major problem is about to use or not to use biometric systems. Because there are many places that biometric security is needed. For example, jails are very good sample for this or airports are very suitable to use biometric security systems. Even social processes can be followed using a biometric system. Otherwise there is a strong resistance to biometric systems. People think that these systems restrict their lives [4] and nobody wants to be watched all day by a computer system. But trends show that security is important than confidentiality.

Another important point for biometric systems is their storage costs. Because everybody has a pattern and a sample pattern is stored in a database. For a huge system it is important to keep data length short. In the Table 2, record lengths are given.

Biometric Method	Data Length (bytes)
Retinal Scan	35
Iris Scan	256
Fingerprints	512 – 1000
Hand Geometry	9

Table 2-Data Lengths

If we norm these record lengths using hand geometry recognition system. We may have got information about recognition systems length. Table 3 shows data lengths of the systems. In this table it is assumed the length of a hand geometry is 1 unit.

Biometric Method	Unit Values
Retina Recognition	4
Iris Recognition	28
Fingerprint Recognition	57-111
Hand Geometry Rec.	1

Table 3-Normed Values

As it can be seen, there are big differences among biometric recognition properties in the storage. Designers should consider this point that is important for system's performance. Nobody wants to make a system design that makes the Network overloaded.

The algorithm that was developed in this study has been tested using a Security System which was designed in GYTE. To test the former a Graphics User login Interface was designed similar to those found in other contemporary systems. In order for a users to logon to our system the user was required to type their "username" and "password". During this process the System learnt the user's biometric parameters. The security of our software was tested when a user entered an existing user's name and passwords but was rejected due to a biometric mismatch. The integrity and repeatability of the biometric recognition algorithm for detecting existing users attempting a login using another identity was also investigated in this report.

2. Biorhythm Identification

Biorhythm is a method that tries to understand peoples' keystroke rhythms. It is also known as keystroke identification. As it was told before it is important to catch a pattern in designing a biometric security system. Up to now, there are many studies have been done to process keystroke rhythms. In 1980 the first study was done by GAINES who showed that Keystroke can be used to supply a security in computer systems [6]. There is an important study which is done by Rick JOYCE and Gopal GUPTA. It is a very large literature study about keystroke identification. In this study seven secretaries were used. It was asked from them to type a paragraph three times in a given period. Taken data analyzed and tried to find a pattern from keystroke latencies. In the study of Rick JOYCE and Gopal GUPTA a very simple and good working method was given to compare users' patterns. JOYCE and GUPTA designed a login screen and took data from users. They produced a latency pattern.[7]

If there are two profiles and n is number of the latencies

$$M=\{m1,m2,m3,...,mn\}$$

T={t1,t2,t3,..........,tn}

T is a training signature which is inputted by the user. Using the mean and standard derivation of the norms‖ M - T ‖, is used to have a criterion to have an acceptable difference vector between M and T.

In the study that was done by JOYCE and GUPTA, it was wanted from a user to type his surname using a keyboard. Keystroke latencies were taken by a program and Figure 10 was drawn. Figure 1 shows that there may be a pattern in keystroke rhythms. If there is an algorithm that compares the patterns, a biometric security system may be initialized as told before.

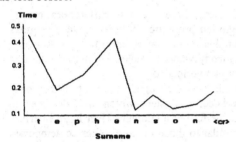

Figure 1- A User Pattern

It is really interesting that there are long times in between t-e and e-n. In this period user spends too long time. On the other hand between n-s, s-o and o-n user types very fast. This information shows that there may be a unique pattern for all computer users.

To process the patterns, there are 2 main groups of algorithms given,

1- Vector Approach
2- Probabilistic Approach

Given algorithm in this study is also a vector algorithm. One of the known methods in Vector Approach is known as "Euclidian Distance Measure". In Euclidian Distance Measure, Distances between pattern vectors are measured. Let's assume that there are two pattern vectors. Mathematical equations of two N-Dimensional vectors can be written as,

$$R = [\, r_1, r_2, r_3, ...,r_n]$$
$$U = [u_1, u_2, u_3, ...,u_n]$$
$$D(R, U) = \left[\sum_{t=1}^{N}(r_t - u_t)^2\right]^{1/2} .$$

For a known U pattern vector Distance between two vectors can be calculated easily. The weakness of this algorithm is that it adds each distances as cumulative. But cumulative addition is not a good way to measure error rates. It is also not sensitive against error. Because this algorithm does not allow us to do any operation on each vector item. Although Cumulative approach is easy, it is difficult to find an exact and good solution. Because of

these disadvantages a new vector based approach has been developed in Gebze Institute of Technology.

Another major approach in Keystroke analysis is using probabilistic method. Probabilistic method can be divided into 2 parts. First one is Non-Weighted probability another is Weighted probability. Their mathematical models are given below [8];

Let U and R be N-dimensional pattern vectors as defined previously.

$$Score(R, U) = \sum_{i=1}^{N} S_{u_i}$$

where,

$$S_{u_i} = \frac{1}{\sigma_{u_i}}\left[\sum_{j=1}^{a_{u_i}} Prob\left(\frac{X_{ij}^{(u)} - \mu_n}{\sigma_n}\right)\right]$$

μ is the mean and σ is standard derivation. $X_{ij}^{(u)}$ is the j th occurrence of the i th feature of U. The Unknown vector is associated with the nearest vector in the database that it makes possibility of the feature vector higher.[MR99]

In English, some letters are used more widely than others, and to compensate a new parameter is added to the Non-Weighted Probabilistic method to improve results.

$$Score(R, U) = \sum_{i=1}^{N} \left(S_{u_i} * w_{u_i}\right),$$

Using weighted probability gives better solution. Given Identification rate for these 3 major methods, for weighted probabilistic method, it is approximately %87.13, for non weighted probabilistic method % 85.63 and Euclidian distance measure, it is %83.22.

Another analysis method in Keystroke pattern recognition uses Neural Network techniques or Genetic Algorithms. There are many researches are being made. Using a well designed model may give effective and acceptable result. In a study done by M. S. Obadiat and B. Sadoun a neural network model was implemented.[9]

3. A New Vector Model Study in Pattern Recognition

In this study, a new approach is given using Vector analysis based algorithms. In the biometric identification systems, there are many classification methods. Given method in this study is a similar method to "**Minimum-Distance Classifiers**" which calculates norms of the vector dimensions for a given 2 vectors to make a decision to compare them. Data of a Biometric property is assigned to a vector. The vector carries all well-known values of the property.

The X vector that is shown in Figure 2 and Figure 3 holds all biometric properties necessary to make a decision. Minimum-Distance Classification gives a method to get a result from vectors. Its logic is very simple. It takes 2 vectors and tries to find distances for each of item. The minimum distance vector gives the minimum error rate that is known as "Template Matching".

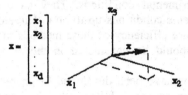

Figure 2- A Sample Pattern Vector

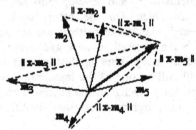

Figure 3-Pattern and Template Vectors

In this study, given method has also same logic. But template vector is stored by the System and real time data for a user is processed using developed algorithm.

3.1 Mathematical Model of the System

Taken parameters from a user is used for generating in 2 special arrays. These arrays are called B and G series. Notation which is used in modeling is given below,

$B(I)$: Spending time during a key pressing.
$G(I)$: Time delay between 2 key.
θb :Difference between reference and real time B vector.
θg : Difference between reference and real time G vector.
Γb : Weighted factor for B .
Γg : Weighted factor for G
ξ : Decision function
Ψb : B vector.
Φg : G vector.
Ω: Weighted factor for ξ

$$B = B(1)+B(2)+B(3)+B(4)+\ldots\ldots+ B(N-\Theta)+\ldots+B(N)$$
$$G=G(1)+G(2)+G(3)+G(4)+\ldots+G(N\Theta)+\ldots\ldots+G(N-1)$$

These series are taken from user inputs and creating vectors using the series.
$\Psi b = \Sigma B(i) Ii;$ Vector form of B Series
$\Phi g = \Sigma G(j) Ij;$ Vector form of G Series

Ψb , Φg vectors are created in real time by the system. There are also 2 reference vectors which come from database. We can name these reference vectors as;

$\Psi br = \Sigma Br(i) Ii;$ Reference vector for B Series
$\Phi gr = \Sigma Gr(j) Ij;$ Reference vector for G Series

We can calculate angle between 2 vector using cosines theory. The theory assumes that for vectors A and B, this formulation is used to find angle.

$$Cos\ \theta = AB / [(\Sigma A^2)(\Sigma B^2)]^{1/2}$$

If it is applied to Keystroke vectors to find angle between real time vector and reference vector, Equation for both B and G series vectors,

$$Cos\theta b = \Psi b\Psi br / [(\Sigma\Psi b^2) (\Sigma\Psi br^2)]^{1/2}$$
$$Cos\theta g = \Phi g\Phi gr / [(\Sigma\Phi g^2)(\Sigma\Phi gr^2)]^{1/2}$$

if Ψb and Ψbr is similar $Cos\theta b$ goes to 1. Because Cos 0 equals to 1. So, ideal value of the $Cos\theta b$ is 1. Same rules exist for Φg, Φgr vectors.

There is also an experimental definition that is weighted multiply for Cos values. Because Φ vector is more reliable than Ψ.
Γb : is weighted multiply for $Cos\theta b$
Γg :is weighted multiply for $Cos\theta g$
Relationship between Γb and Γg is given;

$$\Gamma b+ \Gamma g = 1$$
$$\Gamma g = 1- \Gamma b$$

We may define a decision function as below.
ξ is important to make a decision on understanding a user identity that is derived from user's parameters which was typed before. Every user has a ξ function that points user's identity. In different login processes, ξ values should be similar for a user.
$$\xi = \Gamma g Cos\theta g + \Gamma b\ Cos\theta b$$
$$\xi = \Gamma g\ (Cos\theta g - Cos\theta b)+ Cos\theta b$$

$\xi i-1$: Value of Decision function from last login.
Ω : Deviation which value is between $0< \Omega < 1$

The result formula which is used in the Algorithm is given as below;
$$\xi i-1\ -(\Omega\ \xi i-1)< \ \xi\ <\ \xi i-1\ +(\Omega\ \xi i-1)$$

3.2 Testing of the Algorithm

Keystroke identification systems need too much time to identify users. There are several ways to teach a user to the system. If system learns a user in real time by analyzing user parameters, this method is known as online identification method. [10] To teach keystroke parameters to the system, it is necessary for a user to type very much. [11] For a keystroke identification system like we have, the best is to force users for a while to teach them to the system. Every keystroke system should have an algorithm to capture and learn users' keystroke patterns. During the development of the algorithm users were asked to log on to the system using another user's "username" and "password".

There is an authenticated user's graph for several attempts. According to Figure 4 every computer user has a pattern and that pattern is usually similar.

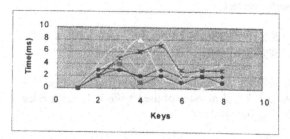

Figure 4- Unauthenticated Attempts

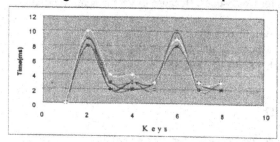

Figure 5- Authenticated Attempts

Although, it can be seen from Figure 5, every user typed the same "text" their patterns are clearly different from each other. This is why keystroke can be used to set up a security system. But, of course, it is not possible to have always same patterns. There may be minor changes in user pattern. The changes may be handled by developed algorithm easily.

4. Conclusion

Since the first studies in research, there have been many algorithms developed by the researchers. It should be noted that keystroke patterns are usually difficult to detect and analyze the patterns and thereby find the optimal solution. In this paper, it has been stated that a biometric property which depends on human behavior always changes. Therefore, analysis has to be considered carefully when a situation arises.

Method	Success
Weighted Probabilistic Method	%87.13
Non-Weighted Probabilistic Method	%85.13
Euclidian Distance Measure	%83.22
Given Method *	%99

Table 4- Recognition Rates

Our results shows to have a higher recognition success rate when compared to the other methods which are used for analyzing keystroke patterns. However it should be

taken into account that these values have been collected in different experimental conditions. They have not been tested in the same conditions up to now. Therefore a new study to measure efficiency of these methods in the same environment should be considered in the next step for research.

New algorithms have been developed for many purposes over time. The concept of "security" has been at the forefront of the minds of companies, organizations and even governments to try and develop more secure systems to protect themselves. On the other hand, Biometric systems, especially keystroke patterns are not just used in the security but also used in new age editors, drawing programs and in many other applications. It shows that keyboards will still be one of the important input devices for computers. User typing on the keyboard can pane the way to make our programs more user friendly and more secure.

References

[1] George I. Davida, Yair Frankel, Brian J. Matt, B. J. *On Enabling Secure Applications Through OffLine Biometric Identification; IEEE Symposium on Security and Privacy*, IEEE Press 1998, pp.148-159.

[2] Chia-Fen Chi, Woei-Shuoh Lan, Jeng-Ru Tsai Ear, eye, gait, keystroke, lip and nailbed biometrics BTT Journal, (2000) pp.8-9

[3] Dawn Song, Peter Venable, Adrian Perrig, "User Recognition by Keystroke Latency Pattern Analysis", http://paris.cs.berkeley.edu/~perrig/projects/keystroke/ ,April 1997

[4] Ken PHILIPS, "Biometrics Identification looms on landscape of network logins., PC Week March, 1997.

[5] Thomas RUGGLES, "Comparison of Biometric techniques",http://biometric-consulting.com/bio.htm

[6] R. Gaines, W. Lisowski, S. Press, N. Shapiro, Authentication by keystroke timing: some prelimary results. Rand Rep. R-2560-NSF, Rand Corporation, 1980.

[7] Rick JOYCE and Gopal GUPTA. "Identity Authorization Based on Keystroke Latencies". Communications of the ACM,168-176, February 1990.

[8] Fabian MONROSE and Aviel RUBIN. "Authentication via Keystroke Dynamics." http://www.acm.org/pubs/articles/proceedings/commsec/266420/p48-monrose/p48-monrose.pdf

[9] A Simulation Evaluation Study of Neural Network Techniques to Computer User Identification INFORMATION SCIENCES 102, 239 258 (1997)

[10] Saleh BLEHA,"Recognition systems based on keystroke dynamics", PH.D. dissertation,Univ. Missouri-Colombia,May 1988

[11] Saleh BLEHA,Charles SLIVINSKY,Bassam HUSSIEN. "Computer-Access Security Systems Using Keystroke Dynamics". IEEE Transactions on Pattern Analysis and Machine Intelligence,VOL 12,NO.12

Session 4–1
Evolutionary Computation

Evolutionary Computation: Current Research and Open Issues

Kenneth De Jong
Computer Science Department
George Mason University
Fairfax, VA 22030
kdejong@gmu.edu

Abstract

The field of evolutionary computation is currently a dynamic and vibrant area of research and applications. In this paper we provide a brief summary of the current state of the field and identify a number of important new directions for research and applications.

1. Introduction

The field of evolutionary computation (EC) is in a stage of tremendous growth as witnessed by the increasing number of conferences, workshops, and journals dedicated to the field. It is becoming increasingly difficult to keep track of and understand the wide variety of new algorithms and new applications. I believe there is, however, there is a coherent structure to the EC field that can help us understand where we are and where we're headed. The purpose of this paper is to present that view, use it to assess the field, and then discuss important new directions for research and applications.

2. A Unifying Perspective

If I am asked what are the basic components of an evolutionary algorithm such that, if I discarded any one of them, I would no longer consider it "evolutionary", my answer is:

- A population of individuals

- A notion of fitness

- A notion of population dynamics (births, deaths) biased by fitness

- A notion of inheritance of properties from parent to child

This, of course, could just as well describe any evolutionary system. In the case of *evolutionary computation*, our goal is to use such algorithms to solve problems, and so there are additional aspects involving the problem domain and how one chooses to use an EA to solve such problems. We explore these basic components in more detail in the following subsections, noting differences in approaches, and identifying some important unanswered questions.

2.1. Modeling the Dynamics of Population Evolution

At a high level of abstraction we think of evolutionary processes in terms of the ability of more fit individuals to have a stronger influence on the future makeup of the population by surviving longer and by producing more offspring which continue to assert influence after the parents have disappeared. How these notions are turned into computational models varies quite dramatically within the EC community. This variance hinges on several important design decisions discussed briefly in the following subsections.

2.1.1. Choosing Population Sizes

Most current EAs assume a constant population size N which is specified as a user-controlled input parameter. So called "steady state" EAs rigidly enforce this limit in the sense that each time an offspring is produced resulting in $N + 1$ individuals, a selection process is invoked to reduce the population size back to N. By contrast, "generational" EAs permit more elasticity in the population size by allowing $K \gg 1$ offspring to be produced before a selection process is invoked to delete K individuals.

Although we understand that the size of an EA's population can affect its ability to solve problems, we have only the beginnings of a theory strong enough to provide *a priori* guidance in choosing an appropriate fixed size (e.g., [1]) or appropriate levels of elasticity K (e.g., [2]), and even less understanding as to the merits of dynamically adjusting the population size.

2.1.2. Deletion Strategies

The processes used to delete individuals varies significantly from one EA to another and includes strategies such as uniform random deletion, deletion of the K worst, and inverse fitness-proportional deletion. It is clear that "elitist" deletion strategies which are too strongly biased towards removing the worst can lead to premature loss of diversity and suboptimal solutions. It is equally clear that too little fitness bias results in unfocused and meandering search. Finding a proper balance is important but difficult to determine *a priori* with current theory.

2.1.3. Parental Selection

Similar issues arise with respect to choosing which parents will produce offspring. Biasing the selection too strongly towards the best individuals results in too narrow a search focus, while too little bias produces a lack of needed focus. Current methods include uniform random selection, rank-proportional selection, and fitness-proportional selection.

We understand these selection strategies in isolation quite well [3]. However, it is clear that parental selection and individual deletion strategies must complement each other in terms of the overall effect they have on the exploration/exploitation balance.

2.1.4. Reproduction and Inheritance

In addition to these selection processes, the mechanisms used for reproduction also affect the balance between exploration and exploitation. At one extreme one can imagine a system in which offspring are exact replicas of parents (asexual reproduction with no mutation) resulting in rapid growth in the proportions of the best individuals in the population, but with no exploration beyond the initial population members. At the other extreme, one can imagine a system in which the offspring have little resemblance to their parents, maximizing exploration at the expense of inheriting useful parental characteristics.

The EC community has focused primarily on two reproductive mechanisms which fall in between these two extremes: 1-parent reproduction with mutation and 2-parent reproduction with recombination and mutation. More recently the virtues of N-parent recombination ($N > 2$) have been explored [4].

As before, we have the tantalizing beginnings of a theory to help understand and guide the use and further development of reproductive mechanisms. However, the rapid growth of the field is pressing these theories hard with new directions not covered by current theory. One of the important issues not well understood is the benefit of adaptive reproductive operators. There are now a wealth of empirical studies which show the effectiveness of adaptive mutation rates (e.g., [5]) as well as adaptive recombination mechanisms (e.g., [6]).

2.2. Choice of Representation

One of the most critical decisions made in applying evolutionary techniques to a particular class of problems is the specification of the space to be explored by an EA. This is accomplished by defining a mapping between points in the problem space and points in an internal representation space.

The EC community differs widely on opinions and strategies for selecting appropriate representations, ranging from universal binary encodings to problem-specific encodings for TSP problems and real-valued parameter optimization problems. The tradeoffs are fairly obvious in that universal encodings have a much broader range of applicability, but are frequently outperformed by problem-specific representations which require extra effort to implement and exploit additional knowledge about a particular problem class (see, for example, [7]).

What is needed, but has been difficult to obtain, are theoretical results on representation theory. Holland's schema analysis [8] and Radcliffe's generalization to formae [9] are examples of how theory can help guide representation choices. Similarly "fitness correlation" [10] and operator-oriented views of internal fitness landscapes [11] emphasize the tightly coupled interaction between choosing a representation for the fitness landscape and the operators used to explore it. Clearly, much more work is required if effective representations are to be easily selectable.

2.3. Properties of Fitness Landscapes

The majority of the EC work to date has been with problem domains in which the fitness landscape is time-invariant and the fitness of individuals can be computed independently from other members of the current population. This is a direct result of the pervasiveness of optimization problems and the usefulness of evolutionary algorithms (EAs) in solving them.

Much of this work has involved optimization problems that are unconstrained or lightly constrained (e.g., upper and lower bounds on the variables). The situation becomes more difficult as the complexity of the constraints increases. The ability to exploit constraint knowledge is frequently the key to successful applications, and that in turn can imply creative, non-standard representations and operators [12]. How to do this effectively is still an interesting and open research issue.

Things become even more interesting and open ended if we attack problem classes in which the fitness landscape varies over time. There are at least three important problem classes of this type for which research results are badly needed: autonomously changing landscapes, the evolution of cooperative behavior, and ecological problems.

The interest in using EAs to solve problems like these which violate traditional assumptions continues to grow. We already have examples of EAs which are are powerful function optimizers, but which are completely ineffective for evolving cooperative behavior or tracking a changing landscape. Modified EAs are now being developed for these new problem classes, but are also much less useful as traditional optimizers. These developments have created both the need and the opportunity to gain a deeper understanding of the behavior of EAs.

3. New and Important Directions for EC Research

In the previous section, we summarized the current state of the art with respect to fundamental EC issues and indicated where additional research on these issues is required. In this section, we discuss some more speculative areas which are likely to play an important role in the near future.

3.1. Representation and Morphogenesis

In the earlier section on representation issues we discussed the tradeoffs between problem-independent and problem-specific representations. Closely related to this is the biological distinction between the more universal genotypic descriptions of individuals in the form of plans for generating them and the phenotypic descriptions of the actual generated structures.

Historically, much of the EA work has involved the evolution of fairly simple structures could be repre sented in phenotypic form or be easily mapped onto simple genotypic representations. However, as we attempt to evolve increasingly more complex structures such as Lisp code [13] or neural networks [14], it becomes increasingly difficult to define forms of mutation and recombination which are capable of producing structurally sound and interesting new individuals. If we look to nature for inspiration, we don't see many evolutionary operators at the phenotype level (e.g., swapping arms and legs!). Rather, changes occur at the genotype level and the effects of those changes instantiated via growth and maturation. If we hope to evolve such complexity, we may need to adopt more universal encodings coupled with a process of morphogenesis (e.g., [15]).

3.2. Inclusion of Lamarckian Properties

Although EAs may be inspired by biological systems, many interesting properties arise when we include features not available to those systems. One common example is the inclusion of Lamarckian operators, which allow the inheritance of characteristics acquired during the lifetime of an individual.

In the EC world this is beginning to show up in the form of hybrid systems in which individuals themselves go through a learning and/or adaptation phase as part of their fitness evaluation, and the results of that adaptation are passed on to their offspring (e.g., see Grefenstette (1991)).

Although initial empirical results are encouraging, we presently have no good way of analyzing such systems at a more abstract level.

3.3. Non-random Mating and Speciation

Currently, most EAs incorporate a random mating scheme in which the species or sex of an individual is not relevant. One problem with this, as with real biological systems, is that the offspring of parents from two species are often not viable. As we move to more complex systems which attempt to evolve cooperating behavior and which may have more than one evolutionary process active simultaneously, the roles of non-random mating and speciation will become an important issue.

Some solutions to these problems have been suggested (e.g, fitness sharing [16]. Unfortunately, these solutions tend to make fairly strong assumptions, such as the number of species and/or the distribution of niches in the environment. For some problems these assumptions are reasonable. However, in many cases such properties are not known *a priori* and must evolve as well [17].

3.4. Decentralized, Parallel Models

Because of the natural parallelism within an EA, much recent work has concentrated on the implementation of EAs on both fine and coarse grained parallel machines. Clearly, such implementations hold promise of significant decreases in the execution time of EAs.

More interestingly, though, for the topic of this paper, are the evolutionary effects that can be naturally implemented with parallel machines, namely, speciation, nicheing, and punctuated equilibria. For example, non-random mating may be easily implemented by enforcing parents to be neighbors with respect to the topology of the parallel architecture. Species emerge as local neighborhoods within that topology. Subpopulations in equilibrium are "punctuated" by easily implemented migration patterns from neighboring subpopulations.

However, each such change to an EA significantly changes its semantics and the resulting behavior. Our admittedly weak theory about traditional EAs needs to be strengthened and extended to help us in better understanding and designing these parallel implementations. In the case of finely grained, neighborhood models some significant progress is being made along these lines [18].

3.5. Self-adapting Systems

Another theme that has been arising with increasing frequency is the inclusion of self-adapting mechanisms with EAs to control parameters involving the internal representation, mutation, recombination, and population size. This trend is due in part to the absence of strong predictive theories which specify such things *a priori*. It is also a reflection of the fact that EAs are being applied to more complex and time-varying fitness landscapes.

Some important issues that need to be solved involve the self-adaptation mechanism itself. For example, do we use an EA or some other mechanism? If we use an EA, how do we use fitness as a performance feedback for self-adaptation?

On a positive note, the EC community has already empirically illustrated the viability of self-adaptation of mutation and recombination as noted earlier, as well as adaptive representations like messy GAs [19],

and dynamic parameter encoding schemes such as Delta coding [20]. Recent work of Turner [21] suggests that simple performance-based mechanisms can be effectively used to dynamically tune parent selection and operator usage.

3.6. Coevolutionary Systems

Hillis' work [22] on the improvements achievable by co-evolving parasites along with the actual individuals of interest gives an exciting glimpse of the behavioral complexity and power of such techniques. More recently, Rosin [23] and Potter [24] have shown the benefits of both "competitive" and "cooperative" co-evolutionary models.

Each of these systems suggests an important future role for co-evolution in EAs, but they raise more questions than they answer concerning a principled method for designing such systems as well as the kinds of problems for which this additional level of complexity is both necessary and effective.

3.7. Theory

One of the most frustrating aspects of evolutionary computation is the difficulty in producing strong theoretical results. EAs are, in general, stochastic non-linear systems for which we have only a limited set of mathematical tools. Progress continues to be made, but slowly, on several fronts including the use of Markov models [25], tools from statistical mechanics [26], and evolutionary game theory [27]. However, there is still a big gap between the simplifying assumptions needed for the analyses and the complexity of the EAs in actual use.

4. Summary and Conclusions

This is an exciting time for the EC field. The increased level of EC activity has resulted in an infusion of new ideas and applications which are challenging old tenets and moving the field well beyond its historical roots. As a result of this rapidly changing EC landscape, a new characterization of the field is required based on core issues and important new directions to be explored.

We have attempted to articulate this new view by summarizing the current state of the field, and also pointing out important open issues which need further research. We believe that a view of this sort is an important and necessary part of the continued growth of the field.

References

[1] D. Goldberg, K. Deb, and J. Clark. Accounting for noise in sizing of populations. In D. Whitley, editor, *Foundations of Genetic Algorithms 2*, pages 127–140. Morgan Kaufmann, 1992.

[2] T. Jansen and K. De Jong. An analysis of the role of offspring population size in eas. In *Proceedings of GECCO2002*, pages 238–246. Morgan Kaufmann, 2002.

[3] T. Bäck. Generalized convergence models for tournament and $(mu, lambda)$ selection. In L. Eshelman, editor, *Proceedings of the Sixth International Conference on Genetic Algorithms*, pages 2–9. Morgan Kaufmann, 1995.

[4] G. Eiben. Multi-parent's niche: N-ary crossovers on nk-landscapes. In *Proceedings of the Fourth International Conference on Parallel Problem Solving from Nature*, pages 319–335. Springer Verlag, 1996.

[5] David B. Fogel. *Evolutionary Computation*. IEEE Press, 1995.

[6] L. Davis. Adapting operator probabilities in genetic algorithms. In J. D. Schaffer, editor, *Proceedings of the Third International Conference on Genetic Algorithms*, pages 60–69. Morgan Kaufmann, 1989.

[7] Z. Michalewicz. *Genetic Algorithms + Data Structures = Evolution Programs*. Springer-Verlag, 1994.

[8] J. Holland. *Adaptation in natural and artificial systems*. University of Michigan Press, 1975.

[9] N. Radcliffe. Forma analysis and random respectful recombination. In R. K. Belew and L. B. Booker, editors, *Proceedings of the Fourth International Conference on Genetic Algorithms*, pages 222–229. Morgan Kaufmann, 1991.

[10] B. Manderick, M. de Weger, and P. Spiessens. The genetic algorithm and the structure of the fitness landscape. In R. K. Belew and L. B. Booker, editors, *Proceedings of the Fourth International Conference on Genetic Algorithms*, pages 143–150. Morgan Kaufmann, 1991.

[11] T. Jones. *Evolutionary algorithms, fitness landscapes, and search*. PhD thesis, University of New Mexico, 1995.

[12] Z. Michalewicz and M. Schoenauer. Evolutionary algorithms for constrained optimization problems. *Evolutionary Computation*, 4(1):1–32, 1996.

[13] J. Koza. *Genetic Programming: On the programming of computers by means of natural selection*. Bradford Books, Cambridge, 1992.

[14] H. de Garis. Genetic programming: modular evolution for darwin machines. In *Proceedings of the International Joint Conference on Neural Networks*, pages 194–197. Lawrence Erlbaum, 1990.

[15] S. Harp, T. Samad, and A. Guha. Towards the genetic synthesis of neural networks. In J. D. Schaffer, editor, *Proceedings of the Third International Conference on Genetic Algorithms*, pages 360–369. Morgan Kaufmann, 1989.

[16] D. Goldberg and J. Richardson. Genetic algorithms with sharing for multimodal function optimization. In J. Grefenstette, editor, *Proceedings of the Second International Conference on Genetic Algorithms*, pages 41–49. Lawrence Erlbaum, 1987.

[17] W. Spears. Simple subpopulation schemes. In *Proceedings of the Evolutionary Programming Conference*, pages 296–307. World Scientific, 1994.

[18] J. Sarma. *An Analysis of Decentralized and Spatially Distributed Genetic Algorithms*. PhD thesis, George Mason University, 1998.

[19] D. Goldberg, K. Deb, and B. Korb. Don't worry, be messy. In R. K. Belew and L. B. Booker, editors, *Proceedings of the Fourth International Conference on Genetic Algorithms*, pages 24–30. Morgan Kaufmann, 1991.

[20] D. Whitley, K. Mathias, and P. Fitzhorn. Delta coding: an iterative search strategy for genetic algorithms. In R. K. Belew and L. B. Booker, editors, *Proceeding of the Fourth International Conference on Genetic Algorithms*, pages 77–84. Morgan Kaufmann, 1991.

[21] M. Turner. *Performance-based Self-adaptive Evolutionary Behavior*. PhD thesis, George Washington University, 1998.

[22] D. Hillis. Co-evolving parasites improve simulated evolution as an optimization procedure. *Physica D*, 42:228–234, 1990.

[23] C. Rosin and R. Belew. Methods for competitive co-evolution: Finding opponents worth beating. In L. Eshelman, editor, *Proceedings of the Sixth International Conference on Genetic Algorithms*, pages 373–380. Morgan Kaufmann, 1995.

[24] M. Potter. *The Design and Analysis of a Computational Model of Cooperative Coevolution*. PhD thesis, George Mason University, 1997.

[25] W. Spears. *The Role of Mutation and Recombination in Evolutionary Algorithms*. PhD thesis, George Mason University, 1998.

[26] J. Shapiro and A. Pruegel-Bennet. Genetic algorithm dynamics in a two-well potential. In M. Vose and D. Whitley, editors, *Foundations of Genetic Algorithms 4*, pages 101–116. Morgan Kaufmann, 1996.

[27] P. Wiegand and K. De Jong. Analyzing cooperative coevolution with evolutionary game theory. In *Proceedings of WCCI-2002*, pages 1600–1605. IEEE Press, 2002.

Mixing of Building Blocks and Single-Point Crossover

Kumara Sastry
Illinois Genetic Algorithms Laboratory,
University of Illinois at Urbana-Champaign,
Urbana, IL
ksastry@uiuc.edu

David E. Goldberg
Illinois Genetic Algorithms Laboratory,
University of Illinois at Urbana-Champaign,
Urbana, IL
deg@uiuc.edu

Abstract

Ensuring building-block (BB) mixing is critical to the success of genetic and evolutionary algorithms. This study develops facetwise models to predict the BB mixing time and the population sizing dictated by BB mixing for single-point crossover. Empirical results are used to validate these models. The population-sizing model suggests that for moderate-to-large problems, BB mixing—instead of BB decision making and BB supply—bounds the population size required to obtain a solution of constant quality. Furthermore, the population sizing for single-point crossover scales as $O(2^k m^{1.5})$, where k is the BB size and m is the number of BB.

1. Introduction

Since the inception of genetic algorithms (GAs), the importance of building blocks (BBs) has been recognized [1,2]. Based on Holland's notion of BBs, Goldberg proposed a design decomposition method for a successful design of GAs [3]. This design decomposition currently consists of seven steps [4] and can be stated as follows: (1) Know what GAs process—building blocks, (2) solve problems of bounded BB difficulty, (3) ensure an adequate supply of raw BBs, (4) ensure increased market share for superior BBs, (5) know BB takeover and convergence times, (6) ensure that BB decisions are well made, and (7) ensure a good mixing of BBs. Significant progress has been made in developing facetwise models for many of the above decomposition steps and the interested reader should consult [4] for further details.

However, researchers have often overlooked the issues of BB identification and mixing, even though studies on selectorecombinative GAs have indicated that they are critical to innovative success. Furthermore, existing models such as convergence-time and population-sizing models *assume* tight linkage. That is, alleles of a BB are assumed to be close to one another, and crossover operators are assumed to ensure necessary exchange of BBs with a high probability. Even though the tight-linkage assumption isolates the phenomenon of interest while bracketing the linkage problem, usually this is not the case, as we don't know which alleles contribute to which BBs.

It is therefore critical to understand the mixing capability of popular recombination operators used in GAs. While models for BB mixing have been developed for uniform crossover [5,6], similar analysis is yet to be done for one- and two-point crossovers [7]. For problems with loosely linked BBs, the mixing model of uniform crossover bounds the mixing behavior of multi-point crossover. On the other hand, for problems with tightly linked BBs, mixing behavior of multi-point crossovers can be different from that of uniform crossover and separate dimensional models have to be developed to predict their BB mixing rates. Therefore the objective of this study is to develop a facetwise model to predict the mixing behavior of single-point crossover and to utilize this model to predict the mixing time and population sizing dictated by BB mixing.

This paper is organized as follows: The following section defines the mixing problem and states the assumptions used in developing the facetwise models. Then a BB mixing model is developed and is used in conjunction with a convergence-time model to develop a population-sizing model bounded by BB mixing. Finally, key conclusions of the study are stated.

2. Problem Definition

The section describes the mixing problem and the assumptions made to facilitate its analysis. Before doing so, it should be noted that there are two ways a crossover can increase the number of BBs on a particular string. One possibility is that the BB at a certain position is *created*. However, the likelihood of BBs being created reduces as the BB size increases. The other possibility is that the BBs are *mixed*. That is, the crossover operator transfers BBs at different positions from both parents to one of the offspring. For instance, a crossover can combine the following two strings, **bb####** and **##b###**, to yield following two offspring, **bbb##**, and **######**. Here **b** refers to a BB and **#** refers to schemata other than the BB.

This aspect of crossover—its ability to recombine BBs in order to find better solutions—is of particular interest to us. Specifically, the rate at which a recombination operator exchanges BBs dictates the success of a GA run. Therefore, we model the mixing rate of single-point crossover on search problems with tightly linked BBs. Specifically, we answer the following question: Given that the individuals in the population have m_c BBs, how long—in number of generations—will it take to obtain individuals with m_c+1 BBs. This time is defined as the *mixing time*, t_x.

To ease the analytical burden, we consider generation-wise selectorecombinative GAs with non-overlapping population of fixed size. The decision variables are encoded into a binary string of fixed length. Furthermore, we consider the class of search problems with uniformly scaled BBs. Uniform scaling implies that the contribution of BBs from different partitions to the overall fitness of the individual is the same. Specifically, we consider fully-deceptive trap functions [8] to validate the mixing models. However, the results should apply to additively decomposable stationary fitness functions of bounded order [4].

Using these assumptions, the following section develops a dimensional model for mixing time. The mixing-time model will be used in conjunction with convergence-time model to develop a population-sizing model dictated by BB mixing.

3. Building-Block Mixing Model

To facilitate the analysis of BB mixing, we blend empirical observations with theory similar to the approach of Thierens and Goldberg [6]. Empirical results on m k-bit deceptive traps indicate two key behavior of one-point crossover: (1) All the BB configurations at a certain *mixing level* have to be discovered before a higher mixing level can be reached. Here a mixing level denotes the number of BBs present in an individual string. For instance an individuals **b#b##**, and **b#bb#** are at mixing levels 2 and 3 respectively. This phenomenon enables us to use the *ladder-climbing* model similar to the one used by Thierens and Goldberg [6]. (2) The proportion of individuals having good BBs at their two ends is higher

than those at other positions. In fact, the proportion gradually reduces along the position and reaches a minimum at the center. This is because the probability of mixing is much higher when mixing two BBs at the extreme points in the string. For example, the mixing probability when recombining **b#···##** and **##···#b** to yield **b#···#b** is *((m-2)k+1)/(mk-1)* as opposed to recombining **b##···#** and **#b#···#** to yield **bb#···#**, in which case the mixing probability is *1/(mk-1)*.

This property of single-point crossover is called the *length-reduction* phenomenon and is what makes the mixing behavior of one-point crossover different from that of uniform crossover. An immediate consequence of the length-reduction phenomenon is that an increase in mixing level leads to a decrease in problem size. For example, when the mixing level is 3, the problem size reduces by two BBs. This is because the majority of the individuals have two BBs at their ends and the third BB can lie anywhere in $m-2$ possible positions.

The combined effect of ladder-climbing and length reduction is illustrated in figure 1. The length-reduction phenomenon suggests that we can consider mixing probability as a function of number of BBs that are not converged at a given time and the BB size. Furthermore, we assume that among the BBs that are not converged the mixing level is always one.

Given that a problem has m BBs and we are currently at mixing level 1, that is, every individual has one BB at some position. There are m^2 total recombination scenarios possible, out of which the following scenarios result in mixing:

Recombination scenario	b##...# #b#...#	b###...# ##b#...#	···	b#...## ##...#b
Events	2(m-1)	2(m-2)	···	2
Mixing prob.	$\dfrac{1}{mk-1}$	$\dfrac{k+1}{mk-1}$	···	$\dfrac{(m-2)k+1}{mk-1}$

Therefore the overall mixing probability can be written as

$$p_{mix}(m_c(t)=1) = \frac{2}{m^2} \sum_{i=1}^{m-1} \frac{(m-i)[(i-1)k+1]}{mk-1}, \quad (1)$$

which can be simplified as follows:

$$p_{mix}(m_c(t)=1) = \frac{2}{3} \frac{(m-1)[(m-2)k+3]}{m(mk-1)}. \quad (2)$$

From the length-reduction phenomenon, we know that, at a given mixing level, m_l, the mixing probability is given by

$$p_{mix}(m_l) = \frac{2}{3} \frac{(m-m_l)[(m-m_l-1)k+3]}{(m-m_l+1)[(m-m_l-1)k-1]}. \quad (3)$$

For moderate-to-large problems, the mixing probability can be assumed to be constant with respect to

233

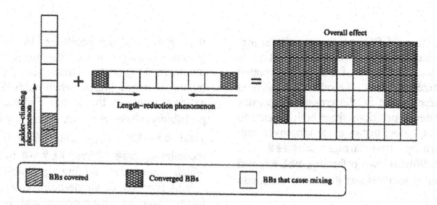

Figure 1 Illustration of the *ladder-climbing* and *length-reduction* phenomena and their combined effect. Ladder-climbing phenomenon suggests that the mixing level increases one step at a time. Length-reduction phenomenon suggests that as the mixing level increases, the problem size dictating mixing shrinks. It also suggests that the BBs at string ends converge faster than those at the middle.

the mixing level and can be approximated by equation (2). That is, $p_{mix} = p_{mix}(m_c = 1)$.

Now the question remains as to how we reach mixing level m_c+1 from mixing level m_c. Assume that after n_x mixing events, we have n_x individuals at mixing level m_c+1. The question to be answered is how many mixing events are needed to have all BBs covered at mixing level m_c+1. Analysis of the ladder-climbing phenomenon answers this question. For brevity, only the final result is presented and details of the analysis are given elsewhere [6, 9]. The number of mixing events required to climb one step of the ladder is proportional to the number of BBs:

$$n_x \approx c_{mx}m/2. \qquad (4)$$

This approximation is slightly conservative, but bounds the mixing behavior of single-point crossover quite accurately as will become clear in the following paragraphs. Recognizing that in a single generations, we have $(n/2)p_c$ recombinations, and using equations (2) and (4), we can calculate the mixing time, t_x:

$$t_x = \frac{n_x}{\frac{n}{2}p_c p_{mix}} = c_{x,m}\frac{m}{np_c}\left[\frac{(m-1)((m-2)k+3)}{m(mk-1)}\right]. \qquad (5)$$

where $c_{x,m} = (2/3)c_{mx}$ is a constant. The above mixing time refers to the time—in number of generations—required to climb one step of the mixing ladder.

However, we are interested in the total mixing time, $t_{x,tot}$, that is, the time required to go from mixing level 1 to mixing level m. Note that there are $m-1$ mixing levels between mixing level 1 and m. Approximating, $m-1 \approx m$, the total mixing time can be written as

$$t_{x,tot} = mt_x = c_{x,m}\frac{m^2}{np_c}. \qquad (6)$$

The model suggests that the total mixing time grows quadratically with the number of BBs and is inversely proportional to the population size and crossover probability. The mixing-time model (Equation (6)) is compared to empirical results in figure 2(a), where the total mixing time is plotted as function of number of BBs, m. The results indicate that the agreement between theoretical and experimental results gets better with the number of BBs.

In the analysis presented above, we have assumed that every individual in the population contains either a BB (all ones) or a deceptive attractor (all zeros). However, in the actual case, the probability of having a BB in a string is 2^{-k}. Therefore, the proportion of crossovers that can result in a mixing event is $2^{-mk}(2^{(m-1)k}-1) \approx 2^k$. With this term as an multiplication factor for the mixing-time model, we are now ready to compare it with the following convergence-time model [10]:

$$t_{conv} = c_c\frac{\sqrt{\ell}}{I}, \qquad (7)$$

where, I is the selection intensity, which is a function of tournament size, and c_c is a constant. Recognizing that for innovative success the mixing time has to be less than the convergence time (recombination has to create the global optimum before the population converges to the local optimum): $t_x < t_{conv}$. Using equations (6) and (7), we get

$$n > c_x\frac{I}{p_c}2^k m\sqrt{\frac{m}{k}}, \qquad (8)$$

where $c_x = c_{x,m}/c_c$ is a constant. The above equation suggest that the population size grows as $O(2^k m^{1.5})$ as opposed to the population sizing predicted by the gambler's ruin model [11] which suggests that population size grows as $O(2^k m^{1/2})$.

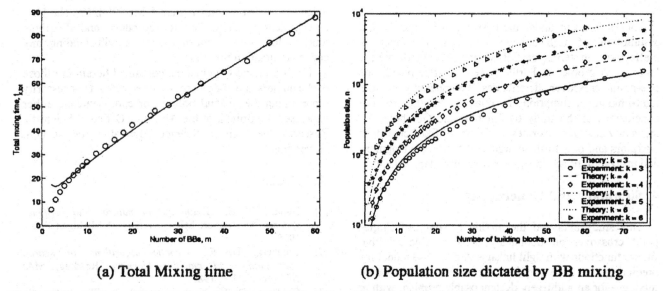

(a) Total Mixing time   (b) Population size dictated by BB mixing

Figure 2 Empirical validation of total mixing-time (Equation (6)) and population-sizing model (Equation (8)). (a) The total mixing time is plotted as a function of number of BBs. The empirical results are for 4-bit deceptive trap function and are averaged over 500 independent runs. (b) Minimum population size required for a GA success is plotted as a function of number of BBs m. The minimum population size is determined by a bisection method and the empirical results are averaged over 25 independent bisection runs.

The BB-mixing based population-sizing model (Equation (8)) is verified with empirical results in figure 2(b). The figure plots the minimum population size required to obtain a solution of desired quality as a function of number of BBs. The empirical results are obtained as follows: A binary tournament selection and single-point crossover with $p_c = 1$ is used. A GA run is terminated when all the individuals in the population converge to the same fitness value. The average number of BBs correctly converged are computed over 50 independent runs. The minimum population required such that the failure probability, α_1, is at most $1/m$ is determined by a bisection method. The results shown in figure 2(b) are averaged over 25 such bisection runs.

The experimental results show good agreement with theoretical predictions, especially for moderate-to-large problems. It is interesting to compare the BB-mixing based and the gambler's ruin based population-sizing models. Two key observations can be made from such a comparison: 1. Gambler's ruin model (BB decision making + BB supply) bounds the population sizing for small problems and the BB mixing bounds population sizing for moderate-to-large problems. (2) The range—in terms of number of BBs—in which decision-making and initial supply bound population sizing is dependent on the BB size. The range increases with the BB size.

Both of these observations are shown in figure 3. From the figure, we can see that there is a boundary that segregates the problem space into two regions: One

where BB decision-making governs the population sizing, and the other where BB-mixing governs the population sizing. This indicates the while one-point crossover is effective—as far as BB mixing in concerned—for small problems, it becomes ineffective as the problem size increases.

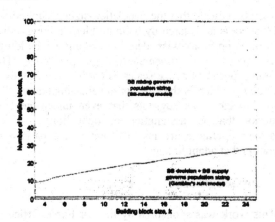

Figure 3 Areas in problem space where BB-mixing and BB decision-making models govern the population sizing required for a GA success. Given a problem with BB-size, k, and m, the gambler's ruin model governs the population sizing if the point (k,m) lies below the boundary line. Otherwise—if the point (k,m) lies above the boundary line—BB-mixing governs population sizing.

Therefore, even under the best scenario—that is, the assumption of tight-linkage—one-point crossover is ineffective—in terms of BB mixing—for moderate-to-large sized problems. Furthermore, the effectiveness of one-point crossover deteriorates exponentially as the tight-linkage assumption is relaxed. Similar to the conclusions of the study by Thierens and Goldberg [6], this study also demonstrates the failure of fixed crossover operators and puts forth an argument for the development and utilization of advanced operators that adapt linkage.

4. Summary and Conclusions

This study analyzed the mixing behavior of single-point crossover on boundedly decomposable additive fitness functions with tight linkage. A facetwise model for predicting the time required for achieving innovative mixing—for an additively decomposable problem with m building blocks—is developed. Two key features of single-point crossover, namely the *ladder-climbing* phenomenon, and the *length-reduction* phenomenon are observed empirically and successfully used in developing the mixing time model.

The resulting mixing time models are compared with existing convergence-time model to investigate scenarios which result in *innovative success*. Using such a comparison, population-sizing model dictated by BB mixing is derived. All the models derived in this study are compared with empirical results. Empirical results show good agreement with theory, thus validating the facetwise models.

Results indicate that the population-sizing required for a GA success is dictated by building-block mixing rather than building-block-wise decision-making or building-block supply for moderate-to-large problems. The minimum population size scales as $O(2^k m^{1.5})$, as opposed to $O(2^k m^{1/2})$ which is the case for advanced operators that adapt linkage. This suggests that even under the best scenario—that is, assumption of tight linkage—fixed crossover operators are less efficient in comparison to operators that adapt linkage.

Acknowledgments

This work was sponsored by the Air Force Office of Scientific Research, Air Force Materiel Command, USAF, under grant F49620-00-0163, and the National Science Foundation under grant DMI-9908252. The U.S. Government is authorized to reproduce and distribute reprints for government purposes notwithstanding any copyright notation thereon.

The views and conclusions contained herein are those of the authors and should not be interpreted as necessarily representing the official policies or endorsements, either expressed or implied, of the Air Force Office of Scientific Research, the National Science Foundation, or the U.S. Government.

References

[1]. Holland, J. H., *Adaptation in natural and artificial systems*. Ann Arbor, MI: University of Michigan Press, 1975.

[2]. Goldberg, D. E., *Genetic algorithms in search optimization and machine learning*. Reading, MA: Addison-Wesley, 1989.

[3]. Goldberg, D. E., K. Deb, and J. H. Clark, "Genetic algorithms, noise, and the sizing of populations," *Complex Systems*, vol. 6, pp. 333–362, 1992.

[4]. Goldberg, D. E., *Design of innovation: Lessons from and for competent genetic algorithms*. Boston, MA: Kluwer Academic Publishers, 2002.

[5]. Goldberg, D. E., D. Thierens, and K. Deb, "Toward a better understanding of mixing in genetic algorithms," *Journal of the Society of Instrument and Control Engineers*, vol. 32, no. 1, pp. 10–16, 1993.

[6]. Thierens, D. and D. E. Goldberg, "Mixing in genetic algorithms," *Proceedings of the Fifth International Conference On Genetic Algorithms*, pp. 38–45, 1993.

[7]. Sastry, K. and D. E. Goldberg, "Analysis of mixing in genetic algorithms: A survey," IlliGAL Rep. No. 2002012, University of Illinois at Urbana-Champaign, Urbana, IL, 2002.

[8]. Deb, K. and D. E. Goldberg, "Analyzing deception in trap functions," Foundations of Genetic Algorithms, vol. 2, pp. 93–108, 1993.

[9]. Sastry, K. and D. E. Goldberg, "How well does a single-point crossover mix building blocks with tight linkage?" IlliGAL Rep. No. 2002013, University of Illinois at Urbana-Champaign, Urbana, IL, 2002.

[10]. Mühlenbein, H. and D. Schlierkamp-Voosen, "Predictive models for the breeder genetic algorithm: I. Continuous parameter optimization," *Evolutionary Computation*, vol. 1, no. 1, pp. 25–49, 1993.

[11]. Harik, G., E. Cantú-Paz, D. E. Goldberg, and B. L. Miller, "The gambler's ruin problem, genetic algorithms, and the sizing of populations," *Evolutionary Computation*, vol. 7, no. 3, pp. 231–253, 1999.

Solution Stability in Evolutionary Computation*

Terence Soule
Computer Science
University of Idaho
Moscow, ID 83844
tsoule@cs.uidaho.edu

Robert B. Heckendorn
Computer Science
University of Idaho
Moscow, ID 83844
heckendo@cs.uidaho.edu

Jian Shen
Computer Science
University of Idaho
Moscow, ID 83844
shen7547@uidaho.edu

Abstract

In this paper we show that evolutionary pressure towards *stable* solutions has a significant impact on the evolutionary process. More stable solutions are less likely to be degraded by variation operators such as crossover and mutation. In particular, our results show that the pressure towards stable solutions has a significant influence on the evolutionary selection of terminals in genetic programming. We solve the same problem using a genetic algorithm with a linear encoding. We observe similar effects with the GA showing that the behavior translates to a variety of evolutionary paradigms.

1 Introduction

The stability of a solution is a measure of the solution's average change in fitness under crossover and/or mutation. The most outstanding evidence of pressure towards stability is the phenomenon of code growth (or bloat) in genetic programming (GP) [1, 2, 3, 4, 5, 6, 7, 3, 8, 9]. Code bloat is a rapid increase in code size that does not result in fitness improvements. The extra code usually consists of introns (code that does not contribute to the program's fitness). It is generally accepted that programs generated using genetic programming grow as a means of protecting the useful code within good solutions. By adding introns the useful code (commonly known as exons) is less likely to be affected by crossover (or other similar operators). However, Luke [7] has argued that introns themselves are not the cause of code growth. Additionally, Smith and Harries have shown that growth can occur in code that does influence fitness (exons) if the exons only have a negligible effect

on performance [10]. Recently, Soule [11] has shown that code growth can occur even with exons that have a significant impact on the programs' fitness. Current research on code growth in GP strongly suggests that it will occur in any evolutionary technique which uses variable size representations [4, 6]. Langdon has shown that growth can occur in non-population based search techniques [12].

Overall code growth can be viewed as a method of making the evolving programs more stable. In this paper we show that the pressure towards stable solutions also influences the selection of primitives, terminals in GP and genes in GA, in the evolutionary process.

2 Experiments

For this experiment we must be able to precisely control what types of exons and introns are possible. This necessitates very simple test problems. For the GP our test problem is to evolve an expression with a fixed target value T using the plus operation and a limited set of terminals. Fitness is the absolute value of the difference between the sum of the terminals and T.

For the GA our test problem is to evolve a set of genes from a limited set of genes who's sum is equal to the target value T. The fitness of the evolved solutions is $1/(|sum - T| + 1)$.

2.1 The Genetic Program

We use a simple, generational GP, written in C++. The programs are tree structured. The only function (internal node) used is a + and the trees are binary. The 90/10 rule is used in selecting crossover points to be consistent with most other GP paradigms. (90% of the selected crossover points are internal nodes, 10% are leaf nodes.) For mutation each node has

---

*This research supported by NIH NCRR P20 RR16448, NSF grant EPS80935, and a generous hardware donation from Micron Technologies.

a probability (P_m) of being mutated into a random node with the same airity. Because only a single non-terminal (+) is used mutation does not change the non-terminals. In practice, the effective mutation rate for terminals is somewhat lower than the given rate because the randomly selected value for a mutated terminal may be the same as the terminal's original value.

2.2 Function and Terminal Sets

In general, the functions and terminals determines what types of exons and introns can evolve. In our experiments the only function is + and we tested two different terminal sets. The first function/terminal set is {+,1.0, 4.0, T = 40}. Introns are not possible, but there is an option between 1's and 4's. Clearly a larger (optimal) program is possible using 1's instead of 4's. In particular, for a target value of 40 an optimal program of all 1's is of size 79 and an optimal program of all 4's is of size 19 (including +'s). Optimal programs with a mix of 1's and 4's will fall somewhere within this range. (The set is essentially identical to one of the test sets used in the paper [11].)

The second function/terminal set is {+,0,1,4, T = 29} This set allows introns in the form of branches consisting of all 0's. Thus, there is no limit on the possible code size.

The target value T is chosen so that the average initial program has a fitness close to T. If this were not the case code growth (or reduction) would occur as the initial, random programs adjusted their sizes to reach the target value. (E.g. consider a very large target value, the initial programs would have to grow rapidly just to reach the target, regardless of other evolutionary pressures.)

The ramped half-and-half generation technique used here results in initial programs whose average (including both functions and terminals) size is 32. For the set {1,4} the average expression value of these programs is 40. For the set {0,1,4} the average expression value of these programs is 29. Thus, 40 and 29 were chosen as the target values for the sets {1,4} and {0,1,4} respectively.

2.3 The GA

The GA is a steady-state GA using a variable length, integer chromosome. Each integer in a chromosome can have one of three values: 0, 1 or 4. The initial length of the chromosomes is fixed at 21. Thus, the average initial value of an individual is 35 (=7*4 +

7*1 + 7*0) and so the target value is 35.

Two point crossover is used. However, to create variable length chromosomes the crossover points are chosen separately in the two parents. Thus, during crossover one parent may lose a much smaller or larger section of chromosome than it gains. This imitates tree based GP in which different sized branches are exchanged during crossover. Mutation is applied to one third of the offspring with a 0.001 probability of changing each gene in the individuals selected for mutation.

The length of the GA individuals grew extremely rapidly. To avoid memory problems individual trials were halted when the average individual length reached 40,000. A total of 94 trials were run. The data is shown for the first 48,000 evaluations. By the 48,000th evaluation 45 of the 94 trials had been halted biasing the statistics towards the surviving trials.

3 Results

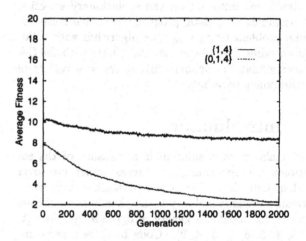

Figure 1: Average fitness for the sets {1,4} and {0,1,4}. Best fitness was zero (perfect) for all trials in all generations. The slow decline in average fitness shows that the programs are becoming more stable, resistant to the deleterious effects of crossover.

Figure 1 shows the average fitness for the terminal sets {1, 4} and {0, 1, 4} averaged across all 50 trials. (The best fitness is not shown because a perfect solution is found in the first generation and kept (elitism) in every generation. Thus, the graph of best fitness is simply a line at zero.) In both cases the average fitness improves (decreases) very rapidly for the first few generations and then improves very slowly.

For both terminal sets the population actually con-

Table 1: Summary of the genetic program and genetic algorithm parameters.

	GP	GA
Objective	Find an expression with the value T	Find integers with sum T
Function Set	+	none
Terminal Set	1, 4 or 0, 1, 4	0, 1, 4
Population Size	800	256
Crossover Probability	0.9	1.0
Mutation Probability	0.001	0.001 (1/3 of the time)
Selection	3 member tournament	3 member tournament
Time	2000 Generations	up to 48000 Evaluations
Maximum Size	None	40,000 (Average size)
Elitism	2 copies of the best individual are preserved	none
Initial Population	Ramped, half-and-half	Random individuals of length 21
Number of trials	50	94
Crossover	Subtree	2 pt. variable length segments

verges on the optimal solution in the first few generations. The average error is non-zero because it is measured after crossover and mutation. Thus, the average error actually measures how far crossover and mutation (the variation operators) move a solution away from the optimal. The decrease in average error shows that over time the solutions are becoming more stable; they are more resistant to the effects of the variation operators.

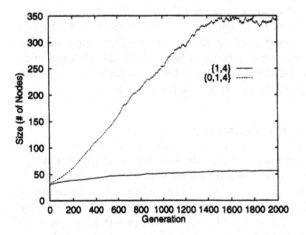

Figure 2: Average program size for the sets {1,4} and {0,1,4}. The slow increase in size for set {1,4} occurs because the 4's are being replaced by multiple 1's. The rapid increase in size for the set {0,1,4} occurs because the 0's are being added to the programs.

Figure 2 shows the average program size for both terminal sets, averaged across all 50 trials. The average size is increasing throughout the evolutionary process, albeit fairly slowly for the set {1 , 4}. For the terminal set {1, 4} this growth can only occur (without creating larger errors) if 4's in the solutions are being replaced by 1's. Thus, the data shows 4's

being replaced by 1's, which leads to progressively more stable solutions.

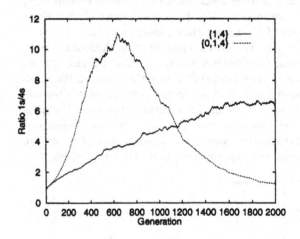

Figure 3: Ratio of 1's to 4's for the sets {1, 4} and {0,1,4}. For the set {1,4} 1's are favored to moderate the effect of crossover. For the set {0,1,4} 1's are also initially favored. However, when a critical number of 0's is reached 4's are favored to reduce the total number of exons (four 1's become a single 4) thereby better 'hiding' the exons from crossover.

This conclusion is confirmed in Figure 3, which shows the average ratio of 1's to 4's in each generation. Clearly the percentage of 1's is increasing while the percentage of 4's decreases. This change produces both the increase in size and the increase in stability.

We hypothesize that 1's are more stable than 4's because crossover is fairly likely to exchange branches with different numbers of terminals, causing a net change in the size of the offspring tree. If the parent tree consists of 4's, then fitness changes by roughly 4 for every terminal gained or lost during crossover, but fitness only changes by 1 per terminal if the terminals are 1's. Thus, 1's are more stable under crossover.

Growth with the set {0,1,4} may occur if 4's are replaced by 1's and if 0's are added. The ongoing growth makes it clear that 0's are being added throughout the evolutionary process. Figure 3 shows the ratio of 1's to 4's for the set {0, 1, 4}. Initially there is a rapid increase in the ratio of 1's to 4's. This accounts for some of the growth seen in Figure 2. However, around generation 400 this increase begins to decline and by generation 700 the trend has reversed itself; 1's are being replaced by 4's.

We hypothesize that the reversal from favoring 1's to favoring 4's occurs because of the changing proportion of 0's. Initially, the programs consist of an equal mix of 0's, 1's and 4's. Crossover is fairly likely to pick a branch that contains some of each of these terminals. As presented earlier 1's, are more stable under crossover than are 4's so there is evolutionary pressure favoring 1's. However, eventually the dominance of 0's means that crossover is fairly likely to affect only 0's. This is ideal (in an evolutionary sense) because the fitness remains unchanged if only 0's are crossed. The probability of only effecting 0's is increased if the number of non-zero terminals (exons) is minimized. (This is a standard argument; the pressure to protect exons leads to increased intron size and decreased exon size.) The number of exons can be minimized by replacing four 1's with a single 4.

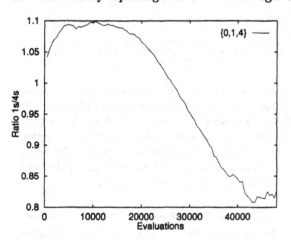

Figure 4: Ratio of 1's to 4's for the GA with 0, 1 and 4 as allowed gene values.

The results with the variable length GA were surprisingly similar. Figure 4 shows the ratio of 1's to 4's for the GA with 0, 1 and 4 as the allowed gene values. The GA chromosomes grew extremely rapidly through the addition of 0's. Initially 1's are favored followed by an eventual shift to 4's. These results are qualitatively very similar to those seen with the GP despite the significant differences between the two algorithms. However, there are some quantitative differences. The maximum ratio of 1's to 4's is much smaller for the GA (1.1:1 for the GA versus 12:1 for the GP) and the minimum ratio of 1's to 4's is smaller for the GA (0.83:1 for the GA versus 1:1 for the GP). Additionally, the changes in the ratio of 1s to 4s occur much sooner for the GA than the GP. For the GA the maximum ratio of 1's to 4's is reached at about 10,000 evaluations (roughly equivalent to 39 generations) versus 600 generations (480,000 evaluations) for the GP.

We believe these differences occur because the GA uses a steady-state model. As noted previously, this is a very simple problem; optimal solutions are found in the first generation and the population converges fairly quickly. In the steady-state model the offspring of crossover replaces the worst individual of the population. As long as a small percentage of the population remains sub optimal the optimal individuals are protected from replacement.

Thus, we believe that the observed results are due to a small sub optimal, subpopulation that is being rapidly modified, combined with a larger, stable subpopulation of optimal solutions. The changes in the ratios are relatively small because the stable subpopulation is skewing the averages. The changes in the ratios occur rapidly compared to the changes with the GP because only a few individuals are actually effected by the evolutionary process.

4 Conclusion

These results clearly demonstrate that there is evolutionary pressure for stable solutions. In both the GP and the GA 0's were rapidly added to the individuals which reduced the effects of crossover. This is a fairly typical example of code growth in GP. However, it is one of the few examples of 'code' growth in a GA.

More interestingly, our results demonstrate that the dynamic pressure for stable solutions influences which terminals are favored in a GP and which 'alleles' are favored in a GA. In both the GP and the GA the favored elements (terminals or alleles) changed during the course of a run, depending on the number of 0's that had been added to the evolving individuals. This represents a fairly complex dynamical change. For more difficult problems involving more and more complex elements we would expect correspondingly more complex dynamics.

Perhaps the most significant feature of these results

is that they demonstrate that the entire search processes is biased by the evolutionary pressure for stable solutions. Elements are being added and removed from the evolving individuals not only to improve fitness, but also to improve stability.

References

[1] John R. Koza. *Genetic Programming: On the Programming of Computers by Means of Natural Selection*. Cambridge, MA: The MIT Press, 1992.

[2] Tobias Blickle and Lothar Thiele. Genetic programming and redundancy. In Jorn Hopf, editor, *Genetic Algorithms within the Framework of Evolutionary Computation*, pages 33 – 38. Saarbrucken, Germany: Max-Planck-Institut fur Informatik, 1994.

[3] Peter Nordin and Wolfgang Banzhaf. Complexity compression and evolution. In Larry J. Eshelman, editor, *Proceedings of the Sixth International Conference on Genetic Algorithms*, pages 310–317. San Francisco, CA: Morgan Kaufmann, 1995.

[4] Nicholas Freitag McPhee and Justin Darwin Miller. Accurate replication in genetic programming. In Larry J. Eshelman, editor, *Proceedings of the Sixth International Conference on Genetic Algorithms*, pages 303–309. San Francisco, CA: Morgan Kaufmann, 1995.

[5] Terence Soule, James A. Foster, and John Dickinson. Code growth in genetic programming. In John R. Koza, David E. Goldberg, David B. Fogel, and Rick R. Riolo, editors, *Genetic Programming 1996: Proceedings of the First Annual Conference*, pages 215–223. Cambridge, MA: MIT Press, 1996.

[6] Terence Soule. *Code Growth in Genetic Programming*. PhD thesis, University of Idaho, University of Idaho, 1998.

[7] Sean Luke. Code growth is not caused by introns. In *Late Breaking Papers, Proceedings of the Genetic and Evolutionary Computation Conference 2000*, pages 228–235, 2000.

[8] Peter Nordin, Wolfgang Banzhaf, and Frank D. Francone. Introns in nature and in simulated structure evolution. In D. Lundh, B. Olsson, and A. Narayanan, editors, *Proceedings BioComputing and Emergent Computation*, pages 22–35. Springer, 1997.

[9] Peter Nordin. *Evolutionary Program Induction of Binary Machine Code and its Application*. Muenster: Krehl Verlag, 1997.

[10] Peter Smith and Kim Harries. Code growth, explicitly defined introns, and alternative selection schemes. *Evolutionary Computation*, 6(4):339–360, 1998.

[11] Terence Soule. Exons and code growth in genetic programming. In James A. Foster, Evelyne Lutton, Julian F. Miller, Conor Ryan, and Andrea Tettamanzi, editors, *Genetic Programming, 5th European Conference, EuroGP 2002*, pages 142–151, 2002.

[12] W. B. Langdon. Fitness causes bloat: Simulated annealing, hill climbing and populations. Technical Report CSRP-97-22, The University of Birmingham, Birmingham, UK, 1997.

A Comparison of Haploidy and Diploidy without Dominance on Integer Representations

Ayse S. Yilmaz
Department of Computer Science
University Of Central Florida
Orlando, FL 32816
selen@cs.ucf.edu

Annie S. Wu
Department of Computer Science
University Of Central Florida
Orlando, FL 32816
aswu@cs.ucf.edu

Abstract

Diploidy and dominance mechanisms have primarily been investigated for binary representations and stationary problems. In this work, we propose a new diploid scheme without a dominance mechanism for integer representations. All diploid individuals evolve without using any haploid stage. The performance of a diploid GA is compared with a haploid GA for both stationary and non-stationary environments. Our test problem is an updated form of Traveling Salesman Problem (TSP). For our integer representation, a simple haploid GA without extra recovery mechanisms appears to outperform our diploid GA in terms of computational overhead, solution quality and storage overhead. Diploidy's ability to maintain diversity slows down its adaptation time to a desired target.

1. Introduction

Diploidy and dominance mechanisms are thought to benefit the GA process by providing memory mechanism. Most of the studies conclude that a diploid GA for binary representations in nonstationary environments improves GA performance [1, 2]. Our interest in understanding the behavior of the diploidy mechanism on different representations has motivated us to investigate integer representation for TSP.

Goldberg [1] proposed the triallelic scheme and showed its superiority to a traditional haploid representation. Ng and Wong [2] prove that the triallelic scheme performs better for an isolated example but can not be generalized. They introduce a mechanism of dominance change to make use of the implicit memory of diploidy; however it fails in cases with more than two targets. The comparative study by Lewis *et al.* [3] shows that for problems with multiple targets, a haploid GA with hyper-mutation

outperforms diploid GA due to its ability to maintain diversity. The mentioned methods have mostly been applied to bit-coding problems where the locus of a determines its meaning. They are inapplicable to the problems where the relative order of characters is significant, as in the TSP. Binary representation typically requires some repair algorithms for the TSP in order to obtain valid paths after operations. Yoshida *et al.* [4] use a technique called pseudo-meiosis to solve the TSP. A haploid chromosome, formed using recombination operators on diploid chromosomes, undergoes genetic operations. Thus the diploid genotype information is not totally maintained after a haploid chromosome is formed.

We investigate the use of diploidy for a sequence based path representation. Our method uses diploidy without a dominance mechanism. Genetic operations are performed directly on the diploid genotype. The phenotype of each diploid individual, however, is formed by applying a recombination operator on a diploid chromosome pair and selection is based on this phenotype. Nevertheless, there is no haploid stage in this work as seen in pseudo-meiosis [4]. The operators used are the corner-stones of the TSP performance. We adopt the *edge-recombination crossover* [5] which performs best among other eight crossover operators for three different test problems [6] and the three best performing mutation types of *displacement mutation* [7], *simple inversion mutation* [8] and *inversion mutation* [9].

2. Designing A Diploid GA

2.1. System Flow

1. Initialize each chromosome of each individual in the population randomly. Calculate the expressed phenotype of each individual.

2. Evaluate the fitness of each individual in current generation using Eq. 1 in section 2.4.

3. Continue until the maximum number of generations is reached.

4. Calculate the expected number of offspring for each individual in current population. The lower the fitness value the greater the number of offspring is.

5. Select the parents of the next generation.

6. Apply genetic operators to reproduce and form the next generation. Generation based reproduction is used where the entire population of chromosomes are replaced by children. Chromosome i of first parent crosses over with the corresponding chromosome i of the second parent with a probability of crossover rate defined. The resulting offspring are then mutated to obtain the final form of the individuals for the new generation.

7. Go to step 2.

2.2. Test Problem

We use a TSP instance consisting of 20 cities. The cost matrix represents the cost (time or price) of travelling between each pair of cities. The cost matrix remains fixed throughout a run of the stationary TSP. The cost matrix changes during the course of the run of the non-stationary TSP to investigate the performance of GAs in terms of adaptivity to environmental changes.

2.3. GA Representation

Path or *Integer Representation* which is considered to be one of the best performing representation for TSP [6] is used to represent the individuals or tours in this work. Each gene on a chromosome represents the label of a city and the entire sequence of genes represent a full tour. While a haploid individual contains only one tour, a diploid individual is composed of two tours in the genotype.

2.4. Fitness Function

Fitness value of each individual is the total length of the tour each individual's phenotype represents. $d(i,j)$ is the cost between city i and city j. Our aim is to minimize this fitness value.

$$fitness_i = \sum_{i=0}^{n-1} d(i, (i+1) \bmod n) \qquad (1)$$

2.5. Operators

2.5.1. Genetic Edge Recombination Crossover.
This operator works by using an edge map that gives the edges for each city

in the parents. This operator always produces valid offspring. The details of the recombination algorithm can be found in Whitley's work [5]. We adopt this operator for the crossover operation occuring between the parents, and we use a modified version of this operator to determine the phenotype of the diploid individual. The modified operator transforms the two "parents" or the two diploid chromosomes into a child which represents the phenotype of the individual. We extend the algorithm so that when the number of entries of the cities in the edge list are equal, the city that has the minimum cost to reach the *current city* is chosen to be the next *current city*. In this way, the diploid mechanism is given the opportunity to express good solutions.

2.5.2. Mutation Operators.
The displacement mutation operator [7] selects a subtour and changes its place randomly. The simple inversion mutation [8] selects a subtour randomly and· reverses the ordering. In the inversion mutation operator [9] a randomly selected tour is removed from the tour and inserted back in a random place in reverse order.

2.6. Parameters

Unless otherwise specified, the default parameter settings are as follows. Haploid GA population has twice as many individuals as the diploid GA to ensure that both GAs have access to the same amount of genotypic information.

Population size	: 300/150 (haploid/diploid)
Genome length	: 20
Parent Selection	: Tournament, size:5
Expected # of offspring	: 0 to 2
Crossover type	: edge-recombination
Crossover rate	: 1.0
Mutation type	: inversion
Mutation rate	: 0.5 (per individual)
Reproduction rate	: 1.0
Max number of generations	: 300
Number of runs	: 100
Oscillation Period	: 100 (non-stationary)

2.7. Test Sets

We compare the performance of our diploid GA with a traditional haploid GA in both stationary and nonstationary environments.

2.7.1. Stationary Environment Tests.
The goals of this set of tests are to investigate:

1. The effects of different mutation & crossover rates.

243

2. How diversity is maintained in both schemes and its effect on the solution quality.

3. The effect of changing population size and mutation types for both GAs.

2.7.2 Non-stationary Environment Tests.
The original cost matrix is composed of the mileage between 20 cities. The minimum cost obtained using the original cost matrix is 9090. In order to simulate changes in the environment we randomly generate cost matrices using uniform distribution. The cost matrix is switched between the different target cost matrices after each oscillation period, i.e. predefined number of generations. The aspects to be investigated are:

1. Diploid GA versus haploid GA under different sudden environmental changes. The minimum cost found for each of the three randomly generated matrices generated are 6976, 6381, 16128 respectively.

2. The effects of increasing the oscillation period. The length of the oscillation period effects the degree to which each GA can converge.The oscillation periods tested are 100, 200 and 400.

3. The effects of varying mutation rate. A haploid GA is solely dependent on mutation operator to adapt to the changes while diploid GA is capable of keeping diversity due to its dual chromosome structure. Using higher mutation rates may increase diversity and eliminate the question of whether results are biased towards diploidy. Mutation rates tested are 0.1, 0.3 and 0.4.

4. The effects of increasing the number of targets. Diploid structure enables a memory mechanism for only two solutions. This test reveals if the diploid mechanism we introduce enables the needed memory mechanism and diversity maintenence to allow for adapting to more than two target changes.

3. Experimental Results

3.1. Stationary Environment

The first set of experiments aims to determine the best mutation and crossover rate combination for the diploid scheme. Table 1 shows that in both the haploid and diploid schemes, a mutation rate of 0.3 and crossover rate of 1 gives us the highest frequency of discovery of the best solution out of 100 runs. In almost all cases however, the diploid GA is not as successful as the haploid GA. We run the second and third set of experiments with the best performing mutation-crossover rate combination.

The second set of experiments compares the abil-

Table 1: Percent optimum found for varying mutation-crossover rates, X:Crossover rate

	Mutation Rates									
	Haploid GA					Diploid GA				
X	0.1	0.3	0.5	0.7	1	0.1	0.2	0.3	0.4	0.5
0.1	24	82	42	67	2	0	1	1	3	0
0.5	38	85	57	80	0	11	23	39	37	6
1	68	93	91	83	1	42	59	61	34	3

Table 2: Percent optimum found for varying mutation types and population size. SIM:Simple inversion, DM:Displacement, IVM:Inversion

	Mutation Types					
	Haploid GA			Diploid GA		
Pop_Size	SIM	DM	IVM	SIM	DM	IVM
100	22	47	71	44	30	35
200	54	64	90	50	46	38
300	62	77	93	54	62	63

ity of haploidy and diploidy in maintaining diversity. The diploid GA clearly excels, with the best fitness over 100 runs levels off after generation 100. The haploid GA levels off as about generation 30. In both GAs, the best fitness continues to improve after leveling off, but at a very slow rate.

In the third set of experiments we test three different population sizes of 100, 200 and 300. Table 2 indicates the number of runs the best solution found out of 100 runs as mutation type and population size varies. For the haploid GA, inversion mutation outperforms other mutation types independently of population size. For the diploid GA, small population sizes appear to be more effective using simple-inversion mutation, while larger population sizes perform better with inversion mutation. In both schemes, increases in the population size result in performance improvement.

3.2. Non-stationary Environment

We test the effectiveness of the diploid integer representation for non-stationary environment. The first set of experiments compare the behavior of diploid and haploid GAs in non-stationary environments with sudden oscillatory changes. We perform the tests with two different sets of cost matrices: the first set oscillate between targets of 6381 and 9090 and the second between 6381 and 16128, both with an oscillation period of 100. The results of the former experiment are given in Figure 1. In both examples, the haploid GA is better at finding the minimum fitness for both targets and shows better behavior in terms of the population average. The diploid GA

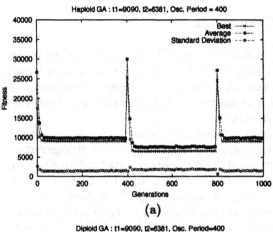

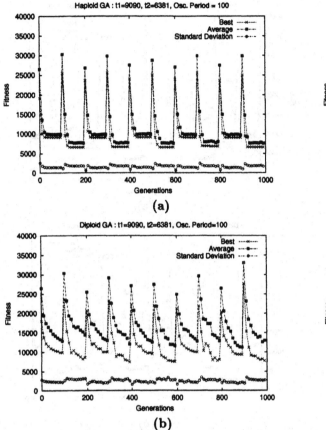

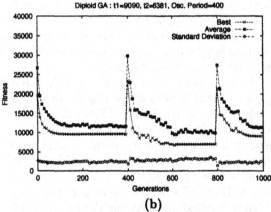

Figure 1: Best/average fitness vs. generation for 2 target oscillating TSP t1=9090, t2=6381. Haploid GA in (a), Diploid GA in (b). Oscillation period=100.

Figure 2: Best/average fitness vs. generation for 2 target oscillating TSP, t1=9090 t2=6381. Haploid GA in (a), Diploid GA in (b). Oscillation period=400.

appears to have slower adaptation which results in worse fitness values at the end of each oscillation period. The variance for diploid GA is higher than that of a haploid GA indicating a greater diversity.

As the diploid GA converges later than the haploid GA, we expect to improve the solution quality for diploidy by increasing the oscillation period. Our second set of experiments focuses on variations in the oscillation period. We alternate between two targets that give the minimum fitness values of 9090 and 6381. The oscillation periods tested are 200 and 400. Figure 2 shows the results for oscillation period of 400. Short oscillation periods do not give the diploid GA a chance to find the best fitness. Increasing the oscillation period results in better solution quality at the time of the target changes. Despite this improvement, we still do not observe an overwhelming performance of the diploid GA over a haploid GA. Haploid GA still has the less variance with better convergence to the two values of 9090 and 6381.

Our third set of experiments focuses on varying mutation rates. Increasing the mutation rate is the only way for a haploid GA to gain diversity while a diploid GA can maintain diversity due to redundancy in representation. We observe that increased mutation rate in a haploid GA does not considerably improve the quality of the best solution obtained. Any deviation from the mutation rate of 0.3 causes both schemes to perform worse in terms of finding good solutions.

Most diploid and dominance mechanisms in binary representations lack the ability to perform well in cases of more than two targets. We examine the performance of both the haploid and diploid schemes on a problem with three targets. We use cost matrices that enable minimum fitness values of 9090, 6138 and 11177. Figure 3 shows that both schemes are able to find all targets but the haploid scheme performs better in finding optimum individuals.

245

4. Conclusion

In binary encoded GAs, diploidy has been shown to improve the GA performance for nonstationary problems while having little apparent benefit in stationary problems. We test this claim on integer representation.

For the stationary version of TSP where the optimum fitness to be achieved does not change during the course of the run, we have tested different parameter settings. We conclude that for the best parameter settings, a diploid GA performs fairly well, but not as good as a haploid GA. The higher diversity achieved by a diploid GA does not appear to help increase its solution quality.

The claimed benefits of diploidy for binary representations in nonstationary environments with [2] and without [1] any extra dominance change mechanism do not appear to extend to the integer representation. What is more interesting about our integer representation GA for the TSP is that a haploid GA can outperform a diploid GA, eliminating the need for additional recovery mechanisms that are commonly required in binary representations immediately after target changes [3]. The use of a haploid GA over a diploid GA leads to significant computational savings including about one third of the storage space required for the diploid scheme, one less chromosome and its associated computational effort. Diploid GA is good at keeping diversity so that it can prevent converging to a local optimum which is not observed frequently for the TSP we tested. Comparison of this diploid scheme versus a haploid scheme on different and larger problems with multiple targets are left as future work.

References

[1] D.E. Goldberg and R.E. Smith, "Nonstationary function optimization using genetic algorithms with dominance and diploidy," in *Proceedings of the second ICGA*, 1987.

[2] Khim Peow Ng and Kok Cheong Wong, "A new diploid scheme and dominance change mechanism for non-stationary function optimization," in *Proceedings of the Sixth International Conference on Genetic Algorithms*, 1995, pp. 159–166.

[3] J. Lewis, E. Hart, and G. Ritchie, "A comparison of dominance mechanisms and simple mutation on non-stationary problems," in *Parallel Problem Solving from Nature*, 1998, vol. 1498, pp. 139–148.

[4] Kukiko Yoshida and Nobue Adachi, "A diploid genetic algorithm for preserving population diversity,"

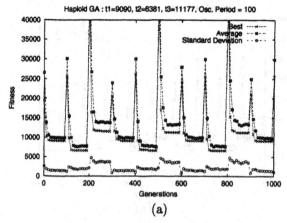

(a)

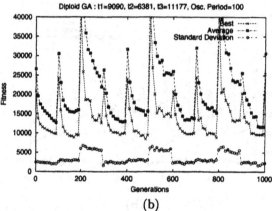

(b)

Figure 3: Best/average fitness of the average of the 100 runs vs generation for 3 targets, haploid GA in (a) and diploid GA in (b). t1=9090 t2=6381 t3=11177

in *Parallel problem solving from nature: PPSN III*, 1994, pp. 36–45.

[5] D.Whitley, T. Starkweather, and D. Shaner, "The travelling salesman and sequence scheduling: Quality solutions using recombination," in *Handbook of Genetic Algorithms*, 1999, pp. 350–372.

[6] P. Larranaga, C. Kuijpers, R. Murga, I. Inzi, and S. Dizdarevic, "Genetic algorithms for travelling salesman problem: a review of representations and operators," *Artificial Intelligence Review*, vol. 13, pp. 129–170, 1999.

[7] Z. Michalewicz, "Genetic algorithms + data structures = evolution programs," in *Springer Verlag, Berlin Heidelberg*, 1992.

[8] J.J. Grefenstette, "Genetic algorithms and their applications," in *Proceedings of the second international conference*, 1987.

[9] D.B. Fogel, "Applying evolutionary programming to selected tsp problems," in *Cybernetics and systems*, 1993, vol. 24, pp. 27–36.

Session 4–2
Computer Networks II

Control of Lightpaths in Heterogeneous Optical Networks

Jing Wu
Communications Research Centre Canada
Ottawa, Ontario, Canada
jingwu@ieee.org

Hussein T. Mouftah
Queen's University
Kingston, Ontario, Canada
mouftah@ee.queensu.ca

Abstract

In order to make the IP layer and/or the routing and control entity independent of the specified implementation of the optical crossconnects, we propose to use an integrated shim layer to hide the implementation details. It integrates the functions of framing, setting up and tearing down lightpaths, performance monitoring, and localised protection switching. These functions traditionally belong to different layers. The integrated shim layer can be implemented as the driver modules (i.e. the controllers) of optical transport systems.

1. Introduction

The fast growing of Internet pushes the evolution of optical transport networks. Wavelength Division Multiplexing (WDM) offers a new dimension of the transportation of IP traffic. By using WDM, the transportation capacity of optical fibres and systems expands greatly. It is of a great importance that WDM provides some new features, i.e. the wavelength routing, and some new protection and restoration features. In order to fully utilise these capabilities, we have to develop new architectures and network control methods to import IP traffic into WDM highways while providing Quality of Service management in a cost effective way.

The interaction of the IP layer and the optical layer is of much concern. The objective is to make the optical layer dynamically adaptive to the change of traffic pattern in the IP layer and eventually to achieve lightpaths on demand. The key issue is how to exchange routing information and control signalling between IP clients and optical networks, and between optical subnetworks, as well as within an optical subnetwork. There are numerous proposals and discussions about this topic in standard bodies, e.g. Internet Engineering Task Force (IETF), Optical Internetworking Forum (OIF), Optical Domain Service Interconnection Coalition (ODSI), Standards Committee T1-Telecommunication (T1X1.5) etc. Examples are listed in references [1-11], and other references can be found in the documents of these standard organisations.

There is a variety of existing optical networks, and at the same time new proposals are coming. They could be catalogued into several dimensions: broadcast-and-select networks versus wavelength routing networks; circuit switching based optical networks versus photonic packet switching networks; optical networks with wavelength converters versus optical networks without wavelength converters; transparent optical networks versus opaque optical networks, etc. In order to apply a unified framework of control of lightpaths in diverse optical networks, it is necessary to define and develop an intermediate layer between the IP layer and the optical layer. The functions of the intermediate layer are to cover the gap between the IP layer and the optical layer. In brief, this intermediate layer is responsible for the local management of resources, in contrast to the non-local management of resources, by the IP layer and/or the optical routing and control signalling entity.

In order to make the general framework work in heterogeneous optical networks, the interface between the IP layer and the intermediate layer has to be standardised. This is important for the practice of network deployment and operation. In reality it is possible to replace one or some of network elements with network elements of different internal structures. Also it is possible to build large-scale networks in several phases. So it is highly desirable for the changes to be localised, which means the changes should result no or minimum effects on the operation of other installed network elements. This can only be achieved by the standardisation of the control interfaces.

This paper focuses on the control of lightpaths in heterogeneous optical networks and proposes a functionally separate intermediate layer between the IP network layer and the WDM optical transport system. First, we summarise the service model of WDM optical networks and the functional models of IP-optical network interaction. Then we describe the definition and the information structure of the proposed integrated shim layer for IP over WDM. As an example, the definitions and the functions of the proposed integrated shim layer in a generic node architecture are illustrated.

2. Service Model of Optical Networks

The service model of optical networks is being studied in standard organisations [6-8]. The service interface between client networks and optical networks is referred to as the User-Network Interface (UNI), while the Network-Network Interface (NNI) is used between optical subnetworks (Figure 1). We prefer to treat this model as a service model (or business model) rather than a control model. This is based on the following reasons. First, the relationship of the parties across UNI or NNI is service relation, i.e. client-service provider relation in the UNI, and co-operation relation in the NNI. Second, the information exchanged through UNI or NNI is not used for the direct control of other parties. We will further clarify this point later.

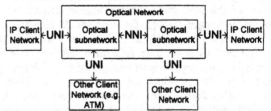

Fig.1. Two types of service interfaces of WDM optical networks

The client networks could be IP networks or other networks, e.g. ATM networks, Time Division Multiplexing (TDM)

networks, etc. However we will only focus on the transportation of Internet traffic in this paper. In most cases the owners of the client networks are different from the owner of the optical network. So the administration and security reasons prohibit the internal topology of these networks/subnetworks from being visible to each other. Moreover, although the re-configuration of the optical network might be as a response of traffic demands from client networks, setting up and tearing down of lightpaths should be managed by optical network operators or the control mechanism of the optical network instead of being directly controlled by client networks. In other words, an IP network in the client side (or user side) has no knowledge of the optical network topology or resources. The control messages in the UNI are limited to simple requests and responses of connection establishment and tear down of lightpaths, as well as status inquiries and reports of lightpaths. A client network specifies the features of a lightpath in its connection request, including the endpoints of a connection, connection bandwidth, directionality (i.e. uni-directional, bi-directional or multi-cast), framing type of a connection, connection time, connection duration, protection class, maximum restoration time tolerance, reserved capacity for restoration, targeted failures in the protection (e.g. single link failure, single node failure, two link failures etc.), reversion strategy (i.e. whether a connection is restored to the original route after failure repair), preemption priority (i.e. the setup and hold priority. A higher setup priority connection could preempt a lower hold priority connection if network resources are scarce during the connection establishment or failure handling.), maximum Bit Error Rate tolerance, routing constraints (e.g. sets of nodes which must / must not be traversed, maximum distance of a single-hop lightpath, maximum number of nodes traversed) [9, 12]. The transportation service providers in the optical network side of the UNI select, reserve and activate resources in response to lightpath requests based on the specified features of lightpaths and Service Level Agreements (SLAs) with client networks.

In the optical network, in addition to the optical layer crossconnection function, we assume some nodes also have the function of IP control message processing and IP traffic bearing according to the proposed framework of the control of lightpaths in an optical network [5]. So the optical network can provide both single-optical-hop and multiple-optical-hop connections. There might be more than one subnetworks in the optical network, which are under the management of different operators. A subnetwork is a trust domain. Within one individual subnetwork, it is supposed that control information is exchanged securely; while between subnetworks, only limited information about topology and resource availability can be distributed. The main goal of the NNI is to provide interoperability, so the information exchanged through the NNI should include more physical parameters to specify the features of lightpaths. The power level and signal-to-noise ratio of a lightpath, and the encoding type of the digital signal transported by a lightpath are examples of parameters, which are important for the design of regeneration. This distinguishes NNI from the control signalling and protocols within an individual optical subnetwork, which will be discussed further in the following sections. So far the NNI for the interoperability between optical subnetworks is still not well defined.

3. Functional Models of IP-Optical Network Interaction

Under the service model discussed in the previous section, we will discuss how to realise the UNI and the NNI, and how to control network elements within an optical subnetwork, i.e. the functional models of IP-optical network interaction, or the control plane of IP over WDM networks.

In this paper, the relation of the functional models and the service model will be clearly addressed. In other words, we will emphasise what kinds of IP-optical network interaction fit whether the UNI, the NNI, or the control within an optical subnetwork. We designate the routers in client IP networks, which act as gateways to the optical network, as border routers. The optical layer crossconnects (OLXCs) connecting to border routers are referred to as border OLXCs. Within the optical network, the routers attaching to OLXCs are referred to as core routers.

Three types of functional models for IP-optical network interaction have been proposed [10]: the overlay model, the integrated/augmented model and the peer model. The major difference is whether there is a single/separate monolithic routing and signalling protocol spanning the IP and the optical domain [11]. In the case of separate instances of routing protocols running for each domain, several aspects distinguish the models. These include what is the interface defined between the two protocol instances, what kind of information can be leaked from one protocol instance to the other, and would one label switching protocol run on both domains.

Under the overlay model, the IP/MPLS routing protocols are independent of the routing and signalling protocols of the optical layer. Figure 2 shows the two separate control planes of the IP and WDM domain. An IP router exchanges information directly with its logical neighbour IP routers and thus indirectly with all the IP routers within the same Autonomous System using Interior Gateway Protocols (IGPs), e.g. Open Shortest Path First (OSPF) and Intermediate System to Intermediate System protocol (IS-IS). The routing protocol between different Autonomous Systems is Border Gateway Protocol (BGP). The routing protocol disseminates the topology of the IP network, and the state of the IP links, which are point-to-point optical channels in the WDM network. In the control plane of the optical domain, an OLXC exchanges information directly with its physically adjacent neighbours and indirectly with all the OLXCs in the same subnetwork in the distributed control mode (refer to Figure 2). Alternatively each OLXC communicates with the central control module of the subnetwork in the centralised control mode (refer to Figure 3). The communicated information includes the state of individual fibres attached to that OLXC, as well as the state of lightpaths or optical channel trails within each fibre. In the distributed control mode, the interaction between a border router and a border OLXC is through the UNI, while in the centralised control mode, their interaction is provisioned through a network management system (NMS). Within an optical subnetwork, the interaction of a core router and an OLXC is via an Application Programming Interface (API).

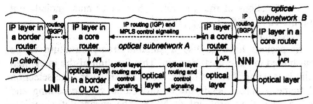

Fig.2. Overlay model in the distributed control mode

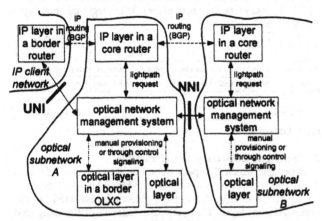

Fig.3. Overlay model in the centralised control mode

The major advantage of the overlay model is the good isolation of information of the IP layer and the optical layer. This makes the implementation of UNI and NNI straightforward. Compared to the integrated model and the peer model, the IP layer does not process physical information, which is meaningless to it, and the optical layer does not process the IP routing table. But the overlay model has some drawbacks. In the distributed control mode, the overlay model has overlapped functions in the IP layer and the optical layer. For example, both layers have the function of topology and reachability discovery. This leads to low efficiency. In addition, the intelligence in both layers might cause co-ordination problem and might do harm to each other. An example is the possible conflict during the protection and restoration. The centralised control mode has a drawback of slow response to the lightpath requests from the IP layer and slow reaction to failures in the optical network.

In the integrated model, a single routing protocol instance runs over both the IP/MPLS and optical domain. A common IGP with appropriate extensions will be used to distribute topology information. Some new features are added to the IP protocol to make it applicable to optical networks, in particular to make it able to control optical networks. An important feature of the integrated model is that each OLXC is accompanied by a core router [5]. In the integrated model, the presence of core routers along with OLXCs is mandatory not optional as in the overlay model (Figure 4). Here IP routers have the intelligence of resource management of both IP network layer resources (e.g. IP link connectivity, IP links bandwidth, etc.) and optical layer resources (e.g. optical layer crossconnects, wavelength converters, etc.). The IP layer is responsible for all non-local management functions, including the management of optical resources, configuration and capacity management, addressing, routing, traffic engineering, topology discovery, exception handling and restoration [13]. In this case, the IP router plays the

role of both traffic bearing and resource management. Actually here the IP router is the functional combination of the traditional packet store and forward engine and the network management agent, while the optical layer in the OLXC provides capacity, dynamic connectivity via switched optical paths.

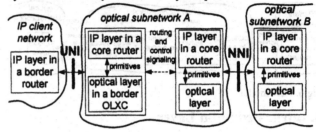

Fig.4. Integrated model

The integrated model has the advantage that only one control signalling and routing information exchange protocol is running across the network. This provides the possibility of better leverage the functions in the IP layer and the optical layer. However the definition of the extensions of IGPs, the interaction between the IP layer and the optical layer, and the algorithms used by the IP layer to allocate the resources are still being developed.

In the augmented model, there are actually separate routing instances in the IP and optical domain, but information from one routing instance is leaked into the other routing instance. For example IP addresses could be assigned to optical network elements and carried by optical routing protocols to allow reachability information to be shared with the IP domain to support some degree of automated discovery.

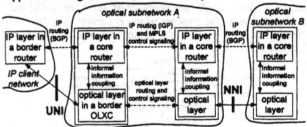

Fig.5. Augmented model

The augmented model is an intermediate model during the migration from the overlay model to the complete integrated model. The benefits of the informal information coupling between the IP layer and the optical layer are still unclear. Moreover it faces the same problem of the overlay model because of two signalling and routing protocols.

As its name suggests, in the peer model the IP layer and the optical layer act as peers. Multi-Protocol Lambda Switching (MPλS) is proposed as the network control architecture of the peer model [1-3]. OSPF/IS-IS with optical extensions is proposed as the routing information exchange protocol for the peer model [14]. The optical Link State Advertisement (LSA) advertises the optical resource information. The resource information, especially the number of available wavelengths, is used by each node to compute accurate and consistent optical paths. Resource reservation protocol (RSVP) or Constraint-based Routing Label Distribution Protocol (CR-LDP) with optical extensions is proposed to be the control signalling mechanism

[15]. The concept of a composite label is important for the establishment of optical label switched paths. A composite label carries the information of specified fibre, lambda, and even time slot. The structure of the revised messages and the processing of the messages are being discussed.

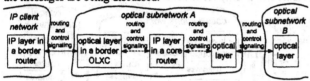

Fig.6. Peer model

4. Integrated Shim Layer

In order to simplify the protocol stack of IP over WDM networks, it may be beneficial to integrate the functions of several traditional layers instead of using several overlay layers for different functions; for example, the SONET/SDH layer for protection and restoration in optical domain, the ATM layer for QoS management. It would be beneficial to make routing and control signalling entities be responsible for all non-local management functions. The proposed integrated shim layer is to hide some implementation details and provide a unified interface to the routing and control signalling entity or NMS. It will localise some functions which are closely dependent on the implementation. So it is important for the generalisation and simplification of non-local management functions of the routing and control signalling entity or NMS. The integrated shim layer is the bottom layer which is intelligent, i.e. we do not add any intelligence into the optical switch fabric to make it do any job other than the crossconnection of optical signals at different granularity (fibre level, wavelength-band level, or individual wavelength level). The presence of the integrated shim layer in different functional models of IP-optical network interaction is illustrated in Figure 7.

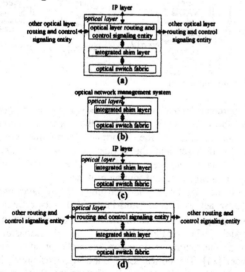

Fig.7. Integrated shim layer
(a) in the overlay model (distributed control mode) or augmented model; (b) in the overlay model (centralised control mode); (c) in the integrated model; (d) in the peer model.

The functions of the integrated shim layer must include but not limited to the following [16].
1.   Framing.

IP packets have to use a suitable frame structure to be transmitted in the optical domain. This function of the integrated shim layer simplifies the operation of the IP layer. The selection of frame structure needs the co-ordination via the routing and control signalling protocol or NMS. The encapsulation or de-encapsulation is performed at the integrated shim layer. Figure 8 shows the data plane (i.e. user plane). The integrated shim layer appears at each node.

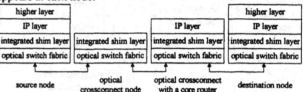

Fig.8. Data plane

2.   Setting up and tearing down lightpaths.

When and which lightpath should be set up or torn down is the decision of the control protocol or NMS, while the process of setting up or tearing down the lightpath is executed by the integrated shim layer. This particular function of the integrated shim layer is also referred to as the mediation device function, i.e. the vendor specified controller function [5]. The operation within the optical switch fabric to set up or tear down lightpaths may include activating or de-activating transceivers, re-tuning of wavelength converters, and re-configuring switch modules.

3.   Performance monitoring.

Local performance monitoring (not end-to-end performance monitoring), which may highly depend on implementation, is another important function of the integrated shim layer. Since the integrated shim layer is likely to act as the driver module of a specified optical switch fabric, it will have more detailed information about the structure and components in the optical switch fabric. This makes it possible to monitor the status of the WDM system more efficiently. It is also the responsibility of the integrated shim layer to interpret physical element parameters and then translate them into the required format of status reports or alarms which is understandable by the control protocol entity or NMS. The operation of performance monitoring may be done continuously, or periodically, or on demand upon receiving a command from the control protocol entity or NMS.

4.   Localised protection switching.

It will be potentially advantageous to implement protection and restoration at different levels; for instance, service restoration at the TCP layer, path protection and restoration at the IP/MPLS layer, optical path or line protection. The integrated shim layer may do some fast localised protection switching within an individual network element without consulting the control protocol entity or NMS. The localised protection switching is triggered by the faults detected by the performance monitoring, and is performed via switching operation to bypass the failure component by the redundant resources within the same node. In order to maintain the consistence of different protection and restoration operations, the integrated shim layer will temporarily lock other protection operations. The timing of localised protection switching of the integrated shim layer must be strictly defined. If within the time bound the protection

252

switching within the node does not finish, the integrated shim layer must give up immediately in order to leave the protection function to other mechanisms. In addition, the consistence of network resource management is maintained by post-operation updates. The co-ordination of localised protection switching and other protection/restoration mechanisms is for further study.

5. Information Structure of the Integrated Shim Layer

Now we define the information structure of the integrated shim layer. Briefly, the information structure should include the dependency and equivalency relations. The dependency is the relation between a lightpath to the related local components in a node. The relation between the quality of a lightpath and the physical parameters of components in a node is also a kind of dependency relation. An example of dependency relation would be that the specified lightpath *(input fibre number, wavelength in the input fibre, output fibre number, wavelength in the output fibre)* depends on the information structure *(plane of fibre crossconnect, address of wavelength-band demultiplexer, plane of wavelength-band crossconnect, address of wavelength-band multiplexer)*.

The equivalency relation reflects the possible alternative internal routes for one lightpath connection, which might be single-optical-hop or multiple-optical-hop. The requirement of the quality of a lightpath connection is the constraint of the equivalency relations. Logically a lot of internal routes are equivalent in a node, but there are only several possible internal routes which satisfy the quality requirement of a lightpath connection; for example the constraint of maximum delay in one node. An example of the equivalency relation would be that *(address of receiver, address of IP router, address of transmitter)* is equivalent to *(address of converter)*.

6. Conclusions

The emerging wavelength routing in DWDM technology has a significant impact on the future network architectures. In the horizontal dimension, there are subnetworks under the management of different operators; while different networking protocols exist in the vertical dimension. The service model of optical networks helps to divide administration borders in multiple-operator environment. In general, the service model provides a view of networks from the horizontal dimension.

In order to achieve tight interaction of the IP layer and the optical layer, several functional models exists. Numerous networking protocols are proposed in standard organisations. They focus on the collection of network information and the distribution of network control messages. In this paper, we suggest to use IP routers in the optical subnetworks to provide not only single-hop lightpaths but also multiple-optical-hop connections for client networks. From this point, the existing functional models are summarised with emphasis on what kind of IP-optical network interaction better fits the UNI, the NNI, or the control architecture within an optical subnetwork.

Then the functions of the controller of optical systems are defined as the integrated shim layer. This layer performs the media access and media control functions such as framing, setting up and tearing down lightpaths, performance monitoring, and localised protection switching within one node. This layer simplifies the interaction of the IP layer and the physical system.

Its importance is in hiding the implementation details and providing a unified interface to the routing and control signalling entity or NMS. Finally the information structure of the proposed integrated shim layer is outlined and its application in a four-tier generic node architecture is illustrated.

References

[1] D. Awduche, Y. Rekhter, J. Drake, and R. Coltun. "Multi-Protocol Lambda Switching: Combining MPLS Traffic Engineering Control with Optical Crossconnects", IETF draft: draft-awduche-mpls-te-optical-02.txt.

[2] D. Basak, D. Awduche, J. Drake, and Y. Rekhter. "Multi-Protocol Lambda Switching: Issues in Combining MPLS Traffic Engineering Control with Optical Cross-connections", IETF draft: draft-basak-mpls-oxc-issues-01.txt.

[3] M. Krishnaswamy, G. Newsome, J. Gajewski, A. Moral, S. Shew, and M. Mayer. "MPLS Control Plane for Switched Optical Networks", IETF draft: draft-krishnaswamy-mpls-son-00.txt.

[4] B. Rajagopalan, D. Saha, B. Tang, and K. Bala. "Signaling Framework for Automated Provisioning and Restoration of Paths in Optical Mesh Networks", IETF draft: draft-rstb-optical-signaling-framework-00.txt.

[5] S. Chaudhuri, G. Hjalmtysson, and J. Yates. "Control of Lightpaths in an Optical Network", IETF draft: draft-chaudhuri-ip-olxc-control-00.txt.

[6] M. Mayer. "First Draft of G.ason", T1X1.5/2000-128 contribution.

[7] J. Ellson. "ASON-the UNI and its Computational Model", T1X1.5/2000-166 contribution.

[8] O. Magd, et al. "Signaling Requirements at the Optical UNI", IETF draft: draft-bala-mpls-optical-uni-signaling-00.txt.

[9] M. Mayer, and O. Magd. "Further Attributes of the ASON User Network Interface", T1X1.5/2000-154 contribution.

[10] B. Rajagopalan, J. Luciani, D. Awduche, B. Cain, and B. Jamoussi. "IP over Optical Networks: A Framework", IETF draft: draft-many-ip-optical-framework-01.txt.

[11] N. Chandhok, A. Durresi, R. Jagannathan, R. Jain, S. Seetharaman, and K. Vinodkrishnan. "IP over Optical Networks: A Summary of Issues", IETF draft: draft-osu-ipo-mpls-issues-00.txt.

[12] G. Bernstein, J. Yates, and D. Saha. "IP-Centric Control and Management of Optical Transport Networks", IEEE Communication Magazine, Vol.38, No.10, Oct.2000, pp.161 –167.

[13] A. Greenberg, G. Hjalmtysson, and J. Yates. "Smart Routers-Simple Optics: A Network Architecture for IP over WDM", Optical Fiber Communication conference, Baltimore, March 2000, ThU3-2.

[14] G. Wang, et al. "Extensions to OSPF/IS-IS for Optical Routing", IETF draft: draft-wang-ospf-isis-lambda-te-routing-00.txt.

[15] Y. Fan, et al. "Extensions to CR-LDP and RSVP-TE for Optical Path Set-up", IETF draft: draft-fan-mpls-lambda-signaling-00.txt.

[16] J. Wu, and H. Mouftah. "Integrated Slim Layer for IP over WDM", IEEE LEOS Summer Topical Meeting, Aventura, Florida, July 2000.

253

The Link-Orientation Problem on Several Practical Networks

W. Chung-Kung Yen
Dept. of Graphic Communications and
Technology
Shih Hsin University, Taipei, Taiwan
(e-mail: ckyen001@ms7.hinet.net)

Shin-Jer Yang
Dept. of Computer and Information Science
Soochow University, Taipei, Taiwan
(e-mail: sjyang@cis.scu.edu.tw)

Abstract

This paper studies the Link-Orientation Problem (LOP), which assigns an orientation to each link of an undirected network $N(V, L)$. First, some practical variations and complexity issues of the LOP are discussed. Then, linear-time algorithms for solving the LOP on several practical networks are designed. These networks include mesh networks, multi-ring networks. The proposed techniques and the computational results can be applied to implement the Weighted Fair Queuing (WFQ) onto the asynchronous link flow and multicast routing in a network. Consequently, identifying the LOP on other classes of networks, including split, permutation, cactus, and interval, can utilize the results of this paper.

Keywords: undirected network, directed network, link-orientation, WFQ, special networks

1. Introduction and Motivations

The major goals of various information services on modern networks are to provide high efficiency, quality, and throughput for people usage. Many basic problems, such as building resources (servers or hosts), multicast routing, loading balancing, as well as traffic controls, have extensive research efforts on them [1, 5]. In [8], the Link-Orientation Problem (LOP) has been defined for assigning flow orientations of links over networks. In flow control of many real environments, each link of a network incident with each switch router is assigned with a weight representing the fair of the buffers. Many useful and powerful approaches for flow control and related asynchronous link flow issues in QoS monitoring have been proposed [2, 4]. One of these approaches, a variation of the Fair Queuing (FQ), termed the *Weighted Fair Queuing (WFQ)* has been studied by many researchers [6]. The WFQ wants to allocate resource in a fairer manner and to enhance link utilization. Basically, a router executing WFQ must decide the weights and the directions to be assigned to each flow (queue) of a network. The direction of message flow through any link $l = (u, v)$ can be oriented from u to v or from v to u. The essential task is to choose an orientation that will be most useful in WFQ or multicast routing on the networks.

Suppose that $N(V, L)$ represents an undirected network [3], where V is the set of nodes and L is the set of links. Consider the situation that we want to place resources at some nodes. The cost of setting up resources at each node will be great different. Thus, each node v is assigned to a real cost for this aspect. Meanwhile, transmission cost within links is another important issue for a computer network. The transmission cost of a link $l = (u, v)$ could be different for u to v and v to u. This causes us to assign an orientation to each link $l = (u, v)$. Let m be the number of links of N. We can have 2^m different ways for assigning the orientations of all links. Each way to assign the orientations of all links is called a *link-orientation scheme*. Determining which one is the best for the WFQ or other network applications is very worthy. This paper proposes efficient algorithms for selecting link-orientation schemes under various network topologies. This issue is called the Link-Orientation Problem.

The Link-Orientation Problem (The LOP)

Let $N(V, L)$ be an undirected connected network. Meanwhile, each node v is associated with a real cost $C(v)$ and each link $l = (u, v)$ is associated with two real weights: $W(u \rightarrow v)$ and $W(v \rightarrow u)$. For any link-orientation scheme A, denote $\mu(A)$ to be the value $\max_{x \in V}\{C(x) + \sum_{x \rightarrow z} W(x \rightarrow z)\}$. The value $\sum_{x \rightarrow z} W(x \rightarrow z)$ is defined to be zero if and only if out-deg$(x) = 0$ within A, where out-deg(x) is the out-degree of the node x. The objective of the problem is to identify a link-orientation scheme A^* such that $\mu(A^*)$ is minimized. We denote $\mu(N)$ as $\min\{\mu(A) \mid A$ is a link-orientation scheme of $N\}$ hereafter.

A special form of the LOP has been defined [8].

The Node-Weighted Only Link-Orientation Problem (The Node-Weighted Only LOP)

Given a network $N(V, L)$ in which each node v is associated with a real cost $C(v)$, for any link-orientation scheme A, denote $\pi(A)$ to be the value $\max_{x \in V}\{C(x) + \text{out-deg}(x)\}$. The aim of the problem is to identify a link-orientation scheme A^* such that $\pi(A^*)$ is minimized. We denote $\pi(N)$ as $\min\{\pi(A) \mid A$ is a link-orientation scheme of $N\}$ hereafter.

The Node-Weighted Only LOP is just the Edge-Direction Assignment problem (the EDA problem), which is originally proposed and studied by the authors in [9]. We have shown that we can effectively and efficiently apply the EDA problem to design linear-time algorithms for solving the Searchlight Guarding Problem (the SGP) on weighted cographs and weighted interval graphs, respectively. In addition, the Node-Weighted Only LOP is the LOP addressed in [8]. We have proposed linear-time algorithms for the problem on weighted complete networks and weighted trees, respectively. Furthermore, to investigate the significance about this research, another useful variation of the LOP has been established in [8].

The Out-Degree Only Link-Orientation Problem (The Out-Degree Only LOP)

Given a connected network $N(V, L)$, for any link-orientation orientation A, let $\theta(A)$ denote the value $\max_{x \in V}\{\text{out-deg}(x)\}$. The objective of the problem is to derive a link-orientation scheme A^* such that $\theta(A^*)$ is minimized. We denote $\theta(N)$ as $\min\{\theta(A) \mid A$ is a link-orientation scheme of $N\}$ hereafter.

The author in [9] has claimed that the Out-Degree Only LOP is the kernel of the Bottleneck Searchlight Guarding Problem (the BSGP). An important strategy for solving bottleneck minimization problems, called the threshold-value binary search has also been proposed. In addition, a linear-time algorithm for solving the LOP on weighted complete-split networks has been designed by the recursive greedy approach [1].

The rest of this paper is organized as follows. Some complexity issues of the LOP are addressed in Section 2. Then, we design linear-time algorithms for solving the LOP on mesh and multi-ring networks in Sections 3 and 4, respectively. Finally, Section 5 draws the concluding remarks and indicates some future research directions.

2. Complexities of the LOPs on General Networks

This section considers the complexities of the LOP on networks. First, based on the discussions in Section 1, the following lemma can be directly established.

Lemma 1: The Out-Degree Only LOP can be polynomially reduced to the Node-Weighted Only LOP; and the Node-Weighted Only LOP can be polynomially reduced to the LOP.

To be further in our discussion, a decision problem corresponding to the Out-Degree Only LOP is introduced.

The Set Constant Out-Degree Link-Orientation Problem (The Set Constant Out-Degree LOP)

Given a connected unweighted network $N(V, L)$, a subset Q of V, and a positive integer constant k, determine whether there exists a link-orientation scheme, A such that $\text{outdeg}(x) = k$, for all $x \in Q$.

A well-known NP-complete problem is introduced.

The One-in-Three Three Satisfiability Problem (The One-in-Three 3SAT problem): Given a set U of variables and a collection C of clauses over U such that each clause $c \in C$ has $|C| = 3$, is there a satisfying truth assignment for C such that each clause has exactly one true literal?

The following lemma can be proved.

Lemma 2: The Set Constant Out-Degree LOP belongs to the class of NP problems.

proof: An NP algorithm for the Set Constant Out-Degree LOP can be designed as follows:

Algorithm NP_Set_Constatnt_Out-Degree_LOP
Input:
A connected unweighted network $N(V, L)$, a subset Q of V, and a positive integer constant k.
Output:
'YES' -- There exists a link-orientation scheme, A, such that $\text{outdeg}(x) = k$, for all $x \in Q$.
'NO' -- Otherwise.
Guessing Phase:
A = empty set;
Let $L = \{l_1, ..., l_m\}$ and $l_i = (v_{i_1}, v_{i_2})$, $i = 1, ..., m$;
for $i \leftarrow 1$ to m
$o_i = \text{choice}(\{ v_{i_1} \rightarrow v_{i_2}, v_{i_2} \rightarrow v_{i_1} \})$;
$A = A \cup o_i$;
endfor
Checking Phase:
Let $V = \{v_1, ..., v_n\}$;
for each vertex $x \in Q$
if out-deg$(x) \neq k$ return 'NO';
endfor
return 'YES';
End NP_Constatnt_Out-Degree_LOP

It is easy to verify that the Checking Phase of the above algorithm can be done in $O(n)$ time. This implies that the Set Constant Out-Degree LOP belongs to the NP class of problems. **Q.E.D.**

Now, suppose that we are given an instance of the One-in-Three 3SAT problem with the h variable-set $U = \{u_1, ..., u_h\}$ and r clause-set $C = \{c_1, ..., c_r\}$. A network $N(V, L)$ is constructed by the following transformation rules.
$V = C \cup U$, and
$L = \{(c_s, u_t) \mid c_s \text{ contains } u_t.\} \cup \{(u_i, \overline{u_i}) \mid i = 1, ..., h.\}$

According to the definition of the One-in-Three 3SAT problem, it is clear that the degree of each c_s is exactly three in the constructed network N. Figure 1 presents a network constructed in this way.

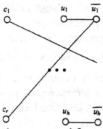

Figure 1. A network constructed from an instance of the One-in-Three 3SAT problem.

Assume that there exists a truth assignment for C. A link-orientation scheme A can be obtained.

For each link (c_s, u_t), the orientation of it is from c_s to u_t if u_t is the true literal in c_s. Otherwise the orientation of the link is from u_t to c_s.

For each link $(u_i, \overline{u}_i)$, the orientation of it is from u_i to $\overline{u}_i$ if u_t is the true literal in some c_s.

Otherwise the orientation of the link is from $\overline{u}_i$ to u_i.

Checking that out-deg$(c_s) = 2$ for all clauses c_s is a simple task.

In another, if there is a link-orientation scheme A such that out-deg$(c_s) = 2$ for all clauses c_s, then a truth assignment for C is just all literals u such that (u, c) is directed from u to c.

Theorem 1: The Set Constant Out-Degree LOP is NP-Complete.

proof: The above reasoning indicates that a solution of the Set Constant Out-Degree LOP with $Q = C$ and $k = 2$ can be derived via solving the One-in-Three 3SAT problem, and vice versa. The time-complexity is clear polynomial. **Q.E.D.**

The following is another NP-Complete problem.

The Monotone Three Satisfiability problem (The M3SAT problem): Given a set C of Boolean clauses in the conjunctive normal form in which each clause can contain either only positive literals, say u_i's, or only negative literals, say $\overline{u}_i$'s, and each clause contains exactly three literals. The task requires determining whether the given Boolean formula is satisfactory or not.

A _bipartite network_ is a network $N(V, L)$, in which V can be separated into two subsets, say X and Y, such that $X \cap Y = \varnothing$ and, X and Y are both independent sets. The following Theorem will resolve The Set Constant Out-Degree LOP on the bipartite networks.

Theorem 2: The Set Constant Out-Degree LOP is NP-Complete on bipartite networks.

proof: The reduction can be achieved from the M3SAT Problem by the same way as in Theorem 1 and the resulted

graphs are bipartite networks. The remaining reasoning is the same.   **Q.E.D**

3. An $O(n)$ Time Algorithm on Weighted Mesh Networks

The class of networks considered in this section is the type of mesh networks. A network $M_{m \bullet n}(V, L)$ is called a $m * n$ _mesh network_ which can be defined as follows:

$$V = \{v_{0,0}, \ldots, v_{0,n-1}, \ldots, v_{m-1,0}, \ldots, v_{m-1,n-1}\} \text{ and}$$
$$L = \{(v_{i,j}, v_{s,t}) \mid |i - s| \leq 1 \text{ and } |j - t| \leq 1\}.$$

A 3 * 4 mesh network is illustrated in Figure 2.

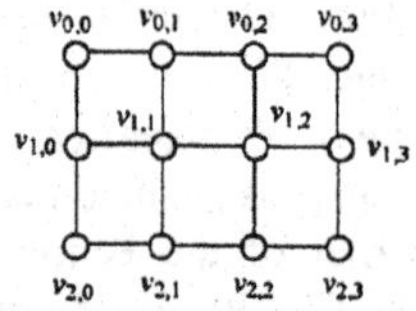

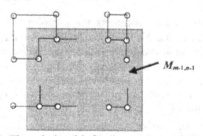

Figure 2. A 3 * 4 mesh network.

Let $M_{(m-1) \bullet (n-1)}$ be the sub-network in which its node-set is $\{v_{1,1}, \ldots, v_{1,n-1}, \ldots, v_{m-1,1}, \ldots, v_{m-1,n-1}\}$ and its link-set is $\{(v_{i,j}, v_{s,t}) \mid |i - s| \leq 1 \text{ and } |j - t| \leq 1, i, j, s, t > 0\}$. The relationship between $M_{m \bullet n}$ and $M_{(m-1) \bullet (n-1)}$ can be illustrated in Figure 3.

Assume that the LOP on $M_{(m-1) \bullet (n-1)}$ has been solved. Define that $K = \{v_{i,j} \mid \mu(v_{i,j}) = \mu(M_{(m-1) \bullet (n-1)}), i = 1, \ldots, m-1, j = 1, \ldots, n-1\}$. We further assume that the size of K of $M_{(m-1) \bullet (n-1)}$ is minimized after we have solved the LOP on $M_{(m-1) \bullet (n-1)}$ recursively. Then, the task required to perform is to assign the orientations of the links connecting between $Q = \{v_{0,0}, \ldots, v_{0,n-1}, v_{1,0}, \ldots, v_{m-1,n-1}\}$ and $M_{(m-1) \bullet (n-1)}$ as shown in Figure 3.

Figure 3. The relationship between $M_{m \bullet n}$ and $M_{(m-1) \bullet (n-1)}$.

Let $W(x)$ is the maximum weight among Q. The following properties can be derived easily.

Property 1: If $W(x) > \mu(M_{(m-1) \bullet (n-1)})$, then the orientations of the links connecting between Q and $M_{(m-1) \bullet (n-1)}$ can be assigned as shown in Figure 4.

256

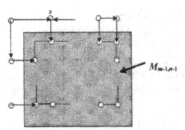

Figure 4. Assigning the link-orientations between Q and $M_{(m-1)\cdot(n-1)}$ under the condition $W(x) > \mu(M_{(m-1)\cdot(n-1)})$.

Property 2: If $W(x) < \mu(M_{(m-1)\cdot(n-1)})$, then the orientations of the links connecting between Q and $M_{(m-1)\cdot(n-1)}$ can be assigned as shown in Figure 5. In Figure 5, the black vertices are the vertices in which their μ values are equal to $\mu(M_{(m-1)\cdot(n-1)})$.

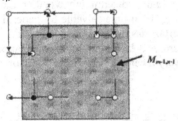

Figure 5. Assigning the link-orientations between Q and $M_{(m-1)\cdot(n-1)}$ under the condition $W(x) < \mu(M_{(m-1)\cdot(n-1)})$.

Property 3: If $W(x) = \mu(M_{(m-1)\cdot(n-1)})$, then the orientations of the links connecting between Q and $M_{(m-1)\cdot(n-1)}$ can be assigned as shown in Figure 6. In Figure 6, the black vertices are the vertices in which their μ values are equal to $\mu(M_{(m-1)\cdot(n-1)})$.

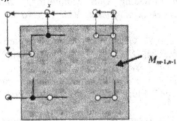

Figure 6. Assigning the link-orientations between Q and $M_{(m-1)\cdot(n-1)}$ under the condition $W(x) = \mu(M_{(m-1)\cdot(n-1)})$.

Algorithm LOP_Mesh
Input: A weighted mesh network $M_{m\cdot n}(V, L)$.
Output: A link-orientation scheme A such that $\mu(A)$ is minimized.
Method:

    recursively solve the LOP on $M_{(m-1)\cdot(n-1)}$;
    $Q = \{v_{0,0}, \ldots, v_{0,n-1}, v_{1,0}, \ldots, v_{m-1,n-1}\}$;
    let $W(x)$ be the maximum weight among Q;
    assign the orientations of the links between Q and $M_{(m-1)\cdot(n-1)}$ based on the comparison of $W(x)$ and $\mu(M_{(m-1)\cdot(n-1)})$ as indicated in properties 1, 2, and 3;
    return;

End LOP_Mesh

    The time-complexity of Algorithm LOP_Mesh can be computed as follows.

Theorem 3: The time-complexity of Algorithm LOP_Mesh is linear, i.e., the LOP can be solved in linear time on weighted mesh networks.
proof: Denote the time-complexity of Algorithm LOP_Mesh as $T(m, n)$. The following recurrence relations can be directly derived from the algorithm.

$$T(m, n)$$
$$= T(m-1, n-1) + O(m+n)$$
$$= T(m-2, n-2) + O((m-1) + (n-1)) + O(m+n)$$
$$= \ldots$$
$$= O(m * n)$$

    Since the number of links of $M_{m\cdot n}(V, L)$ is equal to $m * n$, the time-complexity of the algorithm is linear.

                                        Q.E.D.

4. An $O(n)$ Time Algorithm on Weighted Multi-Ring Networks

    The simplest boundary condition of Multi-Ring is a single ring as shown in Figure 7.

Figure 7. A single ring network with six nodes.

    The LOP on a single ring network can be assigned easily as depicted in Figure 8. Figure 8 implies that only two possible case should be handled if the LOP on the network induced by deleting the link (v_0, v_{n-1}) have been solved.

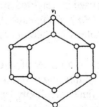

Figure 8. An optimal LOP on a single ring network.

Figure 9. An example of a multi-Ring network.

257

Next, we generalize the results to multi-ring network as shown in Figure 9. Let $MR_{n,k-1}$ be the sub-network in which its node-set is $\{v_1, ..., v_{(k-1)\cdot n}\}$. The relationship between $MR_{n,k}$ and $MR_{n,k-1}$ can be demonstrated in Figure 10.

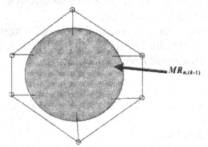

Figure 10. The relationship between $MR_{n\cdot k}$ and $MR_{n\cdot(k-1)}$.

Assume that the LOP on $MR_{n\cdot(k-1)}$ has been recursively solved. Then, the flow orientation schemes of $MR_{n\cdot k}$ can be classified into two types as shown in Figure 11 and Figure 12, respectively.

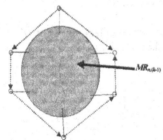

Figure 11. The Type I Flow.

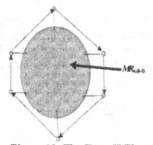

Figure 12. The Type II Flow.

An efficient algorithm for solving the LOP on weighted mlti-rng networks can be easily designed using the similar reasoning used in weighted mesh networks. The time-complexity is $O(m)$ since each link is examined constant times. The following theorem can be established.

Theorem 4: The time-complexity of algorithm for solving the LOP on weighted multi-ring networks is linear.
Proof: Denote the time-complexity of the algorithm as $T(n, k)$. The following recurrence relations can be directly derived from the algorithm.

$$T(n, k)$$

$$= T(n, k-1) + O(k)$$
$$= T(n, k-2) + O(k-1) + O(k)$$
$$= ...$$
$$= O(n * k)$$

Since the number of links of $MR_{n\cdot k}(V, L)$ is equal to $n * k$, the time-complexity of the algorithm is linear. *Q.E.D.*

5. Conclusions

This paper has been proven that the Set Constant Out-Degree LOP is NP-Complete on bipartite networks. Then, we proposed the $O(n)$ time algorithms for solving the LOP on mesh and multi-ring networks, respectively. In addition, the LOP issues can be extended to solve the link flow on the split networks by shortest path rule [7].

In the future, determining whether the LOP is NP-hard or polynomial time solvable on general network is a very important task. We tend to conjecture that the LOP is NP-hard and heuristics for finding approximate solutions is a very meaningful research direction.

References

[1] T. H. Cormen, C. E. Leiserson, and R. L. Rivest, *Introduction to Algorithms*, The MIT Press, New York, 1990.
[2] W. C. Feng, D. D.Kandlur, D. Saha, and K. G. Shin, "Understanding and Improving TCP Performance over Networks with Minimum Rate Guarantees," *IEEEE/ACM Transactions on Networking Journal*, Vol. 7, No. 2, 1999, pp. 173-187.
[3] M. C. Golumbics, *Algorithmic Graph Theory and Perfect Graphs*, Academic Press, Inc., New York, 1980.
[4] Y. Jiang, C. K. Tham, and C. C. Ko, "Challenges and Approaches in Providing QoS Monitoring," *International Journal of Network Management*, Vol. 10, No. 6, 2000, pp.. 323-334.
[5] H. Lorenz and A. Orda, "QoS Routing in Networks with Uncertain Parameters," *IEEE/ACM Transactions on Networking Journal*, Vol. 6, No. 6, June 1998, pp. 768-778.
[6] L. L. Peterson and B. S. Davie, "Computer Networks: A Systems Approach," Morgan Kaufmann Publishers, CA. USA, 2nd Ed., 2000.
[7] S. J. Yang, "An Approach for Finding the Efficient Cost Cores on Weighted Split Networks," In *Proceedings of the ISCA 13th International Conference on Computers and Their Applications*, Honolulu, U.S.A., March 1998, pp. 76-81.
[8] William C. K. Yen and S. J. Yang, "The Link-Orientation on Weighted Networks," In *Proceedings of the 16th International Conference on Computer and Their Applications*, Seattle, Washington, U.S.A., 2001, pp. 325-329.
[9] William C. K. Yen and C. Y. Tang, "The Searchlight Guarding Problem on Weighted Split Graphs and Weighted Cographs," *Networks*, Vol. 35 No. 4, 2000, pp. 195-206.

Peer-to-Peer Cooperative Driving

Alina Bejan
Computer Science Department
University of Iowa
Iowa City, USA
abejan@cs.uiowa.edu

Ramon Lawrence
IDEA Lab
University of Iowa
Iowa City, USA
rlawrenc@cs.uiowa.edu

Abstract

In this paper we address database-related issues in the emerging application field of ITS (Intelligent Transportation Systems). In this context we propose and study two cooperative driving scenarios: on-the-fly highway alert scenario and mutual driving group scenario. Vehicles cooperate and coordinate their actions by exchanging information, hence the need for database technologies such as consistency, replication, and query optimization. Technical requirements and suitability of technologies such as wireless and peer-to-peer communication and mobile ad-hoc networks are discussed. We introduce the notion of a peer-dependent query for the application environment.

1 Introduction

The area of ITS, *Intelligent Transportation Systems*, is a fairly new concept which involves an advanced information and telecommunications network for users, roads, and vehicles [1, 12]. Problems of concern addressed by ITS are road safety, detection and avoidance of traffic accidents or traffic congestion, and safe driving assistance. One direction associated with ITS is cooperative driving, a paradigm involving inter-vehicle communication in which road participants exchange information in order to coordinate and support some of their actions. The existence of ITS is due to developments in several technological areas: navigation systems, electronic toll collection systems (ETC), telecommunications, and wireless communication.

Vehicle-to-vehicle communications in an ITS demonstrates properties of both peer-to-peer (P2P) [6] networks and mobile ad-hoc networks [7, 10]. In peer-to-peer (P2P) [6] systems, participants rely on one another for service, rather than solely relying on a dedicated and centralized infrastructure. Peers in the system both provide and consume services. A mobile ad-hoc network is a collection of mobile hosts with wireless communication capabilities, forming a temporary network without aid of any established infrastructure [7]. In such networks, topological connectivity is subject to frequent, unpredictable change. Given the mobility of vehicles on the road, it is obvious that an ITS network demonstrates properties of both network types. Further, in an ad-hoc network two hosts that want to communicate may not be within wireless range of each other, but could still communicate if other hosts between them are also participating in the ad-hoc network and are willing to forward messages for them. We exploit already existing routing algorithms for inter-vehicle communication.

Our contribution consists in studying how peer-to-peer communication in a mobile ad-hoc network would serve as an architecture for two new cooperative driving scenarios, namely on-the-fly highway alert scenario and mutual driving group scenario, and also demonstrate the role for database management in such an architecture. To the best of our knowledge this is the first comprehensive examination of ITS from a database perspective, even though there exists research on component topics of mobile databases [2] and geographic, network routing [5], and P2P [4]. We demonstrate how ITS merges problems from these diverse areas, and give a practical architecture, based on previous work in these fields.

The paper is structured in five sections as follows. **Section 2** describes the two cooperative driving scenarios, and **Section 3** presents the architecture while addressing the technical and networking issues. Database techniques applicable to our scenarios are discussed in detail in **Section 4**, including materialization of views for query answering as well as location and peer dependent queries. Our concluding remarks and future research directions are summarized in **Section 5**.

2 Problem Description

Before we describe our scenarios, we briefly present the basic concept of ITS communications. There are two basic types of ITS (see Figure 1 [8]):

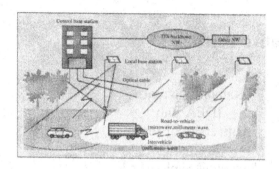

Figure 1. The basic concept of ITS communications

- road-to-vehicle communications

- vehicle-to-vehicle communications

The road-vehicle communication involves base stations located along the road that communicate with the vehicles on the road and are coordinated by several control stations. An example is the warning highway system that warns about congestion or accidents and suggests alternative route(s). Inter-vehicle communication has not been explored in as much detail.

In this paper we present two application scenarios of an ITS, in which vehicles can cooperate and coordinate their actions, and enumerate the database issues involved. In order for a set of vehicles to be engaged in a *cooperative driving* scenario, they have to be able to exchange information about each other. Cooperative driving has been briefly introduced in the literature [3], and we extend the discussion to two different working scenarios and study the database aspects. To this point, ITS technology has been exclusively addressed in the domain of networking and private corporations. However, as the functionality of these systems progresses, the need for database technologies such as consistency, replication, and query optimization will have an increasing role. A description of the two cooperative driving scenarios follows.

In the *on-the-fly highway alert* scenario, vehicles transmit to and receive from other participating vehicles warning messages regarding the state of the road (accidents, traffic congestion, closed roads). Although this service is available in a centralized broadcast fashion, it can be enhanced by allowing the vehicles themselves to be involved in detecting and propagating the road status information. This can be useful when a centralized dispatcher is not available for that specific road segment, or it can be used to improve the accuracy of the centralized information (if available). For this scenario to function properly, a larger number of vehicles need to participate in detecting and passing along the information to upcoming vehicles. Otherwise the information

might be meaningless or not trustworthy. Each vehicle uses this information to decide an alternative route or make different local decisions (depending on the warning type).

The second scenario is a *mutual driving group* of vehicles that plan a trip together. They leave together and plan to reach the same destination. The goal is that vehicles stay in communication as much as possible throughout the entire trip. They may need to communicate in order to make common decisions (such as dynamically deciding which exit to take). Clearly, it is not always possible that vehicles stay in visual contact, and communication disconnections are quite possible. Unlike other approaches [3] that perform real-time cooperative driving, we will allow vehicles to lose communication contact for periods of time, and still be able to track each other. We would like each vehicle of the group to have sufficient information about the rest of the group, at any given time, and also be able to foresee when they will be within communication range again.

3 An ITS Architecture

This section presents the technical requirements for the cooperative driving scenario, summarizes the technologies involved, and enumerates the network and database issues.

3.1 Assumptions

Location information is essential in the scenarios described. Therefore, each vehicle is equipped with a GPS (Global Positioning System) receiver and a corresponding off-line map. For our purpose, the GPS receiver will provide the following functionalities:

- provide location coordinates (x, y) at time t,

- ability to locate (x, y) on a static map stored in the device memory,

- ability to plot a path on the map given the table (x, y, t), and ability to plot multiple paths[1] in a similar form.

Each participating vehicle is equipped with a wireless communication module (transceiver), that has a limited broadcast range R. Initially, assume all have the same range. Each vehicle has a unique identification number *vid* based on its transceiver, for use in communication and tracking. Though security issues are not addressed in this paper, the vehicle *vid* may be encoded using encryption techniques during communication to avoid the effects of potential interference of malicious participants. Our assumption is that all the vehicles are trustworthy.

---

[1]Tracking multiple vehicle routes on the same map is not currently a standard feature of GPS receivers.

3.2 An Ad Hoc Mobile Network

Using the wireless transceivers, vehicles form a *wireless network* given a suitable network protocol. Due to the highly dynamic nature of the environment, vehicles join and leave the network frequently. Therefore, the network is a *mobile ad-hoc network* [7], where hosts travel through physical space and communicate in an opportunistic manner via wireless links. Further, since the communication and control are decentralized, the network can be viewed as a *peer-to-peer network*. Decentralization offers scalability, robustness, and limits requirements for central administration.

The network is characterized by wireless communications, no central control, and cooperation among nodes. These features form a union of P2P, wireless, and ad-hoc networks, therefore our network architecture will be a *peer-to-peer, mobile, ad-hoc, wireless network*.

3.3 Network and Routing Issues

In this section we will look at membership, discovery and routing issues in the context of cooperative driving. These topics have been well studied in the context of system networks. Algorithms exist for routing in ad-hoc networks [7], and group membership management and discovery in peer-to-peer networks [10]. We will be using these results in designing a solution for the cooperative driving problem.

Vehicles periodically broadcast messages containing their location and time information. This will insure basic network connectivity. Each vehicle manages a *routing table*, needed to store information about neighboring vehicles (participating vehicles within its range). Updates in the routing table are triggered by the receipt of a broadcast message. A broadcast message is a quadtuple (vid, x, y, t), where vid is the vehicle identification number, (x, y) is vehicle's current GPS coordinates, and t is the value of the local clock. Note that GPS tells extremely accurately time, so clock synchronization is not an issue.

GPS-enabled vehicles allow for the development of useful location dependent services, such as navigation and automated road assistance. Integrating GPS data into network protocols, such as the Internet protocol, to create such services has been studied in [5]. Addressing based on physical location of nodes instead of a logical address is called *geographic addressing*, and corresponding *GPS-based routing protocols* have been proposed [5]. We make use of existing geographic and ad-hoc routing algorithms to solve the addressing and routing mechanisms for our scenarios.

As with any P2P architecture the system's robustness, availability, performance and accuracy depend on the number of peers: the more participating peers, the more available and accurate the information. Vehicles would not benefit much if the network size is small and if new members join and leave frequently.

3.4 Database Issues

One important aspect in our application is the availability of a *consistent view* of the system to all of the network members. It is not trivial to compute the global network image due to the highly dynamic behavior of the network which may induce *stale* data in the routing tables. The routing table is in fact a database relation that stores information about the neighboring vehicles. This relation can be seen as a view of a distributed database, since all the members of the ad-hoc network contribute information. The entire configuration of the network is most likely not known by each individual node, although this is desirable. Instead, each node has some local information regarding its neighbors. Putting all local information together creates the global view of the system.

A vehicle with a GPS and no transceiver is limited on the types of queries that can be performed. Data from the GPS can be used for static mapping and location-dependent queries. Some examples of such queries are: "*Where am I?*", "*Where is the closest gas station?*", "*How far is the closest restaurant?*". However, by introducing a mechanism for communication between GPS-equipped vehicles, database issues of distribution and consistency arise. From a global-level view, at any point in time, there exists a relation $L(vid, x, y, t)$ storing the current location of all vehicles and the corresponding time information. Further, a global-level historical relation $H(vid, x, y, t)$ stores locations of all vehicles for all times. Each vehicle i has its own local views L_i and H_i of the global relations. The views of both relations are continually dynamic, especially L, whereas H may contain incomplete or inconsistent information. We highlight that views are in fact constructed based upon the information exchanged by the peers and not upon information provided by a central unit. History table management is discussed in detail in Section 4, and Figure 2 provides the system infrastructure.

4 Database Issues in Cooperative Driving

Each time a vehicle receives a message, it accordingly updates the two tables: the tuple corresponding to the vehicle whose vid is in the message received will be updated in both L_i and H_i. On an update from a broadcast, the history table represented by relation $H(vid, x, y, t)$ is updated by inserting the current tuple (vid, x, y, t) in H_i. The routing table is managed by the underlying network protocol.

Important issues are dealing with disconnections, stale data, and garbage collection, which are discussed in the next section.

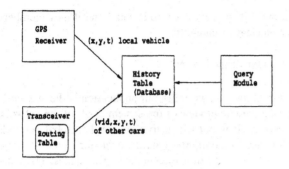

Figure 2. Infrastructure

4.1 View Materialization for Query Answering

In order to compute the global view of the network, individual vehicles need to query other members to gather information about non-neighboring nodes. Dynamic routing protocols are used to re-materialized a view.

The history table is used to store information about all the neighbors throughout the journey. The database queries will be performed on this table. We consider two possible cases: when a node receives the query "*Where is X?*", it can either answer immediately with whatever information that node has by inspecting its history table, or it can itself initiate a look-up process to gather information from its own neighbors. Since the sets of neighbors of these two nodes can be distinct, more valuable information may be collected. A mechanism is used to detect query replication. Suppose vehicle i sends this query to vehicle j. Then j will perform a query like *SELECT * FROM H_j WHERE (SELECT MAX(t) FROM H_j WHERE vid = X) = t* to retrieve the most current record for X. This query is used in constructing and updating the history table, since they are used to provide up-to-date information when *stale* data is detected.

One valid question is how far should the query process go. The number of steps should be finite and also the time allotted to this operation should not exceed a certain threshold, since in that case the answer might be already outdated by the time it reaches the initiator (the queried vehicle had changed its position considerably, making the information useless). To improve efficiency, when a vehicle replies to a query it appends its own current information to the reply. This allows the query initiator to update two tuples when receiving the answer: the one corresponding to the queried vehicle and the one corresponding to the answering neighbor.

In addition to storing time information, derived information such as velocity vector are also useful. By using interpolation techniques, this would allow us to make location-time predictions or answer queries corresponding to time

values for which no records exist in H. Efficient query answering can be achieved using known indexing protocols [9, 11].

4.2 Location Dependent Queries

Queries can be classified into *GPS specific queries* and *location dependent queries* in the context of cooperative driving. Examples of GPS specific queries, that can be answered without peer interaction include make use of base data (current location, speed, time), or derived data (trip time, average speed, estimated arrival time). These queries are simple in nature as they can be answered by applying mathematical formulas to the stored data in the GPS receiver in addition to information from the history. Database techniques are not required.

In addition to these queries *peer-dependent queries* require peer knowledge to be answered, such as:

- *Who are my neighbors?*

- *Where is vehicle X?*

- *Are all the mutual group vehicles within my range?*[2].

Peer-dependent queries can always be "trivially" answered by querying over the history table (relation H). To answer "*Where is vehicle X?*", a vehicle i could check its history table. If it finds the corresponding entry there, and if the tuple's timestamp is *recent enough*[3], then the information is considered valid. If the information is *stale*[4], then a look-up procedure is performed. The protocol for detecting the position of vehicle X is presented in Figure 3.

The answer to the query "*Who are my neighbors?*" can be easily obtained by scanning the routing table. If it is essential that the information is very accurate, a record may be checked for stale data, and appropriate actions should be taken if this is detected. By inputing historical relation H_i into the GPS receiver, one vehicle can monitor the route progress of a predefined set of vehicles.

4.3 Problem Alert Queries

Alert queries involve passing warning messages between vehicles. Instead of drivers initiating and sending warning messages directly, given each vehicle's local view, data mining can be performed on the historical relation H to decide if the traffic ahead has significantly changed in speed

---

[2] Of course this query is a combination of the previous two, because one can check the neighbors list and look for certain vehicle *vids*.

[3] It means that the difference between i's clock and the tuple timestamp is less than a predefine value *tmax*.

[4] It means that the difference between i's clock and the tuple timestamp is greater than *tmax*.

Protocol for vehicle i to detect vehicle X
{ i first checks its own table H_i, then broadcasts }
N_i := { i's set of neighbors };
rec = SELECT * FROM H_i WHERE
    (SELECT MAX(t) FROM H_j WHERE $vid = X$) = t;
if rec = $\emptyset$ then rec := (X, 0, 0, 0); endif;
send "Where is X?" to N_i (broadcast);
receive { $rec_j \mid j$ in N_i };
for each rec_j do
    if $rec_j.t > rec.t$ then
        $H_i := H_i \cup (X, x, y, t)$;
    endif
    $H_i := H_i \cup (j, x_j, y_j, t_j)$;
enddo;

Figure 3. Protocol to answer "Where is X?"

(and maybe direction). A notion of *progress* can be established. Progress occurs when vehicles maintain roughly the same speed and direction. Any changes in this setting signals a potentially wrong event and an alert message is broadcast. The neighbors receive the message and retransmit it further to their neighbors (geographic routing is involved), thus alerting the upcoming vehicles of potential problems ahead. Drivers can then become more cautious, adjust their speed, and make route changing decisions ahead of time if necessary. Such capability contributes to a safer driving environment.

Note that the message propagation wave can reach vehicles located very remotely from the actual incident, and it is possible that these will not be at all affected by a sudden traffic slow down. The vehicles can make local decisions with respect to the importance of the notice, by considering the location, time, gravity of the incident from the broadcast message and their own time, location, and direction of movement.

5 Conclusion and Future Work

In this paper we have studied how protocols that deal with routing in mobile ad-hoc networks and routing based on geographical location can be used in cooperative driving scenarios, where road participants become engaged in offering and consuming services while driving. The environment is a totally decentralized architecture, based on peer-to-peer interaction. The presented scenarios functionality relies entirely on the willingness of the vehicles to cooperate, and on the quality of the information exchanged. In addition to enumerating the issues in the emerging application area, we characterized some of the database issues involved. By moving from static, single vehicle queries to dynamic, multi-vehicle communications, the need for database technologies increases. We also discussed database issues related to history table management, namely constructing materialized views of the system, and how this information can be used in answering location and peer dependent queries. A protocol for answering basic queries by dynamic view materialization using existing network protocols has been proposed.

Our future work will focus on adding security constraints to our scenarios and by optimizing the management of the history table. This table can grow considerably and techniques for reducing its size are important.

References

[1] T. Brinkhoff. Requirements of traffic telematics to spatial databases. In *Proceedings of SSD99*, volume 1651, pages 365–369, 1999.

[2] M. Choy, M.-P. Kwan, and H. Leong. Distributed database design for mobile geographical applications. *Journal of Database Management*.

[3] W. Franz, H. Hartenstein, and B. Bochow. *Internet on the Road via Inter-Vehicle Communications*. Workshop der Informatik 2001: Mobile Communications over Wireless LAN: Research and Applications, 2001.

[4] S. Gribble, A. Halevy, Z. Ives, M. Rodrig, and D. Suciu. What can databases do for peer-to-peer? In *Proceedings of WebDB2001*, 2001.

[5] T. Imielinski and C. Navas. Geographic addressing, routing, and resource discovery with the global positioning system. *Communications of the ACM Journal (CACM)*, 1997.

[6] M. Naraghi-Pour, M. Hegde, and R. Pallapotu. Peer-to-peer communication in wireless local area networks. In *Proceedings of the ICCCN98*, pages 432–437, 1998.

[7] S. Nesargi and R. Prakash. Issues pertaining to service discovery in mobile ad hoc networks. In *Proceedings of POMC2001*, pages 41–48, 2001.

[8] S. Ohmori, Y. Yamao, and N. Nakajima. The future generations of mobile communications based on broadband access technologies. *IEEE Communications*, December 2000.

[9] D. Pfoser, C. Jensen, and Y. Theodoridis. Novel approaches to the indexing of moving object trajectories. In *Proceedings of VLDB2000*, 2000.

[10] G.-C. Roman, Q. Huang, and A. Hazemi. Consistent group membership in ad hoc networks. In *Proceedings of the 23rd International Conference in Software Engineering (ISCE)*, 2001.

[11] S. Saltenis, C. Jensen, S. Leutenegger, and M. Lopez. Indexing the positions of continuously moving objects. In *Proceedings of the 2000 ACM SIGMOD International Conference on Management of Data*, pages 331–342, 2000.

[12] Y. Shiraki, T. Ohyama, S. Nakabayashi, and K. Tokuda. Development of an inter-vehicle communications system. *OKI Technical Review*, 68(3), September 2001. Special Edition on ITS of OKI Electric Industry Co., Ltd.

Fairness in Differentiated Services Architecture

Erhan Asim Ozturk
Aydin Software and Electronics Inc.,
(AYESAS)
Ankara, Turkey
erhano@ayesas.com.tr

Cuneyt F. Bazlamacci
Dep. of Electrical and Electronics Engineering,
Middle East Technical University,
Ankara, Turkey
cuneytb@ metu.edu.tr

Abstract

Recently much attention has been given to the Differentiated Services (Diffserv) Architecture, which is proposed to offer quality of service (QoS) in IP networks. Assured Forwarding (AF) in diffserv provides a better quality of service than best effort to traffic within the assured class under moderate conditions. The present study evaluates the diffserv behavior for the assured and best effort traffic classes in case of responsive (like TCP) and non-responsive (like UDP) traffic mixture with and without an active queue management scheme from the fairness point of view. It also investigates the effect of rate adaptive traffic shaper on fairness.

1. Introduction

Most of the current Internet applications require a certain quality of service (QoS) level but the current Internet structure still provides best effort service and hence user dissatisfaction is inevitable. Internet Service Providers (ISPs) want to be able to provide different services to different users and charge according to the quality of services they provide. As a result, the Internet community proposed two models to provide QoS in the Internet. Integrated Services (intserv) model [1] is based on resource reservation for each flow. Differentiated services (diffserv) model [2], on the other hand, does not make per-flow reservation but uses prioritization. It classifies packets by setting their Differentiated Services Code Point (DSCP) Field in their header and treats these packets according to their DSCP. Therefore, the QoS provision is made not per flow but per groups of flows having the same DSCP. The treatment of a network node to a particular group is called Per Hop Behavior (PHB). There are two main PHBs in addition to Best Effort: Expedited Forwarding and Assured Forwarding [3].

In this paper, Assured Forwarding (AF) PHB is studied. In AF, a Service Level Agreement (SLA) between the user and the service provider determines the service profile. If a user exceeds the SLA, the excess packets, marked as OUT packets, are not guaranteed for delivery but they still enter the network with IN (SLA compliant) packets. Both IN and OUT packets enter the same queue where an active queue management scheme (usually some form of RED variant) is employed.

One of the main issues of Assured Forwarding to be resolved is the fairness issue, which is important in the presence of UDP in addition to TCP. When there is congestion, the RED algorithm drops some packets in the queue randomly. UDP does not respond to congestion and continues to send at the same rate whereas TCP drops its sending rate by decreasing its window size. As a result, UDP packets get more share of the bandwidth and TCP packets are punished by their responsive behavior.

One approach to solve this problem is using "FRED" (Flow Random Early Drop) [4] instead of RED, which improves fairness by keeping state information about flows that have packets in the queue. It is also possible to use a "Rate Adaptive Shaper" (RAS) [5] in conjunction with a marker like Two Rate Three Color Marker (trTCM) [6]. Impact of RAS on performance is already investigated in [7] for all traffic being modeled as TCP. However, in the presence of UDP, neither srTCM nor trTCM can provide fairness.

The present study, first demonstrates the unfairness in the presence of both UDP and TCP flows when trTCM is used as the marking scheme. It also shows the impact of Round Trip Time (RTT) of TCP flows on fairness. Then the effect of using FRED instead of RED is investigated and finally, RAS is employed in conjunction with trTCM and FRED to achieve an improvement in fairness.

In the paper, section 2 reviews some basic mechanisms to provide AF PHB and section 3 presents our simulation study on fairness issue. Finally, section 4 concludes the paper and identifies some possible future work.

2. Assured Forwarding Mechanisms

2.1. Multiple Random Early Drop (MRED)

Random Early Drop (RED) is an active queue management (AQM) scheme to detect upcoming congestion and force the adaptive applications to reduce their sending rate by dropping their packets. It is the basis for other AQM Schemes. When a packet arrives, the router checks the average queue size. If it is below min_{th}, incoming packet is accepted; if it is above max_{th}, all incoming packets are dropped, if it is between min_{th} and max_{th}, incoming packets are dropped with a non-zero probability up to max_p.

Since there are three drop precedence levels in each AF service class in diffserv, a separate RED mechanism should be employed for each drop precedence. In AF, drop precedence levels are named as red, yellow and green; red, having the highest drop precedence and green, having the lowest. In MRED, green, yellow and red packets have different RED parameters and average queue size for a color is calculated as the sum of the average size of that color and the average number of packets of the color with lower drop precedence.

2.2 Flow Random Early Drop (FRED)

FRED (Flow Random Early Drop) was first proposed in [4]. It is a modified form of RED to provide fairness for bandwidth share among all sources.

Bandwidth fairness is an important issue in AF. There are two main reasons for unfairness. Either some flows do not respond to packet loss (non adaptive) but some others respond to it by decreasing their sending rate (adaptive) or all flows are adaptive but they have different RTTs. Both cases lead to an unfair sharing of the bandwidth such that the non-responsive source gets a better share in the first case and low RTT connections get a better share than the high RTT ones in the second case because of a high RTT flow's longer recovery time from a packet loss compared to low RTT ones having all other things being equal.

FRED provides better fairness in the above cases by keeping state information for flows that are present in the queue. It does not allow a flow to buffer more than a maximum value and it counts how many times it tries to exceed this maximum value (called a strike). If it tries to exceed the maximum (makes strike) more than once, the flow is not allowed to buffer packets more than "average queue size / number of flows in the queue". So the packets belonging to non adaptive flows are not accepted beyond a limit and this protects the adaptive flows from non adaptive ones resulting in an improvement in fairness.

On the other hand, FRED allows each flow to buffer a number of packets (min_q) regardless of the state of the queue and then random dropping starts only if the number of packets of that flow is higher than this value. Hence a high RTT flow can buffer the same number of packets as the low RTT flows before random drop occurs and by protecting low RTT flows in this fashion fairness is again improved to a certain extent.

2.3 Two Rate Three Color Marker

A Two Rate Three Color Marker [6] has four parameters: Peak Information Rate (PIR), Peak Burst Size (PBS), Committed Information Rate (CIR), Committed Burst Size (CBS). These are actually the parameters for two token buckets: P (Peak) and C (Committed). The burst sizes are bucket sizes, information rates are token generation rates.

If a packet is not marked before, trTCM operates in color blind mode. When a packet is received, its size is checked. If there are not enough tokens for the packet in P bucket, the packet is marked as red. If there are enough tokens in P bucket but not in C bucket, the packet is marked as yellow and token count for the P bucket is decremented by B. If there are enough tokens both at P and C buckets, the packet is marked as green and both P and C buckets' token counts are decremented by B.

If the packet is marked before, trTCM operates in color aware mode. When a packet of size B is received, if there are not enough tokens at bucket P or the packet is marked as red before, the packet is marked as red. If there are enough tokens in P bucket but not in C bucket, or the packet is marked as yellow before, the packet is marked as yellow and token count for bucket P is decremented by B. Otherwise the packet is marked as green and both T_p and T_c are decremented by B.

2.4 Rate Adaptive Shapers

In AF, the customer can send traffic over the SLA and the excess traffic (usually marked as red) can still get service in this way. Therefore, the shaper should not have a fixed shaping rate since the excess traffic is undetermined. Leaky bucket and token bucket do not satisfy this need so Rate Adaptive Shaper (RA Shaper) and Green Shaper [8] are proposed to be applied to trTCM for TCP traffic only.

RA Shaper has a standard tail drop FIFO queue as in leaky bucket shaper. The shaping rate depends on the occupancy of the queue. If buffer occupancy increases, the shaper increases its shaping rate to prevent possible loss (because the queue can get full) and large delay. The shaping rate is kept at least equal to the estimated average input traffic rate. So $SR(t)=\max(B_f(B_{occ}(t)),EAR)$ where SR is the shaping rate, B_f is a function of buffer occupancy (B_{occ}) and EAR is the estimated arrival rate. B_f is a piecewise linear function.

EAR is calculated using the following formula:

$$EAR_{NEW} = (1 - e^{-t/K}) \cdot \frac{L}{T} + e^{-t/K} \cdot EAR_{OLD}$$

where T is the time between the previous and current packet arrival, L is the length of the newly arrived packet and K is a constant that determines how fast the EAR follows the instantaneous arrival rate.

3. Simulation Experiment

3.1 Traffic Modeling and Simulation Setup

In the experiments, an open source network simulator 'ns' (version 2.1b8) is used after implementing and incorporating the necessary modules, namely MFRED and RAS. The whole network traffic is generated by Assured class and Best Effort class sources. The Assured service users are, one short lived TCP source, three long lived TCP sources and one CBR UDP source. The Best Effort traffic users are identical to Assured users. Unless otherwise specified, TCP traffics have the same RTT but to see the effect of RTT, the RTT of an assured TCP flow is adjustable. Maximum window size of all TCP connections are set to 64K in order not to make the maximum window size the limiting factor.

Short lived TCP sources generate exponential on/off traffic with average on time of 10ms and off time of 100ms. When it is on, it generates 100kbps TCP traffic. Long lived TCP sources are implemented as continuous FTP connections. UDP sources generate CBR traffic at a rate of 1Mbps. All sources generate 1024 bytes long packets. In this experiment, it is assumed that TCP acknowledgments are not lost. Throughout the experiment, PIR is taken as 2 times CIR, CBS and PBS are taken as 5KB.

Figure 1 shows the network topology used in the experiment. The nodes at the left hand side of the figure generate traffic to the destinations at the right hand side of the figure. Sources 0 to 4 generate Assured traffic to destinations 0 to 4, respectively. The remaining sources generate best effort traffic to their corresponding destinations. The bottleneck link capacity is set to 3Mbps.

In all steps, the simulation is run for 80 seconds and the last 73 seconds period to is used to ignore the transient network state. The three steps of the experiment is presented in the following subsections.

3.2 Unfairness in Two Rate Three Color Marker

In the first step of the experiment, trTCM marking scheme is evaluated to show the unfairness problem in trTCM by using the standard diffserv module in 'ns' after

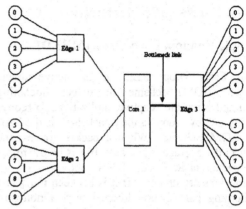

Figure 1. Network Topology in the Experiment

creating the above topology and setting the RED parameter as follows:

Table 1 RED Queue Settings

Virtual Queue	min_{th}	max_{th}	max_p
Green	20	40	0.02
Yellow	10	20	0.1
Red and Best Effort	5	10	0.2

It is observed that Assured long TCP flows having the same drop precedence get similar throughputs whereas Assured UDP flow gets quite a high percentage of the traffic it generates (see Figure 2) and fairness is not achieved among Assured flows.

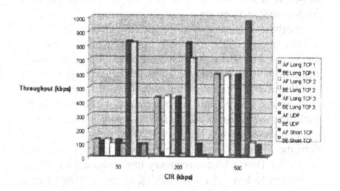

Figure 2. Flow Throughput Versus CIR

This is the case also in Best Effort Class. UDP source gets whole Best Effort service and Best Effort TCP sources starve. When CIR is low, less Assured packets are marked as lower drop precedence so their behaviors get similar to Best Effort class. However, as CIR increases, more packets of Assured TCP flows have lower drop precedence and they get quite a good share of the bottleneck link capacity. Therefore, it can be concluded that, Assured traffic is protected from Best Effort traffic by marking Best Effort as lower drop precedence.

Assured TCP traffic benefits much from this behavior and even Assured UDP increases its bandwidth. However, it is worth to note that the Assured service is still not shared fairly among the UDP and TCP sources within this class.

To see the impact of RTT on TCP throughput, one of the Assured long TCP flow's RTT value is changed.

Figure 3 demonstrates that an increase in RTT of an Assured long TCP reduces the throughput of the corresponding source and increases the throughputs of other TCP flows.

Figure 3. Flow Throughput for Different RTT

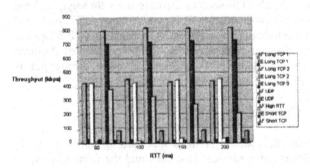

3.3 Effect of Flow Multiple Random Early Drop

In the second step, the effect of using FMRED instead of MRED is evaluated to show the potential improvement in fairness by replacing MRED queues in the original diffserv module of 'ns' by FMRED. In this, we actually have one physical queue but three different virtual queues that operate independently and the packets are placed in virtual queues according to their code points being green, yellow or red. Best effort packets are placed in the virtual queue corresponding to the red code point. For each drop precedence, different threshold values and maximum dropping probabilities are used. In addition, average queue size is calculated separately for each drop precedence and therefore random drop is decided for each drop precedence independently.

Besides, a maximum allowed per flow queue size is kept for each drop precedence separately because otherwise assured packets can not get better service than best effort packets, which is especially important for TCP flows. Finally, the number of active flows is also kept separately for each drop precedence because in FRED algorithm this value is important to decide if the flow is a non-adaptive one or not.

On the other hand, the strike value (number of times a flow tries to exceed its associated buffer's maximum threshold) is not kept separately in order to protect the adaptive flows better. Because in this way, strike of a flow in one of the virtual queues affects the other virtual queues so the non adaptive flow is punished in all virtual queues improving the fairness.

The queue size is 300 packets (of size 1KB). The thresholds and the maximum drop probabilities for virtual queues are set as follows:

Table 2 FMRED Parameters

Virtual Queue	min_{th}	max_{th}	max_p
Green	64	128	0.02
Yellow	32	64	0.1
Red and Best Effort	16	32	0.5

With the above modifications, the simulation produced the following results:

Table 3 Throughput with and without FMRED

Source	Throughput (kbps			
	Same RTT		One RTT is high	
	MRED	FMRED	MRED	FMRED
AF Long TCP 1	373	409	206	313
AF Long TCP 2	373	396	398	456
AF Long TCP 3	368	406	400	455
AF Short TCP	89	90	90	90
AF UDP	860	754	876	654
BE Long TCP 1	26	187	50	204
BE Long TCP 2	35	174	47	193
BE Long TCP 3	30	170	52	199
BE Short TCP	25	85	38	85
BE UDP	779	305	801	330

When all TCP flows have the same RTT, both in AF and BE, UDP throughput decreases whereas TCP throughput increases. This effect is more obvious in BE since the unfairness was more obvious in this class. Here, FMRED improved fairness among TCP and UDP sources. Another interesting result is that, short TCP sources achieve their desired bandwidth even though the network is under provisioned. These results show that using FMRED protects TCP flows from UDP flows of same service class and short TCP flows are protected from other flows by FMRED.

The results that are obtained by increasing the RTT value of one long TCP flow of the Assured class by changing its propagation delay from 20ms to 100ms are also presented in Table 3.

In this case, using FMRED increased high RTT flow's throughput by more than half and fairness is improved. Other Assured long TCP flows' throughputs are also increased while the throughput of the Assured UDP flow decreased by 25%. Still FMRED improves fairness among Best Effort traffic by increasing TCP throughput while decreasing the UDP one.

3.4 Effect of Rate Adaptive Shaper

In the third step of the experiment, Rate Adaptive Shapers with FRED scheme is evaluated. In this part, CIR is set to 200kbps and RA Shaper Parameters are set as:

267

T1: 64KB, T2: 128KB, T3: 192KB.

These values are selected same as the values in the other RA Shaper studies. FMRED parameters are same as the previous step.

First, an Assured Long TCP traffic is shaped with an RA Shaper. Then the shaper is applied to all Assured Long TCP traffic. The results are shown in Figure 4.

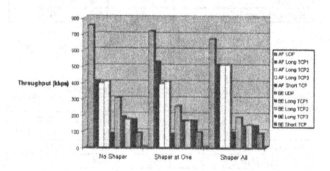

Figure 4. Throughput for Each Flow with RA Shaper

It is observed that applying RA Shaper to a TCP flow increases the corresponding TCP throughput considerably. However, FRED still protects other Assured TCP flows and they get the same bandwidth, whereas Assured UDP flow's throughput is decreased. Also the best effort UDP and long TCP flows lose while FMRED protects short TCP ones.

Similar to the previous experiments, Figure 5 presents the effect of increasing RTT of one long TCP flows in the Assured class.

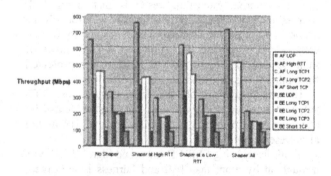

Figure 5. Throughput with RAS with Different RTT

When only high RTT flow is shaped, its throughput increases and the throughput of other Assured long TCP flows decrease since, with the shaper, we mark more packets of high RTT flow as green and yellow so packets of high RTT flow is less likely to be dropped.

At the same time, other long TCP flows experience more drops possibly because their red packets occupy a greater percentage of the queue of red and best effort

packets. The UDP packets are also dropped more frequently but because UDP does not respond to congestion, this effect reduces the throughput of the TCP sources and increases that of UDP.

When shaping is applied to an Assured long TCP with low RTT, we observe that it gets more throughput than the other Assured long TCP with the same RTT. We can also see that Assured TCP sources get the same throughput as the case with no shaper but the throughputs of UDP flows are reduced.

When shaping is applied to all Assured long TCP sources, all TCP sources increase their throughput. This also has an interesting effect on Assured UDP such that its throughput is also increased as much as TCP flows but still fairness is improved as the percentage of Assured UDP throughput in total Assured class throughput is reduced.

4. Conclusions

In this paper, Assured Forwarding (AF) PHB in differentiated services is studied and the fairness issue in AF is investigated in detail.

In a simulation study the unfairness, when trTCM is used in the presence of both UDP and TCP flows, is demonstrated and the impact of Round Trip Time (RTT) of TCP flows on fairness is shown. Then the effect of FRED on fairness is investigated and "Rate Adaptive Shaper" is used with FRED and trTCM to improve fairness further.

As future work, the effect of FMRED and RA Shaper parameters may be investigated further in more detail and the experiment may be repeated by replacing trTCM with FairTC in order to see the effect of using FairTC with RA Shaper.

References

[1] Braden, B., Clark, D., and Shenker, S, "Integrated Services in the Internet Architecture: An Overview", *IETF RFC* 1633 (1994)

[2] Blake, S., Black, D., Carlson, M., Davies, E., Wang, Z., Weiss, W., "An Architecture for Differentiated Services", *IETF RFC* 2475 (1998)

[3] Heinanen, J., Baker, F., Weiss, W., Wroclawski, J., "Assured Forwarding PHB Group", *IETF RFC* 2597 (1998)

[4] Lin, D., Morris,. R. "Dynamics of Random Early Detection", *Proceedings of ACM SIGCOMM* (September 1997), pp. 127-137.

[5] Bonaventure O., "A Rate Adaptive Shaper for Differentiated Services", *IETF RFC* 2963 (2000)

[6] Heinanen, J., Guerin, R., "A Two Rate Three Color Marker", *IETF RFC* 2698 (1999)

[7] Weiss, W., "QoS with Differentiated Services", *Bell Labs Technical Journal*, October-December 1998, pp. 48-62.

[8] Rezende, J., "Assured Service Evaluation", *Proceedings of GLOBECOM'99* (December 1999).

Session 4–3
Databases

Exploiting Semantic Constraints
in a Database Browser

Jie Zhang
Department of Computer Science
Rensselaer Polytechnic Institute
Troy, NY 12180
zhangj2@cs.rpi.edu

David L. Spooner
Department of Computer Science
Rensselaer Polytechnic Institute
Troy, NY 12180
spoonerd@cs.rpi.edu

Abstract

We present a Database Browser tool for the visualization of relational data. The Browser works by exploiting the structural semantic information inherent in a relational database. Specifically, the tool constructs a hierarchical graph among the relations using foreign key and primary key definitions from the database. This graph is used to guide users in selecting "interesting" relations and attributes. No programming is needed. The visualization of the selected data by the Browser is based on a two-dimensional scatter plot. A simple mapping mechanism is provided that allows users to configure this visualization as they wish. The user interface is implemented in Java.

1. Introduction

Database visualization research has been inspired by two different needs. On one hand, the number of non-expert users accessing databases is growing fast. On the other hand, as the quantity of data managed in databases has grown by an order of magnitude or more, even users who are experienced database users may have difficulties finding the "interesting" data in these large databases.

In our research, we try to exploit the semantic information inherent in databases (of any type) to automatically design potential display presentations and select the best presentation for selected data. In this paper, we present the first step of our research: a database browser tool that organizes the visualization of the data in a database by exploiting the structural semantic information inherent in any relational database. This Browser provides a graphical user interface that allows users to access the database without having any SQL knowledge. Our tool uses semantic information (e.g., foreign key relationships and primary keys) in

a database to show users the basic structure of the database so that even users with no database experience can easily use the tool. This tool constructs a hierarchical graph among the relations that guides users to select "interesting" relations and attributes. No data visualization programming is needed. A simple mapping mechanism is provided that allows users to configure the data visualization as they wish. Since the ODBC[1] application program interface is supported by nearly all major commercial database systems, our tool uses ODBC to extract the database semantics and communicate with the underlying database system.

This paper is organized as follows. Section 2 introduces related work and compares it with our Browser. The architecture of our tool is presented in Section 3. Section 4 talks about how to exploit the semantic information for database visualization. Section 5 discusses how the data is visualized. Finally, Section 6 talks about lessons learned and future work.

2. Related Work

The goal of the work presented in this paper is to provide a browser tool that users can customize and apply to any relational database. Other research projects[2,3,4,5,6,7] have had similar goals.

The FilmFinder[2] project uses a star field display to encode multi-attribute database items as dots or colored rectangles on a two-dimensional scatter-gram. Sliders are provided to allow users to dynamically browse the database. There are two limitations in this approach, when considered for a general-purpose database browser tool. First, the user interface can become too crowded, limiting its usefulness. The more important limitation, however, is that the representations of the x-y axes and sliders are static so that the FilmFinder system provides only limited dynamic browsing capability.

271

Tioga-2[3], a DBMS-centric visualization tool, provides a powerful imperative, programming-oriented style for defining visual presentations. To display data in a relation using an X-Y coordinate system, Tioga-2 introduces two extra attributes(called location attributes) and at least one display attribute into each relation to specify how to paint each tuple on a 2D canvas. To display data from different relations in the same view, Tioga-2 overlaps the visualizations of the relations. DEVise[4] introduces a mapping technique to interactively develop a visual representation of data. Visualization in DEVise is based on mapping each source data record to a visual symbol on the screen. A view is the basic display unit. Cursors and Links are mechanisms to operate on one view or coordinate the contents of two views. Each of these operations creates a new view so that it is sometimes necessary to generate many intermediate views to get the desired view.

Both Tioga-2 and DEVise are powerful systems for displaying relational data and provide ways to display attributes in different relations together. Their limitations are that they require extra attributes to be added to a database before visualization is possible and they require users to "program" the visualization before users can browse a database. The goal of the database browser described in this paper is to be able to browse any relational database. Therefore, extra attributes or preprogramming of the visualization are not possible. The browser must be able to extract the information that it needs from the semantics of the database itself, such as primary key attributes and foreign key references between relations. Our tool currently allows users to select attributes from different relations and display them on the screen without the need to compute intermediate results. No programming of the interface is required; only a simple mapping of attributes to shapes, colors, and axes in a two-dimensional grid. These mappings can be changed dynamically to adjust the visualization.

Other visualization systems[5,6,7] have been developed to integrate data from a variety of sources. These systems provide sophisticated techniques for processing the data sources and developing graphical visualization. While some of the ideas from these systems are useful in developing a general-purpose database browser, by themselves they do not provide an easy to use database interface for novice users.

3. Architecture of the tool

Based on the architecture for database visualization developed by Groth and Robertson[8], Figure 1 shows the architecture of the Browser. Users query a rela-

tional database using a graphical user interface provided by the Browser. The Browser uses ODBC to communicate with the database, so it can be used with any database system that supports ODBC.

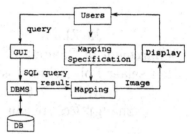

Figure 1: **Architecture of the Browser**

The Browser does not require users to have prior knowledge of the structure of the database. It instead generates and displays the partial structure of the database by using the semantic constraints in the database. From this partial structure, users can easily determine the relationships among the relations and then select the relations of interest for browsing. After that, users construct a mapping specification using the mapping interfaces provided in our tool. Since we design a 2D presentation for the selected data in the Browser, this mapping specification defines how data from the database is visualized in the Browser using visual properties such as shape, color and location in a two-dimensional grid. Based on the users' selections, the Browser generates the required SQL queries and sends them to the database. The mapping specification is then applied to the data resulting from these queries to create the visualization of the database in the Browser window.

4. Exploiting Semantic Information

As we mentioned above, both Tioga-2 and DEVise begin with one relation and require the user to understand the basic structure of the database. We remove the need for most of these restrictions by exploiting foreign-key definitions in our tool.

Initially, our Browser displays a list of all the relations in the database of interest. This information is obtained using an ODBC operation to interrogate the schema of the database. When the user selects one relation from this list, this relation and other relations related to it by foreign-key relationships are depicted graphically in a window on the screen as a hierarchical graph, which is described below. The partial structure of the database is depicted in this graph. Users then select the relation(s) from this graph to browse. This defines the search space for the Browser. At this point, the user completes the data visualization specification by defining mappings that maps the attributes from the selected relations to visual representations on the screen. This is discussed further below.

4.1. Foreign-key Relationships

Foreign-key relationships are part of the SQL standard for relational databases. A foreign-key constraint represents a relationship between two relations in which one relation references tuples in the other relation by recording the primary key values for the referenced tuples. We use this information in the Browser to display a partial structure for the database in order to provide a high-level organization for visualizing the data in the database. The ODBC interface provides a set of function calls that allow a program such as the Browser to interrogate the schema of a database and determine all the foreign-key relationships. Unfortunately, not all implementations of ODBC currently support this set of function calls. However, it is likely in the future that most will since foreign-key definitions are part of the SQL standard and part of the formal definition of ODBC. For database systems that do not support the required ODBC function calls, a new relation can be introduced into a database that records the foreign-key relationships for that database. In such a case, the database cannot be used with the Browser until this new relation is defined. The Browser is written so as to first try the ODBC function calls and then to look for the special relation with the foreign-key definitions if the ODBC function calls fail.

As described above, the data display begins with a list of all the relations in the database. A user selects any one of these relations by clicking on it. This relation and all the relations that have foreign-key relationships with it are then displayed as a hierarchical graph. In this graph, each relation is represented as a rectangle with the relation name inside. Lines between the rectangles show that these two relations have foreign-key relationships. When one or more relations are selected in the current hierarchical graph by double-clicking on their rectangles, all relations that have foreign-key relationships with the selected relations, and are not already in the current graph, are displayed as rectangles with their names inside. Additional lines connecting the rectangles are created to show the relationships. Figure 2 shows a hierarchical graph example.

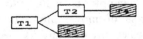

Figure 2: **A hierarchical graph example**

From the hierarchical graph, users select relations of interest for the next step in the browsing process. Only the data attributes in the selected relations are considered for visualization. The Browser needs to construct join conditions for the selected relations in the queries that the Browser generates. There are two cases:

• Two selected relations have a foreign-key relationship.

In this case, only a single join condition is needed that matches the foreign key in one relation with the primary key of the other.

• Two selected relations don't have a foreign-key relationship.

In this case, a more complex join condition will be generated. The Browser searches the hierarchical graph for a path between the two selected relations. A depth first search is used, stopping when the first such path is found. The Browser then constructs a join clause by anding together predicates generated for each pair of relations along the path. Since the relations in each pair have foreign-key relationship, the predicate for each pair matches the foreign-key in one relation with the primary key of the other.

The Browser must be able to generate the required join conditions for any two relations from the hierarchical graph. Using the two cases above, the algorithm to do this is straightforward. In Figure 2, suppose that the user selects two relations of interest, say T3 and T4 (the corresponding rectangles are shaded in the figure). To construct the required join condition for these two relations, we use DFS algorithm to find the path from T4 to T3, which is T4-T2-T1-T3. We collect the conditions through the path and combine them using the "AND" operator to generate the final join condition for querying the database. Here, we get the final join condition: "$T4.a1 = T2.a1$ AND $T2.a2 = T1.a2$ AND $T3.a3 = T1.a3$". All the attributes a1, a2, a3 are the corresponding foreign key/primary key pairs between two relations along the path.

If three or more relations are selected, then any two of the selected relations generate one join condition using the algorithm described above. The Browser generates the final join condition by anding together these preliminary join conditions.

4.2. Conditional Attributes

After generating the basic query as described above, we allow the user to constrain the data to be displayed to a subset of the chosen tuples in the database. FilmFinder uses sliders as query filters to constrain the data to be displayed. Sliders are good for visual presentations, but they have the disadvantage of taking up space in the visual display. In our Browser we simply ask users to set the minimum and/or maximum values for some subset of the attributes in the selected relations. We call these attributes "conditional attributes". To set the minimum/maximum value for an attribute, we must consider the type of the attribute. For ordinal types, we use the default order. For nominal types, we use alphabetical order. Currently, our tool allows users to choose zero or more conditional attributes. All the query conditions generated by these attributes are connected by "AND" operators to form the join condition expression.

4.3. Display Attributes

Display attributes are those attributes whose values will be displayed on the screen. The Browser visualizes data using an x-y coordinate system. It defines four display attributes: X, Y, Shape and Color. The X and Y attributes are also called "location attributes". The Browser provides a graphical user interface for users to choose the display attributes.

The four attributes chosen as display attributes may come from any of the selected relations. A set of related tuples, with one tuple from each of the selected relations, forms the basis for visualization of a single data item. The attributes from these tuples designated as the location attributes, X and Y, define where in the x-y coordinate system the data item is visualized. The two attributes designated as the Shape and Color attributes are used to define the shape and the color of the data item when it is visualized. This is discussed in more detail below.

4.4. Mapping

Mapping the values of the shape and color attributes to visualized shapes and colors is an important step in our tool. Currently, our tool defines a fixed set of shapes and colors. All the values satisfying the conditions generated by the conditional attributes are retrieved from the database. The user selects one of the shapes or colors for each distinct value of a Shape or Color attribute. In other words, the value of a shape or color attribute is mapped to one shape or color, respectively. Multiple distinct values may be mapped to the same shape or color. All these settings are stored as a mapping specification that can be changed at any time. Default shape and color mappings are used if the user does not define his or her own mappings.

Figure 3 shows an example of shape mapping if the user selects attribute "Origin" in the relation "Actors" (represented as "Actors.Origin" in the figure) as the Shape attribute.

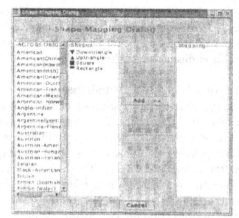

Figure 3: **Shape mapping example**

5. Visualizing the Data

Once the mappings are defined, the Browser is ready to visualize the data from the database. The values for each of the display attributes from each set of related tuples are retrieved from the database and displayed using the designated shape and color as defined by the mappings. The location of the value is defined by the two location attributes. Each distinct value of one of the location attributes is mapped to a spot on the x-axis. Each distinct value of the other location attribute is mapped to a spot on the y-axis. The mappings to the x and y axes preserve the orderings of the values in the appropriate domains for the two location attributes. Since the number of distinct values for the x and y attributes may be large, we partition the visualization into different pages and only display 50 values for x and for y on one page. Buttons are provided to jump to the next and previous pages for x and y values.

Each spot on the x and y axes is labeled with the value of the corresponding location attribute. To avoid clutter, only the first few characters are displayed. Clicking on one of these axis labels causes the entire value of the location attribute to be displayed. A horizontal or vertical line is drawn from that axis label to make it easier to determine which shape in the visualization corresponds to that axis label. Clicking on one of the shapes in the visualization also causes the full values of the corresponding location attributes to be displayed along the axes.

Consider an example of using the Browser on our test database of movie information. At the beginning we select three relations: Actors, Casts and Films, from the 15 relations in the list. Films.TITLE, Casts.AWARDS, Actors.ORGIN and Films.CATEGORY are chosen as the display at-

274

tributes: X, Y, Shape and Color, respectively. Films.YEAR is chosen as a conditional attribute with minimal and maximal values set to 1900 and 2000. The shape and color mapping specifications are listed using pairs of the form (value, shape/color) below:

• shape mapping: (American, Downtriangle), (British, Uptriangle), (French, Square), (Others, Rectangle)

• color mapping: (action, yellow), (adventure, red), (cartoon, pink), (comedy, orange), (drama, magenta), (horror, lightgray), (mystery, gray), (romantic, darkgray), (science fiction, cyan), (Others, blue)

Here, "Others" means all values in the database except those values listed earlier in the list.

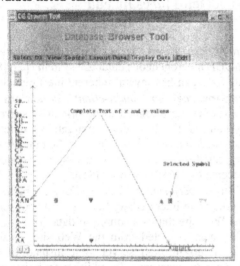

Figure 4: **One data displaying example**

Figure 4 shows one page of the resulting visualization. The values of the x and y axes are displayed next to the axis lines. Since the values are large, we only display the complete text when users select a symbol in this picture. In this example, when the user selects the square symbol, the x and y values are shown completely. The circle symbol means that there is no value of the shape attribute for that particular set of values, so the default shape (i.e., a circle) is used.

6. Future Work

Every existing database system incorporates different semantic information about the databases that it manages. The Browser presented in this paper uses primary keys and foreign-key relationships, and provides a natural way to graphically display data from a possibly large relational database. There are other types of semantic information inherent in a relational database, for example, domain constraints. This additional semantic information can be exploited to provide a more flexible database browser that is able to tailor the visualization of data to the type of data to be displayed. For example, one might wish to organize the display of data with a time component into a time-line for visualization. This could be done for data with domains DATE and TIME in SQL. In future work, we will investigate extensions to the database browser to take advantage of additional semantic information in a database.

The two-dimensional, x-y plot of data currently used by the Browser is only one of many potential visualizations schemes that a database browser might use. For example, an alternate scheme would be to use an indented outline format to represent relationships between data items. The data items themselves might be represented as graphical icons with labels extracted from key attributes. In future work, we will explore alternate visualization schemes for browsing the data.

Finally, object-oriented database systems often contain much more useful semantic information about the data in a database and its structure. Multiple types of associations between objects may be represented in a database. And application-specific objects may be defined to better model an application domain. How to take advantage of these richer semantics for database browsing is an interesting research topic.

References

[1] Kingsley Idehen, "Open Database Connectivity Without Compromise", Technical White Paper, http://www.openlinksw.com/info/docs/odbcwhp/tableof.htm#Table of Contents.

[2] C. Ahlberg and B. Shneiderman, "Visual Information Seeking: Tight Coupling of Dynamic Query Filters with Star field Displays", Proc. of *CHI*, 1994, *ACM*, New York, pp. 313-317.

[3] A. Aiken, J. Chen, M. Stonebraker and A. Woodruff, "Tioga-2: A Direct Manipulation Database Visualization Environment", Proc. of *the 12th International Conference on Data Engineering*, New Orleans, LA, February 1996, pp. 208-217.

[4] M. Livny, R. Ramakrishnan, et. al., "DEVise: Integrated Querying and Visualization of Large Datasets", Proc. of *SIGMOD* Conference, 1997, pp. 301-312.

[5] C. Ahlberg and E. Wistrand, "IVEE: An Information Visualization and Exploration Environment", Proc. of *IEEE Symposium on Information Visualization*, 1995, Atlanta, pp. 66-73.

[6] I. F. Cruz, "Delaunay: a Database Visualization System", Proc. of *ACM SIGMOD*, 1997, pp. 510-513.

[7] I. F. Cruz, "DOODLE: a Visual Language for Object-Oriented Databases", Proc. of *ACM SIGMOD*, 1992, pp. 71-80.

[8] D. P. Groth and E. L. Robertson, "Architecture Support for Database Visualization", Workshop on *New Paradigms in Information Visualization and Manipulation*, *ACM*, 1999, pp. 53-55.

Dispatching Java agents to user for data extraction from third party web sites

Dmitriy Beryoza, Naphtali Rishe, Andrei Selivonenko, Alejandro Roque, Ian De Felipe
High-performance Database Research Center
School of Computer Science
Florida International University
University Park, Miami, FL 33199, USA
+1 (305) 348-1706
{beryozad, rishen, selivona, aroque03, idefel01}@cs.fiu.edu

Abstract

Data retrieval on the World Wide Web has been a focus of intensive research in the past few years. The majority of existing approaches concentrate on mechanisms for data discovery and schema induction. Few researchers, however, address issues of performance of data extraction systems. Thus, centralized, server-based data extraction solutions often suffer from congestion and low speed of execution. In this work we present a mechanism for enhancing performance of data retrieval through distributing its functionality to the client computer using Mobile Data Retrieval Agents (MDRA).

1 Introduction

The amounts of data accessible on the World Wide Web have exploded in the recent years. Unfortunately this increase was not followed by significant improvement in mechanisms for accessing and manipulating this data. It is still accessed by browsing Web pages, entering information in query forms and *reading* the results that Web sites present. No convenient mechanism exist that would give user more power over the data on the Web, by, for example, allowing her to define custom queries to Web sites or to extract the returned data from HTML pages and use it in external applications.

Querying the Web and data extraction on the Web has recently become a popular research topic. A variety of methods for schema discovery and data extraction from HTML documents have been proposed. We have designed Data Extractor system for Web data retrieval [3] that uses wrappers written in Java for posing queries to sites and extracting resulting data sets. Data Extractor allows us to treat virtually any Web site as a data source. It is implemented both as a standalone server solution and a set of functionality that can be embedded in applications and provide them with live data from the Internet. This system is also used as a Web data provider for MSemODB heterogeneous database system ([7], [8]).

Data Extractor has several inherent inefficiencies:

- *Performance in multi-client conditions.* Data Extractor was designed to be primarily server-based system, with the data extraction functionality executed in a central location. As the number of users (especially remote users) grows, the system may become overloaded with requests.

- *Network performance issues.* Data Extractor server works as an intermediary between data consumer and the Web site that is a source of data. This means that after it is extracted from the Web site, data always has to go through server first instead of coming directly to consumer. In addition to being a longer delivery route this can present problems if Data Extractor server is located in a low-bandwidth or highly-congested network segment.

- *Legal issues.* In rare cases Data Extractor server maintainers may be prevented by law from extracting data from certain sites on behalf of the client, as such extraction may constitute a copyright violation. In these same cases giving user ability to extract data directly, without the services of a middleman, may be legal.

Installing local server for exclusive use of a small number of clients may be one solution for these problems, but costs and complexity associated with such an operation could be high. In this work we are defining an alternative - performing data extraction on the client side through *Mobile Data Retrieval Agents (MDRA).*

2 Architecture

The idea of MDRA is in distributing the data extraction functionality to the client computer, close to consumer of extracted data. MDRA approach is different from shipping the complete data extraction functionality

276

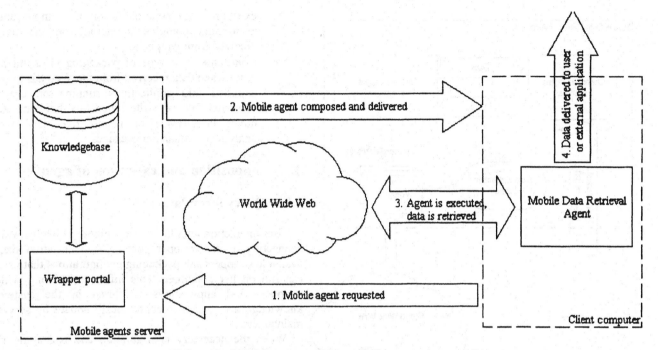

Figure 1   MDRA composition, delivery and execution

to the client side, because agent composition and maintenance mechanisms remain on the server and are managed centrally.

The server, called *mobile agents server,* hosts *wrapper portal* and a *knowledgebase* (see Figure 1). *Wrapper portal* is a Web-based catalog that allows users to select and execute wrappers. Users who subscribe to the MDRA service connect to wrapper portal and request wrapper or application to be executed on the client computer. In response to that request a package containing functionality necessary to perform data extraction for a particular Web source is constructed and shipped to the client computer. It will then be executed there and extract data for the user. Aside from listing and packaging wrappers, portal authenticates users, allows them to change and save their preferences, and save and retrieve previously created *queries* (references to wrappers together with wrapper parameters).

Knowledgebase used in MDRA server system contains information about available wrappers, their parameters and status. It may also contain information required by the wrapper portal. For example, it could store user account information, such as access privileges and preferences. Names and execution parameters of wrappers that users have run so far can also be stored in this database. Using this information, wrappers can be executed with the same settings on a regular basis. Finally, lightweight applications that use wrapper output or act as intermediaries between wrapper and applications on client

computers can be stored in the knowledgebase, together with necessary composition and parameter information.

Architecture of agents generated and packaged by mobile agents server is based on the architecture of Data Extractor system. The internal structure of a Mobile Data Retrieval Agent is shown in Figure 2. It consists of the following components:

- *Mobile wrapper controller.* Wrapper controller is responsible for controlling the behavior of wrappers, passing parameters to them and directing the flow of data from them. In this sense it is very similar to wrapper controller used in Data Extractor system, but, perhaps, optimized for shipment to client computer and execution there.

- *Wrappers.* The same wrappers are used in the Data Extractor and MDRA implementations. They will be created and stored on the server and managed centrally for all users of MDRA service. This significantly simplifies service maintenance, ensures correct operation and makes timely updates available to all users of the system.

- *Data Extraction Library.* Data Extraction Library contains functionality that is essential for performing data extraction and networking operations and has to be shipped with every MDRA. Our implementation of it is very compact and will be transmitted to the client computer quickly even on slow links.

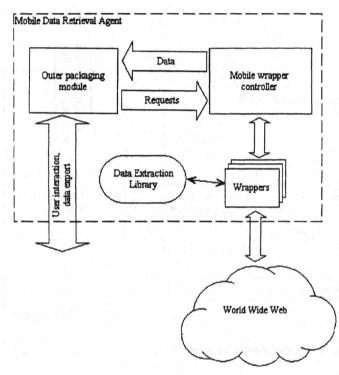

**Figure 2   Architecture of Mobile Data
Retrieval Agent**

- *Outer packaging.* Outer packaging component is a module that unites all other modules in the MDRA. It can be implemented as a Java applet, an application, a browser plugin or take some other form. The job of this component is to communicate user commands to the wrapper controller and receive results generated by the wrapper.

    Packaging component can be implemented to take on one of the following functions:

    ◆ *Browser.* Browser works as a flexible display tool. It displays data that it receives in tabular form, akin to a mini-spreadsheet. Columns can be adjusted, collapsed and sorted. Data can be edited, searched, copied, printed and exported. This mode is useful for browsing and modifying data generated by the wrapper.

    ◆ *Exporter.* This type of packaging is useful for non-interactive mode of operation. It can be configured to automatically generate on user's computer a data file that will contain data output by the wrapper. Data files can be in a variety of formats – plain ASCII, Comma Separated Values, Microsoft Excel, XML and others.

    ◆ *Wrapper-based application.* Lightweight applications can be developed to perform simple operations on data generated by wrappers. Such applications can work interactively with user,

executing wrappers based on user input and performing complex operations on the data received from wrappers.

◆ *Connector.* This type of packaging is useful in cases when data received from the Web has to be exported into applications running on user's computer. We can write connectors that populate tables in DBMSs or import live data into analytical or financial packages.

3   Composition and execution of agents

3.1   Query formulation

User interaction with the system (Figure 1) begins with connecting to the wrapper portal. Wrapper portal lists available wrappers and packaging configurations that user can run on her computer. This information along with wrappers and applications is stored in the system knowledgebase, which is continuously update by server maintainers.

When the necessary configuration and packaging is selected, user optionally can specify execution parameters and save this configuration for future reference. In some cases additional information may be required from user. This information may include usernames, passwords or credit card information for wrappers that access pay-per-use sites. After all necessary information has been collected from the user, she may ask the system to build, deliver and execute the agent.

3.2   Agent construction and delivery

Once the wrapper portal receives the request for an agent it begins packaging it. Several components, including outer packaging module, wrapper parameter information, wrapper controller, wrapper, and Data Extraction Library can be combined in a single package for delivery to client computer. Optionally, components that change frequently (such as wrappers and their parameters) can be packaged separately from the ones that do not change often. With separate packaging the part that does not change may be cached on the client computer. Depending on particular implementation, the package can be compressed and/or digitally signed. When packaging components, special attention must be paid to keeping agent as compact and platform-independent as possible. Once the package is ready for delivery it is sent to the user computer.

3.3   Agent execution

When the agent is delivered to the client computer it is executed based on parameters supplied to it. Parameters can be specified at the portal or through dialogue with the

278

user. Outer packaging component handles the dialogue with the user and controls wrapper execution through commands to wrapper controller. Wrappers interact with the Web sites, extract data and pass it to the outer packaging component module through the controller. Overall agent execution, including stopping and restarting, is controlled through its user interface.

3.4 Data delivery

When the data is retrieved from the Web it can be returned in several forms: it can be fed into other applications, displayed to the user or exported to the file system.

4 Implementation

The prototype of the MDRA system is currently being implemented in Java programming language. Java was chosen for a variety of reasons. Because the mobile agents are based on existing implementation of Data Extractor and Data Extraction Library, which are implemented in Java, compatibility was important, as was reuse of the existing modules. Portability was also an important consideration because MDRA code is shipped to the client side and executed there, and thus has to be supported with no or little modifications on a variety of platforms.

There are, of course, concerns about Java performance, as it is slower than its compiled counterparts, such as C++. Some of the performance problems did indeed manifest themselves at the early stages of implementation of Data Extractor system and Data Extraction Library functionality. These problems primarily appeared when the load on the Data Extractor system increased dramatically because of multiple connected clients. Most of these problems were identified and resolved following techniques described in [6]. In MDRA framework agent execution will be dedicated to a single client and as a result we do not expect any noticeable performance degradation.

4.1 Framework

For MDRA technology to be easy to use it has to be user-friendly. This starts with installation procedures. For the majority of computer users downloading software from the Web site and installing it on their computer is unattractive. There are many reasons for that: the process of software downloading and installation is often inconvenient and confusing; user may be afraid of viruses or have insufficient permissions to install software on her computer.

One of the easiest ways to ship MDRA functionality to the user's computer and execute it there is through a Java applet. Because it starts automatically and integrates with browsers well, even inexperienced users will be able to use it. When user requests the agent the browser will receive a Java applet packaged with all the necessary system components and libraries. The applet will then execute in browser context, querying the Web and supplying data to the user.

Other options for packaging MDRA technology may include ActiveX controls, Netscape plugins, and, in absence of alternatives, downloadable applications. These options, however, are associated with a set of problems, such as limited portability, size, access restrictions and others.

4.2 Performance

In preliminary tests MDRA agents have shown better performance compared to that of Data Extractor implementation, which was expected as the data extraction is done at client site without unnecessary trips to server and server is no longer the performance and bandwidth bottleneck. On average, the time it took to package an agent and extract data from Web pages was negligible in comparison to the time it took to download pages from Web sites. Download times varied significantly depending on the type of link the client computer had, the saturation of the network segment in which it was located, and the responsiveness of the Web site being queried for data.

4.3 Security

One of the strengths of Java applets—security— becomes a challenge in the context of mobile agents. Browsers prohibit Java applets from accessing system on user computer in order to prevent attacks from maliciously written applets.

MDRA, however, need to access system resources and perform other actions that applets are normally prohibited from doing. These actions include accessing network resources (to extract data) and file system and system resources (to save data on the system or feed it into other applications on the system).

A partial solution to this problem is to create a proxy application on the server where the applet came from (applets are allowed to communicate with the home server). Through such proxy (whose role can be played by a standard HTTP proxy server) the applet would be able to download pages from the third party Web sites. This approach, however, does not solve the problem of data export—applet will still be prohibited from exporting the data that it extracts to anywhere on the user's computer. Also, the proxy application will become a bottleneck that will affect system performance in high-volume data extraction applications.

Another solution—*applet signing*—appears to be more feasible. Applet signing allows developer to "sign" the applet with a digital certificate purchased from a certification authority. Signed applets are allowed certain degree of freedom inside the browser. Users can grant them permission to access network resources or the file system. To take advantage of this functionality applet that contains MDRA will be signed before delivery to the client computer, and the code that requests permissions from browser will be inserted in applet initialization routines.

5   Related work

The idea of employing agents for data extraction has been discussed by numerous researchers ([4], [2], [1], [5]). A system similar to MDRA is described in [4]. The mobile agents' framework discussed there uses an approach different from MDRA - it introduces a cooperating set of agents that browse information servers and execute short queries to sites. In MDRA agents do not cooperate but the emphasis is placed on accuracy of extracted information and performance while serving needs of a single user, which we feel is only achievable through use of custom-crafted agents. MDRA also solves a wider variety of problems, allowing us to build Web data-aware applications and extract high volumes of data in a variety of formats.

Mechanisms for performing data extraction at the client site can also be found in business applications, such as downloadable personal shopping bots from GoTo Shopping (http://shop.goto.com/) and R U Sure (http://www.rusure.com). User downloads and installs an application associated with one of these services on her computer and then can use it to perform price comparison for a variety of products by querying Web sites in real time. Up-to-date instructions on how to get prices from a variety of online stores are periodically comparison downloaded by the shopping application from the central location. Technologies used in these services are proprietary and cannot be evaluated to discuss their merits and disadvantages. MDRA is an open platform that is not geared only towards comparison but will support any application that requires data extraction from the Web.

6   Conclusion

We have presented a Mobile Data Retrieval Agents framework, which is an application of Data Extractor Web data retrieval technology. MDRA "lease" data extraction services to users. Using it users modify, download and execute queries to Web sites, and receive extracted datasets. The extracted data can then be imported into other applications and further analyzed and processed. Mobile agents significantly increase performance of the Web data extraction mechanism by moving it off the centralized server and to client site. This distributed approach allows us to free-up server resources and increase overall system performance.

As part of our future research effort we intend to experiment with different implementations of MDRA, both standalone and embedded inside client-side applications. We will also work on improving the performance of client-side agent execution.

7   Acknowledgements

This research was supported in part by NASA (under grants NAG5-9478, NAGW-4080, NAG5-5095, NAS5-97222, and NAG5-6830), NSF (CDA-9711582, IRI-9409661, HRD-9707076, and ANI-9876409), ONR (N00014-99-1-0952), the Department of Interior, and the FSGC.

8   References

[1]   Bauer, M. and Dengler, D.   TrIAs: trainable information assistants for cooperative problem solving. *Proceedings of the 3rd Annual Conference on Autonomous Agents*, 1999, Pages 260 - 267

[2]   Bauer, M., Dengler, D. and Paul, G.   Instructible information agents for Web mining. *Proceedings of the 2000 International Conference on Intelligent User Interfaces*, 2000, Pages 21 - 28

[3]   Beryoza, D., Rishe, N., Graham, S., De Felipe, I. Data Extractor Wrapper System. *Proceedings of the 6th World Multiconference on Systemics, Cybernetics and Informatics*, 2002, Vol. VII, Pages 425-431

[4]   Dharap, C. and Freeman, M.   Information agents for automated browsing. *Proceedings of the 5th International Conference on Information and Knowledge Management*, 1996, Pages 296 - 305

[5]   Frank, M., Szekely, P.   Collapsible user interfaces for information retrieval agents. *Proceedings of the 1999 International Conference on Intelligent User Interfaces*, 1999, Pages 15 - 22

[6]   Heydon, A., and Najork, M.   Performance Limitations of the Java Core Libraries. In *Proceedings of the 1999 ACM Java Grande Conference*, pages 35-41, June, 1999.

[7]   Rishe, N., Athauda, R., Yuan, J. and Chen, S.C. Knowledge Management for Database Interoperability. *International Conference on Information Reuse and Integration*, Honolulu, Hawaii, November 1 - 3, 2000.

[8]   Rishe, N., Yuan, J., Athauda, R., Lu, X., Ma, X., Vaschillo, A., Shaposhnikov, A., Vasilevsky, D. and Chen, S.C. SemanticAccess: Semantic Interface for Querying Databases. *The International Conference on Very Large Data Bases (VLDB 2000)*, September 10-14, 2000.

Incremental Maintenance of Object-Oriented Views in Data Warehouses

Ching-Ming Chao
Department of Computer and Information Science,
Soochow University,
Taipei, Taiwan
chao@cis.scu.edu.tw

Abstract

Object-oriented data warehouses store integrated information as object-oriented materialized views and are well suited for integrating data from modern heterogeneous data sources. Previous work on incremental maintenance of materialized views in data warehouses is confined to the relational setting. Although recently incremental maintenance of object-oriented views has been investigated, the proposed view maintenance algorithms do not work in a warehousing environment. In this paper, we study incremental maintenance of object-oriented views in data warehouses. In particular, we focus on two primary issues. First, we identify which kinds of updates to which classes may cause changes to an object-oriented view. Then, we propose an algorithm that can incrementally maintain an object-oriented view derived from multiple distributed data sources. A prototype system has been implemented and the result of a preliminary performance evaluation shows that our incremental view maintenance algorithm is correct and efficient.

1. Introduction

Data warehousing is an approach to data integration in which integrated information is stored in a *data warehouse* for direct querying and analysis. The data warehouse defines and stores *materialized views* over data from multiple distributed, autonomous, and possibly heterogeneous data sources. *Object-oriented data warehouses* store integrated information as object-oriented materialized views and are well suited for integrating data from modern heterogeneous data sources [4].

Maintaining data consistency between a materialized view and its source data is an important issue in data warehousing. To maintain a materialized view, one has a choice between recomputing the view from scratch and maintaining the view incrementally. *Incremental view maintenance* is generally less expensive when the size of updates to the source data is small compared to the size of the source data. However, it is more difficult.

Previous work on incremental maintenance of materialized views in data warehouses is confined to the relational setting, e.g., [1,5,6]. Because object-oriented databases have many unique features that are absent from relational databases, such as object identity, complex attributes, inter-object reference, class inheritance, etc., existing approaches to incremental maintenance of relational views cannot be directly used to maintain object-oriented views. Although recently incremental maintenance of object-oriented views has been investigated, e.g., [2,3], the proposed view maintenance algorithms do not work in a data-warehousing environment.

In this paper, we study incremental maintenance of object-oriented views in a data warehouse with multiple distributed data sources. In particular, we focus on two primary issues. The first issue is to identify during view compilation time which kinds of updates to which classes may cause changes to an object-oriented view. Such updates are called the *potential updates* to the view. We identify six categories of potential updates to an object-oriented view. The second issue is to maintain an object-oriented view in response to its potential updates. We propose an algorithm that can incrementally maintain an object-oriented view derived from multiple distributed data sources. We have implemented a prototype system for incremental maintenance of object-oriented data warehouses and conducted a preliminary performance evaluation. The result shows that our incremental view maintenance algorithm is correct and efficient.

The rest of this paper is organized as follows. Section 2 describes some background. Section 3 identifies the potential updates to an object-oriented view. Section 4 presents our incremental view maintenance algorithm. Section 5 shows some results of our preliminary performance evaluation. Section 6 concludes this paper.

2. Background

We assume that materialized views of the data warehouse are defined over object-oriented classes. In case that some data sources are not object-oriented databases, the wrapper can be used to perform the transformation. A simplified university data warehouse will be used as the running example throughout this paper. The data warehouse derives data from two data sources, source X and source Y. Figure 1 shows the definition of base classes in which the classes Staff and Department are stored in source Y and the other classes are stored in source X.

```
class Person
{Name: string, Age: integer, Children: set (Person)};
class Student inherits Person
{Major: Department, Year: integer, Courses: set (Course)};
class Staff inherits Person
{Dept: Department, Salary: integer};
class Graduate inherits Student
{Advisor: Staff, Thesis: string};
class Course
{Name: string, Code: string, Credit: integer};
class Department
{Name: string, Head: Staff};
```

Figure 1: Definition of base classes

We study the maintenance of object-oriented views that are defined over one or more classes and whose definition allows path expressions to appear in the SELECT and WHERE clauses. Figure 2 shows the definition of two materialized views in the data warehouse.

```
view    V1 (SN: string, CN: set (string), HN: string,
        HA: integer)
select  Student.Name, Student.Courses.Name,
        Student.Major.Head.Name,
        Student.Major.Head.Age
from    Student
where   Student.Year = 4
and     "BCC" in Student.Courses.Name ;
view    V2 (SN: string, FN: string)
select  Student.Name, Staff.Name
from    Student, Staff
where   Student.Major = Staff.Dept ;
```

Figure 2: Definition of materialized views

3. Potential Updates

Identifying the potential updates to a view is necessary for view maintenance, because one has to know which updates to which classes may cause changes to a view to be able to maintain the view. To improve maintenance efficiency, we identify the potential updates to a view during view compilation time instead of run time.

For the purpose of identifying potential updates, we distinguish four roles that a class may play for a view. A class is a *defining class* of a view if the class appears in the FROM clause of the view definition. For example, Student is the only defining class of the view V1. A class is a *referenced class* of a view if the class is referenced from a defining class within some path expression of the view definition. For example, Course, Department, and Staff are the referenced classes of V1. A class is an *inheriting class* of a view if the class directly or indirectly inherits a defining or referenced class of the view. For

example, Graduate is an inheriting class of V1. A class is an *irrelevant class* of a view if the class does not play any of the three previous roles for the view. For example, Person is an irrelevant class of V1.

Updates to an irrelevant class of a view cannot cause any change to the view. To demonstrate this argument, we enumerate various situations in which a class is regarded as an irrelevant class of a view. First, a class that is inherited by a defining or referenced class of a view is an irrelevant class of the view. For example, Person is inherited by Student (a defining class) and Staff (a referenced class), and therefore is an irrelevant class of V1. Updates to objects of Person that are not also objects of any of its subclasses cannot cause any change to V1. Second, a class that is referenced by a defining class in the class composition hierarchy but not within any path expression of a view is an irrelevant class of the view. For example, Person is referenced by Student in the class composition hierarchy but not within any path expression of V1 and is therefore an irrelevant class of V1. Finally, a class that is not related in any way to a view is an irrelevant class of the view. Updates to such kind of classes obviously cannot cause any change to the view.

Updates to a defining, referenced, or inheriting class of a view may cause changes to the view, but only for certain kinds of updates. Again for the purpose of identifying potential updates, we distinguish five kinds of updates to a class: insertion, deletion, modification of SELECT attributes (i.e., attributes that appear only in the SELECT clause of the view), modification of WHERE attributes (i.e., attributes that appear in the WHERE clause of the view), and modification of other attributes (i.e., attributes that do not appear in the definition of the view). We will discuss the effects of these five kinds of updates to those three kinds of classes on a view in turn.

First, we discuss the effects of updates to a defining class on a view. Inserting an object to a defining class will cause insertion of one or more objects to a view if the WHERE condition evaluates to true on the inserted object. For example, inserting an object to Student will cause insertion of an object to V1 if the inserted Student object makes the WHERE condition of V1 evaluate to true. Deleting an object from a defining class will cause all objects derived from the deleted object, if any, to be deleted from a view. For example, deleting a Student object will cause all objects derived from the deleted Student object, if any, to be deleted from V2. Modifying a SELECT attribute of an object of a defining class will cause one or more attributes of all objects of a view that are derived from the modified object to be modified. For example, modifying the attribute Major of a Student object will cause the attributes HN and HA of the V1 object derived from the modified Student object to be modified. Modifying a WHERE attribute of an object of a defining class may cause insertion to, deletion from, or modification of a view. For example, changing the value of the attribute Year of a Student object from 3 to 4 may cause an object to be inserted to V1. Modifying other attributes of a defining class cannot cause any change to a view.

282

Then we discuss the effects of updates to a referenced class on a view. Inserting an object to a referenced class may cause modification of the defining class of the referenced class but does not by itself cause any change to a view. The same applies to deleting an object from a referenced class. Therefore, we do not consider the insertion to and deletion from a referenced class as the potential updates to a view. Modifying a SELECT attribute of an object of a referenced class will cause one or more attributes of all objects of a view that are derived from the objects of the defining class that reference the modified object to be modified. For example, modifying the attribute Head of a Department object will cause the attributes HN and HA of V1 objects derived from Student objects that reference the modified Department object to be modified. Modifying a WHERE attribute of an object of a referenced class may cause insertion to, deletion from, or modification of a view. For example, changing the value of the attribute Name of a Course object from "BCC" to "IIT" may cause objects to be deleted from V1. Modifying other attributes of a referenced class cannot cause any change to a view.

Finally, we discuss the effects of updates to an inheriting class on a view. The effect of updating an inheriting class on a view is the same as that of updating the defining or referenced class that is inherited by the inheriting class, because an object of an inheriting class is also an object of the inherited class. For example, inserting an object to the class Graduate produces the same result to V1 as inserting an object to the class Student.

In summary, we identify the following six categories of potential updates to an object-oriented view.

1. **Ins**: Insertion to a defining class or an inheriting class that inherits a defining class
2. **Del**: Deletion from a defining class or an inheriting class that inherits a defining class
3. **MDS**: Modification of SELECT attributes of a defining class or an inheriting class that inherits a defining class
4. **MDW**: Modification of WHERE attributes of a defining class or an inheriting class that inherits a defining class
5. **MRS**: Modification of SELECT attributes of a referenced class or an inheriting class that inherits a referenced class
6. **MRW**: Modification of WHERE attributes of a reference class or an inheriting class that inherits a referenced class

For example, the six categories of potential updates to the view V1 are listed below.

1. **Ins** Student   **Ins** Graduate
2. **Del** Student   **Del** Graduate
3. **MDS** Student.Name   **MDS** Student.Major
       MDS Graduate.Name   **MDS** Graduate.Major
4. **MDW** Student.Year   **MDW** Student.Courses
       MDW Graduate.Year   **MDW** Gradate.Courses
5. **MRS** Department.Head
       MRS Staff.Name   **MRS** Staff.Age
6. **MRW** Course.Name

4. View Maintenance Algorithm

In this section, we present an algorithm that can incrementally maintain an object-oriented view derived from multiple distributed data sources. Our algorithm adopts the *immediate update* mode, in which a view is maintained immediately after each update to its source data. With regard to the correctness of a view maintenance algorithm, [6] defined four levels of consistency for warehouse views. Our algorithm achieves *strong consistency*, in which each warehouse state reflects a set of valid source states and the order of the warehouse states matches the order of the source actions.

Our algorithm has several salient features that can improve maintenance efficiency. First, only the potential updates to a view can cause the algorithm to compute the change to the view. This avoids a waste of resources on updates that cannot affect any view. Second, a source modification that only causes modification of a view rather than insertion to or deletion from a view is treated directly. In contrast, most of the previous algorithms treat such a modification as a deletion followed by an insertion. Finally, our algorithm uses two *auxiliary views* to assist in the maintenance of a warehouse view, which can avoid access to source data as much as possible.

As a materialized view V is defined in the data warehouse, two auxiliary views AV1_for_V and AV2_for_V are also defined there. AV1_for_V is materialized but AV2_for_V is not materialized. AV1_for_V has attributes for the OID of objects in the defining classes of V that derive an object of V as well as an attribute for the OID of that object of V. AV2_for_V is almost identical to V except that it includes additional attributes for the OID of objects that derive an object of V, if V does not have those attributes. For example, the definition of auxiliary views for V2 is shown in Figure 3. AV1_for_V is used to find the objects of V and AV1_for_V that are to be deleted or the objects of V that are to be modified without access to source data. AV2_for_V is used to compute the objects to be inserted to V and AV1_for_V.

view	*AV1_for_V2 (SO: Student, FO: Staff, VO: V2)*
select	*Student, Staff, V2*
from	*Student, Staff, V2*
where	*Student.Major = Staff.Dept*
and	*V2.SN = Student.Name*
and	*V2.FN = Staff.Name ;*
view	*AV2_for_V2 (SO: Student, FO: Staff, SN: string, FN: string)*
select	*Student, Staff,* Student.Name, Staff.Name
from	Student, Staff
where	Student.Major = Staff.Dept ;

Figure 3: Definition of auxiliary views for V2

To simplify the presentation, we describe a partial version of our algorithm that handles the first three categories of potential updates. Actually, the complete algorithm can handle all six categories of potential updates. Expanding the partial algorithm to the complete algorithm is straightforward. The fourth category of potential updates is handled by treating it as a deletion followed by an insertion. The fifth and sixth categories of potential updates are handled similarly to the third and fourth categories of potential updates, respectively, with some extension. Figure 4 shows the partial algorithm.

Algorithm Incremental View Maintenance

At each data source:
> Upon detection of an update U, send U to the warehouse.
> Upon receipt of a query Q, evaluate Q in terms of the current source state and send the result to the warehouse.

At the date warehouse:
> Initialize WV and WAV1 with the current state of V and AV1, respectively.
> Upon receipt of an update U_i that is a potential update to V:
  ① If U_i is insert (C_i, ΔC_i)
   → Set PU (U_i) = $\varnothing$;
   → *Source_evaluate* (AV2 [ΔC_i]);
   → Upon completion of evaluating ΔV and $\Delta AV1$, $\forall U_j \in$ PU (U_i),
    ❶ If U_j is delete (C_j, ∇C_j)
     ⇒ Find $\nabla \Delta V$ and $\nabla \Delta AV1$ by searching ∇C_j in $\Delta AV1$;
     ⇒ Execute delete (ΔV, $\nabla \Delta V$) and delete ($\Delta AV1$, $\nabla \Delta AV1$);
    ❷ If U_j is modify (C_j, $\Diamond C_j$, MA (C_j))
     ⇒ Find $\Diamond \Delta V$ by searching $\Diamond C_j$ in $\Delta AV1$;
     ⇒ Determine the affected attributes in ΔV, AA (ΔV), from MA (C_j);
     ⇒ Compute the new value of AA (ΔV) possibly by querying data sources;
     ⇒ Execute modify (ΔV, $\Diamond \Delta V$, AA (ΔV));
   → Execute insert (WV, ΔV) and insert (WAV1, $\Delta AV1$) without inserting duplicate objects;
  ② If U_i is delete (C_i, ∇C_i)
   → $\forall U_k \in$ UUS and U_k is an insertion, add U_i to PU (U_k);
   → Find ∇V and $\nabla AV1$ by searching ∇C_i in WAV1;
   → Execute delete (WV, ∇V) and delete (WAV1, $\nabla AV1$);
  ③ If U_i is modify (C_i, $\Diamond C_i$, MA (C_i))
   → $\forall U_k \in$ UUS and U_k is an insertion, add U_i to PU (U_k);
   → Find $\Diamond V$ by searching $\Diamond C_i$ in WAV1;
   → Determine the affected attributes in V, AA (V), from MA (C_i);
   → Compute the new value of AA (V) possibly by querying data sources;
   → Execute modify (WV, $\Diamond V$, AA (V));
> When UUS = $\varnothing$, replace V and AV1 with WV and WAV1, respectively.

Figure 4: View maintenance algorithm (partial)

First, we define the notations used in the algorithm. V is the view to be maintained. AV1 and AV2 are the auxiliary views of V. WV and WAV1 are the working copies of V and AV1, respectively. If C denotes a base class, the notations ΔC, ∇C, and $\Diamond C$ denote the objects inserted to C, deleted from C, and modified in C, respectively. If C denotes a materialized view, the notations ΔC, ∇C, and $\Diamond C$ denote the objects to be inserted to C, deleted from C, and modified in C, respectively. Let C be a base class or a materialized view. The notation insert (C, ΔC) denotes an update that inserts objects ΔC to C. The notation delete (C, ∇C) denotes an update that deletes objects ∇C from C. The notation modify (C, $\Diamond C$, A) denotes an up-

date that modifies attributes A of objects $\Diamond C$ in C.

UUS is the *unfinished update set*, which contains source updates that have been received at the data warehouse but their effects on V have not been incorporated into WV. Let U be an insertion, PU (U) denotes the set of *pending updates* of U, which contains source updates that are received at the data warehouse while U is still in UUS. PU (U) contains only deletions and modifications, but not insertions. AV2 [ΔC_i] denotes the view defining expression of AV2 in which C_i is replaced with ΔC_i. *Source_evaluate* (AV2 [ΔC_i]) denotes the evaluation of the query AV2 [ΔC_i]. It first checks if the query can be answered with only data available at the data warehouse. If not, it sends queries to data sources to compute the result of the query AV2 [ΔC_i]. After the query AV2 [ΔC_i] is evaluated, ΔV and $\Delta AV1$ can be computed.

Now we explain how the algorithm works. Upon detection of a source update, a data source sends the update to the data warehouse. Upon receipt of a query from the data warehouse, a data source evaluates the query in terms of its current state and sends the result of the query to the data warehouse. Initially, WV and WAV1 have the same value as V and AV1, respectively. Upon receipt of a source update U that is a potential update to V, the data warehouse computes the changes to V and AV1 caused by U. These changes are not applied to V and AV1 immediately; instead, they are applied to WV and WAV1. This prevents V and AV1 from being in an inconsistent state. The data warehouse updates V and AV1 by assigning the value of WV and WAV1 to A and AV1, respectively, only when it is assured that doing so will bring V and AV1 to a consistent state. This occurs when UUS is empty; that is, when the effect of every received update on V has been computed and applied to WV.

When a deletion (the second category of potential update) or a modification (the third category of potential update) is received, the data warehouse finds the objects to be deleted from V or modified in V locally without querying data sources. When an insertion (the first category of potential update) is received, the data warehouse generates a query AV2 [ΔC_i] to compute the objects to be inserted to V, ΔV, and the objects to be inserted to AV1, $\Delta AV1$. To evaluate the query, the data warehouse may need to query data sources. While the query is being evaluated by data sources, concurrent updates may occur at data sources. This causes two problems. The first problem is that applying ΔV and $\Delta AV1$ to V and AV1, respectively, may bring V and AV1 to an inconsistent state. This problem can be solved by the mechanism involving WV, WAV1, and UUS, as described in the previous paragraph. In addition, duplicate objects must not be inserted while inserting ΔV and $\Delta AV1$ to WV and WAV1, respectively. The second problem is that the processing of concurrent deletions or modifications at the data warehouse may miss those objects returned by the query. To remedy the problem, the data warehouse keeps a set PU (U) of deletions or modifications for each insertion U. As a deletion or modification is received at the data warehouse, it is added to PU (U) for each insertion U that is in UUS. After ΔV and ΔAV1 have been computed with AV2 [ΔC$_i$] for an insertion U, each deletion or modification in PU (U) is processed again to delete or modify objects of ΔV and ΔAV1 that were missed. Then the updated ΔV and ΔAV1 are inserted to WV and WAV1, respectively.

Example: Maintain V2 in response to three updates
Assume initially there are five objects in the class Student whose attribute Major has the value "CS" and two objects in the class Staff whose attribute Dept has the value "CS". Two updates U1 and U2 occur at source X. One update U3 occurs at source Y. U1 inserts an object whose attribute Major has the value "CS" to the class Student. U2 deletes the object inserted by U1. U3 inserts an object whose attribute Dept has the value "CS" to the class Staff. Using our algorithm, the following events for maintaining V2 may occur at the data warehouse.

1. The warehouse receives U1 from source X, initializes PU (U1) to be empty, and sends a query Q1 to source Y to compute the changes to V2 and AV1_for_V2 caused by U1.
2. The warehouse receives U2 from source X and adds U2 to PU (U1). Because the answer of Q1 has not been returned, nothing is deleted from both WV2 and WAV1_for_V2 in response to U2.
3. The warehouse receives U3 from source Y and sends a query Q3 to source X to compute the changes to V2 and AV1_for_V2 caused by U3.
4. The warehouse receives the answer of Q1 from source Y with three objects in both ΔV2 and ΔAV1_for_V2. Because U2 is in PU (U1), the processing of U2 causes both ΔV2 and ΔAV1_for_V2 to become empty; therefore, nothing is inserted to both WV2 and WAV1_for_V2.
5. The warehouse receives the answer of Q3 from source X and inserts five objects to both WV2 and WAV1_for_V2.
6. Because UUS is now empty, the warehouse replaces V2 and AV1_for_V2 with WV2 and WAV1_for_V2, respectively. The state of V2 is consistent with the source state after U1, U2, and U3 have occurred.

5. Performance Evaluation

We have implemented a prototype system and conducted a preliminary performance evaluation. Figure 5 compares the execution time between incremental maintenance (IM) and recomputation (RC) of V1 in response to 10 consecutive updates of various kinds to Student. Figure 6 compares the execution time between IM and RC of V2 in response to 10 consecutive updates of various kinds to Staff. The size of the database is varied but only the number of objects in Student is shown in figures. Our experiments show that our incremental maintenance algorithm is more time efficient than recomputation.

6. Conclusion

In this paper, we addressed two primary issues on incremental maintenance of object-oriented views in data warehouses. First, we identified six categories of potential updates to an object-oriented view. Second, we proposed an algorithm that can incrementally maintain an object-oriented view derived from multiple distributed data sources. Our empirical study showed that our view maintenance algorithm is correct and efficient.

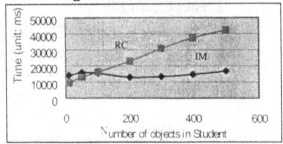

Figure 5: Execution time for maintaining V1

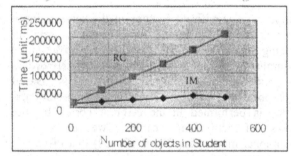

Figure 6: Execution time for maintaining V2

References

[1] Agrawal, D., A. El Abbadi, A. Singh, and T. Yurek, "Efficient View Maintenance at Data Warehouses", In *Proceedings of the 1997 ACM SIGMOD International Conference on Management of Data*, Tucson, Arizona, USA, May 1997, pp. 417-427.

[2] Alhajj, R. and F. Polat, "Incremental View Maintenance in Object-Oriented Databases", *ACM Data Base for Advances in Information Systems*, 39(3), 1998, pp. 52-64.

[3] Ali, M.A., A.A.A. Fernandes, and N.W. Paton, "Incremental Maintenance of Materialized OQL Views", In *Proceedings of 3rd ACM International Workshop on Data Warehousing and OLAP*, Washington D.C., USA, November 2000.

[4] Thomann, J. and D. Wells, "Real World Objects in the Data Warehouse: the Vision", *Journal of Data Warehousing*, 2(2), 1997, pp. 62-65.

[5] Zhuge, Y., H. Garcia-Molina, J. Hammer, and J. Widom, "View Maintenance in a Warehousing Environment", In *Proceedings of the 1995 ACM SIGMOD International Conference on Management of Data*, San Jose, CA, USA, May 1995, pp. 316-327.

[6] Zhuge, Y., H. Garcia-Molina, and J.L. Wiener, "The Strobe Algorithms for Multi-Source Warehouse Consistency", In *Proceedings of the International Conference on Parallel and Distributed Information Systems*, Miami Beach, FL, USA, December 1996, pp. 146-157.

Cortex-Based Mechanism For Discovery of High-Order Features

Olcay Kursun
kursun@cs.ucf.edu

Oleg Favorov
favorov@cs.ucf.edu

School of Electrical Engineering and Computer Science
University of Central Florida
Orlando, FL 32816, USA

Abstract

Recognition of significant features in the sensory input patterns is one of the brain's fundamental information processing tasks. This is a challenging task, since behaviorally significant environmental features are orders of complexity removed from raw sensory inputs. Based on a proposal that learning of significant environmental variables is performed in the cerebral cortex by the dendrites of individual neurons, we describe a computational mechanism (SINBAD cell) that discovers orderly features through a search for different, but nevertheless highly correlated functions over non-overlapping subsets of the available environmental variables. Organized into series of cortex-like layers, such SINBAD cells ought to be able to discover complex orderly features present in the input patterns.

1. Introduction

One of the brain's most remarkable properties is its ability to recognize perceptually and behaviorally significant features of various degrees of complexity in the patterns of its sensory inputs. Based on an idea of Becker and Hinton [1], Ryder and Favorov [6] suggested a basic computational strategy (SINBAD) that might be used by the cerebral cortex in its learning of high-order features characterizing the inhabited environment.

To put the SINBAD idea to practical use, a number of implementation issues will have to be resolved. In this paper we briefly describe the SINBAD idea, review the general design of the SINBAD network, identify the most important unresolved issues and offer their solution. We demonstrate this solution by applying the updated SINBAD design to a task of discovering orderly features in natural images.

2. Sinbad Approach

According to Ryder and Favorov [6], the environmental features recognized by the cerebral cortex are those environmental variables that factor in regularities that obtain in the environment. Such significant environmental variables can be discovered through a search for different, but nevertheless highly correlated functions of any kind over non-overlapping subsets of the known environmental variables. Such *correlated functions* must have a reason for their statistical interdependence, a causal source in the environment, and therefore these functions identify this source. That is, the correlated functions over different sets of environmental variables express a hidden environmental variable (a previously unrecognized *feature* of the environment) that is responsible for the correlation [1, 3, 4, 6].

Such newly discovered variables are very likely to have other effects in the environment, besides the ones that led to their recognition. And once they are recognized, it will become easier to notice their other effects. Furthermore, once a number of hidden variables are discovered, correlated functions can be searched for among *them*, thus discovering higher-order hidden variables, etc.

3. Sinbad Neuron

Favorov and Ryder [3, 6] proposed that the search for significant environmental variables is performed in the cerebral cortex by the dendritic trees of individual pyramidal cells (the main type of neurons there). According to the SINBAD model, the basic function of each pyramidal cell is (1) to discover and represent one of the hidden environmental variables, and (2) to learn to infer the state of its variable from the states of other variables, represented by other pyramidal cells. A network of such cells – each cell just attending to representation of its variable – can function as a sophisticated and useful inferential model of the outside world [3].

In the SINBAD model of pyramidal cells, several dendrites of a cell teach each other to produce correlated outputs to their different inputs. As a result, the cell as a whole tunes to the environmental variable that is responsible for correlation. Since each dendrite should be capable of learning functions over its inputs that are likely to be nonlinear, dendrites are viewed as functional analogs of error backpropagation networks [5], and a pyramidal cell is modeled as a set of two (or more) backprop nets whose outputs are added together to produce the cell's output (Figure 1). The cell's output is also used as the training signal for each dendrite.

The activity of a hidden unit h in dendrite d is computed as a sigmoid function of the activities of its input sources:

$$H_{d,h} = \tanh(\sum_i w_{d,i,h} \cdot A_{d,i}), \qquad (1)$$

where $A_{d,i}$ is the activity of input source d,i and $w_{d,i,h}$ is the weight of its connection onto the hidden unit h of dendrite d. The activity of the output unit, i.e. the output of dendrite d, is:

$$D_d = \sum_{h=1}^{50} w_{d,h} \cdot H_{d,h}, \qquad (2)$$

where $w_{d,h}$ is the weight of the connection from the hidden unit d,h to the output unit. The outputs of the two dendrites are summed to produce the cell's output:

$$A = D_1 + D_2. \qquad (3)$$

The cell's output A is the principal contributor to the training signal T, used to adjust the weights of connections on the three dendrites. Additional factors contributing to the training signal are: (1) the average output activity of the cell, $\bar{A}$, driving the cell to have $\bar{A} = 0$; and (2) deviation of the current output activity from the average, $A - \bar{A}$, designed to expand the dynamic range of output values. Thus,

$$T = A - \alpha \cdot \bar{A} + \beta \cdot (A - \bar{A}), \qquad (4)$$

where, α and β are scaling coefficients. Coefficient β is determined by the variability of the output activity: smaller the variability, greater the value of β. It is computed as:

$$\beta = \left[\beta_{\max} - \gamma \cdot \overline{|A - \bar{A}|}\right]^+, \qquad (5)$$

where $\beta_{\max}$ and γ are controlling parameters, and $[\ \cdot\ ]^+$ indicates that if the quantity is negative, the value is to be taken as zero.

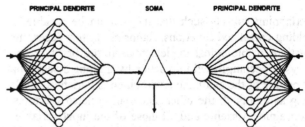

FIGURE 1. The SINBAD model of a cortical pyramidal cell with two dendrites connected to the soma (shown as a triangle). Each dendrite is modeled as an error backpropagation network with one output unit and a single layer of hidden units.

The connections of the hidden units are adjusted according to the error backpropagation algorithm of Rumelhart et al. [13]. Specifically, the error signals δ_d are first computed for the two dendrites as:

$$\delta_d = T - 2 \cdot D_d. \qquad (6)$$

For the hidden units, δ is backpropagated as:

$$\delta_{d,h} = \delta_d \cdot w_{d,h} \cdot (1 - H_{d,h}^2). \qquad (7)$$

Connection weights are adjusted by:

$$\Delta w_{d,i,h} = \mu_i \cdot A_{d,i} \cdot \delta_{d,h}$$

and,

$$\Delta w_{d,h} = \mu_h \cdot H_{d,h} \cdot \delta_d \qquad (8)$$

where μ_i and μ_h are learning rate constants for the input and hidden unit connections.

4. Finding Related Sets of Environmental Variables

In its current form, the SINBAD model describes the principle by which pyramidal cells can discover significant variables in their sensory environment, given that different principal dendrites in a cell are exposed to different sets of environmental variables that carry implicit information about the same hidden environmental variable(s). Thus, for any practical implementation of this principle, the SINBAD design must also address the question of how to choose *related* sets of environmental variables; i.e., sets without any variables in common, but with *implicit* information about the same hidden environmental variable and therefore capable of producing correlated functions. Ideally, these sets should be chosen by some procedure that will maximize the chances that the sets will be related, while minimizing the number of variables in each set.

This problem can be split into two different tasks. The first task is to find an overall set of related variables. The second task is to separate this overall set into non-overlapping subsets such that they would be capable of yielding correlated functions. Ignoring, in this paper, the questions of biological implementation, the first task can be easily accomplished in practice by training a backprop net on one of the available environmental variables, while using as inputs all the other potentially related variables. The training variable and all those of the input variables that the backprop net will learn to rely on in computing its output can then be taken as an overall set of related variables, likely to yield a significant environmental feature.

To accomplish the second task (that of separating the overall set of variables into two subsets), we can give each dendrite of a SINBAD cell *all* the variables in the set, but also expand our definition of the error function, which determines the learning procedure in each of the SINBAD dendrites. That is, in addition to the already used component of the error function, i.e. $(T - 2 \cdot D_d)^2$, we use a second term, which measures the degree to which each of the input variables contributes to *both* dendrites. Specifically,

$$E_d = (T - D_d)^2 + \phi \cdot \sum_i \left[\frac{\Psi_{d,i} \cdot \Psi_{\hat{d},i}}{(\Psi_{d,i} + \Psi_{\hat{d},i})^2} \right], \quad (9)$$

where $\Psi_{d,i} = \sum_h w_{d,i,h}^2$ is the total connection weight from input channel i to the dendrite d, and $\hat{d}$ represents the other principle dendrite. ϕ is a scaling constant controlling the relative strength of the separation term.

Consequently, instead of Eq. 8, the input connection weights are adjusted by:

$$\Delta w_{d,i,h} = \mu_i \cdot A_i \cdot \delta_{d,h} - \phi \cdot w_{d,i,h} \cdot \frac{\Psi_{\hat{d},i} \cdot (\Psi_{\hat{d},i} - \Psi_{d,i})}{(\Psi_{d,i} + \Psi_{\hat{d},i})^3} \quad (10)$$

This modification of the learning procedure automatically drives the dendrites to establish connections with different – nonoverlapping – subsets of environmental variables while searching them for correlated functions.

5. Natural Image Demonstration

The modified SINBAD neuron was tested on natural images. After initially setting all the adjustable connections to randomly chosen strengths w's, the SINBAD cell was exposed to grayscale images of grass,

bushes, and landscapes. The cell was trained on 100000 image exposures. During this time the two dendrites of the cell learned to produce closely correlated outputs, indicating that they tuned to some orderly local image feature. After training, responses of the cell were measured to point light stimuli applied at different locations in the blank image, thus generating a "receptive field" of that cell. Similar procedures are used in neuroscience to map receptive fields of neurons in the cerebral cortex.

Figure 2 shows four examples of receptive fields developed by the SINBAD cell in four different training runs. These receptive fields show a strong resemblance to receptive fields of neurons in the primary visual and somatosensory cortical areas, involved in the early stages of cortical sensory information processing [2]. This similarity of receptive fields suggests that the SINBAD cell learns local spatial features in natural images that are also recognized by neurons in the sensory cortex.

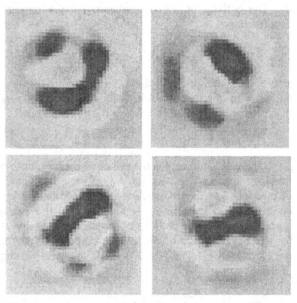

FIGURE 2. Exemplary receptive fields developed by SINBAD cells. These elongated receptive fields indicate that these cells are sensitive to the lines or edges of certain orientations.

FIGURE 3. A. Original image. **B.** Response of a SINBAD cell to the original image (the receptive field is included in the upper-left corner).

An example of visual features recognized by a SINBAD cell is shown in Figure 3. The right panel shows the map of responses of the SINBAD cell to its receptive field positioned over every pixel in one of the images (left panel). Also shown in the inset is the receptive field of this cell. Consistent with the slanted orientation of its receptive field, this cell responded preferentially to similarly oriented lines and edges in the image.

6. Conclusion

Environmental features learnable by SINBAD cells have a number of useful properties. They are *predictable*: that is how they are identified in the first place. They are *informative*: being involved in orderly relations, or regularities, they are predictive of other conditions taking part in those relations. Finally, they can be useful as *building blocks* in the construction - by other SINBAD cells - of higher-order features and the discovery of regularities involving those higher-order variables. Thus, for example, recognition of lines, edges, and textures by some SINBAD cells will enable recognition of surfaces and figures by other cells, which in turn will enable recognition of different types of objects and their states by yet other cells, which will enable recognition of different types of situations (involving interacting objects), etc.

In conclusion, we believe that SINBAD cells are potentially very powerful devices for discovery of orderly features of the environment. An individual SINBAD cell obviously will have a limited ability to recognize orderly features in the information it receives from other cells. But, when organized into sequences of cortical-like networks, SINBAD cells can build their discoveries on the discoveries of the preceding cells, thus gradually recognizing more and more complex features.

References

[1] Becker S, Hinton GE (1992) A self-organizing neural network that discovers surfaces in random-dot stereograms. *Nature* 355: 161-163

[2] DiCarlo, J.J., and Johnson, K.O., 2000, Spatial and temporal structure of receptive fields in primate somatosensory area 3b: effects of stimulus scanning direction and orientation, *Journal of Neuroscience*, 20: 495-510.

[3] Favorov OV, Ryder D (2002) SINBAD: A neocortical mechanism for discovering environmental variables and regularities hidden in sensory input. *Biological Cybernetics* (submitted)

[4] Phillips WA, Singer W (1997) In search of common foundations for cortical computation. *Behavioral and Brain Sciences* 20: 657-722

[5] Rumelhart DE, Hinton GE, Williams RJ (1986) Learning internal representations by error propagation. In: Rumelhart DE, McClelland JL, PDP Research Group (eds) Parallel distributed processing: explorations in the microstructure of cognition, MIT Press, Cambridge, Mass, 1: 318-362

[6] Ryder D, Favorov OV (2001) The new associationism: a neural explanation for the predictive powers of cerebral cortex. *Brain and Mind* 2: 161-194

Session 5–1
Graph Theory

Maximum Alliance-Free and Minimum Alliance-Cover Sets

Khurram H. Shafique and Ronald D. Dutton

School of Computer Science

University of Central Florida

Orlando, FL USA 32816

khurram@cs.ucf.edu, dutton@cs.ucf.edu

Abstract

A *defensive $k-$alliance* in a graph $G = (V, E)$ is a set of vertices $A \subseteq V$ such that for every vertex $v \in A$, the number of neighbors v has in A is at least as large as the number of neighbors it has in $V - S$ plus k (where k is the strength of $k-$alliance). An *offensive $k-$alliance* is a set of vertices $A \subseteq V$ such that for every vertex $v \in \partial A$, the number of neighbors v has in A is at least as large as the number of neighbors it has in $V - S$ plus k. In this paper, we deal with two types of sets associated with these $k-$alliances that we refer to as maximum $k-$alliance free and minimum $k-$alliance cover sets respectively. We define a set $X \subseteq V$ to be *maximum $k-$alliance free* (for some type of $k-$alliance) if X does not contain any $k-$alliance (of that type) and X is a set of largest cardinality among all such sets. A set $Y \subseteq V$ is called *minimum $k-$alliance cover* (for some type of $k-$alliance) if Y contains at least one vertex from each $k-$alliance (of that type) and is a set of minimum cardinality satisfying this property. We present bounds on the cardinality of maximum $k-$alliance free and minimum alliance $k-$cover sets and explore their inter-relation. The existence of forbidden subgraphs for graphs induced by these sets is also questioned.

1   Definitions and Notations

Alliances in graphs were first introduced by Hedetniemi et. al.[2]. They proposed different types of alliances, namely (strong) defensive alliances, (strong) offensive alliances, global alliances etc. In this paper, we consider generalizations of offensive and defensive alliances which refer to as $k-$alliances, where the strength of an alliance can be varied by varying the value of parameter k associated to it. Consider a graph $G = (V, E)$ without loops or multiple edges, and a sub-set A of V. A vertex v in set A is said to be $k-$ satisfied with respect to A if $\deg_A(v) \geq \deg_{V-A}(v) + k$, where $\deg_A(v) = |N(v) \cap A| = |N_A(v)|$. A set A is called *defensive $k-$ alliance* if all vertices in A are $k-$satisfied with respect to A, where $-\Delta < k \leq \Delta$. Note that a defensive$(-1)-$alliance is a "defensive alliance" (as defined in [2]), a defensive $0-$alliance is a "strong defensive alliance" or "cohesive set" [3]. Similarly, a set $A \subseteq V$ is called offensive $k-$alliance if $\forall v \in \partial A, \deg_A(v) \geq \deg_{V-A}(v) + k$, where $-\Delta + 2 < k \leq \Delta$. Hence, an offensive $1-$alliance is an "offensive alliance" and an offensive $2-$alliance is a "strong offensive alliance"[1].

A set $X \subseteq V(G)$ is *defensive $k-$alliance free* ($k-$daf) if for all defensive $k-$alliances A, $A - X \neq \emptyset$ i.e. X does not contain any defensive $k-$alliance. A defensive $k-$alliance free set X is maximal if $\forall v \notin X$, $\exists S \subseteq X$ such that $S \cup \{v\}$ is defensive $k-$alliance. A maximum $k-$daf set is a maximal $k-$daf set of largest cardinality. Let $\phi_k(G)$ be the cardinality of maximum $k-$daf of graph G. For simplicity of notation, we will refer to a maximum $k-$daf set of G as a $\phi_k(G)$-set. If a graph G does not have a defensive $k-$alliance (for some k), we say that $\phi_k(G) = n$, for example, $\phi_k(P_n) = n, \forall k > 1$.

We define a set $Y \subseteq V(G)$ to be *defensive $k-$alliance cover* ($k-$dac) if for all defensive $k-$alliances A, $A \cap Y \neq \emptyset$ i.e. Y contains at least one vertex from each defensive $k-$alliance of G. A $k-$dac Y is minimal if no proper subset of Y is a defensive $k-$alliance cover. A minimum $k-$dac is a minimal cover of smallest cardinality. Let $\zeta_k(G)$ be the cardinality of minimum $k-$dac of graph G. Once again, we will refer to a minimum $k-$dac of G as a $\zeta_k(G)$-set. When G does not have a defensive $k-$alliance (for some k), we say that $\zeta_k(G) = 0$.

For offensive $k-$alliances, we define two types of al-

293

liance free (cover) sets depending on whether or not the boundary vertices of an offensive alliance affect the definition of the set. A set $S \subseteq V$ is *offensive* $k-alliance$ *free* ($k-$oaf) if for all offensive $k-$alliances A, $A - S \neq \emptyset$. S is *weak offensive* $k-$*alliance free* ($k-$woaf) if for all offensive $k-$alliances A, $(A \cup \partial A) - S \neq \emptyset$. Similarly, a set $T \subseteq V$ is *offensive* $k-$*alliance cover* ($k-$oac) if for all offensive $k-$alliances A, $A \cap T \neq \emptyset$. T is *weak offensive* $k-$*alliance cover* ($k-$woac) if for all offensive $k-$alliances A, $(A \cup \partial A) \cap T \neq \emptyset$. The maximum (weak) offensive $k-$alliance free sets and minimum (weak) offensive $k-$alliance cover sets are defined in the same fashion as their defensive counterparts. For a graph G, we define the following invariants

- $\phi_k(G) =$ Size of maximum $k-$daf set of G
- $\zeta_k(G) =$ Size of minimum $k-$dac set of G
- $\phi_k^o(G) =$ Size of maximum $k-$oaf set of G
- $\zeta_k^o(G) =$ Size of minimum $k-$oac set of G
- $\phi_k^w(G) =$ Size of maximum $k-$woaf set of G
- $\zeta_k^w(G) =$ Size of minimum $k-$woac set of G

In this paper, we explore the properties and bounds of the above defined invariants and their relationship with each other. In general we will refer to both offensive and defensive $k-$alliances as $k-$alliances. Similarly, the terms $k-$alliance free set and $k-$alliance cover set will encompass all types of alliance free sets and cover sets defined in this section. For other graph terminology and notations, we follow [5].

2   Basic Properties

Theorem 1. $X \subseteq V(G$ *is a* $k-$*alliance cover if and only if* $V(G) - X$ *is* $k-$*alliance free.*

Proof. X is a defensive $k-$alliance free set if and only if, for every defensive $k-$alliance A, $A - X \neq \emptyset$ if and only if, for every defensive $k-$alliance A, $A \cap (V(G) - X) \neq \emptyset$ if and only if $V(G) - X$ is a defensive $k-$alliance cover.

The justification for the (weak) offensive alliance cover is similar. □

Corollary 2. $\phi_k(G) + \zeta_k(G) = \phi_k^o(G) + \zeta_k^o(G) = \phi_k^w(G) + \zeta_k^w(G) = n(G)$

Corollary 3.

(i) *If* V' *is a minimal* $k-$*dac* ($k-$oac) *then,* $\forall v \in V'$, *there exists a defensive (offensive)* $k-$*alliance* S_v *for which* $S_v \cap V' = \{v\}$.

(ii) *If* V' *is a minimal k-wdac then,* $\forall v \in V'$, *there exists an offensive* $k-$*alliance* S_v *for which* $(S_v \cup \partial S_v) \cap V' = \{v\}$.

Since, $\forall k_1 > k_2$, a k_2-alliance free set is also a k_1-alliance free set and every k_1-oaf set is also a k_1-woaf set, we have the following observation.

Observation 4. *For any graph* G *and* $-\Delta \leq k_2 < k_1 \leq \Delta$,

(i) $0 \leq \phi_{k_2}^o(G) \leq \phi_{k_1}^o(G) \leq \phi_{k_1}^w(G) \leq n(G)$

(ii) $0 \leq \phi_{k_1}^w(G) \leq \phi_{k_2}^w(G) \leq n(G)$

(iii) $0 \leq \phi_{k_2}(G) \leq \phi_{k_1}(G) \leq n(G)$

Also note that every $k-$daf set X is also a $k-$woaf set. Suppose not, then there is an offensive $k-$alliance A such that $A \cup \partial A \subseteq X$. Then $\forall v \in A' = A \cup \partial A$, $\deg_{A'}(v) \geq \deg_{V-A'}(v) + k$, which implies that A' is a defensive $k-$alliance and contradicts X being a $k-$daf set.

Observation 5. $\phi_k^w(G) \geq \phi_k(G)$

Suppose now a minimal k_1-dac set Y and let $A \subseteq Y$ such that A is an offensive k_2-alliance. Let $y \in A$, then by Corollary 3, there exists a defensive k_1-alliance S_y such that $S_y \cap Y = \{y\}$. Hence $\exists x \in \partial A - Y$ such that $\deg_A(x) \leq \deg_{V-A}(x) + 2 - k_1$. Also, since A is an offensive k_2-alliance, $\deg_A(x) \geq \deg_{V-A}(x) + k_2$. Combining the two inequalities, we get, $k_2 \leq 2 - k_1$. This leads to the following observation:

Observation 6. $\forall k_2 > 2 - k_1$, $\phi_{k_2}^o(G) \geq \zeta_{k_1}(G)$

3   Defensive $k-$Alliance Free & Cover Sets

We know that any independent set in a connected graph G is $k-$daf for $k \geq 0$, therefore $\phi_k(G) \geq \beta_0(G)$, $k \geq 0$, where $\beta_0(G)$ is the independence number of graph G. We can further improve this bound by noting that addition of any $\left\lceil \frac{\delta(G)}{2} \right\rceil + \left\lfloor \frac{k}{2} \right\rfloor - 1$ vertices in an independent set will not induce any defensive $k-$alliance in the new set, hence, $\phi_k(G) \geq$

$\beta_0(G) + \left\lceil \frac{\delta(G)}{2} \right\rceil + \left\lfloor \frac{k}{2} \right\rfloor - 1$, $k \geq 0$. Since, $\forall A \subset V(G)$ such that $|A| \geq n(G) - \left\lfloor \frac{\delta(G)}{2} \right\rfloor + \left\lceil \frac{k}{2} \right\rceil$, A is a defensive $k-$alliance, $\phi_k(G) < n(G) - \left\lfloor \frac{\delta(G)}{2} \right\rfloor + \left\lceil \frac{k}{2} \right\rceil$, $k \geq 0$. The above reasoning also holds for $-\delta(G) < k < 0$.

Observation 7. *If G is a connected graph and $-\delta(G) < k < \Delta(G)$ then*

$$\beta_0(G) + \left\lceil \frac{\delta(G)}{2} \right\rceil + \left\lfloor \frac{k}{2} \right\rfloor - 1 \leq \phi_k(G) < n(G) - \left\lfloor \frac{\delta(G)}{2} \right\rfloor + \left\lceil \frac{k}{2} \right\rceil$$

Next we present the values of $\phi_k(G)$ for some of the common graph families.

Observation 8. *If G is an Eulerian graph then $\phi_{2i-1}(G) = \phi_{2i}(G)$, $-\frac{\delta(G)}{2} < i < \frac{\Delta(G)}{2}$*

Observation 9. *For the complete graph K_n, and $-n+1 < k < n$*

$$\phi_k(K_n) = \begin{cases} \left\lfloor \frac{n}{2} \right\rfloor + \left\lceil \frac{k}{2} \right\rceil & \text{for odd } n \\ \left\lfloor \frac{n}{2} \right\rfloor + \left\lfloor \frac{k}{2} \right\rfloor & \text{for even } n \end{cases}$$

Observation 10. *For the complete bipartite graph $K_{p,q}$, $p \leq q$, and $-p < k \leq q$*

$$\phi_k(K_{p,q}) = \begin{cases} q + \left\lceil \frac{p}{2} \right\rceil + \left\lfloor \frac{k}{2} \right\rfloor - 1 & \text{for odd } p \\ q + \left\lceil \frac{p}{2} \right\rceil + \left\lceil \frac{k}{2} \right\rceil - 1 & \text{for even } p \end{cases}$$

Note that both K_{2r} and $K_{2r,q}$, $2r \leq q$ attains the lower and upper bounds of observation 7. We have shown in [4] that the following lower bound holds for $\phi_k(G)$.

Theorem 11. *If G is a connected graph and $0 \leq k \leq \Delta(G)$ then*

$$\phi_k(G) \geq \left\lfloor \frac{n}{2} \right\rfloor + \left\lfloor \frac{k}{2} \right\rfloor$$

where the equality exists if every block of G is either an odd clique or an odd cycle (the converse is also true when $k = 0$).

We believe (but have'nt been able to prove) the following extension of above theorem for $k < 0$ to be true:

Conjecture 1. *If G is a connected graph and $-\delta(G) < k \leq \Delta(G)$ then*

$$\phi_k(G) \geq \left\lfloor \frac{n}{2} \right\rfloor + \left\lfloor \frac{k}{2} \right\rfloor$$

Next, we show that no forbidden subgraph characterization exists for the graphs induced by minimual $k-$dac sets.

Theorem 12. *Let G be any graph and r an integer such that $r \geq 2$. Then there is a graph G' with $\zeta_k(G') = r$, $k \geq 2 - r$, which contains G as an induced subgraph.*

Proof. Let a graph $G = (V, E)$ where $V = \{v_1, v_2, \ldots, v_n\}$ and construct a graph $G' = (V', E')$ as follows: $V' = V \cup X \cup Y$, where $X = \left\{ x_i^j, \ 1 \leq i \leq n, \ 1 \leq j \leq \max\left(2r + k, \Delta(G) - k + 1\right) \right\}$ and $Y = \{y_1, y_2, \ldots, y_{2r+k-2}\}$. $E' = E \cup E_1 \cup E_2$, where $E_1 = \left\{ v_i x_i^j, \ v_i \in V, \ x_i^j \in X \right\}$ and $E_2 = \left\{ x_i^j y_l, \ x_i^j \in X, \ y_l \in Y \right\}$. Thus $\delta(G') = 2r + k - 1$. Since by Observation 7, $\zeta_k(G') \geq \left\lfloor \frac{\delta(G')}{2} \right\rfloor - \left\lceil \frac{k}{2} \right\rceil + 1$, we have $\zeta_k(G') \geq \left\lfloor \frac{2r+k-1}{2} \right\rfloor - \left\lceil \frac{k}{2} \right\rceil + 1 = r$.

Now consider $C \subseteq Y$ such that $|C| = r$. We claim that C is a $k-$dac set of graph G'. Suppose not. Then there exists a defensive $k-$alliance $S \subseteq V' - C$ in G'. Let $v \in S$. Since $\forall x \in X \ \deg(x) = 2r + k - 1$, if $v \in S \cap X$ then $\deg_S(v) \leq r + k - 1 < \deg_C(v) + k = r + k$, which is contrary to S being a defensive $k-$alliance. Hence $S \cap X = \emptyset$. Now let $v \in V$. By construction of graph G', $\forall v \in V$, $\deg_X(v) + k \geq \Delta(G) + 1 > \deg_{V'-X}(v) \geq \deg_S(v)$, again a contradiction. The only remaining case is $S \subset Y$, which is not possible as $\forall v \in S$, $\deg_S(v) = 0 < deg_{V'-S}(y) \leq n(2r + k)$. Hence $S = \emptyset$ and C is a $k-$dac set. Thus $\zeta_k(G') \leq r$.

Combining the two results, we get $\zeta_k(G') = r$. $\square$

4 Offensive $k-$Alliance Free & Cover Sets

In this section, we study the properties of the free sets and cover sets associated with offensive $k-$alliances. We begin by presenting the values of $\phi_k^o(G)$ and $\phi_k^w(G)$ for some special classes of graphs.

Observation 13. *For the complete graph K_n, and $-n + 3 < k < n$*

$$\phi_k^o(K_n) = \phi_k(K_n) - 1 = \begin{cases} \left\lfloor \frac{n}{2} \right\rfloor + \left\lceil \frac{k}{2} \right\rceil - 1 & \text{for odd } n \\ \left\lfloor \frac{n}{2} \right\rfloor + \left\lfloor \frac{k}{2} \right\rfloor - 1 & \text{for even } n \end{cases}$$

$$\phi_k^w(K_n) = n - 1$$

Observation 14. *For the complete bipartite graph $K_{p,q}$, $p \leq q$, and $-p+2 < k \leq q$*

$$\phi_k^o(K_{p,q}) = \begin{cases} \left\lceil \frac{q}{2} \right\rceil + \left\lceil \frac{p}{2} \right\rceil + 2\left\lfloor \frac{k}{2} \right\rfloor - 2 & p \ \& \ q \text{ both odd} \\[2mm] \left\lceil \frac{q}{2} \right\rceil + \left\lceil \frac{p}{2} \right\rceil + 2\left\lceil \frac{k}{2} \right\rceil - 2 & p \ \& \ q \text{ both even} \\[2mm] \left\lceil \frac{q}{2} \right\rceil + \left\lceil \frac{p}{2} \right\rceil + k - 2 & \text{otherwise} \end{cases}$$

$$\phi_k^w(K_{p,q}) = n - 2, \quad p, q \neq 1$$

It is interesting to note that while complete graphs attain the lower bound for $\phi_k(G)$, they have the maximum value for $\phi_k^w(G)$.

Lemma 15. *If S is an offensive k_1- alliance then*

(i) *for all offensive k_2-alliances $S' \subseteq V - S$ such that $k_1 + k_2 > 0$, $\partial S \cap \partial S' = \emptyset$.*

(ii) *for all defensive k_2-alliances $S' \subseteq V - S$ such that $k_1 + k_2 > 0$, $\partial S \cap S' = \emptyset$.*

Theorem 16. *For a connected graph G, if X is a maximal k_1-woaf set and $Y = V - X$ then*

(i) *$\forall k_2 > -k_1$, Y is a k_2-woaf set (and hence, X is a k_2-woac set), and*

(ii) *$\forall k_2 > \max(-k_1, -\delta(G))$, Y is a k_2-daf set (hence, X is a k_2-dac set).*

Proof. For i), let $k_2 > -k_1$ and suppose there exists an offensive k_2-alliance S for which $S \cup \partial S \subseteq Y$. Let $x \in \partial S$. From Corollary 3, there is an offensive k_1-alliance S_x for which $(S_x \cup \partial S_x) \cap Y = \{x\}$. If $x \in \partial S_x$, then from Lemma 15, S and S_x cannot be disjoint, a contradiction. So we must assume that $x \in S_x$. But then, $N(x) \subseteq \partial S_x \subseteq X$, which leads to a contradiction since x must have at least one neighbor in $S \subseteq Y$. Thus, Y is a k_2-woaf set and, from Theorem 1, X is a k_2-woac set.

For ii), let $k_2 > \max(-k_1, -\delta(G))$ and suppose there exists a defensive k_2- alliance $S \subseteq Y$. Let $x \in S$. From Corollary 3, there exists an offensive k_1- alliance S_x for which $(S_x \cup \partial S_x) \cap Y = \{x\}$. If $x \in \partial S_x$ then from Lemma 15, S and S_x cannot be disjoint, a contradiction. So we must assume that $x \in S_x$, but then $N(x) \subseteq \partial S_x \subseteq X$, which is not possible since $\deg_S(x) \geq (\deg(x) + k_2)/2 > 0$. Hence, Y is a k_2-daf set and, from Theorem 1, X is a k_2-dac set. $\square$

Corollary 17.

(i) *Every maximal k_1-woaf set contains a minimal k_2-woac set, $\forall k_2 > -k_1$.*

(ii) *Every maximal k_1-woaf set contains a minimal k_2-dac set, $\forall k_2 > \max(-k_1, -\delta(G))$.*

Since every $k-$woaf is also $l-$woaf $\forall l > k$, by Theorem 1, every $k-$woac is also $l-$woac. This observation leads to the following corollary of Theorem 16.

Corollary 18. *$\forall k > 0$, $\zeta_k^w(G) \leq \left\lfloor \frac{n}{2} \right\rfloor$*

It is easy to prove that $\forall k \leq 0$, $\zeta_k^w(G) = \left\lfloor \frac{n}{2} \right\rfloor$ if and only if $G \approx K_2$ and $k < 2$.

We conclude this section by presenting a result for $\zeta_k^w(G)$ similar to the one for $\zeta_k(G)$ in Theorem 12.

Theorem 19. *Let G be any graph and r an integer such that $r \geq 1$. Then there is a graph G' with $\zeta_k^w(G') = r$, which contains G as an induced subgraph.*

Proof. Let a graph $G = (V, E)$ where $V = \{v_1, v_2, \ldots, v_n\}$ and construct a graph $G' = (V', E')$ as follows: $V' = V \cup X \cup Y$, where $X = \{x_1, x_2, \ldots, x_r\}$ and Y is the union of disjoint sets $Y_1, Y_2, \ldots, Y_r$, such that $\forall i$, $|Y_i| = n - k + 1$. $E' = E \cup E_1 \cup E_2 \cup E_3$, where $E_1 = \{v_i x_j, \ v_i \in V, \ x_j \in X\}$, $E_2 = \{x_i y, \ \forall y \in Y_i, \ 1 \leq i \leq r\}$ and $E_3 = \{yz| \ y, z \in Y_i, \ 1 \leq i \leq r\}$. Hence, G' is obtained by adding r vertex disjoint cliques $Y_i \cup \{x_i\}$, each of order $n - k + 2$ vertices and making each x_i adjacent to every vertex of V.

It is easy to see that X is a $k-$woac set of graph G', i.e. $\zeta_k^w(G') \leq |X| = r$. We claim that $\zeta_k^w(G') = \dot{r}$. Suppose not and let $C \subset V$ be a $k-$woac set of graph G' such that $|C| < r$. By pigeon hole principle, there exists Y_i such that $(Y_i \cup \{x_i\}) \cap C = \emptyset$. Since $\partial Y_i = \{x_i\}$ and $\deg_{Y_i}(x_i) = n + k + 1 > \deg_{V'-Y_i}(x_i) + k = n + k$, Y_i is an offensive $k-$alliance in G' such that $(Y_i \cup \partial Y_i) \subseteq V' - C$, which is contrary to C being a $k-$woac set of graph G'. Hence $\zeta_k^w(G') \geq r$.

Combining the two results, we get $\zeta_k^w(G') = r$. $\square$

5 Open Problems

1. Determine the computational complexity of finding each of $\phi_k(G)$, $\phi_k^o(G)$ and $\phi_k^w(G)$.

2. Find the efficient algorithms for computing $\phi_k(G)$, $\phi_k^o(G)$ and $\phi_k^w(G)$.

3. Determine tight upper and lower bounds for $\phi_k^o(G)$ and $\phi_k^w(G)$ and characterize the extremal graphs.

4. Determine the values of $\phi_k(G)$, $\phi_k^o(G)$ and $\phi_k^w(G)$ for other classes of graphs for example grid graphs.

5. Does a similar result as Theorem 12 and Theorem 19 holds for $\zeta_k^o(G)$?

6. Study the cover and free sets of other alliances like dual alliances and global alliances and their relationship.

References

[1] O. Favaron, G. Fricke, W. Goddard, S. M. Hedetniemi, S. T. Hedetniemi, P. Kristiansen, R. C. Laskar, and D. Skaggs. "Offensive alliances in graphs". Preprint, 2002.

[2] S. M. Hedetniemi, S. T. Hedetniemi, and P. Kristiansen. "Alliances in graphs". Preprint, 2000.

[3] K. H. Shafique and R. D. Dutton. "On satisfactory partitioning of graphs". In *33rd Southeastern International Conference on Combinatorics, Graph Theory, and Computing*, March 2002.

[4] K. H. Shafique and R. D. Dutton. "Alliance-cover and alliance-free sets in graphs". Preprint, 2002.

[5] D. B. West. *Introduction to Graph Theory*. Prentice Hall, NJ.

Offensive Alliances in Graphs

Odile Favaron, Université Paris-Sud
Gerd Fricke, Morehouse State University
Wayne Goddard*, University of Natal, Durban
Sandra M. Hedetniemi, Clemson University
Stephen T. Hedetniemi, Clemson University
Petter Kristiansen, University of Bergen
Renu C. Laskar, Clemson University
Duane Skaggs, Morehouse State University

Abstract

A set S is an offensive alliance if for every vertex v in its boundary $N(S) - S$ it holds that the majority of vertices in v's closed neighbourhood are in S. The offensive alliance number is the minimum cardinality of an offensive alliance. In this paper we explore the bounds on the offensive alliance and the strong offensive alliance numbers (where a strict majority is required). In particular, we show that the offensive alliance number is at most 2/3 the order and the strong offensive alliance number at most 5/6 the order.

1 Introduction

In real life, an alliance is a collection of entities such that the union is stronger than the individual. The alliance can be either to protect against attack, or to assert collective will against others. This motivated the definition of defensive and offensive alliances in graphs, given in [4].

In this paper we study the offensive alliances. Informally, given a graph $G = (V, E)$, we say a set S is an offensive alliance if every other vertex that is adjacent to S is outgunned by S: more of its neighbours are in S than are not. Formally, we denote by $N(v)$ the neighbourhood of a vertex v and $N[v] = \{v\} \cup N(v)$. Similarly, for $S \subseteq V$ we denote $N(S) = \bigcup_{v \in S} N(v)$ and $N[S] = S \cup N(S)$. We define the boundary of ∂S as the set $N(S) - S$. Then S is an *offensive alliance* if:

for all $v \in \partial S$: $|N[v] \cap S| \geq |N[v] - S|$.

It is a *strong offensive alliance* if the inequality is strict for all vertices in the boundary. Equivalently, we define the *excess* of a vertex relative to S by

$$ex(v; S) = |N[v] \cap S| - |N[v] - S|.$$

So for an offensive alliance the excess of each vertex in the boundary is at least 0, and for a strong offensive alliance the excess is at least 1.

Then in [4] the offensive alliance and strong offensive alliance numbers of a graph G were defined as follows:

$a_o(G)$ *is the minimum cardinality of a nonempty offensive alliance, and* $\hat{a}_o(G)$ *is the minimum cardinality of a nonempty strong offensive alliance.*

This definition specifically allows for S to be only local. We say that an offensive alliance is *global* if every vertex is affected. That is, $S \cup \partial S = V$ (S is a dominating set).

This parameter is related to the monopolies introduced by Linial et al. [5] (which have application in distributed and fault-tolerant computing), to the unfriendly graph partition problem introduced by Aharoni et al. [1] and Luby [6], and to signed domination introduced by Dunbar et al. [2].

In this paper we explore the elementary properties of the offensive alliance numbers, including their values for several families of graphs. We then establish upper bounds on the offensive alliance and strong offensive alliance numbers. Thereafter we consider graphical operations and how the alliance numbers for these relate to those of the constituents. We close by noting that these parameters have linear-time algorithms for trees, but are NP-hard even for cubic graphs.

2 Bounds and Calculations

We start with a primitive lower bound in terms of the minimum degree $\delta(G)$. This bound follows from considering any vertex in the boundary.

Observation 1 *For all graphs G, $a_o(G) \geq (\delta(G)+1)/2$ and $\hat{a}_o(G) > (\delta(G)+1)/2$.*

Examples of equality in the above bounds are the complete and complete bipartite graphs (though for the strong offensive alliance number the star is an exception):

Corollary 2 *For $n \geq 1$, $a_o(K_n) = \lceil n/2 \rceil$ and $\hat{a}_o(K_n) = \lceil (n+1)/2 \rceil$.*
For $1 \leq r \leq s$, $a_o(K_{r,s}) = \lceil (r+1)/2 \rceil$.
For $2 \leq r \leq s$, $\hat{a}_o(K_{r,s}) = \lceil r/2 + 1 \rceil$ but $\hat{a}_o(K_{1,s}) = \lceil s/2 + 1 \rceil$.

At the other extreme, there is the following upper bound since every vertex cover is an offensive alliance. We use $\alpha(G)$ to denote the vertex cover number of G.

Observation 3 *For all graphs G, $a_o(G) \leq \alpha(G)$. If $\delta(G) \geq 2$, then $\hat{a}_o(G) \leq VC(G)$.*

In general, $\hat{a}_o(G)$ is at most the minimum cardinality of a vertex cover that contains all end-vertices. If the graph has small maximum degree $\Delta(G)$, there are similar lower bounds.

Observation 4 *Let G be a connected graph. If $\Delta(G) \leq 2$ then $a_o(G) \geq \alpha(G)$, and if $\Delta(G) \leq 3$ then $\hat{a}_o(G) \geq \alpha(G)$.*

One consequence is that $\hat{a}_o(G) = \alpha(G)$ for cubic graphs, and hence the strong offensive alliance number is NP-hard. Other examples of equality in the above bounds are the paths and cycles.

Corollary 5 *For $n \geq 1$, $a_o(P_n) = \lfloor n/2 \rfloor$ and $\hat{a}_o(P_n) = \lfloor n/2 \rfloor + 1$.*
For $n \geq 3$, $a_o(C_n) = \hat{a}_o(C_n) = \lceil n/2 \rceil$.

The two parameters are equal for the cycle and indeed equal for any Eulerian graph, as then every offensive alliance is automatically strong.

Corollary 6 *Let G be a connected graph. Then $a_o(G) = 1$ iff G is a star, and $\hat{a}_o(G) = 1$ iff $G = K_1$.*

In particular, this confirms that there is no upper bound for the strong offensive alliance number in terms of the offensive alliance number.

3 Maximum Values

In this section we consider the maximum offensive alliance and strong offensive alliance numbers of a graph.

Theorem 1 *For all graphs G of order $n \geq 2$,*
$a_o(G) \leq 2n/3.$

PROOF. Let $G = (V, E)$. The result is trivial if G has an isolated vertex. So assume that $\delta(G) \geq 1$. Color the vertex set V with three colors such that the number of monochromatic edges (both ends the same color) is as small as possible. Then any vertex is incident with at least double the number of non-monochromatic edges as monochromatic edges. (If a green vertex has more green neighbours than red neighbours, then we can recolor it red, a contradiction.) So any two colour classes form an offensive alliance. QED

We know of three examples of equality in the above bound: K_3, $K_{2,2,2}$ and the graph formed as follows: take three disjoint triangles T_1, T_2, T_3 and add 3 edges so that there is a triangle containing one vertex of each of T_1, T_2 and T_3.

Asymptotically, the maximum for connected graphs that we know is 5/8 of the order. An example is depicted in Figure 1.

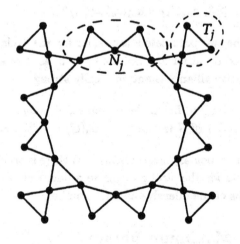

Figure 1: The graph G_4

Using more tedious techniques, one can show:

Theorem 2 *For all graphs G of order $n \geq 3$, $\hat{a}_o(G) \leq 5n/6$. Moreover, if G has minimum degree at least 2, then $\hat{a}_o(G) \leq 3n/4$.*

In general, as the minimum degree increases, the upper bound tends to half the order. A trivial probabilistic method argument, identical to that used by Füredi and Mubayi [3], shows:

Theorem 3 *For graph with order n and minimum degree δ, $a_o(G) \leq \hat{a}_o(G) \leq n(1/2 + o(\delta))$.*

4 Graph Operations

In this section we consider the parameters for the result of various graph operations.

A trivial observation is that the (strong) offensive alliance number is the minimum of the two numbers when the graph is the union of two components:

$$a_o(G \cup H) = \min(a_o(G), a_o(H)) \text{ and}$$
$$\hat{a}_o(G \cup H) = \min(\hat{a}_o(G), \hat{a}_o(H)).$$

We consider next the join. In general there is no upper bound for $a_o(G + H)$ in terms of $a_o(G)$ and $a_o(H)$ (for example, consider the join of two stars). Nor in fact is there an upper bound even if one of the pieces is a single vertex.

However, one can provide bounds if one generalises the definition of an offensive alliance. For an integer k, we define a *k-excess alliance* as a set S where every $v \in \partial S$ has $ex(v; S) \geq k$. It is global if $ex(v; S) \geq k$ for all $v \in V - S$. (For $k \geq 0$ this is equivalent to saying that S dominates.) We define $a_k(G)$ and $a_k^g(G)$ as the minimum cardinality of a nonempty k-excess and global k-excess alliance.

Lemma 7 *Let G be a graph of order n. Then for any integer k, $a_k(G + K_1) \leq a_{k-1}^g(G) + 1$, with equality if $a_{k-1}^g(G) \leq (n + k)/2$.*

Corollary 8 *If $\delta(G) \geq 1$ and $\Delta(G) \leq 2$, then $a_o(G + K_1) = \gamma(G) + 1$.*

This gives the offensive alliance number of the wheel. These results can be extended to adding more than one vertex.

We consider next cartesian products. Again, there is no general upper bound for the parameter for $G \times H$ in terms of the parameters for G and H. So we consider the special case of the grid. We need the following two observations.

Observation 9 *Let $G = C_m \times C_n$ for $m, n \geq 4$ and let S be an offensive alliance. Then each component of $G - S$ is a subgraph of the star on 4 edges.*

The following is an extension of the vertex cover upper bound. The 4-packing number $\rho_4(G)$ is the maximum number of vertices that are pairwise at least distance 4 apart.

Lemma 10 *If G is r-regular for $r \geq 3$ and triangle-free, then $a_o(G) \leq n - (r+1)\rho_4(G)$.*

Theorem 4 *If n and m are both a multiple of 4, then $a_o(C_n \times C_m) = \frac{3}{8}nm$.*

PROOF. A 4-packing of cardinality $nm/8$ is obtained by taking from the even-numbered copies of C_m every fourth vertex (staggered by two each time. (See the doubly ringed vertices in Figure 2.) So the above value is an upper bound.

On the other hand, let S be an offensive alliance, and let M be the number of edges between S and ∂S. Trivially, $|M| \leq 4|S|$. On the other hand, by considering each of the five possible components of $G - S$ in turn, it follows that $|M| \geq 12|V - S|/5$. This means that $|S| \geq 3|V|/8$.   QED

Similar asymptotics hold for grids which are the product of two paths.

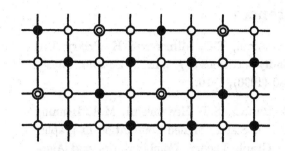

Figure 2: The grid $C_4 \times C_8$: The black vertices form a strong offensive alliance

5   Algorithms and Complexity

Both parameters are NP-hard, even for cubic graphs. Indeed, for a cubic graph G, $a_o(G) = n - \rho(G)$ while $\hat{a}_o(G) = \alpha(G)$. While in a cubic graph every strong offensive alliance is strong, this is not true for normal offensive alliances. The minimum cardinality of a global offensive number is the 2-domination number, but complexity is unknown.

In contrast, standard ideas produce linear-time algorithms for trees.

6   Open Questions

1. What is the real upper bound for the strong offensive alliance number? What are the extremal graphs? What is the maximum asymptotically for the two parameters?

2. The relationship between these parameters and between them and other parameters is important. Under what conditions is every offensive alliance global? When is $a_o(G) = \hat{a}_o(G)$? When is $a_o(G) = \alpha(G)$?

3. Can one determine the exact values for any other classes of graphs (e.g. grids). Or at least good bounds (e.g. outerplanar graphs).

References

[1] R. Aharoni, E.C. Milner and K. Prikry, Un-friendly partitions of graphs, *J. Combin. Theory B* **50** (1990), 1–10.

[2] J.E. Dunbar, S.T. Hedetniemi, M.A. Henning and P.J. Slater, Signed domination in graphs, in: "Graph Theory, Combinatorics and Algorithms" (Y.Alavi and A. Schwenk, Eds.), pp. 311–321, Wiley, 1995.

[3] Z. Füredi and D. Mubayi, Signed domination in regular graphs and set-systems, *J. Combin. Theory Ser. B* **76** (1999), 223–239.

[4] S.M. Hedetniemi, S.T Hedetniemi and P. Kristiansen, Alliances in graphs, submitted.

[5] N. Linial, D. Peleg, Y. Rabinovitch and M. Saks, Sphere packings and local majorities in graphs, In 2nd ISTCS, 141–149. IEEE Computer Soc. Press, June 1993.

[6] M. Luby, A simple parallel algorithm for the maximal independent set problem, *SIAM J. Comput.* **15** (1986), 1036–1053.

302

Global Defensive Alliances

Teresa W. Haynes
Department of Mathematics
East Tennessee State University
Johnson City, TN USA 37614
haynes@mail.etsu.edu

Stephen T. Hedetniemi
Department of Computer Science
Clemson University
Clemson, SC USA 29634
hedet@cs.clemson.edu

Michael A. Henning *
Department of Mathematics
University of Natal
Pietermaritzburg, 3209 South Africa
henning@nu.ac.za

Abstract

A *defensive alliance* in a graph $G = (V, E)$ is a set
of vertices $S \subseteq V$ satisfying the condition that for
every vertex $v \in S$, the number of neighbors v has
in S plus one (counting v) is at least as large as the
number of neighbors it has in $V - S$. Because of such
an alliance, the vertices in S, agreeing to mutually
support each other, have the strength of numbers to
be able to defend themselves from the vertices in $V - S$.
A defensive alliance S is called *global* if it effects every
vertex in $V - S$, that is, every vertex in $V - S$ is
adjacent to at least one member of the alliance S. Note
that a global defensive alliance is a dominating set.
We summarize results and list some open problems on
global defensive alliances in graphs.

1 Introduction

Alliances in graphs were first introduced and studied
by Hedetniemi, Hedetniemi, and Kristiansen in [6].
In this paper we consider specific types of alliances,
namely, global defensive alliances (listed as an open
problem in [6]), but first we give some terminology and
definitions. Let $G = (V, E)$ be a graph with $|V| = n$.
An *endvertex* is a vertex which is adjacent to exactly
one vertex, and its neighbor is called a *support vertex*.
For any vertex $v \in V$, the *open neighborhood of v* is
the set $N(v) = \{u : uv \in E\}$, while the *closed neighborhood of v* is the set $N[v] = N(v) \cup \{v\}$. For a subset
$S \subseteq V$, the *open neighborhood* $N(S) = \cup_{v \in S} N(S)$ and
the *closed neighborhood* $N[S] = N(S) \cup S$. A set S is
a *dominating set* if $N[S] = V$, and is a *total dominating set* or an *open dominating set* if $N(S) = V$. The
minimum cardinality of a dominating set (respectively,
total dominating set) of G is the *domination number*
$\gamma(G)$ (respectively, *total domination number* $\gamma_t(G)$). A
detailed treatment of domination and its many variations is available in the books [2, 3]. For other graph
theory terminology and notation, we follow [1] and [2].

A non-empty set of vertices $S \subseteq V$ is called a
defensive alliance if for every $v \in S$, $|N[v] \cap S| \geq
|N(v) \cap (V - S)|$. In this case, by strength of num-
bers, we say that every vertex in S is *defended* from
possible attack by vertices in $V - S$. A defensive alliance S is called *strong* if for every vertex $v \in S$,
$|N[v] \cap S| > |N(v) \cap V - S|$. In this case we say that
every vertex in S is *strongly defended*.

In this paper, any reference to an alliance will mean
a defensive alliance. An (strong) alliance S is called
critical if no proper subset of S is an (strong) alliance.
The *alliance number* $a(G)$ is the minimum cardinality
of any critical alliance in G, and the *strong alliance
number* $â(G)$ is the minimum cardinality of any critical
strong alliance in G.

An alliance S is *global* if it effects every vertex in
$V - S$, that is, every vertex in $V - S$ is adjacent to at
least one member of the alliance S. In other words, S
is both an alliance and a dominating set. The *global
alliance number* $\gamma_a(G)$ (respectively, *global strong alliance number* $\gamma_â(G)$) is the minimum cardinality of
an alliance (respectively, strong alliance) of G that is
also a dominating set of G. The entire vertex set is
a global (strong) alliance for any graph G, so every
graph G has a global (strong) alliance number. Note
that a global alliance of minimum cardinality is not
necessarily a critical alliance, and a critical alliance is
not necessarily a dominating set. It is observed in [6]
that any critical (strong) alliance S in a graph G must
induce a connected subgraph of G. This is obvious,
since any component of the induced subgraph $\langle S \rangle$ is
a smaller alliance (of the same type). However, for a
global alliance this is not necessarily true. For example, the two endvertices of the path P_4 form a global
alliance. We refer to a minimum dominating set of G

---

*Research supported in part by the South African National
Research Foundation and the University of Natal

as a $\gamma(G)$-set. Similarly, we call a minimum global alliance (respectively, a minimum global strong alliance) of G a $\gamma_a(G)$-set (respectively, $\gamma_{\hat{a}}(G)$-set).

Applications of alliances range from national defense to natural orders in botany. A list of interesting, real world applications is given in [6].

2   Global Alliances

Since every global strong alliance is a global alliance, and every global alliance is both an alliance and dominating, our first observation is immediate.

Observation 1 *For any graph* G,
(i) $1 \leq \gamma(G) \leq \gamma_a(G) \leq \gamma_{\hat{a}}(G) \leq n$,
(ii) $1 \leq a(G) \leq \gamma_a(G) \leq n$, *and*
(iii) $1 \leq a(G) \leq \hat{a}(G) \leq \gamma_{\hat{a}}(G) \leq n$.

To illustrate the concept of global alliance numbers, we give values for specific graph families.

Proposition 2 [4] *For the complete graph* K_n,
(i) $\gamma_a(K_n) = \lfloor \frac{n+1}{2} \rfloor$, *and*
(ii) $\gamma_{\hat{a}}(K_n) = \lceil \frac{n+1}{2} \rceil$.

Proposition 3 [4] *For the complete bipartite graph* $K_{r,s}$,
(i) $\gamma_a(K_{1,s}) = \lfloor \frac{s}{2} \rfloor + 1$,
(ii) $\gamma_a(K_{r,s}) = \lfloor \frac{r}{2} \rfloor + \lfloor \frac{s}{2} \rfloor$ *if* $r, s \geq 2$, *and*
(iii) $\gamma_{\hat{a}}(K_{r,s}) = \lceil \frac{r}{2} \rceil + \lceil \frac{s}{2} \rceil$.

In [4], we showed that the global alliance, global strong alliance, and total domination numbers are the same for graphs with minimum degree at least two and maximum degree at most three.

Lemma 4 [4] *For any graph* G *with* $\delta(G) \geq 2$, $\gamma_t(G) \leq \gamma_a(G)$. *Furthermore, if* $\Delta(G) \leq 3$, *then* $\gamma_t(G) = \gamma_a(G)$.

As a special case of Lemma 4, if G is a cubic graph, then $\gamma_t(G) = \gamma_a(G)$. The total domination number of paths P_n and cycles C_n is well known.

Proposition 5 *For* $n \geq 3$,

$$\gamma_t(P_n) = \gamma_t(C_n) = \begin{cases} \lfloor \frac{n}{2} \rfloor + 1 & \text{for } n \equiv 1, 2, 3 \,(mod\,4) \\ \frac{n}{2} & \text{for } n \equiv 0 \,(mod\,4). \end{cases}$$

Since every total dominating set of a cycle is also a global strong alliance, the following result is an immediate consequence of Lemma 4.

Proposition 6 [4] *For cycles* C_n, $n \geq 3$, $\gamma_a(C_n) = \gamma_{\hat{a}}(C_n) = \gamma_t(C_n)$.

Next we see that for paths, the global strong alliance number equals the total domination number, but the global alliance number of a path is not necessarily equal to its total domination number.

Proposition 7 [4] *For* $n \geq 3$, $\gamma_{\hat{a}}(P_n) = \gamma_t(P_n)$.

Proposition 8 [4] *For* $n \geq 2$, $\gamma_a(P_n) = \gamma_t(P_n)$ *unless* $n \equiv 2 \,(mod\,4)$, *in which case* $\gamma_a(P_n) = \gamma_t(P_n) - 1$.

Note that the minimum degree condition is necessary for Lemma 4 to hold. In fact, there exist connected graphs G for which the difference $\gamma_t(G) - \gamma_a(G)$ can be arbitrarily large. For $2 \leq s \leq k - 1$ and $k \geq 3$, consider the graph G obtained by attaching (with an edge) s disjoint copies of P_3 to each vertex of a complete graph K_k. For $k = 3$ and $s = 2$, the graph G is shown in Figure 1. Since a support vertex must be in every $\gamma_t(G)$-set, it follows that at least two vertices from each attached copy of P_3 must be in every $\gamma_t(G)$-set. Moreover, the set of support vertices of G along with their neighbors of degree two form a $\gamma_{\hat{a}}(G)$-set and a $\gamma_t(G)$-set. Hence, $\gamma_t(G) = 2sk$. But since $s \leq k - 1$, the set of endvertices together with the vertices of K_k form a global alliance of G of minimum cardinality, and so $\gamma_a(G) = (s+1)k$.

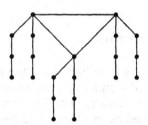

Figure 1: A graph G with $\gamma(G) = 7$, $\gamma_a(G) = 9$, and $\gamma_{\hat{a}}(G) = \gamma_t(G) = 12$.

Our last example in this section is a double star. A *double star* $S_{r,s}$ is a tree that contains exactly two vertices that are not endvertices, where one of these vertices is adjacent to r leaves and the other to s leaves.

Proposition 9 [4] *For* $r, s \geq 1$,

$$\gamma_a(S_{r,s}) = \lfloor (r-1)/2 \rfloor + \lfloor (s-1)/2 \rfloor + 2, \text{ and}$$

$$\gamma_{\hat{a}}(S_{r,s}) = \lfloor r/2 \rfloor + \lfloor s/2 \rfloor + 2.$$

3 Lower Bounds

In this section, we give lower bounds on the global alliance and global strong alliance numbers of a graph. To facilitate in illustrating some of the sharp bounds, we will use the following graph operation. For graphs G and H, the *corona* $G \circ H$ is the graph formed from G and a $V(G)$ copies of H, where the *ith* vertex of G is adjacent to every vertex in the *ith* copy of H.

We begin with bounds for general graphs.

Theorem 10 [4] *If G is a graph of order n, then*

$$\gamma_a(G) \geq (\sqrt{4n+1} - 1)/2,$$

and this bound is sharp.

That the bound of Theorem 10 is sharp may be seen as follows. Let $F_1 = K_2$ and for $k \geq 2$, let $F_k = K_k \circ \overline{K}_k$. Then, F_k for some $k \geq 1$ has order $n = k(k+1)$, and so $k = (\sqrt{4n+1} - 1)/2$. Thus, $\gamma_a(F_1) = 1 = (\sqrt{4n+1} - 1)/2$. If $k \geq 2$, then the k vertices of the complete graph K_k form a global alliance, and so $\gamma_a(F_k) \leq (\sqrt{4n+1} - 1)/2$. Consequently, $\gamma_a(F_k) = (\sqrt{4n+1} - 1)/2$.

Proposition 11 [4] *If G is an r-regular graph of order n, then*

$$\gamma_a(G) \geq \frac{n}{\lceil \frac{r}{2} \rceil + 1}.$$

Corollary 12 [4] *If G is a cubic graph or a 4-regular graph of order n, then $\gamma_a(G) \geq \frac{n}{3}$.*

Theorem 13 [4] *If G is a graph of order n, then*

$$\gamma_{\hat{a}}(G) \geq \sqrt{n},$$

and this bound is sharp.

To see that the bound of Theorem 13 is sharp, let $G_1 = K_1$ and for $k \geq 2$, let G_k be the graph $K_k \circ \overline{K}_{k-1}$. Then, G_k has order $n = k^2$, and so $k = \sqrt{n}$. Moreover, $\gamma_{\hat{a}}(G_1) = 1 = \sqrt{n}$ and for $k \geq 2$, the vertices of the K_k form a global strong alliance, and so $\gamma_{\hat{a}}(G_k) \leq \sqrt{n}$. Hence, $\gamma_{\hat{a}}(G_k) = \sqrt{n}$.

Next we determine a new sharp lower bound.

Theorem 14 *If G is a graph of order n and maximum degree Δ, then*

$$\gamma_a(G) \geq \frac{2n}{\Delta + 3} \text{ if } \Delta \text{ odd,}$$

$$\gamma_a(G) \geq \frac{2n}{\Delta + 2} \text{ if } \Delta \text{ even,}$$

and these bounds are sharp.

Proof. Assume that Δ is even and $\gamma_a(G) = k$. Then for any $\gamma_a(G)$-set S, no vertex in S can have more than $\Delta/2$ neighbors in $V - S$. Thus, $n - k \leq k\Delta/2$. Also, if Δ is odd, then $n - k \leq k(\Delta + 1)/2$. Thus, if Δ is even, $\gamma_a(G) \geq \frac{2n}{\Delta+2}$, and if Δ is odd, $\gamma_a(G) \geq \frac{2n}{\Delta+3}$.

That the bounds are sharp can be seen by the graph $G_t = K_k \circ \overline{K}_t$, where $k \geq 1$ and $t = k - 1$ for Δ even and $t = k$ for Δ odd. In either case, the k vertices of the K_k form a global alliance of G_t. If $t = k - 1$, then G_t has maximum degree $\Delta = 2k - 2$ and order $n = k^2$. If $t = k$, then G_t has $\Delta = 2k - 1$ and $n = k(k+1)$. It follows that $\gamma_a(G_k) = 2n/(\Delta + 3)$ and $\gamma_a(G_{k-1}) = 2n/(\Delta + 2)$. $\square$

A similar argument to the proof of Theorem 14 yields the following bounds for the global strong alliance number.

Theorem 15 *If G is a graph of order n and maximum degree Δ, then*

$$\gamma_{\hat{a}}(G) \geq \frac{2n}{\Delta + 1} \text{ if } \Delta \text{ odd, and}$$

$$\gamma_{\hat{a}}(G) \geq \frac{2n}{\Delta + 2} \text{ if } \Delta \text{ even.}$$

Our final result in this section is for trees.

Theorem 16 [4] *If T is a tree of order n, then*

$$\gamma_a(T) \geq \frac{n+2}{4}, \text{ and}$$

$$\gamma_{\hat{a}}(T) \geq \frac{n+2}{3},$$

and these bounds are sharp.

That the bounds of Theorem 16 are sharp may be seen as follows. For the global alliance number, let T be the tree obtained from a tree F of order k by adding $\deg_F v + 1$ new vertices for each vertex v of F and joining them to v. Then, T has order $n = |V(F)| + \sum_{v \in V(F)}(\deg_F v + 1) = 2k + \sum_{v \in V(F)} \deg_F v = 2k + 2(k - 1) = 4k - 2$. Since $V(F)$ is a global alliance of T, $\gamma_a(T) \leq k = (n + 2)/4$. Consequently, $\gamma_a(T) = (n + 2)/4$. Similarly, a tree built from F by attaching $\deg_F v$ new vertices for each vertex $v \in V(F)$ attains the bound for the global strong alliance number.

4 Upper Bounds

Our aim in this section is to give known upper bounds on the global alliance and global strong alliance numbers of a graph.

Proposition 17 [4] *For any graph G with no isolated vertices and minimum degree δ,*
  (i) $\gamma_a(G) \leq n - \lceil \delta/2 \rceil$, *and*
  (ii) $\gamma_{\hat{a}}(G) \leq n - \lfloor \delta/2 \rfloor$,
and these bounds are sharp.

That both the bounds of Proposition 17 are sharp follows directly from Proposition 2 (take $G = K_n$ with n odd for (i) and $G = K_n$ for (ii)).

Corollary 18 [4] *For any graph G, $\gamma_a(G) = n$ if and only if $G = \overline{K}_n$.*

In order to give a sharp upper bound on the global alliance number of a tree and to characterize the trees achieving this bound, we introduce a family $\mathcal{T}_1$ of trees as follows: Let $T = P_5$ or $T = K_{1,4}$ or let T be the tree obtained from $tK_{1,4}$ (the disjoint union of t copies of $K_{1,4}$) by adding $t - 1$ edges between leaves of these copies of $K_{1,4}$ in such a way that the center of each $K_{1,4}$ is adjacent to exactly three leaves in T. Let $\mathcal{T}_1$ be the family of all such trees T.

Theorem 19 [4] *If T is a tree of order $n \geq 4$, then*

$$\gamma_a(T) \leq \frac{3n}{5},$$

with equality if and only if $T \in \mathcal{T}_1$.

Finally we give sharp upper bound on the global strong alliance number of a tree and a characterization of the trees achieving this bound. Let $\mathcal{T}_2$ be a family of trees T where T is defined as follows. Let T be the tree obtained from the disjoint union $tK_{1,3}$ of $t \geq 1$ copies of $K_{1,3}$ by adding $t - 1$ edges between leaves of these copies of $K_{1,3}$ in such a way that the center of each $K_{1,3}$ is adjacent to at least one leaf in T.

Theorem 20 [4] *If T is a tree of order $n \geq 3$, then*

$$\gamma_{\hat{a}}(T) \leq \frac{3n}{4},$$

with equality if and only if $T \in \mathcal{T}_2$.

5 Trees T with $\gamma(T) = \gamma_{\hat{a}}(T)$

As we have seen in Section 2, for any graph G,

$$\gamma(G) \leq \gamma_a(G) \leq \gamma_{\hat{a}}(G).$$

A constructive characterization of the trees with equal domination and global strong alliance numbers can be found in [5]. For example, the corona $T \circ K_1$ of any nontrivial tree T has $\gamma(T \circ K_1) = |V(T)| = \gamma_{\hat{a}}(T \circ K_1)$. See Figure 2 for another example of a tree T with $\gamma(T) = \gamma_{\hat{a}}(T)$.

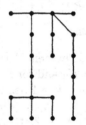

Figure 2: A tree T with $\gamma(T) = \gamma_{\hat{a}}(T) = 9$.

If $\gamma(T) = \gamma_{\hat{a}}(T)$, then clearly, $\gamma(T) = \gamma_a(T)$. It remains an open problem to characterize the trees T with $\gamma(T) = \gamma_a(T) < \gamma_{\hat{a}}(T)$.

6 Open Problems

We conclude with a list of open problems.

1. Characterize the trees T for which $\gamma(T) = \gamma_a(T) < \gamma_{\hat{a}}(T)$.

2. It is obvious that $\gamma_t(G) \leq \gamma_{\hat{a}}(G)$ for any nontrivial connected graph G. Characterize the trees T for which $\gamma_t(T) = \gamma_{\hat{a}}(T)$.

3. Determine relationships between $\gamma_a(G)$ (respectively, $\gamma_{\hat{a}}(G)$) and other domination parameters.

4. Determine the computational complexity of GLOBAL ALLIANCE and GLOBAL STRONG ALLIANCE decision problems.

5. Does there exist a linear algorithm for computing $\gamma_a(T)$ and $\gamma_{\hat{a}}(T)$ for any tree T?

6. Determine the global alliance and global strong alliance numbers of grid graphs.

7. Study the global counterparts for other types of alliances defined in [6].

References

[1] G. Chartrand and L. Lesniak, *Graphs & Digraphs: Third Edition*. Chapman & Hall, London (1996).

[2] T. W. Haynes, S. T. Hedetniemi, and P. J. Slater, *Fundamentals of Domination in Graphs*. Marcel Dekker, Inc. New York (1998).

[3] T. W. Haynes, S. T. Hedetniemi, and P. J. Slater, *Domination in Graphs: Advanced Topics*. Marcel Dekker, Inc. New York (1998).

[4] T. W. Haynes, S. T. Hedetniemi, and M. A. Henning, Global defensive alliances in graphs. Submitted for publication.

[5] T. W. Haynes, S. T. Hedetniemi, and M. A. Henning, A characterization of trees with equal domination and global strong alliance numbers. Submitted for publication.

[6] S. M. Hedetniemi, S. T. Hedetniemi, and P. Kristiansen, Alliances in graphs. Submitted for publication.

Introduction to Alliances in Graphs

Petter Kristiansen
Department of Informatics
University of Bergen
N-5020 Bergen, Norway
Petter.Kristiansen@ii.uib.no

Sandra M. Hedetniemi
Department of Computer Science
Clemson University
Clemson, SC USA 29634
shedet@cs.clemson.edu

Stephen T. Hedetniemi
Department of Computer Science
Clemson University
Clemson, SC USA 29634
hedet@cs.clemson.edu

Abstract

A *defensive alliance* in a graph $G = (V, E)$ is a set of vertices $S \subseteq V$ satisfying the condition that every vertex $v \in S$ has at most one more neighbor in $V - S$ than it has in S. In this paper we introduce this new concept, together with a variety of other kinds of alliances, and initiate the study of their mathematical properties.

1 Introduction

In this paper we introduce the study of alliances in graphs. In its simplest form, an *alliance* is nothing other than a set of vertices having some collective property. But, as in the real world there are different types of alliances, so shall we define different types of alliances.

Alliances are found in many varieties, including those formed:

(i) by people who unite by kinship or friendship;

(ii) by confederations between sovereign states;

(iii) by members of different political parties;

(iv) in botany, by groups of natural orders of plants;

(v) in ecology, by groupings of closely related associations;

(vi) in business, by companies with common economic interests;

(vii) in times of war, by nations for mutual support, usually defensive in nature, where allies are obligated to join forces if one or more of them are attacked, but also offensive, as a means of keeping the peace, e.g. NATO troops in a war-torn country.

2 Alliances in Graphs

Definition 1 A non-empty set of vertices $S \subseteq V$ is called a *defensive alliance* if and only if for every $v \in S$, $|N[v] \cap S| \geq |N(v) \cap (V - S)|$. In this case, by strength of numbers, we say that every vertex in S is *defended* from possible attack by vertices in $V - S$. A defensive alliance is called *strong* if for every vertex $v \in S$, $|N[v] \cap S| > |N(v) \cap (V - S)|$. In this case we say that every vertex in S is *strongly defended*.

Definition 2 A non-empty set of vertices $S \subseteq V$ is called an *offensive alliance* if and only if for every $v \in \partial(S)$, $|N(v) \cap S| \geq |N[v] \cap (V - S)|$. In this case we say that every vertex in $\partial(S)$ is *vulnerable* to possible attack by vertices in S. An offensive alliance is called *strong* if for every vertex $v \in \partial(S)$, $|N(v) \cap S| > |N[v] \cap (V - S)|$.

Any two vertices u, v in an alliance S are called *allies (with respect to S)*; we also say that u and v are *allied*.

An alliance S (defensive or offensive) is called *critical* if no proper subset of S is an alliance (of the same type). Note that the property of being an alliance (of any type) is not necessarily *hereditary*.

For a graph G we will consider the following classes of alliances:

$\mathcal{A}(G)$, the class of critical defensive alliances,

$\hat{\mathcal{A}}(G)$, the class of critical strong defensive alliances,

Associated with each of these classes of critical alliances, are two invariants, as follows:

$$a(G) = \min\{|S| : S \in \mathcal{A}(G)\},$$

the *alliance number of G*,

$$A(G) = \max\{|S| : S \in \mathcal{A}(G)\},$$

the *upper alliance number*,

$$\hat{a}(G) = \min\{|S| : S \in \hat{\mathcal{A}}(G)\},$$

the *strong alliance number*,

$$\hat{A}(G) = \max\{|S| : S \in \hat{\mathcal{A}}(G)\},$$

the *upper strong alliance number*.

In addition to defensive and offensive alliances, there are several other types of alliances that can be considered.

Definition 3 A defensive alliance S is called *global* if it effects every vertex in $V - S$, that is, every vertex in $V - S$ is adjacent to at least one member of the alliance S. In this case, S is a dominating set, and one can define the global alliance number, denoted $\gamma_a(G)$, to equal the minimum cardinality of a global defensive alliance in G.

Definition 4 An offensive alliance S is called *global* if for every vertex $v \in V - S$, $|N(v) \cap S| \geq |N[v] \cap (V - S)|$. Thus, global offensive alliances are also dominating sets, since every vertex in $V - S$ is adjacent to at least one vertex in the alliance S.

Both global defensive alliances and global offensive alliances are new kinds of dominating sets. A fairly complete listing of different kinds of dominating sets can be found in the two books by Haynes, Hedetniemi and Slater [21, 22].

Definition 5 An alliance is called *dual* if it is both defensive and offensive.

Definition 6 An alliance is called *open* if it is defined completely in terms of open neighborhoods, that is, a set $S \subseteq V$ is an *open defensive alliance* if for every vertex $v \in S$, $|N(v) \cap S| \geq |N(v) \cap (V - S)|$.

Notice that every strong alliance is also an open alliance. Notice also that open alliances are *cohesive sets*, as defined in [16, 27].

Definition 7 An alliance S is called *weighted* if associated with every vertex $v \in V$ is a weight (or a strength) $wt(v)$, and we require that for every vertex $v \in S$, $\sum_{u \in N[v] \cap S} wt(u) \geq \sum_{w \in N(v) \cap (V - S)} wt(w)$.

3 Concepts Similar to Alliances

Although the concept of an alliance in a graph is newly defined here, concepts similar to defensive and offensive alliances can be found in the literature. Among the earliest of these is that of an *unfriendly 2-partition* of a graph $G = (V, E)$, which is a partition $\Pi = \{V_0, V_1\}$, having the property that every vertex $v \in V_i$ is adjacent to at least as many vertices in V_{1-i} as it is to vertices in V_i. Stated in terms of alliances, unfriendly 2-partitions almost correspond to a partition of V into two offensive alliances. If the definition of an unfriendly 2-partition is changed as follows, then it corresponds to a partition of V into two global offensive alliances. A 2-partition $\Pi = \{V_0, V_1\}$ is called *very unfriendly* if every vertex $v \in V_i$ is adjacent to *more* vertices in V_{1-i} than it is to vertices in V_i.

Unfriendly 2-partitions were perhaps first introduced by Borodin and Kostochka in [3], and have also been studied by Bernardi [2], Cowan and Emerson [6], Aharoni, Milner and Prikry [1], and Shelah and Milner [28]. Basic to these investigations is the simple observation that every finite graph has an unfriendly 2-partition. Shelah and Milner [28] showed that not all infinite graphs have unfriendly 2-partitions, but all graphs have an unfriendly 3-partition.

A similar concept has been studied by Gerber and Kobler [16], who define a vertex v in a set $A \subset V$ to be *satisfied* if it has at least as many neighbors in A as in $V - A$. A set A is called *cohesive* if every vertex in A is satisfied with respect to A. It is easy to see that every cohesive set is a strong defensive alliance. A graph is said to be *satisfiable* if has a vertex partition into two or more non-empty sets so that every vertex is satisfied with respect to the set in which it occurs. Such a partition is called a *satisfactory partition*. Satisfactory partitions correspond, therefore, to partitions of V into strong defensive alliances. It can be seen that not all graphs have satisfactory partitions, for example complete graphs. Shafique and Dutton [27] present some necessary and sufficient conditions for graphs to be satisfiable, and show that no forbidden subgraph characterization exists for this class of graphs.

Several authors have studied signed and minus dominating functions in graphs, which are defined as follows. A function $f : V \to \{-1, +1\}$ is called a *signed dominating function* if for every vertex $v \in V$, $f(N[v]) \geq 1$. Stated in other words, if $\Pi = \{V_{-1}, V_1\}$ is the 2-partition defined by f^{-1}, then the set V_1 is a global dual alliance. Similarly, a function $f : V \to \{-1, 0, 1\}$ is called a *minus dominating function* if for every vertex $v \in V$, $f(N[v]) \geq 1$. Stated in other

309

words, if $\Pi = \{V_{-1}, V_0, V_1\}$ is the 3-partition defined by f^{-1}, then the set V_1 is a global strong defensive alliance. Signed and minus domination have been studied in [7, 9, 10, 11, 13, 17, 18, 23, 29].

Another concept similar to that of alliances has been studied by Dunbar, Hoffman, Laskar and Markus [12], who define a set $S \subseteq V$ to be an α-*dominating set*, for some α, $0 < \alpha \leq 1$, if every vertex $v \in V - S$ satisfies the inequality: $|N(v) \cap S| \geq \alpha |N(v)|$. Thus, if $\alpha > 1/2$, then every vertex in $V - S$ has more neighbors in S than it has in $V - S$. This means that the set S is a global offensive alliance. However, if $\alpha \leq 1/2$, then every vertex in the set $V - S$ has at least as many neighbors in $V - S$ as it does in S, and therefore, $V - S$ is a strong defensive alliance. Recently, Langley, Merz, Stewart and Ward [25] have studied α-domination in tournaments.

Still another concept similar to that of alliances has been studied by Dunbar, Harris, Hedetniemi, Hedetniemi, Laskar and McRae [8], who define a set $S \subseteq V$ to be *nearly perfect* if for all $v \in V - S$, $|N(v) \cap S| \leq 1$. It is easy to see that if S is a nearly perfect set, then the complement $V - S$ is a defensive alliance.

A *perfect dominating set* is a dominating set having the property that for all $v \in V - S$, $|N(v) \cap S| = 1$. A set $S \subseteq V$ is a 2-*packing* if for all $v \in V$, $|N[v] \cap S| \leq 1$. It follows from these definitions that the complement of every perfect dominating set and the complement of every 2-packing is a defensive alliance (cf. [5, 21, 22] for discussion of perfect dominating sets and 2-packings).

One final type of set leads to alliances. A set $S \subseteq V$ is a *vertex cover* if for every edge $uv \in E$, $S \cap \{u, v\} \neq \emptyset$. It is well known that the complement $V - S$ of any vertex cover S is an independent set. It is easy to see, therefore, that every vertex cover of a connected graph is a global offensive alliance.

Since the introduction of the concept of alliances in graphs by the authors in August, 2001 [24], several papers have been written, and are in preparation, on this topic (cf. [4, 14, 15, 19, 20, 26]).

4 Selected Results

Proposition 1 *For any graph G,*

(i) $a(G) = 1$ *if and only if there exists a vertex $v \in V$ such that* $\deg(v) \leq 1$.

(ii) $\hat{a}(G) = 1$ *if and only if G has an isolated vertex.*

Corollary 2 *For any tree T and path P_n, $a(T) = a(P_n) = 1$.*

Proposition 3 *For any graph G,*

(i) $a(G) = 2$ *if and only if $\delta(G) \geq 2$ and G has two adjacent vertices of degree at most three.*

(ii) $\hat{a}(G) = 2$ *if and only if $\delta(G) \geq 1$ and G has two adjacent vertices of degree at most two.*

Corollary 4 *For any cycle C_n and any wheel W_n,*

(i) $a(C_n) = \hat{a}(P_n) = \hat{a}(C_n) = a(W_n) = 2$.

(ii) $\hat{a}(W_n) = \lceil n/2 \rceil + 1$.

Proposition 5 *For any graph G,*

(i) $a(G) = 3$ *if and only if $a(G) \neq 1$, $a(G) \neq 2$, and G has an induced subgraph isomorphic to either (a) P_3, with vertices, in order, u, v and w, where $\deg(u)$ and $\deg(w)$ are at most three, and $\deg(v)$ is at most five, or (b) isomorphic to K_3, each vertex of which has degree at most five.*

(ii) $\hat{a}(G) = 3$ *if and only if $\hat{a}(G) \neq 1$, $\hat{a}(G) \neq 2$, and G has an induced subgraph isomorphic to either (a) P_3, with vertices, in order, u, v and w, where $\deg(u)$ and $\deg(w)$ are at most two, and $\deg(v)$ is at most four, or (b) isomorphic to K_3, each vertex of which has degree at most four.*

The $m \times n$ *grid graph* is the Cartesian product $G_{m,n} = P_m \,\square\, P_n$.

Theorem 6 *For the $m \times n$ grid graph $G_{m,n}$,*

(i) $1 \leq a(G_{m,n}) \leq 4$ *and*

(ii) $\hat{a}(G_{m,n}) = 4$ *if and only if $\min\{m, n\} \geq 4$.*

Proposition 7 *For the complete graph K_n,*

(i) $a(K_n) = \lceil n/2 \rceil$.

(ii) $\hat{a}(K_n) = \lfloor n/2 \rfloor + 1$.

Theorem 8 *[15] For any graph G of order n,*

(i) $a(G) \leq \lceil n/2 \rceil$,

(ii) $\hat{a}(G) = \lfloor n/2 \rfloor + 1$,

and these bounds are sharp.

For the following class of graphs, the upper bound in Theorem 8 can be improved slightly. Let $\lambda(G)$ denote the *edge connectivity* of a connected graph G, which equals the minimum number of edges in a set, whose removal from G results in a disconnected graph. Note that for any connected graph G, $\lambda(G) \leq \delta(G)$, that

310

is, a connected graph G can always be disconnected by removing all of the edges incident to a vertex of minimum degree $\delta(G)$.

Let $\Pi = \{V_1, V_2\}$ be a bipartition of the vertices of a connected graph G, such that there are $\lambda(G)$ edges between vertices in V_1 and vertices in V_2. If either $|V_1| = 1$ or $|V_2| = 1$, then we say that Π is a *singular λ-bipartition*, while if both V_1 and V_2 have at least two vertices, then we say that Π is a *non-singular λ-bipartition*.

Proposition 9 *For any graph G of order n, for which $\lambda(G) < \delta(G)$,*

$$a(G) \leq \hat{a}(G) \leq \lfloor n/2 \rfloor.$$

Corollary 10 *For any graph G of order n having a non-singular λ-bipartition,*

$$a(G) \leq \hat{a}(G) \leq \lfloor n/2 \rfloor.$$

Table 1 provides an overview of results for $a(G)$ and $\hat{a}(G)$, and for both $A(G)$ and $\hat{A}(G)$. In Table 1, $\mathrm{gr}(G) = \mathrm{girth}(G)$, that is, the length of a smallest cycle in a graph G, and $\mathrm{lcc}(G)$ is the maximum length of a chordless cycle in G.

Class	$a(G)$	$A(G)$	$\hat{a}(G)$	$\hat{A}(G)$
1-reg	1	1	2	2
Paths	1	$2, n \geq 4$	$2, n \geq 3$	$2, n \geq 3$
Trees	1	any k	any k	any k
Cycles	2	2	$2, n \geq 3$	$2, n \geq 3$
3-reg	2	2	$\mathrm{gr}(G)$	$\mathrm{lcc}(G)$
4-reg	$\mathrm{gr}(G)$	$\mathrm{lcc}(G)$	$\mathrm{gr}(G)$	$\mathrm{lcc}(G)$
5-reg	$\mathrm{gr}(G)$	$\mathrm{lcc}(G)$	?	?

Table 1: Alliance numbers for several classes of graphs.

5 Algorithmic Complexity

This paper has not considered any algorithmic complexity issues, but there are many to consider, including, for example, the following NP-completeness questions:

(CRITICAL) ALLIANCE
INSTANCE: graph G, positive integer k.
QUESTION: Does G have a (critical) alliance of size at most k?

(CRITICAL) STRONG ALLIANCE
INSTANCE: graph G, positive integer k.
QUESTION: Does G have a (critical) strong alliance of size at most k?

McRae, Goddard, Hedetniemi, Hedetniemi and Kristiansen have shown that ALLIANCE and STRONG ALLIANCE are both NP-complete, even when restricted to bipartite or chordal graphs [26]. But many complexity questions remain unanswered, including the following:

OFFENSIVE ALLIANCE
INSTANCE: graph G, positive integer k.
QUESTION: Does G have an offensive alliance of size at most k?

GLOBAL ALLIANCE
INSTANCE: graph G, positive integer k.
QUESTION: Does G have a global alliance of size at most k?

DUAL ALLIANCE
INSTANCE: graph G, positive integer k.
QUESTION: Does G have a dual alliance of size at most k?

In addition, the following questions are of some interest:

1. Given a graph G and a vertex $v \in V$, define the *alliance number of v*, $a(v)$, to equal the smallest defensive alliance containing vertex v. How difficult is it to determine $a(v)$?

2. Given a graph G and two vertices $u, v \in V$, what is $a(u, v)$, that is, the smallest cardinality of an alliance containing both u and v?

3. Given a graph G, the *alliance partition number*, $\psi_a(G)$, is the maximum order of a partition $\Pi = \{V_1, V_2, \ldots, V_k\}$ of $V(G)$ into defensive alliances. What is the alliance partition number of a grid graph $G_{m,n}$?

4. Define the *kth alliance number $a_k(G)$* to equal the smallest cardinality of a defensive alliance having the property that it can defend itself from any k simultaneous attacks. What can you say about $a_k(G)$?

References

[1] R. Aharoni, E.C. Milner and K. Prikry, Unfriendly partitions of a graph, *J. Combin. Theory, Ser. B* 50:1-10, 1990.

[2] C. Bernardi, On a theorem about vertex coloring of graphs, *Discrete Math.* 64(1):95-96, 1987.

[3] O.V. Borodin and A.V. Kostochka, On an upper bound of a graph's chromatic number, depending on the graph's degree and density, *J. Combin. Theory Ser. B* 23:247-250, 1977.

[4] R.C. Brigham, R.D. Dutton, T.W. Haynes, and S.T. Hedetniemi, Dual alliances in graphs, in preparation, August, 2002.

[5] E.J. Cockayne, B.L. Hartnell, S.T. Hedetniemi and R. Laskar, Perfect domination in graphs, *J. Combin. Inform. System Sci.* 18(1-2):136-148, 1993.

[6] R. Cowan and W. Emerson, Proportional coloring of graphs, unpublished.

[7] J.E. Dunbar, W. Goddard, S.T. Hedetniemi, M.A. Henning and A.A. McRae, The algorithmic complexity of minus domination in graphs, *Discrete Appl. Math.* 68:73-84, 1996.

[8] J. Dunbar, F. Harris, S.M. Hedetniemi, S.T. Hedetniemi, R. Laskar and A. McRae, Nearly perfect sets in graphs, *Discrete Math.* 138:229-246, 1995.

[9] J.E. Dunbar, S.T. Hedetniemi, M.A. Henning and A.A. McRae, Minus domination in graphs, *Discrete Math.*, 199:35-47, 1999.

[10] J.E. Dunbar, S.T. Hedetniemi, M.A. Henning and A.A. McRae, Minus domination in regular graphs, *Discrete Math.* 149:311-312, 1996.

[11] J.E. Dunbar, S.T. Hedetniemi, M.A. Henning and P.J. Slater, Signed domination in graphs, in Y. Alavi and A.J. Schwenk, Editors, *Graph Theory, Combinatorics, and Applications, Proc. 7th Internat. Conf. Combinatorics, Graph Theory, Applications*, Vol. 1, pp. 311-322, Wiley, 1995.

[12] J.E. Dunbar, D.G. Hoffman, R.C. Laskar and L.R. Markus, α-Domination in graphs, *Discrete Math.* 211:11-26, 2000.

[13] O. Favaron, Signed domination in regular graphs, *Discrete Math.* 158:287-293, 1996.

[14] O. Favaron, G. Fricke, W. Goddard, S.M. Hedetniemi, S.T. Hedetniemi, P. Kristiansen, R.C. Laskar and D. Skaggs, Offensive alliances in graphs, in preparation, August, 2002.

[15] G.H. Fricke, L.M. Lawson, T.W. Haynes, S.M. Hedetniemi .and S.T. Hedetniemi, A note on defensive alliances in graphs, *Bull. ICA*, to appear.

[16] M.U. Gerber and D. Kobler, Algorithmic approach to the satisfactory graph partitioning problem, *European J. Oper. Res.* 125:283-291, 2000.

[17] J.H. Hattingh, M.A. Henning and P.J. Slater, Three-valued k-neighbourhood domination in graphs, *Australas. J. Combin.* :233-242, 1994.

[18] J.H. Hattingh, M.A. Henning and P.J. Slater, On the algorithmic complexity of signed domination in graphs, *Australas. J. Combin.* 12:101-112, 1995.

[19] T.W. Haynes, S.T. Hedetniemi and M.A. Henning, Global defensive alliances in graphs, submitted for publication, .

[20] T.W. Haynes, S.T. Hedetniemi and M.A. Henning, A characterization of trees with equal domination and global domination numbers, in preparation, August, 2002.

[21] T. W. Haynes, S. T. Hedetniemi and P. J. Slater, *Fundamentals of Domination in Graphs*, Marcel Dekker, New York, .

[22] T. W. Haynes, S. T. Hedetniemi and P. J. Slater, Editors, *Domination in Graphs: Advanced Topics*, Marcel Dekker, New York, .

[23] M.A. Henning and P.J. Slater, Inequalities relating domination parameters in cubic graphs, *Discrete Math.* 158:87-98, 1996.

[24] P. Kristiansen, S.M. Hedetniemi and S.T. Hedetniemi, Alliances in graphs, manuscript, August, 2000.

[25] L. Langley, S. Merz, D. Stewart and C. Ward, α-Domination in tournaments, preprint, 2002.

[26] A. McRae, W. Goddard, S.M. Hedetniemi, S.T. Hedetniemi and P. Kristiansen, The algorithmic complexity of alliances in graphs, in preparation, August, 2002.

[27] K.H. Shafique and R.D. Dutton, On satisfactory partitioning of graphs, manuscript, 2001.

[28] S. Shelah and E.C. Milner, Graphs with no unfriendly partitions, *A tribute to Paul Erdös*, 373-384, Cambridge Univ. Press, Cambridge, 1990.

[29] B. Zelinka, Some remarks on domination in cubic graphs, *Discrete Math.* 158:249-255, 1996.

Session 5–2
Computer Networks III

Case-Based Agents for Packet-Level Intrusion Detection in Ad Hoc Networks

R. Guha and O. Kachirski
SEECS - Computer Science
University of Central Florida
Orlando, FL, USA
Contact: guha@cs.ucf.edu

D.G. Schwartz, S. Stoecklin, and E. Yilmaz
Department of Computer Science
Florida State University
Tallahassee, FL, USA
Contact: schwartz@cs.fsu.edu

Abstract

In this paper we propose a distributed agent framework for an intrusion detection system aimed at ad hoc wireless networks. Wireless networks are particularly vulnerable to intrusion, as they operate in an open medium, and use cooperative strategies for network communications. By efficiently merging audit data from multiple security agents, we analyze the entire ad hoc wireless network for intrusions and try to inhibit intrusion attempts. A case-based reasoning approach to our intrusion detection engine provides a framework incorporating sophisticated artificial intelligence techniques that help overcome some of the limitations of other rule-based intrusion detection systems. In contrast to many existing intrusion detection systems, we design and implement an efficient, bandwidth-conscious framework that targets intrusion at multiple levels and takes into account the distributed nature of ad hoc wireless network management and decision policies.

1. Introduction

1.1. Case-Based Reasoning

The basic features of a general case-based reasoning (CBR) system are depicted in Figure 1. The most important component of the system is the case archive where the previously experienced problems are stored with their solutions. Each entry in the case archive is called a "case" which contains (i) the features describing the problem, and (ii) the action or actions that were taken to solve the problem. When a problem is detected in the surrounding environment, it is formulated as a set of case features (step 1.0). Then, this problem description is transferred to a search engine that extracts the similar cases from the case archive, where similarity is measured by the similarity between the matching features of the problem description and the case features of actual cases

in the case archive (step 2.0). The returned cases are ranked according to their degrees of similarity to the given problem. At this moment two different scenarios are possible: either some of the selected cases are decided as a solution to the problem or a new case is formulated to solve the problem based on the returned cases. In either case, the actions recommended by the returned case or cases are taken (step 4.0). Furthermore, the measure of success or failure of the result of the action is reported along with the case into the case archive (step 5.0). In future applications of the case-based reasoner, this information will be taken into account in the similar-case extraction process so that the performance of the system will improve over time.

1.2. Intrusion Detection Systems

Traditionally, intrusion detection systems (IDSs) were divided into two classes: network-based and host-based IDS. Network-based systems (NIDS) listen on the network, and capture and examine individual packets flowing through a network. NIDSs often require dedicated hosts and special equipment, and can be prone to the network attack. A few reliable NIDSs are described in [1, 5, 7, 8]. Host-based intrusion detection systems [1, 2, 3, 6] are concerned with what is happening on each individual host. They are able to detect actions such as repeated failed access attempts or changes to critical system files, and normally operate by accessing log files or monitoring real-time system usage. To ensure effective operation, host IDS clients have to be installed on every host on the network, tailored to specific host configuration. These systems can considerably slow down the hosts that have IDS clients installed.

IDS systems are functionally divided into two categories: anomaly detection and misuse detection systems. Anomaly detection bases its ideas on statistical behavior modeling. This model detects intrusion detections in a very accurate and consistent way, and has a low number of false alarms if the system under surveillance follows static behavioral patterns. Misuse detection systems monitor networks and hosts for known attack patterns. This class of IDS systems is useful in networks with highly dynamic behavioral patterns. However, a frequently updated (and large) database of known attack signatures must be maintained. Both categories of IDS can be used on host-based and network-based IDS systems.

Structural and behavioral differences between wired and wireless mobile networks make existing IDS designs inapplicable to wireless networks. As discussed above, wireless network communications are conducted in an open air environment. Thus, network monitoring in wireless ad hoc networks is performed at every network node [3]. This approach is inefficient due to network bandwidth consumption and increased computations – resources that are highly limited in a wireless network. Host-based monitoring also contributes to a high amount of processing on each host, shortening battery life and slowing down the host. Physical mobile host security is an issue, as each host contains keys used to encrypt information over the network, and if captured, the network is subject to eavesdropping.

Applying functionality-based network IDS models also has limitations. The anomaly detection model is built on a long-term monitoring and classifying of what is a normal system behavior. Ad hoc wireless networks are very dynamic in structure, giving rise to apparently random communication patterns, thus making it challenging to build a reliable behavioral model. Misuse detection requires maintenance of an extensive database of attack signatures, which in the case of an ad hoc network would have to be replicated among all the hosts.

To avoid the problems outlined above, we have designed a modular IDS system [16], based on intelligent mobile agents. We have also developed a case based approach to network intrusion detection [15]. In this paper we incorporate the case-based reasoning engine, proposed in [15] for detecting intrusions at the packet level in the modular IDS system [16] and study the effect of such incorporation.

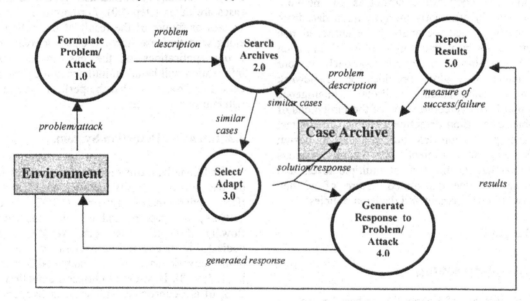

Figure 1. Case-Based Reasoning Process.

2. Case-Based Agent Intrusion Detection System

2.1. Agent-Based IDS architecture

Our IDS is built on a mobile agent framework, as described in [16]. It is a non-monolithic system and employs several sensor types that perform specific functions, such as:

- Network monitoring: Only certain nodes have sensor agents for network packet monitoring, since we are interested in preserving total computational power and battery power of mobile hosts.

- Host monitoring: Every node on the mobile ad hoc network is monitored internally by a host-monitoring agent. This includes monitoring system-level and application-level activities.

- Decision-making: Each node determines on its own degree of intrusion threat. Certain nodes collect intrusion information and make collective decisions about network-level intrusions.

Action: Every node has an action module responsible for resolving intrusion situations on a host.

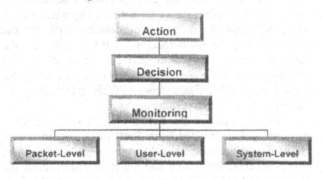

Figure 2. Layered Mobile Agent Architecture.

An advantage of the agent-oriented approach is that one can make the total network load smaller by separating the necessary functional tasks into categories and dedicating different agents to different specific purposes. This way, the workload of the IDS system is distributed among the nodes in such a way as to minimize the power consumption and IDS-related processing time by all nodes. A hierarchy of agents has been devised in order to achieve the above goals. This is depicted in Figure 2. There are three major agent categories: monitoring, decision-making, and action agents. Some are present on all mobile hosts, while others are distributed to only a select group of nodes, as discussed further. The monitoring agent class consists of packet, user, and system-monitoring agents. Hierarchical IDS systems have been proposed in [5, 6, 7].

To save resources, some of the IDS functionality must be distributed efficiently to a (small) number of nodes while providing an adequate degree of intrusion detection. While all the nodes accommodate host-based monitoring sensors of the IDS, we use a distributed algorithm described in [16] to assign a few nodes to serve as host sensors that monitor network packets, and agents that make decisions. We logically divide a mobile network into clusters (similar to the Clustered Gateway Switch Routing protocol described in [9, 10, 11, 12]) with a single cluster head for each cluster that monitors packets within the cluster. This will ensure that the minimal number of nodes is selected for hosting packet-monitoring agents.

Packet-monitoring agents reside on each selected cluster head, collect all packets within communication range, and analyze them for known attacks. As the physical network arrangement changes, cluster membership is dynamically updated. For the case of a one-hop cluster, each node has at least one neighboring node hosting a packet-monitoring agent, and thus the entire network is always being monitored. If the system resources are scarce and security requirements can be relaxed, a two-hop system is more appropriate. At any given time, a few links might not be monitored. This may be acceptable for a highly-dynamic environment, where network configuration changes often. The packet detection mechanism is discussed further in this paper.

Local detection agents are located on each node of an ad-hoc network, and act as user-level and system-level anomaly-based monitoring sensors. These agents look for suspicious activities on the host node, such as unusual process memory allocations, CPU activity, I/O activity, and user operations (invalid login attempts with a certain pattern, super-user actions, etc). If an anomaly is detected with strong evidence, a local detection agent will terminate suspicious processes or lock out a user and initiate re-issue of security keys for the entire network. If some inconclusive anomalous activity is detected on a host node by a monitoring agent, the node is reported to the decision agent of the cluster of which the suspicious node is a member. If more-conclusive evidence is gathered about this node from any source (including packet monitoring results from a network-monitoring agent), the action is undertaken by the action agent on that node, as described above.

2.2. Case-Based Detection Mechanism

2.2.1. Generic Case Based Reasoning

Case-based reasoning systems are designed for a given application domain. But it is possible to abstract out the common aspects of CBR from the domain specific aspects [15]. This leads to a generic case-based reasoner from which any arbitrary domain-specific case-based reasoner can be created as a specific instance.

In order to build the desired generic case-based reasoner, it is required to generalize both the notion of a case and the notion of a similarity metric used for determining the degree of similarity between cases. Since cases are described by their features, the first task is to describe the generic notion of a case feature. The framework proposed in [15] makes it possible to define virtually any type of feature and any type of case.

The similarity metric for cases can be defined as a collection of feature comparison results with a rule specifying how these intermediate results are combined. Moreover, feature comparisons can be generalized into the generic notion of feature comparator of which each specific comparator is an instance. Although each case feature may require a different type of comparison, the result of the comparison should be a similarity assessment between the same case feature of the problem specification and of a case from the case archive.

Therefore for each new type of case feature, it is required to define a comparator that determines the degree of similarity between the problem situation feature and the corresponding feature in the case archive. Since different case features may use the same comparator, the number of comparators in the system will be much smaller than the number of different features. The modular distinction between comparators and case features simplifies the adaptation of the system into different problem domains.

2.2.2. Adaptive Case-Based Reasoning Process

The generic CBR component assumes no knowledge about the application domain regarding case features and their comparison. The system can be tailored into a domain-specific case-based reasoner by defining the data type definition of the XML representation of a domain specific case, together with a metadata dictionary where the data about different case features, such as the required comparator and its value type, are stored. This use of a metadata dictionary and the separation of domain specific knowledge from generic components is an example of "adaptive" or "reflective" architecture. Hence the title for our system The advantage of this software engineering approach is that the same generic CBR source code can used for any application domain – no, or very minimal, additional programming is required.

The adaptive CBR process of an IDS is as follows. A packet is received from the network and fed into the CBR module. The packet is converted into an XML representation as specified in a corresponding DTD file. The search engine in the CBR module searches for similar cases in case archive. In the search process, cases are compared to the received packet's XML representation. For each feature in the packet XML data, the CBR module looks in the metadata dictionary for the type of the required comparator, and the comparator is created by reflection (i.e., during run time). Each comparator determines whether the packet feature matches the corresponding case feature. Once all the features are compared, the CBR module assigns a similarity value for the compared case. Last the CBR module retrieves the matching case or cases and performs the prescribed action.

3. Packet-Level Intrusion Detection

3.1. CBR Implementation of a Packet-Monitoring Agent

In order to implement a packet-monitoring agent using adaptive CBR, we converted the rules of the well-known Snort IDS into a case archive. All the elements in a rule header, as well as the rule options, that are used in

the rule matching process by Snort are treated as case features, and the rule action and its corresponding rule options (such as message element) are treated as the case action.

In the Snort IDS, the corresponding rule action is taken only if all of the elements that make up a rule match with the network packet. This means that in the corresponding domain-specific CBR system, the similarity metric must be bivalent; in other words, the matches must be exact. Hence there is no need for similarity ranking. Thus, from a CBR standpoint, the corresponding system is quite simple.

The entire packet monitoring CBR system, including the case archive created from Snort rules, together with required comparators, is quite small in size. Moreover, due to its modular design and implementation, both the reasoner and case archive components are portable. This is very important for network agent implementation. As explained in the next section, this CBR system can serve as the core of the "decision agents" in their intrusion detection process.

3.2. Packet Monitoring and Evidence Collection Process

Packet-monitoring agents reside on cluster head nodes. Each cluster head monitors packets sent by every member of its cluster, and therefore, the agent subsystem has a low-level access to the underlying operating system's network layer to capture packets that are not intended for the cluster head node. For now, we limit the collection of packets only to those that have as originator any node that belongs to the cluster. This is done to prevent processing of the same packet more than once by any packet-monitoring agent. When packets are captured, they are inserted in a queue (logically), and physically added to a buffer of fixed size (the size depends on the node's available memory). The packets are then dequeued and processed by the agent's case-based reasoning engine for intrusion detection. If a queue becomes full, further packets are dropped until space is available in the queue (see Figure 3). By varying queue size, we limit processing done by a cluster head node, as its resources are also used for performing regular user tasks. Agent subsystem also allows us to limit CPU usage by an agent to a certain level, acceptable by the user. As case-based reasoner scans the packets from the queue, it checks the packet information (network addresses, ports and payload contents) against a known set of rules, as described in the previous section. When a match is detected, alert is raised and forwarded to the decision-making agent (residing on the same host – the cluster head).

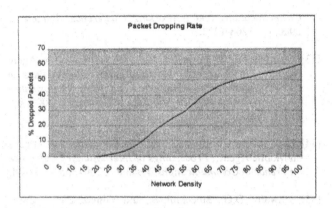

Figure 3. Increase in packet dropping rate as the network density increases.

Our intrusion detection system utilizes an independent decision-making mechanism. Decision agents are located on the same nodes as packet-monitoring agents. Decision agent contains a state machine for all the nodes within the cluster it resides in. As intrusion and anomalous activity evidence is gathered for each node, the agent can decide with a certain confidence that a node has been compromised by looking at reports from the node's own local monitoring agents, and the packet-monitoring information pertaining to that node. When a certain level of threat is reached for a node in question, decision agent dispatches a command that an action must be undertaken by the local agents on that node, as described in section 3. Decision-making agent maintains a "sliding-window" view on the intrusion data for each node within its cluster. This is necessary to account for certain uses of the network node that do not conform to accepted range of normal behavior, yet do not represent a threat to the wireless network as such. Repetitive alerts of the same type within that window will cause an action to be undertaken by a decision agent to secure the breach in a network caused by a certain node or a group of nodes.

4. Concluding Remarks

In this paper, we have proposed a distributed modular intrusion detection system that employs case-based reasoning engine for intrusion detection. The database for CBR engine is distributed to every node of the wireless ad hoc network. The CBR engine is activated by a packet monitoring agent of a cluster-head node. Using our network clustering algorithm, developed in [16], we have simulated the intrusion detection process that uses CBR engine and an intrusion database. The simulation shows that for a single cluster head node processing all the incoming packets, the number of dropped packets increases significantly when the density

of ad hoc wireless network increases. Although each cluster head's processing load due to IDS system is controlled, the reliability of IDS system attack detection decreases. This issue will be addressed in future work, when cluster processing algorithm will be employed, where the monitoring tasks are shared among nodes in a cluster. Current and future work involves investigating the most effective sharing process, resulting in a minimized packet drop rate and providing a high degree of protection, while limiting the load on each node due to intrusion detection processing.

Acknowledgements

This work was supported by the US Army Research Office, grant number DAAD19-01-1-0502. The views and conclusions herein are those of the authors and do not represent the official policies of the funding agency.

References

[1] Lippmann R., et. al., "Evaluating Intrusion Detection Systems: The 1998 DARPA Off-Line Intrusion Detection Evaluation", *Proceedings of DARPA Information Survivability Conference & Exposition II, Volume. 2*, 1999, pp. 12-26.

[2] Haines, J., L. Rossey, R. Lippmann, and R. Cunningham, "Extending the DARPA Off-Line Intrusion Detection Evaluations", *Proceedings of DARPA Information Survivability Conference & Exposition II, Volume 1*, 2001, pp. 35-45.

[3] Zhang, Y. and W. Lee, "Intrusion Detection in Wireless Ad-Hoc Networks", *Proceedings of the 6th Annual International Conference on Mobile Computing and Networking, MobiCom'2000*, pp. 275-283.

[4] Siraj, A., S. Bridges, and R. Vaughn, "Fuzzy Intrusion Detection", *Joint 9th IFSA World Congress and 20th NAFIPS International Conference, Voume 4*, 2001, pp. 2165-2170.

[5] Dasgupta, D. and H. Brian, "Mobile Security Agents for Network Traffic Analysis", *Proceedings of DARPA Information Survivability Conference & Exposition II, DISCEX '01, Volume: 2*, 2001, pp. 332-340.

[6] Bernardes, M.C. and E. Santos Moreira, "Implementation of an Intrusion Detection System based on Mobile Agents", *Proceedings of International Symposium on Software Engineering for Parallel and Distributed Systems*, 2000, pp. 158-164.

[7] Helmer, G., J. Wong, V. Honavar, L, Miller, "Lightweight Agents for Intrusion Detection", Technical Report, Dept. of Computer Science, Iowa State University, 2000.

[8] Tao, J., L. Ji-ren, and Q. Yang, "The Research on Dynamic Self-Adaptive Network Security Model Based on Mobile Agent", *Proceedings of 36th International Conference on Technology of Object-Oriented Languages and Systems*, 2000, pp. 134-139.

[9] Royer, E.and C.-K. Toh, "A Review of Current Routing Protocols for Ad Hoc Mobile Wireless Networks", *IEEE Personal Communications*, Vol. 6, No. 2, April 1999, pp. 46-55.

[10] Chiang, C-C., et. al., "Routing in Clustered Multihop, Mobile Wireless Networks with Fading Channel", *Proceedings of IEEE SICON*, April 1997, pp. 197-211.

[11] Ramanujan, R., A. Ahamad, J. Bonney, R. Hagelstrom, and K. Thurber, "Techniques for Intrusion-Resistant Ad Hoc Routing Algorithms (TIARA)", *Proceedings of 21st Century Military Commu-nications Conference, Volume. 2*, 2000, pp. 660-664.

[12] Venkatraman and L., D. Agrawal, "A Novel Authentication Scheme for Ad Hoc Networks", *Proceedings of Wireless Communications and Networking Conference, Volume 3*, 2000, pp. 1268-1273.

[13] Guan, X., Y. Yang, and J. You, "POM-A Mobile Agent Security Model against Malicious Hosts", *Proceedings of the 4th International Conference on High Performance Computing in the Asia-Pacific Region, Voume. 2*, 2000, pp. 1165-1166.

[14] Chun Man, M. and V. K. Wei, "A Taxonomy for Attacks on Mobile Agent", *Proceedings of International Conference on Trends in Communications, Voume 2*, 2001, pp. 385-388.

[15] Schwartz, D.G., Stoecklin, S., and Yilmaz, E., "A Case-Based Approach to Network Intrusion Detection", *Fifth International Conference on Information Fusion, IF'02*, Annapolis, MD, July 7-11, 2002, pp. 1084--1089.

[16] Kachirski, O. and Guha, R., "Intrusion Detection Using Mobile Agents in Wireless Ad Hoc Networks", *Proceedings of IEEE Knowledge Media Networking Conference, KMN'02*, July 2002

A Routing Solution for a Global, Space-based Multimedia System

M. Guizani and I. G. Schneller
University of West Florida
11000 University Parkway
Pensacola, FL 32514

Abstract

This paper focuses on the Teledesic satellite constellation, which is an attempt to provide high speed, multi-media networking connectivity to any location on the globe. Since the routers (satellites) are in constant motion, this venture is unique and leads to a one-of-a-kind data routing scheme. This concept is still in the design phase, with implementation still a few years away. However, several large companies and capital investors have already committed funds to this venture. Supporters are claiming a full operational capability in roughly 3 years. Our focus in this paper is to develop a routing algorithm for the Teledesic satellite constellation and to model its operation in a simulator. The algorithm is conceptually developed and implemented using a software simulation. Our results, which indicate this algorithm is a viable solution to the routing problem, and our implementation details are presented below.

1. Introduction

Teledesic is a limited license company comprised of Motorola, Boeing, Microsoft, and several other companies and venture capitalists. Their goal is to build a global, broadband Internet-in-the-Sky ™ network [1], which is targeted to begin in 2004. Using satellite technology, Teledesic is creating the world's first network to provide worldwide access to telecommunications services such as multimedia applications, computer networking, and broadband Internet access from any one point on the Earth to any other point, fully independent of any ground-based, cable infrastructure. The current constellation calls for 288 satellites orbiting in a Low Earth Orbit (LEO). The orbits are polar, meaning they travel over the poles of the Earth. The logical structure is similar to a mesh network topology.

Teledesic has two main components [2,3]: the space-based component as described above, and the ground-based component. The space-based component is the satellite constellation itself. The satellites act as routers in the network, moving the data from sender to receiver. The function of each router can be the gateway to an individual's network, or as intermediary between several routers. The ground-based component consists of transceivers either fixed upon or mobile near the surface, which serve as an interface point for messages entering and exiting the satellite constellation. Overall, this entire network is designed to support millions of simultaneous users. The Teledesic architecture must have a robust, redundant routing algorithm if it is to be successful. The algorithm must take into account several factors that traditional networks have not needed to address. The first is the extremely dynamic nature of the routers (satellites) themselves. Because of the orbit, a typical user will only be in the range of a satellite for about 20 minutes [5]. This means that the algorithm must be able to hand off to another router, possibly in the middle of a transaction. Since the orbits are polar, and the Earth is turning, this solution is not as simple as passing the transaction to the next satellite in the same plane. Cross-planar transfers may be needed. Another factor to consider is identifying which router will service which customer. For instance, with the current Internet structure, users know that the router servicing their facility will never move -- the gateway router will physically be the same. The Teledesic routing algorithm will need to identify servicing access points, in addition to the traditional role of routing the messages. While it is true that today's ground-based routers must be dynamic and robust as well, Teledesic is bringing this problem to a new dimension.

2. Teledesic Routing: Possible Solutions

To analyze Teledesic and pick a specific adaptive algorithm, consider the following example. If node A sends a message to node B, which happens to be exactly half-way around the world, the number of equal length paths, considering nodes and physical distance, is exactly equal to the number of planes the satellite constellation uses. To put the example differently, consider the number of equal length lines between the North and South poles -- infinite. If we limit the paths to lines of longitude only, there are 360 paths (one for each degree) from source to destination, with not one taking the same path, yet all are the same length. If one router is busy, the algorithm should take into account other equal length paths. Following this logic, it makes sense for each router to also consider its own internal characteristics to make a routing decision. For these reasons, the chosen algorithm must be a distributed, adaptive routing algorithm [4].

The Teledesic architecture requires the analysis of several characteristics that have never been a factor in conventional routing algorithms. The first is making the bridge from logical to physical addresses. In today's Internet, all devices are assigned an IP address, which is a logical number. With the proper routing configurations, two devices can be located halfway across the world from each other, yet have logical numbers that are practically neighbors. Teledesic routers, on the other hand, only have connectivity to a certain physical location on the Earth at any one time; therefore, we propose the use of physical addresses. An address corresponding to latitude and longitude would meet this requirement. Each ground station must have one such physical address. If the fidelity of the address were carried out to the tenths of a second (degree:minute:second:tenths), the possibility of several ground stations in the same "address space" would be likely. A solution would be to assign an identifying network number to each station in that space. An advantage to this addressing scheme is that anyone could very easily determine their address without going through a controlling authority (InterNIC) to obtain their address. With GPS technologies, mobile ground stations could automatically and quickly update their address whenever needed [4].

Another factor, moving routers, adds significant difficulty to the routing problem. Since the constellation is a low earth orbit (LEO), the satellites are constantly moving in reference to a single location on the Earth. This means that the satellite used to route traffic at the beginning of a transmission may soon move out of range of either ground station. The routing algorithm chosen must handle the possibility that gateway routers will change any number of times during a communication session. Fortunately, the physics to calculate the location of celestial objects based on time is quick, easy and widely available. The challenge is to handle the changes within a communication without having to reset the session every time a satellite moves out of ground station range [4].

3. Problem Solution

Consider the case where ground station (GS) A needs to communicate with GS B. A may determine that its default gateway is Satellite 1. Using a DNS concept, the user will obtain the lat/long pair and unique number of the destination. Also using the destination lat/long pair, our algorithm will determine which satellite is the destination gateway (satellite 2). This process solves the external routing problem. The second problem is the internal routing problem, which will determine a route from router (satellite) 1 to router 2. At this point the message can be successfully delivered to the destination [4].

Ground station addresses

All ground stations will have an address based on their physical location. The address will be in the format Degrees:Minutes:Seconds. By carrying the address out to the tenths of a second, we are allowing one unique address for every 100' square location on the Earth. In addition to the geographic location, a unique number will be assigned to each ground station. This number could be adequately represented with 10 bits, ensuring a maximum of 1024 unique nodes within an area as it is only necessary to identify unique users in each "cell" which is approximately 100' X 100' [4].

Satellite Node Addresses

Each satellite will need a unique identifier. A 2-Byte identifier will provide more than enough unique addresses for the constellation, which currently calls for 288 satellites [3]. This number will be used to identify the sender's and the recipient's gateway. This number will also be used for internal routing within the satellite constellation. [4]

Domain Name Servers

Obviously, a domain naming system will need to be implemented. It would be unrealistic for a user to need to remember lat/long coordinates to use an address. Traditional, land-line, ground based servers would service user's name requests. However, in this case, a lat/long coordinate and unique identification number is returned instead of an IP address. Also, as part of the registration process for mobile users, their DNS entry would be dynamically input and updated as necessary. [4]

Function to calculate satellite positioning given time

Given the current time, a ground station knowing its lat/long coordinates will be able to calculate which satellite will be the optimal gateway to use for transmission. Also, the ground station, knowing the destination lat/long pair, will be able to calculate the destination's gateway. [4]

Determining Local Gateway

Taking the router calculation concept a step further, a static routing table can be built at each ground station, if it is non-mobile. Each entry in the routing table will consist of three numbers: start time, end time and satellite number.

For example, if the current time is 1135, the default gateway would be 61. At this point, one may ask, why do we need to number the default gateway? Why not just send the message and let any satellite in range receive and route it? The message must be addressed to a particular satellite because at any one time, two or more satellites will be within transmission range. Numbering the gateway will remove any ambiguity to which the servicing router will be. If multiple routers are used, multiple copies of the same message will be sent, wasting bandwidth and processing time and convoluting the acknowledgement process. Since the orbital characteristics of the satellite constellation will remain constant, the default gateway routing table for the ground station will remain constant. When a ground station is set up, the local routing table can be built once, and then updated only when necessary. Of course a mobile station could perform these calculations dynamically at the beginning of each transmission with minimal additional overhead.

Handoff Time

Using the proposed routing table solution, a ground station will also know the exact time the current gateway's footprint will leave the ground station's transmission range. This is critical for ensuring an efficient means exists for the destination to reply to the sender. Consider again, the situation where GS A is just sent a message to GS B. If the handoff time is within the timeout period of the current time, *B* will recalculate a new gateway for *A*. When *A* receives the reply, it will notice that it's handoff time has already expired. Therefore, before sending another message back to *B*, it will update its handoff field. Before *B* releases the message, it updates *B*'s own handoff time, using it's own static routing table. After one cycle of send and receive, both fields will be filled. [4]

Internal Routing

Internal routing is concerned with routing a message within the satellite constellation. One favorable characteristic of this satellite constellation is that in reference to itself, it is static. That is, the nodes within its network never move in relation to each other. This is the exact opposite of the case found in the external routing problem. Using this characteristic, the satellite constellation can be represented by a directed graph. The medium is a K-band transmission in outer space, and transmission time between nodes is roughly constant [5]. This leaves the graph as having a distance (or cost) of one for each link. Thus, a shortest path algorithm using node count as the metric will determine the internal route. The time consuming calculations of determining which gateways to use are left to the ground stations. Furthermore, some method of making a choice based on network health should also be implemented. A simple solution would be for a router to include in the header a number indicating it's congestion level. When the next router in the chain receives the message, it will note the congestion level and number of the sending router and update an internal table to reflect the situation. [4]

4. Implementation

This section outlines the operational details and results of implementing the pseudocode in the previous chapter into a working simulation. The main application is the simulator itself. The simulator creates an independent thread for each satellite in the system. This concept is repeated for each ground station in the simulation also. The application waits a tenth of a second between each instantiation to allow for deconfliction of system resources during startup. The rest of the simulation is simply a loop that runs for a user-defined set of time. Until time expires, a random message is generated and sent to a ground station, which calculates its gateway router using a random number. Since each thread is handling all the routing decisions and actions on their own, the only other function needed by the main application is to provide a global structure used to simulate locations of messages.

To simulate the sending of processes from satellite to satellite, or from ground station to ground station, two global linked lists are used, one for the satellite and one for the ground station. This list's relationship with the satellite threads is shown in Figure 1. Each object will be able to write to the queue of the corresponding recipient of a message. For instance, if satellite 4 receives a message to route to satellite 50, it may calculate the next satellite in the path is 5. Therefore, to simulate sending that message from 4 to 5, satellite 4 will place another node in satellite 5's queue

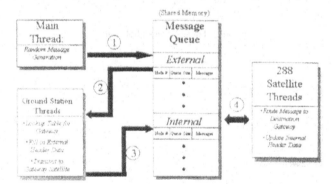

Figure 1. Simulator Architecture

and remove that same node from its own queue. A separate queue will be maintained for each ground station. When a satellite thread is created in the main program, the first thing the newly created thread does is complete a power on setup of the routing table. Initially, all paths have a cost of "one." This is due to the characteristic of the satellites not changing neighbors throughout their orbits. During the exchange of messages, the satellite is responsible for noting the congestion level in the field of the message it receives. If this level has changed, the satellite will change its internal routing table. This data structure was chosen to be implemented separately for each satellite. For this reason, each satellite may have a different routing table in a congested network. Given a unique satellite number, or node, the function GetNeighbors calculates a node's four neighbors. The calculation is trivial if the node in question is in the middle of

323

the graph. The left, right, up and down neighbors are simply as shown in Figure 2.

However, if the selected node resides on a boundary node, then the calculation changes. The neighbors for a bordering side node are shown in Figure 3. Note that in this case, the neighbor isn't simply the first or last node in the same row of the graph. The neighbors are chosen in the manner shown because of the characteristics of "unwrapping" the satellite constellation from a three-dimensional circular object representing the Earth. The neighbors for a bordering node on the top or bottom row of the graph are shown in Figure 4. Since Teledesic calls for 288 satellites, we implemented a 12 X 24 node graph in our simulator.

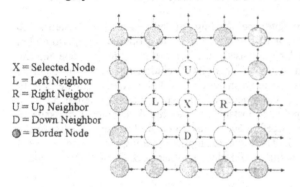

Figure 2. Trivial Neighbor Solution

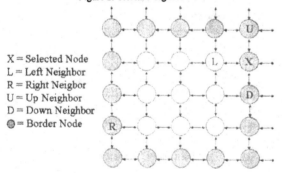

Figure 3. Side Border Neighbor Solution

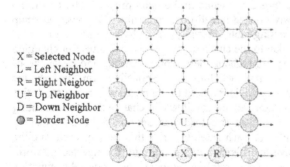

Figure 4. Top/Bottom Border Neighbor Solution

Each satellite node, after startup, runs in a loop constantly searching its row in the linked list for messages. If its "numMessages" field is greater than zero, then the node removes the first message from the queue and recalculates a destination router. If the message structure contained a changed congestion level, then the node will update its own routing table at that point.

5. Implementation Results

Test cases of the simulation implementation have been successful in proving that the algorithm proposed in this study will route a message from ground station to ground station via a network of mobile routing satellites. This section will describe the data collected in addition to an analysis of the results. A total of 126 test cases were created and run, resulting in over 40,600 messages simulated being delivered. In all cases, 10 ground stations were simulated, along with 288 satellite nodes. The following data was collected during each test case:

- *Message Density:* The speed at which the simulation generated messages for delivery. The number roughly translates to the number of milliseconds to wait in between sending the next message. Therefore, a higher number results in a slower delivery rate.
- *Ground Sleep:* The amount of time in milliseconds that a ground station and satellite router will pause if it determines that it's queue is empty before searching it again.
- *Congestion Routing (on or off):* Indicates whether congestion routing was turned on or not during that particular test run.
- *Total Messages Delivered:* The total number of messages successfully delivered during the test case.
- *Total Messages Created:* The total number of messages generated by the simulation of that particular test case.
- *Average Delivery Time:* The average time in seconds that each message needed from creation at the source ground node until delivery at the destination ground node.
- *Average Hops:* The average number of routing decisions needed for each delivered message during the simulation.
- *Number of Handoffs:* The number of times a destination gateway satellite moved out of range during the execution of the simulation.

From the collected data, several data items could then be calculated for each test case:

- *Percent Delivered:* [Number of Messages Delivered] divided over [Number of Messages Created]
- *Time per Hop:* [Average Delivery Time] divided over [Average Hops per Message]
- *Handoffs per Message:* [Number of Handoffs] divided over [Number of Messages Delivered]

We present three testing phases in the remainder of this section.

Phase I: Determine a Baseline. The first phase of testing was designed to find an ideal set of parameters for [Ground Sleep] and [Message Density]. The goal was to find a pair that would generate a large number of messages, without tying up the computer's resources to the point of causing many missed messages. With a broad range of values for ground sleep, the experiments showed that by setting message density to 1000 (1 new message created approximately every 1 second) provided the most stable testing environment, which averaged just over a 91% delivery rate. For the purposes of future test cases, a value of 200 was chosen for a [Ground Sleep]. By setting [Ground Sleep] to 200 and [Message Density] to 1000, tests resulted in an overall average successful delivery rate of 97%.

Phase II: Evaluation of Success of the Algorithm. The second phase of the testing process was to generate and analyze a group of test cases and evaluate whether or not the algorithm in this thesis performed in a manner expected based on various simulation parameters. Figure 5 shows a summary of the results of 58 separate test cases, each simulating the delivery of a random number of messages

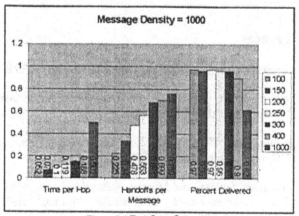

Figure 5.1 Test Case Summary

(minimum: 100, maximum: 1500). In each test, the simulation was set with the [Message Density] parameter to 1000, simulating approximately 1 message every second. Each message was randomly set to consist of between 1 and 10 packets. The legend on the right shows the [Ground Sleep] values. Three main characteristics of each test case are shown for each varying value of [Ground Sleep].

As the [Ground Sleep] time is lengthened, we would expect the characteristics listed below:

- *Time per Hop:* increases by a constant rate (with the exception of the last case). We attribute this anomaly due to errors caused by resource constraints in the testing machine. By setting the [Ground Sleep] to a high value, router queues fill up quickly, exhausting the memory allocated to each thread, causing it to fail and lose its

currently stored messages. To avoid this, we suggest that a machine with a large amount of memory (at least 512 MB) is chosen. If this solution is not feasible, then a choice for [Ground Sleep] must be chosen so as to not allow the queues to grow too large. For the computer in our simulation, setting [Ground Sleep] equal to 1000 was too large, but values between 100 and 400 allowed the simulation to work correctly.

- *Handoffs per Message:* Increases by a constant rate, which is consistent with a longer [ground sleep] time.
- *Percent Delivered:* Fairly constant, with the exception of having a ground sleep of 1000, which simulates the routing thread blocking for 1 second if the queue is empty.

This data supports a stable, consistent and correct simulation of the proposed satellite routing model. A second supporting test is shown in Figure 6, which also demonstrated a consistent operating simulation.

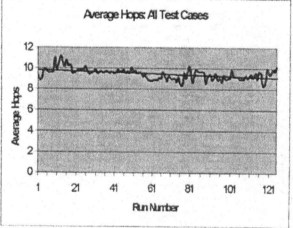

Figure 6 Average Hops Summary

Since the satellite constellation is a 12 by 24 node directed graph, the maximum number of hops needed to transit the internal network can be calculated by adding together half of the maximum x value and the maximum y values: $.5(12) + .5(24) = 6+12 = 18$. With a large number of test cases, one could expect to see an average of 9 hops per test case. Also, the average number of hops should be relatively constant. In fact, an analysis of the data shows this is true, with an approximate value of just under 10 for average number of hops. This observation is shown in Figure 6, with the single straight horizontal line representing the average trend.

Phase III: Congestion Routing. The third and last phase of the data analysis evaluated the congestion routing portion of the algorithm. Several tests were run with congestion routing on and off, with all other parameters of the simulation being the same. Two sets of test cases were run:

- Set 1: [Message Density]=1000 and [Ground Sleep]=200
- Set 2: [Message Density]=250 and [Ground Sleep]=150

In both cases, all of the results are almost identical for all characteristics collected or calculated for the simulation. This is probably due to the complexities that arose in trying to start the simulation with heavily preloaded router queues. The system used to run the simulation would fault whenever

would inappropriately degrade performance due to the extra

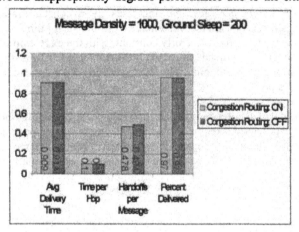

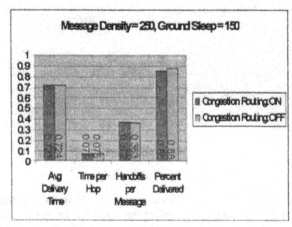

calculations involved. In this implementation, the answer is

a substantial load was applied prior to starting the simulation. However, it is important to note, that with or without congestion routing turned on, the simulation successfully routed messages to their intended recipient. This is an important conclusion since one should reasonably be concerned if using congestion routing on a low-load network that turning congestion routing on has no negative impact on performance even in a low-load system. Figure 7 shows the results of executing both sets of congestion routing test cases.

6. Conclusion

The complexities that arise from the Teledesic concept of networking have spawned a unique and complex problem space to routing high-speed multimedia network operations. To solve this problem, a routing algorithm that uses physical addresses instead of logical addresses can be used, which is a divergence from normal routing operations today. Our tested algorithm breaks away from the traditional logical addressing concept and solves the physical routing problem. Our ideas were tested successfully via a software-based simulator, which indicated high-speed multimedia application data can be efficiently and reliably be routed using our algorithm.

References

[1] Gilder, George, "Ethersphere," *Simon & Schuster*, 1996.

[2] Khare, Rohit, *Reflections on the Teledesic Security Architecture*, CalTech University, 28 March 97.

[3] Motta, Mary, *Teledesic to Roll Out Plan for Battered ICO*, www.space.com, 7 Oct 2000.

[4] Schneller, Guizani and Murray, *A Routing Solution for a Global, Space-based Multimedia System*, IEEE GLOBECOM 2001, 3 Nov 2001.

[5] *Teledesic Technology Overview*, www.teledesic.com, 2000, Teledesic, LLC.

Design and Implementation of Smart Packet Processor for the Cognitive Packet Network Router

Taskin Kocak and Jude Seeber
School of Electrical Engineering and Computer Science,
University of Central Florida, Orlando, FL
tkocak@cs.ucf.edu,   js67854@pegasus.cc.ucf.edu

Abstract

As the Internet expands significantly in numbers of users, servers, IP addresses, and routers, the IP based network architecture must evolve and change. Recently, Cognitive Packet Networks (CPN) was proposed as an alternative packet network architecture, where there is no routing table, instead reinforcement learning (Random Neural Networks) is used to route smart packets [1,2]. CPN routes packets based on QoS, using measurements that are constantly collected by packets and deposited in mailboxes at routers. Previously, CPN is implemented in a software test-bed. In this paper, we present design approaches for CPN network processor chip. Particularly, we discuss implementation details for one of the modules in the chip: The smart packet processor, which includes a neural network hardware design.

1. Introduction

Cognitive Packet Networks (CPN) was proposed recently as an alternative to the IP based network architectures [1,2]. CPN attempts to solve some of the problems associated with the legacy IP networks, such as QoS, never-ending expansion of routing tables and all sorts of issues related to that (e.g., search, update, etc). CPN does not employ a routing table instead it relies on a learning algorithm to route smart or probing packets. There are three types of packets: smart packets, dumb packets, and acknowledgement packets [1]. Smart packets act as network explorers for different QoS-source-destination (QSD) sets. As a smart packet traverses the network, its next hop is determined by the experiences of previous smart packets with the same QSD parameters. When the smart packet arrives at its destination, the destination node generates an acknowledgment that follows the reverse course recorded by the smart packet. As the acknowledgement travels to the smart packet's source, it updates each node with data gained by the smart packet. Dumb packets are source

routed. The path that a dumb packet will follow is determined by the data that the acknowledgement packets return to the source node.

The CPN uses a random neural network (RNN) [3,,4] model with reinforcement learning (RL) [5] to determine the next hop for the smart packets. In this implementation, an n-port CPN router has an n-neuron RNN within it (each neuron corresponds to a particular port). After a smart packet enters the router, the next hop is determined by referencing the neurons of the RNN. The neuron with the highest output value (in RNN terminology, q: the steady-state probability of being excited) represents the outgoing port that the smart packet will use. The acknowledgement packet that returns will carry data, which will either deter or promote the decision to use this port again.

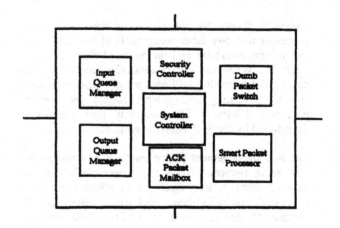

Figure 1: CPN network processor architecture

The rapid expansion of networking applications and data traffic is leading to new specialized network component designs that would keep up with the growing field of networking and communications. We have recently started working on a network processor for a CPN router. In Fig. 1, system architecture for the CPN network processor is illustrated. It is expected that the router be capable of prioritizing packets of varying QoS for each of the three packet types, thus some kind of input and output queue management modules are required. Secure transmission is an unavoidable feature for any kind of network application, and we are currently implementing a elliptic curve cryptography (ECC) based algorithm in a separate work. Dumb packets are source routed and they do not require further processing at each node, hence they can be forwarded to the outgoing port through a switch. ACK packet mailbox is organized as a stack and keeps the information collected by the ACK packets at the intermediate nodes, which they visit.

In this paper, we present the design details for the smart packet processor. Implementation of the smart packet processor is described in the following section. In section 3, we provide simulation results and we conclude the paper with some future work in the fourth section.

2. Smart Packet Processor

Smart packets are routed using a reinforcement learning (RL) algorithm [5]. The RL algorithm for CPN routing requires all decision variables to be mutually related; therefore a recurrent neural network model is needed. In order to guarantee convergence of the RL algorithm to an unique decision (i.e., selecting an outgoing port for a given smart packet), CPN uses the random neural network (RNN) [3,4] which has an unique solution to its internal state for a given set of weights and input variables.

Figure 2 shows the interaction of the smart packet processor with two other components of the CPN router: the system controller and the acknowledgement packet mailbox. When the system controller receives a smart packet, the controller will forward the QSD parameters and the incoming port number to the smart packet processor (SPP). The outgoing port number is determined by the SPP and returned to the controller.

The acknowledgement packet mailbox is a storage and processing element. Acknowledgement packets deposit network data (i.e. delay time) in the mailbox. The data is processed into information and disseminated to CPN components that require it. The SPP receives the QSD parameters, the incoming port number and the reward value from the mailbox. Using this information, the SPP updates its smart packet routing strategy.

In order to provide routing services to smart packets while integrating the data obtained from

acknowledgement packets, the SPP grants simultaneous access for both the system controller and the

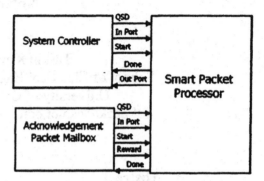

Figure 2: Employment of the smart packet processor

Acknowledgement mailbox. However, since the purpose of the SPP is to efficiently direct smart packet transmission, the processing of the smart packets will be an internal priority of the SPP. This is achieved by optimizing the state machines with regards to the number of clock cycles required to service a smart packet.

Another issue addressed in the SPP design is the simplification of the RNN structure. According to the original software design specifications, within each router there is a separate RNN with $2n^2$ weight terms for each QSD combination. An equivalent hardware design is unfeasible. Instead, the SPP design incorporates a table to store the characteristic parameters of the RNN and the RL. Additionally, an analysis of the reinforcement learning algorithm permits for the number of weight terms to be reduced to $2n$. In addition to yielding significant memory savings, the calculations for the steady state probabilities are also simplified.

Figure 3 shows the completed SPP design. The RL component is the most complex state machine in the design. When the SPP receives the start signal from the ACK mailbox, the RL component requests the RNN parameters relative to the QSD from the table. If the entry is not present in the table, then the initial default values are used. Next, the RL device updates the weights based upon the reward value.

Once the weights are determined, they are supplied to the neuron array for calculating the q (neuron output) values. Originally, these calculations were initiated when a smart packet was being serviced by the SP interface. The SP interface would retrieve the weights from the table and invoke the neurons to calculate the q values. Then the SP interface would direct the SP through the port whose corresponding neuron had the highest q. Performing these calculations in conjunction with the RL algorithm yields faster service to the SP's. In the current design, the RL component stores the port numbers at the end of its cycle. The SP interface simply reads this information and applies it to the SP.

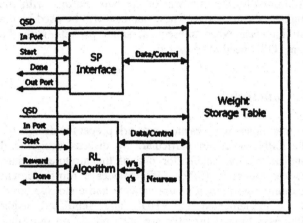

Figure 3: Composition of the smart packet processor

Figure 4 depicts the neuron composition with its original configuration as described in the previous work. Λ and r are constants that are determined by the number of ports in the router. Figure 5 shows the same neuron with the benefits of our weight term analysis.

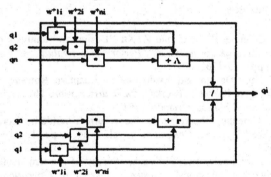

Figure 4: Neuron i

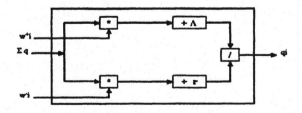

Figure 5: Neuron i after weight term reduction

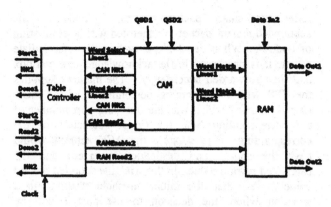

Figure 6: Composition of the weight storage table

The table consists of three components: a table controller, a content addressable memory, and a random access memory. Figure 6 depicts the internal composition of the table. The weight storage table is a dual port memory structure that maintains the characteristics of multiple RNN models. The table's dual port configuration allows for simultaneous read/read and read/write operations. Port 1 is for read operations only and is dedicated to smart packet processing. Port 2 is capable of read and write operations as required by the processing of the acknowledgement packets. As shown in Figure 6, the inputs for port 1 consist of a start signal and the quality of service, source, and destination (QSD) parameters. The outputs are a done and a hit signal as well as the requested data, if available. In addition to the interface incorporated by port 1, port 2 has a read/write signal and data inputs. Both ports are synchronized to an external clock source.

3. Simulation Results

An SPP for a 4-port CPN router has been implemented in VHDL. Simulated inputs from the system controller and acknowledgement mailbox have been applied to the design. Figures 7 and 8 show some of the results from the simulations.

In figure 7, the SPP has been initialized with no network information. The first smart packet arrives through port *0* (*inc_port_sp*) and the system controller queries the SPP for the next destination. The SP originated from node *4* with a destination of node *6* and a QoS requirement of *1* (*qsd_sp* = 10000000400000006). Since the SPP does not contain a relevant RNN model within its table, the device responds with a random outgoing port assignment (*out_port_sp*) that is not the same direction from where the packet came. In this case, the packet is routed out through port *1*.

After the smart packet arrives at node *6*, the acknowledgement packet is generated with a destination of node *4*. When the ACK arrives at the intermediate router, it is processed in the acknowledgement mailbox and then forwarded accordingly. The mailbox supplies the SPP with the incoming port number of the ACK (*inc_port_ack* - which was the outgoing port number of the corresponding SP), the QSD parameters of the corresponding SP (*qsd_ack* – the ACK actually would have the source and destination reversed) and the calculated reward value. In this trial, the supplied reward value is less than the initial threshold resulting in a situation where the decision to use port *1* will be punished.

Still in Fig. 7, a second smart packet with the same QSD parameters enters the router from port *0*. In this instance, the SPP uses the experience of the previous smart packet to change its decision. This new smart packet is routed out through port *2*.

The simulation results in Fig. 8 show the low level execution of the reinforcement learning algorithm. Once the SPP receives the start signal (*start_ack*) from the acknowledgement mailbox, the RL component attempts to read the weights and threshold related to the given QSD from the table. In this case, the table responds with a miss. This resets the weight (w_p and w_m) and threshold terms to their default values. For this implementation, the weight, threshold and q terms each have 15 bits to the right of the ones position. Therefore, the hexadecimal value 08000 is equivalent to 1.0000. In this brief examination, the exact values are not as important as being able to identify the correct trends in the simulation.

After the terms are reset, the threshold is compared to the reward value from the mailbox. Since the reward value is greater, the RL component must now reward the previous decision (*inc_port_ack* represents the previous decision). To increase the probability of assigning port *0* again, the excitation weight w_{p0} is increased. In addition, the inhibition weights w_m associated with the other ports are incremented. This decreases the probability of one of the other ports being selected. Next, the weight terms are normalized to prevent them from growing unbounded.

Once the weights are determined, they are used by the neuron array to calculate the steady state probabilities q. As seen in the figure, this iterative process enables the values to converge. Neuron *0* has the highest q at 4A0F (an actual probability of 0.578). After those calculations are complete, the RL component determines which two neurons had the highest q. The final calculation performed in this sequence is the adjustment of the

threshold value. The new threshold, 017B, is significant increase over the previous value, 0100, due to the large reward that was received, 3FF9.

The final step is to store the necessary RNN characteristics into the table. The threshold and weights terms are saved for future use by the RL component. Additionally, the numbers of the two neurons with the highest q's are stored. These numbers will be used by the SP interface when subsequent smart packets with the same QSD need to be routed.

4. Conclusion

In this paper, we present a network processor design for the CPN router. In particular, we discuss design and implementation details for one of the modules: Smart packet processor (SPP). SPP includes a reinforcement learning algorithm, a neural network and a storage table. It is implemented in VHDL and simulated using Synopsys tools. Currently, we are working on the other parts of the network processor. In the second phase of the project, we plan to incorporate all the modules and synthesize for FPGA to form a test bed with several boards. Eventually, we plan to design a full-custom ASIC CPN network processor, and we would like to form a test bed from the fabricated chips.

References

[1] E. Gelenbe, R. Lent, and Z. Xu ``Design and analysis of cognitive packet networks'', *Performance Evaluation*, Vol. 46, pp. 155-176, 2001.
[2] Z. Xu, "Design and Evaluation of Adaptive Routing in Cognitive Packet Networks", *Ph.D. dissertation*, University of Central Florida, Orlando, 2001.
[3] E. Gelenbe, "Learning in the recurrent random neural network", *Neural Computation*, vol. 5, no. 1, pp. 154-164, 1993.
[4] H. Bakircioglu, and T. Kocak, "Survey of random neural network applications", *European Journal of Operational Research*, Volume 126, Issue 2, October 2000, pp. 319-330.
[5] R. Viswanathan and K.S. Narendra, "Comparison of expedient and optimal reinforcement schemes for learning systems", *J. Cybernetics.*, vol. 2, pp. 21-37, 1972.

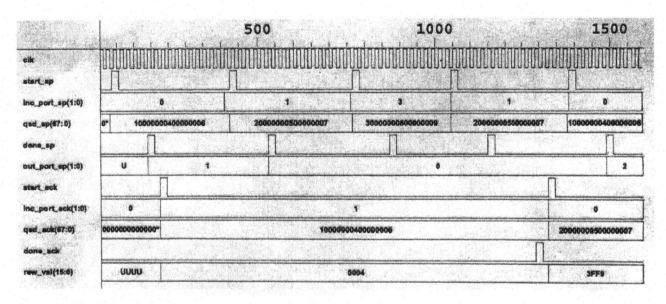

Figure 7: Simulation results for smart packet processing

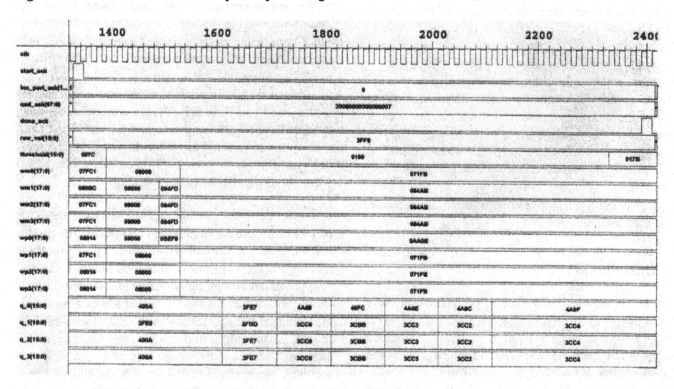

Figure 8: Low-level execution of the reinforcement learning algorithm

Dynamic Shortest Path Routing in 2-circulants

Tomaž Dobravec, Borut Robič, Boštjan Vilfan
Faculty of Computer and Information Science
University of Ljubljana, Tržaška 25, Ljubljana, Slovenia
{*tomaz.dobravec, borut.robic, bostjan.vilfan*} *@fri.uni-lj.si*

Abstract

A *k-circulant* network $G(n; h_1, h_2, \ldots, h_k)$ is undirected graph where the node set is $\mathbb{Z}_n$ and the edge set is the union of sets $E_i = \{(u, u + h_i \pmod{n}) | u \in \mathbb{Z}_n\}$, for $i \in \{1, 2, \ldots, k\}$. In the paper we present an optimal (i.e. using shortest paths) dynamic two-terminal routing algorithm for 2-circulant networks. The algorithm dynamically routes a message along one of the shortest paths to its destination, i.e. at each node where the message has stopped the algorithm determines the next node to which the message will be sent in order to remain on the shortest path to its destination.

Key words: *distributed systems, circulant network, message routing*

1. Introduction

Let $k \geq 2$ and let $n, h_1, \ldots, h_k$ be positive integers such that $0 < h_1 < h_2 < \ldots < h_k < n/2$. A *k-loop* network $G(n; h_1, h_2, \ldots, h_k)$ is a directed graph where the node set is $\mathbb{Z}_n$ and the edge set is the union of sets $E_i = \{(u, u + h_i \pmod{n}) \mid u \in \mathbb{Z}_n\}$, for $i \in \{1, 2, \ldots, k\}$. In the undirected case, which is known as a *k-circulant network* and is denoted by $G(n; \pm h_1, \pm h_2, \ldots, \pm h_k)$, arcs are changed into (undirected) edges. It is well known that $G(n; h_1, h_2, \ldots, h_k)$ and $G(n; \pm h_1, \pm h_2, \ldots, \pm h_k)$ are connected *iff* $\gcd(n, h_1, h_2, \ldots, h_k) = 1$ [2]. We will therefore assume $\gcd(n, h_1, h_2, \ldots, h_k) = 1$. Informally, a *k*-loop network contains *k* interleaved rings. Note that rings, fully connected networks,

twisted tori, and recursive circulant graphs are special cases of *k*-loop networks (Fig. 1).

We are interested in the case where $k = 2$. The corresponding networks are called double-loops and 2-circulants. Both have been extensively studied as topologies for computer networks and distributed memory multiprocessor systems [1, 2, 3, 5, 6, 7, 9, 11, 15, 16]. While in double-loops a link can transfer messages in one direction only, in 2-circulants a link is capable of transferring data in a *forward* direction (i.e. from u to $u + h_i$) as well as in a *backward* direction (i.e. from $u + h_i$ to u). It is usually assumed in 2-circulants that links are not full duplex.

In the *two-terminal* routing problem a message is to be routed from its source node to its destination node according to the conditions imposed by the routing model [10, 13, 14]. For double-loop networks Guan [10] presented an optimal dynamic two-terminal routing algorithm, i.e. an algorithm that routes a message along one of the shortest paths to its destination. Although Guan's algorithm can be used to route messages in 2-circulant networks, it is no longer optimal for these networks (because it uses the links of the undirected network as they were directed).

In this paper we present a new optimal (i.e. using shortest paths) dynamic two-terminal routing algorithm for 2-circulant networks based on Guan's algorithm for double-loops. We briefly describe the new algorithm in Section 2.. In Section 3 we prove the optimality of the algorithm and discuss its time complexity.

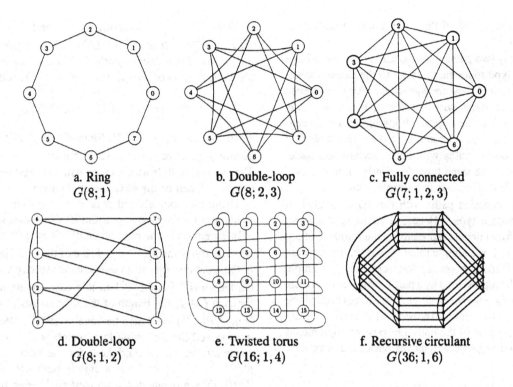

a. Ring
$G(8;1)$

b. Double-loop
$G(8;2,3)$

c. Fully connected
$G(7;1,2,3)$

d. Double-loop
$G(8;1,2)$

e. Twisted torus
$G(16;1,4)$

f. Recursive circulant
$G(36;1,6)$

Figure 1: Several k-loop networks

2. Routing algorithm, informally

Let us first informally describe the basic idea of our algorithm (Fig. 2). Suppose that in a particular routing step a message with its final destination v is at some node u. The algorithm first determines the candidates for the next node where the message can be sent from u so that it still remains on one of the shortest paths to its destination v. The algorithm then selects one of the candidates and sends the message to it. To determine the candidates, our algorithm computes paths $p_1^{(u,v)}$, $p_{-1}^{(u,v)}$, $p_2^{(u,v)}$ and $p_{-2}^{(u,v)}$, where $p_i^{(u,v)}$ denotes a shortest path from u to v having no links from E_i. The key observation is that if the path $p_i^{(u,v)}$ is longer than the path $p_j^{(u,v)}$ for some i, j, then the shortest path from u to v (with no restrictions on allowed links) must contain at least one link from E_i. Since any permutation of the links along a path in 2-circulants routes the message to the same final destination v (which is informally due to the symmetry of 2-circulants [10, 12]), the neighbor node $u + \text{sign}(i) * h_{|i|}$ is one of the candidates for the next node. The possible existence of several candidates allows our algorithm to dynamically solve or even avoid potential routing problems that may arise from node/link faults [4, 8] (or from congestions if several messages were routed through the

network simultaneously).

3. Routing algorithm in detail

In the following we describe our routing algorithm in detail.

3.1. Preliminaries

At each routing step a message can proceed using one of four possible links, i.e. by making a *hop* of one of the four possible types $\mathcal{E}_1, \mathcal{E}_{-1}, \mathcal{E}_2$ or $\mathcal{E}_{-2}$. Let $I = \{1, -1, 2, -2\}$.

A *hop of type* $\mathcal{E}_i$ (also called $\mathcal{E}_i$-*hop*), $i \in I$, is the move of a message from a node u to node $u + \text{sign}(i) * h_{|i|} \pmod{n}$. The hop is said to be *forward* (resp. *backward*) if $i > 0$ (resp. $i < 0$). An $\mathcal{E}_i$-hop from u is denoted by e_i^u. Hence, even though there is only one link connecting u and $u + \text{sign}(i) * h_{|i|} \pmod{n}, i \in I$, this link can be used for two opposite hops (i.e. forward and backward).

In any given network a message can be routed through one of (possibly many) paths connecting its source and destination. In 2-circulant networks these paths can be classified into several equivalence classes. For each path from u to v containing an $\mathcal{E}_i$-hop ($i \in I$),

333

there is another path of the same length starting with the $\mathcal{E}_i$-hop [10].

Since any two paths with the same number of hops of certain type route the message to the same destination, we say that they are *equivalent*. An equivalence class of such paths will be referred to as the *route*. Notice also that the opposite hops along a path cancel each other out. A route is said to be *simple* if it does not contain paths with both forward and backward hops of the same type. Similarly, a path is said to be simple if it belongs to a simple route.

A route contains paths with the same number of hops of certain type. Hence, a route is characterized with four integers representing the numbers of $\mathcal{E}_i$-hops, $i \in I$. For a simple route, however, a maximum of two of these integers are non-zero. Thus, a simple route can be represented by a pair (s, b), where s (resp. b) denotes the number of short (resp. long) hops along the paths in the route. The sign of s and b will denote the direction of the hops, i.e. positive sign means forward and negative sign means backward direction.

3.2. Computing the candidates

Next, we introduce paths $p_i^{(u,v)}$ that are used at each routing step to determine the candidates for the next hop. Let $P_{\bar{i}}^{(u,v)}$ be the set of all simple paths from u to v containing no $\mathcal{E}_i$-hops. Then we define $p_i^{(u,v)}$ to be one of the (possibly many) shortest paths of $P_{\bar{i}}^{(u,v)}$.

The length of $p_i^{(u,v)}$ will be denoted by $d_i^{(u,v)}$. Clearly $d_i^{(u,v)} > 0$ when $u \neq v$. Notice also that $d_i^{(u,v)} < \infty$ because 2-circulants are connected by assumption.

Every shortest path from u to v is simple and is in the set $\bigcup_{i \in I} P_{\bar{i}}^{(u,v)}$. To see this, let p be a shortest path from u to v. Since $u \neq v$, the path p contains at least one hop, say an $\mathcal{E}_j$-hop. If p contained an $\mathcal{E}_{-j}$-hop, it would not be the shortest path, contradicting the assumption. Thus, p is simple. Furthermore, $p \in P_{-j}^{(u,v)}$ which implies $p \in \bigcup_{i \in I} P_{\bar{i}}^{(u,v)}$.

We can now state the conditions when a shortest path contains hops of certain type. *If for any $i, j \in I$ the path $p_i^{(u,v)}$ is longer than the path $p_j^{(u,v)}$ (i.e. $d_i^{(u,v)} > d_j^{(u,v)}$), then any shortest path from u to v contains at least one $\mathcal{E}_i$-hop.* Suppose that a shortest path from u to v (say p) contains no $\mathcal{E}_i$-hops. Then $p \in P_{\bar{i}}^{(u,v)}$ and consequently $|p| = d_{\bar{i}}^{(u,v)} \leq d_j^{(u,v)}$. This contradicts the assumption that $d_i^{(u,v)} > d_j^{(u,v)}$.

Now, let $d^{(u,v)} = \min_{i \in I} d_i^{(u,v)}$ and $D^{(u,v)} = \max_{i \in I} d_i^{(u,v)}$. *If $d^{(u,v)} \neq D^{(u,v)}$ then, in order to follow one of the shortest paths from u to v, a message should make any of the candidate hops e_i^u from the set*

$$C^{(u,v)} := \{e_i^u; \, d_i^{(u,v)} = D^{(u,v)}\}.$$

To see this, let $e_i^u \in C^{(u,v)}$. Since $d^{(u,v)} \neq D^{(u,v)}$ by assumption, there exists j, such that $d_i^{(u,v)} > d_j^{(u,v)}$. The shortest path from u to v contains at least one $\mathcal{E}_i$-hop, which can be the next hop on the path.

Using this, our algorithm is able to determine the candidates for the next hop in almost all the cases. The only exception is the case when $d^{(u,v)} = D^{(u,v)}$, i.e. when all the paths $p_i^{(u,v)}$, $i \in I$, are of the same length. In this case our algorithm uses another strategy. Since the length $d_i^{(u,v)}$ of $p_i^{(u,v)}$ in this case equals $d^{(u,v)}$, for each $i \in I$, the length of the shortest path (which is in $\cup_i P_{\bar{i}}^{(u,v)}$) must also be equal to $d^{(u,v)}$. We have thus proved the following fact, which is also used to construct the set of candidates for the next hop. *If $d^{(u,v)} = D^{(u,v)}$ and p is a simple path with length $d^{(u,v)}$, then p is one of the shortest paths from u to v. In order to follow one of the shortest paths from u to v, the message should make any of the candidate hops e_i^u from the set*

$$C^{(u,v)} := \{e_j^u; \, e_j^u \text{ is a hop on any } p_i^{(u,v)}; i \in I\}.$$

At each routing step our algorithm first calculates the paths $p_i^{(u,v)}$, then it determines the candidates for the next hop and finally sends the message along one of the determined candidates.

3.3. Optimality of the algorithm

The optimality of the algorithm (Fig. 2) is stated by the following theorem.

Theorem *Algorithm in Fig. 2 is an optimal (i.e. using shortest paths) dynamic two-terminal message routing algorithm.*

Proof: At each routing step the algorithm takes into account the two possible cases, viz. the case when all the lengths of the paths $p_i^{(u,v)}$ are equal (Fig. 2, line 7) and the case when they are not (line 9). In both cases the algorithm determines the set C of candidate hops for the next hop by applying the facts from Subsection 3.2. These facts guarantee that C is not empty and that it contains only hops that are parts of the shortest

```
begin
1:   for $i \in I$ do
2:       $p_i^{(u,v)} :=$ the shortest path from $P_i^{(u,v)}$;
3:       $d_i^{(u,v)} :=$ the length of $p_i^{(u,v)}$;
4:   endfor;
5:   $d^{(u,v)} := \min\{d_i^{(u,v)}; i \in I\}$;
6:   $D^{(u,v)} := \max\{d_i^{(u,v)}; i \in I\}$;
7:   if $d^{(u,v)} \neq D^{(u,v)}$ then
8:       $C := \{e_i^u; i \in I; d_i = D^{(u,v)}\}$;
9:   else
10:      $C := \{e_j^u; e_j^u$ is a hop on any $p_i^{(u,v)}; i \in I\}$
11:  endif;
12:  send the message along one of the hops from $C$.
end
```

Figure 2: The message routing algorithm for each node u

paths from the current node to the final destination. Thus, taking any of the hops from C (Fig. 2, line 12) guarantees that the message will stay on one of the shortest paths to the final destination. Consequently, the algorithm is optimal. $\square$

3.4. Time complexity of the algorithm

The time complexity of the algorithm depends on the time needed to calculate paths $p_i^{(u,v)}, i \in I$. A brute force approach finds $p_i^{(u,v)}$ by finding a shortest path in the set $P_i^{(u,v)}$ of all simple paths from u to v containing no $\mathcal{E}_i$-hops. Using *breadth-first search*, this can be done in $\mathcal{O}(|E(G)|)$ which, in case of 2-circulants, equals to $\mathcal{O}(n)$. Thus the overall time complexity of the algorithm is bounded above by $\mathcal{O}(l*n)$ and below by $\Omega(l)$, where l is the distance between the source and the destination of the message. Notice also that $l \leq \operatorname{diam}(G(n; \pm h_1, \pm h_2)) = \mathcal{O}(\sqrt{n})$ [2].

4. Conclusion

In this paper we discussed the two-terminal routing problem in 2-circulant networks, i.e. the problem of routing messages from the source node to the destination node satisfying given conditions. For double-loop networks, which can be viewed as directed version of 2-circulants, Guan presented an optimal two-terminal routing algorithm, which is dynamic, i.e. at each node where the message has stopped it determines the next node to which the message will be sent in order to remain on the shortest path to its destination. Although

Guan's algorithm can also be used to route messages in 2-circulant networks, it is no longer optimal for these networks. In our paper we present a new optimal (i.e. using shortest paths) dynamic two-terminal routing algorithm for 2-circulant networks based on Guan's algorithm for double-loops. Our algorithm also offers the flexibility needed to avoid potential routing problems arising from congestion or node/link faults. This is especially important and useful in *permutation routing* where several messages have to be routed through the network from their sources to their destinations.

References

[1] F. Aguilo and M. A. Filo. An efficient algorithm to find optimal double loop networks. *Discrete Mathematics*, 138:15–29, 1995.

[2] J.C. Bermond, F. Comellas, and D.F. Hsu. Distributed loop computer networks: A survey. *Journal of Parallel and Distributed Computing*, 24:2–10, 1995.

[3] Y. Cheng and F. K. Hwang. Diameters of weighted double loop networks. *Journal of Algorithms*, 9:401–410, 1988.

[4] C. Chou, D. J. Guan, and K. Wang. A dynamic fault-tolerant message routing algorithm for double-loop networks. *Information Processing Letters*, 70:259–264, 1999.

[5] B. Codenotti, I. Gerace, and S. Vigna. On some combinatorial questions related to circulant graphs. *Linear Algebra and its Applications*, 285:123–142, 1998.

[6] T. Dobravec, B. Robič, and B. Vilfan. Routing in double-loop networks. In *Proceedings of the IASTED International Symposia Applied Informatics*, pages 408–411, Innsbruck, Austria, February 2001.

[7] D. Z. Du, D. F. Hsu, Q. Li, and J. Xu. A combinatorial problem related to distributed loop networks. *Networks*, 20:173–180, 1990.

[8] M. Escudero, J. Fiabrea, and P. Morillo. Fault-tolerant routing in double-loop networks. *Ars Combin.*, 25A:187–198, 1988.

[9] M.A. Fiol, J.L.A. Yebra, I. Alegre, and M. Valero. A discrete optimization problem in local networks and data alignment. *IEEE Transactions On Computers*, C-36(6), 1987.

[10] D.J. Guan. An optimal message routing algorithm for double-loop networks. *Information Processing Letters*, 65:255–260, 1998.

335

[11] F. K. Hwang and W. C. W. Li. Reliabilities of double-loop networks. *Probability in the Engineering and Information Science*, 5:255–272, 1991.

[12] F.T. Leighton. *Introduction to Parallel Algorithms and Architectures*. Morgan Kaufmann Publishers, San Mateo, California, 1992.

[13] B. Robič. Optimal routing in 2-jump circulant networks. Technical Report 397, University of Cambridge, U.K., Computer Laboratory, 1996.

[14] B. Robič and J. Žerovnik. Minimum 2-terminal routing in 2-jump circular graphs. *Computers and Artificial Intelligence*, 19(1):37–46, 2000.

[15] J. Žerovnik and T. Pisanski. Computing the diameter in multiple-loop networks. *J. Algorithms*, 14:226–243, 1993.

[16] J. Žerovnik, B. Robič, and T. Dobravec. Optimal permutation routing in 2-jump circulant networks. In *Proc. ACIS 1st International Conference on Software Engineering Applied to Networking and Parallel/Distributed Computing SNPD*, pages 175–180, Reims, France, May 18-21 2000.

Session 5-3
Software Engineering

Measuring the Size of Object-Oriented Software Applications

Jing-Chiou Liou
AT&T Labs.
200 S. Laurel Ave.
Middletown, NJ 07748, USA
Email: jing@att.com

Abstract

In measuring the software size, feature Points and Function Points are two examples of metric methodology. The Function Point Analysis (FPA) is by far the most popular counting method for software development used in industry. However, when applying the IFPUG standard to count the Object-Oriented software application, the resulting function points are insignificant or inaccurately low. In this paper, we present a methodology, called Object Point Analysis (OPA), for counting the object points for the Object-Oriented software application. The OPA has been used by multi-million-dollar software projects for more than six years. The positive results received from these projects provide a preliminary study on sizing of OO software application. Comparing to the FPA, the OPA not only produces a more accurate size measurement for OO software applications, but also provides a means for sizing automation, which reduces the human errors often found in FPA.

1   Introduction

Software size is in general the magnitude of the software work products. Although they are related, software size is easily confused with the amount of the functionality the software project carries out or the complexity and difficulty of the software product. To avoid the confusion, we adopt the definition of software size given in [5].

Given a system $S = <E, R>$, where E represents the set of elements of S, and R is a binary relation on E ($R \subseteq E \times E$) representing the relationships between S's elements, the size of a software system S is a function $Size(S)$ that is characterized by the following properties:

(1) Nonnegativity. The Size of a software system $S = <E,R>$ is nonnegative

$$Size(S) \geq 0 \qquad (1)$$

(2) Null Value: The size of a software system $S = <E,R>$ is null if E is empty.

$$E = \varnothing \Rightarrow Size(S) = 0 \qquad (2)$$

(3) Module Additivity: The size of a software system $S = <E,R>$ is equal to the sum of the sizes of two of its modules $m_1 = <E_{m1}, R_{m1}>$ and $m_2 = <E_{m2}, R_{m2}>$ such that any element of S is an element of either m_1 or m_2.

$$(m_1 \subseteq S \text{ and } m_2 \subseteq S \text{ and } E = E_{m1} \cup E_{m2} \text{ and } E_{m1} \cap E_{m2} = \varnothing) \Rightarrow Size(S)$$
$$= Size(m_1) + Size(m_2) \qquad (3)$$

The formula for calculating the attribute Size can now be shown to be:

$$Size(S) = \sum_{e \in E} Size(m_e) \qquad (4)$$

In estimating/measuring the software size, there are some methodologies that meet the properties. These methodologies can be either simply counting the source lines of code (SLOC) [2] or using metric methodology. Feature Points and Function Points are two examples of metric methodology [13]. Traditionally, system size has been measured in SLOC estimates. Although easiest to count, there is no standard definition for SLOC. As a result, SLOC no longer measures what developers directly create [8]. It is also discovered in [9] that SLOC measures are poor estimating tools because they are highly language, environment, and programmer dependent and estimation is most needed before any language decision have been made

The Function Point Analysis (FPA) is by far the most popular counting methodology for software development [9]. However, when applying the IFPUG standard to count the Object-Oriented software application, the resulting function points are insignificant or inaccurately low. Furthermore, according to [9], "function point counts, ..., suffer because of the labor-intensive process required to collect them and their poor mapping onto object-oriented systems, ..., GUIs and the like."

In this paper, we present a methodology, called Object Point Analysis (OPA), for counting the object points for the Object-Oriented software application. The OPA has been used by software projects, with totally over twenty millions US dollar annual budgets, for more than six years. The positive results received from these projects provide a preliminary study on sizing of OO software application. Comparing to the FPA, the OPA not only produces a more accurate size measurement for OO software applications, but also provides a means for sizing automation, which reduces the human errors often found in FPA.

2 Background

The Object Point Analysis presented in the paper was originally developed in 1996 to size a Rule Data development under the OO environment in the Telecommunication Management Network (TMN) model [1]. With the constraint of modern multi-vendor network environment, the issue of "reuse" must be addressed in designing the application.

While using the Object-Oriented paradigm in designing the application, the following design strategy was used to support software reuse between different application scenarios [4]:

- Building application functions and architect by recognizing the commonality between scenarios.
- Separating the commonality found (core aspects) from the network specific aspects.

Therefore, it was determined that all of the basic network management functionality could be "generalized" to a set of primary object classes, while the rest are "special" classes supporting the definition of *Rules* to drive the application behavior. Whenever a core operation is initiated, the application accesses the appropriate rules to determine the constraints for establishing relationship between objects.

In order to achieve the optimizing level of process maturity, software estimation and measurement metrics are required for Total Quality Management (TQM) which is originated from the principles of statistical quality control [6]. The goal of TQM is to meet the needs of the customer, now and in the future. What are the needs of customer? The software quality, the development and maintenance cost, and the delivery schedule are the three elements of customer satisfaction [3].

Among all types of estimates for a software project, software size is the most important one, and yet the basis of other estimates. If the software size estimate is incorrect, then the cost and schedule estimates can be also incorrect, not to mention the prediction of quality metrics, such as the reliability or the total number of defects.

When the Function Point Analysis was firstly applied to size our Object-Oriented software application, it was discovered that the counting methodology of FPA could not correctly size the Rules Data development of the OO software application. While looking for solution to accurately size our application, we found that no metric methodologies reported in the literatures can correctly size the OO software development. Therefore, we started to develop a new methodology that links the concept of FPA and the information model in the Object-Oriented paradigm.

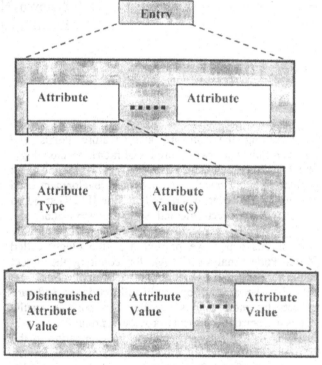

Figure 1 Object Entry in Information Model

The Object Point Analysis methodology was firstly developed under an Object -Oriented (OO) programming environment. In OO software application, many objects may have state dependencies and these objects may interact with each other [14].

In the initial stages of Object-Oriented Analysis (OOA), it is typical to define a set of primary object classes (superclasses). Then, an inheritance hierarchy based on "attribute" information that allows categorization of the class is developed.

An object entry in information model [12] is shown in the Figure 1. The object entry carries some attributes that can be distinguish from each other. Each attribute can be used to form a new object class that inherits the attribute. That object class can have instances and each instance carries an attribute value or multiple attribute values.

340

3 Object Point Analysis

The concept of developing "*Object Point*" Analysis that is comparable to the Function Point Analysis has been started in 1996. The methodology was firstly called "*Equivalent Function Point.*" The basic idea behind the concept is that we can adopt the way that counts function points for the data function types, especially for the internal logical files, for those object classes [10]. In other words, we would treat those object classes as internal logical files.

The application object modeling drove the definition of the table structures in the relational database. Using the Rumbaugh's techniques, the tables closely resemble the objects themselves [8]. The mapping of object classes to the internal logical files gives us a jump start and an advantage that the methodology is easily organized and understood.

For example, an equipment profile table (an object class) shown in the Table 1 establishes combination of port descriptions and sd_ids. The sd_ids are for a valid link that can connect to specific ports within or between pieces of equipment. Those equipment complexes that terminate services identified in a service description table would be further identified here to the specific port level.

Description	Data Element	Populated Values	Impact
Numeric id of the A side port	prof_port_desc_id	38 numeric	The id of the port as it appears in the data field - prof_port_desc_id - of the prof_port_desc table.
sd_id of the terminating link.	sd_id	6 alpha numeric	The id of the port as it appears in the data field - prof_port_desc_id - of the prof_port_desc table.
Numeric id of the Z side port	rel_prof_port_desc_id	38 numeric	The id of the port as it appears in the data field - prof_port_desc_id - of the prof_port_desc table.

Table 1: Structure of an Equipment Profile Table

Common scenarios of operations in a software application can be observed and impacted object classes can be summarized. These common scenarios and their related object classes form the basis of the Object Point Analysis.

To compute the object points, rule developer identifies rule tables (internal logic files) for each scenario, for instance, to add a cabling service. For each scenario, each impacted rule table is marked as requiring changes ("X") or potentially requiring changes ("O"). Potential changes are resolved only after detailed analysis and design (i.e., final count).

The number of object class (tables) involved in each scenario (Record Element Type, "RET") and the number of elements (columns or data fields) in each object class (Data Element Type, "DET") are counted. The minimum and maximum RET and DET are computed by counting entries marked "X" and entries marked "X" and "O", respectively. An instance (object attribute values) for such set of DET and RET is called a *rule*. An example is illustrated in Table 2.

ID	Object Class (Rule Table)	RET	D1 Scenario name 1	D2 Scenario name 2	...	DN Scenario name N
R01	Rule Table name 1	13		X	...	
R02	Rule Table name 2	4	X			...
...	...	2			...	
RNN	Rule Table name N	6	O	O	...	X
	Min. RET		37	48	52	7
	Min. DET		2	4	5	1
	Max. RET		50	59	63	50
	Max. DET		4	7	8	4
	Min. OPs		10	10	10	7
	Max. OPs		10	15	15	10
	Min. Adj. OPs		13.1	13.1	13.1	13.1
	Max. Adj. OPs		13.1	19.65	19.65	19.65
	Minimum Effort (PDs)		4.4	4.4	4.4	3.1
	Maximum Effort (PDs)		4.4	6.5	6.5	4.4
	Average Effort (PDs)		4.4	5.5	5.5	3.8

Notes:

X: Rules must be added
O: Rules may need to be added
DET: Number of rule tables to which rules need to be added/modified for a particular rule customization scenario
RET: Total number of rule columns for all the rule tables that have one or more rules needed to be added/modified for a particular rule customization scenario

Table 2: Object Points counting metrics based on development scenarios

The Table 2 can be divided into 4 parts in a top-down manner. The first part that has "X" and "O" are the matrix for object point analysis as described in the previous paragraphs. The second part of the table shows the resulting minimum and maximum RET/DET for the scenario. The third part of the table shows the object points resulting from the second part of the table. In other words, the minimum RET/DET produces minimum "raw" object points, while the maximum RET/DET generates maximum "raw" object points. The minimum (and maximum) adjusted object points is the result of multiplying a Value Adjustment Factor (GSC) to the minimum (and maximum) "raw" object points. The forth part of the table 2 is actually not part of the Object Point Analysis, but a historical data of effort (person days, PDs) for the scenarios. This historical data of effort may be collected and used later for effort estimating purpose.

A *GSC* (General System Characteristics) is used to calculate the Value Adjustment Factor that is defined as:

Value Adjustment Factor

$$= (GSC \text{ total rating} \times 0.1) + 0.65 \qquad (5)$$

There are 14 characteristics in the GSC [7]. Each has a score from 0 to 5. Therefore, depending on the software characteristics, the bound for the value is $0.65 \leq$ Value Adjustment Factor ≤ 1.35.

The actions carried by each scenario can be ADD, CHANGE, or DELETE. For adding rules in a specific scenario, object points are counted and the software size increases. If the rules got changed in a scenario, object points are counted and the software size is re-calculated with the difference. Finally, if rules got deleted, the software size decreases with the amount of object points counted for the rules.

3.1 Weights of the ILF

Table 3 shows the weights of the Internal Logical file defined in the IFPUG 4.1 standard. There are only three levels of weights: Low (7), Average (10) and High (15). The definition of weights of the ILF worked fine when we first developed the object point methodology.

Record Type	Data Element Type		
	1 - 19	20 - 50	51+
1	7	7	10
2 to 5	7	10	15
6+	10	15	15

Table 3: Weights of the Internal Logical File

We have applied the methodology of Object Point Analysis to the rule related object classes of our application (totally 218 object classes). Currently, there are 22 scenarios of rule development. Each of them produces a different amount of object points. Table 1 also shows possible effort estimates based on the historical data acquired from 4 OO software projects' rule deliveries (projects U1, U2, A, and C) from 1996 to 1997.

From 1996 to 1998, the methodology of Object Point Analysis has been used to estimate the rule developments for customers of 4 OO software projects. The estimates produced by the methodology prove that the Object Point Analysis is very successful and precise. However, when delivering rule data to customer for a new project (project N) in 1998, it was discovered that the object points generated by the methodology were a bit inflated.

For the rapid development pattern in the Project N, the requirements for each service or equipment profile were usually requested separately and rules were delivered in different timeframes. The requirements were partially complete in a development cycle, and hence an equipment element can be profiled in several development cycles to its completeness. Therefore, the size of the rules for an equipment element can be counted several times, each time with a minimum of 7 object points.

Another problem caused by the current set of weights of object point methodology is that the points are not normalized with the size of development work. For a specific scenario of rule development, populating one instance of 40 columns (DET) in an object class (RET) can generate 7 object points, while populating a total of 1000 instances of 40 columns in 6 object classes produces 15 object points. The ration is only 2 which does not reflect the difference of the actual development effort.

3.2 Complexity Factor

In the concept of "Equivalent function point" (the same as in the ILF in the FPA), it does not take into account of the complexity of implementation. In other words, for the same function, a developer could write a five-hundred-line source code, while another developer could write a one-thousand-line source code. Both would produce the same amount of function points.

This is generally true for functional programming. However, In many cases of the object-oriented programming, feature has significant impact on determining the complexity of implementation.

In the information model of OO design, a rule development for the most complicated object class would produce 15 object points. It is not difficult to find that, for the same 15 object points, a object class may require one hundred rules (instance of object attribute values set) while another may have four hundreds rules developed for it. No matter who is doing the work, apparently the efforts dedicated into the rule development of these two network equipments are different.

3.3 Weights for Object Point Analysis

We have reviewed the historical data and current OO development paradigm and calibrated the weights such that the weight system can represent different levels of complexity and effort.

A new weight system is shown in Table 4. In the new weight system of OPA, weights are classified into 5 levels: Very Low (3), Low (5), Average (8), High (11), and Very High (15). For the cases of changing few rules for some object classes, 3 object points are counted. To develop rules, say for a complete equipment element, that would touch many object classes, 15 object points are produced.

Record Type	Data Element Type			
	1 - 15	16 - 30	31 - 45	46+
1	3	3	5	8
2 to 4	3	5	8	11
5 to 7	5	8	11	15
8+	8	11	15	15

Table 4 : Weights for the Object Point Analysis

As one can see, the weights system has a max-to-min ration of 5, comparing to 2 in the ILF weights system. This weight system, by taking into account of complexity factor, allows OPA to more precisely measure the size of object-oriented development.

3.4 *Software Sizing Automation*

One of the advantages for OPA methodology, comparing with other methodology, is that the OPA can be easily automated into a tool so anyone will produce the same size for the same software. Also, with very little training, anyone can use the sizing automation tool to count the object points for any project.

In FPA, the function point counting must be performed by a certified FP specialist (CFPS). Moreover, it is also known that, for the same software, different people, even they are certified, could produce different count. This is not the case for OPA. Since the object classes can be grouped into super class or formed into scenario, Table 2 can be easily turned into a tool for software sizing automation. For each scenario, it has some known required attributes and some optional attributes. Hence the size of the scenario can be:

Size(S) = Size(required attributes) + Size(optional attribute) (6)

Therefore, the maximum (with optional attributes) and minimum (without optional attributes) OP count can be estimated right away. Unless any attribute is mistakenly missed from the tool, no one will produce different OP count for the scenario. And the size of a software is nothing but the sum of the size of all scenarios plus some components that cannot be grouped into scenario.

4 Conclusion

Details of theoretical validation and data analysis can be found in full paper [11]. The Object Point Analysis was firstly developed in 1996 and had been recommended as a standard software sizing methodology for the organization that the pilot projects reside in. Comparing to FPA, the Object Point Analysis provide an accurate and efficient means to measure the amount of the functionality in Object-Oriented paradigm.

Reference

[1] S. Aidarous and T. Plevyak, *Telecommunications Network Management into the 21st Century: Techniques, Standards, Technologies and Applications*, IEEE Press, Piscataway, NJ, 1996.

[2] A.J. Albrecht and J.E. Gaffney, Jr., "Software Function, Source Lines of Code, Development Effort Prediction: A Software Science Validation," *IEEE Transactions on Software Engineering*, 9:6:639-648, 1983.

[3] E.M. Bennatan, *On Time, Within Budget: Software Project Management Practices and Techniques*, 2nd ed. John Wiley & Son, Inc, 1995

[4] J. O. Bergholm, etc. Service Design And Inventory System - SDI WhiteSheet. http://nina.mt.att.com/sdi_web/about_sdi/

[5] L. C. Briand, S. Morasca, and V. R. Basili, "Property-Based Software Engineering Measurement," ," *IEEE Transactions on Software Engineering*, 22:1:68-85, 1996.

[6] Carnegie Mellon University, Software Engineering Institute, *The Capability Maturity Model: Guidelines for Improving the Software Process*, Addison-Wesley, 1995.

[7] D. Garmus and D. Herron, "Measuring the Software Process: A Practical guide to functional measurements," Prentice Hall, Englewood Cliffs, NJ, 1996.

[8] A. Goldberg and K. S. Rubin, *Succeeding with Objects: Decesion Frameworks for Project Management*, Addison-Wesley, Reading, MA, 1995

[9] I. Graham, Migrating to Object Technology, Addison-Wesley, Wokingham, England, 1995

[10] J.-C. Liou and Y. Tsay, "Object Point Analysis and Measurement," Version 1.0, AT&T, 200 Laurel Ave. Middletown, NJ 07748, 1999.

[11] J.-C. Liou "On Sizing the Rule Development for Object Classes in OO Software Applications", Submitted to *IEEE Transactions on Software Engineering*.

[12] J. Rumbaugh, etc. Object-Oriented Modeling and Design, Prentice Hall, Englewood Cliffs, NJ, 1991.

[13] R.D. Stutzke, Software Estimating Technology: A Survey. in *Software Engineering Project Management*, 2nd ed. (R. H. Thayer ed.), Los Alamitos, CA: IEEE Computer Society Press, 1997.

[14] N. Wilde and R. Huitt, "Maintenance support for object-Oriented Programs," *IEEE Transactions on Software Engineering*, 18:12:1038-1044, 1992.

'Net-Class',
A Multilingual
Web based Learning Management Tool

Seren Başaran, Neşe Yalabık, Ümit Kızıloğlu
Informatics Institute, METU, Ankara, TURKEY
sbasaran@ii.metu.edu.tr, yalabik@ii.metu.edu.tr, umk@ii.metu.edu.tr

Abstract

This paper presents a web based multilingual learning management system (LMS) 'Net-Class'. The Net-Class software provides online course management facilities for instructors, students and administrators. Even though it is designed for web-based asynchronous distance learning, it may also be used as a supplementary teaching-learning tool for traditional face-to-face courses. Net-Class features many facilities for communication, motivation building, assessment and course administration. Especially designed to be used in two languages (namely, Turkish and English) simultaneously, it offers a convenient facility for educational institutions and companies that may use both languages in different applications. The system gradually evolved to a professional tool in a few years of use with continuous student and faculty feedback in several programs and individual courses in Middle East Technical University.

Keywords

Web based education, multilingual learning management tool, asynchronous learning, Net-Class.

1. Introduction

Web based learning technologies are rapidly evolving at our information era where learning anytime, any place and any age is in great demand. Globally dispersed educational institutions and organizations are inclined to use web-based learning management systems (LMS) more and more to supply the needed education [1,2,3,4].

LMS are software platforms for online courses and programs but they may also be used as supplementary tools for traditional classroom environment.

LMS feature a wide variety of facilities for the educational aspects of online learning. These include: *effective communications between the instructor and students, motivation building tools for students such as self-scheduling, course management tools for the instructor such as testing and grading, student follow up.* In addition, they also provide tools for the administrator, *such as course and student registration.*

Many LMS are commercially available today, including WebCT, Learning Space (by IBM), and Blackboard. Many of these are very new and became available recently. Companies started to show great interest in LMS for in-service training activities, which might have different aspects compared to the university applications. For example, self-learning facilities are more in demand. This means LMS developers should include university and in-service training versions of these tools.

'Net-Class' started to be developed a few years ago in METU Informatics Institute, to be used in many web based learning projects in METU. These include online certificate and degree programs. It is in constant evolution with respect to the demands of faculty and students for improvements. 'Multilinguality' is in constant demand in Turkey since education in English in addition to Turkish may be desired for many reasons. Net-Class has a multilinguality feature that allows users to switch to either of the two languages online and it differs from other tools in this aspect in addition to some other unique features.

First web based education activities in Middle East Technical University begun in 1997 with a campus wide project (supported by DPT-Government Planning Organization) called METU-Online where the first version of the Net-Class software was used to support courses lectured throughout the campus. Today, there are approximately 890 students enrolled to 11 courses during each academic semester. Net-Class is used as a support tool for more than a 100 courses/semester, with a growing demand.

The current version of the Net-Class is in the service of the *Informatics Online* Masters degree program that is started at the spring 2001. A growing number of universities and companies are among the users of the Net-Class.

A comparison of the earlier version of Net-Class with other commercially available tools is given in [3].

This paper discusses the educational and technical features of the current version of Net-Class, including some usage statistics.

1.1. Net-Class System

Net-Class software works with web-based graphical interfaces and any web browser at its client-side can be used to operate. The entire client-side interaction is based on HTML pages and forms. Since the users of the system may be working on various platforms, great care has been taken to include minimum amount of browser specific code because one of the major aims was to provide maximum availability.

Net-Class is developed in **Java servlet** environment, which provides platform independence, ease of maintenance and increased reusability. At the server side, a web server, a servlet engine, and a relational database server are required to establish the Net-Class system. A three-tiered architecture is used in developing the Net-Class. The design characteristics of Net-Class allow platform independence and load balancing by supporting distribution of all servers onto distinct physical machines. However, this is not compulsory, as you may have all servers running on the same machine. The current system architecture is depicted in Diagram – 1.

Diagram-1 Net-Class System Architecture

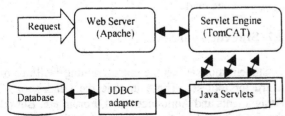

The Apache Tom-CAT web server initially receives the client-side requests. Then these requests are sent to the corresponding Java servlet of the Net-Class. Related information is either extracted from the related tables of the database or stored to the related tables consequently. Java servlets communicate via JDBC adapter that enables

the use of any relational database. Currently PostGre-SQL is been used as a database.

More detailed diagram of Java-Servlets communication of Net-Class can be represented in Diagram-2:

Diagram-2: Java Servlet Communication

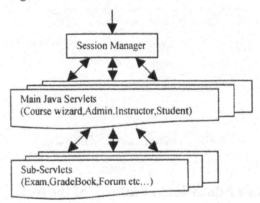

Requests arriving to the Tom-CAT server is received and managed by the Session Manager servlet. This servlet obtains the users' user-id, password and language option by the existing cookie technology for every user request consequently then passes these arguments to the corresponding second level sub-servlets.

Net-Class recognizes three types of statically defined users, **instructor**, **student**, and **administrator** in the system. The other type, **assistant**, may have changing privileges that are defined by the instructor of the course, to which the teaching assistant is assigned. The system serves the users the relevant functionality by determining the type of the user during the authorization process.

Net-Class is currently in wide-range use throughout METU campus under the name 'METU-Online'. A demo version is also available for testing from the website (http://online.metu.edu.tr). The screenshots of METU-Online and a typical course main page are given in Figure-1 and Figure-2 below:

Figure-1: METU-Online main page

Figure-2: Course main page for instructor

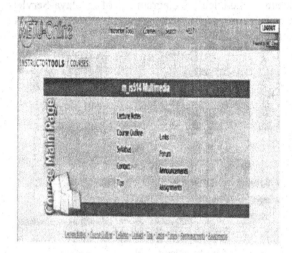

2. Some Educational Features of the Net-Class

Some standards on the educational features of LMS's are developed, such as Advanced Distributed Learning (ADL) [5] in which ADL defines a typical LMS as follows:
"*LMS* refers to a suite of functionality designed to deliver, report on, and administer learning content, student progress, and student interactions." (ADL is standards is established by the the Department of Defense (DoD) to develop a DoD-wide strategy for using learning and information technologies to modernize education and training.) Net-Class's educational properties that are in line with these are highlighted as follows:

2.1. Instructor Tool Set

1. *Gradebook*: Enables online self-automated grading, easing the work of tracking student success and competency. This module provides the instructor the means to inform the students about the results of the quizzes, homework and other student works hich needs to be graded. This feature is important in **motivation building** since students can follow their own progress. It also lets the instructor follow the students' progress and construct final grades quickly with the various facilities.
2. *Online Exam*: This module provides flexibility for an instructor to create her/his own exams by choosing previously prepared questions from the question pool. Online exams are mostly used for **self-evaluation** for students. Currently, only multiple choice test types are available. The

results of the tests are automatically added to the gradebook.
3. *Student tracking*: Identifies the student performance and enables to view class competency. This module enables the instructor to view the number of access times and location of course lecture notes between the chosen date range. By entering the student **user id** or **name** the instructor can follow the student's interest in the course materials. The instructor can follow student's accesses to the pages, the time of access and time spent on each of the pages, and contributions to the group projects. This constructs the **skeleton** of **progress tracking**. Histograms showing the statistics of page access per student and as a whole are also available to the instructor, who can look at most recently visited pages and time spent on each page.
4. *Forum*: Helps instructor to initiate course related group discussions. The instructor can also view the individual student participation to the discussion of a specific subject here. Instructor can define **student discussion groups** or **project groups** by using this module. Students in the same group have the facility of conducting and starting discussions, asking questions and receiving answers in an asynchronous environment. These discussion notes can be **archived**. Instructor can **delete** and **deactivate** each group. To enlarge the discussion environment and increase the sharing of ideas instructor can also **combine** the groups. Archived discussion notes can be searched and **feedback** can be supplied when necessary. Upload and attachment facilities are also available for this module.
5. *E-mail*: Provides an easy to use communication medium between the tutors and the students. Instructors can do group mailing to the selected students. His tool is especially useful when an urgent announcement to all or some students is to be made.

2.2. Student Tool Set

Student tool set has the corresponding facilities of the instructor tool set. These include the Gradebook, Test, Assignments and Announcements, Forum etc. But one of the most important for the student is the lecture notes browsing., which of course should contain well written notes for online courses , which might be the subject of another paper.

346

2.3. Administrator Tool Set

1. *User Enrollment*: enables to enroll/assign/delete users (instructor, student, assistant) to the system and to the related courses.
2. *Course creation, course data backup and deletion*: Backups are later used for statistical purposes.

3. Technical Features of the Net-Class

3.1. Security

1. Secure Socket Layer can be maintained upon request during the first level of access to the system.
2. The **authorization** that is provided by the tool in assigning access and other privileges to specific users and user groups, and the **basic authentication** is provided by the TomCAT Apache web-server that is used to prevent unauthorized access and/or any modification within the data.
3. Each Net-Class user has a standard UNIX **DES** encrypted password for the accessing to the system.
4. Server Side Security: Server-Side security is achieved by the operating system that is established on the server where Net-Class is operating on. The course accounts where course data are kept and the instructor user accounts are reserved by the server. Since Java technology is used in developing Net-Class learning management tool, it is platform independent. Net-Class is currently operating on Digital Unix and Red Hat Linux operating systems.

3.2. Database

1. Net-Class is communicating with the relational database via JDBC. All web based course related records except the course's HTML pages (i.e. lecture notes) are reserved within this relational database. System modules are coded and implemented in Java Servlet environment and they are communicating with each other through a main servlet in the position of a gateway to the system. Since JDBC technology is used, Net-Class LMS is entirely independent from the relational database. Any other relational database will be equally welcomed and compatible with the tool.

2. Net-Class is currently using Post-GreSQL version 7.1 as a relational database.

3.3. Multilingualty

As previously mentioned Net-Class supports the multilingual option provided for all users where every user can select the language during the first accessing to the system with which s/he is most comfortable. Once the desired language is selected, all the interfaces are shown dynamically in the desired language during the session. Currently Net-Class has two optional languages: Turkish and English. Other languages can be also set upon request. This flexibility of language provides Net-Class a more effective interface whereas the general commercial learning management tools have different packages for the desired languages. There exists a document preserving a keyword and a reference to this keyword and a corresponding image directory for every language option/document. Once the user has selected the desired language, the Session Manager servlet obtains the language parameter and communicates with the related servlets passing this parameter and letting the necessary interfaces to be presented to the user. In other words, bilingualty process can be described more technically as follows:

Every sub-servlet consists of a method called "match" that enables the handling of the language option. There exists a document namely a dictionary file for every language used within Net-Class, which includes the original word or a sentence and the corresponding meaning of these groups of words in the selected language in a parametric way. When a certain language is set (either to Turkish or English) every servlet extracts the regarding word/words from these dictionary files and the preferred language is presented to the user via browser. Similarly for every language option there is a corresponding image directory that operates synchronously according to the above process.

4. Some Statistics

Some statistical data of the academic programs which are currently using Net-Class, are given in the tables Table-1 and Table-2 below:

Table-1 Net-Class Statistics

Name	Type	No. of Courses	Total registered students	Start year
METU-Online	Online → Traditional→	23 100	6000	1998
Informatics Online	M.S. program	19	160	2001

The word 'Traditional' states that the course's medium of instruction is both face-to-face and online.

'Online' represents the whole lecture is taught in fully online format.

Table-2:Informatics Online Student opinions

	Yes (%)	No (%)	Neutral (%)
Ease of usability	68.2	9.1	22.7
Graphical interface is functional	68.0	12.0	20.0
Technical Support is satisfactory	69.6	13.0	17.4
Operates efficiently on various browsers and on client-side operating platforms	60.8	34.8	4.3
Network connection is satisfactory	60.0	16.0	24.0

4. Results and Conclusions

Refering to the 'Student opinions' and the statistical data given above, Net-Class LMS's benefits can be summarized in general as follows:

1. *Instructor Tools*: Powerful gradebook, a forum with group facility, e-mail to selected students, bilinguality, student tracking
2. *Student Tools*: Powerful grade reporting, forum, homework upload, bilinguality
3. *Technical Infrastructure*: platform independence. Unix and NT based versions available. Highly secure environment.
4. Eye appealing and user-friendly graphical interface for users.
5. Net-Class is platform free i.e. it can be easily transportable to another operating platform.
6. By the asynchronous two sided communication tools provided by Net-Class remarkably reduces the use of any other tools.

The missing features with room for improvement are:
1. A course planner for instructors and students
2. Synchronous communications
3. Student scratch book.

Acknowledgments

Many people participated in the development process of the Net-Class software. Onur Tortamış, Işıl Yamaç, and Alpay Karagöz contributed as programmers and developers. Bige Çetinoğlu designed the main web-graphic interface of the Net-Class software. Tevfik Aytekin coordinated the development process. We would also like to thank Ferda Alpaslan for comments and valuable discussions.

References

[1] Hanna, D.E. *Higher Education in an Era of Digital Competition: Emerging Organizational Models*, Journal of Asynchronous Learning Networks, Vol. 2, 1998.

[2] B. Henderson, *The components of Online Education: Higher Education on the Internet*, University Saskatchewan, Saskatoon, Canada, 1998.

[3] Yılmaz, B., Yalabık N., Karagöz A., *A Comparison of the Web Based Course Management Tools with 'Net-Class'*, Informing Science Conference, Krakov, Poland 2001.

[4] ADL Sharable Courseware Object Reference Model, Advanced Distributed Learning, Version 1.0, January 31, 2000.

[5] ADL Sharable Courseware Object Reference Model (SCORM) Documentation http://ww.adlnet.org

Biographies

Neşe Yalabık is a professor at Middle East Technical University, Computer Engineering Department. She is also the Director of the Informatics Institute, Middle East Technical University.

Ümit Kızıloğlu is a professor at Middle East Technical University, Physics Department. He is also the Associate Director of the Informatics Institute, Middle East Technical University.

Seren Başaran is working at the Informatics Institute of Middle East Technical University since 1998, as a member of distance education unit.

How Human Factors Impact on Software Process Maturity

Jing-Chiou Liou
AT&T Laboratories.
200 S. Laurel Ave.
Middletwon, NJ 07748, USA
Email: jing@att.com

Abstract

Software process is a repeatable path toward the final goals of a software project and is also one of the most important subjects on building a high quality software. Better process not only ensures the quality of the software, but also improves the productivity of the project. Among the Capability Maturity Model (CMM), the ISO9000 series, and best practices, the CMM is the one specially focusing on the software development. In this paper, we demonstrate that the process maturity of software development organizations can be negatively affected by leadership and other human factors. Even for those organizations that are assessed for certain levels of process maturity, with no periodical audit from CMM assessors, their process maturity still under influence of these factors. These human factors, based on the industry experience, are identified and possible resolutions are discussed.

1   Introduction

There are three essential objectives for a project: *Cost, Schedule*, and *Quality*. During the development of a software application, it is very common for a project team to be under pressure of meeting schedule and lowering cost. Achieving these two objectives may please customer at the first place, but the quality is the key to the customer satisfaction. However, this does not mean a software project manager should focus only on quality. Because building a software application involves *product, people*, and *process*. Focusing on quality manages the scope of the "product." Project management manages "people" for the schedule and cost. And the software engineering "process" management and improvement optimizes the balance of previous two. In other words, "process" finds a smooth path for "people" to build quality software "product" on time and within budget.

There are some existing standards or guidelines to help software development organizations to establish the processes that suit their needs. The Capability Maturity Model (CMM) [3], the ISO9000 series [8], and best practices [7] are well known parts of the process management and improvement. Among them, the CMM is the one specially focusing on the software development.

But to establish software process must start from focusing on quality. Only those organizations that focus on quality can institutionalize the process they wish to establish. In this paper, we demonstrate that leadership and other human factors can negatively affect the process maturity of software development organizations. Even for those organizations that are assessed for certain levels of process maturity, with no periodical audit from CMM assessors, their process maturity still under influence of these factors. These human factors, based on the industry experience, are identified and possible resolutions are discussed.

The rest of this paper is organized as the followings: Section 2 discusses some background of this work. Section 3 reviews industrial experience of human factors impacting on software process maturity by discussing three case studies. And finally section 4 presents the conclusion.

2   Background

During the last decade, software engineering researchers have tried to identify the success and obstacle factors to the software development. Many researches have presented surveys [7, 13] and proposed methodologies [2, 9, 12], tools [10], and guidelines [3, 7, 8] on this issue. Conclusions from most of the researches related to the issue show that software process is one of the most important subjects contributing into the success or failure to the software development.

2.1   Software Process and Quality

Schedule press is very common for software development organization. Unfortunately, the interaction of software schedules and software quality is poorly understood by many software managers and technical personnel as well [7]. Software engineering is employed when a software organization rests on the commitment to quality. Software engineering is a layered technology [12]. It is built on top of a quality focus. The next layer is the software process that holds all software technologies together and enables the efficient software product development by people.

The term process may be referred to different things to people in different disciple. Version 1.1 of the CMM views a process as a "sequence of steps" performed by people with the aids of tools and equipment to transform raw material into a product [3, 4]. By the definition, process defines a set of key process areas (KPAs) [3] that forms the basis of management control for software projects. The key process areas also help projects to produce desire deliverables (e.g., documentation, forms), establish milestones for quality assurance and manage change control.

The goal of Total Quality Management (TQM) is to meet the needs of the customer, now and in the future [1]. What are the needs of customer? The software quality, the development/maintenance cost, and the delivery schedule are the three elements of customer satisfaction [1]. In order to achieve the optimizing level of the TQM that is originated from the principles of statistical quality control [4], a process management and improvement culture must be fostered.

2.2 Process Improvement and Maturity

In general, a software development organization wants to be competitive, improve quality, and increase productivity, the following actions are required [4]:

- Focus on the processes that develop the software to improve quality and productivity.
- Ensure that the processes are properly supported.
- Manage poorly behaving processes by fixing the processes, not blaming the people.
- Process improvement comes from reducing variation in all processes.
- Management action uses data from the process to guide decisions.

Even quality has such dependence with process, however, as we can see later in the case studies, many of these required actions are easily broken by human factors such as leadership problems. Nonetheless, process management and improvement are necessary to ensure the process serving its purpose.

Process management is to define, measure, and control the process. When a process is clearly defined, well measured, and under control, the process can reach a certain level of maturity. In that maturity level, a software development organization can achieve its goals by employing the software process as the policy of

development. However, as the scope of the goals promotional changed (E.g., meeting customer's needs), the process has to be accordingly improved. In other words, the process maturity has to be improved by improving its capabilities or replacing existing sub-processes with other more efficient ones.

Continue process improvement is based on many small, evolutionary steps rather than revolutionary innovations [3]. The CMM provides a framework for organizing these evolutionary steps into five maturity levels that lay successive foundations for continuous process improvement:

1. *Initial*
2. *Repeatable*
3. *Defined*
4. *Managed*
5. *Optimizing*

The CMM supports measurement of the software process by providing a framework for performing reliable and consistent appraisals. According to the Capability Maturity Model, a software process assessment is an appraisal by a trained team of software professionals to determine the state of an organization's current software process to determine the high-priority software process-related issues facing an organization, and to obtain the organizational support for software process improvement. An assessment from SEI also certifies an organization as in a certain maturity level.

3 Case Studies of Human Factor Impacting on Process Maturity

The Capability Maturity Model assumes only an upward path. In other words, a software development organization shall hold the maturity level once it is assessed, provided that the organization keeps doing what they did during the maturity assessment. Therefore, there is no need for periodical audit from the SEI appraisal team. Ideally, this is true. The CMM was partially developed to eliminate the human factors in an immature (CMM level 1) software organization. But the assumption ignores the factors originated from *human being* and *business trends* that may affect the software organization after the assessment. Both of them can be referred as human factors.

In this section, we will present three case studies based on industry experience. In the cases we presented here, we demonstrate that process maturity can be negative impacted by the human factors, either intentionally or unintentionally. All of the cases were actually experienced in two telecommunication software applications development organizations, one called SDS, with about 1,800 staffs, another called NMS, with about 800 staffs. These cases are studied in a period of time from 1997 to 2001.

350

3.1 Change of Maturity Level

The request of focusing on quality of products may come from any level of management. However, the request for an accomplishment of achieving specific process maturity level (e.g., change from CMM level 1 to level 2) usually come from the upper management of an organization. This is the case when the director of the SDS organization formed a Process Improvement Initiative (PII) team in 1997. The initial goal was to achieve CMM level 2 in 1998. Following that as a more aggressive goal to achieve CMM level 3 in 1999.

The goals may seems simple, but the whole SDS organization faced the following issues:

- *Balancing the product delivery schedule and the CMM related effort*: The low-level (district) managers in the SDS organization must decided how to balance the product delivery schedule and the CMM related effort. In 1997, many managers responded to the issue with the followings:
  - Forming a CMM core team: In every project, staffs were assigned to form a CMM core team to deal with the CMM related issues. The core team was the main working force to achieve the CMM maturity level 2 (and 3).
  - Protecting key persons from the CMM related effort: Those development key persons were kept away from the CMM related effort, except for the required training, and focused on the product delivery.
  - Doing what the CMM consultants recommended to do: CMM subject experts were employed to consult the project team for preparing the software process assessment. The CMM core team would follow the CMM consultant's recommendation for any actions.
- *Resources funding for the CMM related activities*: At the directorate level, the resources for the CMM related activities were funded. But no specific resources were funded at the project level.
- *Staff training for CMM Level-related KPAs*: All staffs were required to receive CMM Level-related KPAs training. There were about 5 hours of training in 1998 and 26.5 to 52.5 hours, depending on staff's job function, in 1999.
- *Obtaining buy-in of the CMM activities from project sponsors (customers)*: Some sponsors even believe that the CMM activities of the SDS organization prevent their requested products from efficient delivery.

Although having those existing issues, the SDS organization finally accomplished their goals: achieved CMM level 2 in 1998, and level 3 in 1999. However, following factors that had influence on the process maturity were identified during and after the assessment:

- *Negligence from low-level management*: With no funding to the CMM effort, low-level managers rely on the CMM consultant to recommend the minimum requirements to achieve the maturity level. And the CMM core team was expected to satisfy all of the key practices of KPAs.
- *Resistance from staffs*: With such a short timeframe to accomplish the goals, some recommendations (fixed formulas and checklists) were produced. When the organization followed the checklist strategy, piles of documents and mountains of paper were generated to "prove" that the software processes are at some prescribed level. The staffs would resist doing more "process work" if the core team suggested to them. Even they followed the suggestion, they would prefer not to execute the process completely.
- *Miscommunication between the directorate process team and project team*: In the CMM level 3, a Software Engineering Process Group (SEPG) is recommended in the key practice of the "Organization Process Focus" KPA. The group, consisting of assigned full time staffs and voluntary project representatives, is responsible for the organization's software process activities. While the project representatives is not a very popular assignment, not many projects in the directorate sent their representatives to the SEPG. The result is that many negative feedback would be sent back to SEPG once the process was effective and projects were asked to follow. Some of the typical comments were:
  - Some (or our) project has already a very good process for this.
  - The process will not work for our project.
  - Why my project was not invited in developing the process.

3.2 Change of Development Structure

Re-organization is a very common phenomenon in the software industry. A case is studied here to examine the influence of human factor on the software process during the organization re-structure.

A software engineering group (district level), called W team, was assigned to develop telecommunication software applications for three customers. The group manager was very process-oriented and the group has established some well defined software processes even before the previously mentioned CMM maturity level assessment. These processes were not documented in standard formats. These defined processes were completely executed during the development cycle:

- *Detailed project planning and management*.
- *Complete configuration management*.
- *Focusing on Quality*: Statistical methodologies and heuristics [9, 10] were used for performance analysis.

- *Emphasizing on process management and improvement.*

When the re-structure happened in 1998, another software engineering group, the B team, was assigned to development a similar telecommunication application for a new and bigger market customer. With the two teams developing almost the same function of application in parallel, the levels of process maturity of these two teams are totally different.

While the manager of the B team does not focus on the process management, in order to meet the schedule, the B team was prototyping the development. The best description of the development concept is: "Let us just get the job done by due day, and if there are any production problems, we can fix them later."

The B team's development process consists of:

- *Strong customer focus team*: The B team maintains a group of people, called Customer Focus Team (CFT), to deal with customer.
- *Minor project planning and management.*
- *Minimum project tracking and oversight.*
- *Weak configuration management*: Work product was delivered to production from individual's personal file(s).
- *Incomplete quality gates certification*: Quality Gates (QGs) sign-off was performed only for Q11 (for business requirement) and Q1 (for installation) that require signatures from both customer and the development organization.

Table 1 shows a metrics for these two teams in the period from 1997 to 1999 when they develop applications in parallel. In Table 1, the second column shows the software release number that team delivered to customer. The software size, in terms of Object Points (OPs) [9], is shown in the third column. The development cycle time (in months) is listed in column four. The fifth column shows the effort spent for development as in staff-month (130 effort-hours per month). Finally, the last column shows the total number of defects reported through the development cycle and delivery into production.

Team	Rel.	Software Size	Cycle Time	Effort (S-M)	No. of Defects
W team	R1	1170	10.7	33.3	61
	R2	2318	13.6	41.7	35
B team	R1	1712	15	118.6	173

Table 1: Performance metrics for W and B teams

Table 2 summarizes a performance metrics based on metrics data in Table 1. The cost ($/unit size)shown in column 3 is calculated based on the following formula:

$$\text{Cost} = \text{Effort} * 130 * (\$ \text{ Hourly Rate}) / (\text{Software Size}) \quad (1)$$

The Defect Density (# of defects/unit size) shown in column 4 is defined as:

$$DD = (\text{No. of defects}) / (\text{Software Size}) \quad (2)$$

And the Productivity is defined as:

$$P = (\text{Software Size}) / (\text{Effort}) \quad (3)$$

Team	Rel.	Cost	Defect Density	Productivity
W team	R1	254	0.052	35.1
	R2	161	0.015	55.6
Bteam	R1	618	0.101	14.5

Table 2: Performance metrics based on metrics data in Table 1

From Table 2, we can see that the effort the W team put into process management and improvement did pay. Not only the cost reduced from $254/OP in R1 to. $161/OP in R2 (37% reduction), but the Defect Density is also dramatically reduced (71% improvement). Comparing to what the W team achieved, the cost for B team is at least 1.4 times higher while the defect density is 94% worse. And to the production defects (defect found in production), comparing to 1 production defect for a software application of 3488 object points (unit of measuring the size of an Object-Oriented application [9]) that the W team developed, the B team produced 11 production defects for the software of 1712 object points.

Factors that influence the software process in this case were identified during the period from 1998 to mid-year of 2000:

- *Acknowledgement for the meaning of the "customer satisfaction".*
- *Previous experience with the software processes.*
- *Focusing on quality or something else.*

3.3 Change in Leadership

Change in leadership could be either a part of the re-structure or simply a change in someone's personal career plan. With different personal management styles, sometimes change in leadership means totally different software process in the organization.

In the case studied here, a software development group, called J team, was assigned to develop a telecommunication software application. The first manager of the group had over 15 years of management experience and was very process-oriented in his management style. The J team performed almost everything the W team did mentioned in the section 3.2 when the first manager was in charge. After the CMM assessment to the SDS organization, the J team documented and followed the standard processes.

When the first manager retired in 1999, a new promoted (the second) manager took the leadership of the group. With additional function assigned, new staffs were brought into the group. Those new staffs were mostly younger and no previous experience of the software processes. The second manager of the group did not involve before with the CMM level assessment. After the change in leadership, software project behaviors also changed.

In this case, most of the factors that impacts on software process are the same as those identified in the case of "Change of Development Structure." However, there is one big different:

- *Management style affects the efficiency of process execution*: The manager in the previous case focused on customer relationship and let his staffs taking care their own technical responsibilities (very coarse grain macro management). On the contrary, the manager in this case was doing his best to tack care almost everything that is from planning down to technical details (a good example of micro management). Due to the fact of micro management, technical decision made by staffs based on the process often superseded by manager's judgements. Superseding itself is not an issue, but too many times the superseding was not made according to the process, but heroic actions. In other words, the manager would use what he believes the best way to do the job learned from personal experiences, regardless what the process would recommend. This is exactly what the CMM describes as level 1 process.

4 Conclusion

For existing standards or guidelines of process management, the CMM is the one specially focusing on the software development. However, CMM does not guarantee that the software organization can actually keep up the maturity level after the organization is assessed, since it does not require audit from outside of the organization. The study presented in this paper has identified some human factors that can negatively impact to the existing process maturity. Among them, leadership is the most mentioned factor. From low level managers to the senior management, the leadership shows such a major influence to the process maturity of a software development organization. Other factors, such as adequate training and resource allocation, were also identified to have impact. In addition to maturity level assessment, it is also conclude that the software development organization should receive periodical CMM audit in order to keep its maturity level certification.

Please referring to [11] for detailed discussion and lesson learned of this research.

Reference

[1] E.M. Bennatan, *On Time, Within Budget: Software Project Management Practices and Techniques*, 2nd ed. John Wiley & Son, Inc, 1995

[2] L. C. Briand, S. Morasca, and V. R. Basili, "Property-Based Software Engineering Measurement," *IEEE Transactions on Software Engineering*, 22:1:68-85, 1996.

[3] Carnegie Mellon University, Software Engineering Institute, *The Capability Maturity Model: Guidelines for Improving the Software Process*, Addison-Wesley, 1995.

[4] W. A. Florac and A. D. Carleton, Measuring the Software Process: Statistical Process Control for Software Process Improvement, Addison-Wesley, Reading, MA, 1999.

[5] D. Garmus and D. Herron, Measuring the Software Process: A Practical guide to functional measurements, Prentice Hall, Englewood Cliffs, NJ, 1996.

[6] A. Goldberg and K. S. Rubin, *Succeeding with Objects: Decesion Frameworks for Project Management*, Addison-Wesley, Reading, MA, 1995

[7] C. Jones, Software Quality: Analysis and Guidelines for Success, International Thomson Computer Press, 1997.

[8] R. Kehoe and A. Jarvis, ISO 9000-3: A Tool for Software Product and Process Improvement, Springer, 1995.

[9] J.-C. Liou, Measuring the Size of Object-Oriented Software Applications. To appear in Proc. 17th International Symposium on Computer and Information Science.

[10] J.-C. Liou and S.-C. Tsay, Estimate Your Software Testing Right. Proc. The Fifth International Conference on Computer Science and Informatics 2000, pp. 615 - 618, Atlantic City, NJ, USA, March, 2000.

[11] J.-C. Liou, CMM and Software Process Maturity - An Industry Experience. Submitted to Project Management Journal.

[12] R.S. Pressman, Software Engineering. in *Software Engineering Project Management*, 2nd ed. (R. H. Thayer ed.), Los Alamitos, CA: IEEE Computer Society Press, 1997.

[13] R.D. Stutzke, Software Estimating Technology: A Survey. in *Software Engineering Project Management*, 2nd ed. (R. H. Thayer ed.), Los Alamitos, CA: IEEE Computer Society Press, 1997.

A Mathematical Formalism for Specifying Design Patterns

Denver R. E. Williams, Charles E. Hughes and Ali Orooji
School of Electrical Engineering and Computer Science
University of Central Florida
Orlando, FL 32816-2362, USA
{dwilliam@cs.ucf.edu, ceh@cs.ucf.edu, orooji@cs.ucf.edu}

Abstract

Model based software development uses design patterns to capture successful designs and micro-architectures. This paper presents the essential constructs of a mathematical formalism for the specification of design patterns. The specification constitutes an extension of basic concepts from many-sorted algebra. The approach can be used to determine efforts for component reuse, facilitate automatic program verification, and aid complex software development by providing the developer with design alternatives.

1. Introduction

Model based software development is the latest episode in the object technology revolution [1,3]. This is an approach to raise the abstraction level at which application developers work and to automate the process of translation from an application model to its corresponding distributable runtime component. The basic thesis here is that we can effectively reverse the division of effort in the software development process in which about 80% of the work goes into the development of infrastructure services and 20% into the development of application logic [2]. This would allow software professionals to approach the order of magnitude speedup in the software development process that has been eluding this community for over three decades.

Design patterns [4] are a promising technique for capturing and articulating proven techniques for developing extensible large-scale software systems. Design patterns express the static and dynamic structures and collaborations of components in software architectures. Patterns aid the development of extensible distributed system components and frameworks by expressing the structure and collaboration of participants in software architectures at a level higher than source code components or object-oriented design models that focus on individual objects and classes. The structural aspects of design patterns are usually described using UML, an OMG adapted standard [6].

The MOF is the OMG adopted technology for defining metadata [5,7,8]. The MOF supports any kind of metadata that can be described using Object Modeling techniques. Recently, the OMG introduced the Model-Drive Architecture (MDA) initiative as an approach to systems-specification and interoperability based on the use of formal models [1,3]. UML and the MOF are the centerpieces of the four-layer modeling stack of the MDA.

The MDA has significant implications for the disciplines of Metamodeling and Adaptive Object Models (AOMs). Metamodeling is the primary activity in the specifications, or modeling, of metadata. Interoperability in heterogeneous environments is ultimately achieved via shared metadata, and the overall strategy for sharing and understanding metadata consists of the automated development, publishing, management, and interpretation of models. AOM technology provides dynamic systems behavior based on run-time interpretation of such models. Architectures based on AOMs are highly interoperable, easily extended at run-time, and completely dynamic in terms of their overall behavioral specifications.

Any reasonable approach to addressing the large-scale software reuse problem and dynamic systems behavior must provide an inherent mechanism for raising abstraction. An architecture approach to software development enables the imposition of an overarching structure that rationalizes, arranges, and connects components to produce the desired functionality. Design patterns facilitate an architectural approach to software development and promote reuse of interface specification through the principles of composition. A composite module specification must guarantee syntactic non-interference and semantic context independence among the different modules. Using a suitable terminology, we have to show a *modularization theorem* for the composition.

Design patterns are micro-architectures that can play a very effective role in the construction of models and metamodels. The automated generation processes to which these models will be subjected can be made more reliable if built on a consistent theoretical framework. In this paper, we propose such a framework.

2. Design Pattern and Knowledge

Informally, a design pattern or micro-architecture software artifact is an aggregate of abstract data types (ADTs). The class of objects corresponding to each of the ADTs is represented by a Σ-algebra [9]. Assuming that the components are linearly independent, we can represent a design pattern as a vector of Σ-algebras [9,2]. One of the major attributes of a design pattern is that it captures knowledge from past experience. Thus, the relationship between the component ADTs must be made explicit in any reasonable representation of a design pattern [2].

One reasonable representation is to extend the n-tuple of Σ-algebras by including a *relation* that is capable of encoding the requisite knowledge [2]. That is, the relation must be able to encode, at a minimum, the relationship, roles, and multiplicity between entities in a design pattern. The relation depicted below is capable of encoding the requisite knowledge in a design pattern

$$R \subseteq L(Alpha) \times L(Alpha) \times A\lg(\Sigma_v) \times A\lg(\Sigma_v) \times$$

$$L(Alpha) \times L(Alpha) \times Nat \times Nat$$

where

$L(Alpha)$ depicts a set of alphabetic strings representing the names of relationships between entities,

$Alg(\Sigma_v)$ is the class of Σ-algebra corresponding to the vector signature Σ_v,

Nat is the set of natural numbers

The components for the relation R are defined as follows: the first component of R depicts the name of the relationship or association between two entities. The second component depicts the type of relationship. The third and forth components depict the entities that the relation is defined between. Components five and six define the roles of the relationship. Components seven and eight define the multiplicity of the relationship.

3. Definitions and Concepts

Within the context of software engineering the nomenclature pertaining to object-oriented methodologies depicts an *object* as an instance of a *class*. An object is a self-contained entity that is complete with its sets of data and associated operations. A class is a specification of an abstract data type. Many-sorted algebra is the mathematical formalism used for the specification of abstract data types and represents a straightforward generalization of classical algebras [9].

The mathematical formalism presented for the specification of design patterns constitutes an extension of the basic concepts from many-sorted algebra. In

particular, the notion of signature is extended to that of a vector, consisting of a set of linearly independent signatures. The linearly independence property is necessary to satisfy non-interference that is essential for compositional based construction [9,10,11]. This is of fundamental concern in the building of large-scale software systems where we have the composition of smaller components to form larger components. Finally, the specification for design patterns is developed as an extension to a loose module specification [2]

3.1 Signatures

A many-sorted algebra consists of sets and functions. A signature may be viewed as the syntax of an algebra for fixing the names of the sorts and functions. A many sorted algebra assigns a meaning to a signature by associating a set of data to each sort and a function to each operation.

Definition 1: Signature
A *signature* Σ is a pair $\Sigma = (S, F)$ of sets, the element of which are called *sorts* and *operations* respectively Each operation consists of a $(k+2)$-tuple $n = s_1 \times s_2 \times \ldots \times s_k \rightarrow s$ with $s_1, s_2, \ldots, s_k, s \in S$ and $k \geq 0$; n is called the *operation name* of the operation and $s_1, s_2, \ldots, s_k \rightarrow s$ its arity; the sorts $s_1, s_2, \ldots, s_k$ are called argument sorts of the operation and the sort s its target sort. In the case $k = 0$ the operation $n: \rightarrow s$ is called a constant of sort s. □

Definition 2: Vector Signature, extension of signature
A *vector signature* Σ_v is an *n*-tuple of linearly independent (Σ-) signatures represented as $\Sigma_v = (\Sigma_1, \Sigma_2, \ldots, \Sigma_n)$, such that $\Sigma_i = (S_i, F_i)$ and S_i represents the set of sorts for Σ_i and F_i represents the set of operations for Σ_i. The linearly independent property states that $S_i \cap S_j = \phi$ for $i \neq j$ and $F_i \cap F_j = \phi$. An operation of Σ_v is a vector. For example the vector w is defined as $w = (w_1, w_2, \ldots, w_n)$ such that $w_i \in F_i$ with $w_i = S_1^j \times S_2^j \times \ldots \times S_k^j \rightarrow S^j$ and $S_1^j, S_2^j, \ldots, S_k^j, S^j \in S_j$ and $k \geq 0$ and $1 \leq i, j \leq n$. □

3.2 Homomorphism

Vector homomorhpisms represent mappings between the carrier sets of vector algebras. The mappings *respect* the functions of the corresponding vector signature.

355

Definition 3: Vector Homomorphism, extension of homomorphism

Let $A = (A_1, A_2, \ldots, A_n)$, $B = (B_1, B_2, \ldots, B_n)$ be two Σ_v–algebras, $\Sigma_v = (\Sigma_1, \Sigma_2, \ldots, \Sigma_n)$, $\Sigma_i = (S_i, F_i)$. A Σ_v–homomorphism $H: A \to B$ is a vector of Σ–homomorhpisms represented as $H = (h_{s^i})_{i=1..n} = (h_{s^1}, h_{s^2}, \ldots, h_{s^n})$ where h_i is a homomorphism from A_i to B_i over Σ_i given by the mapping $h_i \colon A_i \to B_i$. For any operation $w \in \Sigma_v = (\Sigma_1, \Sigma_2, \ldots, \Sigma_n)$, say $w = (w_1, w_2, \ldots, w_n)$, such that $w_i \in F_i$ with $w_i = S_1^i \times S_2^i \times \ldots \times S_k^i \to S^i$ and $S_1^i, S_2^i, \ldots, S_k^i, S^i \in S_i$ and $\Sigma_i = (S_i, F_i)$ and $k \geq 0$ and $1 \leq i \leq n$, the following conditions hold:

$H(A)(w)(\bar{a}_1, \bar{a}_2, \ldots, \bar{a}_n)$

$= B(w)(H(\bar{a}_1), H(\bar{a}_2), \ldots, H(\bar{a}_n))$

$\equiv H(A_1)(w_1)(\bar{a}_1), H(A_2)(w_2)(\bar{a}_2), \ldots, H(A_n)(w_n)(\bar{a}_n)$

$= B_1(w_1)(H(\bar{a}_1)), B_2(w_2)(H(\bar{a}_2)), \ldots, B_n(w_n)(H(\bar{a}_n))$ (3)

The above equation (3), is called the homomorphism condition for the vector homomorphism H for the operation w. In the case when $k = 0$, the condition simply states:

$H(A_1)(w_1), H(A_2)(w_2), \ldots, H(A_n)(w_n)$

$= B_1(w_1), B_2(w_2), \ldots, B_n(w_n)$

$\equiv h_{s^1}(A_i(w_i)), h_{s^2}(A_2(w_2)), \ldots, h_{s^n}(A_n(w_n))$

$= B_i(w_i), B_2(w_2), \ldots, B_n(w_n)$ ⊔

3.3 Formal Specification for Design Pattern

It is now possible to introduce a formal notion of the *syntactic specification* for design pattern. Three dimensions of design pattern are characterized: the major classes forming the body or realization of the pattern, the interface or specification of the pattern, and the relationship between the classes in the body and interface of the pattern.

Definition 4: Module Vector Signature, extension of Module Signature

A *module vector signature* is a 3-tuple consisting of a pair of signatures and the knowledge relation discussed above. This is represented as follows: $(\Sigma_i^v, \Sigma_e^v, R^+)$ where Σ_i^v represents the vector signature corresponding to abstract data types depicting the main classes in the body or realization of the design pattern. Σ_e^v represents the vector signature corresponding to the abstract data views

(ADVs) depicting the main classes in the interface or specification of the design pattern [10,12,13,14]. R is the relation that captures the inter-relationship between the classes in Σ_i^v and Σ_e^v. □

Definition 5: Modularized Vector Abstract Data Type, extension of modularized ADT

A *modularized vector abstract data type* for the module vector signature $(\Sigma_i^v, \Sigma_e^v, R^+)$ is a family of total functions that define the relationships between the various classes in a design pattern. $\Sigma_i^v = (\Sigma_1, \Sigma_2, \ldots, \Sigma_m)$ and $\Sigma_e^v = (\Sigma_1, \Sigma_2, \ldots, \Sigma_n)$ are vector signatures representing abstract data types corresponding to classes in the main body (realization part) and interface (specification part) of a design pattern respectively.

i. The *realization part* of the *modularized vector abstract data type* for the module signature $(\Sigma_i^v, \Sigma_e^v, R^+)$ is defined by the following function:

$$M_1 : Alg(\Sigma_k) \to \wp(Alg(\Sigma_l))$$

where the following conditions hold: $1 \leq k, l \leq m$ and $k \neq l$ and $\Sigma_k, \Sigma_l \in \Sigma_i^v$ and for each algebra $A \in Alg(\Sigma_k)$ the class $M_1(A) \subseteq Alg(\Sigma_l)$ is an abstract data type.

ii. The *specification part* of the *modularized vector abstract data type* for the module signature $(\Sigma_i^v, \Sigma_e^v, R)$ is defined by the following function:

$$M_2 : \bigcup_{1 \leq k \leq m} Alg(\Sigma_k) \to \bigcup_{1 \leq l \leq n} \wp(Alg(\Sigma_l))$$

where the following conditions hold: $1 \leq k \leq m$, $\Sigma_k \in \Sigma_i^v$ and $1 \leq l \leq n$, $\Sigma_l \in \Sigma_e^v$ and for $A \in \wp(Alg(\Sigma_k))$ the class $M_2(A) \subseteq \wp(Alg(\Sigma_l))$ is an abstract data view. □

The function M_1 effectively defines the use of object-oriented design principles such as inheritance, composition, and aggregation in the progressive build up of the realization part of design patterns. The mapping allows subsets of the component ADTs of the design pattern to present their interfaces through a combined abstract data view. The ADV can be used to specialized or extend the functionality provided by the component ADTs comprising the realization part of the design pattern [2].

Definition 6: Design Pattern Specification, Extension of Loose Module Specification

Let L be a logic.

i. *Abstract Syntax*

A *design pattern specification* in L is a pair

$$dpsp = ((\Sigma_i^v, \Sigma_e^v, R^+), \Phi) \text{ where } (\Sigma_i^v, \Sigma_e^v, R^+) \text{ is a}$$

vector module signature with $R = \bigcup_{1 \leq i \leq 3} R_i^+$ and

$$(R_1 modifies \Sigma_i^v), (R_2 modifies \Sigma_e^v),$$

$(R_3 modifies(\Sigma_i^v \cup \Sigma_e^v))$ and $\Phi = \Phi_1 \cup \Phi_2$

with $\Phi_1 \subseteq L(\Sigma_i^v)$ and $\Phi_2 \subseteq L(\Sigma_e^v)$. Φ is a set of formulas that defines the derivation sequence to establish a relationship between two instances (entities) of the abstract data types corresponding to the vector signatures. R is the resultant static relationship that is determined by Φ.

ii. *Semantics*

The meaning $M(dpsp)$ of the design pattern specification $dpsp = ((\Sigma_i^v, \Sigma_e^v, R^+), \Phi)$ is the $(\Sigma_i^v, \Sigma_e^v, R^+)$ -module defined by the following set of mappings:

1. The meaning of the relationships in the realization part of the design pattern specification is given by:

$$M(dpsp)(A) = \{ B \in \mathrm{Alg}(\Sigma_l) \mid A \models_{\Phi_1} B, \textit{ iff } \text{for}$$

each $op_i \in \Phi_1$,

$A_i' \models_{op_i} A_{i+1}'$, implies $(A_i', A_{i+1}') \in R_1^+$ and

$op_i(A_i') = A_{i+1}' \}$

for each algebra $A \in Alg(\Sigma_k)$ and $1 \leq k, l \leq m$ and $k \neq l$ and $\Sigma_k, \Sigma_l \in \Sigma_i^v$ and $A_i', A_{i+1}' \in Alg(\Sigma_i^v)$.

Note: $A \models_{\Phi_1} B \equiv B \models \Phi_1$.

2. The meaning of the relationships in the interface part of the design pattern specification is given by:

$$M(dpsp)(A) = \{ B \in \wp(Alg(\Sigma_l)) \mid A \models_{\Phi_2} B, \textit{iff}$$

for each $op_i \in \Phi_2$,

$A_i' \models_{op_2} A_{i+1}'$, implies $(A_i', A_{i+1}') \in R_2^+$ and

$op_i(A_i') = A_{i+1}' \}$

for each $A \in \wp(Alg(\Sigma_k))$ and

$1 \leq k \leq m, 1 \leq l \leq n, \Sigma_k \in \Sigma_i^v$ and $\Sigma_l \in \Sigma_e^v$. $\square$

The set of formulas represented by Φ_1 characterizes the nature of the relationship between abstract data types constituting the realization part of the design pattern that is consistent with the mapping defined by M_1 of definition 5. Φ_1 is depicted as follows:

$$\Phi_1 \subseteq L(\Sigma_i^v) \equiv (\bigcup_{i \leq l \leq m} L(\Sigma_l))$$

The set of formulas represented by Φ_2 characterizes the nature of the relationship between the specification part and realization part of the design pattern that is consistent with the mapping defined by M_2 of definition 5. Φ_2 is depicted as follows:

$$\Phi_2 \subseteq L(\Sigma_e^v) \equiv (\bigcup_{i \leq l \leq n} L(\Sigma_l))$$

We can think of $A \models_\Phi B$ as having the meaning of abstract data type B derived from abstract data type A through a sequence of *formulas* or operations belonging to Φ. In addition, an operation is only permissible if the resulting relationships between the abstract data types for each of the derivation steps are contained in the transitive closure of R. That is, if the following relationship holds:

$$A_i' \models_{op_i} A_{i+1}', \text{ iff } (A_i', A_{i+1}') \in R^+$$

and $op_i \in \Phi$ and

$$A_i', A_{i+1}' \in \wp(A \lg(\Sigma_i^v)) \cup \wp(A \lg(\Sigma_e^v))$$

This process of deriving abstract data type B from abstract data type A can be interpreted using a derivation tree for the operations in Φ. The process of building the derivation tree is constrained by the relationship set depicted by R^+.

It is conceivable to have more than one derivation tree for a design pattern. Each derivation tree will result in a difference structural version of the pattern. This variation could account for differences in implementation approaches. For example, one implementation may favor delegation over an inheritance-based strategy.

4. Closure of Patterns under Composition

Let $\Sigma_v = (\Sigma_1, \Sigma_2, .., \Sigma_n)$ be a vector signature. The composition of two Σ_v-homomorphisms, say $H: A \to B$ and $G: B \to C$, yields a Σ_v-homomorphism $G \circ H: A \to C$ that is a family of functions of the form $G \circ H = (g_{s_i} \circ h_{s_i})_{i=1..n}$.

357

Theorem 1: For any vector signature Σ_v the composition of two Σ_v-homomorphisms yields a Σ_v-homomorphism. Given a vector signature $\Sigma_v = (\Sigma_1, \Sigma_2, \ldots, \Sigma_n)$ and the two Σ_v-homomorphisms

$$H : A \to B \quad \text{and} \quad G : B \to C, \quad G \circ H : A \to C$$

satisfies the vector homomorphism condition, thus

$$G \circ H(A(w)(\bar{a}_1, \bar{a}_2, \ldots, \bar{a}_n) = C(w)(G \circ H(\bar{a}_1), G \circ H(\bar{a}_2), \ldots, G \circ H(\bar{a}_n))$$

That is,

$$g \circ h_{s_1}(A_1)(w_1)(\bar{a}_1), g \circ h_{s_2}(A_2)(w_2)(\bar{a}_2), \ldots, g \circ h_{s_n}(A_n)(w_n)(\bar{a}_n)$$
$$= C_1(w_1)(g \circ h_{s_1}(\bar{a}_1)), C_2(w_2)(g \circ h_{s_2}(\bar{a}_2)), \ldots, C_n(w_n)(g \circ h_{s_n}(\bar{a}_n))$$

5. Concluding Remarks and Future Work

The collective wisdom about building complex distributed software over the past decade or so is that the software construction process must be iterative and incremental. A tool environment that takes advantage of the above mentioned formal principles will give the practitioner the ability to quickly build scenarios with very complex module specifications and therefore help to guide the development process. Since the set of elemental operations needed to build a component is finite then we can use the aggregate of the sequence of operations as a quantitative measure of the effort to reuse a component

The applicability of the formal principles explored in this paper to automatic program verification can be put into the format of a theorem prover based on the principle of *interpretation between theories* [11]. The vector signature concept can be incorporated into a logic based on predicate calculus. This can then be used to represent a design pattern as a *theory*, to which the principle of interpretation between theories can be applied. Thus, we can develop a formal mathematical basis for the theorem prover [2].

References

[1] OMG Architecture Board MAD Drafting Team, "Model-Driven Architecture: A Technical Perspective", ftp://ftp.omg.org/pub/docs/ab/01-02-01.pdf

[2] Denver R.E. Williams, "An Adaptive Integration Architecture for Software Reuse," PhD dissertation, University of Central Florida, Orlando Florida, August 2001.

[3] OMG Architecture Board ORMSC, "Model Driven Architecture", OMG, July 2001.

[4] Erich Gamma, Richard Helm, Ralph Johnson, and John Vlissides, "Design Patterns: Elements of Reusable Object-Oriented Software", Addison-Wesley Publishing Company, Inc., Reading, MA, December 1996.

[5] OMG, "*Meta Object Facility (MOF) Specification: Version 1.3*", OMG, March 2000.

[6] OMG, "*OMG Unified Modeling Language (UML) Specification: Version 1.3*", OMG, March 2000.

[7] Colin Atkinson, "Meta-Modeling for Distributed Object Environments," *Proceedings of the 1st International Enterprise Distributed Object Computing Conference*, pp. 90-101, 1997.

[8] OMG, "*OMG XML Metadata Interchange (XMI) Specification: Version 1.1*", OMG, November 2000.

[9] Jacques Loeckx, Hans-Dieter Ehrich, and Markus Wolf, "Specification of Abstract Data Types", John Wiley & Sons, Inc., New York, NY, 1996.

[10] D. D. Cowan, R. Ierusalimschy, C. J. P. Lucena, and T. M. Stepien, "Abstract Data Views", Structured Programming, Volume 14, January 1993, pp. 1-13.

[11] H. B. Enderton, "A mathematical Introduction to Logic", Academic Press, New York, NY, 1972.

[12] L. M. F. Carneiro, D. D. Cowan, and C. J. P. Lucena, "ADVcharts: A visual formalism for interactive systems", SIGCHI Bulletin, 1993, pp. 74-77.

[13] L. M. F. Carneiro, M. H. Coffin, D. D. Cowan, C. J. P. Lucena, "User interface higher-order architectural models", Technical Report 93-14, Computer Science Department, University of Waterloo, Waterloo, Ontario, Canada, 1993.

[14] A. Alencar, L. Carneiro, D. D. Cowan, and C. Lucena, "Towards a formal theory of abstract data views", Technical Report 94-18, Computer Science Department, University of Waterloo, Waterloo, Ontario, Canada, April 1994.

[15] A. Alencar, L. Carneiro, D. D. Cowan, and C. Lucena, "The semantics of abstracts data views: A design concept to support reuse-in-the-large", Proc. Colloquium Object-Orientation in Database and Software Engineering. Kluwer Press, May 1994.

[16] D. D. Cowan, "Application Integration: Constructing composite applications from interactive components," *Software Practice and Experience*, Volume 23, March 1993, pp. 255-276.

[17] C. W. Krueger, "Software Reuse," *ACM Computing Surveys*, Volume 24, Number 2, June 1992.

[18] OMG, *The Common Object Request Broker Architecture: Architecture and Specification: Version 2.4.2*, OMG, February 2001.

[19] Martin Wirsing, "Algebraic Specification," Handbook of Theoretical Computer Science, 1990, pp. 675-788.

Session 6–1
New Issues in Networking

A New Wireless Architecture for QoS, Security and Mobility

Hakima Chaouchi and Guy Pujolle
LIP6, University of Paris 6,
8 rue du Capitaine Scott, 75015, Paris, France

Abstract

This paper introduces a policy-based management framework within an IP wireless network. It describes how a policy-based approach can be applied to deal with QoS, security, access control, mobility, etc. The framework presented here is derived from 3GPP and IETF works in different working groups and mainly in Resource Allocation Protocol working group of the IETF. Finally, we present some new evolutions that could be part of the future global policy-based networking architecture.

1. Introduction

The policy-based networking concepts are born from the need to get an overall end-to-end strategy to correlate the business with the overall network actions. Policy-based networking objectives are to deliver a comprehensive architecture that allows the merging of users, applications and resource policy information with network policy actions. The goals of policy-based networking architecture are to address the enforcement of policies in the nodes of the network and to globally manage the system.

A policy may be defined following two perspectives: an explicit goal and actions to guide and determine present and future decisions. Policies are a set of rules to control and manage network resources.

A policy-based networking system defines two main components: a policy decision point (PDP) and policy enforcement points (PEP). The signaling protocol COPS (Common Open Policy Service) is used to communicate policy information between policy enforcement points (PEP) and a remote policy decision point (PDP) within the context of a particular type of client. To get local policy decisions in the absence of a PDP, the PEP can use the optional local policy decision point (LPDP).

This architecture is described in different RFCs [1-8] mainly coming from the work of the rap (Resource Allocation Protocol) and policy (Policy Framework) working groups.

In this paper, we present policy-based networking operations and some new ideas that could be developed to reach a homogeneous structure to control future IP networks. In section 2, we describe the classical policy-based networking (PBN) architecture. In section 3, we describe the 3GPP architecture based on these concepts. In section 4, we present some applications that could be handled by policy-based systems. In section 5, some specific extensions that we developed in our laboratory are introduced. Finally we present some concluding remarks.

2. The Basic Architecture

A policy-based networking (PBN) system needs several components:
- a policy management tool,
- a policy repository,
- a policy decision point (PDP),
- policy enforcement points (PEP).

These components are shown in Figure 1. The policy management tool assists the network manager in the task of constructing and deploying policies, and monitoring status of the policy-managed environment. The policy management tool may be seen as an interface between the network manager and the policy repository.

The policy repository can be defined from two perspectives. First, it can be a specific data store that holds policy rules, their conditions and actions, and related policy data. A database or directory would be an example of such a store. Second, the policy repository may be seen as a logical container representing the administrative scope and naming of policy rules, their conditions and actions, and related policy data. A QoS policy, a security policy or a mobility domain would be an example of such a container.

The policy decision point (PDP) is a logical entity that produces policy decisions for itself or for other network elements that request such decisions. A decision involves actions for enforcement when the conditions of a policy rule are true. Policy enforcement points (PEP) are logical entities that enforce policy decisions.

The PEP may also have the capability to select a local policy decision via its local policy decision point (LPDP). However, the PDP remains the authoritative decision point at all times. This means that the relevant local

361

decision information must be relayed to the PDP. That is, the PDP must be granted access to all relevant information to select a final policy decision. To facilitate this functionality, the PEP must send its local decision information (using its LPDP) to the remote PDP.

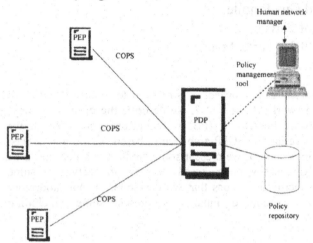

Figure 1 – The basic PBN architecture

The signaling protocol, COPS, is a simple query/response TCP-based protocol that can be used to exchange policy information between a PDP and its clients, the PEPs. Then, a PEP is responsible for initiating a persistent TCP connection to a PDP. The PEP uses this TCP connection to send requests to and receive decisions from the remote PDP. Communication between the PEP and remote PDP is mainly in the form of a stateful request/decision exchange, though the remote PDP may occasionally send unsolicited decisions to the PEP to force changes in previously approved request states. The PEP also has the capacity to report to the remote PDP that it has successfully completed performing the PDP's decision locally. This capability is useful for accounting and monitoring purposes. The PEP is responsible for notifying the PDP when a request state has changed on the PEP. Finally, the PEP is responsible for the deletion of any state that is no longer applicable due to events on the client side or decisions issued by the PDP. When the PEP sends a configuration request, it expects the PDP to send configuration data via decision messages as applicable for the configuration request. When a policy is successfully installed on the PEP, the PEP has to send a report message to the PDP confirming the installation. The server may then update or remove the configuration information via a new decision message. When the PDP sends a decision to remove a configuration from the PEP, the PEP will delete the specified configuration and send a report message to the PDP as a confirmation.

COPS protocol is designed to communicate self-identifying objects which contain the data necessary for identifying request states, establishing the context for a request, identifying the type of request, referencing previously installed requests, relaying policy decisions, reporting errors, providing message integrity, and transferring client specific/namespace information.

To distinguish between different kinds of clients, the type of client is identified in each message. Different types of clients may have different client specific data and may require different kinds of policy decisions. It is expected that each new client-type will have a corresponding usage RFC specifying its interaction within COPS protocol.

The COPS context object identifies the type of request and message that triggered a policy event via its message type and request type fields. COPS identifies three types of outsourcing events: (1) the arrival of an incoming message (2) the allocation of local resources, and (3) the forwarding of an outgoing message. Each of these events may require different decisions to be complete. The content of a COPS request/decision message depends on the context. A fourth type of event is useful for types of clients that wish to receive configuration information from the PDP. This allows a PEP to issue a configuration request for a specific named device or module that requires configuration information to be installed.

There are two mechanisms by which resources may be allocated: configured (or provisioned, or pre-defined, or pro-active) and signaled (or on-demand, or reactive). Each solution has their strengths and weaknesses. With configured mechanisms, traffic treatment (such as classification, priority, shaping, etc.) can be specified as well as the characteristics of the traffic to receive that treatment. An administrator would observe traffic patterns on the network, compare that with the desired state (based on business or operational needs), and then choose policies that allocate resources accordingly. Such mechanisms may work quite well for traffic such as HTTP, telnet, or FTP, which are tolerant to the variance in flow quality (jitter, packet reordering, etc.).

The outsourcing model is totally different. A policy enforcement device issues a request to ask for a decision for a specific request coming from a user, a program or a process. For example, the arrival of an RSVP message to a PEP requires a fast policy decision to avoid a long delay for an end-to-end set-up. The PEP may use COPS-RSVP to send a request to the PDP, soliciting for a policy decision.

Note that the outsourcing policy scheme differs with configuring policy scheme, but they are not mutually exclusive and operational systems may combine both.

The strength of signaling is that it enables the network to offer QoS guarantees, and to simultaneously be used efficiently. Without signaling, it is necessary either to compromise the quality of the guarantees, or to overprovision the network. In some networks, over provisioning may be a viable option. However, in other networks it may not. If the network manager wants to have the flexibility to not overprovision the network then, an end to end signaling must be available to be used for policy-based admission control decisions.

Signaling mechanisms can provide information beyond the QoS needs to handle the traffic. User information and application identification that could be hidden by IPsec can be provided, thus allowing higher quality information on the traffic.

One of the most difficult parts of PBN concerns policy translations: transformation of a policy from a representation or from a level of abstraction, to another representation or level of abstraction. For example, it may be necessary to convert a PIB data (Policy Information Base, e.g., a named data structure) to a command line format. In this conversion, the translation to the new representation is likely to require a change in the level of abstraction. Although these are logically distinct tasks, they are in most cases hidden in the acts of translating or converting or mapping. Therefore, policy conversion or policy mapping is an important problem that we do not look at in this paper.

3. The 3GPP architecture

Figure 2 introduces the generic model for session

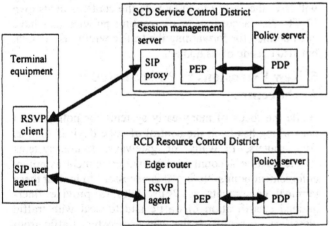

establishment, QoS and policy enforcement proposed by the 3GPP and submitted to the IETF [9, 10].

Figure 2 – The generic 3GPP network model

The terminal equipment is a device used by a client to access network services. The terminal equipment includes a client for requesting network services (e.g. through SIP) and a client for requesting network resources (e.g. through RSVP). The edge router is a network element connecting the end host to the rest of the resource control district. The edge router contains a PEP to enforce policies related to resource usage in the resource control district by the terminal equipment. It also contains an RSVP agent for handling resource reservation requests from the terminal equipment. The policy server is a network element that includes a PDP. Note that there may be a policy server in the service control district to control use of services and there may be a separate policy server in the resource

control district to control use of resources along the packet forwarding path. Note also that network topology may require multiple policy servers within either district, however they provide consistent policy decisions to offer the appearance of a single PDP in each district.

The resource control district (RCD) is a logical grouping of elements that provide connectivity along the packet forwarding paths to and from terminal equipment. The RCD contains edge router and policy server entities whose responsibilities include management of resources along the packet forwarding paths. The service control district (SCD) is a logical grouping of elements that offer applications and content to subscribers of their services. The session management server resides in the SCD along with a policy server. The session management server is a network element providing session management services. This server contains a PEP to enforce policies related to use of services by the terminal equipment. It also contains a SIP proxy for handling service requests from the end terminal.

In this system, the terminal equipment issues a session set-up request (e.g. SIP INVITE) to the session manager indicating, among other things, the media streams to be used in the session. As part of this step, the terminal equipment may authenticate itself to the session manager. The session manager, possibly after waiting for negotiation of the media streams to be completed, sends a policy decision request (e.g. COPS REQ) to the SCD policy server in order to determine if the session set-up request should be allowed to proceed. The policy server sends a decision (e.g. COPS DEC) to the session manager, possibly after modifying the parameters of the media to be used. The session manager sends a response to the terminal equipment indicating that session set-up is complete or is progressing. Included in this response is a description of the negotiated media.

Then, the terminal equipment issues a request (e.g. RSVP PATH) to reserve the resources necessary to provide the required QoS for the media stream. The edge router intercepts the reservation request and sends a policy decision request (e.g. COPS REQ) to the RCD policy server in order to determine if the resource reservation request should be allowed to proceed. The RCD policy server sends a decision (e.g. COPS DEC) to the edge router, possibly after modifying the parameters of the resources to be reserved. The edge router, possibly after waiting for end-to-end negotiation for resources to be completed, sends a response to the terminal equipment (e.g. RSVP RESV) indicating that resource reservation is complete or is progressing.

We can note in this model the use of three signaling systems: SIP, RSVP and COPS.

4. Examples of Policy-based Networking Architecture

Policy-based systems may be used to manage and control different types of functionalities. In this section we will have a look at different examples where PBN may be applied. A first example concerns admission control schemes. These schemes are responsible for ensuring that the requested resources are available. Moreover, these schemes must take care of temporal constraints, identification and permission.

Policy-based admission control is able to express and enforce rules with temporal dependencies. For example, a group of users might be allowed to make reservations at certain levels only during off-peak hours. In addition, the policy-based admission control should also be able to support policies that take into account identity or credentials of users requesting a particular service or resource. For example, through a PBN scheme, an RSVP reservation request may be denied or accepted based on the credentials or identity supplied in the request.

A second example concerns Authentication, Authorization, Accounting (AAA) schemes. AAA deals with control, authentication, authorization and accounting of systems and environments. The schemes may be based on policies set by the administrator and users of the systems. The use of policy may be implicit or explicit. For example, a network access server can send dial-user credentials to an AAA server, and receives authentication that the user is who he claims, along with a set of attribute-value pairs authorizing various service features. Policy may be implied in both the authentication, which can be restricted by time of day, number of sessions, calling number, etc., and the attribute-values authorized.

A third example concerns quality of service (QoS). QoS refers to the ability to deliver network services according to the parameters specified in a Service Level Agreement. Quality of service is characterized by service availability, delay, jitter, throughput and packet loss ratio. At a network resource level, quality of service refers to a set of capabilities that allow a service provider to prioritize traffic, control bandwidth, and network latency. There are two different approaches to the quality of service on IP networks: Integrated Services (IntServ), and Differentiated Service DiffServ. IntServ approaches require policy control over the creation of signaled reservations, which provide specific quantitative end-to-end behavior for a flow. In contrast, DiffServ approaches require policy to define the correspondence between codepoints in the IP packet DS-field and individual per-hop behaviors to achieve a specified per-domain behavior. A maximum of 64 per-hop behaviors limit the number of classes of service traffic that can be marked at any point in a domain. These classes of service signal the treatment of the packets with respect to various QoS aspects such as flow priority and packet drop precedence. In addition, policy can be used to specify the forwarding of packets based on various classification criteria. The policy controls the set of configuration parameters and forwarding for each class in DiffServ, and the admission conditions for reservations in IntServ.

Another example is provided with VPN configuration. Let us first recall VPN meaning since the term has been widely used with a great deal of confusion. VPN is a set of terminal equipments that can communicate with each other. More formally, a VPN is defined by a set of administrative policies that control connectivity, quality of service, security, etc. among terminal equipment. A classical use of VPNs is security. Rather than impose the network manager to set security mechanisms for individual terminal equipment, policy-based management system can consolidate and synchronize access control lists and related policy information to promote a consistent security policy across the enterprise. For example, the network manager can use a policy-based management system to set policies for selection of tunneling protocols and to update client configuration instead of configuring each security device and each terminal equipment, making the management of the VPN system more scalable.

This approach clearly assumes that each service provider will have the ability to instantiate the contents of its own IP TE PIB, according to the routing policies that have been defined for forwarding the traffic within its domain, but also outside of its domain.

5. New Extensions to Policy-based Architecture

While the focus of many early systems for policy-based networking has been the control of edge devices such as edge routers, firewalls, or gateways, future systems should have to account for terminal equipment as policy enforcement points. In fact, it is necessary to look at these terminal equipments as PEPs, both to provide finer-grained classification of traffic and to deal with traffic classification problems that can arise when traffic from the user terminal is encrypted. Problems with network congestion and QoS adaptation will be solved by enforcing policies at the terminal equipment, requiring this terminal to be well aware with regards to the network traffic it generates. We believe that in the future the enforcement points could not be edge routers except complicating the way to enforce the policy on these machines. Another advantage is to reduce the number of different signaling systems to just one instead of two or three as in 3GPP architecture.

So, we think that COPS is able to take place in this new architecture as a homogenization element to take care directly of the terminal equipment in its quality of service, its mobility, its security, etc. We can define a new client type that would permit to interface directly the customer with the PDP.

To get a direct negotiation with the PDP, we have proposed an Internet draft [11] using COPS protocol for supporting SLS (Service Level Specification) negotiation. COPS-SLS is an extension of COPS protocol. The advantage when using COPS for SLS negotiation is the inherent flexible characteristic of COPS protocol. COPS may support multiple client-types. So, COPS-SLS protocol needs only to specify corresponding new objects used in this client-type (COPS-SLS). The client-handle object defined by the COPS protocol gives a mechanism for handling various requests in a single PEP. This capability will be used to handle several SLS negotiations from a single PEP.

The PEP in COPS-SLS is just a logical entity which requests network resources for itself or possibly on behalf of other entities. So, the client may be an end-host, or a gateway of a local network or another ISP. The model we have implemented is illustrated in Figure 3.

To negotiate a level of service, COPS-SLS has two phases: Configuration phase and Negotiation phase. The communication starts with the Configuration phase. The PDP uses the Configuration model to configure the Negotiation phase. After that, in the Negotiation phase, the client use the Outsourcing model to request a level of service with parameters conforming to the configuration installed in the Configuration phase. This organization in two phases makes the SLS negotiation dynamic. At any time, when the network sends a new configuration to the client, the Negotiation process will apply these policies in subsequent service level requests.

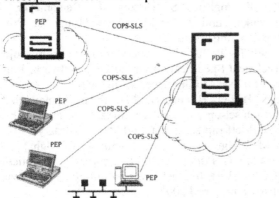

Figure 3 – The COPS-SLS model

To negotiate a level of service, the client sends a request indicating its desired service level under the form of instances of PIB classes. Using PIB to represent SLS information makes COPS-SLS flexible and adapted to desired negotiation parameters of network providers. COPS-SLS protocol is designed to permit basic activities in SLS negotiation. The client can request, modify or terminate a level of service. The network can accept or reject a service level request, propose another service level to the client or degrade a service level when necessary.

With COPS-SLS protocol, it is easy for a company to install an Intranet with a policy-based control. This policy-based control may allow some applications to get a good quality of service and some others to be delayed. Packets of these applications may be given a very low level of priority within the company or even may be discarded as a non-appropriate traffic. This solution could be used as a basis for a security system using a firewall.

COPS-SLS is suitable for the negotiation of SLS between network providers. A domain may negotiate with another domain to obtain a level of service for inter-domain communications. For example, a DiffServ domain may request another DiffServ domain to guarantee a level of service for all packets having a specific DSCP.

Another application of the policy-based architecture we developed concerns the management of the mobility of the terminal or the mobility of the user. COPS extension for Mobile IP policy registration control was proposed in [12]. This proposal deals with terminal mobility management. We introduce a policy-based architecture to support mobile user and mobile terminal registration, service portability, and QoS negotiation in fixed and wireless network access. The first challenge of this work is to define a policy based architecture to support user and terminal registration to achieve location management. The second challenge is to define a policy based architecture to support fixed or mobile service portability and QoS negotiation. To achieve these challenging goals, we introduce new components in the IETF policy-based architecture (e.g., Figure 4) and we introduce two COPS extensions called COPS-MU (Mobile User) and COPS-MT (Mobile Terminal), which define new policy objects to support user and terminal registration, service portability, and QoS negotiation.

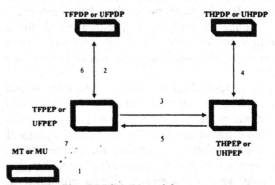

Figure 4 – The COPS-MU model

Figure 4 describes the new components used in the COPS-MU or COPS-MT architecture related to mobile terminal and mobile user. Some mobile IP terms used in this figure are explained below:

TFPDP/UFPDP Terminal/User Foreign Policy Decision Point

TFPEP/UFPEP Terminal/User Foreign Policy Enforcement Point

THPDP/UHPDP Terminal/User Home Policy Decision Point
THPDP/UHPDP Terminal/User Home Policy Enforcement Point.

The process represented by the sequence 1 to 7, in Figure 4, permits to treat registration, service portability, QoS assignment and mobility for terminal and user mobility [13]. Both techniques, COPS-SLS and COPS-MU, may be combined to avoid T/UFPEPs and T/UHPDPs devices in COPS-MU.

Associated with these policies, it is possible to address allocation schemes using DHCP protocol. Policies can dictate how sets of IP addresses are to be allocated and for what duration. It is also possible to address routing policies, VPN policies and many others IP protocols management schemes. Some extensions have been provided in [14].

6. Conclusion

This paper presented an introduction to policy-based management within an IP network. It also looked at different proposals to use efficiently policy-based management techniques. This management is related to translating high-level user needs to device-specific configuration. An important problem concerns the dynamic of the system. Adaptive policies could handle the changes in the network. Rules reflecting a change can be placed in the policy repository. The change may happen from a threshold or simply from the time of day. Agents on PEPs may indicate these changes to the PDP. The PDP decides about the set of policies that need to be applied. PDP may also choose the policy that satisfies the requirement of a high-level policy determined by a business needs. Another way to consider the problem is to support a policy discovery system that should determine the best policy to apply to a user requesting for a transmission. For example, the policy discovery system may decide to use IPsec if the flow has to traverse the Internet.

The policy is applied on an administrative domain and another challenge concerns interdomain policies. It would be interesting to see how the notion of policies applies across administrative domains. The use of COPS protocol is an available solution to correlate the policies to be chosen when a flow has to cross several administrative domains. An agent negotiation is another possibility to settle the policies to be applied.

Finally, policy monitoring has also to be determined to verify that the network is meeting the desired business needs. The monitoring system checks that the implementation of the policy complies with what was expected by the PDP. Indeed, the high-level policies reflect the SLAs, and the monitoring system must confirm that these SLAs are performed.

As a conclusion, we think that the most important function of policy-based networking systems is to simplify network management and operations in complex networks. These systems provide QoS, security, mobility and much more functions within a homogeneous way.

References

[1] RFC 2748 – D. Durham, J. Boyle, R. Cohen, S Herzog, R. Rajan, A. Sastry, The COPS (Common Open Policy Service) Protocol, January 2000.

[2] RFC 2749 – J. Boyle, R. Cohen, D. Durham, S Herzog, R. Rajan, and A. Sastry, COPS usage for RSVP, January 2000.

[3] RFC 2750 – S. Herzog, RSVP Extensions for Policy Control, January 2000.

[4] RFC 2751 – S. Herzog, Signaled Preemption Priority Policy Element, January 2000.

[5] RFC 2753 – R. Yavatkar, D. Pendarakis, R. Guerin, A Framework for Policy-based Admission Control January 2000.

[6] RFC 2872 – Y. Bernet et R. Pabbati, Application and Sub Application Identity Policy Element for Use with RSVP, June 2000.

[7] RFC 2940 – A. Smith, D. Partain, J. Seligson Definitions of Managed Objects for Common Oper Policy Service (COPS) Protocol Clients, October 2000.

[8] RFC 3084 – K. Chan, J. Seligson, D. Durham, S. Gai K. McCloghrie, S. Herzog, F. Reichmeyer, R Yavatkar, and A. Smith, COPS Usage for Policy Provisioning, March 2001.

[9] 3GPP TS 29.207, 3rd Generation Partnership project Technical Specification Group Core Network; Policy control over Go Interface, April 2002.

[10] L.N. Hamer, B. Gage, and H. Shieh, Framework for session set-up with media autjorization, Internet Draft <draft-ietf-rap-session-auth-03.txt>, February 2002.

[11] T.M.T. Nguyen, N. Boukhatem, Y. El Mghazli, N Charton, G. Pujolle, COPS Usage for SLS negotiatior (COPS-SLS), Internet Draft, <draft-nguyen-rap-copsn sls-02.txt>, April 2002.

[12] M. Jaseemuddin, A. Lakas, COPS usage for Mobile IP, Internet draft, draft-jaseem-rap-cops-mip-00.txt October 2000.

[13] H. Chaouchi, G. Pujolle, COPS-MU: Policy based user mobility management, Proceeding IEEE Conference on Applications and Services In the Wireless Public Infrastructure, Evry, France, July 2001.

[14] T.M.T. Nguyen, N. Boukhatem, Y. Ghami Doudane G. Pujolle, COPS SLS: A Service Level Negotiation Protocol for the Internet, IEEE Communications Magazincs May 2002.

Bandwidth Allocation in Bluetooth Scatternets

Ulf Körner
Department of Communication Systems
Lund University,
Lund, Sweden
Ulf.Korner@telecom.lth.se

Niklas Johansson
Ericsson Research,
Ericsson AB,
Stockholm, Sweden
Niklas.Johansson@era.ericsson.se

Abstract

This paper deals with bandwidth allocation in a Bluetooth scatternet. The proposed assignment of transmission rights provides a controlled traffic transfer between Bluetooth piconets and represents a key component in an ad-hoc wireless Bluetooth network in order to provide with efficient data packet passing within and across piconets. This assignment is obtained by executing a distributed algorithm in each node. The algorithm works for unrestricted topologies of both stationary and mobile networks and also deals with assignment changes caused by network re-configurations without the use of a centralized factor. The effect of this re-assignment can be limited to the locality of that topology change. The construction of a link schedule of minimum length in a Bluetooth scatternet is NP-complete.

1. Introduction

Bluetooth, as a default radio interface in a number of different types of handheld electronic devices, will provide new means to rapidly interconnect these into ad-hoc networks. Ad-hoc networks, i.e. multi-hop packet radio networks, are an ideal technology to provide a seamless extension of the Internet to the wireless mobile environment. In ad-hoc networks, nodes can be mobile and communicate with one another either directly or through intermediate nodes, without relying on any preexisting network infrastructure. The self-configuring, dynamic-connectivity, multi-hop-propagation and fully-distributed nature of ad-hoc networks make them very attractive for many new applications but also introduce difficult problems at the link and network level. Building Bluetooth ad-hoc networks introduces a number of new challenges, partly stemming from the fact that Bluetooth was developed for single hop wireless connections. In this paper we study the scheduling problems in a Bluetooth scatternet and propose a heuristic, conflict free scheduling algorithm with the ability to support Quality of Service (QoS) requirements.

Bluetooth is a short-range radio technology operating in the unlicensed ISM (Industrial-Scientific-Medical) band at 2.45 GHz. Two or more units sharing the same channel form a piconet, where one unit acts as a *master* and the other units act as *slaves*. Communication in Bluetooth is always between master and slave nodes, i.e. there is no direct transmission between slaves in a Bluetooth piconet, only between the master and a slave, and vice versa. Within each piconet there may be only one master (and there must always be one) and up to seven active slaves. To make the link robust to interference, it employs a Frequency Hopping Spread Spectrum (FHSS) technique, with carrier frequency changed at any packet transmission. A Gaussian-shaped Frequency Shift Keying (GFSK) modulation is applied to minimize transceiver complexity and the system offers a gross data rate of 1 Mbps. The terms master and slave are defined as logical states, in that any particular device can be a master or a slave. The Bluetooth system provides full-duplex transmission based on a slotted Time Division Duplex scheme, where each slot is 0.625 ms long. Master-to-slave transmission, always starts in an even-numbered time slot, while a slave-to-master transmission always starts in an odd-numbered time slot. An even-numbered time slot and its subsequent odd-numbered time slot form a so called frame. The master unit controls the link bandwidth by polling the slaves for any data to be exchanged and thus, performs bandwidth allocation to each slave. According to the polling rules, a slave is only allowed to transmit in the slave-to-master slot if it has been polled in the previous master-to-slave slot. The master may or may not include data in the packet used to poll a slave.

Several piconets can be established and linked together in an ad-hoc fashion, thus forming a *scatternet* in which each piconet is identified by a unique frequency hopping sequence. Scatternets are formed when a Bluetooth unit participates in more than one piconet at the same time, thus functioning as a bridge. Scatternets may be used for a number of reasons. First, this is a way to extend the rather limited coverage that Bluetooth provides. Second, the partition of a network into several piconets may give an overall gain in capacity for the same area. For instance, if two slave nodes in different piconets have a sustained traffic between them, it may be a better choice to create a new piconet containing only the two nodes, and the resulting scatternet has an improved performance. We define *bridging degree* as the number of piconets a bridging node is member of. A Bluetooth unit may simultaneously be a slave member of multiple piconets, but it may be master in only one piconet. Since Bluetooth units only have one transceiver, bridging units may only be active in one piconet at any given instant and thereby, bridging units must switch between piconets on a time division basis. One of the most technically challenging issues with respect to bridging units lies in the fact that their presence needs to be scheduled in an efficient manner. Since the bridging unit cannot receive information from more than one piconet at a time, the need to co-ordinate the presence of masters and bridging devices in each piconet is a necessity to achieve a controlled service. Furthermore, due to the fact that different piconets are not synchronized in time, a bridging unit necessarily looses some time while switching from one piconet to another. For further information regarding the Bluetooth technology the reader is referred to [1], [2].

Even though the Bluetooth specifications at hand do describe mechanisms how to create piconets and form scatternets, the methods to do this with a controlled Quality of Service (QoS) for the participating units, have been considered very briefly. In particular, the rules to communicate between piconets in a scatternet with controlled delay and throughput have not yet been addressed in the specifications. This type of communication typically needs a *schedule*, i.e. a sequence of fixed length time slots, where each possible transmission is assigned a time slot in such a way that transmissions assigned to the same time slot do not collide.

In this paper we present a new algorithm for "distributed link scheduling for a Bluetooth scatternet" based on the allocation of transmission rights to links in timeslots, which are organized in recurring identical cycles. This allocation provides each link with a guaranteed, conflict free (with respect to primary interference) access to the shared channel. The proposed algorithm is completely distributed and allows parallel allocations involving only the locality of each node, both in stationary and mobile networks. The resulting allocation offers an efficient use of the bandwidth by constructing a short TDMA cycle. Specifically, each time slot may be simultaneously shared by several nodes, so that spatial reuse is accomplished. Conflict free communication is guaranteed in the network in the face of mobility and under any combination of one or more simultaneous topology changes. The execution of the algorithm is invoked at network initiation or following a topological change which may result from failures, node movements, altered link requirements, etc. Lastly, while by reduction to the graph-coloring problem, it is shown that finding the optimal (minimal) cycle length is an NP-complete problem, the time and message complexity of the proposed algorithm is polynomial in the number of nodes. It also limits the effect of a topological change on the assignment to a local subset (sub graph) of network nodes. See [3].

The scheduling problem for multi-hop packet radio networks has been extensively studied in the literature. Most of these studies concentrate on finding fair conflict free algorithms, which maximize the system throughput by using graph theory. However, none of these algorithms is applicable in a Bluetooth scatternet network. The scheduling problem here is augmented by the need to coordinate the presence of bridges such that timing mismatches are avoided.

A number of researchers has addressed the issue of scheduling in Bluetooth. See for e.g. [4] and [5]. Most of these studies have, however, been restricted to the single piconet environment, where the fundamental question is the polling discipline used by the piconet master to poll its slaves. Although the above studies have revealed a number of important performance aspects of scheduling in Bluetooth piconets, the algorithms developed therein are not applicable for scatternet scheduling.

Up to the authors' knowledge no thorough analysis is available in the literature regarding the scheduling of a Bluetooth *scatternet*, but there is an ongoing work in the Personal Area Networking (PAN) working group of the Bluetooh Special Interest Group (SIG) to define an appropriate scheduling algorithm for Bluetooth scatternets

2. Scheduling

A *schedule* is a sequence of fixed length time slots, where each possible transmission is assigned a time slot in such a way that transmissions assigned to the same time slot are not in conflict with one another. In a scheduled access method, time is divided into fixed length slots, which are organized cyclically. In a packet radio network, transmissions may collide in two ways - these are typically referred to as primary and secondary interference. Primary interference occurs when the schedule is such that a station must do more than one thing in a single timeslot - for instance, transmit and receive, or communicate with multiple sources, in the same timeslot. Accordingly, we define primary conflict, for a Bluetooth network, as the cases when a bridging node is assumed to be active in more than one piconet at the same time and when a node is expected to communicate with more than one neighbor at the same time. There is an overlap between the two cases since a node that is a slave in two piconets, i.e. a bridge, is required to be active in both piconets at the same time in order to be able to communicate with its neighbors. To completely describe the notion of primary conflict in a Bluetooth network we also have to add the case where only one of the two transceivers of a link assumes the link to be active, i.e. we have a timing mismatch, to the description. An example of this would be the case where a master sends a packet to a bridging node that is not active in this piconet. Secondary interference occurs when a receiver R tuned to a particular transmitter T is within range of another transmitter whose transmissions, though not intended for R, interfere with the transmission of T. Since Bluetooth uses a polling scheme at the *Medium Access Control (MAC) layer* (part of the *Baseband Layer* in the Bluetooth specification), which implies that no collisions can occur within a piconet, and the frequency hopping scheme is expected to be robust against interference, it is assumed that only primary interference has to be considered.

Compared to random access methods, scheduled access provides channel control by explicit scheduling of transmissions, leading to better channel utilization, handling of priorities, coping with different types of traffic, etc. It has been proven analytically that any link utilization that is achievable by any collision resolution technique, including all random access methods, is also achievable by time division scheduled access. Further, although efforts have been made to guarantee QoS in CSMA based MAC, dynamic methods are in general inherently inappropriate for providing QoS guarantees.

The problem when scheduling a Bluetooth scatternet is augmented by the need to coordinate the presence of bridges such that timing mismatches are avoided. One also has to take into account that a bridge, switching between two piconets, will consume at least one slot before any traffic may be sent, due to the fact that piconets are not aligned. That is, the slot boundaries of different piconets do not match in general. This results in a switching overhead that should be taken into account in

the design of the scatternet scheduler. The slot boundary difference between two piconets will henceforth be referred to as the *phase difference* between these piconets. At most two slots equivalent to 2*0.625 ms, i.e. a full frame, are lost.

3. A Heuristic Distributed Scheduling Algorithm

In constructing a practical heuristic scheduling algorithm we are guided by the following considerations. **1)** The number of messages and its computation time must be polynomial in the number of nodes in the scatternet, **2)** the solution must be easy to implement by a distributed algorithm and **3)** it must remain correct in a mobile environment.

Accordingly, the proposed solution is based on two principles: **1)** The scheduling process, based on polling, is managed by the masters of the scatternet. All information regarding a piconet is gathered in the master and thereby makes it a natural choice for scheduling the links of its piconet which leads to robustness, and **2)** the reduction of the algorithm's input, from considering all nodes by each node, to that where each master is only considering its slaves. Since only primary interference is a concern in Bluetooth, information regarding neighboring node schedules is sufficient to find a conflict free schedule. This leads to ease of implementation.

The outline of the distributed solution can be given as follows. It is assumed that nodes have distinct identities; each Bluetooth unit has a globally unique 48-bit IEEE 802 address, and is aware of the identities and traffic requirements of their neighbors. During connection setup the identities are exchanged and hence, one hop away connectivity is given. The traffic requirements are also assumed to be negotiated during connection setup. On entering the algorithm each *master* needs the permission of all its neighbors to schedule its piconet. *A neighboring master* is a node that is both a neighbor and a master, i.e. neighboring masters is a subset of neighbors. Permission is granted to the neighboring master with the highest ID among those neighboring masters that have not yet scheduled their piconets. Permissions are passed in messages together with a set of restrictions specifying which frames that are not possible to allocate due to previous assignments performed by other neighboring masters. After receiving the permission rights from all neighbors, the master assigns timeslots to its slaves. This is done by allocating timeslots for a slave from those timeslots that are known not to be previously assigned, by some other master or the node itself (the slave may be a master in another piconet), for that particular slave. The algorithm terminates when all masters have scheduled their piconets.

It should be noted that: **1)** The information propagation is always limited to a one-hop radius. **2)** Due to the locality property, the adaptation of slot assignment triggered by topological changes can also be executed locally. This permits fast network adaptation and concurrent execution of multiple changes. **3)** The original cycle can be reduced to the maximum slot number selected in the network. To reduce the size of the cycle the nodes need to agree on the new size and on the time in which the new cycle should go into effect simultaneously at all nodes. The methods for reaching such a consensus are discussed in [6].

The network operational assumptions underlying the construction of the algorithm are given (some of them have been elaborated on above):

- The nodes have distinct identities and know the identities of their neighbors.
- The network topology does not change during the algorithm execution.
- Each node is aware of changes in its set of neighbors due to its own movement and loss of contact with its neighbors due to other reasons, and
- at network initiation an initial schedule has been formed so that information exchange can take place.

3.1 The Distributed Scatternet Scheduling

In this Subsection we present the Distributed Scatternet Scheduling Algorithm (DSSA), which is distributed in the sense that it requires no centrally stored information, no global knowledge of the topology and there is no special central station. The algorithm is continuously adaptive to topological changes and can be executed in parallel. The algorithm works for a static network but with smaller changes, the algorithm can be executed in a dynamic, mobile environment.

Before we formally present the proposed algorithm we need to define the following *functionality sets*, as seen from a master's perspective regarding the slaves in its piconet.

Set 1: Slaves that are masters in other piconets,
Set 2: Slaves that are active in several piconets, i.e. bridges, but not masters, and
Set 3: slaves that are only active in the master's piconet.

The algorithm is message driven and four types of messages are used. On entering the algorithm each node has the following lists (some of these lists are not used by all nodes as explained below). 1) LOCAL.Neighbors, which contains the identities, functionalities and degrees of all its neighbors. It also contains two flags for every neighbor, j: PERMISSION_Received, indicating whether a PERMISSION has been received from node j and Piconet_Scheduled, indicating whether the slot assignment has been accomplished for j's piconet. Note that if node j belongs to the second or third functionality set, this flag is set at initialization. 2) LOCAL.Schedule, which lists its status, busy or idle, during each slot in the scheduling frame. A node is not only busy when it is transmitting and receiving *but also when it is switching between different piconets*. 3) NEIGHBOR.Schedules stores the LOCAL.Schedule for each neighbor and is used to update the LOCAL.Schedule and, in case the node is a master, to construct the LOCAL.Schedule. The node also has a LOCAL.ID, a LOCAL.Degree (the degree of a node i, corresponds to the total amount of traffic that it handles) and a LOCAL.Functionality.

A node starts participating in the algorithm either on receiving a WAKE message from an upper layer algorithm (protocol) or by the first reception of some message sent by another node executing the algorithm. Each slave entering the algorithm sends a message to all neighboring masters. This message contains the so called LOCAL(LOCAL.Degree, LOCAL.Functionality). Each master entering the algorithm sends a WAKE message to each slave in its piconet and the slaves respond with the same LOCAL message as in the previous phrase. In case a slave caused the master to start participating in the algorithm by sending a LOCAL message to it, no WAKE message is sent to this slave. This information is used by the master to fill in the degree and functionality in LOCAL.Neighbors. On completion of this list, the master is waiting for the proper conditions for scheduling its piconet. At a master this condition is obtained when it has received a PERMISSION message from all neighboring units, i.e. when the flag PERMISSION_Received is raised for all its neighbors. PERMISSION messages are sent together with a set of restrictions (LOCAL.Schedule) specifying frames that the master is not allowed to assign itself for this particular node. The master collects these restrictions in NEIGHBOR.Schedules, initially empty, and they are used by the master when constructing its schedule. The PERMISSION message is sent to the node with the highest ID in LOCAL.Neighbors, i.e. in its network locality, whose Piconet_Scheduled flag is false. In general, a master, that has received the PERMISSION message from all its neighbors, can schedule its piconet, taking the accumulated restrictions into account when doing so. After the schedule has been completed, a message SCHEDULE(LOCAL.Schedule) is transmitted to all slaves in the piconet. Upon reception of the SCHEDULE message, the LOCAL.Schedule and LOCAL.Neighbors.Piconet_Scheduled are updated and the PERMISSION message is sent to the next master in line, that has not scheduled its piconet, if any.

It is easy to see that we now can form a conflict free schedule based on the information given in the different lists mentioned above. The following rules are used by the masters to find their LOCAL.Schedules. The slaves are first prioritized according to their functionality set belonging (set one has the highest priority). Within a functionality set, slaves are prioritized according to their degree, i.e. the slave with the highest degree within the functionality set has the highest priority and so on. Going through all slaves (according to their priorities) in descending order, the first frames, i.e. the frames with lowest frame number, which can be found in master i's LOCAL.Schedule, that does not conflict with j's LOCAL.Schedule (stored in NEIGHBORS.Schedules in the master), are assigned to slave j. The ordinary polling protocol, e.g. FEP [4], could also be used to allocate capacity for slaves in the last functionality set. The advantage of such an approach is that some multiplexing gain could be achieved, and thereby only a fraction of the sum of the link requirements for the nodes in the last functionality set has to be accounted for in the schedule. How big this fraction should be and how to do this in a flexible manner is left for future work.

The reason for prioritizing the slaves is that we want to minimize the impact of switching overhead by first scheduling the switching nodes and thereafter let the non-switching nodes, so to say, "fill in the gaps". By allocating the first non-conflicting frames encountered, we are striving toward finding maximal transmission sets, i.e. to maximize the spatial reuse. Notice, that the selected frames is the final decision unless topological changes occur in the node's locality.

The algorithm has been tested on a number of generated sample networks. We have used a standard random graph generator with inputs like the number of vertices in the network, and the average degree of the network. Once the random graph has been generated, another algorithm sees to that master and slave roles are allocated to complete the scatternet graph.

Our algorithm has shown very good performance in supporting the Quality of Service requirements set up by the communication nodes.

4. Summary and Concluding Remarks

We have presented a scheduling algorithm for a Bluetooth scatternet, which provides a conflict free access to the shared medium. Graph theory was used to illustrate the complexity of finding an optimal schedule for such a network. While the optimal solution is intractable, it was shown that the presented algorithm has provable bounds for any network topology. An extension, which enables the algorithm to operate correctly under any topological changes, was also presented. The proposed algorithm is completely distributed and its execution time is polynomial in the number of nodes in the network.

The adaptation process to topological changes in the proposed algorithm is event driven. If this was not the case, periodic updates would have been required and thereby would adaptation to topological changes be slow due to the need for waiting a time O(period) for the adaptation to start. Moreover, since a significant number of changes can accumulate within each period, the protocol concurrency becomes a crucial issue. Typically, the easiest solution is a complete re-computation of the slot assignment resulting in a periodic suspension of transmission activities. In the proposed protocol the adaptation is triggered by events, such that no additional delay of execution is enforced and no nodes outside the piconet in which the change took place are affected.

References

[1] Specification of the Bluetooth System, ver. 1.0 B, October 2000.

[2] J. Haartsen, BLUETOOTH - the Universal Radio Interface for Ad-hoc, Wireless Connectivity, Ericsson Review, no. 3, 1998.

[3] N. Johansson, U. Körner and L. Tassiulas, A Distributed Algorithm for a Bluetooth Scatternet, In "Teletraffic Engineering in the Internet Era", Elsevier, 2001

[4] N. Johansson, U. Körner and P.Johansson, Performance Evaluation of Scheduling Algorithms for Bluetooth, In Proc. IFIP TC6 Fifth Int. Conf. Broadband Commun'99, Hong-Kong, Nov. 1999.

[5] M. Kalia, S. Garg and R. Shorey, Efficient policies for increasing capacity in Bluetooth: An indoor pico-cellular wireless system, In Proc. VTC2000-Spring, Tokyo, Japan, May 2000.

[6] M. J. Fischer, The Consensus Problem in Unreliable Distributed Systems (A Brief Survey), In Proc. Int. Conf. Found. Comput. Theory, Sweden, Aug. 1983.

Mobility and Multicast: Protocol Design and Analysis

Rolland Vida   Luís H. M. K. Costa   Serge Fdida

Laboratoire d'Informatique de Paris 6 – Université Pierre et Marie Curie
8, rue du Capitaine Scott – 75015 – Paris, France
`{Rolland.Vida, Luis.Costa, Serge.Fdida}@lip6.fr`

Abstract

With the emergence of a wide variety of mobile devices, providing an efficient multicast service in a mobile environment became important. Traditional solutions based on remote subscription are not efficient for highly mobile nodes, as the multicast tree must be frequently reconstructed. On the other hand, solutions based on bi-directional tunneling introduce triangular routing.

Performance losses due to triangular routing are highly dependent on network topology. In this paper we analyze these losses for different theoretical models, such as k-ary and self-similar trees. Then we compare them with simulation results obtained on realistic, Internet-like topologies.

1. Introduction

With the emergence of a variety of mobile devices, such as laptops and PDAs, handling user mobility became an important network service requirement. On the other hand, a growing number of applications (Internet TV, videoconferencing, distributed games and simulations) are based on multicast distribution.

There are two traditional solutions to handle host mobility in IP multicast: *remote subscription* and *bi-directional tunneling* [7, 8, 12, 16]. Each of these solutions has its drawbacks. Remote subscription is not efficient for highly mobile receivers, as it requires frequent grafts and prunes of branches in the multicast distribution tree. Moreover, in case of source mobility for a source-based multicast tree, not only branches, but the entire distribution tree must be reconstructed.

On the other hand, bi-directional tunneling introduces triangular routing. Efficiency losses due to this phenomenon are highly dependent on the network topology. We show that, by eliminating routing triangles, performance can be improved significantly.

This paper is organized as follows: section 2 shows that the relative gains in performance, obtained through the elimination of routing triangles, are dependent on the shape and particular characteristics of the multicast tree.

Section 3 analyzes these characteristics for two different theoretical models: k-ary and self-similar trees. Section 4 compares these models to realistic Internet-like topologies through simulation. Section 5 concludes the paper.

2. Triangular Routing

The performance degradation due to triangular routing depends heavily on the network topology and thus on the multicast tree shape. Figure 1 presents the routing triangles introduced by bi-directional tunneling. In a companion paper [15], we propose *M-HBH* (*Multicast Hop-By-Hop routing*), a protocol which optimizes the paths from the source to the first branching node (*fbn*) of the tree, as well as from a receiver to its corresponding last branching node (*lbn*), short-cutting the routing triangles. The present paper gives a mathematical analysis of the performance gains expected from this type of solution.

First, we define the delivery delay of a packet as the number of hops the packet traverses from the source to a receiver. This definition ignores processing and queuing delays, and it assumes that all links have the same unitary propagation delay.

Consider that the source S leaves its home network, and acquires a care-of address S' in the network visited. Let $AvDel_{BT}(S, S')$ denote the average delivery delay for bi-directional tunneling, and $AvDel_{NRT}(S, S')$ the average delay with no routing triangle. If there are m receivers, and $d(S, r_i)$ is the distance in number of hops from the source S to the receiver r_i, then the *relative gains in average delivery delay* are defined as:

$$\Delta AvDel(S, S') = \frac{AvDel_{BT}(S,S') - AvDel_{NRT}(S,S')}{AvDel_{BT}(S,S')}$$

$$= \frac{x_S + y_S - z_S}{y_S + \sum_{i=1..m} d(S,r_i)/m}, \quad (1)$$

where x_S is the distance between the source S and *fbn*, y_S is the length of the tunnel between S and S', and z_S is the length of the direct path from S' to *fbn*.

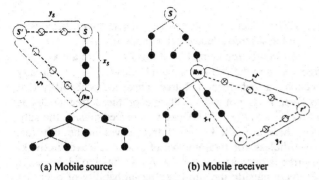

(a) Mobile source   (b) Mobile receiver

Figure 1: Eliminating triangular routing.

Note that x_S depends on the size of the multicast group. The larger the number of receivers, the higher is the probability of a branching node close to the source. This is because the receivers are uniformly distributed in the network. In practice, however, receiver distributions are not uniform, as the network connectivity is variable. Nevertheless, this scenario provides us a worst case.

The length of the other two sides of the routing triangle, y_S and z_S, depends on the new location of the source. Intuitively, the farther the source moves from its home network, the smaller the difference $y_S - z_S$. Moreover, y_S and z_S tend to be similar even if the source is near its home network. This is because the source moves between edge networks that may not be directly connected. Therefore, the tunnel from S to S' must pass through intermediate "core" routers. On the other hand, the first branching node is usually in the core of the network, thus the length of z_S is not biased by the shape of the topology.

Thus, for a fixed tunnel size $y_S = c_1$, a fixed average distance c_2 between the source and the receivers, and considering that $y_S \sim z_S$, we obtain:

$$\Delta AvDel(S, S') \sim \alpha x_S, \qquad (2)$$

where $\alpha = (c_1 + c_2)^{-1}$. Thus, the relative gains in average delay are dependent of x_S, i.e. the number of links between the source and the first branching node of the tree.

The case of receiver mobility can be treated similarly. We consider that receiver r leaves its home network and acquires a care-of address r' in the visited network (Figure 1(b)). The delivery path can be optimized through the elimination of the routing triangle between the mobile receiver r and lbn. If $Del_{BT}(r, r')$ denotes the delivery delay in case of bi-directional tunneling and $Del_{NRT}(r, r')$ the delivery delay with no routing triangle, then the *relative gains in delivery delay* for a mobile receiver are:

$$\Delta Del(r, r') = \frac{Del_{BT}(r, r') - Del_{NRT}(r, r')}{Del_{BT}(r, r')} = \frac{x_r + y_r - z_r}{d(S, r) + y_r}, \quad (3)$$

where x_r is the distance between the home network of receiver r and its last branching node, y_r is the length of

the tunnel between r and r', and z_r is the length of the direct path between r' and lbn.

As for source mobility, x_r depends on the size of the multicast group. The larger the number of receivers, the higher is the probability of a late branching in the tree. The length of the other two sides of the triangle, y_r and z_r, can also be estimated as in the case of source mobility. Thus, for a fixed tunnel size $y_r = c_1$, a fixed distance c_2 between the source and the receiver's home network, and considering that $y_r \sim z_r$, we obtain:

$$\Delta Del(r, r') \sim \beta x_r, \qquad (4)$$

where $\beta = (c_1 + c_2)^{-1}$. The relative gains in delivery delay for a mobile receiver r depend therefore on x_r, i.e. the number of hops between its home network and lbn.

In the following we evaluate x_S and x_r for two different mathematical models: k-ary and self-similar trees. We then compare these theoretical results with simulation results obtained on more realistic topologies.

3. Theoretical Model Analysis

3.1. K-ary trees

In [13] and [14] multicast trees are modeled as subsets of perfect k-ary trees. Consider a k-ary tree of depth D, where the source S is the root and all receivers are placed at the leaves. We randomly pick m distinct leaves, and construct the corresponding multicast tree. We then evaluate x_S and x_r (we assume that $m > 1$).

Consider a node N at level j in the k-ary tree; k^j such nodes exist. For each receiver r_i, there is a branch $b(r_i)$ in the tree that connects r_i to S. Each $b(r_i)$ includes one of the k^j nodes from level j. Therefore, $b(r_1)$ includes N if r_1 is placed at one of the leaves of the sub-tree situated below N. As this sub-tree has k^{D-j} leaves, the probability that receiver r_1 is placed at one of these nodes is k^{D-j} / k^D. Thus, $P(N \in b(r_1)) = k^{D-j} / k^D$. Once r_1 is placed, $k^{D-j} - 1$ leaves are still available in the sub-tree. Consequently, $P(N \in b(r_2) \mid N \in b(r_1)) = (k^{D-j} - 1) / (k^D - 1)$. Then, the probability that N is included in all $b(r_i)$, $i = 1..m$ is:

$$P\left(N \in \bigcap_{i=1}^{m} b(r_i)\right) = \prod_{i=0}^{m-1} \frac{k^{D-j} - i}{k^D - i}. \qquad (5)$$

Proposition 1: For a given tree, *fbn* is situated at level j ($j < D$), if the following events occur simultaneously:

- $e1(j)$: "All branches, corresponding to the m receivers, include the same node at level j";
- $e2(j)$: "From the k child nodes of the common node at level j, no node is included in all $b(r_i)$, $i = 1..m$ ".

As $m > 1$, *fbn* cannot be located at level D. The probability of event $e1$ can be calculated using Equation (5). There are k^j nodes at level j, and the events $e(N_h) =$

"node N_h is included in all $b(r_i)$, $i = 1..m$", $h = 1.. k^j$, are mutually exclusive. Therefore,

$$P(e1(j)) = P\left(\bigcup_{h=1}^{k^j} e(N_h)\right) = \sum_{h=1}^{k^j} P(e(N_h))$$

(6)

$$= \sum_{h=1}^{k^j} P\left(N_h \in \bigcap_{i=1}^{m} b(r_i)\right) = k^j \prod_{i=0}^{m-1} \frac{k^{D-j} - i}{k^D - i},$$

The probability of event $e2$ is also deduced from Equation (5). We pick a node N at level j so that there is a receiver r for which $N \in b(r)$. If event $e1$ occurs, then all the m receivers are included in the sub-tree situated below N. We are interested in the probability of having no node at level 1 of this sub-tree that is included in all $b(r_i)$, $i=1..m$. As the sub-tree is a k-ary tree of depth $D - j$, we obtain:

$$P(e2(j)|e1(j)) = 1 - k \prod_{i=0}^{m-1} \frac{k^{D-j-1} - i}{k^{D-j} - i}.$$

(7)

Some special cases have to be considered. Indeed, we cannot place more than k^{D-j} receivers on the leaves of a k-ary sub-tree of depth $D - j$. Therefore, if $m > k^{D-j}$, then $P(e1(i)) = 0$, $\forall i = j..D$. In other words, $P(e1(j)) = 0$, $\forall j > D - \ln m / \ln k$. Finally, from Proposition 1 we conclude that if $P(e1(j)) = 0$ then $P(e2(j-1)) = 1$, $\forall j > 0$. Therefore, the probability that fbn is situated at level j is:

$$P(x_s = j) = P(e1(j))P(e2(j)|e1(j)) =$$

$$\begin{cases} k^j \left(1 - k \prod_{i=0}^{m-1} \frac{k^{D-j-1} - i}{k^{D-j} - i}\right) \prod_{i=0}^{m-1} \frac{k^{D-j} - i}{k^D - i}, & 0 \le j \le D-1 - \frac{\ln m}{\ln k}; \\ k^j \prod_{i=0}^{m-1} \frac{k^{D-j} - i}{k^D - i}, & D-1 - \frac{\ln m}{\ln k} < j \le D - \frac{\ln m}{\ln k}; \\ 0, & D - \frac{\ln m}{\ln k} < j \le D. \end{cases}$$

(8)

We then compute x_s as a weighted average:

$$x_s = \sum_{j=0}^{D-1} jP(x_s = j).$$

(9)

The computation of x_r is similar. Consider that receiver r is placed at one of the m distinct leaf nodes selected on the k-ary tree. Let N_i denote the node that is included in the branch $b(r)$ at level i.

Proposition 2. $d(r, lbn) = j$ ($j > 0$) if both of the following events occur:

- $e1(j)$: "There is no receiver, except r, in the sub-tree situated below node N_{D-j+1} ($j > 1$)";

- $e2(j)$: "There is at least one other receiver, besides r, in the subtree situated below node N_{D-j}".

As $m > 1$, lbn cannot be at level D. There are $k^{j-1} - 1$ free leaves in the sub-tree situated below N_{D-j+1} (r already occupies a leaf of the sub-tree. Thus, the probability that receiver r_1 is not placed at one of these free nodes is $1 - (k^{j-1} - 1) / (k^D - 1)$. Once r_1 is placed outside the sub-tree, there are still $k^{j-1} - 1$ free leaves in the sub-tree. Nevertheless, the total number of available leaves in the k-ary tree is decreased to $k^D - 2$. As we have to place $m - 1$ receivers outside the sub-tree, the probability of event $e1$ can be calculated as follows:

$$P(e1(j)) = \prod_{i=1}^{m-1} \left(1 - \frac{k^{j-1} - 1}{k^D - i}\right).$$

(10)

If we assume that event $e1$ occurs, for event $e2$ to occur we have to place at least one of the $m-1$ receivers on the $k^j - k^{j-1}$ remaining leaves of the sub-tree situated below node N_{D-j}. Therefore, we obtain:

$$P(e2(j)|e1(j)) = 1 - \prod_{i=0}^{m-2} \left(1 - \frac{k^j - k^{j-1}}{k^D - k^{j-1} - i}\right).$$

(11)

Thus,

$$P(x_r = j) = P(e1(j))P(e2(j)|e1(j)) =$$

$$\left[1 - \prod_{i=0}^{m-2} \left(1 - \frac{k^j - k^{j-1}}{k^D - k^{j-1} - i}\right)\right] \prod_{i=1}^{m-1} \left(1 - \frac{k^{j-1} - 1}{k^D - i}\right).$$

(12)

We then calculate x_r as a weighted average:

$$x_r = \sum_{j=1}^{D} jP(x_r = j).$$

(13)

3.2. Self-similar trees

In [1] authors argue that self similar k-ary trees model better real Internet trees than simple k-ary trees do. Therefore, consider a k-ary tree of depth D, with all the receivers located at the leaves of the tree. We assume that the link connecting a node at level $l - 1$ with a node at level l is a concatenation of a random number of links. Let t_l denote the average number of these links. Then, a self-similar tree with similarity factor θ, is a tree for which:

$$t_{l-1} = \theta t_l, \quad \theta \ge 1, l = 2..D.$$

(14)

Therefore, $t_l = \theta^{D-l} t_D$. For simplicity, we assume that $t_D = 1$. Note that if $\theta = 1$ we have a regular k-ary tree. In such a self-similar tree, if fbn is at level j ($j > 0$) then the number of links between S and fbn is:

$$\sum_{i=1..j} t_i = \sum_{i=1..j} \theta^{D-i} = \theta^{D-j}\left(\frac{\theta^j - 1}{\theta - 1}\right). \qquad (15)$$

Adapting Equation (9) to these conditions, we obtain:

$$x_S = \sum_{j=1}^{D-1} \theta^{D-j}\left(\frac{\theta^j - 1}{\theta - 1}\right) P(x_S = j), \qquad (16)$$

where $P(x_S = j)$ is obtained from Equation (8). Similarly, if there are j levels between receiver r and lbn, then the number of intermediate links is:

$$\sum_{i=0..j-1} t_{D-i} = \sum_{i=0..j-1} \theta^i = \frac{\theta^j - 1}{\theta - 1}. \qquad (17)$$

Adapting Equation (13) to these conditions, we obtain:

$$x_r = \sum_{j=1}^{D}\left(\frac{\theta^j - 1}{\theta - 1}\right) P(x_r = j), \qquad (18)$$

where $P(x_r = j)$ is obtained from Equation (12).

4. Theoretical Models vs. Realistic Topologies

In the previous section we mathematically analyzed the gains obtained from the elimination of routing triangles, for k-ary and self-similar trees. To complement these results, we simulate more realistic Internet-like topologies.

Different researchers studied the properties of the Internet topology. A number of power-law relationships were observed on real Internet maps [5]. Thus, the quality of a topology generator can be measured from its ability to reproduce these properties [10]. In this work, we have chosen *nem* [11]. *Nem* is an Internet topology generator that creates topologies by sampling a real Internet map and produces a sub-graph that preserves the properties of the original map. We used *nem* to extract a topology with 2000 nodes from a recent Internet map obtained by Govindan *et al.* [6] and Burch *et al.* [2] (284772 nodes). We then used the Dijkstra algorithm to generate shortest path trees of different sizes.

Figure 2 compares the theoretical results obtained for k-ary and self-similar trees with the simulation results obtained with the topology generator. The values of k and D were chosen in a way to obtain trees of a comparable size with the generated topology. We observe that the mathematical model gives a reasonable approximation for the average value of x_r (Figure 2(b)). In order to verify the correctness of our model, we generated a k-ary topology and used the Dijsktra algorithm to compute shortest path trees. Note that the curve obtained through this simulation corresponds almost perfectly to the curve obtained from Equation (13). The introduction of the similarity factor θ does not influence the shape of the results in this case.

On the other hand, Figure 2(a) shows that the theoretical models are imprecise on the average value of x_S. The correctness of the calculus for k-ary trees is verified through simulation, but the obtained curves rapidly converge to zero, as opposed to that corresponding to the Internet-like topology. By introducing the similarity factor, the approximation improves, but the rapid convergence to zero persists. This behavior is explained by the fact that for x_r we calculated an average value over all the receivers. On the other hand, there is only one source in the multicast tree and a "badly" placed receiver can result in the first branching node being the source itself. As in the uniformly connected mathematical models the probability of such a "bad" placement is strong, the value of x_S rapidly converges to zero. Nevertheless, the simulation results show that on realistic topologies, where connectivity is not uniform and certain regions are more densely populated than others, this convergence is much slower. Thus, in practice, the elimination of the routing triangle improves performance also for source mobility.

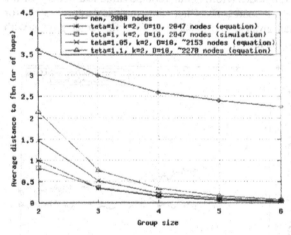

(a) Average distance from S to *fbn*

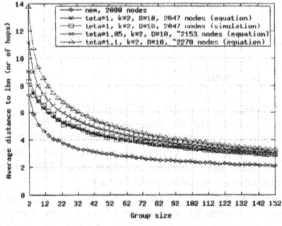

(b) Average distance from r to *lbn*

Figure 2: Theoretical models vs. sampling topologies.

The shape of a multicast tree is influenced by the network connectivity and thus by the shape of the general topology it is mapped on. Chalmers *et al.* observed that the skewed distributions and the power laws that characterize the Internet can also be applied to multicast trees [3]. Pansiot *et al.* verified this hypothesis by measurements realized on real multicast trees comprising nearly 4000 nodes and 5000 edges [12]. These studies also show that in real multicast trees receivers are placed throughout the whole height of the tree. Adapting the mathematical models to this behavior is the object of our current work.

Figure 3 shows the relative gains in delivery delay obtained through the elimination of the routing triangle for the *nem*-generated topology. Note that the receiver mobility curve is similar in shape to the one representing simulation results for x_r in Figure 2(b), confirming Equation (4). We see that the elimination of the routing triangle leads to a relative gain in delivery delay of about 40% for small groups, and about 20% for groups as large as 150 nodes (from about 1000 possible leaf nodes). In the case of source mobility, gains are as large as 30% for small groups, and as large as 15% for larger groups with 150 members.

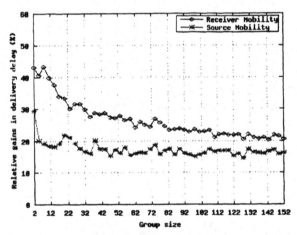

Figure 3: Relative gains in delivery delay.

5. Conclusion

Providing an efficient multicast service for mobile hosts is currently an important problem. Traditional solutions based on remote subscription are not efficient for highly mobile nodes. On the other hand, solutions based on bi-directional tunneling introduce triangular routing that reduces the data delivery efficiency.

In this paper we analyzed the performance gains obtained through the elimination of the routing triangles for source and receiver mobility. As the performance depends on the shape of the multicast tree, we compared different theoretical models with Internet-like generated topologies. Results showed that the potential performance

gains can be as large as 20% for receiver mobility and 15% for source mobility for relatively large groups. These promising results prove the importance of the multicast mobility routing problem.

References

[1] C. Adjih, L. Georgiadis, P. Jacquet, W. Szapankowski, "Is the Internet Fractal? The Multicast Power Law Revisited", Research Report 4157, Hipercom Project, INRIA, April 2001.

[2] H. Burch, and B. Cheswick, "Mapping the Internet", *IEEE Computer*, vol. 32, no. 4, April 1999, pp. 97-98.

[3] R. Chalmers and K. Almeroth, "Modeling the Branching Characteristics and Efficiency Gains of Global Multicast Trees", In *Proceedings of IEEE INFOCOM'01*, Anchorage, Alaska, USA, April 2001.

[4] L. H. M. K. Costa, S. Fdida, and O. C. M. B. Duarte, "Hop By Hop Multicast Routing Protocol", In *Proceedings of ACM SIGCOMM 2001*, San Diego, CA, USA, August 2001, pp. 249-259.

[5] C. Faloutsos, M. Faloutsos, and P. Faloutsos, "On power-law relationships of the internet topology", In *Proceedings of ACM SIGCOMM '99*, Cambridge, MA, USA, August 1999, pp. 251-262.

[6] R. Govindan and H. Tangmunarunkit, "Heuristics for Internet Map Discovery", In *Proceedings of IEEE INFOCOM'00*, Tel Aviv, Israel, March 2000, pp. 1371-1380.

[7] T. G. Harrison, C. L. Williamson, W. L. Mackrell and R. B. Bunt, "Mobile Multicast (MoM) Protocol: Multicast Support for Mobile Hosts", In *Proceedings of ACM/IEEE Mobicom'97*, Budapest, Hungary, September 1997, pp. 151-160.

[8] C.R. Lin and K-M. Wang., "Mobile Multicast Support in IP Networks", In *Proceedings of IEEE INFOCOM'00*, Tel Aviv, Israel, March 2000.

[9] D. Magoni and J.-J. Pansiot, "Analysis and Comparison of Internet Topology Generators", In *Proceedings of IFIP-TC6 Networking'02*, Pisa, Italy, May 2002, pp. 364-375.

[10] D. Magoni and J.-J. Pansiot, "Internet Topology Modeler Based on Map Sampling", *IEEE Symposium on Computers and Communications*, Taormina, Italy, July 2002.

[11] J.-J. Pansiot and D. Grad, "On routes and multicast trees in the Internet", *ACM Computer Communication Review*, vol. 28, no. 1, January 1998, pp. 41--50,.

[12] C. Perkins, "IP Mobility Support for IPv4", RFC 3220, January 2002.

[13] G. Phillips, S. Shenker and H. Tangmunarunkit, "Scaling of Multicast Trees: Comments on the Chuang-Sirbu Scaling Law", In *Proceedings of ACM SIGCOMM'99*, Cambridge, MA, USA, August 1999, pp. 41-51.

[14] P. Van Mieghem, G. Hooghiemstra, and R. Van der Hofstad, "On the Efficiency of Multicast", *IEEE/ACM Transactions on Networking*, vol. 9, No. 6, December 2001, pp. 719-732.

[15] R. Vida, L. H. M. K. Costa, S. Fdida, "The M-HBH Protocol", Technical Report, June 2002, Work in progress, (http://www-rp.lip6.fr/~vida/mhbh_techrep.pdf).

[16] Y. Wang and W. Chen, "Supporting IP Multicast for Mobile Hosts", *ACM/Kluwer Mobile Networks and Applications, Special Issue on Wireless Internet and Intranet Access*, vol. 6, no. 1, January 2001, pp. 57-66.

Performance Modeling of an Edge Optical Burst Switching Node

Lisong Xu, Harry G. Perros, George N. Rouskas
Computer Science Department
North Carolina State University
Raleigh, NC 27695-7534
E-mail: {lxu2,hp,rouskas}@csc.ncsu.edu

Abstract

We consider an edge optical burst switching (OBS) node with or without converters. The OBS node serves a number of users, each connected to the switch over a fiber link that supports multiple wavelengths. Each wavelength is associated with a 3-state Markovian burst arrival process. The arrival process permits short and long bursts to be modeled. We model the edge OBS node as a closed non-product-form queueing network, and we develop a suite of approximate algorithms to analyze it. Our approximate algorithms have a good accuracy, and they provide insight into the effect of various system parameters on the performance of the edge OBS node.

1 Introduction

Optical burst switching (OBS) [5, 7] is a dWDM-based technology positioned between wavelength routing (i.e., circuit switching) and optical packet switching. The unit of transmission is a burst whose length in time is arbitrary. The transmission of each burst is preceded by the transmission of a control packet on a separate signaling channel. A source node starts transmitting a data burst after a delay (referred to as *offset*), following the transmission of the control packet.

JumpStart [1, 2] is an ARDA-supported research project between NCSU and MCNC that is investigating issues associated with *control protocols* for OBS networks. The signaling protocol follows the just-in-time (JIT) approach, and is based on the work by Wei and McFarland [6]. The JumpStart project represents an important first step in bringing OBS networks beyond the "paper concept" stage and into reality. The scope of project includes the development of a specification for a JIT signaling protocol, an implementation of the specifications in hardware and software, and an evaluation of the implementation in a testbed network environment. The defined protocol supports point-to-point and multicast communications, and the control message format is optimized to permit protocol implementation in hardware.

In this paper, we develop for the first time a queueing network model of an edge OBS node with burst arrival processes described by a general Markov process. Below, we describe briefly the operation of an edge OBS node in Section 2. In Section 3, we present the burst arrival process used in the queueing network model described in this paper. In Section 4, we describe a queueing network model of the edge OBS node. Section 5 describes a method for analyzing this queueing network. We validate the accuracy of the approximation algorithm in Section 6 by comparing it to simulation results, and we conclude the paper in Section 7.

2 The Edge OBS Node

We consider an OBS network consisting of OBS nodes (switches) interconnected by bidirectional fiber links. Each fiber link between a user and an OBS edge node, or between two adjacent OBS nodes, can support $W+1$ wavelengths. Of these, one wavelength (referred to as *control wavelength*) is used to transmit control packets, and the other W wavelengths (referred to as *burst wavelengths*) are used to transmit data bursts. A user is equipped with $W + 1$ pairs of optical transceivers, each fixed tuned to one of the $W + 1$ wavelengths.

Following the JumpStart JIT signaling protocol [2], a user first sends a setup message to its edge OBS node. The setup message includes the source and destination addresses, the wavelength on which the source prefers to transmit the burst, and other information. We assume that an OBS node consists of a non-blocking space-division switch fabric, with no optical buffers. If the edge node can switch the burst on the specified wavelength, it returns a setup ack message to the user. The setup ack message contains the offset field that informs the user how long it should wait before transmitting its burst. It is possible, however, that a setup message be refused if the preferred wave-

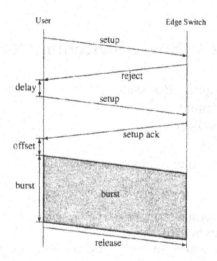

Figure 1: Signaling messages in JumpStart

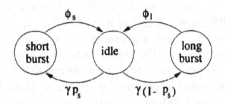

Figure 2: The burst arrival process

length on the destination output port is busy, or in the case of full wavelength converters, if all the wavelengths on the destination output port are busy. In this case, the edge node returns a reject message. The user goes through a random delay, and it then re-transmits the setup message. In our model, we assume that the user continues to re-transmit the setup message until it receives a setup ack message, although this assumption can be easily removed.

3 The Burst Arrival Process

Each burst wavelength from a user to an OBS edge switch is associated with a burst arrival process. We use the three-state Markov process shown in Figure 2 to model arrivals on a given burst wavelength. The arrival process may be in one of three states: **short burst**, **long burst**, or **idle**. If it is in the **short burst** (respectively, **long burst**) state, then the user is in the process of transmitting a short (respectively, long) burst on this wavelength. If it is in the **idle** state, then the user is not transmitting any burst on this wavelength. The duration of a burst, whether short or long, is assumed to be exponentially distributed.

The burst arrival process of Figure 2 is characterized

completely by the following parameters: $1/\gamma$, the mean duration of the **idle** state; $1/\phi_s$ and $1/\phi_l$, the mean durations of the **short burst** and **long burst** states, respectively; p_s, the probability that a burst is a small burst, and p_i, the probability that a burst from the user has output port $i, i = 1, \cdots, P$, as its destination.

We use the squared coefficient of variation of the inter-arrival time of successive bursts (short or long), $c^2(A)$, as a measure of the burstiness of the arrival process. Unlike the Poisson process which is smooth ($c^2(A) = 1$), one may introduce any degree of burstiness into the arrival process by appropriately selecting the parameters of the three-state Markov process. For more details, the interested reader is referred to [8].

4 A Queueing Network Model of an Edge OBS Node

An edge OBS node is connected to a number of users and to a number of other OBS nodes. Consequently, it receives bursts both from users and other OBS nodes. In this work, we assume that there is no burst traffic from other OBS nodes to the edge OBS node, and we only consider the burst traffic from the users to the edge node. Let P and N denote the number of input (or output) ports of an edge node and the number of the users connected to the edge node, respectively. Note that, $P \geq N$.

4.1 Edge OBS Node Without Converters

Let us first consider an edge OBS node with no converters. In this case, a burst on an incoming wavelength can only be switched to the *same* wavelength on each output port, and user bursts arriving to the edge switch on different wavelengths do not interfere with each other. Consequently, the edge node can be decomposed into W sub-systems, one per burst wavelength, and this decomposition is exact. Each sub-system $w, w = 1, \cdots, W$, is a $P \times P$ switch with N users, but each input and output port has a single wavelength, which corresponds to wavelength w of the original edge switch. Therefore, each sub-system has N burst arrival processes.

The queueing network model of a sub-system is shown in Figure 3; it consists of $P + 1$ nodes numbered $0, 1, \cdots, P$. Node 0 is an infinite server node, and it represents the burst arrival processes which are in the **idle** state. Node $i, i = 1, \cdots, P$, represents the (single) wavelength on output port i. Each node i consists of a single *transmission server* and an *infinite server*. The customer (if any) occupying the transmis-

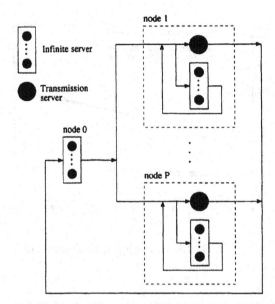

Figure 3: Queueing network model of a sub-system of an edge switch without converters

sion server represents the burst arrival process whose burst is being transmitted by output port i. The customers (if any) in the infinite server represent those burst arrival processes which are undergoing a delay before their users re-transmit the corresponding **setup** messages. The customers in the infinite server are often referred to in the literature as *orbiting* customers. The total number of customers in this closed queueing network model of a sub-system is equal to N (i.e., it is equal to the total number of burst arrival processes in the sub-system).

4.2 Edge OBS Node With Converters

Let us now consider an edge OBS switch with converters. In this case, a **setup** message for output port i of the switch is accepted as long as at least one wavelength is free on this output port. Otherwise, the **setup** message is rejected, and the user undergoes a delay before retransmitting the message. Clearly, the above decomposition of an edge switch into sub-systems per wavelength is no longer possible, since user bursts arriving on different wavelengths may interfere with each other. However, the edge switch *as a whole* can be modeled by a closed queueing network very similar to the one shown in Figure 3. The new queueing network consists of $P + 1$ nodes and a total of NW customers (since there are now NW arrival processes). Node 0 in the new queueing network is identical to node 0 in the network of Figure 3. Similarly, each node $i, i = 1, \cdots, P$, in the new queueing network corresponds to each of the

output ports of the edge switch. The main difference is that each node $i, i = 1, \cdots, P$, consists of an infinite server and W (rather than one) transmission servers, each corresponding to one of the W wavelengths of output port i.

5   Analysis of the Queueing Network

The queueing network shown in Figure 3 is a non-product-form queueing network with Coxian service times. It consists of a single class of customers if all customers are associated with the same arrival process. Otherwise, it becomes a multi-class queueing network. The single class queueing network with or without converters was analyzed using Marie's algorithm [3]. To this end, we need to construct a *flow equivalent server* for each node $i, i = 1, \cdots, P$. Node 0 is an infinite server (i.e., a BCMP node), so we do not need to construct a flow equivalent node for it. We note that, to the best of our knowledge, Marie's method has not been applied to nodes with orbiting customers. Consequently, the derivation of a flow equivalent server for such a node is a new contribution. For an edge OBS switch without converters, we obtained the closed-form expression of the conditional throughput of the special node with orbiting customers. In the case of converters, we cannot obtain a closed-form solution, and we solve each node i numerically using the Gauss-Seidel method [4]. The multi-class queueing network was analyzed by decomposing it into a set of two-class networks. For more details, the interested reader is referred to [8].

6   Numerical Results

In this section, we present results to illustrate how the different system parameters affect the performance of the edge OBS node. In order to investigate the accuracy of our approximation algorithms, we also compare the approximate results to results obtained from a simulation program of an edge OBS switch.

We show results for $P = 16$ (i.e., a 16×16 edge switch) with $W = 32$ wavelengths per fiber and a hotspot traffic pattern such that 10% of all arriving traffic has output port 16 as its destination, while the remaining traffic is uniformly distributed among the other 15 output ports (i.e., $p_{16} = 0.1$, and $p_i = 0.06 \ \forall \ i \neq 16$). We assume that all customers are associated with the same arrival process. That is, our queueing network is a single class queueing network. We consider the following three performance measures: *switch throughput*, which is the sum over all output ports of the port throughput; *switch utilization*, i.e., the average across all output ports of the port utilization; and *mean waiting time of a user*, that is, the average waiting time until a user transmits a burst to the switch.

Figures 4–6 plot the three performance measures, respectively, against the number N of users attached to the edge switch; these figures show results for an OBS switch *without* converters. Two sets of plots are presented, each set corresponding to a different burst arrival process. For both arrival processes, the mean burst size has been set to 1, and the mean burst inter-arrival time has been set to 1.2. However, the squared coefficient of variation $c^2(A)$ of the burst interarrival times is set to 1 for one process, and to 100 for the other. The burst arrival process with $c^2(A) = 1$ is very smooth, while the one with $c^2(A) = 100$ is extremely bursty. Each set consists of two plots, one corresponding to simulation results and one corresponding to results obtained using the approximate analytical model we developed in Section 5.

From the three figures, we observe that there is a good agreement between the analytical and simulation results. We also observe that as the number of users increases, the switch throughput, switch utilization, and mean user waiting time all increase. We also see the dramatic effect that the burstiness of the arrival process can have on the performance of the edge OBS node. Specifically, for the smooth arrival process $(c^2(A) = 1)$, the switch throughput and utilization increase with the number of users, while the mean waiting time remains low. When the arrival process is extremely bursty $(c^2(A) = 100)$, on the other hand, increasing the traffic load by increasing the number of users has minimal effect on switch throughput or utilization, which remain at low levels, while it severely affects the mean waiting time.

Figures 7–9 are similar to Figures 4–6, respectively, but present results for an edge OBS node *with* converters. We consider two arrival processes as before, with the same parameters. We note again that there is a good agreement between the analytical and simulation results. We also observe two important differences compared to the results for a switch with no converters. First, for the same traffic load (i.e., number N of users), all performance measures are significantly improved. The second important observation is that, for all three measures considered here, there is little difference in the performance when the squared coefficient of variation (i.e., the burstiness) of the arrival process increases from 1 to 100 (compare to the switch with no converters where burstiness severely affects performance). Overall, the results indicate that, in addition to their well-known benefits, wavelength converters may also mitigate the adverse effects of even

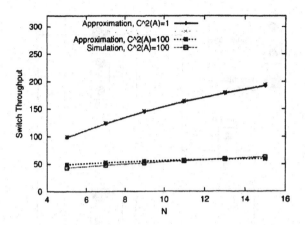

Figure 4: Switch throughput, no converters

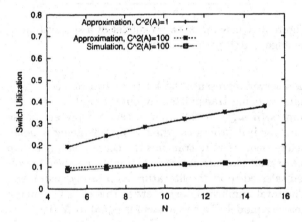

Figure 5: Switch utilization, no converters

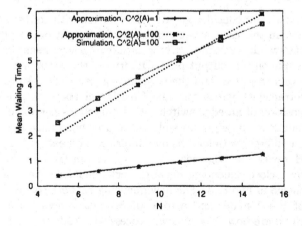

Figure 6: Mean waiting time, no converters

extremely bursty traffic on switch performance. This observation is quite important given the fact that, by definition, OBS networks will have to deal with bursty traffic.

7 Concluding Remarks

We have presented a new queueing network model of an edge OBS node. The model is quite general, and it permits us to study the performance of an edge switch under a wide range of traffic and operational scenarios, including: an arrival process with any desired degree of burstiness, and output ports with or without converters. We have developed approximate algorithms for each variant of the model, and we have presented numerical results which demonstrate the accuracy of our approximations. We are currently working on extensions of the queueing network models presented here to analyze a network of OBS nodes, including edge and core switches.

References

[1] The JumpStart project. http://jumpstart.anr.mcnc.org.

[2] I. Baldine, G. N. Rouskas, H. G. Perros, and D. Stevenson. JumpStart: A just-in-time signaling architecture for WDM burst-switched networks. *IEEE Communications Magazine*, 40(2):82–89, February 2002.

[3] R. Marie. An approximate analytical method for general queueing networks. *IEEE Trans. Software Eng.*, 5(5):530–538, Sep. 1979.

[4] H. Perros. *Queueing Networks with Blocking: Exact and Approximate Solutions*. Oxford University Press, 1994.

[5] C. Qiao and M. Yoo. Optical burst switching (OBS)-A new paradigm for an optical Internet. *J. High Speed Networks*, 8(1):69–84, January 1999.

[6] J. Y. Wei and R. I. McFarland. Just-in-time signaling for WDM optical burst switching networks. *J. Lightwave Tech.*, 18(12):2019–2037, Dec. 2000.

[7] Y. Xiong, M. Vandenhoute, and H.C. Cankaya. Control architecture in optical burst-switched WDM networks. *IEEE Journal on Selected Areas in Communications*, 18(10):1838–1851, October 2000.

[8] Lisong Xu. *Performance Analysis of Optical Burst Switched Networks*. PhD thesis, North Carolina State University, Raleigh, NC, July 2002.

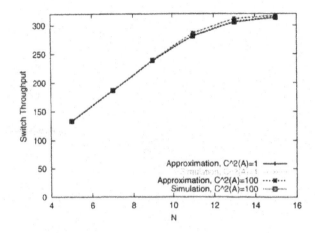

Figure 7: Switch throughput, with converters

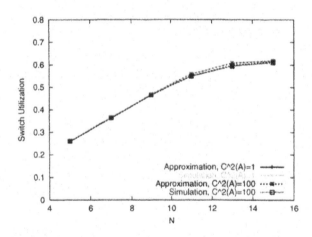

Figure 8: Switch utilization, with converters

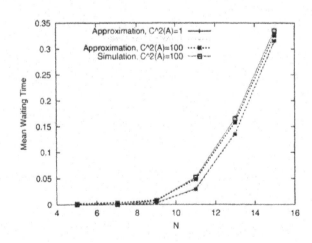

Figure 9: Mean waiting time, with converters

Session 6–2
Web-Based Simulation

Educational Application of an
Online Context Sensitive Speech Dictionary

G. Bengu[1],Guangyu Liu, Ritesh Adval,Frank Shih

New Jersey Institute of Technology
University Heights, Newark, New Jersey07102

bengu@njit.edu

Abstract—As part of an online freshmen courseware, a context sensitive speech dictionary is implemented to improve learning efficiency of scientific terminologies. The meaning system is based on WordNet, a context sensitive semantic database developed in Princeton University. Speech functionality is achieved by implementing a Java speech interface for the TTS (Text-To-Speech) engine. These features are targeted to help the students to understand the online reading material more accurately and more efficiently. Microsoft SAPI (Speech Application Programming Interface) and TTS (Text to Speech) engine are selected as the audio driver. A server program is implemented based on Component Object Model (COM) standard and provides a simple online speech interface. The interface can also be easily used for other software to provide fast and reliable speech service on the Internet. The toolkit is prepared for the general chemistry education courseware in New Jersey Institute of Technology (NJIT).

Index Terms—Dictionary, WordNet, Speech, TTS, Java, Microsoft SAPI, COM (Common Object Model)

I. INTRODUCTION

The objective of this study is to enhance the comprehension of Internet based Educational courseware. Its main features are context sensitive meaning extraction and real time pronunciation functionality.

The online context sensitive dictionary is implemented for Freshman Chemistry Education web site in NJIT with the support of *NJCMR* (New Jersey Center for Multimedia Research)[2], NJIT. Using *WordNet*, a semantic database developed in Princeton University. With the help of this context sensitive dictionary, readers can achieve more accurate understanding of the context and higher efficiency in learning than traditional on-line dictionaries. Traditional dictionaries provide all possible meanings of a given word and the user must search over alternatives and comprehend the meanings before deciding about the appropriate definition. The higher efficiency provided by this unique

system, is attributable to the fact that the students are able to stay focused more on the task while easily finding accurate scientific explanations. They can concentrate without being distracted by loading their cognition to search over unrelated information.

Originally, the WordNet database provided no pronunciation functionality. An enhancement with Text-To-Speech (TTS) technology is created to pronounce the words from plain text input of a web courseware. TTS technology is considered as "the most successful computer simulation of a complex human mental function". It analyzes linguistic information and converts it into audio output. It also deals with stress, rhythm, intonation and various pronunciation phenomenons in a phrase, sentence or paragraph in the way of human being. Based on the advance over the past 40 years, TTS technology now can provide the intelligibility nearly as the real human voice [1,2]. Addition of Text-To-Speech technology is intended to provide this context sensitive dictionary to communicate in ways that come naturally to humans. The overall objective is to improve the efficiency of learning process by incorporating effective use of senses related to learning new terms in vocabulary.

II. SYSTEM DESCRIPTION

A. WordNet - Context Sensitive Dictionary Database

The dictionary uses WordNet database to provide word meaning *[3]*. WorldNet was developed by the Cognitive Science Laboratory at Princeton University under the direction of Professor George A. Miller.

WordNet is a lexical reference system whose design is inspired by current psycholinguistic theories of human lexical memory. English nouns, verbs, adjectives and adverbs are organized into synonym sets, each representing one underlying lexical concept. The synonym sets are linked by different kinds of relationship *[4]*.

The advantage of WordNet is that words are organized semantically rather than alphabetically. So the fundamental differences in the semantic organization of these syntactic categories can be clearly revealed and systematically exploited.

Wordnet Database has 3 kinds of files: data file, index file, sense file. Tagged file is used to provide context sensitive meaning within the paragraph. All these files are *ASCII*

---
[1]Correspondence and offprint requests to: Prof. G. Bengu, Department of I&M Engineering, NJ Institute of Technology, University Heights, NJ 07102, USA
[2]This work is supported by a grant from NJ Commission on Science and Technology via NJCMR.

385

(American Standard Character for Information Interchange) files that are readable for machine and human being although it's difficult to understand because of many special symbols and offset values.

For the purpose of context sensitive meaning, text paragraphs are processed using Wordnet database tools and tagged files are created to cooperate with the database.

The four kinds of files are related with each other. There are 4 kinds of index file and data file corresponding to noun, verb, adjective and adverb. For example, the data file for noun is "noun.dat" and index file "noun.idx". The data file contains the content of synonym sets. The index file is an alphabetized list of all the words in a category and one or more byte offsets related with each word that indicate the starting addresses of synonym sets in the data file [3].

The organization of index files focuses on words. Wordnet database provides the sense file "sense.idx" that focus on the meaning. On each line it consists of a sense key and an offset into the data file to which a word belongs.

For the purpose of context sensitive meaning, the text page needs to be converted into a tagged file. The tagged file contains the paragraph, line, and position information of a word and connects this word with a sense key. From the sense key, we can find the context sensitive meaning in the data file through the sense file and the index file [3].

Upon the theory and concepts of WordNet, a Web Based Interface has been developed in Brandeis University. This interface is independent from WordNet (as API), and is usable over Internet with a Web browser [5].

B. TTS Speech Service

TTS technology is used to provide speech service in this toolkit [6]. TTS engines convert plain text to audio files or code. For the most part, all TTS conversion engines can be broken out into one of three methods used to convert phonemes into audible sounds [7,8,9].

a. Concatenation of Words

This method works by joining previously recorded phrases and words' waveform to construct a complete sentence. Its advantage is that it keeps precisely the waveform of human speech because of the direct recording. But the speech signal has large frequency redundancies because the frequency ranges of our hearing are restricted by the physical mechanism of our auditory organs. So this method will occupy more bandwidth to transmit and more capacity to store than necessary because it records the raw waveform exactly. On the other hand, if the speech engine need to adjust the features of the speech, such as the tone, it will be difficult to do so using this method. The reason is that the waveform is static and has no dynamic mechanism to control its features.

b. Analysis-Synthesis of Words

This method generates "synthetic" words by electronically applying mathematical algorithms to simulate throat length, mouth cavity, lip shape, and tongue position. Since the sound units are stored by using speech production model parameters such as spectral envelope parameters, the amount of information is much less than with the previous method of storing by waveform, although the naturalness of synthesized speech is slightly degraded. The typical bit rate is 2.4-4.8 kbps in this method, whereas the bit rate for the previous method is 9.6-64 kbps [7]. Additionally, this method is more flexible to change the speech features. The speech engine can control the parameters to change the speaking rate or smooth the pitch transition between phonemes easily. Various DSP (Digital Signal Processing) technologies are applied in the procedure of Analysis-Synthesis to decrease the bit rate while keeping the speech quality. The model parameters are adjusted in a loop of feedback control system to minimize the error and optimize the speech quality. Channel vocoders and speech synthesizers based on digital processing algorithms like Line Spectrum Pair (LSP) analysis or PARtial auto-CORrelation (PARCOR) analysis methods are used to improve the quality of synthetic speech [7]. Because of its reduced storage, it is especially suitable to be implemented in software speech engines. It is used in Microsoft speech engine that we used for this project.

c. Diphone Concatenation

This method concatenates short digital-audio segments together and mathematically smoothes out the gaps to produce a continuous sound. These short segments are called diphones. This method is different from the first one in that it divides a word into smaller units to decrease the total number of the units. This method is also different from the second method in that mathematical algorithm is only used to process the transition between sound units rather than creating the speech phonemes. The advantage is that the algorithm needed for this method is relatively simple because it does not need to create the phonemes. But it lacks the flexible control ability of the second method to adjust the speech features.

As we can see, Analysis-Synthesis method has lower byte rate, parametric quality control and DSP improvement potential. The disadvantage of it is the complexity of speech production algorithm. Fortunately, the modern computers provide the powerful calculation ability to host the software implementation needed for this method.

In this project, we select Microsoft TTS engine that falls into the second type. The system is comprised of a server and a number of clients. The server is on Windows NT platform and stores the database. The clients is required to use :

- Win32 Operating System
- Sound card, a speaker that can play Microsoft WAV audio file
- Microsoft Internet Explorer 5.0 or higher

III. IMPLEMENTATION

The system provides 3 sets of functions for the user:

1. **context sensitive dictionary functions are provided.** *i)* The user can click on a word in the paragraph and then get the exact meaning within the context. *ii)* He or she can also acquire all other possible meanings of this word. *iii)* Previously selected words (history) can be

listed. *iv)* The list(history) result can be cleared to restart with a new list. *v)* the speech functions can be disabled to continue reading alone, *vi)* selected words can be highlighted to see the occurrences of it in the current page etc.

2. Second, **speech functions are provided** such as *i)* TTS conversion, *ii)* playback and fast replaying of the sound files and *iii)* selection of a speaker. When the user clicks on a word in the frame, he or she can hear the pronunciation and standard windows wav file is created locally. The user can replay the word fast using the saved audio files. The user can also select different speakers who are of different genders, ages and voice characteristics.

3. The automatic downloading and installation functions are provided to configure the runtime environment.

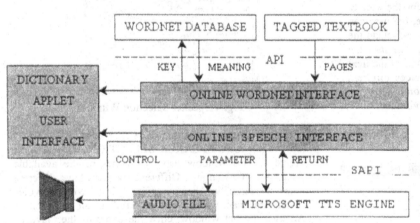

Fig.1 Configuration Chart

Figure 1 shows the system configuration. The shaded parts are implemented in this project while other blocks indicate external resources.

"ONLINE WORDNET INTERFACE" is a set of Java modules to provide context sensitive meaning functionality. Java Socket is used to communicate between the server database and clients. Java Applet provides the user interface in the browser of the client *[10,11]*. A tagged chemistry textbook file is the context resource. Wordnet Database stores word meanings in synonym sets.

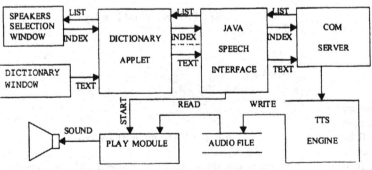

Fig.2 Online Speech Interface Structure

The tagged textbook file contains every word with their position in lines, paragraphs and pages. It also contains an index of meaning for Wordnet Database called "sense key". The content of the textbook file is read from the server and displayed for a user when the user accesses the dictionary toolkit. Then the user can click a word to request explanation. Dictionary applet then finds out the sense key associated with the word clicked. WordNet database is searched using the above sense key to get the word meaning. Word meaning found in above step is sent to Applet to display. The meaning entries are stored to enable the review at some time later. The user can also request all the meanings of one word rather than the context sensitive meaning. In this case, the word is sent to WordNet Database to query all its meaning indexes from an index file. Then the meaning entries are queried by the use of these indexes *[3]*.

"ONLINE SPEECH INTERFACE" is comprised of 3 parts: i) *Java Speech Interface*, ii) *Play Module* and iii) *Com Server*. It retrieves the word clicked by the user and control TTS engine to create the audio file for this word. The audio file is then played or replayed by the *Play Module*. It also provides selection of dialect speakers based on the choice available in the TTS engine.

Java Speech Interface manages all the work related with speech service. It imports the interface package of in-proc *Com Server* to manipulate the functions of TTS ENGINE. It also has a reference to PLAY MODULE to play or replay the audio file. *Com Server* is a Dynamic Link Library (DLL) written in Visual C++. It contains a set of COM interfaces exposed by TTS ENGINE to provide functions like speech site initialization, TTS conversion, speakers selection et al. TTS ENGINE receives the commands of the *Com Server* and creates the audio file for the specific word *[6]*.

Figure 2 shows the structure of *Online Speech Interface*. When the user clicks a word in the *Dictionary Window*, the text is sent to a *Java Speech Interface* class. Then the word is transferred to *Com Server* that starts up the TTS function of TTS engine. An audio file is created as a local file. Then *Com Server* activates PLAY MODULE to play the sound. Generally, the user will replay the sound to listen to the pronunciation. Because the audio file exists as a local file, replay will be quite fast.

When the DICTIONARY APPLET is downloaded at the beginning, a request is sent to query the speakers list available in TTS engine. Since the list depends on the configuration of TTS engine, it will be constant during the run time of the process. When the user clicks the SPEAKERS icon, SPEAKERS SELECTION WINDOW displays the list of speakers. After the user selects the speaker, an index is passed to COM SERVER through the JAVA SPEECH INTERFACE class. COM SERVER controls TTS ENGINE to change the speaker option. COM SERVER is implemented using automation as a Dynamic Link Library (DLL). It hides the complex detail of

SAPI programming and exposes a set of practical speech functions with simple signature. These functions can be used in JAVA, Visual Basic, Visual C++ or any language that supports COM standard. Software vendors can also use it to construct extended speech functions [12,13,14].

A standard setup package is created so that the user can download and install the required Java Virtual Machine (JVM) version and speech environment. Code signing technology is used to get the permission to create audio files in the local file system.

WordNet and TTS functionality are integrated seamlessly under a unique simple user interface. All the user needs to do is to click a specific word. The system will then spawn 2 threads to process meaning and pronunciation request asynchronously. It results in the optimal responsive performance that will accelerate the learning process. Efficient overview techniques are provided for the user to master the knowledge obtained. For example, the user can replay the pronunciation very fast. He or she can reload the previous selected words with their meanings and save the information to the particular user profile for use at the next time logon. Speaker selection function provides different dialect pronunciation to give the impressive comparison and provide interested variants for the learning environment.

IV. RESULTS

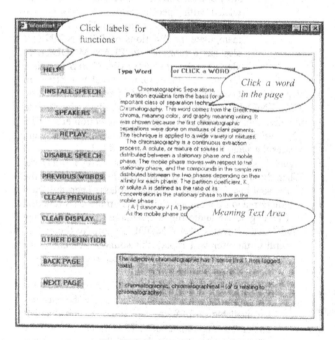

Fig.3 Dictionary User Interface

Figure3 shows the run time screen snapshot of Dictionary toolkit. When the user clicks one word, for example "chromatographic", the context sensitive meaning will be displayed in the text area, an audio file will be created in drive C and the sound will be played out by the speaker. It will take 2 to 4 seconds depending on the number of syllables of different words. For example, word "phase"

will be faster than "chromatographic" to be explained and pronounced. The service speed is 3 to 5 times faster than using some TTS conversion sites on Internet that are using CGI method (Common Gateway Interface). This speedy performance enables this system to be used as a practical tool in education.

Fig. 4 Speaker Selection Window

In order to change the speaker, first click the "SPEAKERS" label to pop up a SPEAKER SELECTION WINDOW as Figure 4. This window lists the names of the available speakers in TTS engine. Different speakers have different voice characteristics. For example, "Mary" with the voice of an American woman while "Sam" is an old man in America. In that window, click the name of the favorite and click the button "SELECT DONE". The window will disappear and the speaker type will be changed.

The dictionary provides many other features for the efficiency of learning. Figure 5 displays previous selected words and their meanings for review. Figure 6 displays all the meaning of one word for the user.

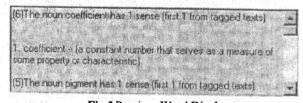

Fig.5 Previous Word Display

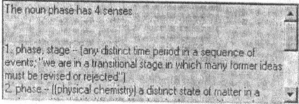

Fig. 6. All Meanings of a Word

The test results show the satisfied speed and performance that are acceptable for education practice. The user interface is compact and consistent. The performance is reliable. The

388

system has been demonstrated on-line in some official conferences[NSF Gateway Coalition Conference, NJIT, Mar24 2000 and NJCS&T Review Conference, Princeton, Apr 3 2000].

The use of this dictionary service can benefit both the teachers and the learners in education community. It can help users master the information more efficiently. To test the above objectives, this application is used in the Freshman Chemistry Laboratory courses, Chem. 124 in NJIT. The assessment and evaluation studies are ongoing. Upon conforming positive results as expected, it can be extended to other fields easily.

V. CONCLUSION

The application of ONLINE CONTEXT SENSITIVE SPEECH DICTIONARY provides an innovative education tool. It makes the user more efficient to catch directly the meaning of a terminology within the specific content. Enhanced with a web based multimedia instructions, the speaking dictionary service provides the user to have a better understanding of the subject matter while providing more impressive memory. The comprehensive instruction by both text and sound is more natural and provides a better advantage for learning ability of human beings.

The embedded ONLINE SPEECH INTERFACE completes the middle layer architecture and the application package between Java programs and Microsoft TTS ENGINES in efficient way.

This study is also flexible for other application purposes since a set of simple and functional sound methods are completed to perform general speech services such as creation of audio files, play of sound and change of speaker characteristic.

In summary, the system functions are designed for specific educational- environment and provided in an efficient and speedy way and in detail [15]. For example, for reusability and speed, system provides a mechanism that saves audio files.

A user-friendly interface has been implemented to make the usage convenient by providing an elaborately designed GUI and an automatic installation procedure.

ACKNOWLEDGEMENT

We would like to thank to Princeton Univ - Prof. George Miller for his permission to use the database and Princeton Univ.-Dr. Jack Gelfand and NJIT, Prof. Frank Shih for their valuable suggestions and the NJ Commission on Science and Technology for their support.

VI. BIBLIOGRAPHY

[1] Michael H. O'Malley, "Text-To-Speech Conversion Technology", IEEE Computer, Vol.23, No. 8,pp. 17-23, August 1990

[2]Mikio Kitai, Kazuo Hakoda, and Shigeki Sagayama, "Trends of ASR and TTS Application in Japan", IEEE 1996

[3] Ritesh Adval, "On-line Semantic Dictionary Interface in JAVA using WordNet Database", Master project report, New Jersey Institute of Technology, Newark, New Jersey, August 1999.

[4] George A. Miller, Richard Beckwith, Christiane Fellbaum, Derek Gross, and Katherine Miller, "Introduction to WordNet: An On-line Lexical Database", August 1993 http://www.cogsci.princeton.edu/~wn/

[5] Oliver Steele, Java routine to access WordNet database http://www.cs.brandeis.edu/~steele/sources/JWordNet.html

[6] Guangyu Liu, "On-line Speech Service Interface Using COM Model", Master project report, New Jersey Institute of Technology, Newark, New Jersey, May 2000.

[7] Geoff Bristow, Electronic Speech Synthesis Techniques, Technology and Application, McGRAW-HILL, New York, 1984

[8] Robert Coleridge, "A High-Level Look at Text-to-Speech via the Microsoft Voice Text Object", MSDN Content Development Group, Redmond, Washington, 1998

[9] Sadaoki Furui, Digital Speech Processing, Synthesis, and Recognition, Musashino, Tokyo, Japan, 1995

(10) Cay S. Horstmann, Gary Cornell, Core JAVA 2, Vol I-Fundamental, PRENTICE HALL, New Jersey

(11) Cay S. Horstmann, Gary Cornell, Core JAVA 1.1, Vol II-Advanced Features, PRENTICE HALL, New Jersey

(12) Dale Rogerson, Inside COM, Microsoft Press , Redmond, Washington

(13) Don Box, Essential COM, Addison-wesley, Massachusetts

(14) Dino Esposito, "The Microsoft Speech SDK", Microsoft Internet Developer, February 1999

[15] William K. Poston Jr. "Factors Impacting Perceived Quality In School Education", Education Policy Analysis Archive , 19 , 5(September 1997), pp34-39

USING COMPUTER SIMULATION TO OPTIMIZE THE OPERATIONS FOR AN AUTOMOTIVE MANUFACTURING FACILITY

Haldun Çelik
SELCO Systems Engineering and
Logistics Consulting Office
Istanbul, Turkey
www.selco.cc

Murat Güventürk
SELCO Systems Engineering and
Logistics Consulting Office
Istanbul, Turkey
www.selco.cc

ABSTRACT

This study describes an application of discrete-process simulation to an instrument panel (IP) assembly process within the automotive industry and to demonstrate the ability of AutoMOD simulation package as a flexible modeling tool. Material flow in a typical manufacturing facility is a critical activity in accomplishing timely product deliveries. There are many dynamic factors that impact the movement of material within a facility. Among those factors, delivery schedules, availability of material handling equipment, routes of movement, aisle utilization are the important ones. Simulation is the most suitable tool to capture such dynamic nature of operations.

1. INTRODUCTION

Simulation models of material handling systems like those found in automotive assembly systems often require many variables and complex operation logic. These systems have many different variables associated with them. The most important ones are: conveyor speeds, material handling equipment quantities, routing information, active and inactive station (dock) information, station operation times, and shift schedules. Material flow systems show many common characteristics for particularly systems that are characterized by discrete moves of a given quantity of material with a transport unit. A transport unit may be in a variety of forms from a human operator to an automated vehicle but the nature of the operation remains the same. In this paper, we present a generic modeling framework in Automod for modeling such systems. The model described in the paper can be used for analyzing similar systems by tailoring to a particular layout. The paper also includes some of the benefits of using simulation for analyzing material flow in a manufacturing plant.

In order for a simulation analyst to control or experiment with a material handling system, he or she will usually have to vary one or more of these variables. In the past, this has meant that these "hard-coded" variables would have to be changed one by one through menus for each material handling segment or system. This paper will address how users can use external data files to control these traditionally "hard-coded" variables, thereby allowing simulation analysts and their customers to drive their material handling systems as they have traditionally used external files to provide process information for their models.

The approach was to create a flexible and robust model that imports all of these system parameters from external data files. This allows for an increase in model efficiency if model experimentation is large and involves many different physical changes. Using this method, a potential customer can modify these parameters for experimentation with a run-time version of AutoMOD simulation software.

In this paper, we first state the benefits of the generic simulation model, and then provide an overview of the production system under study and then describe the development of the simulation model. We conclude by describing the use of simulation model for future analysis.

2. BENEFITS OF THE GENERIC SIMULATION MODEL

Discrete event simulation can be one of the most powerful tools available to industrial engineers. Simulation programs allow us to predict overall system performance like the throughput of a system. It is also beneficial in identifying bottlenecks, evaluating proposed alternatives for eliminating bottlenecks, identifying under utilized resources, and determining buffer sizes just to name a few. Simulation tools like AutoMOD offer users the ability to investigate many diverse process systems from automotive manufacturing plants to hospital operating wings.

Traditionally, simulations are developed based on a pre-determined base layout with appropriate assumptions and data. However, in the past few years, companies are starting to use simulation in the very early stages of process design. In this phase, many of the parameters that simulation modelers have come to expect to be available for use as an input to model are unavailable. During this phase, system variables such as location of conveyors or stations, operation times, pallet or carries counts, shift patterns, etc. are changing continuously. If all these variables and parameters are hard-coded into the model, too much time, resources, and overhead will be spent to make changes in the model. To prevent this, a flexible and reusable simulation model should be developed by simulation engineers.

Even if the model is created later in the design phase, creating flexible models becomes an important issue. Here more information is known about the process layout; however, behavior of that system under many different parameters may not be known. During the experimentation phase of an analysis, for example, most simulation engineers have to conduct different what-if scenarios and alternatives to determine the effect on system performance measures like the throughput of the system. Based on the findings and result of experiments, the customers may want to run more scenarios by changing the speed of a conveyor, the path of the material handling equipment, or the cycle time of the operator. With most software packages, the simulation engineer has to update many dialog boxes or menus to vary even the simplest parameters of a model. The probability of making errors can be very high leading to faulty results. In addition, if there is a gap between the time the model was originally created and the next time it is used, there is a greater possibility that the simulation engineer will not remember how to modify the simulation model. This will also increase the likelihood of an error.

3. OVERVIEW OF THE PRODUCTION SYSTEM

The production system under study comprises the plastic extrusion, component assembly, and final assembly operations within an instrument panel (IP) assembly plant. The client was reengineering its production, warehouse, and vehicle distribution system over North American automotive assembly plant network. The study was conducted to develop computer models of the production plant and distribution channels and to recommend and evaluate improvements in before mentioned systems.

The main objectives for this study were:

1. Create a flexible and robust simulation model of IP Production System that can be handed off to the client for use via a run-time only version of AutoMOD simulation software.
2. In this model, utilize appropriate variables to allow key parameters to be changed and experimented with model runs. The initially

determined questions to answer using the model were:

a) the comparison of the push and pull material replenishment system in the facility
b) the optimum number of the material handling equipments (forklifts, tow trucks, etc.) for each department for the proposed replenishment system
c) the optimum routing of the each material handling equipment in order to get equally congested aisles to prevent accidents in the facility
d) the optimal number of docks and schedules for the incoming and outgoing delivery trucks which transports raw material, semi-finished, and finished products.
e) The best storage locations and quantities for all materials and products traveling in the system
f) The optimal reorder point quantity for each material used in the assembly lines
g) The optimum speed of 18 instrument panel assembly lines
h) The number of finished-good shipments per week for each instrument panel type

In order to satisfy these objectives, it is decided to include following parameters and variables as an input data in the simulation model:

A) System Variables
1) Part Types
2) Part Volume
3) Container specifications (# of parts in a box, box type, # of parts in a container, container type)
4) Material handling device quantity
5) Material handling device route for each part (intersection by intersection)
6) Parking and empties location of each part in the system
7) Dedicated material handling devices for each part type or area
8) Material handling device capacity
9) Material handling device speed
10) Valuable versus non-valuable time for material handling devices (Delivery time vs. battery charge time)
11) Storage system or buffer area locations and capacities for each part
12) Loading and unloading time of each material handling device for each part
13) Assembly line names, types and speeds
14) Assembly line scheduled start and finished times
15) Transportation supplier name, # of trucks dedicated for the facility, trucks capacities,

16) Docks and gates supplier trucks may approach for receiving and shipping of parts
17) Transportation supplier tardiness frequency, tardiness amount, under-delivery frequency and under-delivery percentage
18) Push or pull replenishment system switch toggle

B) Station(Pick-Up & Drop-off Points) Variables
1) Pick-Up & Drop-off Points for each part
2) Active/Inactive station toggle effect
3) Station load/unload cycle times
4) Intersection control logic

C) Shift Variables
1) Shift operating patterns
2) Individual shift events (shift lengths, breaks, time between shifts)
3) Model run length (up to X day run length)

D) Output Reporting
1) M.H device utilization, # of times each material handling device was used throughout specified time period
2) Path utilization
3) Congestion rates
4) Dock utilization
5) Buffer utilization
6) Intersection utilization
7) Path locations for each part (TBD)
8) Load/unload station rates

In addition, it was agreed that the data would be entered in to the model by using Microsoft Excel Spread Sheet including macro for user-friendly interface. 3D Animation of the model including layout of the facility, material handling equipment movements and storage area dynamics were output of the study.

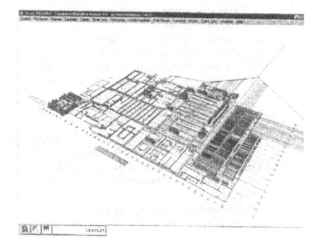

4. USE OF SIMULATION MODEL

After development stage of the model, in order to capture optimal facility design parameters and to satisfy material flow requirements, several scenarios were conducted. The client used the simulation to understand the relationships between a layout and the material flow in a facility, the movements of material from receiving docks to intermediate storage and to consumption points analyzed by considering the distances and the volumes. Then, by analyzing the frequency of movements between various points of a plant layout, a quantitative assessment of its efficiency were made in relation to the flow of materials. Production schedules, variation in product mixes, availability of material handling equipment, routings, transportation supplier capacity and delivery schedules created varying loads on the system. A simulation model were built to study the effectiveness of different forms of material handling equipment by considering their detailed parameters such as speed, acceleration, movement paths, and traffic and control logic. In addition, simulation also helped to make dynamic analyses of aisle congestion, buffer space utilization, and traffic congestion at critical intersections. Clearly, dynamic analyses were utilized in evaluating the efficiency of a layout in terms of flow of materials for complete, accurate, and timely analyses.

An appropriately designed flexible simulation helped to do the analysis quickly and easily. The model creator also handed off their work to non-simulation experts. These attributes were particularly attractive to customers who have only a runtime simulation. It was also beneficial when the same model must be reused for future investigations. The software should also have the ability to update the animation of the model as the data values change. This will help the end user to understand the results of particular scenarios and minimize confusion associated with model data changes.

APPENDIX: TRADEMARKS

AutoMOD is a registered trademark of AutoSimulations, Incorporated.

REFERENCES

Banks, Jerry, and Randall Gibson. 1996. Getting started in simulation modeling. *Industrial Engineering Solutions* 28(11):34-39.
Gunal, Ali K., Shigeru Sadakane, and Edward J. Williams. 1996. Modeling of chain conveyors and their equipment interfaces. In *Proceedings of the 1996 Winter Simulation Conference*, eds.

John M. Charnes, Douglas J. Morrice, Daniel T. Brunner, and James J. Swain, 1107-1114.

Langnau, Leslie. 1997. Simulation and emulation fine-tune material handling. *Material Handling Engineering* (May 1997), 41-45.

Law, Averill M., and Michael G. McComas. 1997. Simulation of manufacturing systems. In *Proceedings of the 1997 Winter Simulation Conference*, eds. Sigrún Andradóttir, Kevin J. Healy, David H. Withers, and Barry L. Nelson, 86-89.

Rohrer, Matthew W. 1997. AutoMod tutorial. In *Proceedings of the 1997 Winter Simulation Conference*, eds. Sigrún Andradóttir, Kevin J. Healy, David H. Withers, and Barry L. Nelson, 657-662.

Williams, Edward J. 1997. How simulation gains acceptance as a manufacturing productivity improvement tool. In *Proceedings of the 1997 European Simulation Multiconference*, eds. Ali Rıza Kaylan and Axel Lehmann, P-3 – P-7.

Williams, Thomas A. 1997. Changing the conveyor 'picture'. *Assembly* 40(8):34-40.

AUTHOR BIOGRAPHIES

HALDÙN ÇELİK holds a bachelor's degree in Mechanical Engineering (İstanbul Technical University- İstanbul, Turkey - 1993) and master's degree in Engineering Management (University of Michigan-Ann Arbor 2000). He worked at Seta Engineering, İstanbul, Turkey as the leader of the Automation Department from 1993 to 1995. From January 1996 to 2000, he had been a Project Manager at Production Modeling Corporation, Dearborn, Michigan. In this position, he had become highly expert in simulation and facilities-layout optimization systems, including AutoMOD, Taylor II, LayOPT, and ROBCAD. His work emphasized real-time simulation using WONDERWARE, STEEPLECHASE, and PLC control programming tools. He founded SELCO, a consulting company together with two partners continue to work as a logistics consultant.

MURAT GUVENTÜRK holds a bachelor's degree in Mechanical Engineering (Bogazici University- İstanbul, Turkey - 1990) and M.S. degree in Systems Engineering (University of Pennsylvania, 1992). He was the general manager of Seta Engineering, İstanbul, a materials handling engineering firm, before starting up a consulting company, SELCO. He is the lecturer of simulation course at Istanbul Kultur University and an advisor at various logistics training programmes.

A Web-based Framework with Experimental Design Approach to Simulation Optimization

Osman Nuri Darcan and Ali Rıza Kaylan
Department of Industrial Engineering,
Bogaziçi University, Istanbul, Turkey
E-mail: darcan@boun.edu.tr, kaylan@boun.edu.tr

Abstract

This paper discusses a framework for web-accessible simulation environment. The framework mainly consists of a web-based graphical user interface and a simulation engine. It allows creating simulation models and performing simple analysis on the results. The system integrates the power of experimental design methodology and response surface based optimisation techniques to a simulation environment using the SC method. The use of the system is explained through a manufacturing system example

1. Introduction

A system is a collection of entities that act and interact toward the accomplishment of a logical end. In order to analyze the system, it is modeled in the form of logical and mathematical relationships. For complex systems, the model can be studied by using discrete event simulation, to which we refer to as simulation in the remaining part of this paper. Once the model is ready, the simulation approach to problem solving can be used to guide the selection of parameters and operating strategies of that model. For this purpose, the simulation of a number of parametric variants of the same model has to be experimented. It typically involves a series of trials in which changes are made to the input variables so that resulting changes in the output variables (responses or system performances) can be observed and identified. The problem known as simulation optimization is that of finding the values for the input parameters such that an expected system performance is optimized.

The standard Clock (SC) method introduced by Vakili is a time synchronous approach that is convenient for simulation of parametrically different and structurally similar variants of a single model [1]. It is first experimented on massively parallel computers [2,3] and later it is demonstrated that a linear speedup can be reached with the same method on the networks of computers [4, 5]. Even though the SC method is an efficient method, the distributed simulation of all variants may be time consuming and expensive in terms of computation if the search space of the problem under study is large. Since the simulation studies are conducted within a time and budget limit, the requirement of the study can be reduced by carefully choosing the simulation runs that will be carried out. This can be accomplished by applying the design of experiment techniques that provide a way of planning which variants to simulate. Based on the results of the current simulation runs, the optimization process may be carried out using the well-known response surface methodology to determine the new set of variants.

This study is an extension of the web-accessible system simulation system reported in [6] in such ways that it integrates the power of experimental design methodology and response surface based optimisation techniques to a simulation environment using the SC method. Even though SC method is originally designed to perform several experiments simultaneously, we believe that such a coupling will help the analyst/experimenter to reach the optimal solution by doing fewer experiments rather than experimenting on the exhaustive search space. In this paper, we mainly focus on the functionality rather than the run-time performance such an approach.

This paper is organized as follows. In the next section, we briefly outline simulation optimisation and two fundamental techniques employed this study; experimental design and response surface methodology. This is followed by the description of the web-based experimental framework that integrates these techniques. In Section 4, we illustrate the use of the system in detail through an example problem from the same area. Section 5 concludes the paper and gives a short outlook on further research.

2. Background

2.1. Simulation Optimization

A simulation optimization problem could simply be defined as an optimization problem where the objective function consists of a set of responses that can be evaluated by computer simulation. For a simulation model, with N input variables (X_1, X_2, ... X_N) and M output variables (Y_1, Y_2, ... Y_M), the objective of the simulation optimization is to find the optimum values (X_1^*, X_2^* ... X_N^*) for the input variables (X_1, X_2,....X_N) that minimize or maximize the output variable(s). In order to solve the simulation optimization problem, both the simulation model implemented on the computer and an optimization procedure are needed. The optimization procedure uses the outputs from the simulation model that evaluates the outcomes of the inputs that are fed into the model. On the basis of the past evaluations and current simulation outputs, the optimization procedure decides on the new set of input values until an appropriate termination criterion is satisfied. Therefore, the process of a simulation optimization is to orchestrate the simulation of a sequence of system configurations so that a system configuration is eventually obtained that provides an optimal or near optimal solution.

2.2. Design of Experiment

The main goal of design of experiments (DOE) applied to simulation is to estimate how changes in input parameters affect the performance measures of a simulation experiment [7]. It provides a way of planning which configurations to simulate so that the desired information can be obtained with the computational burden. In the DOE terminology, the input parameters are called *factors* and the performance measures or outputs are called *responses*. The "experiment" is the execution of a simulation model with the factors fixed at certain values. Each factor takes at least two values or levels, during the experiment. A carefully planned design of experiments can provide us with valuable data from which to extract the relations between factors and responses. Hence, DOE can be defined as selecting the combinations of factor and levels that will be actually simulated in an experiment with the simulation model.

Factorial designs are the most commonly used class of designs because they are easy to visualize and they permit the estimation of cross-product terms. The basic example of this class is the 2^N full-factorial design, in which for 2 levels and N factors, 2^N different combinations of the factors, each defining one experiment of the model, are obtained. There is no general prescription on how to set these levels but they are usually set to be "opposite" in nature and referred as the low and the high levels.

The responses of the experiments can be used to determine, (1) main effect of each factor, which is defined as the average difference in response from its low level to its high level, and (2) interaction effects between the factors, i.e. dependence of the effect of one factor in some way on the level of other factors. Interaction effect is important in the sense that significant interactions cloud the interpretation of main effects, since the presence of the cross product causes the main effect no longer to be an accurate measure of the effect. One way to remedy this limitation is to use more than two levels for each factor. However, this results in more complex designs, which must be set up and analyzed in more sophisticated ways. Depending on the complexity of the model, available time, and computational resources, acceptable designs may be 2N or 3N factorial designs.

2.3. Response Surface Methodology (RSM)

The RSM is mainly a collection of statistical and mathematical techniques useful for optimizing functions [8]. Most experimental designs are based on an algebraic regression-model assumption about the way the factors affect the outputs. Hence, one can create a regression model as an approximation to the simulation model. If there are two factors, say X_1 and X_2, that are thought to affect the objective function Y of the simulation model, one might approximate this relationship by the regression model

$$Y = \beta_0 + \beta_1 X_1 + \beta_2 X_2 + \beta_{12} X_1 X_2 + \beta_{11} X_1^2 + \beta_{22} X_2^2 + \varepsilon$$

where the β_j coefficients are unknown to be estimated somehow, and ε is a random error term representing whatever inaccuracy such a model might have in approximating Y.

An important application of RSM is for optimizing a simulated system. [9,10,11] When simulation runs are expensive, the RSM permits the user to develop an inexpensive substitute to facilitate the understanding as well as the optimization of the system being studied. When applied to simulation optimization, RSM is based on the procedure of fitting a series of regression models to the objective function formed from responses of the simulation model evaluated at several points and trying to optimize the resulting regression model. The regression models typically fall into one of the following three classes: (i) a first-order polynomial, which consists of main effects only, and the overall mean; (ii) a first-order polynomial augmented with interactions between pairs of factors (two-factor interactions); and (iii) a second-order polynomial, which also includes purely quadratic terms.

The optimization process is usually carried out by a two-stage version of the sequential RSM, which can be outlined as follows. The process, usually referred as the first phase, starts on a small subregion of the domain, described by a current point of interest and the step size. Simulation runs are carried out at points of an experimental design on this subregion. A first-order regression is performed to characterize the response surface around the current point. A line search is carried out in the direction of steepest descent/ascent to determine the next region of interest. This process is repeated until the first-order fit shows a significant lack-of-fit. In the second phase, the objective function is approximated by a second order polynomial.

3. The prototype

The framework for the simulation optimization system can roughly be split into four phases of model building, experiment design, experiment execution and simulation optimization. First, the user selects or develops the simulation model. Configurations to be evaluated are determined by using the classical experimental design. Upon execution of the selected experiments, the results are analyzed using the ANOVA table in order to determine the important factors and the objective function is approximated by a regression model. The optimization of the model defines the new region of interest.

3.1. Architecture

The work presented in this paper aims at optimizing simulation models which are evaluated through distributed executions of several experiments. The system is mainly based on the client/server system. The proposed architecture includes the simulation engine, a Simulation and Storage Manager (SSM) hosted by the web server and a rather thin web client interface. The overall system architecture is depicted in Figure 1.

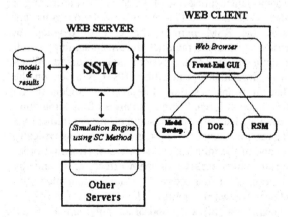

Figure 1. The Architecture of the Web-Accessible Distributed Simulation System

3.1.1. SSM and Simulation Engine. The SSM component controls the entire simulation process and manages the

storage and retrieval operations. It directly communicates with the simulation client and the Web client. The SSM component performs the simulation experiments by using the simulation engine after the simulation parameters have been received from the web client. When the simulation is finished, it stores results in a database and transmits them to the web client. The simulation engine uses the distributed implementation of the Standard Clock approach on networks of heterogeneous UNIX workstations as explained in detail in [5].

3.1.2. The Web Client. The user interface in the Web client, referred as Front-end GUI, is provided by a Java applet running within a browser. The user accesses remotely the simulation environment from applet running in a Java-enabled environment. It consists of a single applet that resides on the web server that is loaded and executed on demand of the user's client computer. The applet only communicates with the SSM component in the Web server for diverse purposes. The phases other than the model execution are carried out using the Web client. The proposed client module consists of the three different modules: model development module, experiment design module and the optimizer module. The following sections explain the details of the modules.

3.1.3. Model Development Module. Model development phase is carried out in the by using the model development module that allows the user to build up the model through a graphical user interface window. The model is pictorially represented by a set of constructs that are diagramed as simple graphical shapes. The current implementation contains five constructs; these are source, service, queue, sink and connector. The user builds up the model by inserting these constructs into draw area and supplies parameters through a dialogue window appropriate for the current construct. The user may also specify the ranges over which the factors will be varied by some specific amount for an exhaustive search of the entire experimental region.

3.1.4. DOE Module. The experimental design phase is carried out through in the DOE module. This module lets the user define various technical parameters related with the design, and analyze the results. All steps of this phase are carried out through a sequence of user-friendly interface windows. They are

- entering the design parameters (i.e. type of the design, number of factors, center points and/or replications),
- selecting the factor from the model parameters such as service or arrival rate, queue length or number of servers. They can be chosen among the input parameters that are specified in the development phase,
- setting the levels of the selected factors if default values will not be used,

- setting the objective function (e.g. cost function), the objective function may be composed of one or more performance measure as well as the input parameters,
- analyzing the effects of factors and their interaction after the experiments are executed.

Present status of the DOE module is capable of handling all full and fractional factorial designs up to 5 factors. The DOE module determines the input factors and/or their interactions, which have significant effect on the objective function. These factors or interactions are then considered as input of the regression analysis in conjunction with the response surface methodology to fit the relationship between the objective function and the factors.

3.1.5. RSM Module. The optimization phase is carried out through in the RSM module through sequence of user-friendly interface windows. This module lets the user to choose the type of the regression model that will be used for the approximation. The current prototype of the module supports three different types of regression models; they are linear, pure quadratic and the combination. For all models, the user has the opportunity to select the factor for which the coefficient of the main and the interaction are calculated and the significance level. The results are given in an ANOVA table that is especially designed for RSM. For the selected regression model and the lack-of-fit of the interaction effects dropped from the model, it displays their sum of squares, degree of freedom, Mean Square, F-ratio, computed using the residual mean square, and critical F-ratio. In addition, the best model fit that describes the behavior of the objective function is given below the table to help the analyst. For the accepted model, the regression equation can be solved by the optimizer. It provides a set of runs for a first-order model or solves the equation for the second order model.

4. Application Example

We consider the manufacturing system consisting of four workstations and three buffers (queues)[12]. Processing times have exponential distribution with means 0.333, 0.5, 0.2 and 0.25 respectively and a server cannot discharge a part if the succeeding buffer is full. The objective of the study is to maximize f (profit), which is defined as follows:

$$f = (\$200 \cdot X_1) - (\$25,000 \cdot X_2) - (\$1000 \cdot X_3)$$

where
- X_1 = throughput
- X_2 = the total number of machines in all workstations
- X_3 = the total number of positions in all buffers

The problem consists of seven decision variables. Each workstation can have up to 3 servers but the total number of servers can not exceed 10. Each buffer position can hold up to 10 parts.

From the load balancing consideration, one can heuristically conclude that 3, 3, 2, and 2 servers at stations 1, 2, 3, and 4, respectively, are optimal. The objective of the problem in this study is reduced to determining the optimal number of buffer positions at each station. We attempt to approximate the objective function by a first-order model. Therefore, we consider three factors at two level each, i.e. a 2^3 factorial experimental design. Factors A, B, and C correspond to the queue size associated with node 1, node 2 and node 3, respectively. The design domain is given the set integer values 1 through 10 for all factors. Full exhaustive search of this domain would require 1000 simulation runs. As the stating region of interest, we selected for all factors the set of integer values 1 through 3 which is centered at 2 and five replications was made for each system configuration. The Figure 2 depicts the set of windows used in defining the design parameters. As to the response function, the profit f, is specified by selecting the corresponding performance measure and its associated component from the list in the "Objective Function" window.

Figure 2. The set of windows used to define the design parameters

After the model and the design parameters have been specified, the set of responses are computed by the simulation engine. From the Anova Table given Figure 3 main factors A, B, and C are significant for the dependent variable at %10 level of significance (for A, $22.657 > F_{0.1, 1, 32} = 2.87$). However, table shows that interaction BC is significant while the other interaction effects are not and they can be neglected or added to the error. The significance is based on a user dependent confidence level. The Anova table is flexible in the sense that user can modify the confidence level or select the main factors or their interactions from the list that appears on the top-right part of the window. If the $\alpha = 0.5$ level of significance has been selected, BC would be insignificant ($F_{0.05, 1, 30} = 4.17$).

Based on the design in the previous section, we present a snapshot of model fitting process in Figure 4. We choose the first-order model given by $Y = \beta_0 + \beta_1 A + \beta_2 B + \beta_3 C$. The values of β_i (i=0,1,2,3) are estimated as

β_0=545095, β_1=71850, β_2=11195, and β_3=5295. The ANOVA table in the "Regression Results" window is especially designed for RSM. For the selected regression model, includes its sum of squares (SUMSQ), degree of freedom (DF), Mean Square (MEAN SQ), F-ratio (F), computed using the residual mean square, and critical F-ratio (F-Crit) obtained from the table for the chosen significance level. The lack-of-fit row is composed of the sum of the squares of the interaction effects dropped from the model. The interaction effect results an insignificant lack-of-fit for estimated model $(0.9 > F_{0.1, 4, 32} = 2.1$, indicated by the symbol NS). The best model fit that describes the behavior of the objective function is given below the table.

Figure 3. Anova Table of 2^3 factorial design

By accepting the first model, "Optimizer" component helps the user to perform a line search from the center point of the current region of interest. To end the line search, the user has to select the number of consecutive observation that is less/higher than the preceding observations. As seen in Figure 5, seven experiments are proposed for the path steepest ascent. Since the stopping number of experiment is selected as 2, execution is stopped after run number 6 and the new region of interest is centered at the point (5,7,4) and with the step size 2. It is described by the set of integer values 3 through 7, 5 through 9 and 2 through 6 for factors A, B, and C respectively.

In the second first order fit, model parameters are estimated as β_1=11000, β_2=1700, and β_3=1140, which leads to a maximum estimated profit of 590,980 at configuration 7,7,4.

5. Conclusion and Future Work

Conceptually, we discussed in the paper a simple simulation optimization system. The current prototype is non-autonomous system based on experimental design and response surface methodology for optimization.

The system is essentially a server and a thin client configuration. Although, Internet technology is improving to allow more files to run on client browsers using Java, the system could be modified to implement the Design and Optimizer components on the server site. Hence, an automated RSM algorithm with no user intervention can then be included in the system.

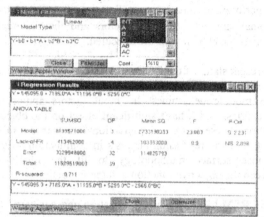

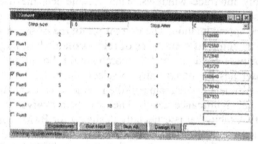

Figure 4. Model Selection and Anova Table of the model

Figure 5. Proposed experiments for the Line Search

6. References

[1] Vakili, P., "Massively Parallel and Distributed Simulation of a Class of Discrete Event Systems: A Different Perspective." *ACM Trans. on Modeling and Computer Simulation*, Vol. 2, No.3, pp 214-238, 1992.

[2] Strickland, S. G., Phelan, R. G., "Massively Parallel SIMD Simulation of Markovian DEDS: Event and Time Synchronous Methods." *Discrete Event Dynamic Systems: Theory and App.*, Vol. 5, pp 141-166, 1995.

[3] Hu, J. Q. "Parallel Simulation of DEDS Via Event Synchronization," *Discrete Event Dyn. Sys: Theory and App.*, Vol. 5, pp 167-186, 1995.

[4] Mollamustafaoğlu, L. "DISCS: An Object Oriented Framework for Distributed Discrete-Event Simulation with the Standard Clock Method." *Simulation*, Vol.70, No. 2, pp 75-89, 1998.

[5] Darcan, O., Kaylan, A. R. "Load Balanced Implementation of Standard Clock Method." *Simulation Practice and Theory*, Vol. 8, No. 3-4, pp 177-199, 2000.

[6] Darcan, O., Kaylan, A. R. "A Web-Accessible Simulation Platform For Parallel Simulation Of *Deds* By Using Standard Clock Method." submitted to *Simulation* for review.

[7] Kelton, W. D. "Experimental Design for Simulation" *in Proceedings of the Winter Simulation Conference*, pp 32-38, 2000

[8] Myers, R. H. Montgomery, D. C. "Response surface methodology: process and product optimization using designed experiments." New York: J.W & Sons. 1995

[9] Kleijnen, J.P.C. "Experimental design for sensitivity analysis, optimization, and validation of simulation models". Handbook of Simulation, Wiley, New York, 1998, pp. 173-223, 1998

[10] Law, M A, and Kelton W.D. "Simulation Modeling and Analysis", 3rd Edition. NewYork, McGraw Hill, 2000

[11] Neddermeijer, H. G, Oortmarssen, G. J., Piersma N. and Dckker, R. "A Framework For Response Surface Methodology For Simulation Optimization" in *Proc. of the Winter Sim.n Conf.*, pp 129-135, 2000

[12] Law, M. A., McComas, M. G. "Simulation Based Optimization", *Proceedings. of the Winter Simulation Conference*, pp 46-48, 2000

Evaluation of the Adaptivity of a Continuous Review Inventory Control Model

Aslı Sencer Erdem   Nuri Başoğlu

Department of Management Information Systems, Boğaziçi University,
80815-Bebek, İstanbul, Turkey.

Abstract

In this study the issues of robustness and adaptiveness are discussed in the EOQ context. Based on a former research by Erdem and Doğrusöz (1994), a continuous review inventory control policy is developed with random demand rate and tested with respect to associated costs in the long run.

1. Introduction

The concepts of "robust" and "adaptive" are widely used in many disciplines and theories. In the statistical theory, robust tests and estimators are well known topics (Huber, 1985). Similarly the property of adaptiveness is attributed to a large class of systems in many theories and systems (Hüseyin et. al., 1982 and Ikeda and Siljak, 1990). On the other hand in management and operations research, these concepts have not received that much attention (Erdem and Doğrusöz, 1994). Little (1970) was among the earliest who used the term robustness where he meant "hard to get absurd answers from".

In the inventory theory robustness of Economic Order Quantity is widely tested, resulting in the conclusion that EOQ is insensitive to the changes in its parameters, namely the setup cost, fixed demand rate and the unit inventory holding cost. The control theoreticians define robust control as "the one that secures stability of the system controlled in spite of the parameter estimation errors or assumption errors about the behavior of the system and its environment". However in almost all of these models, stability is concieved as the insensivity of the decision variable, namely the optimal order quantity in the EOQ model to estimation errors. As discussed by Erdem and Doğrusöz (1994), a robust model leads to a design of a system which does not cause a significant loss, if any change occurs in the parameter of concern. Thus the robustness of the model is due to the adaptiveness of the system designed. Here adaptiveness is relative to the objective of concern, i.e., the cost minimization. In other words, although the optimal value of the decision variable significantly changes with the value of an estimated parameter, if the cost associated with such an error is relatively insignificant, such a system shows adaptive behavior, hence the model must be conceived as a robust model.

In their study a robust production and inventory control model and an adaptive control system which they call "SPIL model" is developed by using the classical EOQ model with fixed production rate. The key conclusion is that when the loss generated by a demand estimation error is concerned, the classical EOQ model with fixed production rate is not adaptive, consequently not robust. However by using the "peak inventory level" -rather than the traditional "order quantity"- as the decision variable, a much more robust model is generated.

This study is based on the former research by Erdem and Doğrusöz (1994). In the next section, the cost of an error in the classical EOQ model is revised. In section three, a simulation study is provided and it is shown that the theoretical results based on a fixed demand rate assumption can still be valid if the demand rate is random. The concluding remarks are given in section four.

2. Cost of an Error

The expected cost function, $TC(Q, D)$ of the well known classical EOQ model with fixed production rate, r and demand rate, D is

$$TC(Q,D) = SD/Q + hQ(r-D)/(2r) \qquad (1)$$

where
Q: Production quantity per cycle
S: Setup cost,
D: Demand rate,
h: Unit inventory holding cost per unit time,
r: Production rate.

Here the control policy is to produce Q units in each cycle with a fixed production rate and then stop production until the invenory levels goes back to zero. In this model if the decision variable is changed to the peak inventory level, I, then the cost function takes the form

$$TC(I,D) = SD(r-D)/(Ir) + hI/2 \qquad (2)$$

where $I = Q(r-D)/r$. Here, in each cycle the production continues until the inventory level reaches the peak inventory level, I. Then the production is stopped until the inventory level goes down to zero. This production policy is named as SPIL, Stop Production Inventory Level (Erdem and Doğrusöz, 1994).

In equations (1) and (2), the optimal values of the decision variables which minimize the cost functions are

$$Q^* = \sqrt{2SDr/(h(r-D))} \qquad \text{and}$$
$$I^* = \sqrt{2SD(r-D)/(rh)} \qquad (3)$$

respectively. Although the cost functions in (1) and (2) seem to be identical in terms of the optimal costs generated by each, where

$$TC(Q^*,D) = TC(I^*,D) = \sqrt{2SDh(r-D)/r} \qquad (4)$$

the SPIL model is more robust than the EOQ model, if the cost of a demand estimation error is concerned.

The cost of a demand estimation error in the EOQ model, $CEOQ$ is defined as

$$CEOQ = TC(\hat{Q},D) - TC(Q^*,D)$$
$$= SD/\hat{Q} + (1/2)h\hat{Q}(r-D)/r - \sqrt{2SDh(r-D)/r} \qquad (5)$$

by using (1) and (4). Here, D is the true demand rate and $\hat{D}$ is the estimated demand rate. Accordingly, Q^* and $\hat{Q}$ are the true and the assumed optimal order quantities, found by substituting D and $\hat{D}$ in (3) respectively.

Similarly, the cost of a demand estimation error in the SPIL model, CSPIL is defined as

$$CSPIL = TC(\hat{I},D) - TC(I^*,D)$$
$$= SD(r-D)/(\hat{I}r) + h\hat{I}/2 - \sqrt{2SDh(r-D)/r} \qquad (6)$$

by using (2) and (4). Here, I^* and $\hat{I}$ are the true and the assumed optimal peak inventory levels, found by substituting D and $\hat{D}$ in (3) respectively. Noting that $CSPIL \leq CEOQ$ for all D and $\hat{D}$, Erdem and Doğrusöz (1994) conclude with mathematical proofs that if the control policy is based on the peak inventory level rather than the production quantity in a cycle, the loss associated with a demand estimation error is much more smaller. In the next section these models are tested for the random demand rate and their robustness is experimented by a simulation analysis.

3. Tests with Random Demand Rate

The major conclusions given in the previous section are valid under the assumption that the demand rate, D is fixed. Thus the inventory cycles are identical. In this study we compare the adaptiveness of the EOQ and the SPIL model when there is a random demand rate, D with a known distribution function, $F(D)$, $D \geq 0$, which will further lead to unidentical inventory cycles.

At the beginning of the planning horizon, the demand rate, $\hat{D}$ is estimated and inventory control policy is determined, i.e., either produce $\hat{Q}$ (EOQ Policy) or produce up to $\hat{I}$ (SPIL Policy) in each cycle as defined in the previous section. However if the true demand rate is random with a different mean, say D, then being unaware of this randomness, we apply an assumed optimal policy, based on $\hat{Q}$ and $\hat{I}$, which will incur extra losses. Note that if the true demand rate is D, then the control policy should be based on Q^* or I^* as defined in (3) and the optimal total cost, $TC(Q^*,D) = TC(I^*,D)$ is as given in (4).

The behavior of the EOQ and SPIL models under the random demand rate is experimented by simulation for 1000 days. Here, the following examples can be given in Table 1 for the uniformly distributed true demand rate between $D_{\min} = 0.9D$ and $D_{\max} = 1.1D$ where $D = 5$, 10, 20, 30, 40, 45 units/day. The demand rate is estimated as $\hat{D} = 10$ units/day and accordingly $\hat{Q}$=250 units/cycle and $\hat{I}$ =200 units/cycle. The other parameters are S=\$2500/setup, h=\$1/unit/day, r=50 units/day.

Table 1: Simulation Experiments with Uniform Demand Rate with Different Means

D (units/ day)	Q* (units/ cycle)	I* (units/ cycle)	TC(Q*,D) ($/day)	TC($\hat{Q}$,D) ($/day)	TC($\hat{I}$,D) ($/day)
5	167	150	150	160	155
10	250	200	200	196	196
20	408	245	245	266	238
30	612	245	245	337	237
40	2000	200	200	411	185
45	1500	150	150	417	141

$TC(Q^*,D)=TC(I^*,D)$

Apparently, the total costs associated with the EOQ policy is always greater than that of the SPIL policy. If the demand rate is random with a different mean than what is expected, the SPIL policy can adapt itself to the new situation and the total costs are not affected much by the changes in the mean demand rate. One should note that if there is only randomness in the demand rate without any change in the mean demand rate, both models seem to be adaptive. We recognize that the total cost of the random demand model converge to the total cost of the fixed demand rate model in the long run as can be seen in $D=\hat{D}=10$ units/day case in the above table.

4. Conclusions

In this study, we try to show that by changing the decision variable in the EOQ policy, the system can be made more adaptive to demand estimation errors. An inventory control policy based on the peak inventory level seems to be more adaptive than the classical EOQ approach. Actually this type of modeling may give way to several further improvements. The efficiency of the system can be improved if this model is embedded in an information system where the mean demand rate is updated after certain number of periods and the control policy is adapted accordingly. Furthermore, one may also need to experiment with the changing production rates or the backorder/stockout cases.

5. References

[1] Erdem, A.S., Doğrusöz, H., "*A Robust Production and Inventory Control Model: An Adaptive Control System*", Boğaziçi University Working Paper, FBE-IE-07/94-08.

[2] Huber, P.J., "*Robust Statistical Procedures*", J.W., Arrowsmith Ltd., England, 1985.

[3] Hüseyin Ö., Sezer M.E., Siljak D.D., "*Robust Decentralized Control Using Output Feedback*", IEEE Proc., Vol. 129, No. 6, 1982.

[4] Ikeda, I., Siljak, D., "*Optimality and Robustness of Linear Quadratic Control for Nonlinear Systems*", Automatica, Vol. 26, No. 3, pp. 490-512, 1990.

[5] Little, J., "*Models and Managers: The Concept of a Decision Calculus*", Management Science, Vol. 16, No. 8, 1970.

Acknowledgement:

This research is partially supported by the research project 02N301 of Boğaziçi University, İstanbul, Turkey.

402

Session 6–3

Software Performance Engineering

Performance Engineering based on UML & SPN's: A software performance tool*

Juan Pablo López-Grao, José Merseguer, Javier Campos

Dpto. de Informática e Ingeniería de Sistemas

Universidad de Zaragoza

Zaragoza, Spain

{jpablo,jmerse,jcampos}@posta.unizar.es

Abstract

The increasing relevance of UML as a semi-formal modelling paradigm has entailed the need for an adjustment of the classical performance evaluation methods within the scope of the new working environment. Under these circumstances, a formal semantics for the UML language and a strong mathematical substratum are required in order to be able to compute performance estimates and validate logical properties in the first stages of the software life-cycle. We believe that stochastic Petri nets are specially suited for this aim. A compositional approach for the translation of several UML diagrams into analyzable Petri net models has therefore been considered in previous papers. Following this approach, we will focus here in the depiction of a model case study from the perspective of our new performance-oriented CASE tool.

1. Introduction

Achieving a balance between the usage of strong, well-known performance formalisms and the usability of the method for non-experienced end-users may be one of the most challenging tasks the software performance engineering (SPE) [18] community has to face nowadays. Performance evaluation often requires wide knowledge in queuing theory [13] and formal performance models. Thus, a successful deployment in industrial terms depends on the degree of integration of this kind of techniques into the regular work of the software analyst or developer.

In line with these considerations, the Unified Modeling Language (UML) [5] has progressively spread as the current universal standard in software modeling. UML is a semi-formal language maintained by the Object Management Group (OMG) [16] consortium and used to specify,

visualize and document artifacts of discrete event systems, being particularly suited for software development environments.

Our proposal is based on taking advantage of UML for SPE purposes. Providing a fully UML-complaint modelling framework ensures an efficient communication between software architects whereas performance issues are integrated in their everyday work in a consistent way. In previous papers [12, 11, 4, 9], this approach has been widely presented. According to that work, the performance evaluation process basically takes three steps: extension of UML diagrams with performance annotations, translation of extended UML diagrams to labelled stochastic Petri net modules [1, 6] and a final composition of the modules into a single model representing the whole system behavior. This model can be used either for validation or performance evaluation means, even though this paper focuses in the last perspective.

Currently, three different classes of UML diagrams have already been studied. All these classes belong to the set of behavioral diagrams of UML: UML statecharts (SCs) were studied in [11] by means of the UML State Machines (SMs) package, UML sequence diagrams (SDs) were discussed in [4] (as well as their relationship with SCs) and UML activity diagrams (ADs) were recently analyzed in [9].

Nevertheless, other kinds of UML diagrams may be taken into consideration in the future. That includes behavioral diagrams (as the Use Case diagram) as well as some structural (as the Class diagram) and implementation diagrams (Deployment and Component diagrams), which will allow us to avoid the infinite resource assumption. Collaboration diagrams may not need further study anyhow, as they are isomorphic to SDs.

In addition, previous work has been developed [12] to illustrate the link between SDs and SCs in the context of a real-world case study. In particular, the software retrieval service in the ANTARCTICA system [12] was profusely discussed and compared with other non-agent-based alternatives thanks to a performance analysis based on our pro-

*This work has been developed within the project P084/2001 of the Gobierno de Aragón and the project UZ00-TEC-03 of the Universidad de Zaragoza.

405

posal.

Our main goal in this paper is to focus in our most recent work, so as to clarify and establish the connection between ADs and the previously studied diagrams through a realistic test problem. Obviously, the whole process will be reflected in this framework.

Furthermore, our new CASE tool prototype will be presented. Its main features will be depicted, as well as the main topics to be considered in future versions. This prototype automatizes the process described below, letting the analyst model performance issues in an intuitive way. That also enables a perfect coordination between the software architect or developer and the performance engineer, establishing well-defined roles. The performance engineer would then be able to perform a profuse analysis based on the system specification without being concerned about details.

This paper is organized as follows: Section 2 recalls the main aspects of the process given in [4, 9]. Section 3 traces the guidelines of the sample case study and applies the concepts stated in the previous section to it. Section 4 presents our CASE tool prototype. Finally, section 5 concludes the paper summarizing its most relevant points besides discussing related and future work.

2. Process

Although the main rules of our SPE process were briefly considered in Section 1, there are a number of points that should be clarified regarding these guidelines. Moreover, we must specify which role is taken by each UML diagram according to the present system description potential. All these issues will be discussed in this section.

As it was previously stated, three steps are taken to obtain directly analyzable models. Firstly, our UML model is (at least) extended with a temporal interpretation of its dynamics, usually based on estimations. In particular, adding performance annotations to UML diagrams lets us define a stochastic interpretation according to their associated semantics. Tagged values will be used to ensure full UML compatibility.

In [9], our proposal for performance annotations in ADs is broadly discussed. Similarly, our performance annotations in SCs and SDs have been studied in previous works, such as the description of the ANTARCTICA Software Retrieval Service [12]. Hence, we will have recourse to the syntax illustrated in those papers.

Secondly, every UML diagram is translated into an analyzable formal model. In particular, we use a specific class of stochastic Petri nets: the labeled Generalized Stochastic Petri Nets (LGSPNs) [6] . LGSPNs are specially suitable for this task, as they allow a compositional (bottom-up) approach to construct a unique analyzable model describing the whole system behaviour.

The reader is assumed to know basic definitions of GSPN and LGSPN systems. Here we follow the notation given in [1, 6]. Note that, with respect to the definition of labeled GSPN system given in [6] both places and transitions can be labeled, moreover, the same label can be assigned to place(s) and to transition(s) since it is not required that L^T and L^P are disjoint. The particular translation rules for SCs, SDs and ADs have already been considered in [4, 11, 9], respectively, and thus they will not be discussed here.

Finally, the whole system is composed from the LGSPNs obtained in the previous step. At our current research status, the system can be described through n SDs, m SCs and o ADs, being $n \in \{0,1\}, m \geq 1, n, m, o \in \mathbf{N}$. That means we have $n + m + o$ nets to be composed. Every diagram belonging to a same diagram class must be composed together (as explained on [4, 11, 9]) to form a unique LGSPN system (either by synchronization or fusion of places).

Hence, we will have (at most) three LGSPNs called $\mathcal{LS}_{sd}$, $\mathcal{LS}_{sc}$, $\mathcal{LS}_{ad}$ (for SDs, SCs and ADs, respectively). The diagram corresponding to ADs will then be composed with that for SCs through superposition of places (i.e., fusion of modules) and elimination of some spare *acknowledge* places. The resulting LGSPN system $\mathcal{LS}_{ad-sc}$ describes the whole system behavior.

As far as the SD is concerned, it lets us consider the behavior of the system under certain restrictions. That is, in terms of the resulting LGSPN, it constrains the firable sequences of $\mathcal{LS}_{ad-sc}$ (composition by synchronization). Paper [11] defines two different approaches (the 'full' case and the 'constrained' case), depending on the interpretation given to the scenario described by the SD.

Concretely, SDs are used to model patterns of interaction between classes within a particular scenario (e.g., in the depiction of a use case). Meanwhile, SCs are used to model the life-cycle for instances of a particular class and ADs to model activities performed in a particular state of a SM (that includes ADs and SCs). This latest task could be accomplished by SCs too, but ADs are rather more suitable for activities that are not dependable of external events. Notice that the system is always modelled at class level. Otherwise, we may require other kinds of formal models, as Stochastic Well-formed Nets (SWN), in order to be able to distinguish between different instances of a class (or classes) [12].

It must be noted that, after composing the entire LGSPN, there exist a lot of unnecessary elements on the net. Thus, it would be useful to apply some proper reduction techniques so as to obtain a more compact model. This matter will be a subject of future research.

3. Case study

In order to shine a light on the process outlined in section 2 a test problem will be analyzed below. The analytical results will be stated in section 4, as well as the facilities our CASE tool provides to obtain them.

The problem consists in modelling a basic mail client. Here we will focus in the first Use Case (UC) showed in figure 1: checking mail from a server using the POP3 [14] protocol.

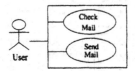

Figure 1. Use Case view of the 'mail client' model

The behavior of the referred client is rather intuitive for this UC. First, the client tries to establish a TCP connection with the server via port 110. If succeeds (reception of a greeting message), both (client and server) begin the authentication (authorization) phase. The client sends the username and his/her password through a USER and PASS command combination. For the sake of simplicity, usage of the APOP command has not been contemplated here.

If the server has answered with a positive status indicator ("+OK") to both messages, then the POP3 session enters the transaction state (phase). Otherwise (e.g., the password doesn't match the one specified for the username), it returns to the beginning of the authorization phase.

In the transaction phase, the client checks for new mail using the LIST command. If there is any, the client obtains every e-mail by means of the RETR and DELE commands. It must be noted that, for simplicity, potential errors have not been considered here; thus, no negative status messages ("-ERR") are modelled.

Once every e-mail has been downloaded, the mail client issues a QUIT command to end the interaction. This provokes the POP3 server to enter the update state and release any resource acquired during the transaction phase. The protocol is ended with a goodbye ("+OK") message.

A SC has been used to depict the mail client behavior (MailClient class) for the referred UC, concretely in figure 2. Notice that the resulting GSPN for the SC has been included right below the SC. Similarly, figure 3 illustrates the server host and user behaviors via two SCs describing the POP3Server class and User actor dynamics. Nonetheless, it should be noted that it is not always possible to apply an stochastic interpretation to the user behavior.

In the original proposal [11] usage of guards in UML transitions was avoided. However, not-event-driven decisions have been considered in this example by modelling guards with its success probability. Concretely, a combination of guards and events has been used in some SC transitions. That probability will be represented in the Petri net using an immediate transition. This has lead to some minor adjustments to the translation rules expressed in [11]. Due

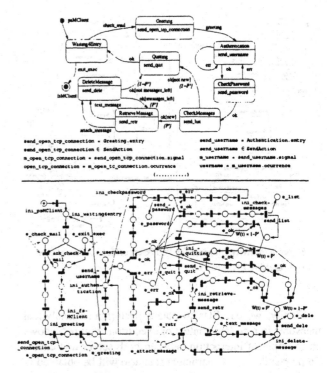

Figure 2. Statechart and resulting LGSPN for the dynamics of the class ClientHost

to the fact that these details do not fit the scope of the paper, they will be commented in future work.

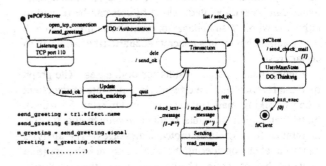

Figure 3. Statecharts for the dynamics of the classes ServerHost and User (actor)

Apart from being necessary to complete system description, the activity Authenticate associated to the state Authorization in the SC for ServerHost (figure 3) is rather relevant to the system performance. Therefore, it is necessary to model the actions performed within. Here we will use an AD (see figure 4), although it may be more useful in cases where there is not such a strong external event dependence (e.g., 'internal' operations). The activity could have been described extending the SC but, in general, ADs provide some additional expresiveness [9] for certain tasks.

407

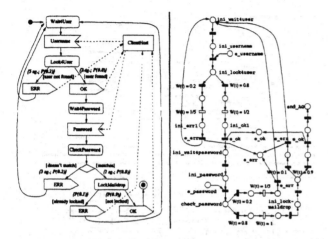

Figure 4. Activity Diagram for POP3ServerHost::Authenticate and resulting LGSPN

Finally, we use SDs to obtain performance analytical measures in a certain context of execution. Figure 5 shows an example of interaction between both server and client. Some results for this particular scenario will be obtained in section 4.

4. Final performance model & analysis

Once the final LGSPN models are obtained (following the composition rules given in [9, 11]) performance estimates can be extrapolated. These figures can be related to either the whole system behavior (somehow unrestricted) or the system behavior in a concrete scenario (thus adjusted to certain restrictions).

Figure 6 shows some results for both cases. The graph on the left represents the effective transfer rate of the client when checking mail (maximum transfer rate: 56 Kbps). Note that higher amounts of data minimize the relative amount of time spent by protocol messages. The analysis has been taken considering the whole system behavior (that is, using the net obtained by composition of the ones corresponding to the SCs and the AD).

Meanwhile, the graph on the right represents the time cost of executing the interaction illustrated in figure 5 in function of different attach file sizes and maximum network speeds. The analysis has been taken using the SD to construct the net for the constrained case [9, 11]. In general, SDs can be extremely useful to check the behaviour of the system for a particular use case. Moreover, analysts may use them to model test conditions in an easy way.

In section 1, our proposal for the establishment of a UML-complaint performance modelling framework was pointed out. The advantages of this approach have been previously discussed in this paper, and they are especially

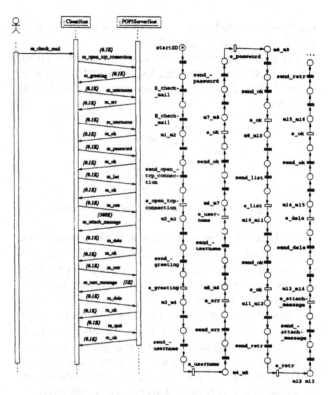

Figure 5. Sequence Diagram describing scenario, and corresponding LGSPN

strong if the process itself is automatizable. To fulfill this objective, a CASE tool prototype based in our own process has been developed.

Some features of this CASE tool (as the possibility to model and translate SDs and SCs) are currently in development phase. However, it is already possible to model ADs (full syntax support) and translate them into GSPNs, as according to [9]. Moreover, importation of models in XMI format is also being implemented. This enables the usage of the tool as a performance analysis front-end for other CASE tools or environments, such as Rational Rose® [17].

Furthermore, tool and files are fully project-oriented (in the sense that every UML element or diagram belongs to a project). This facilitates the construction (and further trans-

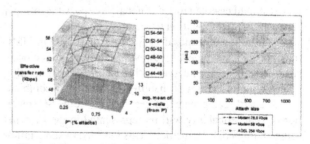

Figure 6. Some analytical results for the presented case study

lation) of complex UML models. The tool also performs basic checking of the diagrams syntax (based on the current UML specification [5]) and provides an intuitive and highly flexible GUI.

The GSPNs generated by the tool are saved in Great-SPN [7] format. These nets are subsequently processed in the referred tool in order to obtain analytical results. Figure 7 shows a snapshot of our tool (the traditional *coffeepot* sample AD, which appears in the UML specification [5], with performance annotations) and its resulting translation in GreatSPN, as it was obtained originally. Note that an special effort has been made to avoid superposition of places and transitions in the resulting nets. Support for other GSPN tools may be part of future work.

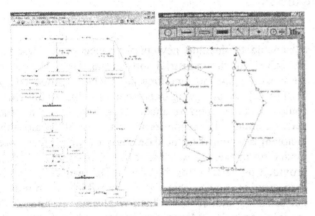

Figure 7. Tool - Extended coffeepot example and results in GreatSPN

5. Concluding remarks

In the present paper, a sample test problem has been studied so as to take a longer view on our UML-based SPE process. Moreover, our new CASE tool prototype has been presented, which supports and automatizes this process. The approach lets the software architect model the system along with performance issues in an easy, consistent fashion whereas performance models can be automatically obtained.

Concerning related work, we are unable to compare our tool due to the fact that, as far as we know, there exist four SPE tools [3, 2, 10, 15] based on UML and none of them uses stochastic Petri nets as performance model. On the other hand, we do not consider DSPNExpress2000 [8] a really UML-based SPE tool as it seems that only rather simple SCs can be used to model the system. Meanwhile, in SimML [3], simulation queuing networks (QN) models [13] for SPE are obtained from UML class diagram and SDs, while in the PERMABASE project [2] models for simulation are obtained from UML SDs and class and deploy-

ment diagrams. Finally, PROGRES [15] is a graph rewriting tool that captures XMI descriptions of UML models (using ADs, collaboration and deployment diagrams) and translates them into layered QNs.

References

[1] M. Ajmone Marsan, G. Balbo, G. Conte, S. Donatelli, and G. Franceschinis. *Modelling with Generalized Stochastic Petri Nets.* John Wiley Series in Parallel Computing, 1995.

[2] D. Akehurst, G. Waters, P. Utton, and G. Martin. Predictive Performance Analysis for Distributed Systems - PERMABASE position. In *Workshop on Software Performance Prediction*, Heriot-Watt University, November 1999.

[3] L. Arief and N. Speirs. A UML tool for an automatic generation of simulation programs. In *2nd International Workshop on Software and Performance*, pp. 71–76, Ottawa, September 2000. ACM.

[4] S. Bernardi, S. Donatelli, and J. Merseguer. From UML sequence diagrams and statecharts to analysable Petri net models. In *3rd International Workshop on Software and Performance*, Rome, July 2002. ACM. To appear.

[5] G. Booch, I. Jacobson, and J. Rumbaugh. OMG Unified Modeling Language specification, v. 1.4, September 2001.

[6] S. Donatelli and G. Franceschinis. PSR Methodology: integrating hardware and software models. In *LNCS 1091*, pp. 133–152. Springer-Verlag, June 1996.

[7] The GreatSPN tool. http://www.di.unito.it/˜greatspn.

[8] C. Lindemann, A. Thummler, A. Klemm, M. Lohmann, and O. Waldhorst. Quantitative system evaluation with DSPNexpress 2000. In *2nd International Workshop on Software and Performance*, pp. 12–17, Ottawa, September 2000. ACM.

[9] J. P. López-Grao, J. Merseguer, and J. Campos. From UML activity diagrams to stochastic PNs: Application to software performance analysis. Technical report, April 2002.

[10] J. Medina, M. González, and J. M. Drake. MAST-UML: Visual modeling and analysis suite for real-time applications with UML. http://mast.unican.es/umlmast/.

[11] J. Merseguer, S. Bernardi, J. Campos, and S. Donatelli. A compositional semantics for UML state machines aimed at performance evaluation. In *6th International Workshop on Discrete Event Systems*, October 2002. To appear.

[12] J. Merseguer, J. Campos, and E. Mena. Performance evaluation for the design of agent-based systems: A Petri net approach. In M. Pezzé and S. M. Shatz, editors, *Proceedings of the Workshop on Software Engineering and PNs*, pp. 1–20, Aarhus, June 2000.

[13] M. Molloy. *Fundamentals of Performance Modelling.* Macmillan, 1989.

[14] J. Myers and M. Rose. RFC 1725: Post Office Protocol - version 3, November 1994.

[15] D. C. Petriu and H. Shen. Applying the UML performance profile: Graph grammar based derivation of LQN models from UML specifications. In *LNCS 2324*, pp. 159–177. Springer-Verlag, 2002.

[16] Object Management Group. http://www.omg.org.

[17] Rational Software Corporation. http://www.rational.com.

[18] C. U. Smith. *Performance Engineering of Software Systems.* Addison–Wesley, 1990.

Extending MASCOT to a Component-based Software Performance Engineering Methodology

Onofre Munar, Carlos Juiz and Ramon Puigjaner
Department of Mathematics and Computer Science,
Universitat de les Illes Balears,
Spain
{cjuiz, putxi}@uib.es

Abstract

The usual approach to most large software design methodologies is to carry out a modular decomposition of the system, which divides the future system into components. However, performance would be normally considered afterwards, even it is an important aspect of any model component-based development. MASCOT provides a systematic component-based design method for real-time systems that does not also provide performance facilities. This paper presents the case study of the performance modelling of the *Track Management Sub-System* (TMS), provided by MBDA for the SUCSEDE project. This design example illustrates the efforts addressed to extend MASCOT to a component-based software performance engineering methodology based on interaction protocols.

1. Introduction

High quality systems must be useful, reliable, flexible, affordable and available. However, these desirable objectives partially fail because performance attributes not covered from software design. On the other hand, one of the usual approaches to most large software designs is to carry out a modular decomposition of the system, which divides the system into components. Then, each component itself is broken down into processes, and the function and interfaces among them are closely defined. However, performance would be normally considered afterwards. Successful industrial practices on system design seem to need performance annotations to be improved. One of them is MASCOT (*Modular Approach to Software Construction Operation and Test*), which provides a systematic design method for real-time systems [1]. This methodology is used for MBDA *Missile Systems* (formerly known as *Matra Bae Dynamics*) to construct complex software systems. Therefore, it seems

reasonable to develop new performance extensions for MASCOT for the industrial software artifacts. Based on the newest real-time functional architecture proposed by MBDA [2], we are going to present how this architecture could include performance measurements in the corresponding interaction protocols. We illustrate this incipient research with the case study of the performance modelling of the *Track Management Sub-System* (TMS), provided by MBDA for the SUCSEDE project [3]. This case study proves that it is possible to build a performance model of a hard real-time system with random arrivals. Moreover, it also shows how to construct a component-based performance model through an object-oriented manner. This suggests that it is possible to translate an extended MASCOT (annotated) functional model into an executable and simulation performance model.

2. MASCOT

MASCOT software structure is based on independent parallel activities that communicate with one another through *Intercommunication Data Areas* (known as IDAs). IDAs conventionally fall into two broad classes: *channels*, which are used to pass data messages between producer activities on one side to consumer activities on the other, and *pools* which are used to hold refreshed data. A network of activities interconnected through IDAs and shown on an *Activity-Channel-Pool* (ACP) diagram represents the overall structure of a software design. Using *windows* and *ports*, a simple mechanism to specify contracts and interfaces in component-oriented designs carries out connection between MASCOT components. Functionally related activities and IDAs may be grouped into subsystems. ACP diagrams can show the relationship between software design elements and hardware devices of particular importance in embedded system design.

MASCOT introduces the notion of templates and instances for all of its design components. In this sense, templates can be seen as a highly practical form of *Object-Oriented Design* (OOD). Figure 1 shows an example of a MASCOT-based system design (example_sys) which interacts with three external data providers (dev1, dev2, and dev3). The system is made up of three subsystems (s1, s2 and s3 which are instances of templates subsys_1, subsys_2, and subsys_3) which exchange data through the channel si1 and the pool si2.

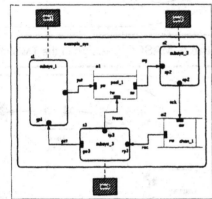

Figure 1. MASCOT Activity Channel Pool Diagram

3. Architecture based on Interaction Protocols

Even though MASCOT provides basic IDAs, these components may result incomplete in order to characterize other ways of communication. Therefore the first step on extending MASCOT to a performance engineering design method was defining an interaction protocol taxonomy. The interaction protocols derive from the explicit representation of intermediate data and from the realization that such data can only be destructively or non-destructively written or read. These temporal effects are the dynamics of the interaction form; in fact, they show the relation between temporal effects and shared data concepts, and that's the interest for their performance modelling and engineering of a software system. The basic interaction protocols are four: *pool*, *signal*, *channel* and *constant*. Thus, these components constitute a superset of the IDAs of the classical MASCOT methodology. A *pool* allows reference data to be passed from one process to another. A *signal* allows event data to be passed from one process to another. A *channel* allows message data to be passed from one process to another. And finally, a *constant* can be regarded as a configuration datum.

3.1. Protocol Extensions
MBDA proposes only two ways in which the four basic protocols are extended: the number of intermediate items (capacity) and the void values (null). The capacity

constraint means varying the buffering. Whatever the degree of buffering, items are always read in the order they are written, so items are queued. This is an important feature from the performance analyst viewpoint. However, if the value of the item can be explicitly identified as being void (stimulus function) or not, has no interest for the performance analysis. That is, although the void value protocols have particular functional significance, they need not be given any special treatment; their timing and synchronization properties can be taken to be identical to their non-void counterparts. Thus, we will only mention the void value protocols when the non-void ones are going to be explained.

At this point, it is convenient to introduce the notion of a protocol family. Every basic protocol defines a protocol family. Thus the *channel* family is regarded as all the protocols derived from the *channel* (including the void extensions) e.g.: *rendezvous, bounded buffer, directional handshake, dataless channel* and *bounded stimulus buffer*. Likewise the *signal* family comprises protocols derived from the *signal*: *flash data, overwriting buffer, prod, stimulus* and *overwriting stimulus buffer*. Neither of the two extensions has any meaning when applied to the *pool* or the *constant* because both have the non-destructive reading property so items cannot be removed to expose the items behind. Also the concept of an unconsumable void has no useful purpose. In spite of this fact, we are going to consider these basic protocols as one-member families. The reason of this consideration is the new extensions not included yet. Simpson (MBDA) proposed this functional taxonomy of interaction protocols as it is shown in figure 2.

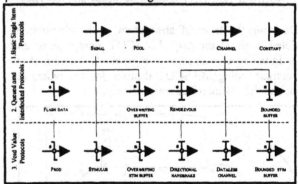

Figure 2. Interaction protocol taxonomy by MBDA

Even the importance of the capacity extension, not only the buffering (or void values) can be considered as the unique feature to build software components. We define new interaction protocols as variants of the members of a protocol family taking into account other features as item classification, scheduling (priority) and many others [4].

4. Case Study: TMS

This case study consists on a *Track Management Sub-System* (TMS). This probabilistic hard real-time system analyses the incoming data received on radar, process the data with other that the user includes and finally, sends the response to the user again. Therefore, the TMS is composed by the radar, the I/O device and the core subsystem. The radar obtains independently the environment information required by the core subsystem and also reacts to commands in order to correct the antenna angle. The I/O device communicates the core subsystem and the user. Therefore, the user asks to and receives information from the system through the I/O device. The core subsystem manages a track, informs to the user about the antenna orientation. In addition, when the user sends commands, the core get the data received from the radar, process them and answers properly though the I/O device.

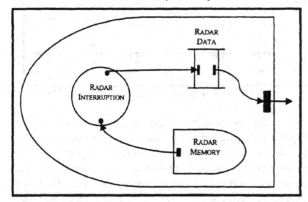

Figure 3. MASCOT diagram representing the TMS

Downing the level of abstraction, each subsystem is modeled with elementary MASCOT components and other lower level subsystems. Figures, 4, 5 and 6 show the corresponding MASCOT designs for the radar, the clock and the I/O interface, respectively.

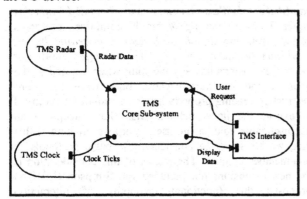

Figure 4. MASCOT design of the TMS radar

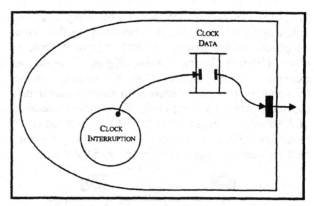

Figure 5. MASCOT design of the TMS clock

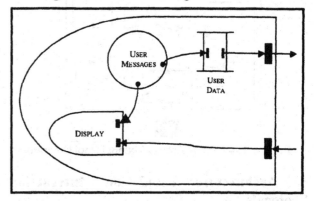

Figure 6. MASCOT design of the TMS I/O interface

The core subsystem stores the incoming data from other subsystems, process this information and responses to the user. Figure 7 shows the four activities that are composing the core subsystem: the radar manager, the antenna manager, the track manager and the display manager. These activities are interacting each other through several channels and one pool.

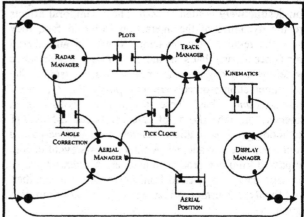

Figure 7. MASCOT design the TMS core

The execution of the radar manager starts with the reception of a message on its channel. This message is processed and analyzed. The nature of the message could be either about the environment or about the antenna. Therefore, the subsequent information is sent to the corresponding managers via their channels. This process is repeated for every message.

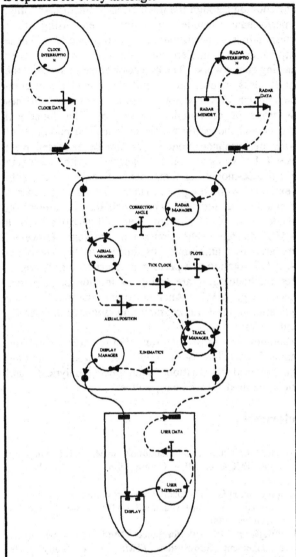

Figure 8. Extended MASCOT design of the core

The track manager activity starts with an event in the tick-clock channel. The user asks information to the system via the corresponding channel in the I/O interface subsystem. The messages providing from the radar manager via the plots channel. Once this information is processed, the antenna position is read from the corresponding pool. Finally, the result of the track manager activity is sent to the display manager via the kinematics tactic channel. This process is repeated continuously. The display manager activity acts with the messages that are coming from the kinematics tactic channel. The messages are transmitted directly to the I/O interface subsystem. The angle correction channel is representing the interaction between the radar manager activity and the antenna manager activity. In a similar manner are acting the plots channel and the kinematics channel. The position antenna pool is representing data storage. The data could be modified by the antenna manager activity and read by the track manager activity. Order of arrival to the pool is essential to guarantee consistence of the data. In order to construct a performance model from the functional model devised above through an interaction protocol taxonomy and the object-oriented performance library, the input data of the model should be known. This input data is comprised by the workload, the capacity of the channels and pools and the read/write relationship interaction. In fact, these are the data that relates the functional and the performance models. The utilization of a protocol interaction taxonomy and its directly associated object-oriented library eases the selection of the right kind of this relationship among activities in comparison with an ad hoc performance model construction. In addition, the taxonomy provides different interaction phenomena to select by the analyst in order to find the convenient alternative of system design. The application of the selected interaction protocols to the initial design results on the extended MASCOT diagram of figure 8. The analyst may ignore the protocol behaviour and only use the components in the right way. Basically, the analyst uses the protocol interaction components for connecting different activities (processes) and submits them to the time and capacity constraints imposed by the designer. Therefore, the resulting performance model will be solved with the queueing network formalism via discrete-event simulation. There are several steps to build the performance model from the extended MASCOT functional model. Every activity in the functional model is converted into two queues. One queue represents the activity process; i.e. the server of this queue represents the time actions of the activity (process queue). Another queue represents the buffering process, i.e. the memory that process uses for the activity actions (memory queue).

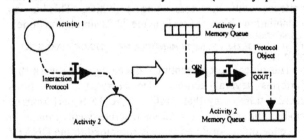

Figure 9. Performance interaction protocols

Every interaction protocol in the functional model is converted into a performance component as it is shown in figure 9. Each performance component encapsulates a queueing network that represents the protocol interaction.

It's necessary to employ auxiliary queues to join the interaction protocols to the activities [5], in this case those are memory queues.

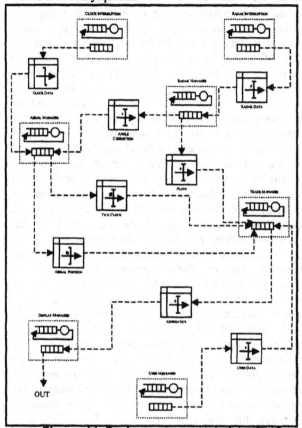

Figure 11. Performance model of the TMS

The specific implementation language to simulate the performance model should include an object library with the interaction protocol taxonomy. In this way, any component will be simply used through instantiation in the specific simulation program code. Each instantiation will differ in their parameters that are representing the time and capacity constraints of the particular interaction protocol with the connecting activities. This is an instantiation object example in the TMS simulation code:

```
BOUNDEDBUFFER
(4,0.1,0.1,MEM_RADAR_MANAGER,MEM_TRACK_MANAGER)
PLOTS;
```

This object is representing a queueing subnetwork that performs several actions. The corresponding actions cause a time delay that conforms the TMS performance model. The model is solved via discrete-event simulation since the object-oriented code is submitted to the QNAP2 solver [6].

5. Conclusions and Open Problems

This paper has presented the initial research on extending MASCOT methodology to be used also a

software performance-engineering methodology. The expected result of this extension has been illustrated through the case study of the TMS design. From the functional model of the extended MASCOT representation through the interaction protocol taxonomy, a performance model is constructed using their corresponding performance components. These components are implemented through object-oriented queueing subnetworks. The object-oriented code eases the analyst tasks in order to submit the model to different time and capacity constraints. This process establishes new ways of communication between the functional designer and the performance analyst. The paradigm of having performance models that can be extracted from MASCOT designs and merged with existing performance-modelling components give the capability to be extended with new performance models. This paper is presented as an incipient workbench that transforms an extended MASCOT design with annotations into a QNAP2 discrete-event simulation program. However, there are other ambitious possibilities as to extend the MASCOT notation to a performance-oriented notation, as other methodologies are trying to include performance aspects, e.g. UML. Another open question is the application of the Java programming language in discrete-event simulation. This language offers several advantages, the most important being thread handling, graphical user interfaces (GUI), and web computing. Also, hybrid evaluation strategies (analytical and simulation models) are being studied.

References

[1] Bate, G., The Official Handbook of MASCOT, Suppliers Joint IECCA & MUF Comm., Great Malvern, Worcs., 1987

[2] Simpson, H.G., "Protocols for Process Interaction, Part 1 – Rationale and Specification", Matra Bae Dynamics, December 2000

[3] Puigjaner, R. "Performance Model of the Track Management Sub-System (TMS) Case Study", The SUCSEDE project, UIB038-1.0, int. doc.

[4] Juiz, C., Puigjaner, R. and K. Jackson, "Performance Modeling of Interaction Protocols", in *Performance Engineering*, Dumke, R. et al. (eds.), LNCS 2047, Springer-Verlag, 2001, pp. 300-316

[5] Savino-Vázquez, N. and R. Puigjaner, "A Component Model for Object-Oriented Queuing Networks and its Integration in a Design Technique for Performance Models". *Proceedings Symposium on Performance Evaluation of Computer and Telecommunication Systems*, SPECTS'01, SCS, July 2001, pp. 364-371

[6] Potier, D. and M. Veran, M., "QNAP2: A portable Environment for Queuing System Modelling", In Proceedings. of the First International Conference on Modelling Techniques and Tools for Performance Analysis, 1984, (May), pp. 25-63

Qualitative and Quantitative Evaluation using Process Algebra

Abdelmalek Benzekri
Institut de Recherche en Informatique de Toulouse,
Université Paul Sabatier,
Toulouse, France
benzekri@irit.fr

Abstract

Performance evaluation should be dealt with early in the development life-cycle of distributed systems to avoid costly redesigns. When integrated with traditional qualitative methods it improves the development productivity. But engineers are often faced to learn skills about different methods and the links between them lack a formal semantic. In this paper, we present a stochastic process algebra which provides a whole integrated formalism to tackle both qualitative and quantitative properties of systems under design.

1. Introduction

Aware of the increasing use of formal description languages for the development of distributed systems, we studied their application in the field of Telecommunication systems. Functiunal requirements or at least behavioural requirements are well covered by the vast majority of formal techniques and so independently of the underlying verification techniques.

Amongst specification languages dedicated to the analysis of communication protocols, none was proposing a quantitative evaluation in the early 90s. Two approaches were developed. The first consisted to extend the formalism with timing concerns [1][2]. The second recommended the integration of adequate formalisms to tackle both functiunal and performance requirements [3][4].

In 1991, within the Esprit II COMPLEMENT n°5409 project, we proposed an integrated solution as the formal languages of interest were international standards and the timing extension work is still ongoing today [5]. In order to enhance the development of real-time systems, we studied how to augment LOTOS with performance annotations [6]. LOTOS, a process algebra language based, is considered powerful thanks to the various description styles it offers allowing the full coverage of the development life-cycle. The related verification techniques are funded on the elaboration of a model finite in general (action tree) reprenting all the behaviours of the modelled system.

The analysis of qualitative properties is conducted by an exhaustive course of the "model" – model checking. The quantitative evaluation has been made possible thanks to the annotation of the systems descriptions with time and propability decorations. A prototype of a QNAP2 model generator allowed to obtain QNAP2 queueing networks performance models directly from annotated LOTOS designs [7]. Dependability and performance estimates such as the frequency of anomalous behaviour, or correct and timely packet delivery guaranteed in at least 95% of all cases, were provided to the designer by the execution of the QNAP2 models – only by simulation.

But the formal semantics chain was broken. Ten years after, meanwhile the standardisation of an extension formalism is still ongoing, another sound idea was proposed [8]. It consists in the application of model specification and analysis techniques from concurrency theory to performance evaluation. Continuous-time Markov chains (CTMCs) are widely used in practice to determine system performance and reliability properties. The specification of CTMCs is supported by a stochastic process algebra, while the quantitative analysis of these models is tackled by the means of model checking.

2. Continuous-time Markov chains (CTMCs)

CTMCs are a widely used performance evaluation model. They can be viewed as transition systems, where the transition labels – rates of exponential distributions – indicate the speed of the system evolving from one state to another. CTMCs had been extensively used by specification techniques like queueing networks or stochastic Petri nets. Both steady-state and transient-state probabilities computations allow for typical performance measures analysis.

The theory of CTMC with finite states and the performance measures that can be obtained are recalled hereafter [9].

Let S be a finite state set. Let the transition rate from state i to state j be q_{ij} and $q_{ii}=-\sum_{i\neq j} q_{ij}$. The resulting matrix $Q=[q_{ij}]_{i,j\in S}$ is called the infinitesimal generator and it is possible to compute the steady state probability distribution solving the usual matrix equation $\pi.Q=0$ with the additional constraint $\sum_{i\in S} \pi_i=1$.

From the steady state distribution π, it is possible to obtain quantitative estimates of the behaviour of the system in the long run. Steady-state do suffice for the evaluation of the performance of most systems. But when dealing with reliability and availability properties, failure-prone systems are of no interest in steady-state, since they are completely failed. So the transient behaviour is of interest.

We assume as usual that the transition probabilities are stationary, i.e., $P_{ij}(t)=\Pr\{X_{t+s}=j|X_s=i\}$.

The Markovian property asserts that $P_{ij}(t)$ satisfies:

(a) $P_{ij}(t)\geq 0$,

(b) $\sum_{j=1,|S|} P_{ij}(t)=1$ $i,j\in S$

(c) $P_{ik}(s+t)=\sum_{j=0,|S|} P_{ij}(s) P_{jk}(t)$ $t,s\geq 0$
(Chapman-Kolmogorov relation)

(d) Given the postulat that: $\lim_{t\to 0+} P_{ij}(t)=\begin{cases}1, & i=j\\ 0, & i\neq j\end{cases}$

If $\pi(t)$ denotes the matrix $\|P_{ij}(t)\|_{i,j=0,|S|}$, then the property (c) can be written compactly in matrix notation as

(e) $\pi(t+s)=\pi(t).\pi(s)$ $t,s\geq 0$

Property (d) asserts that $\pi(t)$ is continuous at t=0 since $\pi(0)=I$ (identity matrix).

As it is proven (differentiability properties of continuous Markov chains) that $\lim_{h\to 0+} [\pi(h)-I]/h=Q$

With the aid of this formula and referring to (e), we obtain: $\pi'(t)=\pi(t).Q$. The solution to this equation under the initial condition $\pi(0)=I$ by the standard methods of systems of ordinary differential equations to yield the formula: $\pi(t)=e^{Qt}=I+\sum_{n=1,\infty} Q^n t^n/n!$

In practical terms we determine the eigenvalues $\lambda_0, \lambda_1,\ldots, \lambda_{|S|}$ of Q and a complete system of associated right eigenvectors $u^{(0)},u^{(1)},\ldots,u^{(|S|)}$ when possible. Then we have the represetation $\pi(t)=U.\Lambda(t).U^{-1}$,

Where U is the matrix whose column vectors are, respectively, $u^{(0)},u^{(1)},\ldots,u^{(|S|)}$ and $\Lambda(t)$ is the diagonal matrix $\| e^{\lambda_i t}\|_{i=0,|S|}$.

To illustrate the use of CTMCs [10], we will consider the M|M|1|K queue. A single server accepts requests to be processed in first-come-first-served discipline. The processing time is assumed to be exponentially distributed with rate μ and the interaarival times are exponentially distributed with rate λ. The state of the server is, due to the involved memoryless distributions, completely given by the number of requests in the server. If we consider that the server can hold at most K requests, (including the one actually being processed), the state of the server is governed by a CTMC.

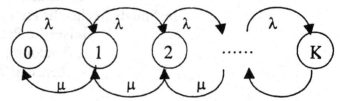

By the fact that the CTMC has a structure in which only left and right "neighbouring" states can be reached, this type of CTMC is called birth-death process. The $(K+1)\times(K+1)$ generator matrix for the CTMC is given as follows:

$$Q=\begin{pmatrix} -\lambda & \lambda & 0 & \ldots\ldots \\ \mu & -(\lambda+\mu) & \lambda & 0 & \ldots \\ 0 & 0 & \ldots\ldots & 0 & \mu & -\mu \end{pmatrix}$$

Exploiting the birth-death structure of the CTMC, we can solve the equation $\pi.Q=0$ at the steady-state explicitly to reveal that $\pi_i=\pi_0.\rho^i$, $i=1,\ldots,K$ and $\pi_0=1-\rho/1-\rho^{K+1}$.

Here $\rho=\lambda/\mu$ is the ratio of the arrival rate and the service rate, which is also called the traffic intensity or the utilisation. Furthermore, the transient probabilities can only be obtained nemerically.

3. Process algebra

Process algebras [11] have been introduced within the concurrency theory framework such as CCS or CSP. They have a complete and formal definition, and offer means to specify the behaviour of systems in a structured way simplifying the analysis. The central concept is the process concept. A process performs internal actions and is able to interact with other processes which form its environment.

Complex interactions between processes are built up out of elementary units of synchronisation which are atomic actions, occuring instantaneously, without consuming time.

An elegant, tractable and rich set of operators allows the composition of processes out of smaller ones, reducing the internal complexity and leading to a manageable modelling of complex systems.

Let a be an observable action, I the unobservable action, A a set of synchronisation actions and B and C be behaviors. Sequential behaviours can be expressed thanks to the inaction –stop–, action-prefix –a;B or i;B– and choice –B+C or $\sum_i B_i$– operators. Parallelism and synchronisation operators –B||$_A$C or B|[A]|C– offer means to composition with the interleaving semantics – i.e. transforming parrallelism into choices. The hiding operator - B\A or hide A in B– allows not only abstraction to avoid from unnecessary details, but reinforces the non-determinism.

The operational semantics provides a means to systematically derive the actions that a process may perform from the structure of the expression itself. Labelled transition systems –also called action trees – are hence built and can be analysed. The analysis may consist in demonstrating that a more detailed description is an implementation of an abstract one. Theories of equivalence – observational, bisimulation…– turned out to be very useful, allowing one not only to prove that an implementation is correct with respect to a given specification but also to replace complex subsystems wit simpler, equivalent ones, within a large system, thus simplifying the analysis of the latter. Equivalences induce algebraic laws such as:

B+C=C+B   a;i;B=a;B
(B+C)+D=(B+C)+D   B+i;B=i;B
B+stop=B   a;(B+i;C)+a;C=a;(B+i;C)
B+B=B
B||$_A$C = C||$_A$B
(B||$_A$C) ||$_A$D = B||$_A$(C||$_A$D)

4. Stochastic Process algebra

Stochastic process algebra are extensions of process algebras in which behaviours may be delayed according to a negative exponential distribution. Different approaches exist [12] and we will present results achieved so far in Markov chains (MC) and interactive Markov chains (IMC) algebras [8]. The central idea is to link labelled transition systems to CTMCs formally.

Process algebraic settings provides a specification formalism for describing CTMCs in an unambiguous and modular way. The equivalence theory has been proven to minimise CTMCs – lumpability – in an efficient and automated way. Large CTMCs performance evaluation is then enhanced, a result that was for a long time based on modeller's ingenuity and experience.

Behaviours are decorated with distribution functions: $(\lambda).B$ denotes a process that evolves into B within t time units according to an exponential distribution of rate λ. In other words it behaves like B after a certain delay D that is determined by Prob(D≤t)=1-e$^{-\lambda t}$ for positive t. This stands for introducing a delay like operator which syntax can be $(\lambda);B$.

The term $\sum_{i \in I}(\lambda_i).B_i$ offers a timed probabilistic choice among processes B_i. As in CTMC, a race is assumed between competing delays. Intuitively, a behaviour Bj is selected with probability $\lambda_j/\sum_{i \in I}\lambda_i$ and the time until this happens is exponentially distributed with rate $\sum_{i \in I}\lambda_i$.

An M/M/1/c queue behaviour can then be expressed with this formalim in the following terms. Given exponential distributions, say λ for the arrival rate and μ for the service rate, we have:

Process MM1KQueue(i):=
  [i<K]-> (λ) ; MM1KQueue(i+1)
  + [i>0] -> (μ) ; MM1KQueue(i-1)
endproc

The labelled transition system is a Continuous time Markov chain and the various classical measures of performance can be obtained as the mean number of customers waiting in the queue, the mean time a customer has to wait, the number of customers lost…

The interleaving operator (parallel composition of independent behaviours) can easily be stated. $(\lambda).B$ ||| $(\mu).C$ can evolve while either B evolves or C independently from each other and in parallel. If ever the delay of process B finishes first with rate λ, the remaining delay of process C is still determined by the exponential distribution with rate μ. This interleaving semantic allows for the expansion law:

$\sum(\lambda_i).B_i$ ||| $\sum(\mu_j).C_j$ =
  $\sum(\lambda_i).(\sum(\mu_j).(B_i|||C_j) + \sum(\mu_j).(\sum(\lambda_i).(B_i|||C_j))$

As in this extension formalism actions are not decorated, that means no rule was given for the synchronisation operator. Issues to describe adequatly how two different chains can interact are raised . Delays may be associated to actions in the sense that after a delay governed by an exponential distribution the action occurs. Another approach considering delays as orthogonal entities is preferred within the IMC framework.

The standard action prefix known from process algebra is added to CTMC algebra, to complement the existing delay prefix $(\lambda).B$ with separate means to specify actions.

Algebraic laws for the IMC algebra are given below:

a;B + a;B = a;B   (λ);i;B =(λ);B
(λ);B + (μ);B=($\lambda+\mu$);B   i;B+(λ);C=i;B

The last equation stands for the maximal progress assumption which ensures that internal (or hidden) events, that is those events that can no longer be inflenced by the environment, occur "as soon as possible" before the passage of time.

A specification of a system involving three interacting processes – the incoming customers with arrival rate λ, the server process serving the customers with rate μ, and the queue with capacity limited to 3 customers - using the whole set of operators defined in the IMC framework is given below [12].

hide req,rsp in customer[req] \[req]\ queue[req,rsp](0)
                  \[rsp]\ server[rsp]
where
process   customer[in]:=(λ);in;customer[in]   endproc
Process Queue[in,out](i):=
[i<K]-> in ; Queue(i+1)
+ [i>0] -> out ; Queue(i-1)
endproc
process server[out]:=out; (μ);server[out] endproc

The CTMC that can be automatically derived from the algebraic laws is:

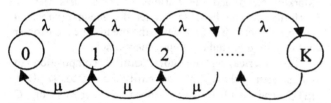

5. Research perspectives

This paper has presented the application of theoretical foundations on how process algebras can be exploited for performance and dependability modelling and analysis.

The stochastic process algebra provides a sound formalism to describe systems in a precise and modular way. A CTMC is hence generated. To evaluate the performance estimates, ongoing works tackle the use of temporal logic to express the constraints on such measures as well as model-checking techniques benefits for an automated analysis of these constraints.

Developers will be provided with a formalism with a powerful power of expressiveness and analysis, which will allow them tackle in an integrated manner both qualitative and quantitative properties of reactive systems.

References

[1] Oxford University Timed CSP Group, Timed CSP : Theory and Practice. Programming Research Group, Oxford University Computing Lab, 11 Keble Road, Oxford OX1 3QD. Groupe animé par S.R. Blamey, J. Davies, D.M. Jackcon, A. Kay, M.W. Mislove, G.M. & J.N. Reed, A.W. Roscoe, B. Scattergood, S.A. Schneider, R. Stamper, S. Superville et A. Wallace.

[2] ISO, Enhancements to LOTOS, ISO/IEC JTC 1/SC21/WG7, Project WI 1.21.20.2.3 Working draft, January 1997. Travaux menés par les équipes de Juan Quemada, Guy Leduc, Allan Jeffrey, Hubert Garavel, Charles Pecheur, Mihaela Sighiream, Giovani Lucero.

[3] P. Dembinski, Queuing network model for Estelle. In Proceedings of Forte'92, Lannion, Fr, Oct. 1992.

[4] Alberto Valderruten Vidal. Modélisation des Performances et Développement de Systèmes Informatiques : une étude d'intégration. Thèse d'Université, IRIT/SIERA, UMR CNRS 5505, Université Paul Sabatier, Toulouse, 2 Novembre 1993.

[5] ISO, Information Processing Systems – Open Distributed Processing – ELOTOS – Extended LOTOS – Committee Draft, International Organisation for Standardisation, Geneva, Switzerland, May 1998 ftp://ftp.dit.upm.es/pub/lotos/elotos/Working.Docs/

[6] A. Valderruten Vidal, O. Hjiej, A. Benzekri, D. Gazal. " *Deriving Queueing Networks Performance Models from Annotated LOTOS Specifications* ", 6th Int. Conf. On Modelling Techniques and Tools for Performance Evaluation, Edinburgh University Press, August 93, pp. 120-130.

[7] O.Hjiej, A. Benzekri, A. Valderruten Vidal. " *From Annotated LOTOS Specifications To Queueing Networks : Performance Models Derivation* ". Int. Conf. On Decentralized and Distributed Systems, ICDDS93, Palma de Mallorca, september 93.

[8] H. Hermanns, J-P. Katoen, "Performance Evaluation := (Process Algebra + Model Checking) × Markov Chains" – Invited paper in Proc. CONCUR 2001, Springer LNCS 2165, pp; 59-81, 2001.

[9] S. Karlin, "A first course in stochastic processes",Academic Press – Fifth Pinting, 1972 – ISBN 0-12-398550-1.

[10] B. Haverkort, " Markovian Models for Performance and Dependability Evaluation", Springer LNCS 2090, 2001

[11] T. Bolognesi, E. Brinksma, "Introduction to the ISO Specification Language LOTOS", Computer Networks and ISDN Systems 14 (1987) 25-59, Elsevier Science Publishers B.V. (North Holland).

[12] E. Brinksma, H. Hermanns, "Stochastic Process Algebra: linking process description with performance", Tutorial presented at FORTE/PSTV 1999, Beijing, China, October 5. http://wwwhome.cs.utwente.nl/~brinksma/FORTEPSTV99/

Modeling nodes of communication networks at the bit and packet levels

Gerardo RUBINO

Irisa / Inria / EnstB

Irisa

Campus de Beaulieu

35042 Rennes Cedex, France

rubino@irisa.fr

Abstract

When analyzing the behavior of a node in a packet switching network using a queuing model in the standard way, we can commit an error since we usually don't take into account the way memory is handled. We illustrate this through some analytical and numerical results in specific simple cases. As a side-effect of this work, we generalize the concept of the power of a queue, given by L. Kleinrock, to queuing networks.

1 Introduction

This paper discusses some basic implicit assumptions done when we use classical queuing theory to analyze a communication system. Perhaps the simplest example to start with is to consider a "$M/M/1$ situation". Assume that packets arrive at some link inside an IP network, and that we need to have an idea about the backlog in the buffer associated with the link, for dimensioning purposes. Our (standard) modeling assumptions are then the following. We assume that the packets have an exponential (real) length with mean B (and we call "bit" the unit length) and that they arrive to the link according to a Poisson process having rate λ in packets per second (pps). The channel speed is constant and denoted by c in bits per second (bps). In order to dimension the FIFO buffer associated with the link, we want to know the average memory occupied by the packets waiting for transmission or being transmitted. This is an introductory exercise in basic queuing theory: we consider the link *at*

the packet level, and observe that at that level, the transmission speed is no more constant but random, exponentially distributed and with parameter $\mu = c\,B$ pps. We make a new modeling step, by assuming that the packet are *dimensionless* objects (in queuing theory, we speak about *customers*), and that at the point in time they access the channel for transmission (that is, when they access the server in the queuing model terminology), possibly after waiting in the queue, they randomly choose a service time according to the exponential distribution with parameter μ. All this means that we have a classic $M/M/1$ queue. Calling $\overline{Q}_{\mathrm{PLM}}$ the mean queue length in the buffer in bits (PLM stands for Packet Level Model), and under the stability condition $\varrho = \lambda/\mu < 1$ (plus the usual independence assumptions on the sequence of service times and between them and the arrival process), we have

$$\overline{Q}_{\mathrm{PLM}} = B\frac{\varrho}{1-\varrho}.$$

This paper wants to point out that this can be wrong because it implicitly implies a specific behavior in the managing of the queue, more precisely in the way memory is handled, and that this assumption doesn't hold, in general, in a communication node.

We continue here the work started in [1] where the claim at the end of previous paragraph is supported. In this paper we complete the results of [1] with some supplementary elements, according to the following structure. In Section 2 we define two other possible models of the same system (a link in a packet network and its associated buffer), and in Section 3 we recall the main analytical results of [1], which we complete with some new elements in the same section and also in Section 4. Section 5 concludes the paper.

2 Modeling discussion

Consider again the model of a communication link, without making any specific assumption about the packets' length and the arrival process. In previous section, we called this view of the system a Packet Level Model (PLM) one, leading in the general case to a classical $G/G/1$ queue to be analyzed.

Assume now that we look at the system at the bit level. Call L_n the length of the nth packet arrived at the link, and A_n its arrival instant, $n \geq 1$. Suppose that the whole packet arrives instantaneously at the buffer (which is reasonable, since it is usually stored in a small buffer while arriving and then put in negligible time into memory). Knowing the speed c of the channel, the pair (A_n, L_n) (a marked stochastic process) characterizes some of the properties of the system such as the waiting time of each customer or its response time. For instance, the waiting time of the nth customer, W_n, defined as the period of time going from A_n to the starting of transmission, is given by the following Lindley recurrence (we assume, for simplicity, that the system is initially empty):

$$W_n = (A_{n-1} - A_n + L_n/c)^+, \text{ for } n \geq 2,$$

with $W_1 = 0$. The response time of the nth packet, R_n, is then given by $R_n = W_n + L_n/c$ since it is defined as the difference between the instant of the end of the transmission and A_n.

Concerning the backlog in the buffer *measured in bits*, however, things are different. The previous considered marked point process is not enough to define it. Let us consider two possibilities. We call the first one a BLMC view, which stands for "Bit Level Model with memory freed Continuously". As its name suggests, in this model the space occupied by the packet in memory is freed continuously, that is, if between time t and $t + dt$ an amount δ of some packet is transmitted, and if no packet arrives at the buffer in that period, the backlog at $t + dt$ is δ bits less than at time t. In the second view, memory is freed only when the packet's transmission finishes, instantaneously. We denote by *BLMF* this second view of the same system. Clearly, this is closer to the behavior of a buffer in a router than the BLMC view: the usual way a link works is to complete transmission first and then, to make a "free" on the space occupied by the packet in memory (for simplicity and for dependability purposes)[1].

---

[1]In fact, the managing of memory is much complex than that,

Now, consider the BLMC model, and, to make things more specific, let's go back to the "M/M/1 situation" considered in the Introduction. Denote by $Q_{\text{BLMC}}(t)$ the backlog at t in the BLMC model. This is a well known random variable in queuing theory called the "unfinished work" at t, because it is the time needed to finish the service (the transmission) active at t and all the units waiting at t. Another usual quantity in queuing theory is the "virtual waiting time" at t, $V(t)$, which is the time that a packet arriving at t must wait for transmission (of course, in the FIFO case). Clearly, $Q_{\text{BLMC}}(t) = cV(t)$. A basic result in queuing theory says that, in the ergodic case, when $\varrho < 1$,

$$\lim_{t \to \infty} U(t) = U(\infty) = B\frac{\varrho}{1-\varrho} = \overline{Q}_{\text{PLM}}.$$

In other words, the standard approach usually followed consists, in the $M/M/1$ case, of assuming that memory is freed continuously. As we discussed before, in communication nodes the second view is closer to reality. In [1] we proved that in the $M/M/1$ case,

$$Q_{\text{BLMC}} = B\frac{\varrho(2-\varrho)}{1-\varrho}.$$

This is done in [1] for $M/GI/1$ queues. In the following section, we recall and complete these results.

3 Some results on $M/G/1$ and $G/M/1$ models

Consider a $M/GI/1$ case, and denote by C the coefficient of variation of the packet length (thus, of the packet transmission time). To derive the quantities $\overline{Q}_{\text{BLMC}}$ and $\overline{Q}_{\text{BLMF}}$, the analysis goes as follows. First, we must observe that departure times of packets (that is, the instant of the transmission of "the last bit of each packet") does not depend on the fact that we deal with a BLMC or a BLMF model. So, the ergodicity conditions are the same as for the PLM view: $\varrho < 1$, where here $\varrho = \lambda B/c$. Second, knowing that $\overline{Q}_{\text{BLMC}} = U(\infty)$ is equal to B times the mean number of units in the PLM, given by the Pollaczek-Khintchine formulas, we have

$$\overline{Q}_{\text{BLMC}} = B\frac{\varrho}{2(1-\varrho)}(1 + C^2).$$

for instance in real routers. Moreover, the architecture of communication nodes can also be quite complex. The goal here is to support the global claim about the effect of freeing memory at the end of transmission only.

For the third step, we denote by $I_n(t)$ (respectively by $J_n(t)$) the r.v. equal to the quantity of memory occupied by the nth packet at t in the BLMF model (respectively in the BLMC one). Observing that

$$Q_{\mathrm{BLMC}}(t) = \sum_{n=1}^{\infty} J_n(t) \quad \text{and} \quad Q_{\mathrm{BLMF}}(t) = \sum_{n=1}^{\infty} I_n(t),$$

we write

$$\overline{Q}_{\mathrm{BLMF}} - \overline{Q}_{\mathrm{BLMC}} = \lim_{t \to \infty} \frac{1}{t} \int_0^t \sum_{n=1}^{\infty} [I_n(x) - J_n(x)] dx.$$

Denote by T_k the instant of departure of packet n (in all models), and by $D(t)$ is the number of departures between 0 and t. We have

$$\frac{1}{T_k} \int_0^{T_k} \sum_{n=1}^{\infty} [I_n(x) - J_n(x)] dx = \frac{1}{T_k} \sum_{n=1}^{D(T_k)} \frac{L_n^2}{2c}.$$

Multiplying and dividing the r.h.s. by $D(T_k)$ and using the equality between temporal and spatial limits (by ergodicity) we have

$$\lim_{k \to \infty} \frac{D(T_k)}{T_k} \frac{1}{D(T_k)} \sum_{n=1}^{D(T_k)} \frac{L_n^2}{2c} = \lambda \mathrm{E}\left(\frac{L_1^2}{2c}\right).$$

We obtain then

$$\overline{Q}_{\mathrm{BLMF}} - \overline{Q}_{\mathrm{BLMC}} = \lambda \mathrm{E}\left(\frac{L_1^2}{2c}\right) = \varrho B \frac{1 + C^2}{2}.$$

The analysis of these formulas says that in the general case, the three models (PLM, BLMC and BLMF) give different results. More precisely, see in Table 3 the relative positions of the three mean backlogs as a function of the coefficient of variation of the packet length distribution.

$M/M/1$	$\overline{Q}_{\mathrm{PLM}} = \overline{Q}_{\mathrm{BLMC}} < \overline{Q}_{\mathrm{BLMF}}$
$M/D/1$	$\overline{Q}_{\mathrm{BLMC}} < \overline{Q}_{\mathrm{PLM}} = \overline{Q}_{\mathrm{BLMF}}$
$M/GI/1, \ C > 1$	$\overline{Q}_{\mathrm{PLM}} < \overline{Q}_{\mathrm{BLMC}} < \overline{Q}_{\mathrm{BLMF}}$
$M/GI/1, \ 0 < C < 1$	$\overline{Q}_{\mathrm{BLMC}} < \overline{Q}_{\mathrm{PLM}} < \overline{Q}_{\mathrm{BLMF}}$

Table 1. Relative positions of the averages $\overline{Q}_{\mathrm{PLM}}$, $\overline{Q}_{\mathrm{BLMC}}$ and $\overline{Q}_{\mathrm{BLMF}}$, as a function of the coefficient of variation of the packet length distribution.

Observe that $\overline{Q}_{\mathrm{BLMF}}$ is always the highest value. In [1] we discuss on the differences between these values,

and about the relative error we have when using the standard theory (that is, $\overline{Q}_{\mathrm{PLM}}$) instead of $\overline{Q}_{\mathrm{BLMF}}$. Observe that $\overline{Q}_{\mathrm{BLMF}} - \overline{Q}_{\mathrm{PLM}} = B\varrho C^2$, saying that the absolute error is unbounded as C can be arbitrary large. An important point is that when C is high, so is $\overline{Q}_{\mathrm{PLM}}$, a direct consequence of Pollaczek-Khintchine formulas, and so is $\overline{Q}_{\mathrm{BLMF}}$. In relative terms, then, the error is much less: in [1] it is shown that it remains always bounded between 0% and 100%.

See that in the case of a $M/M/1$ model, we have

$$\overline{Q}_{\mathrm{BLMF}} = B\left(\frac{\varrho}{1 - \varrho} + \varrho\right),$$

saying that the absolute difference between both views is bounded by the average size of a packet and, most important, that it is higher when the load is high, and so, when the backlog is high.

A simple observation now is that the analysis described in this section leading to the result

$$\overline{Q}_{\mathrm{BLMF}} - \overline{Q}_{\mathrm{BLMC}} = \varrho B \frac{1 + C^2}{2}$$

holds in fact for any ergodic $G/G/1$ system, λ being now interpreted as the mean arrival rate, which is not necessarily Poisson. The point is then to be able to compute one of those quantities, the previous expression allowing to obtain the other one.

Here, we complete the discussion of the section using a more recent model having many applications in modern systems. It gives another way of obtaining more variability in the backlog process than with the basic $M/M/1$ model.

Let us thus consider an On-Off/$M/1$ model. We have an exponential server (that is, we keep the assumption of packets having an exponential length as in the introduction, for tractability reasons) but we consider a more general arrival process by assuming that the packets are sent by a source of the "on-off" type. This means that the source has two "states" called "on" and "off", The evolution of the state of the source obeys to a continuous time Markov chain with transition rate α from "on" to "off" and β from "off" to "on". While it is "on", the source sends packets according to a Poisson process having rate λ; no packet is sent if the source state is "off".

The packet level analysis of this queuing system is straightforward (see the Annex for some details) because we kept the service time exponential. A similar analysis can be done for an On-Off/PH/1 model using, for instance, a matrix geometric approach leading to numerical procedures. Here, we can proceed to obtain a closed-form expression. Let us first normalize the parameters by denoting $\varrho = \lambda/\mu$, $a = \alpha/\mu$ and $b = \beta/\mu$. Under the stability condition $b\varrho < a + b$, the model is ergodic, and we denote by $\pi_0 = 1 - b\varrho/(a+b)$ the steady-state probability of an empty system. Then, the backlog in equilibrium, $\mathrm{E}(N_\infty)$, can be written

$$\mathrm{E}(N_\infty) = \frac{2b\varrho\pi_0}{a+b(1-\varrho)} \frac{1}{1-a-b-\sqrt{\Delta}},$$

where $\Delta = (a+b+1+\varrho)^2 - 4(1+b)\varrho$. The mean throughput of this system is $T = \lambda b/(a+b)$. It can be observed that the mean backlog in equilibrium, $\mathrm{E}(N_\infty)$, is always greater than the mean backlog in equilibrium of an $M/M/1$ queue with arrival rate T (that is to say, than $T/(\mu - T)$). More precisely, if we denote by ϕ the "burstiness factor" $\phi = a/(a+b)$, if we keep μ and T fixed and move ϕ from 0 to 1, $\mathrm{E}(N_\infty)$ goes from $T/(\mu - T)$ to infinity. So, even if the load is low, the mean number of packets here can be more important than in the $M/M/1$ model having arrival rate T.

Observe that if $p_n(t)$ denotes the probability of having n packets at time t, we have, due to the lack of memory of the exponential distribution

$$V(t) = \sum_{n=1}^{\infty} p_n(t) n \frac{B}{c},$$

leading to $\overline{Q}_{\mathrm{BLMC}} = cV(\infty) = \overline{Q}_{\mathrm{PLM}}$.

To illustrate the preceding remarks by a numerical example, assume that the packets are 1000 bits long, on the average, and that the offered traffic (the mean arrival rate) is 500 pps. Also assume that the link speed is 1 Mbps. This means that $\mu = 1000$ pps and that $\varrho = 0.5$. In the $M/M/1$ case, this leads to a mean queue length of 1 packet. If we consider now an Off-On source with burstiness factor 0.1, the arrival rate in the "on" state must be equal to 5000 pps, and the mean queue length is now equal to 4.696 packets. This means $\overline{Q}_{\mathrm{PLM}} = 4696$ bits and $\overline{Q}_{\mathrm{BLMF}} = 5196$ bits, which roughly means a 10% error if we use the first value instead of the second one.

In the next section we discuss two other situations where the difference in using the standard and the new analysis proposed here, can be explicitly calculated.

4 Supplementary analytical results

Let us consider again the way we derived the difference between $\overline{Q}_{\mathrm{BLMF}}$ and $\overline{Q}_{\mathrm{BLMC}}$. We can see that the analysis still holds for an ergodic $G/G/c$ model, where ϱ represents now the mean number of servers that are busy, in steady state. This immediately suggests to consider the $M/M/c$ model, for which analytical expressions of the mean number of units in equilibrium are simple to obtain. We then have $\overline{Q}_{\mathrm{BLMF}} = \overline{Q}_{\mathrm{BLMC}} + B\varrho$ and we also have in this case $\overline{Q}_{\mathrm{BLMC}} = \overline{Q}_{\mathrm{PLM}}$ (same reasoning as in the On-Off/M/1 case).

In the $M/M/c$ model with arrival rate λ and service rate μ, writing $\varrho = \lambda/\mu$ and under the stability condition $\varrho < c$, the mean number of packets (standard packet level, or dimensionless view) can be written

$$\mathrm{E}(N_\infty) = \varrho + \frac{\varrho}{c-\varrho}\frac{A}{A+B},$$

where

$$A = \frac{\varrho^c}{c!}\frac{c}{c-\varrho} \quad \text{and} \quad B = \sum_{n=0}^{c-1}\frac{\varrho^n}{n!}.$$

This allows to check that the relative error when using $\overline{Q}_{\mathrm{PLM}}$ instead of $\overline{Q}_{\mathrm{BLMF}}$ satisfies

$$\frac{c-\varrho}{2(c-\varrho)+1} < \text{rel. error} < \frac{1}{2},$$

that is, in particular, that the relative error is less than 50%. It is interesting to give a numerical illustration. In Table 4 we put both values $\overline{Q}_{\mathrm{PLM}}$ and $\overline{Q}_{\mathrm{BLMF}}$ for a $M/M/20$ model, for some values of ϱ. We can see that the difference between the mean backlogs for the two views is not negligible.

The previous discussion argues that the difference between the two extreme views (PLM and BLMF) can be important. A last discussion now, concerning a moderate load case, is related to the following observation. Consider a network of queues of the Jackson type used to evaluate an IP network by means of the Kleinrock's independence assumption. We have then M queues of the $./M/1$ type, and our analysis at the bit level again holds: we know $\overline{Q}_{\mathrm{PLM}}$ (this is Jackson's result) and we also know the difference between $\overline{Q}_{\mathrm{BLMF}}$ and $\overline{Q}_{\mathrm{PLM}}$ (which is here equal to $B\varrho_i$ at node i, ϱ_i being the load factor at that node). Now, with the exponential assumption on the length of the packets, the absolute difference between the backlog in these two

ϱ	$\overline{Q}_{\text{BLMC}}$	$\overline{Q}_{\text{BLMF}}$
2	2.00	4.00
4	4.00	8.00
6	6.00	12.00
8	8.00	16.00
10	10.00	20.00
12	12.04	28.22
14	14.22	28.22
16	17.02	33.02
18	22.96	40.96

Table 2. Mean backlogs in multiples of B (or, equivalently, for the value $B = 1$), in the $M/M/20$ context and for both PLM and BLMF, as a function of ϱ.

views of the system is not large, especially if the load factors are themselves not high. An interesting connection can then be made here with the concept of *power* of a queue also proposed by Kleinrock (see [2] and the references there, or the more recent [3]).

The power of queue i is the ratio between the utilization factor of the queue and the normalized mean response time, or equivalently, between the utilization factor squared and the mean backlog. In symbols, consider a stable $G/G/1$ queue in equilibrium, where A is the mean inter-arrival length (in sec), S the mean service time (in sec), T is the mean throughput in pps, U is the utilization factor ($U = TS$), R is the mean response time and L is the mean queue length (service subsystem included). As the manager of the system modeled by this queue, you usually want T to be high but R to be low. To handle this contradictory goals, it is useful to consider the power metric P, defined as

$$P = \frac{TS}{R/S},$$

where, for scaling purposes, we use U as a normalized throughput and R/S as a normalized mean response time. Using the Little property $TR = L$ we can also write $P = U^2/N$. The goal for the manager will be here to have P maximal.

In the case of a $M/M/1$ queue with load factor ϱ, we immediately obtain $P = \varrho(1 - \varrho)$, which has its maxi-

mum for $\varrho = 1/2$; the maximal value is 1/4. Observe that when the power is maximal, the mean backlog is $L = 1$. The optimal operation point of the system is when there is no waiting time at all, that is, when there is only one unit at a time. This result also holds in the case of a $M/GI/1$ model: P is maximal when $L = 1$.

Now, consider a network of the Jackson type, leading to a product-form result. Let λ be the total arrival rate to the network. We propose to define the power of the network as the ratio

$$P = \frac{\left(\sum_{i=1}^{M} \varrho_i\right)^2}{\sum_{j=1}^{M} \frac{\varrho_j}{1 - \varrho_j}}.$$

This comes from the observation that the mean total service TS received by a customer is

$$TS = \frac{\sum_{i=1}^{M} \varrho_i}{\lambda}$$

and that the global mean response time GR is

$$GR = \frac{\sum_{i=1}^{M} \frac{\varrho_i}{1 - \varrho_i}}{\lambda}.$$

leading to the proposal $P = \lambda TS/(GR/TS)$. Observe that if the network consists only of one queue the proposed definition reduces to Kleinrock's one. It can also be shown that, again, P is maximal if for all node i, $\varrho_i = 1/2$. In this case, the maximal power value is $M/4$. This says, as for the single node case, that the optimal operation point of the system (following [2]) is the one where only one packet is in the queue at a time. Looking with care at the space occupied in this optimal configuration, leads to a total space of MB bits in the PLM case, and equal to $3MB/2$ if we adopt the BLMF one.

5 Conclusions

We point out that the standard assumptions done when we use classic queuing models to analyze communication systems can be inaccurate, without modifying those standard assumptions. The problem appears when we ask for backlogs measured in bits instead of in packets. This presentation focused in analytical results, and in open models.

Finite buffer systems are more difficult to evaluate. In [1] some complex models of audio and data transmission through a network of nodes is discussed, using simulation. It is shown that if we look at losses, now, the differences between the PLM and the BLMF views can be of several orders of magnitude. The analysis of finite buffer situation is an interesting research direction for the continuation of the research effort presented here.

6 Acknowledgments.

I thank my colleagues at the Tuileries d'Auffiac Research Center and the wonderful conditions found there, where most of this work was done.

References

[1] J. Incera and G. Rubino. On modeling the nodes of a packet communication system: bit-level versus packet-level. Technical Report 1471, IRISA, 2002. Submitted.

[2] L. Kleinrock. On the modeling and analysis of computer networks. In *Special Issue of IEEE Proceedings*, pages 1179–1191, August 1993.

[3] L. Kleinrock. The power function as a performance and comparison measure for atm switches. In *Globecom'98*, November 1998.

Annex: equilibrium analysis of the On-Off/M/1 model

Let us code by 1 state "on", by 0 state "off", and say that the system is in state (n, i), with $n \geq 0$ and $i = 1$ or 0 if there are n customers in it and the source is in state i. If $\pi_{n,i}$ is the associated steady-state probability, and if π_n is simply the steady-state probability of having n customers in the system (that is, $\pi_n = \pi_{n,1} + \pi_{n,0}$), a standard way to compute the main performance parameters is to look for the generating function $G(z) = \sum_{n \geq 0} \pi_n z^n$. Starting from the balance equations of the corresponding Markov chain, we obtain, for instance, the expression

$$G(z) = \frac{\pi_0 - (c\pi_0 + \varrho\pi_{0,0})z + \varrho\pi_{0,0}z^2}{1 - (c + \varrho)z + (b+1)\varrho z^2}.$$

By elementary algebraic manipulations, it is easy to verify that the roots of the denominator are both real. Denoting them z_1 and z_2 where

$$z_1 = \frac{c + \varrho - \sqrt{\Delta}}{2(b+1)\varrho} \quad \text{and} \quad z_2 = \frac{c + \varrho + \sqrt{\Delta}}{2(b+1)\varrho},$$

we also have $0 < z_1 < 1 < z_2$. Since by construction $G()$ is analytical on the disk $\{z : |z| \leq 1\}$, z_1 must be also a root of the numerator giving us $\pi_{0,0}$:

$$\pi_{0,0} = \frac{\pi_0(1 - cz_1)}{\varrho z_1(1 - z_1)}.$$

Thus, $G(z)$ can be written

$$G(z) = \frac{\pi_{0,0}}{b+1} \frac{z - z_3}{z - z_2},$$

where z_3 is the remaining root in the numerator of the first expression given for $G(z)$; it can be obtained for instance using

$$z_3 = \frac{c\pi_0 + \varrho\pi_{0,0}}{\varrho\pi_{0,0}} - z_1 = \frac{1 - z_1}{1 - cz_1}.$$

The mean number of customers is then $G'(1)$ given by

$$G'(1) = \frac{\pi_{0,0}}{b+1} \frac{z_3 - z_2}{(1 - z_2)^2}$$

which can be simplified into the expression given in the paper.

Author Index

Acar, Dogal 187
Adval, Ritesh. 385
Akleman, Ergun 137, 142, 147
Alexander, Khary 25
Alpaslan, Ferda N. 181
Altan, Zeynep 187
Altintas, Kemal 192
Asprey, S. 93
Atalay, Volkan 76, 81, 210, 215
Atmaca, Tulin 98

Basaran, Seren. 344
Basoglu, Nuri 399
Bazlamacci, Cuneyt F. 264
Beaumont, O. 18, 115
Bejan, Alina. 259
Bengu, G. 385
Benzekri, Abdelmalek. 415
Beryoza, Dmitriy. 276
Borrero, A. 103

Campos, Javier 405
Cao, Xi-Ren 3
Cassandras, Christos G. 8
Çelik, Haldun 390
Celikel, Ebru 130
Çetin, A. Enis 81, 210
Chao, Ching-Ming 281
Chaouchi, Hakima. 361
Chen, Jianer. 147
Chen, Yih-Farn 159
Chien, Sang-Fong 54
Choa, Fow-Sen 31
Cicekli, Ilyas. 192
Cicekli, Nihan K. 181
Costa, Luís H.M.K. 372

Dalkilic, Mehmet Emin. 130
Darcan, Osman Nuri 394
Davis, Larry 152
De Felipe, Ian 276
De Jong, Kenneth 227
Dobravec, Tomaz 332
Dutton, Ronald S. 293

El-Sayed, Mazen. 197
Erdem, Asli Sencer 399
Erdem, Aykut 210
Erdem, Erkut. 210

Fang, Yuguang. 164
Favaron, Odile. 298
Favorov, Oleg 286

Fdida, Serge 372
Fonseka, John P. 174
Fourneau, Jean Michel 103
Fricke, Gerd 298

Gavirneni, Vasavi 49
Gerek, Öner Nezih 81
Gilfeather, Patricia 36
Goddard, Wayne 296
Goldberg, David E. 232
Guha, R. 315
Guizani, M. 321
Gunes, Hatice 71
Guven, Aykut 220
Güventürk, Murat 390

Hamza-Lup, Felix G. 152
Harrison, Peter G. 12, 108
Hassanpour, Reza 215
Haynes, Teresa W. 303
Heckendorn, Robert B. 237
Hedetniemi, Sandra M. 298, 308
Hedetniemi, Stephen T. 298, 303, 308
Henning, Michael A. 303
Hiltunen, Matti 159
Hua, Kien A. 64
Hughes, Charles E. 152, 354

Jana, Rittwik 159
Johansson, Niklas 367
Juiz, Carlos 410

Kachirski, O. 315
Karri, Ramesh. 25
Karsligil, M. Yahya 71
Kaylan, Ali Riza 394
Keutzer, Kurt. 41
Kiziloglu, Ümit 344
Koç, Özcan 181
Kocak, Taskin 327
Korn, Isreal 174
Körner, Ulf 367
Korosec, Peter. 120
Kristiansen, Petter. 298, 308
Kursun, Olcay 286
Kwon, Younggoo 164
Kwong, Raymond 205

Lang, S.D. 64, 115
Lasker, Renu C. 298
Latchman, Haniph. 164
Lawrence, Ramon 259
Lee, Jaemin 142

Legrand, A.. 18
Li, Xuan 25
Lin, Jie. 31
Lin, Ping-Yi. 54
Liou, Jing-Chiou 339, 349
Liu, Guangyu 385
Lopez-Grao, Juan Pablo 405

Maccabe, Arthur B. 36
Merseguer, José. 405
Minkin, Igor 25
Mishra, Piyush 25
Mouftah, Hussein T. 249
Mülayim, Adem Y. 76
Munar, Onofre. 410

Oh, Jung Hwan 49
Orooji, Ali. 354
Ozturk, Erhan Asim 264

Pacholczyk, Daniel 197
Palmer, James Dean 147
Perros, Harry G. 377
Popa, Daniel 98
Puigjaner, Ramon 410
Pujolle, Guy 361

Quessette, F. 103

Rishe, Naphtali 276
Robert, Y.. . . . . 18, 115
Robic, Borut 120, 332
Rolland, Jannick P. 152
Roque, Alejandro 276
Rouskas, George N. 377
Rubino, Gerardo 419
Rustem, B.. 93

Sastri, Suneil 205
Sastry, Kumara 232
Schlegel, Christian 169
Schneller, I.G. 321
Schwartz, D.G. 315
Seeber, Jude 327
Selivonenko, Andrei 276
Shafique, Khurram H.. 293
Shah, Niraj 41
Shen, Jian 237
Sheu, Simon 54
Shih, Frank 385
Silc, Juriz. 120
Skaggs, Duane. 298
Sogukpinar, Ibrahim 220

Soule, Terence 237
Spooner, David L. 271
Srinivasan, Vinod 137
Stoecklin, S. 315

Tavanapong, Wallapak 59
Thornley, David 108
Tran, Minh 59
Türker, Mustafa 81

Vida, Rolland 372
Vilfan, Bostjan 332

Vu, Khanh 64

Williams, Denver R.E. 354
Wu, Annie S. 242
Wu, Jing 249
Wu, Kaijie 25

Xu, Lisong. 377

Yakut, Mehmet 86
Yalabik, Nese 344
Yaman, Mustafa 81

Yang, Shin-Jer. 254
Yen, W. Chung-Kung 125, 254
Yin, Yunjing 174
Yilmaz, Ayse S. 242
Yilmaz, E. 315
Yilmaz, Ulas 76

Zakovic, S. 93
Zatschler, Harf 108
Zhang, Jie 271